CITY HALL AND PARK OF NEW YORK.

A

GEOGRAPHICAL HISTORY

OF THE STATE OF

NEW YORK:

EMBRACING ITS

HISTORY, GOVERNMENT, PHYSICAL FEATURES, CLIMATE,

GEOLOGY, MINERALOGY, BOTANY, ZOOLOGY,

EDUCATION, INTERNAL IMPROVEMENTS, &c

WITH A SEPARATE

MAP OF EACH COUNTY.

THE WHOLE FORMING

A COMPLETE HISTORY OF THE STATE.

BY J. H. MATHER and L. P. BROCKETT, M. D.

UTICA:
PUBLISHED BY H. H. HAWLEY & CO.
1848.

Entered according to Act of Congress in the year 1848, by
H. H. HAWLEY & CO.,
in the Clerk's office of the District Court of the Northern District of New York.

ISBN 978-1-60135-507-2

PREFACE.

This Work has been prepared with great care and labor and presents the following claims to the patronage of the people of New York.

It gives historical sketches of the first settlement of the state, and of each County, compiled from the most authentic sources, also the date of the settlement of each town, in chronological order.

It presents the Geography of the State, accompanied by Maps of the State, and of each County,—correctly delineating the county and town lines of boundary, and representing the localities of the most important cities and villages.

These maps are of very great importance to the scholar and reader of this work, aiding him in his knowledge of locality, without which all geographical research is only superficial.

In the absence of a reference map, they serve as a substitute to a good degree, especially in defining the boundaries of counties and towns, being free from names, they are perfectly distinct to the eye.

It also gives all the most valuable particulars of the late Geological Survey, not only in relation to the Geology and Mineralogy, but also to the Botany and Zoology of the State.

To the Politician it is a valuable manual, furnishing him with the new Constitution, the organization of the different departments of the State Government, the history of the land purchases, which have been the source of much controversy in the State, and the Statistics of wealth, manufactures and population in each County.

To the friend of education, this book is valuable on account of its full and accurate statistics of the history, progress, and present condition of the Public Schools, the Normal School, the Universities, Colleges and Academies in the state, together with the Common School System.*

It is emphatically a book FOR THE FAMILY, and as such we offer it to the people of the State of New York.

---

*Soon after this work went to press the office of County Superintendant of Schools was abolished by the Legislature.

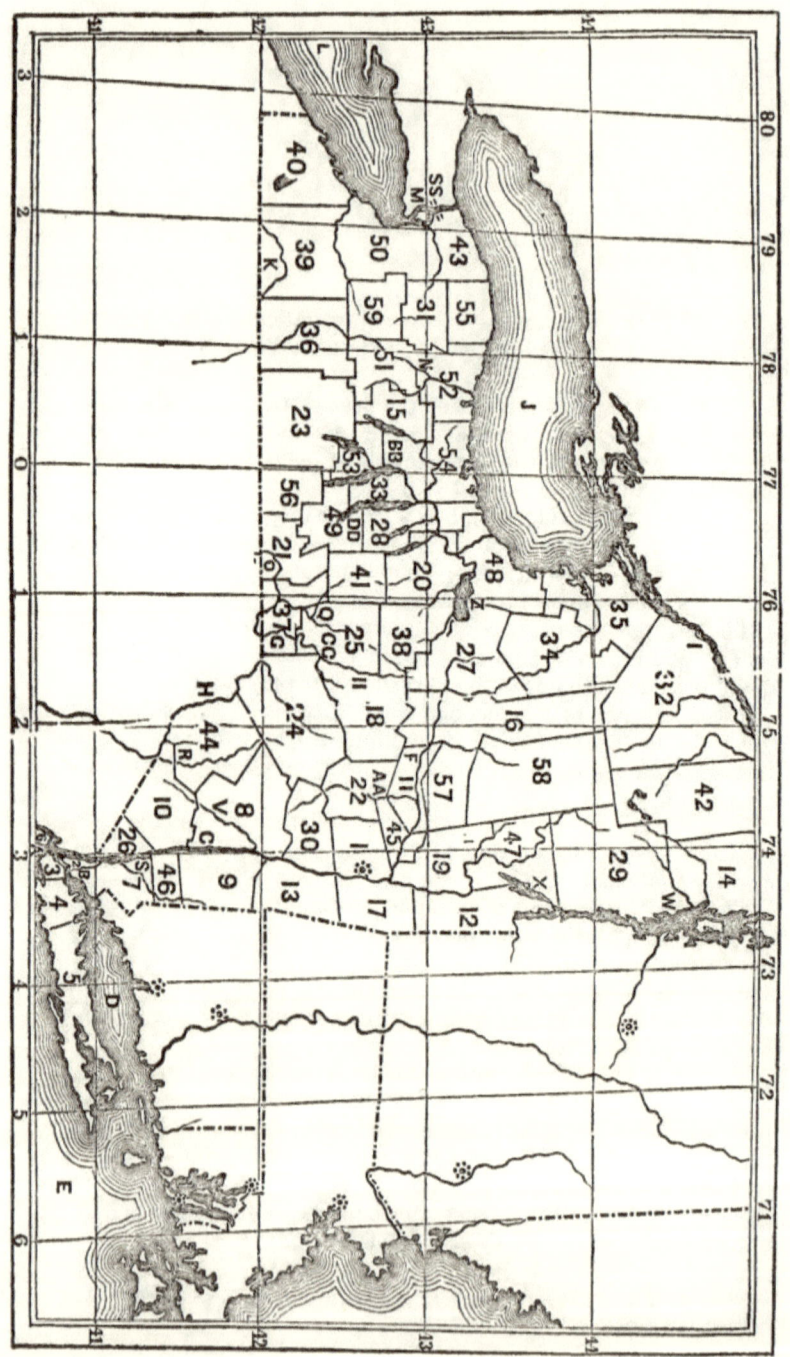

CONTENTS.

PHYSICAL FEATURES OF NEW YORK, 13. Lakes, 15.
   Boundaries, 13. Rivers, 17.
   General Features, 13. CLIMATE OF NEW YORK, 18.

NATURAL HISTORY OF NEW YORK.

GEOLOGY AND MINERALOGY, 21.
   Tabular View of the Rocks of New York, 24.
   Mineralogy, 29.
   Mineral Springs, 30.
BOTANY, 32.
ZOOLOGY, 39.
   Class I Mammalia, 39.
   Class II Aves—birds, 39.
   Class III Reptiles, 43.
   Class IV Amphibia, 43.
   Class V Fishes, 43.
   Class VII Crustacea, 46.
   Class VIII Mollusca, 46.
   Class IX Insects, 47.

CIVIL HISTORY OF NEW YORK.

DUTCH COLONIAL ADMINISTRATION, 48.
   Discovery and Settlement, 48.
   Director Minuit's Administration, 50.
   Director Van Twiller's Administration, 52.
   Director Kieft's Administration, 53.
   Governor Stuyvesant's Administration, 58.
ENGLISH COLONIAL GOVERNMENT, 62.
   The State Administration, 77.
INTERNAL IMPROVEMENTS, 94.
PURSUITS OF THE PEOPLE, 100.
   Agriculture, 100.
   Commerce, 100.
   Manufactures, 101.
   Mines, 101.
GOVERNMENT OF NEW YORK, 102.
   Constitution of New York, 102.
   Government of Counties, Towns, and Villages, 119.
PUBLIC EDUCATION, 120.
   Origin and History of the Common School System, 120.
   Present Condition of Common Schools, 121.
   State Normal School, 123.
   City School Organization, 124.
   Universities, Colleges, and Academies, 126.

GEOGRAPHY AND HISTORY OF THE COUNTIES.

   Land Purchases, 129.
I Albany County, 131.
II New York County, 139.
   Long Island, 152.
III Kings County, 154.
IV Qeens, 159.
V Suffolk, 164.
VI Richmond, 169.
VII Westchester, 173.
VIII Ulster, 181.
IX Dutchess, 186.
X Orange, 191.
XI Montgomery, 199.
XII Washington, 204.

CONTENTS.

XIII Columbia, 209.
XIV Clinton, 214.
XV Ontario, 219.
XVI Herkimer, 223.
XVII Rensselaer, 228.
XVIII Otsego, 233.
XIX Saratoga, 239.
XX Onondaga, 248.
XXI Tioga, 254.
XXII Schoharie, 257.
XXIII Steuben, 262.
XXIV Delaware, 266.
XXV Chenango, 269.
XXVI Rockland, 273.
XXVII Oneida, 277.
XXVIII Cayuga, 286.
XXIX Essex, 290.
XXX Greene, 295.
XXXI Genesee, 299.
XXXII St. Lawrence, 302.
XXXIII Seneca, 307.
XXXIV Lewis, 310.
XXXV Jefferson, 313.
XXXVI Allegany, 320.

XXXVII Broome, 323.
XXXVIII Madison, 326.
XXXIX Cattaraugus, 330.
XL Chautauque, 334.
XLI Cortland, 340.
XLII Franklin, 343.
XLIII Niagara, 347.
XLIV Sullivan, 354.
XLV Schenectady, 357.
XLVI Putnam, 361.
XLVII Warren, 364.
XLVIII Oswego, 369.
XLIX Tompkins, 373.
L Erie, 377.
LI Livingston, 382.
LII Monroe, 388.
LIII Yates, 393.
LIV Wayne, 396.
LV Orleans, 399.
LVI Chemung, 402.
LVII Fulton, 406.
LVIII Hamilton, 410.
LIX Wyoming, 413.

STATISTICAL TABLES.

Table I 417.
Table II 420.
Table III 423.

Table IV 430.
Table V 431.
Table VI Governors of the state, 432.

SIGNS USED ON THE MAPS.

 Capital of the State.

 County Seats.

 Villages not County Seats.

 Universities and Colleges.

 Forts.

 Battle Fields.

Falls.

STATE OF NEW YORK.

TOPOGRAPHICAL GEOGRAPHY.

PHYSICAL FEATURES OF NEW YORK.

Square Miles, 45,658, (exclusive of the Lakes.) Population, 2,603,995.
Date of discovery, 1609. Valuation in 1845, $605.646,095.

Boundaries. New York is bounded North by Lake Ontario, the river St. Lawrence and Canada; East by Vermont, Massachusetts and Connecticut; South by the Atlantic Ocean, New Jersey and Pennsylvania; West by Pennsylvania, Lake Erie and the Niagara river.

Its extreme length from North to South is 310 miles; from East to West, including Long Island, 408 miles; exclusive of that island 340 miles. It extends from 40° 30' to 45° North Latitude, and from 5° 05' East to 2° 55' West Longitude from Washington.

General Features. The Hudson and Mohawk rivers naturally divide the State into three sections, of unequal size.

The first comprises Long Island, and that portion of the State lying east of the Hudson river and Lake George. The second embraces all of the State lying north of the Mohawk and Oswego rivers; and the third and largest, the vast, fertile tract, south of those two rivers. These three sections may be called the Eastern, Northern and Southern.

The ranges of mountains of these different sections are numerous, and some of them quite elevated.

In the Eastern division, the Taghkanic range forms the eastern boundary of the state, from Lake Champlain to Putnam county. At this point it turns southwestward, and the Hudson forces a passage through it.

On the west side of the Hudson it assumes the name of the Kittating mountains, and continues its course, into New Jersey and Pennsylvania, under that name.

The Northern section, comprising that portion of the State lying north of the Mohawk and Oswego rivers, has six ranges of mountains running northeasterly.

1. The Palmertown range, some portions of which have also received the names of Black, and Tongue mountains.

This range rises in the northern part of Saratoga Co., runs northeast through the tongue of land which separates Lake George from Lake Champlain, and finally terminates in bold and precipitous cliffs, at the shore of the latter lake, south of Ticonderoga.

2. The Kayaderosseras, or Luzerne mountains.

These are about six miles wide and seventy long, running from Montgomery Co., through Saratoga and Warren counties, along the Western side of Lake George to Ticonderoga.

The Hudson breaks through it on the line of Warren and Saratoga counties.

3. The Clinton range.

This extends from Montgomery Co. northeast, through Fulton, Hamilton, Saratoga, Warren and Essex counties, to Point Trembleau on Lake Champlain. It is the largest range of mountains lying north of the Mohawk. At its most elevated portion there are numerous distinct peaks, forming a remarkable group, known as the Adirondack. The Mohawk forces a passage through its southwestern extremity. This range divides the waters flowing into the St. Lawrence, from those flowing into the Mohawk and Hudson. Its principal peaks are Mounts Marcy, McIntyre, McMartin and Dial mountain. The first is the highest in the State, being 5467 feet above tide water.

4. The Au Sable, or Peru range.

This range commences in Montgomery Co., and, running parallel with the others through Fulton, Hamilton and Essex counties, terminates in the south part of Clinton county.

It is one hundred and sixty miles long, and higher than the preceding ranges. White Face, its loftiest peak, is 2000 feet in height.

5. The Chateaugay range.

This is the longest and highest range in the state. Commencing on the line of the Kaa'sbergs, in Herkimer Co., it maintains an altitude of nearly 2000 feet through the counties of Hamilton, Franklin and Clinton; and crossing the Canada line terminates upon the Canada plains.

6. A range commencing ten or twelve miles from the northern extremity of the Chateaugay range, and trending along the slope of the St. Lawrence.

This has been little explored, and is of less extent than the last. The St. Regis, Grasse and other rivers descending into the St. Lawrence divide it into several distinct portions.

The Northern section has also two smaller ridges worthy of notice.

1. The Highlands of Black river.

This ridge extends from the sources of Black creek, west, and northwest, about sixty miles, covering much of the country between Black river on one side, and the plains north of Oneida Lake on the other. Its altitude is given at from twelve to sixteen hundred feet; and it has frequently a rolling surface upon its top of several miles in width.

2. The Hassencleaver mountain.

Hassencleaver ridge, extending from Herkimer county into Oneida, occupies the space between the Highlands and the Mohawk river. It is twenty miles long —about nine miles broad at its base—and has an altitude varying from eight to nine hundred feet, with a rolling surface.

PHYSICAL FEATURES.

The third, or Southern section may be subdivided into two distinct portions—the Eastern and the Western.

The Eastern division has three distinct ranges of mountains.

1. The Highlands of Orange and Putnam counties, running to the northeast.

2. The Shawangunk, running in a similar direction, and skirting the valley of the Rondout.

3. The Catskill, or Kaatsberg, whose direction is northwest through the counties of Ulster, Albany and Schoharie, to the valley of the Mohawk. Those portions of this range lying in the counties of Albany and Schoharie, are called the Helderberg mountains.

The southwestern section, also called western New York, gradually rises, from the shore of Lake Ontario, till it obtains its highest elevation, in the southern tier of counties.

The first of the terraces, composing this ascent, extends from the Genesee river, near Rochester, to the falls of Niagara, at Lewistown, a distance of eighty miles, and from six to ten miles in width. It is called the Ridge Road, and is supposed once to have formed the shore of Lake Ontario. It is about three hundred feet above the surface of the Lake.

The second extends from this ridge road to the falls of the Genesee, at Nunda and Portageville, where there is another abrupt declivity of nearly 300 feet.

This surmounted, the ascent is gradual to the summit level, at a height of 1500 to 2000 feet in the southern portion of Chautauque, Cattaraugus, Allegany and Steuben counties.

These terraces, though all quite fertile, are each characterized by a difference of soil and of forest trees.

NOTE. The following table presents the names, situation and elevation of the principal summits of these different ranges.

	Feet.
Mount Marcy, Adirondack Group, Essex county,	5,467
" McIntyre, " " "	5,183
" McMartin, " " " about	5,000
Dial Mountain or Nipple Top, " "	4,900
White Face,	4,855
Mount Seward, Adirondack group, Franklin county,	4,000
Round Top, Catskill mountains, Greene county,	3,804
High Peak, " " "	3,718
Pine Orchard, " " "	3,000
Shawangunk, Orange "	1,866
New Beacon, or Grand Sachem, Highlands,	1,685
Butter Hill, "	1,520
Old Beacon, "	1,471
Breakneck Hill, "	1,187
Anthony's Nose, "	1,128
Mount Defiance, near Ticonderoga,	750
Palisades,	550
Fort Putnam, near West Point,	500
Harbor Hill, Long Island,	319
Richmond Hill, Staten Island,	307

LAKES. New York abounds in lakes of great beauty and surrounded by the most lovely scenery.

Lake Erie, lying on the western border of the state, is the most extensive. It is 268 miles in length, and from 30 to 50 in breadth.

Its surface is greatly elevated, being 565 feet above tide water, and 334 above Lake Ontario. Its greatest depth is 270 feet, though its mean depth does not exceed 120. Only 60 miles of its coast lie within the state, and these afford but three good harbors, viz: Buffalo, Black Rock, and Dunkirk. The amount of its navigation, however, is very great, and rapidly increasing. During the autumnal months, it is subject to storms of great violence. Area of the lake 8030 sq. miles.

NOTE. The amount of business on Lake Erie is much greater than that upon any other of our inland seas. In 1845 the amount of shipping, registered, enrolled and licensed, for the district of Buffalo alone, was about 25,000 tons; and this was but a small portion of that employed upon the lake.

In 1844 more than 40,000 tons of shipping were owned by the American ports on that lake, aside from the English shipping, and that coming from other lakes. The increase is estimated at not less than 10 per cent. per annum.

The entire lake trade of 1845 was estimated at $122,000,000, of which probably three-fourths passed over Lake Erie.

Several of the steamers (of which there are some hundreds), employed on this lake, are of more than 1000 tons burthen; and for convenience and excellence of accommodations are unrivalled.

Lake Ontario is the second in size and importance, lying upon the northwest of the State.

It is of a very regular, elliptical form, 190 miles in length, 55 in its extreme width, and about 485 in circumference.

It is in some places over 600 feet in depth, having a mean depth of 492 feet, and in every part sufficient water for the largest vessels. Its surface is 334 feet lower than that of Lake Erie, and 231 feet above the level of the Atlantic.

The commerce of Lake Ontario is extensive; and its ports open usually earlier than those of Lake Erie. Of these, the principal, lying in the state of New York, are Oswego, Sacketts Harbor, and Port Genesee or Charlotte. It is less subject to violent storms and heavy swells than Lake Erie. Its area is 5400 sq. miles.

Lake Champlain, forming a portion of the eastern boundary, is a long and narrow sheet of water, of great beauty and containing a number of fine islands. Of these, Valcour and Schuyler, besides several smaller islets, belong to New York; the others to Vermont.

Its extreme length is 134 miles; its breadth varies from 40 rods to 14 miles; and its depth from 54 to 282 feet. In the winter it is usually entirely closed by ice for about two months. During the remainder of the year, large steamers and sloops navigate its waters, richly freighted with the produce of the counties along its shores.

Lake George, or Horicon, named by the French, Lac Sacrament, on account of the purity of its waters, lies south of Lake Champlain.

It is two or three miles in breadth and thirty-six in length. Its surface is 243 feet above tide water. It discharges itself into Lake Champlain by a descent of 150 feet. A steamboat plies upon its waters during the summer.

The lake is surrounded by hills, towering to the height of 1200 or 1500 feet. The numerous islands which stud its placid surface; the transparency of its waters, which reveals the pebbles beneath, at a depth of 40 feet; and the rich and varied scenery which surrounds it, all combine to render it one of the most delightful resorts in the state, to the invalid or the man of business.

The northern portion of the State abounds with small lakes, seldom exceeding six or eight miles in length, and two or three in breadth. Their number is probably not less than 200.

Some of these, among the Adirondack group of mountains, are greatly elevated. Avalanche lake, in Essex county, is 2900 feet, Colden lake, in the same county, 2750 feet, and Racket lake, in Hamilton county, 1731 feet above tide water.

The central portion has a chain of lakes of considerable size and importance.

PHYSICAL FEATURES. 17

They extend through the counties of Oneida, Oswego, Onondaga, Cayuga, Seneca, Yates, Ontario and Livingston; and are hardly surpassed in beautiful and picturesque scenery.

The principal lakes in this chain are Seneca, Cayuga, Oneida, Crooked and Canandaigua.

The first four are navigated by steam and canal boats. They are generally from 300 to 600 feet deep, and from 400 to 700 feet above the surface of the Atlantic.

The other lakes, connected with this chain, are Onondaga, Cross, Otisco, Cazenovia, Skeneateles, Owasco, Honeoye, Canadice and Conesus.

These are all small, but are worthy of notice, for the beautiful scenery which surrounds them. Extensive salt springs abound on the shores of the Onondaga, whose waters are, notwithstanding, fresh.

The only other lakes of importance are Otsego and Canaderaga in Otsego county, and Chautauque, in Chautauque county.

RIVERS. The Hudson, 320 miles in length, is the largest river lying wholly in the State, and one of the finest navigable streams in the United States. It rises among the Adirondack group of mountains, and flows almost directly South to the bay of New York. It is navigable for steamboats of the largest size, and sloops, to Troy, 160 miles from its mouth.

In the number and magnificence of its steamers, and in the extent of business done upon its waters, it is probably surpassed only by the Ohio and Mississippi rivers.

The principal branches of the Hudson are, the Hoosick on the east side, and the Mohawk on the west.

The Hoosick, rising in Berkshire county, Mass., runs northwest and west, and furnishes many fine mill seats.

The Mohawk takes its rise in Oneida and Lewis counties. It pursues at first a southerly course; then, changing to east southeast, it forms the valley of the Mohawk. Its length is about 130 miles.

The other tributaries of the Hudson are, on the east, Schroon branch, the outlet of Schroon lake; Battenkill, Kinderhook and Croton rivers; on the west, Wallkill, Rondout, Esopus, Kaaterskill and Sacandaga, besides several smaller streams.

The St. Lawrence forms the northwestern boundary of New York, for a hundred miles; and is the outlet of the great American lakes.

It conveys to the ocean a larger body of water than any other river in the world, except the Amazon. It is navigable for sloops as far as Ogdensburg, 60 miles from Lake Ontario. Below this point, the frequent rapids render navigation difficult and dangerous.

The Thousand Islands lie near its junction with Lake Ontario, a portion of which, and some others belong to the United States. This group actually exceeds 1500 in number.

The Oswego is the next in importance in the State. Its whole length is 120 miles.

Under the name of Mud creek, it rises in Ontario county, and flowing easterly receives, through the Canandaigua outlet, the waters of Canandaigua lake. Proceeding eastwardly under the name of the Clyde, it receives the waters of Seneca and Cayuga lakes through their common outlet, and assumes the name of Seneca river. After a still farther enlargement by the waters of Onondaga lake, it takes the title of Oswego river; and suddenly curving towards the northwest, collects from the Oneida river its tribute of the waters of Oneida lake, and discharges itself into Lake Ontario. It has about 100 feet fall after assuming the name of Oswego river, and furnishes, by its constant supply of water, valuable mill privileges. Seven thousand square miles of territory are drained by its waters; and, by means of the Oswego Canal and locks, it is navigable for its whole extent.

The Allegany river, one of the sources of the Ohio, takes its rise in Allegany county, and is navigable for steamers of small draft from Olean, a distance of about 40 miles, to the state line.

The Susquehanna and Delaware both take their rise in this state, and, though not navigable to any considerable extent, afford fine seats for mills.

The other principal rivers of the state are, the Niagara, which is the connecting link between Lakes Erie and Ontario, and forms the celebrated falls of the same name;

The Genesee, distinguished for its immense water power, and for being the feeder of the Genesee Valley Canal;

It is navigable almost to Rochester, and is 145 miles in length, emptying into Lake Ontario.

The Black, the third river in size, lying wholly in the state, and also discharging its waters into Lake Ontario; it is 120 miles in length, and navigable for 40 miles.

The Chenango and the Chemung, important tributaries of the Susquehanna;

The Oswegatchie, rising in Herkimer county, the principal tributary of the St. Lawrence.

The other streams flowing into the St. Lawrence are Indian, Grasse, Racket, St. Regis and Salmon rivers.

Chazy and Saranac are the chief streams flowing into Lake Champlain.

CLIMATE OF NEW YORK.*

From the extent and diversity of its surface, it is impossible to give a general description of the climate of New York, which would apply with equal truth to each section of the state. We can only say that it is subject to great extremes of heat and cold; and that, although in the same latitude, which in Europe produces the fig, the olive and the grape, its more severe climate admits only of the culture of the hardier plants and grains.

The state, though subject to sudden and severe changes, may be considered healthy. The number of deaths to the population is not greater than in the other states; nor do malignant diseases prevail to any considerable extent.

* The facts on which this article is based have been collected from a chapter on the climate of the state in Gordon's Gazetteer; from the reports of the Regents of the University; and from a paper in the Quarterly Journal of Agriculture.

CLIMATE.

In the eastern counties, consumption and other diseases of the lungs are the prevailing maladies; in the western counties, bilious affections are more prevalent. Cholera Infantum is a common and fatal disease with children in the cities and large towns, during the summer and autumn.

It has been ascertained, by numerous observations made in this state and New England, that an elevation of surface of 350 feet produces a diminution of heat, equal to the addition of a degree of latitude. Hence we see the influence of our mountain systems upon the climate of the state.

In order to present more clearly the peculiar characteristics of the climate to the scholar, we shall divide the state into six districts, viz. 1st, Long Island; 2d, The valley of the Hudson; 3d, The valley of the Mohawk; 4th, The district north, and north east of the Mohawk, extending from Lake Ontario to Lake Champlain; 5th, The district south and south west of the valley of the Mohawk, extending from the valley of the Hudson to the smaller Lakes; and 6th, The country west of the smaller Lakes.

The following table, prepared with great care, exhibits the mean, or average temperature; the mean annual maximum, or highest degree of heat; the mean annual minimum, or lowest degree of temperature; the average annual range of the Thermometer; and several other particulars, which show the length and forwardness of the seasons, and the progress of vegetation. It contains the results of observations made at 59 different places, for a period of 15 years.

TABLE OF THE CLIMATE OF NEW YORK.

Facts observed.	Average Date.	No. of Locations of Observations.	No. of Observations.
Robins first seen,	March 19,	44	266
Shadbush in bloom,	May 1,	48	168
*Peach in bloom,	May 2,	57	175
Currants in bloom,	May 4,	58	269
Plum in bloom,	May 6,	52	264
Cherry in bloom,	May 7,	52	250
Apple in bloom,	May 15,	59	374
Lilac in bloom,	May 15,	45	151
Strawberries ripe,	June 12,	58	210
Hay harvest commenced,	July 8,	34	127
Wheat harvest commenced,	July 25,	45	186
First killing frost,	Sept. 23	57	471
First fall of snow,	Nov. 5,		536
Mean, or average temperature,	46° 49'	59	577
Mean annual maximum of heat,	92° 00'	59	550
Mean annual minimum, below zero,	12° 00'	59	551
Mean ann. range of the thermometer,	104° 00'	59	550

We will now proceed to consider the climate of the several districts, into which we have divided the state, in their order.

1st District. *Long Island.*

The climate of this district is remarkable for the uniformity of its temperature. The greatest heat of summer is on an average 1½° less, and the greatest cold of winter from 10° to 18° less, than in other parts of the state.

The spring is somewhat backward, trees blooming a week later than in the interior of the state; yet strawberries ripen, and the wheat harvest commences earlier than the average of the state.

---

* This is the average for the southern and middle portion of the state only.

Frost occurs at a much later period in autumn, than in any other section. At East Hampton, it is a full month, and at Jamaica and Flatbush, nearly three weeks, later than the average of the state.

2d District. *The Valley of the Hudson.*

This valley is remarkable for the great annual range of the thermometer; the heat of summer and the cold of winter being equally intense. The average temperature of Albany is nearly 2° higher than that of the state. The extreme cold of winter at Kinderhook, Lansingburgh, Cambridge, Salem and Granville, causes the mercury to sink 10° lower than in the southern towns of the valley. The spring opens a week or ten days later, at Albany, and above that city, than at the city of New York.

3d District. *Valley of the Mohawk.*

The average annual temperature of this valley is 1° less than that of the state. Northerly and easterly winds prevail in this section. The latter seems to be a diversion of the south, or south west wind, which prevails in the valley of the Hudson.

Utica, in this district, may be considered as a fair representative of the general climate of the state, as its temperature is about the average temperature of the whole state.

4th District. *North and North East of the Valley of the Mohawk.*

The climate of this region is characterized by a low average temperature, extreme cold in winter, great range of the thermometer, backward seasons, and early frosts.

Gouverneur, in St. Lawrence Co. reports a lower degree of temperature in winter, and with one exception, a lower annual average of temperature, than any other town in the state, from which meteorological records have been received.

The average annual temperature of the whole district is more than 2° lower than that of the remainder of the state.

5th District. *The Region South of the Mohawk, extending to the smaller Lakes.*

The average annual temperature of this section is about 2° lower than that of the state, and the autumnal frosts occur from 4 to 13 days earlier. Vegetation is uniformly backward, yet the robin appears earlier than in other sections.

Pompey, in Onondaga county, is the coldest place reported, its annual temperature being $3\frac{1}{2}$° lower than that of the state; yet the cold of winter is not so intense, nor do the autumnal frosts occur as early there, as in the state generally.

6th District. *That portion of the State West of the small Lakes.*

The climate of this section, like that of Long Island, is characterized by uniformity. The mean temperature does not differ materially from that of the whole state, but the average annual range of the thermometer is only 96°, while that of the state is 104°.

Vegetation in the spring is somewhat in advance of the state generally, corresponding with that of Albany.

The prevalent local wind of this region is from the southwest. In the autumn it is violent throughout the whole section, and frequently attended with rain; but on Lake Erie, probably owing to its meeting with other currents of wind, it frequently manifests extraordinary fury in September and October, and occasionally produces disastrous shipwrecks.

The extreme heat of summer is very uniform throughout the state. Only 5 places, out of 55, show a difference of over 3° from the average of the state, which is 92°.

The average time throughout the whole state, from the blooming of the apple tree, to the first killing frost in autumn, is 174 days. On the west end of Long Island it is $12\frac{1}{4}$ days more; and in St Lawrence county 22 days less. These are the extremes.

NATURAL HISTORY OF NEW YORK.

I. GEOLOGY AND MINERALOGY.

Geology may be defined as that science which treats of the structure of the earth, and the substances which compose it.

An examination of the banks of rivers, the sides of precipices, &c., shows that there are two kinds, or classes of rocks; the one being deposited in layers, or strata, of variable thickness, are called *stratified rocks*, and bear evidence of having been, at some remote period, deposited as a sediment, from water; the other irregular in shape, containing numerous crystals, and most of the metals in common use, and forming the basis of the lofty mountain chains, are termed *unstratified rocks*, and were undoubtedly brought into their present form by the action of fire, which then existed, and probably still exists, in the interior of the earth.

Granite is the principal constituent of the unstratified rocks, and probably formed the original crust of the earth. It still exists below all the other rocks. Owing, however, to violent convulsions of nature, (such as earthquakes, volcanic eruptions, &c.,) which have occurred since the layers above it were deposited, it has in many places been forced up through fissures in these layers, so as to appear on the surface, or has raised them up, so as to form mountains or hills. If these were still covered with water, or became again submerged by a subsequent convulsion, new layers were again deposited, frequently at considerable angles with the first deposit.

The figure represents such an occurrence.

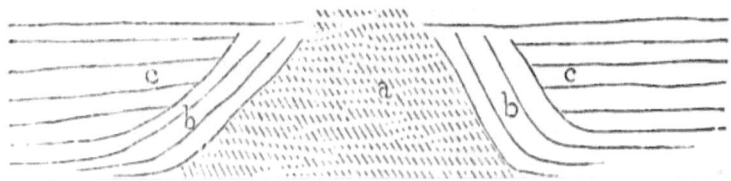

a, represents the unstratified rock upon which the layers *b*, *b*, had been deposited in a horizontal position; but by a convulsion of nature, the whole mass had been upheaved, and the granite had forced its way to the surface; being however still submerged, new layers c, c, were deposited, at an angle of nearly 45º with the first.

Hypersthene and primitive limestone also occur among the unstratified rocks.

The Stratified Rocks are divided into six orders or systems, as they are called; viz.,—beginning at the lowest strata, or those next succeeding the unstratified rocks, we have,

I. The Primary, or Primitive System, consisting of disintegrated granite, deposited by the waters; and probably again modified by the action of the subterranean heat.

The rocks, composing this system, are known as gneiss, mica schist, and hornblende. There is no evidence of the existence of either animal or vegetable life, during the period while this strata were depositing. Nearly all the metals, used in the arts, are found in these rocks, and in the granite on which they rest.

II. The Transition System. This system embraces a great variety of formations, and occupies a large portion of the crust of the earth. Its lower strata consist of limestones, sandstones, and shales or slaty rocks. Above these, is a layer of sandstone, known as the old red sandstone, which is succeeded by a limestone, forming the bed of the vast coal formations, which furnish so large an amount of fuel to the world. Over these is deposited a magnesian limestone, and another layer of red sandstone, distinguished as the new red sandstone.

The period, when these deposits were made, was characterized by extraordinary luxuriance of vegetable life. The coal deposits are all of vegetable origin, and were reduced to their present form, by the influence of heat, decay and pressure. In the rocks belonging to this system are also found, in immense quantities, the lower orders of animals, shell fish, snails, and a few fishes, and amphibious reptiles. None of them, however, belong to species now known to be in existence.

III. The Secondary System, composed of oolitic limestone, greensand, and chalk. This system contains a large number of fossils, both animal and vegetable. Among the former are those gigantic amphibious animals, mostly belonging to the lizard and crocodile tribes, whose skeletons, found both on this continent and in Europe, have excited so much attention. There are also many shells, fishes, insects, and a few quadrupeds. Several hundreds of species of plants have been found in the secondary rocks. These fossils, vegetable and animal, with scarcely an exception, belong to extinct species.

IV. The Tertiary System. This consists of deposits of clay, sand and gravel, in some instances hardened into rock, but generally containing evidence of the comparative recentness of its deposition. It contains an immense number of fossils, both animal and vegetable; of these about 12 per cent. have been identified as belonging to existing species, and the remainder generally bear a marked resemblance to plants and animals now in existence, which the fossils of the earlier periods do not.

V. The Diluvial Deposits, called also the *erratic block group.* In thi system are included the boulders, scattered so abundantly over many sections of the earth's surface, and many of the more extensive deposits of sand, gravel and clay, which are evidently the result of the resistless action of an overwhelming deluge. These deposits contain numerous animal and vegetable forms, the greater part of which belong to existing species, although occasionally extinct races are found.

VI. The Alluvial Deposits, including the deltas, or earthy deposits at the mouths of rivers, the beds of lakes which have become drained, the valleys of rivers subject to periodical inundations, the shores of oceans, seas, &c.

These also contain, in untold quantities, relics of animal and vegetable existence, but, with very few exceptions belonging to races now known. The gigantic mastodon has been found in these deposits.

We have been thus particular in noticing the fossils belonging to each system, because they serve as way-marks, by the aid of which, even the most unlettered may read the progress of the earth's history, from the period, when it was first set in motion, a vast mass of molten granite, devoid of vegetable or animal life, to the present time, when its green fields, and its innumerable hosts of living and moving beings, attest with myriad voices, the power and wisdom of the great Creator.

The whole of these formations do not exist in every part of the world; but wherever geological explorations have been made, it has been found that the same order is observed; and, that, although some one, or more, of these systems are absent, those which are present follow the arrangement we have described.

In the state of New York the secondary formation is wanting,* as well as the upper members of the transition system,* and in most parts of the state the tertiary system.

It will be seen, by the following table, that coal is not laid down among the formations of the state. All the formations of New York, except the alluvial and diluvial deposits, and the beds of tertiary, on the St. Lawrence, are below the coal measures; the Catskill group, which is the highest member of the transition system in New York, being the layer immediately beneath it.

It is true that there are layers of Anthracite, an inch or two in thickness, and extending over a few feet of surface, between the strata of rocks of an earlier era, in various parts of the state; but coal does not exist in the state, in sufficient quantities to be of any practical value. This deficiency, however, is abundantly made up by the vast coal fields of Pennsylvania and Ohio, which, by means of the extended systems of internal improvement, are rendered so easily accessible.

The prevalence of limestone in nearly all the formations is worthy of notice, affording, as it does, the basis rock best adapted to yield the materials for fertilizing the soil.

The table exhibits the geological formations of the state, according to the arrangement adopted by the state geologists in their late survey.

III., IV. and V. of this arrangement are comprised under the general head of the Transition system, heretofore described.

---

* The existence of a small bed of oolite in Saratoga county, and the somewhat doubtful era of the red sandstone of Rockland county, can scarcely be considered as exceptions to this statement.

TABULAR VIEW OF THE ROCKS OF NEW YORK, ARRANGED IN
SYSTEMS, GROUPS AND FORMATIONS.

Systems.	Groups.	Formations.
I. Alluvial.	Alluvial.	
II. Diluvial.	Diluvial, including boulders, &c. Clays and sands.	
III. Old Red sandstone system.	Old Red sandstone, or Catskill group.	Conglomerate, Old Red sandstone.
IV. New York transition system.	Erie group,	Chemung sandstones and flagstones, Ludlowville shales.
	Helderberg series,	Helderberg limestone, Schoharie grit, Brown argillaceous sandstone, Encrinal limestone, Oriskany sandstone, Green shaly limestone, Pentamerus limestone.
	Ontario group,	Onondaga salt and gypseous rocks, Limestone and green shales, Argillaceous iron ore, Medina sandstone, soft, green and variegated.
	Champlain group,	Grey sandstone and conglomerate, Lorraine shales and roofing slates, Utica slate, Trenton limestone, Birdseye limestone, Chazy limestone, Calciferous sandrock, Potsdam sandstone.
V. Taghkanic, or Taconic system.		Light green shales, sometimes dark and plumbaginous. Grey and clouded limestone, Brown sandstone.
VI. Gneiss, or Primary system.		Gneiss, hornblende, and mica slate, Talcose slate and steatite.
VII. Superincumbent rocks.		Greenstone, trap and porphyry.
VIII. Unstratified rocks.		Granite, Hypersthene rock. Primary limestone, serpentine, Magnetic iron ore.

There are in the state two tracts of *primary* and *unstratified rocks*. The first is nearly circular in form, and occupies the counties of Essex, Warren and Hamilton, and portions of Saratoga, Fulton, Herkimer, Oneida, Lewis, Jefferson, St. Lawrence, Franklin and Clinton. The Black river forms its southwestern boundary, from Wilna, in Jefferson, to Remsen, in Oneida county.

The second is in the southeastern part of the state, of a somewhat triangular form, and comprises Putnam and Westchester, together with the larger part of New York, and part of Rockland, Orange and Dutchess counties.

These two sections together occupy nearly one third of the state.

They contain extensive and valuable mines of iron, lead and plumbago, both in the northeastern and southeastern portions of the state. Their surface is generally broken and elevated, towering up to the height of more than a mile above tide water, in the Adirondack group, and attaining a considerable, though less lofty altitude in the beetling cliffs which overlook the waters of the Hudson.

The soil is less arable and fertile than in the lands of the limestone formations, but is covered, except in the older counties, with a gigantic growth of oak, pine and hemlock timber.

The gneiss of this system furnishes a fine building material, and under the name of granite, is abundantly quarried for that purpose. The serpentine, primitive limestone, and steatite, are also largely quarried for the purposes of the arts.

These rocks abound in minerals of great interest to the mineralogist. Garnet, beryl, chrysoberyl, pyroxene, sphene, tourmaline, apatite, colophonite, scapolite, Labradorite, epidote, &c. &c.

Geologists differ in opinion, on the question, whether the Taghkanic, or Taconic system should be ranked with the Primary, or the Transition system. It is composed of brown sandstone, limestone and green shales, or slaty rocks. It contains some minerals, and furnishes a fine limestone for building, but has few, or no fossils. The soil which overlays this system is generally good, and often highly fertile.

Its range is quite extensive, although frequently of no great width. It comprises nearly the whole of the counties of Washington, Rensselaer and Columbia, part of Dutchess, Ulster, Greene, Albany and Saratoga, and trending westward occupies a narrow tract in Schenectady, Montgomery, Herkimer and Oneida, and expands more widely in Oswego and Jefferson counties.

We next come to the New York system, as it has been appropriately named, comprising, according to the table, four distinct groups. We commence with the lowest of these, the Champlain Group. The constituents of this group are various kinds of sandstone and limestone, slate, conglomerate, and a peculiar stone, compounded of lime and sandstone, and hence called calciferous (or limebearing) sandrock.

Of these the Potsdam sandstone furnishes a beautiful and durable building material, and is also used in the manufacture of glass, and the preparation of sand paper. The Trenton and birdseye* limestones are used for the purposes of the arts. The Lorraine shales, and the Utica slate are employed for roofing, and to some extent for writing slates. The grey sandstone and conglomerate furnish stone suitable for grindstones.

The rocks of this group, and particularly the limestones and slates, abound in fossils of the earlier periods; encrinites, trilobites and numerous others, unlike any of the crustaceous animals now in existence.

The soil, throughout the territory occupied by this group, is generally good, and much of it is highly fertile, being constantly enriched by the decomposition of the limestone, slate and sandstone, which is

---

* This limestone receives its name from the abundance of encrinites which it contains, which give it, when polished, an appearance somewhat resembling birdseye maple.

effected by the combined action of air and water. The group occupies a very considerable, but irregular territory. It appears occasionally in small beds, then dips beneath the surface, and again appears, as the surface rock, over an extensive tract. In the forms of Potsdam sandstone, calciferous sandrock, birdseye and Trenton limestone, and Utica slate, it bounds the great primary region of the northeast in every direction, varying in width from two to fifty miles. It also makes its appearance in narrow beds on either side of the Hudson.

The Ontario Group, which comes next in order, consists of three distinct portions; the lowest a marly sandstone, generally soft, and either red, green, brown, or variegated,—decomposing rapidly, when exposed to the atmosphere, and denominated Medina sandstone; next, a series of soft, green, slaty rocks, also easily decomposed, and overlaid by clayey and flinty limestones, alternating with each other, and finally terminating in the limestone over which the Niagara pours its resistless cataract; and lastly a group of limestones, containing gypsum or plaster of Paris, water lime and salt, known as the Onondaga salt group.

This group, considered with reference to practical purposes, is the most valuable of the transition system in the state. It includes the salt springs in Salina and its vicinity, and at Montezuma, which yield so large an amount of revenue to the state; the gypsum beds, which furnish such inexhaustible resources for the fertilization of the soil, as well as for the various purposes of the arts, to which this valuable mineral is applied; and the water lime, called, after its preparation, *hydraulic cement*, a material indispensable to the proper construction of canals, aqueducts, cisterns, and other masonry exposed to the action of water, and one which has proved of the greatest service in the construction of the public works of the state.

The fossils of this group are numerous and interesting. Shells of bivalve molluscous animals, corallines and madrepores, together with unequivocal traces of vegetable existence, mark this era.

Its minerals are not numerous. The clayey limestones contain iron ore; fluor spar and selenite appear occasionally, and sulphur springs gush up from different sections. Its soil is of unsurpassed and perpetual fertility, being constantly enriched by the slowly decomposing lime and gypsum. It is the granary of the state, and before the wide prairies of the west waved with the golden grain, it supplied nearly the whole country with bread-stuffs. The oak, beech, maple, elm, butternut, hickory and black walnut, are the principal forest trees. The Ontario group commences at the southwestern extremity of Lake Ontario in Canada, and extends eastward with a medium breadth of twenty miles to its termination in Montgomery county.

The Helderberg series comprises four kinds of limestone and three of sandstone. Of these the Helderberg limestone is extensively used as a flagging stone, under various local names; it is also employed to some extent as a building material; the Oriskany sandstone is also used as a building material; it occasionally contains lime. Of the remaining layers, one of the sandstones is dark, shaly and brittle; the other calcareous and abounding in fossils. Two of the limestones contain large quantities of fossils, and derive their names from that fact ; in one the encrinite, one of the most beautiful of the crustaceous fossils, is predominant ; in the other, the pentamerus, whose shell bears some resemblance, in form, to that of the common oyster. The remaining limestone is slaty and easily decomposed.

The Helderberg limestone is cavernous, and many of its caves have been explored for a considerable distance. They contain stalactites and stalagmites of great beauty.

The principal minerals of this formation are bog iron ore, calcareous and fluor spar, jasper, sulphate of strontian, in great abundance, satin spar, alum, bitumen and small veins of anthracite. The soil, overlying these rocks, is generally either a fine clay, or sand lying upon clay. Marl occurs quite frequently. By suitable cultivation it yields good crops of wheat and other grains. The timber is usually oak, chestnut, hickory, pine and hemlock.

This group occupies a narrow tract, commencing in the western part of Orange county, and passing northeasterly through Ulster to the Hudson ; thence along the banks of that river, to Albany county, where it turns westwardly, passes through the centre of the state immediately south of the Ontario group, forming the bed of most of the small lakes in western New York, and terminates on the shores of Lake Erie.

The Erie Group is divisible into two portions, the lower, denominated Ludlowville shales, is composed of soft slaty rocks, alternating with thin beds of limestone, and is easily decomposed ; the upper, called the Chemung group, consists of thin, even beds of gray sandstone, with intervening shales, or beds of slate.

Some of the fossils, found in this group, possess great beauty, and show the approach to that period of vegetable luxuriance, which marks the coal formation. Ferns, and other vegetable fossils frequently occur, and the avicula, delthyris and other shell fish, strongly resembling some living species, are found imbedded in the rocks.

The minerals of this group are few, and of no great importance. Petroleum, or mineral oil, called, in some parts of the state, Seneca oil, occurs in several localities, and the shale is often so strongly impregnated with it as to burn quite freely. Carburetted hydrogen, or inflammable gas, also issues from the surface in a number of places, and in such quantities, as to be used, in one or two instances, for illuminating villages, light houses, &c.

The soil where the Ludlowville shales form the surface rock, though apparently rough and broken, is rendered fertile by the constant decomposition of the rock. It is well adapted to the culture of wheat and other grains. As we ascend, to the more elevated surface of the Chemung sandstone, we find a marked change in the character of the soil ; the white pine and hemlock take the place of the oak, maple and beech of the lower lands, and attain a gigantic growth. These lands produce the grasses luxuriantly, and, as they become cleared, will afford pasturage to vast herds of cattle and sheep.

The Erie group covers nearly the whole of Chautauque, Cattaraugus, Wyoming, Allegany, Steuben, Yates, Tompkins, Chemung and Tioga counties, together with portions of Broome, Chenango, Cortland, Ontario, Livingston, Genesee and Erie, as well as a narrow tract in Sullivan, Ulster, Greene, Schoharie and Otsego counties.

This completes what, for convenience, has been termed the New

York Transition system. The remaining group properly belongs to the Transition system of the English Geologists, and is by them denominated the Old Red sandstone, that rock being its principal constituent. The State Geologists, from the fact of its being the predominant rock of the Catskill mountains, have given it the name of the Catskill group.

It consists of two distinct formations, viz., the Old Red sandstone overlying the Chemung sandstone, and the conglomerate strata, which are immediately beneath the coal bearing limestone of Pennsylvania. Between the layers of the former are interposed soft shales combined with mica.

The sandstone is generally of a deep red color, and imparts the same hue to the soil which covers it. It contains comparatively few fossils; the scales and bones of some lizard-like fish have been discovered in it.

The minerals of this group are few, and of but little importance. Bog iron ore and calcareous spar are those most worthy of notice. The conglomerate affords fine grindstones, and has been used to some extent for millstones.

The soil is generally good; the sandstone decomposing readily under atmospheric influence, mingles with the vegetable mould and renders it fertile. Hemlock, beech, maple, elm, basswood, butternut, &c. are the principal timber trees; the oak is seldom found in this formation.

The Red sandstone of the Catskill group is mostly confined to the vicinity of the Kaatsbergs; occupying the county of Delaware, and portions of Sullivan, Ulster, Greene, Otsego, Chenango and Broome; but the conglomerate extends westward, and caps the highest hills of the southwestern counties.

The Diluvial deposits skirt the shores of the St. Lawrence, Lake Champlain, and the Hudson, and compose the surface of the northern half of Long Island. They consist of a stiff blue clay beneath, a yellowish brown clay above this, and sand on the surface. The marine shells, found in these clays, belonging in some instances to extinct species, show that these deposits were made at an earlier period than those thrown down by rivers or oceans, in modern times. To this system belong also the boulders, scattered so widely over the state.

The Alluvial deposits, consisting of gravel, sand, loam, &c. thrown up by the waves, or deposited on the shores of lakes, and the banks of rivers, and still in the process of aggregation, constitute the last of the geological formations of the state. To these belong portions of the valleys of the rivers and lakes and the southern half of Long Island. The soil of both these classes of deposits is usually fertile.

The class of rocks known as trap and porphyry, do not, in this state, constitute a separate formation. They occur either in columnar masses like the Palisades, on the west bank of the Hudson, near New York, or in narrow veins or dikes, traversing rocks of an entirely different constitution. They are evidently the result of the action of subterranean fire. Porphyry is only found occupying a tract of a few miles in length, on Lake Champlain.

In connexion with the Geology of the state, the "Ridge road" is deserving of notice. This road consists of a bank of sand, gravel and other alluvial and diluvial deposits, varying in height from 100 to 150 feet, and extending along the whole southern coast of Lake Ontario, at a distance of six or eight miles from it, forming a natural highway. It is said that a somewhat similar ridge exists along the northern shore of the Lake.

That this ridge once, and at no very distant period, formed the southern shore of the lake, is proved, by the existence of small sand hillocks, evidently heaped up by the action of the waves; by the entire absence of Indian mounds and fortifications, on the north side of the ridge, and their frequent appearance, immediately south of it; and above all, by the structure and composition of the ridge itself.

The deep channels, cut in the rocks, by many of the rivers of the state, are also a subject of geological interest. The Hudson, St. Lawrence, Oswego, and some of the northern streams, either have banks regularly sloping to the water's edge, or, if they occasionally pass through narrow and precipitous defiles, have not won for themselves a passage, by the action of their waters upon the rocky barrier which opposed them, but have availed themselves of a route opened by some convulsion of nature.

Such is not the case with the Mohawk, the Chenango, the Genesee, and the Niagara. Descending from elevated table lands, they have, by their ceaseless flow, hewn out a channel through the shales, slates and marly sand and limestones, in some instances 400 or 500 feet below the level of the surrounding country. The constant action of the waters upon these decomposing rocks has also caused the falls of Niagara to recede, as some geologists conjecture, a distance of five or six miles, and this recession is still in progress.

MINERALOGY. We have already adverted to the minerals, peculiar to the different formations, but a somewhat more particular description of the mineral wealth of the state seems requisite, in a work like ours.

Among the useful metals, *Iron* is most abundant in New York. It is found in five forms.

1st. *The Magnetic Oxide*, most abundant in Essex, Clinton, Franklin, Warren, Orange and Putnam counties, but occurring also in considerable quantities in Lewis, St. Lawrence and Jefferson. This variety is adapted to the production of malleable iron and steel, and for this purpose is superior to any in the United States, and equal to most of the foreign ores. The quantity is immense, a single vein (the Sandford vein in Newcomb, Essex county,) being estimated by Prof. Emmons to contain ore sufficient to yield at least three millions of tons, of malleable iron; several other veins, in the same neighborhood, contain nearly as much more, and the mines of Orange county, though worked for nearly a century, are still very productive. This ore is confined to primary rocks.

2d. *The Specular Oxide*, found in St. Lawrence, Jefferson and Franklin counties, imbedded in sandstone. This variety is well adapted to castings. Though less abundant than the preceding, it is found in large quantities.

3d. *The Argillaceous ore*, called also *bog iron ore*, found in various parts of the state, evidently deposited by alluvial and diluvial action, in the clay or gravel. It is principally used for castings.

4th. *The Hematitic ore*, frequently occurring in crystals of fantastic and beautiful forms. This ore occurs extensively in Richmond, Orange, Ulster, Putnam, Dutchess, Columbia, Warren and Wayne counties. It is also found in smaller quantities in Rockland and Westchester. It usually makes its appearance in the lower limestones of the transition system. When combined with the magnetic oxide, it improves its quality.

5th. *The Carburet of Iron*, called also Black lead, Plumbago and graphite, occurs abundantly in Dutchess county, and in considerable quantities in Essex and Clinton counties.

Lead is found, in immense quantities, at Rossie and its vicinity, in St. Lawrence county, and less abundantly in the Shawangunk mountains, in Sullivan and Ulster, and in Dutchess, Columbia, Lewis and Monroe counties. It does not seem to be confined to any particular geological era, occurring in nearly all the formations.

Zinc and *Copper* occur in various parts of the state, but not in sufficient quantities to be of much practical value.

Arsenic has been discovered in Putnam county.

Manganese, in the form of manganese wad, occurs in Columbia, Lewis and Dutchess counties, and is used to some extent for bleaching. Manganesian garnet is found in New York county.

Barytes and *Strontian* are abundant in Schoharie and Jefferson, and probably exist in some of the other counties.

Alum, principally in the form of efflorescence, is found in several parts of the state.

The existence and value of the deposits of *gypsum*, and *water lime*, has already been noticed, in speaking of the Onondaga salt group.

Serpentine and its allied minerals, *soapstone, talc, carbonate, hydrate* and *sulphate* of *magnesia*, (Epsom salts,) together with *asbestus* and *amianthus*, occur abundantly in Putnam, Orange, Westchester, Jefferson and St. Lawrence, and in considerable quantities in Monroe, Orleans, Genesee, Albany, Cayuga, Essex, Rensselaer and Niagara counties.

Those minerals, which are only of interest to the mineralogist, are enumerated under the counties in which they occur.

MINERAL SPRINGS. These are of various kinds.

1. *Chalybeate Springs.* The most celebrated of these, are those of Saratoga county, which are fully described in another part of the work. There are a few, but of no great strength or notoriety, in other parts of the state.

2. *Sulphur Springs.* These are widely disseminated. Those at Avon, in Livingston county, have attained the greatest celebrity. Those in the vicinity of Rochester, Monroe county, and Chittenango, Madison county, are perhaps next in importance. The State Geologists report sulphur springs in twenty-eight counties of the state

3. *Brine Springs* occur in every part of the Onondaga salt formation, and are also found, though of less strength, in other parts of the state. They are supposed to be impregnated by deposits of rock salt, at some distance below the surface. Those in the towns of Salina and Montezuma are the most important and valuable.

4. *Acid Springs*, or those in which the water is strongly impregnated with sulphuric acid, are found in Genesee, Erie and Orleans counties.

GEOLOGY AND MINERALOGY. 31

5. *Petrifying Springs*, so highly charged with carbonate of lime as to deposit it upon whatever the water falls, and thus give it a coating of limestone, are found in Madison and Saratoga counties.

6. *Oil Springs*, the waters of which are covered with a thick pellicle of Petroleum, or mineral oil, are found in Cattaraugus and Allegany counties.

7. *Springs evolving Nitrogen Gas.* The most celebrated of these are those of New Lebanon, in Columbia county, and of Hoosick, in Rensselaer county. There is also one, of some note, near Canoga, in Seneca county.

8. *Springs evolving Carburetted Hydrogen, or inflammable gas.* These abound in the neighborhood of Lake Erie, and the Niagara river. The village of Fredonia, and the light house at Barcelona, in Chautauque county, are illuminated by them. Springs of the same character are also found in Dutchess, Oneida and Monroe counties.

Marl, a valuable fertilizing agent, exists in vast beds in Madison, Monroe, Columbia, Dutchess, Greene, Onondaga, Ontario, Orange and Wayne counties, and in considerable abundance in Rensselaer, Washington, Saratoga, Albany, Schoharie, Herkimer, Cortland, Oneida, St. Lawrence, Niagara and Erie counties.

Peat is less widely distributed. It occurs, however, on Long Island, and in Richmond, Rockland, Orange, Sullivan, Putnam, Westchester, Columbia, Clinton, Oneida and Cattaraugus counties. The attention of farmers should be directed to this, on account of its value, both for fuel, and as a manure.

The *gneiss* and *granite* of the primary region, as we have already remarked, form elegant and durable building materials. The *Potsdam sandstone*, from its power of resisting atmospheric influence, and the facility with which it may be cut in any desired shape, is highly valued for building. The *Chemung gray sandstone* and the *red sandstone* of Rockland county are also prized by builders. The *Medina sandstone* is more liable to decomposition, but is used to some extent.

The limestone formations furnish a great number of varieties of *marble*, suitable not only for architectural purposes, but for the arts. The most celebrated ornamental varieties are the black marble of Glen's falls, which equals any of the foreign varieties; the Chazy black marble, considered as fully equal to the best Irish; the variegated marbles of St. Lawrence and Rockland counties; the slate and dove colored of Otsego, Oneida and Onondaga; the birdseye of the Champlain group; and the white marble of Westchester, Dutchess, Columbia, Washington and St. Lawrence counties. The Singsing marble is largely employed, as a building stone, in New York city. The *serpentine* rocks, in several parts of the state, afford slabs, of sufficient size, to be used for the manufacture of furniture. The Utica *slate*, and some of the slate formations in the northern part of the state, furnish slates of excellent quality, both for roofing and writing.

The gray sandstones and conglomerate of the Champlain and Erie groups, furnish *grindstones* of superior quality, and from the Shawangunk grits, *millstones* have been manufactured, which compared well with the French buhrstone.

It will be seen, by the brief sketch we have given of the Geology and Mineralogy of the state of New York, that her mineral resources are equal to her agricultural, commercial and manufacturing facilities. True, she does not possess coal, or so far as has yet been ascertained, the precious metals; but the former is abundantly supplied by the neighboring states of Pennsylvania and Ohio; and the latter, paradoxical as it may seem, have never conduced to the wealth, or prosperity of any state, which has possessed them.

Her mines of iron, lead and plumbago; her salt-springs and beds of water lime and gypsum; and her quarries of granite, sandstone and marble are, to her citizens, a more valuable inheritance than the gold and silver mines of Mexico, and will confer upon them a greater and more lasting prosperity.

II. BOTANY.

It would be entering into a far more elaborate view of the subject than the limits of this work permit, to trace out even an abstract of the vegetable wealth of New York. From its geographical position, diversity of soil, surface, and climate; its holding a middle place between the north and south, nearly all the great features of the United States flora are here produced. Immense forests still occupy the uncultivated regions north and west, consisting mainly of pine, oak and beech, while the chestnut, hickory and maple, with a host of other less numerous, but not less valuable trees, are scattered over its territory.

The mountain sides and woods are clothed with an undergrowth of shrubs; as the whortleberry, rhododendron and mountain laurel; under whose shade, and in the open fields, flourish hundreds of more humble herbaceous plants, among which will be found many that are rare and curious, as well as of great beauty and utility.

Anemone, Ranunculus, and Violets, often before the snow has entirely disappeared, put forth their blossoms in every sheltered nook of wood and meadow. These, with the cowslip (*Caltha palustris*), the woodbine (*Aquilegia*), bloodroot (*Sanguinaria*), and many of that wide spread tribe, the *Cruciferae*, or crosslike plants, serve to mark the opening spring. As the season advances, nature assumes much gayer colors. The beautiful blue Lupine (*Lupinus perennis*), Desmodiums, and the wild Sensitive plant (*Cassia nictitans*), whose leaves close together, when touched by the hand, are frequent on sandy soils.

Common in our swamps and boggy ground, is the Side Saddle flower, or Hunter's cup (*Sarracenia*), bearing a single, nodding, dark red flower, a wonder by itself, but more so, when viewed in connection with the singular structure of its leaves. These are not flat, as in other plants, but hollow, and somewhat pitcher shaped, arranged in a circle around the base of the stem, their open mouths turned upwards to catch the falling rains. At the orifice of each leaf is a broad lip, furnished with short stiff hairs pointing downwards, and forming a trap, for numerous insects, that seek the water, always contained in them. A luckless fly once entered, it is impossible for him to return; and he is forced to go onwards, until dropping, he perishes in the water beneath. Of what use, in the economy of the plant, these dead insects are (the cup being often half filled with them) is not, as yet, well known; but possibly they serve in some degree as nutriment.

Another plant well worthy of notice for its elegance and exquisite fragrance, is the white Pond Lily (*Nymphæa odorata*). The roots, which are rough and knotty, creep along the muddy bottoms of ponds and slow-flowing streams; while the large round leaves, of a bright and glossy green, cover the water above, in many instances for acres, contrasting well with the pure white flowers. Like the primrose and wonderful four o'clock, which almost serve to mark the hour, Nymphæa expands its buds early in the morning, and whether the day be clear or cloudy, before noon, regularly closes, and sinks beneath the surface. The leaf stalks are long and flexile, varying with the depth of water, and forming, as every wandering school boy knows, a secure retreat for fish.

Spatter Dock, or Yellow Pond Lily (*Nuphar advena*), is common in every ditch, but an allied genus (*Nelumbium*), or Sacred Bean, is rare; Big Sodus Bay, Lake Ontario, is the only known locality in the state.

In shallow water, along the Hudson, above the Highlands, and through the western counties, is the *Vallisneria* or Tape Grass, remarkable for the peculiar spiral form of its stems, which always permit the flower to float upon the surface whatever may be the rise of tide.

Besides those just mentioned, the more frequent plants of low grounds and margins of streams are the Iris, Sweet Flag, or Calamus root (*Acorus calamus*), Yellow Lily, (*Lilium Canadense*), Forget-me-not (*Myosotis*), whose bright blue flowers continue from early spring till frost, Arrow leaf (*Sagittaria*), Cat-tail flag (*Typha palustris*), with numerous varieties of Rush (*Juncus*), and Sedges (*Carex*), the last sometimes eaten by cattle, for want of more nutritious food. Virgin's bower (*Clematis Virginiana*), a handsome, indigenous vine creeping over bushes and fences is often cultivated for its quick growth and abundant blossoms.

In the Lobelia tribe, we have the Cardinal Flower (*L. Cardinalis*), noted for the splendor of its scarlet blossoms; Indian Tobacco (*L. Inflata*), the grand panacea of the Thompsonians; the *L. Syphilitica*, also used by them; Water Gladiole (*L. Dortmanni*), much less common than either of the preceding, and *L. Nuttallii*, confined to the sandy swamps of Long Island.

In the deep recesses of woods and swamps, the Arum and the Orchis tribes are met with. Of the former, Indian Turnip (*Arum triphyllum*), well known for its acrid root, and Water Arum (*Calla palustris*), are good examples.

The Orchids, from the strange forms and brilliant colors of their contorted flowers, are well worth the trouble it takes to cultivate them. *Platanthera grandiflora*, or tall purple Orchis, is one of the most beautiful, although *Arethusa*, *Pogonia*, our three species of Lady's Slipper (*Cypripedium*), and the graceful White Lady's Tress, are not less deserving a place in the garden.

Plants of the great group *Compositæ*, to which the Asters and Goldenrods belong, forming one ninth of our entire flora, are characteristic of the autumnal vegetation. Some Asters are fine garden plants, but, like the whole class, chiefly interesting for their gorgeous appearance. From the sweet scented golden-rod (*Solidago odora*), a fragrant volatile oil, sometimes used in medicine, is distilled. Yarrow (*Achillea*), Boneset (*Eupatorium perfoliatum*), Tansy (*Tanacetum vulgare*), and some few others are medicinal; most of the order, however, are but weeds, as every farmer who has had his lands overrun with Canada thistle and pigweed, can testify. The seeds of the Sunflower (*Helianthus annuus*) yield, under pressure, an oil similar in quality and uses to that of linseed. Jerusalem Artichokes are the tuberous roots of the *Helianthus tuberosus*. They are too watery to be used as food. Neither of the two last are natives of the state, but they are occasionally found in waste places near habitations.

Angelica, Sweet Cicely (*Osmorrhiza*), Sanicle (*Sanicula*), Cicuta (*Cicuta maculata*), types of the order of umbelliferous plants are well known; Wild Carrot (*Daucus carota*), poisonous in its wild state, is, when cultivated, the esculent carrot of the garden.

Poison Hemlock (*Conium maculatum*), by a draught of which Socrates is related to have died, with some other introduced and native plants, as the Milkweed (*Asclepias*), Plantain, Canada Thistle, Poke weed (*Phytolacca decandra*), Thorn Apple (*Datura Stramonium*), Oxeye Daisy (*Chrysanthemum*), and Dandelion (*Leontodon*), belong to a class that might be named "wayside plants," from their commonly occupying a position beside the roads and fences.

Plantain (*Plantago major*) has been called by the Indians "white man's footstep," because it is found wherever he has placed his dwelling; and with a faithfulness not equalled in the human race, is constantly in his path. The more it is trodden down the wider does it spread, and the more luxuriantly does it grow.

The Eglantine or Sweet Brier (*Rosa Rubiginosa*), such a general favorite with the old and young, is a member of the large family *Rosaceæ*, of which our state can boast many representatives. Among these are the Rose, seven or eight species of Blackberry (*Rubus*), Strawberry (*Fragaria*), Fivefinger (*Potentilla*), (one species of which (*P. tridentata*) is a little Alpine plant found only on the summits of the mountains), Thornbush (*Cratægus*), Service berry or Shad bush (*Amelanchier*), Wild Plum and lofty Wild Cherry. The last is used in cabinet work, being as dark and heavy as some inferior kinds of mahogany.

Of Labiatæ or the mint tribe, Spearmint, or Julep weed (*Mentha Viridis*), Peppermint (*M. Piperita*), Penny Royal, Catnep, Balm, (*Melissa*) and Mountain mint (*Pycnanthemum incanum*), are very generally known.

A few of the Nightshade tribe (*Solanaceæ*), are natives of the state, such as Bittersweet (*Solanum dulcamara*), deadly Nightshade (*S. Nigrum*), and Winter Cherry (*Physalis*), which are all of suspicious appearance, and reputed poisonous.

Buckwheat is one of the *Polygonaceæ*; and of the same order are the common Sorrel (*Rumex acetosella*), Water Dock (*R. crispus*), and Smart weed (*Polygonum*).

Shrubby plants are numerous; many species are highly ornamental; others, from their virtues, are admitted into the Pharmacopœas; others, again, are poisonous. Of this latter class are some of the species of Sumach (*Rhus*); the most virulent of these, is the Swamp Sumach (*Rhus venenata*), simple contact with which, or mere exposure to its effluvium, being sufficient in many cases to cause a most painful eruption on the skin. Mercury, or Poison Oak, is less active than the preceding, but sufficiently so, to cause all those who are easily affected by vegetable poisons to shun its neighborhood. The leaves of the common Sumach (*R. glabra*), are used in the manufacture of morocco.

The large flowering Rose bay (*Rhododendron maximum*) is a shrub from six to twelve feet in height, with broad and thick leaves, growing in tufts from the extremities of the branches; and large showy flowers, in dense terminal clusters. It is said to be the most beautiful flowering shrub in the United States, and is sometimes cultivated in lawns and door-yards.

The wild upright Honeysuckle (*Azalea*, or *Rhododendron nudiflorum*), and the broad leaved Laurel (*Kalmia latifolia*) make the woods gay by the profusion of their purple blossoms. The dwarf Laurel (*Kalmia angustifolia*), known also by the names sheep-poison and lamb-kill, is a pretty little bush, but has a bad reputation, the leaves being said to poison sheep. The last two are common in the southern counties, while in the west the glaucous Kalmia takes their place.

The Elder (*Sambucus Canadensis*) and the Hazel (*Corylus Americanus*), prized for its nuts, which, though sweeter, do not equal in size, the filbert of Europe, are to be seen in every coppice. Whortleberries are the product of several species of *Vaccinium*. The earliest in the market is the dwarf blue Whortleberry (*V. Pennsylvanica*), growing in sandy woods, and on hill sides and summits of the mountains. The Bilberry (*V. corymbosum*) is frequent in swamps and wet shady woods. The agreeably acid Cranberry, an almost indispensable article of food, is the fruit of two species of *Vaccinium*, (*V. oxycoccus and V. macrocarpon*). The former abounds in the northern and western parts of the state, and the latter, which is the common American cranberry seen in the market, is most frequent in the south.

The banks of every stream and rivulet are fringed with the Willow (*Salix*), Alder (*Alnus*), and Spice wood (*Laurus Benzoin*). This last is a shrub easily recognized, by its smooth brittle branches and glossy foliage. The bark has an agreeably spicy taste; and a decoction of the young twigs is often used, as a medicinal drink, in the spring of the year. In the moist thickets, conspicuous from its red fruit, is the Winter berry (*Prinos*), once used for the cure of fever and ague; but, for this purpose, it is much inferior to the Dogwood (*Cornus florida*), which possesses many of the peculiar properties of Peruvian Bark.

Witch Hazel (*Hamamelis Virginica*) is, in the eyes of the superstitious, a most notable shrub, because, in the moment of parting with its foliage, it puts forth a profusion of gaudy yellow blossoms, giving to November, the counterfeited appearance of spring.

The most important vegetable productions of the state are undoubtedly the forest trees, of which we can boast numerous species. The cone bearers (*Coniferae*), which are nearly all evergreen trees, are well represented in our Flora. We have no less than nine species of Pines. Pitch Pine (*Pinus rigida*) forms nearly all the woodland of Long Island, and covers a great extent of barren country, west of Albany; it is serviceable for little else than fuel and making charcoal. White, or Weymouth pine (*P. strobus*) is met with in most parts of the state, but chiefly on the head waters of the Hudson, Delaware, Allegany, and rivers entering into Lake Ontario: indeed nearly all the western counties were once covered with dense forests of this noble tree, nor can we wonder that it is rapidly disappearing beneath the axe, when 65,000 acres must be annually cleared, to meet the demand for lumber, 650,000,000 feet of which are obtained from New York alone. Hemlock Spruce (*P. Canadensis*) affords an inferior kind of timber, lasting well if protected from the weather; but in exposed situations it warps, splits and soon decays. The bark is extensively employed in tanning, and although inferior to oak, it makes very good leather. Balm of Gilead, or Balsam Fir (*P. Balsamea*), is not found lower than the Catskill mountains; but is abundant in the northern counties, especially among the Essex mountains. The turpentine, sold under the name of *Canada Balsam*, is obtained by opening the blisters which form beneath the bark. Black Spruce (*P. nigra*) is employed principally for the yards and lighter spars of vessels, for which purpose it is admirably fitted by its lightness and strength. White Spruce (*P. alba*) is a small tree found in swamps, and on the sides of the northern mountains; rarely south of Catskill. The Indians split the small tough roots into fibres for sewing their bark canoes. Tamarack (*P. Pendula*) differs from all other pines, in its leaves, which fall at the approach of winter.

Belonging to the same natural family (*Coniferæ*) are the Red Cedar (*Juniperus Virginiana*), noted for its great durability; White cedar (*Cupressus Thuyoides*) constituting the cedar swamps of Long Island; Arbor Vitæ (*Thuya occidentalis*), conspicuous along the banks of the Hudson for its cone like growth; although it is sometimes found in swampy places, and then is known by the name of White cedar. We have also the Yew (*Taxus Canadensis*), which is very different from the yew tree of Europe, though identical in Botanical character—with us it is a shrub of humble growth, trailing over rocks, and found in woods, beneath the shelter of taller evergreens.

The Oaks are almost, if not quite, equal in value to the Pines, and much more numerous, as regards species. White Oak (*Quercus alba*) is always considered one of our most valuable timber trees. The wood is of great strength and durability, and is used when these qualities are required, as in ship building and heavy frame work for machinery. When sawed into plank, the wheelwright, the wagon-maker, and indeed, almost every mechanic, uses it more or less in his labor. Black Oak (*Q. tinctoria*) furnishes Quercitron bark, an article of export, and used in dyeing; Scarlet Oak (*Q. coccinea*), and Black Chestnut Oak (*Q. montana*), are much prized by the tanner. Other species are Willow Oak (*Q. phellos*), with narrow leaves; Chinquapin (*Q. prinos*), a dwarf species bearing edible acorns; Swamp White Oak (*Q. bicolor*); Mossy Cup Oak (*Q. olivæformis*); Pin Oak (*Q. palustris*) and Black Jack (*Q. nigra*); the last is indigenous to Long Island only.

The White Elm (*Ulmus Americana*) is a most graceful species, and when growing in moist rich soil one of the largest of our forest trees. The Slippery Elm (*U. fulva*), a smaller tree, growing on higher ground, is well known for the mucilaginous properties of its inner bark. Thomas' Elm (*U. racemosa*), so named from the person who first described it, is rather frequent on river banks in the middle and western parts of the state.

Of the Ash (*Fraxinus*), we have only three species, the White, Black and Grey. White Ash (*F. Americana*) has elastic, tough wood, and is used in the manufacture of carriages, agricultural implements, &c. From its splitting freely, it is much employed by the cooper for hoops.

Sugar Maple (*Acer saccharinum*) is a large and handsome tree, well known as furnishing the maple sugar which is obtained, by boiling down the sap, procured from the trees, during the months of February and March—Birdseye and Curled Maple are accidental varieties in the wood of this species. Red Maple (*A. rubrum*), White or Silver leaved Maple (*A. dasycarpum*), Mountain Maple, or Moose wood (*A. Spicatum and A. Pennsylvanicum*), are the only other species.

The Walnut tribe are valuable, both for food and timber. Black Walnut (*Juglans nigra*), and Butternut (*J. cinerea*), occur in most parts of the state. Shell bark Hickory (*Carya alba*) bears the common white walnut, so pleasant to crack by the winter fireside. The bark of this tree separates in long flat scales, with loose, detached ends, giving the trunk a ragged appearance; Moker-nut (*C. tomentosa*), Pig-nut (*C. porcina*) and Bitter-nut (*C. amara*) are the only remaining New York species.

The Beech (*Fagus*) and Chestnut (*Castanea*) are both noble growing trees. The wood of the Beech is heavy and compact, but not durable. Chestnut, on the contrary, though light and open grained, bears exposure, for a great length of time, without decay. The American Chestnut is considered a variety of the European, differing only in its smaller and sweeter nuts.

The Canoe Birch is the *Betula papyracea*. From the bark of this species, which readily peels off in long thin sheets, and slips of cedar, the Indians manufacture their canoes. The wood of the Black Birch (*Betula lenta*), is considerably used in cabinet making. The Dwarf Birch (*Betula nana*) is an Alpine shrub, found only on the high mountains of Essex county. The Sycamore (*Platanus*), the Poplars, and the Willows, are of little value, except as shade trees. Not so the Locust (*Robinia pseudo-acacia*), a tree of rapid growth and graceful form. Its wood is exceedingly hard and nearly indestructible, and is mostly used for trenails, and gate posts, and in ship-building. It is not a native of the state, but is cultivated for sale, and as an ornamental tree.

The Tulip tree (*Liriodendron Tulipifera*) is the pride of our northern forests for its majestic growth, symmetrical form, and handsome foliage. It not unfrequently rises to the height of seventy feet without a branch, and is covered in May or June with innumerable tulip shaped flowers. The Magnolia (*Magnolia glauca*) is found only in the swamps of Long Island, and there but sparingly. Its flowers exhale a heavy, but not unpleasant, perfume. One other species, the Cucumber tree (*M. acuminata*), is not uncommon in the western parts of the state, and is thus named from the appearance of the seed cone.

Of vast importance, as furnishing directly or indirectly the food of man and animals, are the grasses; and no class of plants is so widely distributed as this. They form the principal portion of the herbage of the earth, giving to the hills and plains their lovely green.

Though our Flora contains many native species, only a small number are of value, our meadow grasses being, with few exceptions, of foreign origin. The principal of these are, Timothy (*Phleum pratense*), making the best of hay; Sweet Vernal grass (*Anthoxanthum odoratum*), which, when half withered, gives out a pleasant odor of vanilla; Meadow grass (*Poa pratensis*), Blue grass (*P. compressa*) and Rough grass (*P. trivialis*), most of which have spread over all our pasture grounds. Wheat (*Triticum*), Rye (*Secale*) and Oats (*Avena*), are extensively cultivated in all parts of the state. *Zizania aquatica*, or wild rice, a favorite food of the Indians, and affording sustenance to myriads of wild fowl, is a native of the northern counties.

The Wild Oat and Chess (*Bromus*), into which our farmers wrongly believe that wheat and rye degenerate, are common. *Phragmites*, the largest grass of the northern states, looking at a distance like broom corn, grows by the river side, and borders of swamps and ponds.

Some grasses are peculiar to the sands; their matted roots, forming a thick sod, prevent the loose soil from being carried away, by the water or wind. Many others, by their annual decay, aid in fertilizing the soil, that would otherwise be arid and unproductive.

Ferns and Fernlike plants occupy a wide extent of territory. Most common of all is the Brake (*Pteris*), under cover of which the sportsman is sure to find the rabbit, or the partridge. Maiden Hair (*Adiantum*), a delicate fern, with dark brown polished stems, is not uncommon. The Walking Fern (*Asplenium rhizophyllum*) is remarkable for striking root from the extremities of the fronds. The Climbing Fern (*Lygodium*) is the only species of the tribe, with a twining stem, found in so high a latitude. The tall Osmunda (*O. cinnamomea*) grows in large bunches, in damp woods and low grounds; sometimes attaining the height of a man.

Club Moss (*Lycopodium*), a creeping evergreen, is in great request at Christmas time, to form festoons and wreaths.

The Scouring Rush (*Equisetum*) is used for polishing wood and metals.

In the report of the recent Geological and Botanical survey, ordered by the legislature, the whole number of species of flowering plants, in the state, is said to be about 1450. Of these, 1200 are herbaceous, and 150 may be regarded as ornamental. Of woody plants there are 250 species, including about 80 that attain to the stature of trees. Of plants that are reputed medicinal, we have (native and naturalized) 160 species. The naturalized plants exceed 160 species.

We must here leave this short notice of New York plants, though we have, by no means, exhausted the materials, nor even touched upon many, that are most frequently met with, in a morning walk. Those who would pursue the study must seek their information in two large volumes, written by Dr. Torrey, which form the Botanical part of the Natural History of New York.

III. ZOOLOGY.
Class I. *Mammalia*.

By mammalia are meant, all those animals having warm blood, a double heart, that is, one with two auricles and two ventricles, and bringing forth their young alive and suckling them. Being, with a few exceptions, four footed animals, they are frequently called quadrupeds. Naturalists have divided these into a number of distinct orders, of which only *five* are found in this state.

These are 1st, *Marsupiata*, or pouched animals. One species, only, belonging to this order, is found in the state, viz. the opossum.

2d, *Carnivora*, or flesh eaters. Of these we have five species of bats; the mole and shrew mole; six species of shrews; the black bear; the raccoon; wolverine; skunk; fisher; weasel, or black cat, called also Pennant's martin; the pine martin, or American sable; the small and the brown weasel; the New York ermine, or ermine weasel; the mink, or minx otter; the common otter; the dog, about thirty varieties, five of which are native; the common wolf, two varieties, the grey, and the black; the panther; the northern, or Canada lynx; the wild cat, or bay lynx; the seal; the hooded seal; and perhaps, the walrus.

3d, *Rodentia*, or gnawers. Among these are the grey fox; the red, striped, and flying squirrel; the woodchuck, or Maryland marmot; the deer mouse, or Labrador rat; the beaver; the musquash, or muskrat; the porcupine; the Norway, or brown rat; two species of black rat; the common mouse; the jumping mouse; six species of meadow mice; the grey rabbit; and the northern, or prairie hare.

4th, *Ungulata:* animals whose toes are covered with a horny case, or hoof. Of these, we have the hog; the horse; the ass; the ox; the goat, the sheep; the American or fallow deer; the moose; the stag, and the reindeer.

5th, *Cetacea*, or the whale tribe. The only species of this order, known to exist in the waters of the state, are, the right whale; the sperm whale; the beaked whale, or rorqual; the broad nosed whale; the social whale, or black whale-fish, called also the howling whale, and bottle head; the common porpoise; the grampus, or thrasher, also called the blackfish whale; and the sea porpoise.

Fossil Mammalia. Of these, but three species, it is believed, have been found, viz, 1st the fossil elephant, of which but a single tooth has been discovered.

2d, The American elephant, of which several teeth have been found in Monroe county.

3d, The mastodon, frequently, but improperly, called mammoth. Remains of this animal, and indeed skeletons nearly entire have been discovered in some 15 or 20 localities in the state, in Orange, Ulster, Monroe, Suffolk, Livingston, Chautauque, Albany, Cattaraugus, Genesee, and Niagara counties,

Class II. *Aves—Birds.*

Six orders of birds are found in the state, viz. 1st, *Accipitres*, birds of prey, including eagles, hawks, vultures, and owls.

2d, **Passeres**, birds of passage. These include most of those birds with which we are familiar, and whose departure for a more southern clime in autumn, renders winter more cheerless, as their return in spring, makes the approaching summer more joyous and delightful.

3d, *Gallinæ*, the cock tribe, including not only our domesticated fowls, but the wild turkey, grouse, prairie hen, &c.

4th, *Grallæ*, waders. This includes all those long legged birds which obtain their subsistence on the borders of streams; the plover, crane, heron, poke, &c.

5th, *Lobipedes*, lobefooted birds; the coot, dipper, &c.

6th, *Natatores*, swimmers. This includes loons, gulls, gannets, wild ducks and geese, &c.

The following catalogue embraces all the birds, of these different orders, known to exist in the state.

Order I. ACCIPITRES.
[Birds of prey,]

Family 1. *Vulturidæ.*
Vulture tribe.
Turkey buzzard.
Family 2. *Falconidæ.*
Falcon tribe.
Golden eagle.
Brown or bald eagle,
American fish hawk,
Rough legged buzzard,
Red tailed "
Red shouldered "
Broad winged "
Swallow tailed hawk,
Duck "
Pigeon "
American sparrow "
Slate colored "
Cooper's "
American goshawk,
Marsh harrier,
Family 3. *Strigidæ.*
Owl tribe.
Great horned owl,
Snowy "
Hawk "
Little screech "
Great grey, "
Long eared "
Short eared "
Barred "
Acadian "
American barn "

Order II. PASSERES.
[Birds of passage.]

Family 1. *Caprimulgidæ.*
Whippoorwill tribe.
Whippoorwill,
Night hawk.
Family 2 *Hirundinæ.*
Swallow tribe.
Chimney swallow,
Purple martin,
White bellied swallow,
Bank "
Barn "
Cliff "
Family 3. *Ampelidæ.*
Fruit eaters.
Black throated waxwing,
Cedar bird.

Family 4. *Alcedinidæ.*
King fisher tribe.
Belted king fisher.
Family 5. *Trochilidæ.*
Humming bird tribe.
Red throated humming bird
Family 6. *Certhidæ.*
Wren tribe.
White breasted nuthatch,
Red bellied "
Brown creeper,
Varied creeping Warbler,
House Wren,
Wood "
Mocking "
Marsh "
Winter "
Short billed "
Family 7. *Paridæ.*
Tomtit tribe.
Crested tit,
Black cap "
Carolina "
Family 8. *Sylviadæ.*
Blue bird tribe.
Golden crested kinglet,
Ruby crowned "
Blue bird.
Family 9. *Merulidæ.*
Thrush tribe.
Common mocking bird,
Brown thrush,
Cat bird,
American Robin,
Wood thrush,
Hermit "
Olive backed "
Wilson's "
Family 10. *Motacillidæ.*
Titlark tribe.
American titlark,
New York water thrush,
{Oven bird, or
{Golden crowned wagtail.
Family 11. *Sylvicolidæ.*
Warblers.
Yellow throat,
Mourning Warbler,
Worm eating "
Whistling "
Blue winged, "
Golden "
Tennessee "
Nashville "
Orange crowned, "
Myrtle bird, "
Red poll "

Spotted Canada Warbler,
Spotted "
Blue grey "
Blackburnian "
Bay breasted "
Black poll "
Prairie "
Blue, yellow backed "
Black throated, blue, "
Summer yellow bird,
Black throated green "
Pine "
Chestnut sided "
Hemlock "
Cape May "
Kentucky, "
Hooded "
Green, black capped "
Blue grey gnat-catcher,
Family 12. *Muscicapidæ.*
Fly catchers.
American redstart,
Small green crested fly catcher,
Yellow bellied fly catcher,
Wood pewee,
Phebe bird,
Olive sided kingbird,
Great crested "
Family 13. *Vireonidæ.*
Greenlet tribe.
Yellow throated greenlet,
Solitary "
White eyed "
Warbling "
Red eyed "
Yellow breasted chat.
Family 14. *Laniidæ.*
Shrikes.
Northern butcherbird.
Family 15. *Corvidæ.*
Crow tribe.
Blue jay,
Canada "
Magpie,
Common crow,
Raven,
Fish crow,
Family 16. *Quiscalidæ.*
Oriole tribe.
Common crow blackbird,
Rusty " "
Meadow lark.
Golden oriole,
Orchard "
Red winged "
Cow bunting,

ZOOLOGY. 41

Boblink, or Ricebird.
Family 17. *Fringillidæ.*
  Finches.
Blue Grosbeak,
Rose breasted grosbeak,
Snowbird,
Fox colored sparrow,
Song   "
{ Bay winged, "
{ or grassbird,
White throated "
White crowned "
Black throated bunting,
Yellow winged "
Varied   "
Field   "
Chippingbird,
Tree bunting,
Savannah   "
Blue striped "
Seaside finch,
Quail head,
Swamp Finch,
{ Yellowbird or
{ American gold finch,
Pine finch,
Lesser redpole,
Mealy   "
Crested purple finch,
Cardinal Grosbeak,
{ Chewink or
{ Ground robin,
Indigo bird,
Red   "
Black winged red bird,
Lapland snow "
White   "
Horned lark,
Pine bull finch,
American crossbill,
White winged "
  Family 18. *Picidæ.*
    [Borers.]
    Woodpecker tribe.
Crested woodpecker
Red headed "
Hairy   "
Downy   "
Yellow billed "
Red   "
Arctic   "
Banded   "
{ Golden winged "
{ or High hole.
  Family 19. *Cuculidæ.*
    Cuckoo tribe.
Yellow billed cuckoo,
Black   "   "
  Family 20. *Columbidæ*
    Pigeon tribe.
Wild Pigeon,
Carolina turtle dove.

Order III. GALLINÆ.

Family 1. *Phasianidæ.*
  Pheasant tribe.
Wild Turkey.
  Introduced and domesticated.
Peacock,
Guinea fowl,
Common cock.
Family 2. *Tetraonidæ.*
  Grouse tribe.
American quail,
Common partridge,
Ruffed grouse,

{ Pinnated grouse,
{ or Heath hen, prairie hen,
Spruce grouse.

Order IV. GRALLÆ.
  [Waders.]

Family 1. *Charadridæ.*
  Plovers.
American ring plover,
Piping   "
Wilson's   "
Kill deer   "
Golden   "
Whistling   "
Turnstone   "
American oyster catcher.
  Family 2. *Gruidæ.*
    Crane tribe.
American crane,
Great blue heron,
Great white   "
{ White crested "
{ or White poke,
Blue heron,
Lousiana   "
Green   "
Small bittern,
American   "
Black crowned night heron,
Yellow   "   "   "
  Family 3. *Tantalidæ.*
    Stork tribe.
White ibis,
Glossy   "
  Family 4. *Scolopacidæ,*
    Curlew tribe.
Long billed curlew,
Jack   "
Small Esquimaux "
Long legged sandpiper,
Semi palmated "
Purple   "
Buff breasted "
Curlew   "
Black breasted "
Schinz's   "
Pectoral   "
Red breasted "
Wilson's   "
Sanderling,
Spotted sand lark,
Grey   "
Yellow leg,
{ Solitary Tatler
{ or Jack snipe,
Varied Tatler,
Willet or stone curlew,
Marlin,
Ring tailed marlin,
{ Dowitchee or
{ Red breasted snipe,
Common American snipe,
American wood cock.
  Family 5. *Rallidæ.*
    Rail tribe.
Salt water meadow hen,
Fresh   "   "   "
Mud hen,
New York rail,
Sora   "
Florida Gallinule,
  Family 6. *Recurvirostridæ.*
    Avoset tribe.
Lawyer,
American Avoset.

Family 7. *Phalaropodidæ.*
Red Phalarope,
{ Hyperborean lobefoot, or
{ Sea goose,
Wilson's Holopode.

Order V. LOBIPEDES.
  [Lobe footed birds.]

Family 1. *Podicipidæ.*
  Coot or Dipper tribe.
American coot,
Horned grebe or dipper,
Crested grebe,
Red necked "
Dipper or pied dobchick.

Order VI. NATATORES.
  [Swimmers.]

Family 1, *Alcidæ.*
  Puffin tribe.
Black Guillemot,
Foolish   " or Murre,
Sea Dove,
Arctic Puffin,
Razor bill,
  Family 2. *Colymbidæ.*
    Loon tribe.
Great loon or diver,
Red throated loon
  Family 3. *Procellaridæ.*
    Petrels.
{ Large shearwater, or
{ Puffin,
Little   "
{ Wilson's Petrel, or
{ Mother Carey's chicken,
Fork tailed Petrel.
  Family 4. *Pelicanidæ.*
    Pelican tribe.
Cormorant,
Double crested cormorant,
Brown Pelican,
American Gannet.
  Family 5. *Laridæ.*
    Gull tribe.
Black Skimmer,
Common tern,
Cayenne,   "
Black   "
Marsh   "
Arctic   "
Sandwich   "
Roseate   "
Silvery   "
Winter gull,
Great black backed gull,
Common American "
Laughing   "
Bonaparte's "
Fork tailed "
{ Three toed   " or
{ Killiwake,
Arctic hawk gull,
Pomarine   "
  Family 6. *Anatidæ.*
    Goose and Duck tribes.
Buff breasted shelldrake,
Red   "   "
Hooded   "
Canvass back duck,
Red head   "
Broad bill   "
Creek   "
Bastard   "

Pied   duck,
Ruddy   "
Old wife   "
Buffle headed "
Whistler,
Harlequin   "
Eider   "
King   "
Surf duck or coot,

Broad billed coot, or Butter bill,
White winged coot,
Wood duck,
Blue winged teal,
Green   "   "
Pintailed duck,
Shoveller, or spoonbill,
Grey duck, or Gadwall,

Black duck,
American widgeon, or Bald pate,
European widgeon,
Wild goose,
White fronted goose,
Brant,
American swan.

Class III. *Reptiles.*

There are but three orders of reptiles found in the state, viz.

1st, *Chelonia.* The turtle tribe. Among the animals belonging to this order are the green turtle, which, though a native of warm climates, occasionally makes its appearance in the waters of New York bay, and Long Island sound; the leather turtle, a gigantic species; the soft shell turtle found in the Mohawk, and in the lakes; the snapping turtle; the salt water terrapin, or mud turtle; the smooth terrapin, which resembles the preceding in its appearance and habits; the painted tortoise; the spotted tortoise or speckled turtle; the wood or fresh water terrapin; the red bellied terrapin; Muhlenburg's tortoise; the geographic, and the pseudo-geographic tortoise, both distinguished by the geometric lines upon their shells; the mud tortoise, found only in the southern counties; the musk tortoise, also called mud turtle, and mud terrapin; the common box, or checkered, tortoise, also called box turtle; and Blanding's box tortoise.

2d, *Sauria.* The lizard tribe. There are but two species of this tribe, known to exist in this state, viz. the blue tailed skink or lizard, called also the striped lizard, found in the southern counties; and the brown swift, frequenting the woods, in every part of the state.

3d, *Ophidia.* The serpent tribe. Most of these are harmless, only two species being venomous.

Of the harmless species, we have the common black snake, from three to six feet long; the pilot black snake, or racer, found in the Highlands and Fishkill mountains; the chain snake, also called racer; the milk or chicken snake, also called house snake, checkered adder, &c.; the striped snake; the ring snake, black and red, small; the grass or green snake; the brown water snake, or water adder—this snake has its tail tipped with horn, and is frequently regarded with dread, but without cause; the striped water, green water, or water garter snake; the yellow bellied snake; the small brown snake: the ribbon snake; the red snake, very small, and found under stones and logs; the hog nosed snake, called also deaf adder, spreading adder, &c

The two venomous species are, the copper head, called also red adder, dumb rattlesnake, red viper, &c.; and the northern rattlesnake. The popular belief that the latter add a new rattle every year is erroneous. Instances have been known where there were forty-four of these fibulæ or rattles on the tail of a single snake, and that not of a very large size. They are found abundantly, in the rocky and unsettled portions of the state. The deer and the hog destroy them rapidly—the latter eating them.

Class IV. *Amphibia.*

Animals living both on the land, and in the water. There are but four families of amphibia, in the state.

1st, *Ranidæ.* The frog tribe. The following are all the species of this family in the state: The common bull frog; the large northern bull frog, found in lakes George and Champlain, and their tributaries; the spring frog, the kind most usually eaten; the marsh or pickerel frog, used for bait, and called also, from its spots, tiger, and leopard frog; the shad frog, which makes its appearance in the early spring; the wood frog, a very nimble animal; the hermit spadefoot, a singular animal, between a frog and a toad; the common American toad, a harmless and useful animal; Pickering's hylodes, a very small toad; the peeper or cricket frog, called in Savannah, the Savannah cricket; the northern, or common tree toad; and the squirrel tree toad.

2d, *Salamandridæ.* The salamander tribe. These are usually, though incorrectly, called lizards. Among them are the yellow bellied salamander; the violet colored, the red backed, the painted, the salmon colored, the blotched, the long tailed, the granulated, the striped back, the red, the scarlet, and the blue spotted salamander.

3d, *Sirenidæ.* The triton tribe. Of these we have the tiger triton, with a tongue like a fish; the common spotted; the dusky, and the grey triton.

4th, *Amphiumidæ.* The proteus tribe. The banded proteus, or great water lizard, a very singular animal, having the body of a lizard, and the gills of a fish; and the Alleghany hell-bender, another curious amphibious animal, very voracious, and from 12 to 24 inches in length, are the only species of this family in New York.

Class V. *Fishes.*

The fishes, belonging to the state, are very numerous.

Fishes are divided into two sub-classes, BONY and CARTILAGINOUS. The first sub-class has six orders, viz.

1st, *Pectinibranchi,* having gills arranged regularly, like the teeth of a comb. This order embraces many of our common fish, both in fresh and salt water. Those best known are the perch, bass, bullhead, sheepshead, porgee, pilot fish, mullet, black fish or tautaug, cunner, sucker, mackerel, &c. &c. In all the fishes belonging to this order the rays of the fin are bony. The same arrangement of the gills occurs in the three succeeding orders.

2d, *Abdominal,* those having belly fins and ventrals. This order includes the shad, herring, salmon, trout, catfish, pipe fish, dace, shiner, carp, pike, pickerel, minnow, &c.

This, and the four succeeding orders, have soft rayed fins.

3d, *Jugular,* having shoulder fins, and ventrals attached to the bones of the shoulder. It includes the cod, haddock, hake, halibut, flatfish, flounder, turbot, sole, lumpfish, &c.

4th, *Apodal,* without fins. This order includes the eel and conger.

5th, *Lophobranchi,* those having tufted gills. This order is small, comprising two species of pipe fish and the Hudson river sea horse.

6th, *Plectognathi,* those having the gills concealed under the skin. The balloon fish, puffer, and globe fish are examples of this order.

Sub-class II. CARTILAGINOUS FISHES. These are divided into three orders, viz.

1st. *Eleutheropomi*, those having free gills. This order is represented in the state only by the sturgeon.

2d, *Plagiostoma*, those having the gills attached. This includes the shark and ray tribes.

3d, *Cyclostomi*, those having circular openings on each side of the neck for respiration. This includes the lamprey, frequently called lamper eel.

FOSSIL FISHES. Twenty-five species of these have been enumerated by the Messrs. Redfield. A number of them are extinct species.

The following catalogue contains the names of all the fishes as yet discovered in the waters of this state:

Sub-class I. *Bony Fishes.*

Order I. PECTINIBRANCHI.

[Spine rayed.]
Family 1. *Percidæ.*
Perch family.
American yellow perch,
Rough "
Rough headed " "
Sharp nosed " "
Slender " "
Striped sea bass,
Ruddy "
Little white "
Small black "
White lake "
Black Huron or black bass,
Champlain pickering,
Yellow pike perch,
Grey " "
Tesselated darter,
Groper,
Black sea bass,
Growler,
Fresh water bass,
Black do. "
Obscure do. "
Common pond fish,
Black eared " "
Coachman,
Spineless perch,
Unarmed Uranoscope,
Northern Barracuta,
Cirrous Lepisoma.
Family 2. *Triglidæ.*
Gurnard family.
Web fingered gurnard,
Red "
Banded "
Spinous "
Sea swallow,
Common bullhead,
Brazen "
Smooth browed "
Greenland "
American sea raven,
Small sea scorpion,
Spotted " "
Northern sebastes,
Little star gazer,
American Aspidophore,
Spotted wrymouth,
Two spined stickleback,
New York "

Four spined stickleback,
Many spined "
Family 3. *Scienidæ.*
Sheepshead family.
Lafayette,
Weakfish,
Lake sheepshead,
Silvery Corvina,
Branded "
Sharpfinned "
Black sheepshead,
King fish,
Big drum,
Banded "
Banded Corvina,
Speckled redmouth,
Yellow finned "
Squirrel fish,
Banded pristipoma,
Black triple tail.
Family 4. *Sparidæ.*
Porgee family.
Sheepshead,
Sand porgee,
Rhomboidal "
Aculeated gilthead,
{ Big porgee, or
{ Scup.
Family 5. *Chetodontidæ.*
{ Banded Ephippus, or
{ Three tailed porgee,
Moon fish,
Razor fish.
Family 6. *Scombridæ.*
Mackerel tribe.
Spring Mackerel,
Fall "
Spanish "
Common tunny,
Striped bonito,
Spotted cybium,
{ Silvery hair tail, or
{ Ribbon fish.
Common sword fish,
New York pilot fish,
Northern crab-eater,
Carolina lichia,
Silvery trachinote,
{ Spinous " or
{ Spinous dory,
Black pilot,
Southern caranx,
Yellow "

Spotted caranx,
{ Hair finned blepharis, or
{ Hair finned dory,
{ Rostrate argyreiose or
{ Dory,
Hair finned "
{ Blunt nosed shiner, or
{ Bristly dory,
Banded seriole,
Blue fish,
Bottle headed dolphin,
Spotted lampugus,
Long finned harvest fish,
Short finned "
Family 7. *Teuthidæ.*
Surgeon.
Family 8. *Atherinidæ.*
Dotted silverside,
Slender "
Family 9. *Mugilidæ.*
Mullet family.
Striped mullet,
White "
Rock "
Spotted "
Family 10. *Gobidæ.*
Goby family,
Sea weed blenny,
Radiated shanny,
Six banded chasmodes,
American butter fish,
Thick lipped eel pout,
Bordered " "
Sea wolf,
Variegated goby.
Family 11. *Lophidæ.*
Toad fish family.
American angler,
Gibbous mouse fish,
Smooth "
Short nosed malthea,
Dotted "
Bat "
Common toad fish,
Two spined toad fish.
Family 12. *Labridæ.*
{ Common bergall, or
{ Cunner,
Spotted do.
{ New York tautaug, or
{ Black fish.

ZOOLOGY.

Order II. ABDOMINAL.
[Soft rayed fishes.]

Family 1. *Siluridæ.*
Catfish family.
Oceanic catfish,
Milbert's arius,
Great lake catfish,
Common " or
Horn pout—minister,
Brown catfish,
Black "

Family 2. *Cyprinidæ.*
Carp family.
Common carp,
Gold "
Variegated Bream,
New York chubsucker,
Brilliant "
Long finned "
Gibbous "
Round backed "
Common sucker,
Oneida "
Horned "
Pale "
Mullet "
Black "
Large scaled "
New York shiner,
Black nosed dace,
Spawn eater,
Redfin,
Roach dace,
Shining "
Black headed "
Silvery "
Banded "
Pigmy "
Bay shiner,
Corporaalen,
Sheepshead leblas,
Striped killifish,
Barred "
Big "
Transparent minnow,
Barred "
Champlain "

Family 3. *Esocidæ.*
Pickerel family.
Muskellunge,
Common pickerel,
Varied "
Federation pike,
Banded Garfish,
Bill fish,
New York flying fish,
Single bearded " "
Double " "

Family 4. *Fistularidæ.*
Pipe fish family.
American pipe fish.

Spotted pipe fish,

Family 5. *Salmonidæ.*
Salmon Family,
Brook trout,
Red bellied "
Lake "
Mackinaw Salmon,
Common sea "
American smelt,
Spotted Troutlet,
Argentine,
Lake white fish,
Common shad salmon,
Otsego "

Family 6. *Clupidæ.*
Herring family.
Common herring,
Striped "
Green "
Little "
Satin striped "
Blue "
Brit,
American shad,
American Alewife,
Mossbonker,
Autumnal Herring,
Slender "
Spotted shadine,
Spotted thread herring,
River moon-eye,
Lake "
Saury,
Western Mudfish.

Family 7. *Sauridæ.*
Bony Pikes.
Buffalo bony pike,
Flat nosed " "

Order III. JUGULAR.

Family 1. *Gadidæ.*
Cod family.
American cod,
Power "
Tom "
Haddock,
American hake,
Plain burbot,
Spotted "
Compressed "
New York Pollack,
Green "
Coal fish,
Cusk,
American Codling,
Spotted "

Family 2. *Planidæ.*
Flatfish family.
Halibut,
New York flat fish,
Pigmy "

Rusty flat fish,
Toothed, "
Oblong Flounder,
Long toothed "
Spotted Turbot,
New York sole.

Family 3. *Cyclopteridæ.*
Lump fish.

Family 4. *Echineidæ.*
White tailed remora,
Indian "
Common "

Order IV. APODAL.

Family 1. *Anguillidæ.*
Eel family,
Common eel,
New York "
Beaked "
Sea "
Bullhead "
American conger,
New York ophidium,
American sand launce,
Banded "

Order V. LOPHOBRANCHI.

Family 1. *Syngnathidæ.*
Banded pipe fish,
Green "
Hudson river sea horse.

Order VI. PLECTOGNATHI.

Family 1. *Gymnodontidæ.*
Balloon fish family.
Spot-striped balloon fish,
Unspotted " "
Warty " "
Hairy " "
Common puffer,
Curved "
Lineated "
Small globe fish,
Short head fish,

Family 2. *Balistidæ.*
File fish family.
Orange file fish,
Long finned " "
Massachusetts " "
Thread " "
Long tailed unicorn fish,
Dusky balistes.

Family 3. *Ostraceonidæ.*
Dromedary,
Yale's trunk fish.

Sub-class II. *Cartilaginous Fishes.*

Order I. ELEUTHEROPOMA.

Family *Sturionidæ.*
Lake sturgeon,
Short nosed "
Sharp " "

Order II. PLAGIOSTOMA.

Family 1. *Squalidæ.*
Shark Family.
Threshing shark,
Small blue "
Dusky "
Ground "

Mackerel porbeagle,
Long tailed "
American houndfish,
Basking shark,
Spinous dog fish,
Nurse, "
Hammer head shark,
American angel fish, or
Sea devil,
Common saw fish.

Family 2. *Raiadæ.*
Ray family.
Clear nosed ray,
Spotted sting "
Prickly "

Broad sting ray,
Cow nose "
Hedge hog " "
Whip "
Smooth skate,
Sea devil.

Order III. CYCLOSTOMI.

Family *Petronyzidæ.*
American sea lamprey,
Bluish "
Small lamprey,
Colored mud lamprey,
Plain "

Class VII. *Crustacea.*

The class *Crustacea* embraces those animals having a covering of a dense calcareous substance, adapted to their form, which they usually shed every year, and which is replaced by an exudation from the surface of the animal's body. Ten orders of this class of animals are supposed to exist in the state, though the existence of two of the ten is not determined with certainty.

Order 1st, *Decapoda*, those having ten feet, is the most numerous and best known. It embraces the various species of crab, lobster, fresh-water lobster, and most of the prawns or shrimps. There are in all twenty-seven species of this order.

Order 2d, *Stomapoda*, those having the feet converging towards the jaws, is less numerous, containing but three species. It embraces the opossum shrimp and the squill.

Order 3d, *Amphipoda*, those having feet connected with both divisions of the body, comprising the sand flea, beach flea, and fresh-water shrimp. It has but four species.

Order 4th, *Læmipoda*, has but two species, the whale louse and the sea measuring worm.

Order 5th, *Isopoda*, is considerably numerous, containing fourteen species. Seven of these are parasitic animals which obtain a subsistence by attachment to other animals. Among them are the salt and fresh-water barnacle; two species of sow bug; the pill bug; and a genus resembling the trilobite.

Order 6th, *Pœcilopoda*, contains five species, and embraces the horsefoot, or king crab, so abundant on the sea coast; and parasites peculiar to the shark, the rock bass, and the alewife.

Orders 7th and 8th, *Phyllopoda* and *Lophyropa*, are not certainly known to exist in the state.

Orders 9th and 10th, *Branchiopoda* and *Ostrapoda*, have but one species each, and those not known, except to the zoologist.

Class VIII. *Mollusca.*

Mollusca is the name given to the class of animals whose bodies are encased in shells. Many of these are known by the name of shell fish.

There are six orders, embracing a large number of genera and species, in the state.

The 1st order is *Cephalopoda*, those having the head surrounded by feet. The cuttle fish, or squid, and the syphon formed spirula, belong to this order.

The 2d order is *Pteropoda*, having fins on each side of the mouth, and without feet. To this order belongs the clio, the food of the whale.

The 3d order is *Gasteropoda*, having the feet under the body. The mollusca, belonging to this order, are very numerous in the state, and are arranged into eight sections or subdivisions, according to the structure of their gills or breathing apparatus.

It comprises, in addition to many species known only to the naturalist, the family of slugs or snails, the animals inhabiting the turbinated shells, and those which yield the famous Tyrian purple dye.

The 4th order, *Acephala*, those having no distinct head, is divided into three sections, and comprises by far the greater number of shell fish with which we are familiar.

In the 2d section, *Lamellibranchia,* those having leaf-like gills, of a semicircular form, we find the oyster, scallop, bloody clam, mussel, and the fresh-water clam and mussel.

In the third section, *Conchifera,* those having single and distinct shells, we find the quahog, or common round clam, and the long clam.

The 5th and 6th orders, *Cirrhopoda,* those having filamentous or thread-like feet, and *Tunicata,* those covered with a leathery or membranous tunic instead of a shell, contain no species of general interest.

The researches of the state geologists have brought to light numerous genera and species of fossil mollusca, imbedded in the lime and sand stones of the state. The most remarkable and common of these are the various species of trilobite, the encrinite, the pentamerus, &c.

Class IX. *Insects.*

No full account of the insects of this state has yet appeared. The naturalists of the adjacent states, of Massachusetts and Pennsylvania, have described most of those, which are inhabitants of the state—and relying upon their descriptions, we shall mention some of those best known.

The order *Coleoptera,* beetles, is very numerous. In Pennsylvania more than 1500 species have been discovered. The boring beetle, hammering beetle, tumble bug, ground beetle, horn bug, goldsmith beetle, and some others of brilliant colors, are the most common.

The order *Orthoptera,* includes the cockroaches, crickets and grasshoppers, of which there are many species. The katydid, so well known by the peculiar sound produced by its wing covers, belongs to the latter family.

The order *Homoptera* comprises the locusts; one species of these is remarkable for remaining seventeen years in the grub state.

The order *Hemiptera,* bugs, comprises many of those insects injurious to vegetation, particularly the May bug, the lady bug, the apple tree blight, &c.

The order *Lepidoptera,* butterflies, are very numerous, probably numbering not less than 1000 species. Among those that fly during the day, those best known are, the small yellow winged butterfly, and the large yellow and black butter-fly. The variety, and beauty of their colors, attract universal attention. Some of the nocturnal species are very large.

The order *Arachnidæ,* spiders, though now usually considered as a separate class, may come in here with propriety. There are probably between one and two hundred species of these in the state. Some of them are very large, and possessed of great beauty. The long legs, the clawed spider, the tick, mite, louse, &c, also belong to this order.

The *worms* of the state, and its *animalcules,* have not yet been made subjects of general investigation.

CIVIL HISTORY OF NEW YORK.

DUTCH COLONIAL ADMINISTRATION.

DISCOVERY AND SETTLEMENT.

The bay of New York was first discovered in 1524, by Jean de Verrazano, a Florentine in the service of France. It does not appear, however, that Francis I. the monarch under whom this discovery was made, ever took advantage of it, or laid claim to the territory adjacent, in consequence of Verrazano's exploration.

On the 4th of Sept. 1609, Henry Hudson, an Englishman, in the service of the States General of Holland, again discovered it, and ascended the river, which now bears his name, to a point a little below the present city of Albany. His ship, or yacht, was of about eighty tons burthen, and was called the Half Moon.

Landing in England on his return, he despatched an account of his adventures to the Dutch East India Company, with the request, that they would furnish him with the means of making another voyage. The English Government, however, determining to secure his services, forbade his sailing again in the service of Holland.

Shortly after, he received the command of a ship, with directions to explore the Northern coast of America, in the hope of finding a North West passage. Having discovered and entered the bay which now bears his name, his crew mutinied, and putting him with some of his men into a small boat, abandoned them to their fate. Whether they perished by the waves, by hunger, or by the inclemency of the climate, is unknown.

The country thus discovered by Hudson, was inhabited by numerous roving tribes of Indians, of whom the Maquaas or Mohawks were the most formidable and warlike. The Manhattans, who inhabited the island on which New York is situated, were also a fierce and warlike nation. Between thirty and forty of these tribes occupied Long Island and the country watered by the Hudson and Delaware rivers and their branches.

In 1610, a ship was sent by some merchants in Amsterdam, to trade with the Indians of Hudson river, for furs, &c. Other voyages were made during the succeeding years. In 1613, one or two small trading forts were erected on the river; and four houses were built on Manhattan Island, under the superintendence of Hendrick Corstiaensen, who visited with his trading boats every creek, inlet and bay in the vicinity, for the purpose of securing for his employers, the furs and produce of the country.

On the 29th of March, 1614, the States General of the United Netherlands passed an ordinance, granting to all original discoverers of lands in North America, the exclusive privilege of making four voyages to such lands as they had discovered, for the purposes of trade. Under this ordinance, five ships were despatched, by a company of merchants, the same year. The command of these vessels was given to Adriaen Blok, Hendrick Corstiaensen and Cornelis Jacobsen Mey. They explored extensively the coast near New York.

Blok discovered and named Block Island, south of Rhode Island, and also the East river, to which he gave the name of Hellegat, from the Hellegat river in East Flanders.

Captain Mey proceeding southward, discovered and named Capes May and Henlopen, or Hindlopen. On the return of these ships, a Capt. Hendrickson was left on the coast, to prosecute discoveries.

The tract of country extending from the Connecticut to the Delaware river, received the name of New Netherlands; and the exclusive right to trade there for three years from that date, Oct. 11, 1614, was granted to the discoverers by the States General.

The discoverers, upon the passage of this grant, formed themselves into a company, called the United New Netherlands Company. This company erected, the same year, a fort and a trading house at an island, near the head of navigation on the Hudson, just below the present city of Albany, and garrisoned it with ten or twelve men. Another fort was erected at the southern point of Manhattan Island; and men were despatched in every direction among the Indian tribes, to induce them to trade with the company.

In 1618, a flood in the North river, or Mauritius, as it was called, injured the company's fort at Castle Island, near Albany, so much that it was deemed best to remove it to another position. Accordingly, a site was chosen on the Normanskill, or creek, a few miles below. Here they made a treaty with the Five Nations. The charter granted to the New Netherlands Company, by the States General, having expired this year, (1618,) they petitioned for its renewal, but in vain. Private traders, principally the former partners of that company, continued, however, to visit the country for the purposes of traffic.

At this period the attention of the Puritans, who afterwards settled at Plymouth, was attracted to this fertile and beautiful country. Having in vain applied to England, for grants of territory in the New World, they intimated, in the beginning of the year 1620, to the prominent individuals concerned in the trade to the New Netherlands, their desire to emigrate thither. This intimation was readily and willingly received by these traders, and a petition presented by them to the States General, for their approval of the project. War existing, however, between the States General and Spain, that body thought best, not to approve this proposition.

In June, 1621, was passed the charter of the Dutch West India Company, an armed Mercantile Association, which was designed to extend the fame and power of the Netherlands; and to render them formidable upon the seas to Spain, their old and sanguinary enemy. This charter, though not particularly favorable to freedom, was as liberal in its provisions, as that of any other commercial association of that period.

The West India Company having been fully organized, sent out a ship called the New Netherlands, on the 20th of June, 1623, to their newly acquired possessions, under the direction of Capt. Mey already noticed, and Adriaen Joriszen Tienpont. The former of these, proceeded immediately to the Delaware, then called the South, or Prince Hendrick's river, and there established a fort, near the present town of Gloucester, which he named fort Nassau. The same year a fortified post, called Fort Orange, was erected within the limits of the present city of Albany, a few miles above that erected in 1618, on the Normanskill.

DIRECTOR MINUIT'S ADMINISTRATION.

In 1624, Peter Minuit, of Wesel, in Westphalia, having been appointed director of New Netherlands, arrived in the country, bringing with him several families of Walloons, inhabitants of the frontier between Belgium and France.

These settled on a bay of Long Island, near Manhattan Island, called from them Wahlebocht, or the bay of the foreigners, a name since corrupted into Wallabout. Here Sarah de Rapelje, the first child of European parentage, whose birth occurred in the colony, was born in June, 1625.

The government of this newly established colony was vested in the director, and a council of five, who possessed supreme executive, legislative and judicial authority in the colony. The only other important officer of the government was the Schout Fiscal, who filled both the offices of Sheriff and Attorney General. Under the superintendence of these authorities, the trade of the colony prospered.

In 1626, Staten Island was purchased of the Indians; and in the same year, the island of Manhattan was bought for the sum of twenty-four dollars. The fort, upon this latter island, received the title of Fort Amsterdam, and the colony that of New Amsterdam.

An affray occurred between some of Minuit's farm servants and an Indian, in which the latter was killed. No attempts were made to punish the murderers; and this outrage afterwards led to serious consequences. The exports of the colony this year amounted to about $19,000.

In the ensuing year, 1627, amicable correspondence was opened between the Dutch authorities at New Amsterdam, and the Pilgrim settlers at Plymouth. In this correspondence the English authority was set up by the Plymouth colonists over the region watered by the Connecticut, and denied by the Dutch.

Up to the year 1629, no colonies, properly so called, can be said to have been established in the New Netherlands. The settlements were simply trading establishments, in which the traffic in furs was the principal employment; and the soil was hardly cultivated in sufficient quantities to supply the wants of the traders.

In Sept. 1628, Admiral Heyn, who had charge of the West India Company's fleet, captured the Spanish Plate ships, containing gold, silver, &c. to the value of five millions of dollars. The directors of the company, elated by such unexpected good fortune, were disposed to yield to any measure apparently calculated to increase their wealth; and at the meeting of the company's council (commonly known as the XIX,) on the 7th of June, 1626, a measure was adopted, the effects of which are yet felt in the state.

This measure was, the passage of a grant to certain individuals, of extensive seignories, or tracts of land, with feudal rights, giving them power over the lives and persons of their subjects. Certain restrictions and limitations were made in this grant, which was called "The Freedoms and Exceptions, granted by the Assembly of the XIX, of the Priviliged West India Company, to all such as shall plant any colonies in New Netherlands."

Under this grant Samuel Godyn and Samuel Bloemmaert purchased, soon after, a tract of land, thirty-two miles long, and two miles wide, on the south-west side of Delaware Bay; and on the 18th of April, 1630, Kiliaen Van Rensselaer, a pearl merchant of Amsterdam, secured a tract on the west side of the North river, embracing the site of the present city of Albany.

By subsequent purchase, in this year and in 1637, Mr. Van

Rensselaer became proprietor of a tract of land, twenty-four miles long, and forty-eight broad, now composing the counties of Albany, Rensselaer, and part of the county of Columbia.

In 1630, Godyn and Bloemmaert also secured a tract, on the opposite shore of the Delaware Bay, making a territory of sixty-four miles in circumference. Another of the company's directors, Michael Paauw, purchased Staten Island, Jersey City and Ahasimus, now called Harsimus, with the lands adjacent.

This colony was called Pavonia: that on the Delaware, Zwanendal, or the valley of swans, and Mr. Van Rensselaer's, Rensselaerwyck.

Active exertions were forthwith made to colonize these vast estates. Colonies were sent to Rensselaerwyck and Zwanendal; and fortifications erected. Anxious, however, to participate in the very profitable trade in furs and peltries, the Patroons, in the opinion of the other directors, soon transcended the limits prescribed, in the bill of Freedoms and Exceptions. Hence difficulties arose between the two parties, which materially embarrassed the prosperity of the infant colonies. Minuit the director, was recalled, partly probably from the machinations of Wouter Van Twiller, who, in the capacity of agent of the company, had visited the colony two years before, (1632.)

On his way home in March, 1632, Director Minuit was forced, by stress of weather, to put into the port of Plymouth, England. The vessel was immediately seized, on her arrival, on a charge of having traded and obtained her cargo in countries subject to Her Brittanic Majesty. Considerable diplomatic correspondence ensued between the State officers of England and the Netherlands; and finally, the object of the English government, (the assertion of their title,) having been attained, the vessel was released.

During this period the dispute between the Patroons and the colony continued. In the latter part of the year, the Indians in the neighborhood of the Delaware Bay, considering themselves injured, came suddenly upon the colony of Zwanendal, and butchered in cold blood all the colonists, thirty-four persons in number. The next year, Captain de Vries, the founder of the colony, returned from Holland, and, finding himself unable to punish the treachery of the Indians, made a peace with them.

DIRECTOR VAN TWILLER'S ADMINISTRATION.

In April, 1633, Wouter Van Twiller, a relation of the Patroon Van Rensselaer, having been appointed director of the settlement, arrived at New Amsterdam. About this time also Rev. Everardus Bogardus, the first minister, and Adam Roelandsen, the first schoolmaster, arrived in the colony. Van

DUTCH ADMINISTRATION. 53

Twiller seems to have been ill calculated to govern the colony, at so stormy a period as this. Addicted to the use of intoxicating liquors, he only resorted to heavier potations, when the emergency called for sober and vigorous action.

In the early part of his administration, the Dutch settlements, on the Connecticut, were established. In 1614, Adrien Blok, one of the most enterprising captains in the employ of the New Netherlands Company, had discovered this river, and named it the Fresh Water River.

In 1632, Hans Encluys, one of the servants of the West India Company, had set up the arms of the States General at Kievits Hoeck, now Saybrook Point, thus formally taking possession of the river. He had also purchased a tract of land, at that point, for the company, from the Indians.

On the 8th of June, 1633, Jacob Van Curler, under the direction of Van Twiller, purchased territory along the Connecticut river, embracing most of the site of the present city of Hartford, and several of the adjacent towns, of Tattoepan, chief of Sickenam (Little) River. On this territory he erected a fort or trading post, which he fortified with two pieces of cannon.

On the 16th of September following, a vessel commanded by Capt. Wm. Holmes, and sent by the Plymouth Colony, who had settled about Massachusetts Bay, ascended the Connecticut. On passing the fort, Capt. Holmes was ordered to stop; but being in stronger force than the Dutch, he persisted; and proceeded, (though not without repeated protests from the Dutch authorities at New Amsterdam,) to erect, a little above, the frame of a house which he had brought round in his vessel.

During this and the succeeding year, the contest between the Patroons and the Company continued to the manifest disadvantage of both parties.

In 1635, the English at Plymouth and Massachusetts Bay, sent several new colonies to the Connecticut river, one of which, under the command of Governor Winthrop, landing at Saybrook Point, tore down the arms of the States General, and carved a buffoon's face in its stead. They also refused to let the Dutch land, on the tract they had purchased in 1632; and erected on the very same tract, Saybrook fort.

At the present site of Springfield, Mass., Mr. Pynchon established a trading house and a plantation: and the next year, 1636, Hooker and his followers located themselves in Hartford.

DIRECTOR KIEFT'S ADMINISTRATION.

In 1637, the mal-administration of Director Van Twiller having come to the ears of the company, William Kieft was appointed in his place. Director Kieft arrived in New Amsterdam in March, 1638, and found the fort greatly dilapidated; the company's property wretchedly managed, and every thing betokening the prevalence of disorder. Director Van Twiller, however, had not suffered his own interests to be neglected; his farms were well stocked, and his houses in good repair.

The new director began, with a strong hand, to reform abuses, and to improve his colony; but he was a man of headstrong temper, who would not brook control or advice, and possessed, at the same time, a weak and ill balanced mind. Like his predecessor, he was addicted to intemperate habits.

In 1638, Peter Minuit, the first Director of the New Netherlands, who had, after his dismission from that station, gone to Sweden, arrived on the coast with a Swedish colony, and settled upon the banks of the Delaware, within the limits of the territory claimed by the Dutch.

Having erected a fort there, which he named Fort Christina, after the Swedish queen, Kieft protested against his course, as an invasion of his territory : but from the weakness of his own colony, he was obliged to content himself with protesting.

In the latter part of the year 1638, the restrictions which hitherto had been placed, by the company, upon the trade to the New Netherlands, were taken off, and free traffic encouraged. This measure gave a new impulse to trade and emigration; new farms were taken up; and a number of gentlemen of wealth and distinction removed to the colony.

Persecution, too, drove many, from New England and Virginia, to settle among the more tolerant Dutch, who, though firm in their adherence to their own creed, did not deem it necessary to persecute those who differed from them in religious tenets.

In the mean time the aggressive disposition of the English settlers still continued. They founded a colony at New Haven, notwithstanding Director Kieft's protests; they occupied the fertile valley of the Tunxis (Farmington) river; and even went so far as to plough and sow the company's lands around the Fort of Good Hope at Hartford, assaulting and severely wounding some of the men in charge of that post, whom they found at work in the fields.

The commander of the fort, Gyshert Op Dyck, promptly remonstrated against this unwarrantable procedure, but the English justified themselves on the ground, that as the lands were uncultivated, and the Dutch did nothing to improve them, "it was a sin to let such fine lands lie waste."

Not satisfied with these aggressions, the Plymouth company proceeded to grant the whole of Long Island, to the Earl of Stirling; and a settlement was soon afterwards effected, by Lyon Gardiner, at Gardiner's Island.

DUTCH ADMINISTRATION.

The Dutch, meantime, were active in establishing settlements, at the western extremity of the island. Lands were granted to settlers in Brooklyn, then called Breuckelen; at Gowanus, and at Gravenzande, now called Gravesend.

In May, 1640, a company of emigrants from Lynn, Mass., claiming authority under the Earl of Stirling's patent, commenced a settlement near Cow Neck. The Director having learned this fact, despatched the Schout, or Sheriff, with a band of soldiers, to investigate the matter; and, if they had actually commenced a settlement, to take them prisoners. This was accomplished; and after examination, they were dismissed, on condition, that they should leave the territory of their High Mightinesses, the States General.

In the autumn of the same year they returned, and founded the town of Southampton, L. I. Other settlers, from the same quarter, soon after founded Southold. These settlements were not disturbed by the Dutch.

This year, a most sanguinary contest commenced, with the Indians, which continued to disturb the colony for five years; and had well nigh depopulated it. The causes of this war were many. The Indians saw, with daily increasing envy and dislike, the heritage of their fathers occupied by strangers. The settlers, often arrogant and selfish, deprived them of their real or imagined rights.

In addition to this, Director Kieft, acting, as he alleged, under instructions received from Holland, proceeded to lay a tax on the Indian tribes for the support of the colony. This aroused their indignation; and unfortunately, about this time, a robbery, committed by some of the servants of the colonists, was attributed to the Indians. Kieft's imprudent disposition led him to send a body of soldiers, to execute summary vengeance upon the supposed offenders. A number of them were inhumanly butchered, and their crops destroyed.

This produced deep hostility of feeling, on the part of the Indians; and the following season, with the cunning characteristic of their race, they took measures for revenge. Unexpectedly, they attacked Staten Island, and killed several planters. Kieft sought satisfaction, by exciting a war between the Indian tribes.

Early in 1642, he determined to avenge a murder, which had been committed by one of the Indians. He accordingly called a council of twelve men, from among the citizens of New Amsterdam, to aid him, in deciding upon the proper course to be pursued.

This council advised patience and forbearance; and then proceeded to take up the abuses of his government, and to ask for reforms. Kieft soon dismissed them, forbade their meeting again, and disregarding their advice, sent a company of soldiers to attack the Indians. They were unsuccessful in finding them, and a hollow peace was concluded between the two parties. This however did not long continue.

In 1643, one of the Hackensack tribe, having been robbed by some of the Dutch, killed two of them in revenge. Kieft demanded the murderer, but the Indians refused to deliver him up. At this juncture the Mohawks, the most formidable tribe, in the territory bordering on the Hudson and the Lakes, descended the river for the purpose of levying tribute from the weaker tribes, in the neighborhood of New Amsterdam.

These, terror stricken, fled to the Dutch for protection, and might have been won to sincere friendship, by kindness; but having been received kindly for a few days, they left the colony, and scattered themselves among the adjacent tribes.

It was at this period that Kieft, forgetful of the dictates of humanity, suffered himself to authorize a transaction which stains, most foully, his whole administration. At a drunken revel on the 22d of February, 1643, a petition was presented to him by some of the most blood thirsty of the inhabitants, requesting him to order the extermination of these Indians, thus deprived of a shelter and a home. Kieft readily complied, and when the season of debauchery was past, refused to recall his order.

Two parties of soldiers were sent out at night to surprise and destroy the unsuspecting red men. One hundred and ten were killed, and thirty taken prisoners. Nor were these all warriors, who were thus butchered in their sleep. Women and children were cut to pieces, by the swords of these ruthless exterminators; and neither age, nor sex were spared.

The consequences, as might have been expected, were, that the farms and buildings of the Dutch were burned by the exasperated Indians; numbers of the settlers were killed; and in a few weeks Kieft was compelled to receive the inhabitants into the fort, as the only place which afforded protection, against the assaults of the savages. His course aroused the prejudices of the people against him; and endeavoring to throw the blame of it upon others, he was threatened with assassination.

In the autumn of 1643, the savages united together to drive the Dutch from New Amsterdam; and almost daily, murders were committed by them. Kieft was again compelled to submit to the association of the representatives of the people, with himself in the government.

Having received a reinforcement, from the English settlers at Westchester, in 1644, under the command of Capt. Underhill, several expeditions were undertaken against their common enemy, in which some eight hundred were slain. These results led the Indian tribes of Long Island, and the shore adjacent, (east of New Amsterdam,) to sue for peace; but it was not of long continuance. In 1645, however, a treaty was concluded, through the powerful intervention of the Mohawks, with most of the Indian tribes.

During this whole period, from 1640 to 1645, the English colonists were constantly pursuing a course of aggression, upon the territories claimed by the Dutch. Determined to harass the commander of the fort at Hartford, till he should be compelled to leave his post, they neglected no means of carrying into effect their resolution. They also proceeded to establish settlements, west of the Connecticut, wherever they could obtain a foothold.

On their southern frontier, too, the Swedes were depriving them of their trade with the Indians, and securing the fairest lands, watered by the Delaware and its tributaries, for their farms, notwithstanding these had been previously purchased of the native proprietors, by the Dutch.

The "Colonie" of Rensselaerwyck, meanwhile, removed from these troubles, and cultivating a friendly relation with the Indian tribes, was peaceful and prosperous. The Patroon complained, indeed, that his rents were not punctually paid; but the number of his bouweries, or farms under cultivation, and the amount of exports, showed conclusively, that its interests were, on the whole, well managed.

Mindful of the religious improvement of his colonists, the Patroon sent over in 1642, the Rev. Johannes Megapolensis, as minister of the "Colonie," who labored among them efficiently and successfully for many years.

Mr. Van Rensselaer never resided in his colony; but confided its management to a Commissary General, or Superintendent; which office was filled by Arendt Van Curler or Corlaer, a most worthy and excellent man; and after him by Anthony de Hooges.

The office of Schout Fiscal or Sheriff and Attorney General, was also one of great importance, and was filled by Jacob Albertsen Planck, and afterwards by Adriaen Van der Donck.

In 1643, a church was erected on what is now Church street, near Market street, or Broadway, Albany.

In 1646, the venerable Patroon, Kiliaen Van Rensselaer, died at Amsterdam. His son Johannes succeeded him as Patroon.

In 1647, two whales ascended the Hudson, one of which grounded on an island at the mouth of the Mohawk, causing great consternation among the honest burghers.

The Assembly of the XIX. finding their colony at New Amsterdam decreasing in numbers and wealth, and verging towards destruction, under the mismanagement of Director Kieft, resolved to recall him; and in 1645 appointed in his place General Peter Stuyvesant, formerly Director of the Island of Curacoa.

GOVERNOR STUYVESANT'S ADMINISTRATION.

Peter Stuyvesant, the successor of Kieft, in the government of New Netherlands, had been Director of the Dutch settlement at Curacoa and the adjacent islands; and had acquired a high reputation for military prowess. Having been wounded in the siege of St. Martins, in 1644, he returned to Holland for surgical aid. In 1645, his health having been partially restored, the West India Company appointed him Director of their colony of New Netherlands.

Changes, however, made at his suggestion, in the organization of the colony, and the difference of opinion which existed between the different chambers of the company, relative to the propriety of these changes, prevented him from proceeding immediately to take charge of his post; and it was not till the 27th of May, 1647, that he entered upon the duties of his office. Meanwhile, the colony continued under the misrule of Director Kieft.

Though possessed of stern integrity and honesty of purpose, yet the strict military education which he had received, had impressed Governor Stuyvesant, with ideas of the necessity of rigid discipline, which soon involved him in contentions with the citizens. These, having tasted in their own country, some of the blessings of freedom, and witnessing, daily, the liberty enjoyed by their English neighbors, were desirous of making trial of a liberal form of government.

His first controversy was with the guardians of Johannes Van Rensselaer, son of the first Patroon, Kiliaen Van Rensselaer, who had deceased in 1646, leaving his son Johannes, then a minor, to the guardianship of Wouter Van Twiller, (the second Director,) and one Van Sleightenhorst. This controversy was kept up for a long period, and finally terminated, by a reference to the States General.

While it was pending, in 1649 and 1650, the Gemeente, or Commonalty of New Netherlands, instigated by Adriaen Van der Donck,* already mentioned as the first Attorney General of Rensselaerwyck, sent repeated remonstrances to the States General, concerning the administration of Stuyvesant, and earnestly solicited his recall.

The States General, unwilling to act hastily, in a matter of so much importance, repeatedly appointed committees to investigate the charges made against him; and on the 27th of April,

---

* Van der Donck seems to have been a man of considerable ability and learning, but possessed of a restless and ambitious spirit. He had, previously to this period, created some disturbance at Rensselaerwyck. He evidently possessed the art of enlisting the populace in his schemes.

DUTCH ADMINISTRATION.

1652, passed an order for his recall. Just at this juncture, a war with England commenced, and the States General, esteeming it highly important, that their interests in the New World should be protected, by an officer of courage and ability, on the 16th of May, rescinded their resolution of the 27th of April, and Stuyvesant retained his station.

In order to compensate, as far as possible, for this slighting the wishes of the people, the States General, in 1652, granted to the city of New Amsterdam, a charter of incorporation, making the city officers elective, and giving them jurisdiction, except in capital cases.

During this period the English, against whom Kieft had so often protested, encroached still farther upon the bounds of the Dutch. They established settlements upon the Housatonic river, and at Greenwich, upon the main land; and crossing over to Long Island, organized colony after colony, upon its fertile lands.

In vain Stuyvesant remonstrated; in vain he attempted to remove their settlements by force, or compelled the inhabitants to swear allegiance to Holland. For every remonstrance they had a reply; and against the employment of force they made threats, which the more flourishing state of their colonies, he well knew, would enable them to fulfil. They seemed as much offended at his resistance, as the Dutch were by their aggressions; and frequently, in their controversies, laid claim to the whole territory under the king's patent, or on account of Cabot's discovery.

Wearied with these protracted disputes, Governor Stuyvesant repaired to Hartford, in September, 1650, where the commissioners of the colonies were in session, to adjust their difficulties, by a personal interview. Unsuccessful in this, he left the settlement in the hands of four deputies, two to be chosen by each party; and, secure in the justice of his cause, appointed as his commissioners, two Englishmen, Willet and Baxter.

On the 29th of September, the commissioners reported articles of agreement, relinquishing to the English, half of Long Island, and all the lands on the Connecticut, except those actually occupied by the Dutch, and prohibiting the Connecticut colonists from settling within ten miles of the Hudson.

Hard as were these conditions, Stuyvesant having once agreed to them, determined to maintain them in good faith, and obtained their ratification, from the States General, in February, 1656. The English government never ratified them, nor did the English colonists pay much regard to them, in their subsequent treatment of the Dutch, for in 1655 they seized, (under Cromwell's orders,) the fort at Hartford, with all its effects; thus terminating, by force, the existence of that colony.

In 1653, a charge of conspiracy between Governor Stuyvesant and the Indians, to massacre the inhabitants of all the New England colonies, was falsely preferred, by Connecticut and New Haven; and but for the firm resistance of Massachusetts, to so iniquitous a transaction, they would have proceeded immediately to destroy New Amsterdam. When this foul charge reached the ears of Governor Stuyvesant, it met with an indignant denial; a denial, to the truth of which, his whole life gave the fullest evidence.

In 1659, Massachusetts, pretending that the agreement made at Hartford, did not extend farther than twenty miles from the coast, claimed the land on the Hudson, above the parallel of 42°, and demanded the right of free navigation of that river.

On the southern frontier, too, the Swedes were not idle. To prevent their encroachments, Stuyvesant, in 1654, erected and garrisoned fort Casimir, on the Delaware, at the site of the present town of New Castle. Risingh, the Swedish governor, soon visited it; and, having, under the guise of friendship, obtained admission, treacherously possessed himself of the fort.

The West India company, indignant at this perfidious act, sent orders to Stuyvesant, to reduce the Swedish settlements on the Delaware. Accordingly, in September, 1655, he left New Amsterdam, at the head of a force of nearly 700 men; and on the 16th, Fort Casimir, and on the 25th of September, Fort Christina, the head quarters of the Swedish governor, capitulated, without bloodshed. The terms offered by the Dutch, to the conquered, were so favorable, that most of them remained in the colony.

During Governor Stuyvesant's absence, upon this expedition, a large body of Indians, deeming it a favorable opportunity to plunder, came upon the defenceless plantations, murdered a number of the inhabitants, and robbed several farms. The return of the Governor, however, put an end to their incursions.

Fort Casimir, after its recapture, became the nucleus of a colony, founded by the city of Amsterdam, and called New Amstel. The terms offered to emigrants were so favorable, that it soon became a place of importance; and in 1657, one Alricks, was appointed Lieutenant Governor of that, and the other Dutch possessions, on the Delaware.

In 1656, Governor Stuyvesant, who was a zealous and somewhat bigoted supporter of the Reformed Dutch church, imprisoned some Lutherans, who had come into the colony, and persisted in the observance of their own forms of worship. In 1658, he banished from the colony, a Lutheran preacher, who attempted to establish a church of his own persuasion. At Vlissingen, (now Flushing,) where the doctrines of the Quakers had made some progress, he attempted, but, of course, un-

DUTCH ADMINISTRATION.

successfully, to eradicate them by fines, imprisonment, and banishment. Their numbers increased with their persecution.

In 1659, Lord Baltimore protested against the settlements on the Delaware, as being within the bounds of his patent. To this protest, Stuyvesant replied on the 6th of October, setting forth the claims of the Dutch to the South, or Delaware river, and its coasts.

In 1663, a body of Indians attacked Fort Esopus, now Kingston, and killed sixty-five persons. Suspecting that several tribes were leagued together in these hostilities against the colonists, Stuyvesant assembled the magistrates of the adjacent towns, to confer on the measures necessary for the defence of the colony. Having recommended such measures as they thought advisable, the magistrates turned their attention to the civil condition of the colony, and urged in forcible language, upon the governor, and the West India Company, the right of the people to a share, in the administration of the government.

In 1653, a convention of delegates from the different towns had met in New Amsterdam, and in similar terms had remonstrated with the Governor and Company, against the abridgement of their rights, as citizens of Holland. But Stuyvesant, true to his military education, regarded such remonstrances, or petitions, with little favor.

On the 30th of March, 1664, Charles II., King of England, regardless of the rights of Holland, granted to his brother James, Duke of Albany and York, the whole of the New Netherlands. The Duke forthwith despatched Colonel Nicolls, with three ships of war, and a sufficient force, to conquer his province.

Governor Stuyvesant hearing of their approach, attempted to put the fort and town in a state of defence, but the sturdy burghers, tired of an arbitrary and despotic government, refused to second his exertions. When, therefore, the fleet appeared before the city, and offered favorable terms, they insisted upon a capitulation. Governor Stuyvesant, angry at their want of spirit, tore the letter of Colonel Nicolls in pieces before them; nor could he be induced to sign the articles of capitulation, till the 6th of September, (1664,) two days after they were prepared.

These terms were, perhaps, the most favorable ever offered to a captured city. The inhabitants were permitted to remain in the colony, if they chose, upon taking the oath of allegiance to the English crown; to retain or dispose of their property; to elect their own local magistrates; and to enjoy their own forms of religious worship. The name of the colony and city was changed to New York.

Governor Stuyvesant, soon after the capitulation, went to Holland, but returned to New York in a few years, and spent the remainder of his life there.

THE ENGLISH COLONIAL GOVERNMENT.

COLONEL NICOLLS having thus acquired the peaceable possession of the New Netherlands, was appointed by the Duke, Governor of the province, in the autumn of 1664.

He appears to have been a man of prudence, moderation, and justice; and though vested with almost absolute authority, used it in promoting the good of the province. During his administration, an effort was made, but unsuccessfully, to determine the boundary between New York and Connecticut.

In January, 1665, a law was passed, requiring the approval and signature of the Governor, to all deeds of lands purchased from the Indians, in order to render the titles valid. This was necessary, as the Indians frequently sold the same tract of land to different individuals.

On the 12th of June, 1666, Governor Nicolls granted a charter to the city of New York.

In 1667, he gave place to Colonel Francis Lovelace, who held the reins of government till 1673, when it was recaptured by the Dutch.

Though somewhat arbitrary, and disposed to burden the people with heavy taxes, the urbanity of his manners, and his desire for the welfare of the colony, caused Col. Lovelace to be regarded as a good governor. In 1670, on the petition of the Dutch inhabitants of the colony, he granted them permission to send to Holland for a minister, and guarantied his support from the public treasury.

On the 7th of August (New Style) Captains Evertsen and Binckes, the commanders of a Dutch squadron, which had been cruising off the American coast, entered the harbor of New York. Governor Lovelace was absent in New England; and the fort and city were under the command of Captain Manning. The fort appears to have been much dilapidated, and scantily supplied with ammunition.

The Dutch squadron demanded its immediate surrender. Captain Manning asked for delay; but the invaders replied that he should have but half an hour. At the end of that period they opened their fire upon the fort, which Captain Manning returned, as well as he was able, until his ammunition was exhausted. The Dutch, meantime, had succeeded in effecting a landing upon the island, in the rear of the fort; and perceiving that further resistance was useless, Captain Manning surrendered, without formal terms of capitulation.*

---

* The above account of the capture of New York differs materially from that of Smith, which has been copied by all succeeding historians; but is fully substantiated by the documents obtained in England, by J. R. Brodhead, Esq. Captain Manning was not, perhaps, a very efficient officer, but he certainly did not merit the epithets of *coward* and *traitor*, which have been so freely bestowed upon him. The affidavits of the witnesses in his trial, prove that his punishment [the breaking of his sword over his head, and incapacitation to hold office] was sufficiently severe for his offence.

ENGLISH ADMINISTRATION.

Fortunately for the city, the Dutch commanders were men of liberal feelings; and mindful of the courteous treatment their countrymen had received in 1664, they granted every privilege of citizens, to the inhabitants.

The name of New York, they changed to New Orange, that of Albany to Williamstadt, and the fort previously called Fort James, to William Hendrick. Captain Anthony Colve was appointed Governor. Connecticut protested against this invasion, but with as little success, as Governors Stuyvesant and Kieft had formerly done, to her usurpations. By the treaty of February 9th, 1674, New York was restored to the English. It was not, however, given up by the Dutch, till the following autumn.

Some doubts existing, relative to the validity of the Duke of York's patent, both on account of the Dutch occupation, and the fact, that it was wrested from that nation in time of peace, he deemed it advisable to obtain a new patent, from his brother, in 1674.

In the autumn of this year, Major Edmond Andross, afterwards so well known as the tyrant of New England, arrived in New York, and assumed the office of governor.

His administration in New York seems to have been marked by few striking events. He won neither the love nor the hatred of the citizens; and being absent a part of the time, attending to the more refractory New England colonies, he did not manifest, in his own state, the tyranny, which subsequently rendered him so odious.

In 1675, Nicolaus Van Rensselaer, a younger son of the first Patroon—came over to New York, with a recommendation from the Duke of York, whose favor he had obtained, and wished to settle as minister in Albany. Niewenhyt, who was, at the time, pastor of the Reformed Dutch church, in that city, refused to recognize him, on the ground that he had received Episcopal ordination. In the difficulty resulting from this refusal, Andross took sides, though unsuccessfully, with Van Rensselaer.

During Governor Andross' frequent absences, Mr. Brockholst, the Lieutenant Governor, officiated.

In August, 1683, Colonel Dongan succeeded Andross in the government of the colony; and among his first acts, was one, granting permission to the people to elect an assembly, consisting of a council of ten persons, named by the proprietor or his deputy, and a house of representatives, eighteen in number, elected by the freeholders, to aid in the administration of government.

In this year, the ten original counties were organized.

In February, 1685, the Duke of York, on the death of his brother Charles II., ascended the throne, under the title of James II. Among the first acts of this bigoted and shortsighted monarch, were his instructions to Dongan, to allow no printing press to be established in the colony.

Colonel Dongan, mindful of the necessity of keeping up friendly relations with the powerful confederation of the Iroquois, visited them in person, and by presents and addresses, won their friendship and alliance. The Jesuit priests, sent by the French among the Indians, were, however, a formidable obstacle to his complete success, in his negotiations with the savage tribes; for, residing among them, and conforming to their habits, they exerted a powerful influence in favor of the French, who had been the hereditary enemies of the confederated tribes.

Colonel Dongan, though himself a Roman Catholic, was too shrewd a statesman not to perceive the injurious influence exerted by the priests upon these Indians, and accordingly attempted to prevent their continuing among the tribes. But James, infatuated by his zeal for Catholicism, forbade him to molest them, and ordered that he should rather aid them, in their efforts, to convert the Indians to the Catholic faith.

In vain, Dongan remonstrated; he only irritated his royal master, and in 1688 was recalled.

Andross, who had preceded him, was designated as his successor, and New England was added to his jurisdiction.

Preferring to locate himself, where he could more easily inspect the conduct of his New England subjects, Governor Andross made Boston his residence, committing the care of the colony of New York, to his Lieutenant Governor, Colonel Nicholson. The latter seems to have been much more mild in his administration than his chief, whose enormities so exasperated the people of Massachusetts, that, on the arrival of the news, at Boston, of the accession of William, Prince of Orange, to the throne, they immediately imprisoned Andross, and sent him to England for trial.

In New York, the intelligence of the accession of the Prince of Orange did not, at first, produce a civil commotion. After a short time, however, a portion of the populace selected Jacob Leisler, a merchant of New York, of Dutch extraction, and the senior captain of the militia, as their leader, and proclaimed William and Mary. This movement, though popular with the masses, was discountenanced by most of the prominent citizens, who were unwilling to acknowledge Leisler, as a leader. Colonel Nicholson, apprehending popular violence, escaped on board a vessel in the harbor, and sailed for England.

On the 3d of June, 1689, finding himself surrounded by a large number of adherents, Leisler assumed the reins of government, associating with himself in the cares of state, his son-in-law, Jacob Milborne.

In the spring of 1690, Milborne, at the head of a considerable force, went to Albany, to reduce that town [which had hitherto remained refractory], to allegiance to the government of his father-in-law. At his first visit he was unsuccessful, but, at a subsequent period their fears of an Indian invasion, led them to submit to his jurisdiction. His confiscation of the estates of some of those who opposed him, excited prejudices which terminated in the ruin of both Milborne and Leisler.

During Milborne's absence at Albany, a letter from the English ministry arrived, addressed to "Francis Nicholson, Esq.: or, in his absence, to such as, for the time being, take care for the preserving of the peace, and administering the laws, in his majesty's province of New York, in America." This letter empowered the person addressed, to take charge of the government, calling in the aid of such of the inhabitants, as he should think proper, until farther orders.

Leisler, being by popular election acting governor, very properly assumed, that this letter was addressed to himself; and consequently, by advice of the citizens, who constituted a committee of safety, selected a council from each of the counties, except Ulster and Albany, which had not yet submitted to his authority.

He also summoned a convention of deputies from those portions of the province over which his influence extended. This convention laid some taxes, and adopted other measures, for the temporary government of the colony; and thus, for the first time in its existence, was the colony of New York under a free government. The strong prejudices, however, which had been awakened by Leisler's measures, soon produced in the minds of his adversaries, a rancor and bitterness, which was perhaps never surpassed in the annals of any political controversy.

This condition of things existed for nearly two years. To the horrors of civil commotion, were added the miseries of foreign war, and hostile invasion. The French Court, being at war with England, had placed over its colonies in Canada, the aged but enterprising Count de Frontenac, the ablest and most formidable governor of their American possessions.

This wily veteran at once determined to annoy his English neighbors, and accordingly despatched a force against Schenectady, in mid winter, which, after enduring extreme hardships, reached that place in the dead of night, and with the utmost barbarity, butchered its sleeping inhabitants, in cold blood.

Attempts were made to revenge this barbarous invasion, by an expedition against Quebec, of which Sir William Phipps and Fitz-John Winthrop, afterward governor of Connecticut, were the commanders; but through mismanagement, and the sickness of the troops, the expedition was unsuccessful.

Colonel Henry Sloughter, who had been appointed governor of New York, by King William, in 1689, arrived in 1691. His coming had been heralded, a few weeks before, by one Ingoldsby, a captain of foot, who, without credentials of any kind, demanded that the fort should be surrendered to him.

This demand, Leisler, with propriety, refused to obey; and when Colonel Sloughter, on his arrival, sent this same Ingoldsby, to demand the surrender of the fort, Leisler asked a personal interview with him. His enemies, who had determined upon his ruin, seized upon this imprudent hesitation, as evidence of treason, and filling the ears of the weak-minded Sloughter with charges against him, they demanded his arrest. The next day he surrendered the fort, and was immediately arrested, and with his son-in-law, after a mock trial, condemned to death for high treason.

Sloughter, however, hesitated to execute the sentence, and

wrote to the English ministry, for directions how to dispose of them. Their enemies, thirsting for their blood, were determined not to be thus foiled, and, persuasions having failed, they availed themselves of the known intemperate habits of the governor, invited him to a banquet, and when he was completely intoxicated, induced him to sign the death warrant. Ere he was recovered from his debauch, the unfortunate prisoners were executed. They met death with heroic fortitude, and Leisler exhibited a martyr's spirit.

Their estates were confiscated, but their adherents were soon after pardoned, by an act of general indemnity. The circumstances of Leisler's execution, roused the indignation of those who had attached themselves to his party, and for many years after, the citizens of the state were divided into Leislerians and Anti-Leislerians.*

In June, 1691, Colonel Sloughter went to Albany, to hold a conference with the Indians. On his return he died, very suddenly, in July, 1691; and, until the English government could appoint a successor, Ingoldsby, the lieutenant governor, assumed the government. The only event of importance, during his administration, was a conference with the Indians, with whom he concluded a treaty.

In August, 1692, he was superseded by Colonel Benjamin Fletcher, who soon exhibited the unamiable traits of his character. In his intercouse with the Indians, he fortunately suffered himself to be advised by Major Peter Schuyler, a man, whose influence over them was unbounded, and who, in his interviews with them, gave them a favorable impression of the English.

During most of Fletcher's administration, he was engaged in controversies with the assembly, principally in regard to appropriations for his expenses. He was empowered, by his commission, to take command of the militia of New England, as well as of New York; but proceeding to Hartford for this purpose, he found himself thwarted, by the stubborn resistance of the people of Connecticut.

Richard, Earl of Bellomont, appointed in 1695, arrived as his successor in April, 1698. He was a man of great dignity, resolution and moral worth; and was sent out by the king to take measures for the suppression of piracy, which had at that period reached a fearful height. For this purpose the earl, before leaving England, at the recommendation of Mr. Livingston, commissioned Captain William Kidd, to sail in pursuit of the pirates, and endeavor to rid the seas of them.

---

* Historians have differed materially in their estimate of the character of Leisler. By some he has been denounced as weak and vain; by others extolled for his firmness and integrity. It is apparent from a careful examination of his administration, that he was a man of honesty and integrity of purpose, but strongly prejudiced against the Roman Catholic faith, and not possessed of those traits of character, which would qualify him for a successful governor, in the troublous times in which he lived.

Milborne was a man of considerable education, and undoubtedly possessed greater abilities, and perhaps less integrity, than his father-in-law. It is alleged that Leisler was very much influenced by him in his measures.

ENGLISH ADMINISTRATION.

Captain Kidd accordingly sailed for New York in April, 1696, but after cruising for a while, himself turned pirate, and became the most ferocious and daring of all the ocean marauders. Returning to America, in 1701, he sold his ship, and boldly appeared in Boston, where he was arrested, and sent to England for trial and execution.

Lord Bellomont died in 1701, and John Nanfan, who had been his lieutenant governor in New York, succeeded him in the government.

The administration of Lord Bellomont is stained by the enactment of one law, which, for its bigotry and intolerance, is deserving of notice. In 1700, a law was passed, directing that every Catholic priest who came into the colony, should be hanged. The design of this law was alleged to be, to prevent the Catholic priests from exerting an influence upon the Indians, hostile to the English.

The earl, as well as Nanfan, who was his kinsman, had espoused the cause of the friends of Leisler, and already two distinct parties had been arrayed against each other.

In 1701, on the petition of the family of Leisler, to the queen, the attainder was reversed, and £1000 granted his heirs, as a compensation for their losses.

Nicholas Bayard, one of the most active of those who had procured the death of Leisler, having attacked Governor Nanfan, and his measures in public, and exhibited insubordination to the government, was arrested, in 1702, tried, convicted of high treason, and sentenced to death. But his prosecutors did not urge his immediate execution; and on the accession of Lord Cornbury, he was liberated from prison, and the attainder reversed.

On the 3d of May, 1702, Lord Cornbury, grandson of the Earl of Clarendon, and first cousin to the queen, arrived as governor.

Of all the Governors of the colony under the English crown, Lord Cornbury received the unenviable distinction, of being the worst. Rapacious without a parallel, he hesitated not to apply the public money to his own private purposes; and though notoriously vicious, yet he was so intolerant, that he sought to establish the Episcopacy at all hazards, imprisoning and prohibiting ministers of other denominations, from exercising their functions, without his special license. He was, moreover, as destitute of gratitude, as of courtesy, injuring those most, from whom he had received the greatest benefits. His manners were as ignoble and undignified, as his conduct was base, and when this hopeful scion of royalty wandered about the streets clothed as a woman, [which was a common practice with him] the people felt that he had taken Caligula for a model.

So urgent were the complaints against him, that the queen, in December, 1708, felt herself compelled to revoke his commission. No sooner was he deposed from office, than his creditors put him in jail, where he remained, till the death of his father, by elevating him to the peerage, procured his liberation. He had attached himself to the Anti-Leislerian party.

He was succeeded, in December, 1708, by John, Lord Lovelace, Baron of Hurley. The cheering hopes, to which the appointment of this excellent man gave rise, were doomed to sudden disappointment, as he died on the 5th of May, 1709.

He was succeeded by the lieutenant governor, Ingoldsby, whose administration, of eleven months, is only remarkable for another unsuccessful attempt upon the French possessions in Canada, under the direction of Colonel Nicholson. This occurred in 1709.

After the failure of this attempt, Colonel Schuyler visited England with five of the Iroquois sachems, in order to rouse the people to greater exertions, in defending the colonies.

In April, 1710, Lieutenant Governor Ingoldsby was removed from office, and Gerardus Beekman, the senior councillor, officiated as governor, till the arrival of General Hunter, in June, 1710. Three thousand Palatines, from Germany, flying from religious persecution in their own country, came over with Governor Hunter.

The ensuing year, another expedition was commenced against Canada, by land and water. The squadron destined for its reduction was under the command of Sir Hoveden Walker, and the troops under Brigadier General Hill. Owing to mismanagement, they did not enter the St. Lawrence sufficiently early in the season, and having unskilful pilots, several of the ships were wrecked in that river, and 800 soldiers lost. The whole expedition proved a failure.

As was to be expected, the assembly did not feel inclined in all cases to pay implicit deference to the governor's mandates; and, in the earlier years of his administration, Governor Hunter had several unpleasant collisions with that body. After a time, however, both parties exercised a spirit of mutual forbearance, which made their intercourse pleasant and advantageous to the colony.

Measures were adopted, during his administration, to adjust the boundaries between the colony and the adjacent colonies of New Jersey and Connecticut; but no definite settlement was made.

Few of the colonial governors resigned their office more generally beloved, or more ardently attached to the interests of the colony, than Governor Hunter. The address of the assembly to him, at his departure, in 1719, in its tone of affection and regard, stands forth alone, in these times of distraction, like a green and fertile oasis, amid the shifting and arid sands of Sahara.

During the period (a little more than a year) which elapsed between the departure of Governor Hunter, and the arrival of his successor, Colonel Schuyler, as senior member of the council, officiated in the place of the governor. Under his administration, a treaty, offensive and defensive, was again concluded with the Iroquois.

Governor Burnet arrived in September, 1720, and continued in office till his death, in April, 1728.

One of the first acts of his administration, was one prohibiting the sale of goods, suitable for the Indian trade, to the French from Quebec and Montreal.

This, though a very just and necessary measure, excited great bitterness of feeling on the part of the merchants who were engaged in this traffic, and of course in the minds of their adherents. They petitioned Parliament for its repeal; but were foiled, by the able manner in which their false statements were exposed, by Dr. Colden, then a member of the council.

During this excitement, another transaction affected Governor Burnet's popularity. He interfered, at the request of one of the parties concerned, in an ecclesiastical difficulty, in the French church in New York city, and of course drew upon himself the opposition of the other party.

ENGLISH ADMINISTRATION.

The French in Canada, under the vigorous government of the aged, but ambitious Count Frontenac, had formed the design of erecting a chain of military posts to the Ohio river, and along its banks; thus confining the English to the coast east of the Alleganies. In pursuance of this design, they proceeded, in 1725, though not without the most strenuous opposition, on the part of Governor Burnet and Colonel Schuyler, to erect a fort on Niagara river, which they called Fort Niagara.

The next year, with equally violent opposition on the part of the French, Governor Burnet erected Fort Oswego, at the present site of the village of Oswego.

The new assembly convened in 1727, were of a different political complexion from their predecessors; and between them and the governor, there were frequent and unpleasant contentions. These contentions continued till the period of his death. His fine talents, profound learning, and unaffected kindness of heart, caused him to be esteemed even by his enemies, and his faults were entombed with him.

Colonel Montgomery succeeded Governor Burnet, in 1728, and remained in office till his death, which occurred in 1731. During his government, viz., in October, 1728, the good will of the Iroquois was secured, and they were engaged to aid in the defence of Fort Oswego. In December, 1729, the king, contrary to the wishes and representations of the best citizens in the colony, repealed the law, prohibiting the sale of Indian goods to the French. The boundary between Connecticut and New York was fully settled, and the line run, in May, 1731.

In July of the same year, Colonel Montgomery having deceased, Rip Van Dam, the senior councillor, administered the government, till August, 1732. During his administration, the French erected a fort at Crown Point, without any resistance on the part of the feeble and inefficient acting governor.

On the first of August, 1732, Rip Van Dam was superseded by the arrival of Colonel Cosby, who remained in office till March, 1736, the period of his death.

Historians have been much divided in their views of Governor Cosby. Some represent him as an arbitrary, tyrannical and unjust ruler. Others regard him as a man of mild manners, but necessarily driven to harsh measures, by the turbulent spirits with whom he had to deal.

The act which caused the most serious difficulties in his administration, was his demand that Rip Van Dam, who had officiated as lieutenant governor, previous to his arrival, should divide with him, the emoluments of his office. Mr. Van Dam offered to do this, provided Governor Cosby would also divide what he had received from the colonies, before coming to this country. Governor Cosby, who appears to have been somewhat avaricious, refused to do this, and commenced a suit against Van Dam, for the half of his salary. Mr. Van Dam attempted to bring a counter suit, but the judges, who were in the governor's interest, declined entertaining it.

The newspapers took up the controversy, and one, conducted by a man named Zenger, defended Van Dam. The attacks of this journal against the governor, provoked the latter and his council, to such a degree, that they directed copies of the paper to be burned by the hangman, and indicted Zenger for libel. At the

4*

trial, his counsel, Messrs. Alexander and Smith, disputed the jurisdiction of the court, and were stricken from the roll of attorneys in consequence.

Andrew Hamilton, of Philadelphia, was employed to defend Zenger, and the jury, without leaving their seats, gave a verdict of acquital. Hamilton was presented with the freedom of the city, in a gold box, as an acknowledgement of his services, in upholding the liberties of the people, against a gove-nor appointed by the crown.

During Governor Cosby's administration, a Latin grammar school was founded in New York, by the assembly.

But a few days previous to his decease, Governor Cosby suspended Rip Van Dam from the council, thereby preventing his acting as lieutenant governor, in the event of his death. This act had well nigh produced serious troubles in the colony; for Mr. Clarke, who was next in order of seniority, having assumed the government, Van Dam opposed him, and himself appointed various officers.

The two parties soon came into collision, and a civil war seemed inevitable. Each party prepared for such a result, when, on the very eve of a conflict, a commission arrived from England, confirming Mr. Clarke, in the office of lieutenant governor, and president of the council.

This, of course, left the other party no alternative but submission. Governor Clarke exerted himself, to remove all just ground of complaint, from the people. He sought every occasion to conciliate those who were hostile to him; and during the seven years he was in power, rendered himself highly popular.

In 1737, a company of Highlanders offered to settle on the shores of Lakes Champlain and George, if they could be countenanced and aided by the assembly. As the colony would prove an effectual barrier to the French, on the northern frontier, the proposition was cheerfully met, by many of the citizens; but the assembly withheld the necessary aid, and the poor colonists were obliged to leave their lands, almost in a state of starvation.

In 1741, occurred the Negro plot, so famous in the annals of New York.

The evidence of the existence of such a plot seems to be meagre and insufficient. It is not improbable that a few profligate wretches, whites as well as blacks, had meditated arson; but the only proof of a plot to burn the city, was the testimony of a single abandoned woman, whose statements often contradicted each other, and were not corroborated by any of her associates. Yet such was the alarm and infatuation of the citizens, that on this woman's testimony, 154 Negroes and twenty Whites were imprisoned, thirteen Negroes were burned at the stake, eighteen or twenty persons hanged, seventy transported to foreign countries, and fifty discharged.

The people, always suspicious of the Roman Catholics, arrested and executed several Irishmen, who professed that faith, and who happened to arrive in the colony about this time. Among others who were hanged, was one Ury, a Catholic priest, who was condemned on two charges; one, that he was concerned in the conspiracy, and the other, that he was a Catholic priest. The charge of conspiracy, he protested was untrue, nor was it proved against him.

In September, 1743, George Clinton, son of the Earl of Lincoln, arrived in the colony, with a commission as governor.

The ensuing year, war was declared, between England and France, and the colonists prepared to carry it on with vigor.

In 1745, the colonies of New England and New York united in an attack upon the French fortress, at Louisburg; and New York furnished ten pieces of cannon, and £8000 towards the expedition. It was surrendered in June, of that year.

The colonies were seriously molested, during the year 1746, by the Indians, in the pay of the French, who attacked and reduced the English fort at Hoosick, and also made an incursion upon the settlement at Saratoga, murdering and plundering all who fell in their way. It was therefore determined to make a vigorous attack upon the French fortresses at Crown Point and Niagara, and also to send an army to capture Quebec. For this purpose New York raised £40,000, and solicited aid from England, which was promised, but not furnished. The enterprise proved unsuccessful.

The peace of Aix la Chapelle was concluded in 1748, and the colony, in the prosperity which followed for a few years, began to recover from its losses by the wars.

In 1746, the assembly appropriated £2250. towards founding a college.

During the years 1746—9, there were constant contentions, between the governor and assembly; but in 1750 both parties manifested a more conciliating spirit, and during the remainder of Governor Clinton's administration, they were on better terms.

Governor Clinton resigned in 1753, and in October of that year, Sir Danvers Osborne arrived, as his successor. Deeply afflicted at the loss of an excellent and amiable wife, the cares of the government seemed, to this unfortunate gentleman, an intolerable burden; and on the 12th of October, 1753, five days after his arrival, he put a period to his own existence.

Mr. De Lancy, the chief justice, was appointed lieutenant governor, a short time previous to Governor Clinton's resignation, and now assumed the reins of government.

Desirous of retaining the affections of the people, and disposed to side with their representatives in those measures which were advantageous to the colony, while at the same time he held his office at the will of the English government, Mr. De Lancy had a difficult task to perform; but the skill with which he conciliated both parties, does honor to his ability, as a statesman.

In 1754 a convention of delegates from the colonies of New Hampshire, Massachusetts, Connecticut, Rhode Island, Pennsylvania, Maryland and New York, met at Albany, to devise some plan of common defence against the French, who had again commenced hostilities.

At this convention Dr. Franklin, afterwards so eminent in the history of the Revolution, proposed a plan for political union, which was rejected by the provincial assemblies, on the ground that it gave too much power to the crown, and by the English government, because it gave too much power to the people.

In September, 1755, Sir Charles Hardy, an admiral in the British navy, arrived in New York, as governor. Being unacquainted with civil affairs, he gave the management of these to Mr. De Lancy. In the spring of this year, the colonies had made extensive preparations for an attack on the enemy, but, owing to the ignorance of the commanders of the English forces, of the tactics of Indian warfare, the campaign was utterly unsuccessful. Braddock, who was sent against Fort Du Quesne, (now Pittsburgh,) was killed, and his army routed, by a small body of Indians. Crown Point, and Niagara, both French posts, although assailed, were not captured.

Nor was the campaign of 1756 more successful. The English fort at Oswego was captured, 1600 men taken prisoners, and a large quantity of stores seized, by the French.

The campaign of 1757 was still more unsuccessful. Fort William Henry, on Lake George, with a garrison of 3000 men, was compelled to surrender. These repeated misfortunes awakened the energies of the English.

In 1758, William Pitt (Lord Chatham) was placed at the head of government, in England, and a new impulse was given to the energies of the nation. Success soon followed. In July, Louisburg, which at the former peace had been restored to the French, was recaptured. Fort Frontenac, on Lake Ontario, (now Kingston, C. W.) was captured soon after, and the French compelled to abandon Fort Du Quesne. General Abercrombie attacked Fort Ticonderoga, but unsuccessfully.

Stimulated by this success, New York, in 1759, exerted herself to the utmost, and raised $625,000 in five months, and levied a force of 2680 men. Ticonderoga was captured by General Amherst, early in the season, and Crown Point surrendered a few days later. In July, General Prideaux invested Fort Niagara, and though he was killed in the attack, Sir William Johnson, his successor in the command, succeeded in reducing it. On the 13th of September, the brave General Wolfe laid down his life, in the moment of victory, when the English banners floated over the towers of Quebec.

The ensuing year the French, made an unsuccessful effort to recapture Quebec; and on the 8th of September of that year, all the French possessions in Canada were surrendered to the British Government, and the French power extinguished there. Two small islands at the mouth of the St. Lawrence, St. Pierre and Miquelon, alone were preserved to them, of their former vast possessions.

During the progress of these events, in July, 1760, Governor De Lancy suddenly deceased. He was succeeded by Dr. Cadwallader Colden, the president of the council, who in August, 1761, was appointed Lieutenant Governor. In October of the

ENGLISH ADMINISTRATION. 73

same year, General Robert Monkton arrived, with a Governor's commission, but left on the 15th of the ensuing month, to command an expedition against Martinique, and the government again devolved upon Dr. Colden.

It was during his administration, that the difficulties between New Hampshire and New York commenced, relative to the territory, now known as the state of Vermont.

By the original patent, granted to the Duke of York, this tract was included. New Hampshire, however, claimed it under her charter; and, contending that the charter of the Duke of York was obsolete, proceeded to make extensive grants of land, to the settlers on the west side of the Connecticut. Emigration progressed rapidly, and in 1763, 138 townships had been granted, by New Hampshire, covering a large portion of the present state of Vermont.

Governor Colden was not the man to sit by, and tamely submit, to what he deemed injustice to his colony. He issued a proclamation, claiming jurisdiction as far east as the Connecticut, and ordered the sheriff to make returns to him, of any persons, who had taken possession, under the authority of New Hampshire.

The Governor of New Hampshire issued a counter proclamation, and the matter was referred to the Crown, which decided in favor of New York. The attempt to enforce this decision, and to induce the inhabitants to take out new deeds under New York, was, with some exceptions, ineffective, and led to constant hostilities between the Vermont settlers, and the government of New York.

In 1764 the news of the passage of the Stamp Act, (which rendered all deeds, bonds, notes, &c., invalid, unless written on stamped paper, which should pay a duty to the Crown,) excited universal indignation among the people. An organization was soon formed in this, as well as some of the adjacent states, called "The Sons of Liberty," which offered the most daring resistance, to this aggression upon the rights of the people.

Governor Colden attempted to enforce the act, but the attempt called down the hostility of the people upon him, and but for his age, he would undoubtedly have suffered in person. As it was, his effigy was carried about the city, and hung upon a gallows erected for the purpose, and his carriage and other property destroyed.

When the stamps arrived, he was obliged to surrender them to the city corporation, and await the action of the Governor, Sir Henry Moore, who arrived in July, 1765, and by the advice of his council, was deterred from attempting farther to enforce the act.

On the 1st Tuesday in October, 1765, a Congress composed of delegates from Massachusetts, Rhode Island, Connecticut, New York, Pennsylvania, New Jersey, Delaware, Maryland, and South Carolina, met at New York, to take into consideration, the invasion of the rights of the colonies, by the Stamp Act.

New Hampshire, Virginia, North Carolina and Georgia, did not send delegates, but two of them expressed their sympathy with the Congress, and the others had no meeting of their legislatures, in time to appoint delegates. This Congress made a declaration of the rights and privileges of the colonies, and petitioned for redress.

The Stamp Act was repealed on the 18th of March, 1766; but

the offensive declaration accompanied the repeal, that "Parliament possessed the power, to bind the colonies in all cases, whatsoever."

In 1767, Charles Townsend, chancellor of the English exchequer, proposed a new bill, levying duties on glass, paper, paints and tea. This passed, and the inhabitants entered, as they had previously done, into non-importation agreements, by which they pledged themselves to use none of these articles, nor, so far as it could be avoided, other articles of British manufacture. In 1769, five-sixths of these duties, and in 1770, all of them, were repealed, except the duty on tea. The people of New York, as well as of the other colonies, rigidly abstaining from the use of this beverage, no excitement was produced; and from 1770 to 1774 a period of calmness ensued, although the English government and the colonists regarded each other with jealousy.

Attempts were made, in 1767, to settle the boundary between Massachusetts and New York. Massachusetts, under her charter, claimed to the Pacific Ocean, and had repeatedly attempted to make settlements within the bounds of New York. The attempt to establish these settlements, had produced collision, and in several instances, bloodshed. Commissioners from the two colonies met at New Haven, in October, 1767, and determined that the Massachusetts line should run twenty miles east of Hudson river, but could not agree in regard to the manner of running that line.

In September, 1769, Sir Henry Moore deceased. His course, during the period in which he acted as Governor, had been prudent, mild, and dignified. He had, as far as possible, abstained from controversy with the assembly and people, interpreting his instructions from the government in England, as liberally as lay in his power. His death was much lamented. Governor Colden again occupied his place, although very much advanced in years.

Governor Dunmore assumed the government in November, 1770; but his administration continued only a few months, and was marked by no important event. He was the first Governor supported by the Crown, a measure against which New York protested, as calculated to make the executive independent of the popular branch of the government. During his short continuance in office, a contest took place with the legislature, in regard to quartering the King's troops, to which the assembly were wholly averse, but to which, under the threats of the British government, they were obliged to submit.

Liberty poles had, at this period, been frequently erected in New York city, and as often cut down and destroyed by the British soldiery, who entertained the bitterest hostility to the citizens. After repeated efforts, the inhabitants erected one upon private grounds, so frmly encased in iron, that the soldiers could not destroy it.

Lord Dunmore having been appointed Governor of Virginia, Governor Tryon succeeded him on the 8th of July, 1771.

In 1772, the New Hampshire grants became a renewed source of serious disquietude to the colony. Governor Tryon offered a reward of fifty pounds for the apprehension of Ethan Allen, Seth Warner, and six others of the most obnoxious of the settlers; and the New York assembly passed an act, declaring the opposition of these citizens to the government of New York, *felony*. Allen and his coadjutors, in return, hurled their defiance at the Governor, and those who were sent to arrest them.

In the Spring of 1775, matters appeared to be approaching a crisis, in regard to this territory. A collision took place, between the officers of New York, and the citizens of Westminster county, Vermont, in which one man was killed, and several wounded. But for the occurrence of the battle of Lexington, at this juncture, probably a serious civil war would have ensued.

The British government resolved, in 1773, to accomplish by cunning, what they had failed to attain by force. They remitted to the East India Company, the customary English duties on tea, and permitted them to ship it for America, with only a duty of three pence per pound, to be paid, on landing it, at any American port. They supposed that as this would make the price of tea lower than in England, the colonists would not object to it; but the colonists saw, in this measure, the same principle, against which they had been contending.

The course adopted by the different colonies, is well known. In New York, a meeting of "The Sons of Liberty" was called, on the receipt of the intelligence, and resolutions passed, that the tea should not be landed. Accordingly, when, in April, 1774, the tea ship, (the Nancy, commanded by Captain Lockyier,) arrived off Sandy Hook, the pilots, who had already received their instructions, refused to bring her any nearer the city. The captain however came up, and was waited upon, by a committee, who informed him, that he must return immediately to England, with his cargo; and for the purpose of preventing his sailors from deserting, a strong guard was stationed near his ship at Sandy Hook. Finding it useless to resist, he submitted to their commands.

Meanwhile information was received that Captain Chambers, of the ship London, a man loud in his professions of patriotism, had brought out eighteen chests of tea, as a private venture. Being questioned by the committee, he denied it; but upon their assuring him, that their evidence was so strong that they should search the ship, he confessed it, but attempted to apologize. His apologies did not avail. His tea was emptied into the harbor forthwith, and he permitted to withdraw. Embarking on board Lockyier's ship, he sailed for England, to hide his shame and disgrace.

About this period a committee of observation was organized in New York, consisting of fifty persons, who were invested with discretionary powers, with regard to the administration of government.

On the 5th of September, 1774, a congress from the different colonies, met at Philadelphia. They adopted several resolutions, and prepared addresses to the King and both houses of Parliament, and to the people of Great Britain and Canada.

To these addresses and resolutions prepared by Congress, the assembly of New York refused to give their assent. On the contrary, they addressed an exceedingly loyal and humble letter to the King, in which they represented their grievances, but without seeming much afflicted by them. They were undoubtedly influenced to this course, by Governor Tryon, a man of very popular manners, and artful insinuating address, who had the skill, to mould the assembly to his will.

This step of New York exerted a very important influence upon the future destiny of the colonies; for the British Ministry were upon the point of yielding to their just demands, when the news of the defection of New York reached them. Stimulated by this, they continued that course of aggression, which ultimately led to the establishment of our liberties.

Governor Tryon sailed for England in April, 1774, and returned in June, 1775.

In April, 1775, a provincial convention was convened at New York, and elected delegates to the 2d Congress, which assembled at Philadelphia in May, 1775.

The news of the battle of Lexington, (Mass,) on the 19th of April the same year, caused great excitement in the city of New York. At the desire of the committee of observation, a committee of superintendence was elected by the citizens, consisting of 100 of the most respectable citizens; and the arms in the city arsenal, and others about to be shipped to Boston, were seized.

Ticonderoga, Crown Point, and Skenesborough, (now Whitehall,) were captured in May, by Colonels Ethan Allen and Benedict Arnold, and the entire command of Lake Champlain obtained.

Governor Tryon returned, in June, from England and was welcomed by the citizens; but his strenuous exertions to promote the royal cause, soon rendered him unpopular, and in October, considering his personal safety endangered, he took refuge on board the Asia, a ship of war lying in the harbor.

On the 22d of May, 1775, a *provincial* Congress was convened at New York, and efficient measures were taken for the military organization, and defence of the country. Two regiments were authorized to be raised, bounties were offered for the manufacture of gunpowder and muskets in the province, fortifications were projected at Kingsbridge and the Highlands, and Philip Schuyler and Richard Montgomery were recommended to the Continental Congress for appointment, the first as a Major General, and the second as Brigadier General.

Upon the adjournment of this Congress in September, for a month, they delegated their powers to a *committee of safety*, composed of three members from the city, and one, from each of the other counties.

Generals Schuyler and Montgomery, at the direction of Congress, undertook an expedition against Quebec, which, though at first, promising a favorable result, finally terminated unfortunately, in the death of Montgomery, and the repulse of the army.

Many of the inhabitants of Tryon county espoused the side of the mother country, under the direction of Sir John Johnson, son of Sir William, already mentioned, and made preparations to fight against the colony. General Schuyler was ordered by Congress to disarm them; and calling out the Albany militia, who rallied around his standard to the number of 3000, he proceeded into that county, and dispersed about 600 loyalists. The loyalists on Long Island also entrenched themselves, but were disarmed, and their leaders secured, by the Jersey militia. These events occurred in the winter of 1775.

July 9th, 1776, the provincial Congress met at White Plains, and took the title of "*The Representatives of the State of New York.*" On the first day of their meeting, they received the Declaration of Independence, and immediately passed a resolution, approving it. Soon after, they enacted a law, that all persons, residing in the state, and enjoying the protection of its laws, who should be found guilty of aiding its enemies, should suffer death.

THE STATE OF NEW YORK.

In July, 1776, General Howe, and Admiral Howe, his brother, the British commanders of the land and naval forces, arrived at Staten Island. The inhabitants, at once, took the oath of allegiance to the British Crown, and, together with a considerable number of loyalists, from New Jersey and Long Island, were embodied as a part of the British forces.

At this period, the troops under Washington were unaccustomed to discipline, not well clothed, nor prepared for efficient military duty; and consequently not to be relied upon, in a direct battle with the highly disciplined, and well appointed troops of England. From this fact, General Washington determined not to risk a general action, until his forces, by constant military exercise, and occasional skirmishes with the enemy, should acquire greater confidence in their own prowess.

It would have been fortunate, had he been able to maintain this position; but unhappily, in a conflict on Brooklyn Heights, on the 27th of August of this year, in which, at first, only a portion of the army were engaged, the entire troops finally became enlisted, and the Americans were routed with severe loss both in killed and prisoners. As the result of this unfortunate battle, Washington was compelled to evacuate New York city, and retreat towards Philadelphia, with one division of his army, while the other made its way northward, along the banks of the

Hudson. This event took place on the 12th of September, 1776. Previous to Washington's evacuating the city of New York, the public stores were removed to Dobb's ferry.

On the 15th of September, the American General attempted to oppose the landing of the British forces, at Kip's and Turtle bays, but unsuccessfully, and with shameful demonstrations of cowardice on the part of the American soldiery. On the 16th of September occurred the battle of Harlaem heights, in which, though but few troops were engaged, the action was close, and the Americans recovered their courage and spirit. Washington having retreated into Westchester Co., a partial action took place at White Plains, on the 28th of October, in which the Americans suffered some loss.

Forts Washington and Lee, the former on the upper part of New York Island, the latter nearly opposite on the Jersey shore, were garrisoned by the Americans; but by too small a force to resist successfully the British troops; and on the 16th of November, after a closely contested action, in which the enemy met with a severe loss, the American garrison was compelled to surrender. With the remnant of his army, dispirited and disheartened, Washington retreated towards Philadelphia; but soon after, by his bold attack upon the Hessian forces at Trenton, he infused new courage into his troops, retrieved his own reputation, and turned the tide of war.

Amid all the discouragements under which the cause of liberty labored, the New York provincial Congress did not despair. On the 23d of December, 1776, they put forth an address to the people, the production of the gifted, patriotic, and pure minded Jay, which was admirably adapted to encourage and animate the zeal of the friends of freedom.

In May, 1777, Colonel Meigs, by a well devised and happily executed enterprise, took possession of, and destroyed a large quantity of the enemy's stores at Sag Harbor, L. I., and captured ninety men. This enterprise was accomplished with a force of only 234 men. Congress voted him a sword, for this gallant exploit.

In January, 1777, the territory known as the New Hampshire grants, assumed the title of the *State of Vermont*, and soon after adopted a constitution. On the 12th of March, a constitution, for the state of New York, was reported by a committee of the provincial Congress, which, on the 20th of April, 1777, was adopted.

A few of its more important provisions should be here noticed. They were, 1st, the requirement of a property qualification in the electors and the elected. 2d, The appointing power was vested in the Governor, and a council, of four persons, chosen from the senate. By this council, sheriffs, coroners, justices of the peace, judges, both of the superior and inferior courts, mayors and recorders of the cities, and all the officers of state, were appointed. This immense amount of patronage, thus thrown into the hands of five individuals, proved a very serious evil. 3d, The Governor was invested with the power of proroguing the legislature when he saw fit. This constitution was revised and amended in 1821.

STATE ADMINISTRATION. 79

On the 22d of March, 1777, a detachment of 800 British troops landed at Peekskill, and set fire to the principal storehouses there; but finding that a large force of Americans were approaching, they retreated. On the 26th of April, Governor Tryon, with 2000 troops, tories and regulars, proceeded to Danbury, Ct., and burned eighteen houses, and a quantity of stores; but was attacked by the Americans, and compelled to retire with considerable loss.

Under the new constitution, George Clinton was elected Governor; but, being at that time in the service of Congress, he did not meet the assembly, at its session. John Jay was appointed Chief Justice, C. R. Livingston, Chancellor, John Morin Scott, Secretary of State, and Comfort Sands, Auditor General.

At the adoption of the state constitution, there were fourteen counties in the state, viz. New York, Richmond, King's, Queen's, Suffolk, Westchester, Dutchess, Orange, Ulster, Albany, Tryon, Charlotte, Cumberland, and Gloucester. The last two, together with part of Albany and Charlotte counties, were within the limits of the present state of Vermont. The first six were mostly under the dominion of the British, the Highlands being the limit, and were governed by General Tryon till 1778, when he was succeeded by General Robertson. The British had garrisoned most of the border posts, from which they kept up a sanguinary and relentless warfare, upon the settlers, during the whole struggle.

General Schuyler and Rev. Mr. Kirkland were, about this time deputed to hold a conference with the Iroquois, who, under the instigation of Sir John, and Colonel Guy Johnson, and the Butlers, as well as the famous Indian chief Brant, were making serious ravages on the frontier settlements. As the result of this conference, the Oneidas remained faithful to the Americans, while the remainder of the tribes, under the influence of the Johnsons, took up arms, on the side of the British.

Determined to leave nothing undone, to effect the entire subjugation of the rebel colonies, the English Ministers sent out a well appointed army, the flower of the English soldiery, together with a numerous body of German troops, under the command of General Burgoyne, an experienced officer, of known bravery, and of high reputation.

General Burgoyne was directed to start from Quebec, and, scouring the country with his Indian allies, to effect a junction with Howe, at some point on the Hudson. As this would cut off all communication between New England and the other colonies, it was thought, that the work of subduing that section, would be comparatively easy.

For the purpose of effecting this object, General Burgoyne detached Colonel St. Leger, with 1600 regular troops, tories, and Indians, to harass and destroy the frontier settlements. St Leger arrived, without opposition, before Fort Schuyler, which he besieged.

Meantime, he despatched Sir John Johnson, with a body of

tories and Indians, against General Herkimer, who was advancing to the aid of Colonel Gansevoort, the commander of the fort. They met at Oriskany. Herkimer's force was small and undisciplined. The battle was a severe one; Herkimer was wounded at the first fire; but the British were obliged to withdraw, defeated. Soon after, by a successful artifice, Arnold compelled St. Leger to raise the siege of Fort Schuyler, and retreat into Canada, with the loss of his Indian allies.

Burgoyne had pursued his march, with the main body of his army, thus far, in triumph; but soon, his fortune began to change. The Americans, under General Schuyler, had obstructed his progress, from Lake Champlain to the Hudson, by felling trees, destroying the roads, &c., so that he was necessarily a long time employed, in the transportation of his artillery and stores.

<small>Finding that these were not sufficient, to last through the campaign, he dispatched Colonels Baum and Breyman, with more than 1500 chosen troops, to obtain stores at Bennington. These were met, and defeated, on the 16th of August, 1777, by the Green Mountain boys, under General Stark, and Colonel Warner, and over 1000 killed, wounded, and taken prisoners. This loss materially impeded Burgoyne's progress, disheartened his army, and prepared the way for his defeat and surrender.</small>

On the 19th of September, a fierce and bloody battle was fought between the American forces, under General Gates, (who had now succeeded General Schuyler,) and Burgoyne's army, which resulted in severe loss on both sides, and the maintenance of their ground by both armies. The loss of the British, however, was much the largest. In this contest, General Arnold and Colonel Morgan distinguished themselves, by acts of the most daring personal bravery.

Burgoyne now fortified his position, and sent to Sir Henry Clinton, for reinforcements and supplies. The American army also entrenched themselves strongly, on Bemis' Heights, Saratoga Co. On the 7th of October, Burgoyne, finding his stores failing, and receiving no intelligence from Sir Henry Clinton, resolved to attack the American entrenchments, and attempt to force his passage through to the Hudson. The battle was a severe one, but he was defeated, with the loss of 200 killed and wounded, and about the same number taken prisoners.

On the 17th of the same month, after repeated attempts to escape from his perilous position, finding himself surrounded on every side by a victorious enemy, General Burgoyne surrendered to General Gates, his entire army, consisting of 5792 men, together with 5000 stands of arms, 42 field pieces, and large quantities of ammunition. This splendid victory did much towards achieving our nation's independence.

On the 17th of November following, Congress adopted the articles of confederation, for the different states. These were approved, by the legislature of New York, February 6th, 1778.

The repeated incursions of the Indians upon the frontier settlements, particularly the cruel outrage at Wyoming, called loudly for retributive justice. But their crimes were still to assume a deeper dye. In November, 1778, Colonel Alden, the commander at Cherry Valley, received intelligence that an attack was intended, upon that place. With a fatal and unaccountable stupidity, he paid no attention to the report. On the 10th, the Indians and tories, under the command of the bloodthirsty Walter Butler, and the Indian chieftain Brant, approached the settlement, killed Colonel Alden, butchered about twenty of the inhabitants, mostly women and children, took nearly forty prisoners, and, after plundering and burning all their houses, departed.

To punish these depredations, General Sullivan, in August, 1778, at the head of an efficient force, visited the country of the Senecas, destroyed eighteen of their villages, laid waste their whole territory, and most signally defeated them.

In April of the same year, Colonel Van Schaick attacked the Onondagas, who had been the most troublesome of the border tribes, destroyed their villages, took between thirty and forty prisoners, and killed twelve of the Indians. These severe blows, for a time, put these tribes in check.

On the 28th of September, 1778, two detachments of the enemy's troops, sent by Sir Henry Clinton, surprised a part of Colonel Baylor's regiment of cavalry, stationed at Tappan, by night, and butchered sixty-seven out of one hundred and four men, unresisting and asking for quarter.

In May, 1779, Sir Henry Clinton made an expedition in person, up the Hudson, compelled the garrison at Verplanck's Point to surrender, after a short but spirited resistance, and took possession of Stoney Point, which was abandoned by the Americans. At his return, he garrisoned both forts.

On the 16th of July, 1778, General Washington commissioned General Anthony Wayne to storm the British fort at Stoney Point, a strong fortress, which was the resort of tory refugees, who sallied out occasionally, and ravaged the neighboring settlements. The fort was carried at the point of the bayonet, and with trifling loss. Owing to the weakness of the American force, however, it was soon found necessary to abandon it, and it was afterwards re-occupied by the enemy.

Soon after, Major Lee made a daring and successful expedition against Paulus Hook, (Powles Hook,) now Jersey City, and captured the British garrison, consisting of 150 men, directly under the guns of the British ships of war, lying in the Hudson river.

General Arnold had been, thus far, distinguished in the Revolution, for his reckless daring, his chivalric bravery, and his apparently ardent patriotism; but amid all, the private character of the man was known to be vicious and corrupt. His reputation was stained by dishonesty, rapacity, and meanness. In consequence of a severe wound, received in the last battle with Burgoyne, he was disabled from active service, and in the summer of 1778, General Washington assigned to him the command of the city of Philadelphia. His extravagance, recklessness, and dishonesty, drew down upon him the displeasure of the citizens, who were loud in their complaints against him; and in March, 1779, he resigned his command.

In April, he married Miss Shippen, a lady who had been a distinguished belle, had received the attentions of the British officers, during their occupancy of that city, and was at heart a loyalist. Through her correspondence with some of the British officers, an opportunity was offered to Arnold, to communicate with the enemy; and he finally took the resolution to sell himself, and his country, for British gold, in order to rid himself of his pecuniary embarrassments. To make his treachery more valuable, in August, 1780, he solicited, and obtained the command of the strong and important post of West Point, the key of the Hudson.

In order to settle finally the terms of his treachery, Sir Henry Clinton despatched Major Andre, an Adjutant General in his army, (who had been Mrs. Arnold's correspondent, and with whom, over a feigned signature, Arnold had also corresponded,) to have an interview with the traitor, and agree upon the details of his infamous treason. They met, made their arrangements, and parted; Arnold to return to his post, and Andre to New York.

Before reaching that city, however, the latter was arrested by three militia men, and having been convicted by a Court Martial, was hanged as a spy. Arnold succeeded in making his escape, though not in surrendering the important post which he commanded, and his base treachery was rewarded by the British Government, with the office of a Brigadier General, and the sum of £10,000 sterling. But he was never trusted implicitly by the British, and so strong was the feeling of loathing, on the part of the British officers, of his meanness, that many of them refused to serve under him.

In the hope of securing him and bringing him to a just punishment; and with a view to save the gifted, but unfortunate Andre, from the fate he had brought upon himself, General Washington commissioned Mr. Champe, a Sergeant Major in Major Lee's regiment, to proceed to the British camp, professedly as a deserter, and to endeavor to seize the person of Arnold. The attempt was unsuccessful.

In 1780, 81, Brant, the Mohawk chief, in conjunction with Sir John Johnson nd Walter Butler, made several incursions upon the frontier settlements, in the Schoharie and Mohawk valleys. In August, a force under Colonel Marinus Willet pursued and routed these marauders, and killed Butler, whose savage cruelties had rendered him notorious. The remaining scenes of the war of the Revolution, mostly occurred in the southern states, and therefore do not come within the scope of this historical sketch.

In 1782, the English Government resolved to relinquish the hopeless contest with their colonies. On the 30th of November of that year, provisional articles of peace were agreed upon; and on the 25th of November, 1783, the British troops evacuated New York, and Washi g , with his army, entered in triumph. On the 4th of December, Washington took an affectionate farewell of his officers; and after resigning to Congress, then in session at Annapolis, Maryland, his commission, retired to Mount Vernon, to spend the remainder of his days in retirement and domestic felicity.

Events which transpired, soon after the Revolution, demonstrated, most conclusively, that the compact, which had connected the different states of the Union together, during the war, would not suffice, to maintain that connection, in time of peace. In 1787, therefore, in accordance with a resolution of Congress, delegates were elected from this state to meet those of the other states, in convention at Philadelphia, in May, to frame a new constitution. The delegates chosen from this state, were Messrs. Yates, Lansing, and Alexander Hamilton.

<small>The constitution prepared by this convention was not at first satisfactory to a majority of the citizens of New York. But the powerful exposition and defence of it, by Mr. Hamilton, John Jay and others, in the essays published under the title of "The Federalist," tended to bring about a change of feeling, in regard to it; and on the 26th of July, 1788, it was ratified, in convention, by the state, not, however, without the recommendation of several amendments, which were not adopted.</small>

During this period, and until 1795, George Clinton, whose services in the Revolution had been so eminent and valuable, held the office of Governor.

A general organization act was passed, in 1788, by the legislature, dividing the state into fourteen counties, which were subdivided into townships. The western and central portions of the state, now free from the hostile inroads of savages, prospered, and rapidly increased in population and wealth.

In 1790, the difficulties, which for twenty-six years, had existed between New York and Vermont, and which had been the cause of bloodshed and bitter hostility, between the citizens of the two states, were amicably adjusted.

But for the patriotism and prudence of her leaders, Vermont would probably have been, to this day, an integral portion of the British empire. In addition to other and more patriotic motives, it cannot be denied that the jealousy of the increasing influence of the southern states in Congress, tended to predispose New York favorably, to a settlement.

Commissioners having been appointed, by both states, in 1789, met and reported in October, 1790, in favor of the payment, by Vermont, to New York, of the sum of $30,000, for the extinction of the land claims, held by the latter; and that New York, upon such payment, should relinquish all claims, either to land, or jurisdiction, in Vermont, and acquiesce in her admission to the Union. This report was approved by both states, and in 1791, Vermont was received into the confederacy.

In 1791, the agriculture of the state received a new impulse, from the organization of a society for the promotion of agriculture, arts and manufactures.

The same year, a committee was appointed by the legislature, to inquire into the most eligible method, of removing obstructions from the Hudson and Mohawk rivers. The next year, (1792,) two companies were formed, styled the Northern and Western Inland Lock Navigation companies, to improve the navigation of the Hudson and Mohawk, and to connect the Oneida and Ontario lakes with the latter, and Lake Champlain with the former. For the purpose of aiding them in this enterprise, the state became a subscriber to their stock, to the amount of $92,000. This, though productive of no great practical results, was the first step, in that system of internal improvement, so ably advocated and carried out, by the genius and perseverance of De Witt Clinton.

During this period manufactures did not prosper; and our country was supplied with most of the products of art, from England and France. In 1785, Governor Clinton having declined being a candidate for re-election to the office of Governor, John Jay, whose patriotic services in the Revolution, as a statesman, have been already noticed, was chosen his successor.

The legislature, in 1796, granted to the Oneida, Cayuga, Onondaga, and Brothertown Indians, $9852, to extinguish their title, to certain lands previously possessed by them. In 1798, Governor Jay was re-elected, and continued in office till 1801. The legislature passed, in 1801, another general organization act, by which the state was divided into thirty counties.

In 1801, a convention was called, by an act of the legislature, to amend the constitution. Colonel Aaron Burr was elected President of the convention. By the act, under which the convention assembled, they were limited, in their amendments, to two points: the first, as to the number of the members of each house of the legislature, and the second, the determination of the question, whether the right of nomination to office, should be vested exclusively in the Governor, or in the Governor and Council jointly. The convention decided upon the latter interpretation of the constitution.

The same year, 1801, Governor Jay having refused to be again a candidate for office, Governor Clinton was again elect-

STATE ADMINISTRATION. 85

ed to the chief magistracy. In 1804, Governor Clinton being elected Vice President of the United States, Morgan Lewis was chosen as his successor. Daniel D. Tompkins succeeded Mr. Lewis as Governor, in 1807. The same year, Albany was made the capital of the State.

In August, 1807, Robert Fulton made his first trip with the Clermont, the first steamboat which ever plied successfully the waters of the World.* In this enterprise he was aided by Robert R. Livingston, one of the most distinguished statesmen of the state or nation.

_{The embargo laid this year by Congress, on all American shipping, at Mr. Jefferson's recommendation, in order to counteract the injurious effects of the British orders in council, and Napoleon's Berlin and Milan decrees, bore hard upon New York, and excited much opposition, for a period.}

Governor Tompkins was re-elected in 1810.

The difficulties between Great Britain and our own country, to which we have already alluded, had for several years been the subject of anxiety and bitter feeling; and every year they had assumed a more unpleasant character. In addition to the injuries already inflicted by England, on our commerce, as a neutral power, she claimed the right to search our merchant vessels; and if her officers found on board of them, men, whom they chose to regard as British subjects, they seized them and compelled them to serve in their navy.

Our government remonstrated, but remonstrances proved unavailing; the outrage upon our national flag was repeated. Under these circumstances our statesmen conceived that they had no alternative, but to declare war upon that nation. Accordingly, on the 19th of June, 1812, the President, being duly authorized by Congress, proclaimed war against Great Britain.

Deeming it of the greatest importance to subjugate the Canadas, and thus deprive the enemy of their strong holds, measures were taken to concentrate a large force on the northern frontier of this state, and the eastern border of Michigan.

General Dearborne was appointed to the command of the forces, and by his direction, General Harrison assumed the command of the north western division, making Detroit his headquarters. General Stephen Van Rensselaer, having his headquarters at Lewistown, commanded the central division, and the commander-in-chief, the eastern, making Plattsburg his place of rendezvous.

---

* There are three other competitors for the honor of introducing steamboat navigation to the notice of the world, viz. John Fitch, of Hartford, Conn., Robert L. Stevens, of New York, and Mr. Evans, of Philadelphia. All undoubtedly deserve credit for the construction of vessels propelled by steam; but it is believed that to Fulton and Livingston belongs the honor of having demonstrated the practicability and advantages of this mode of navigation.

Experience soon proved that, unfortunately, pride of opinion is sometimes stronger than love of country. A large minority of the citizens of this, and the adjacent states, were loud in their denunciations of the war; and if they did not afford direct aid to the foe, they weakened the hands, and discouraged the hearts of those who were to contend with the enemy ; and furnished grounds of scruple, by which the timorous and faint-hearted justified their cowardice. Under such adverse influences, officers of known spirit, and tried courage, faltered in meeting the foe, and surrendered to a force inferior to their own.

The first considerable action of the war was disgraceful to our boasted prowess. General Hull, deputed to carry aggressive war into Canada, and to take the British post at Malden, seemed panic-struck at the approach of the enemy. Forgetting his former renown, as a brave soldier, he returned to Detroit without striking a blow; and on the 16th of August, 1812, surrendered his whole force, consisting of about 2000 troops, occupying a strongly fortified garrison, together with the whole territory of Michigan, to General Brock, whose entire army consisted of only 700 British troops, and 600 Indians.

General Van Rensselaer, with his command, was stationed at Lewiston, below the Falls. His troops, (principally militia,) often urged him to give them an opportunity of displaying their prowess by facing the enemy. Determining not to remain inactive, he despatched his aid-de-camp, Lieutenant Colonel Van Rensselaer, a brave and meritorious, but somewhat rash officer, with about 225 men, to attack the British post of Queenstown, on the opposite shore of the Niagara river.

The attack was successful at the outset, and but for the shameful cowardice of the troops remaining upon the American shore, would undoubtedly have terminated in a brilliant victory.

Such were the pretended constitutional scruples of the remaining troops as to the propriety of crossing over to the enemy's territory, that when ordered to reinforce Lieutenant Colonel Van Rensselaer, they preferred to see their brethren in arms cut to pieces, rather than move to their relief; and thus nearly the whole force which had crossed the river, were either killed, or taken prisoners.

General Van Rensselaer, disgusted with his army, soon after resigned his commission, and was succeeded by General Alexander Smyth, of Virginia.

This officer appears to have been a mere braggart, for after issuing a proclamation, announcing the wonderful deeds he intended to perform, he finally ordered his troops into winter quarters, without accomplishing any thing.

In January, 1813, occurred the battle of the River Raisin, in Michigan, one of the most sanguinary contests of the war. In this conflict, the British General, Proctor, acquired lasting infamy from his inhumanity to the American troops, who had surrendered; giving them up to the savages for torture and massacre, in violation of his solemn pledge to General Winchester, the American commander.

STATE ADMINISTRATION. 87

In February, 1813, Captain Forsyth, commander of the American forces at Ogdensburg, crossed the St. Lawrence, in pursuit of some prisoners whom the English had taken from his vicinity, and succeeded in capturing some military stores and about fifty prisoners. In revenge for this act, the British, on the 22d of February, 1813, crossed the St. Lawrence with a considerable force, and took Ogdensburg. Forsyth, however, with his forces, made good their retreat.

On the 27th of April, 1813, General Dearborne made a successful attack upon York, now Toronto, (Canada West), aided by the squadron of Commodore Chauncey. After a short resistance, it was captured, together with a large quantity of military stores. The force detailed for this service, consisted of about 1700 troops, under the command of General Z. M. Pike.

The enemy, in their retreat, laid a train of combustibles to their magazine, with the fiendish design of thus destroying the invaders. The scheme was, in part, successful; and the brave and noble hearted Pike was killed, by the explosion, at the head of his troops, in the moment of triumph. The troops faltered for a moment, but rallied instantly, and drove the foe from the field. The British lost in this action, in killed, wounded, and prisoners, about 750. The Americans, about 300.

Early in May, 1813, the Americans evacuated the fort at York. They removed to Four mile creek, a short distance below Fort Niagara, and, in connection with a force of 100 men, who were landed from two armed schooners despatched to cooperate with them, took possession of some military stores, at that place, belonging to the enemy, and then proceeded in safety to Fort Niagara.

On the 27th of May, a descent was made, by Commodore Chauncey, upon Fort George, which surrendered, after a short contest. The American loss in killed and wounded, was 150: the British, in killed, wounded, and prisoners, 386, beside 507 militia men, released on their parole.

On the 23d of June, General Dearborne sent Lieutenant Colonel Boerstler with 570 men, to Beaver Dam, to disperse a body of the enemy. When within about two miles of that place, he was attacked by the foe, who, in ambuscade, had awaited his approach. After a short contest, he succeeded in driving them into an open field, and sent an express to General Dearborne for reinforcements; but before they could arrive, he was surrounded by a superior force, and compelled to surrender.

During the period occupied by these enterprises, the enemy were not idle. About the last of May, Commodore Chauncey's fleet having left Sackett's Harbor, for Fort George, Sir George Prevost made a descent upon the town, with 1000 troops, but was repulsed with considerable loss. On the 19th of June, the British landed and burned the village of Sodus, where some military stores were deposited. On the following day, they made an unsuccessful attempt to land at Oswego. On the 2d of July, they again attacked Sackett's Harbor, but with no better success than before. On the 11th, they crossed over to Black Rock, and succeeded in capturing some stores.

Meantime, both parties were seeking to secure the exclusive control of Lake Erie. Commodore Perry, by extraordinary exertion, had built and equipped an American squadron of nine vessels. carrying fifty-four guns; and Commodore Barclay had prepared a British squadron of six vessels, mounting sixty-three guns.

The two squadrons met on the 10th of September, 1813, near the western extremity of the lake. Owing to a calm at the commencement of the action, the Lawrence, Commodore Perry's flag-ship, was exposed to almost the whole fire of the enemy, and soon disabled.

At this juncture, when the foe were ready to triumph, Perry, with four of his men, leaped into a boat, flag in hand, and a gentle breeze springing up at the time, brought the Niagara, to which he had transferred his flag, into action. Through the exertions of Captain Elliot, her commander, the remainder of the vessels were brought up, and the Niagara led the way through the enemy's line, supported by the rest of the squadron, pouring successive broadsides into five of their vessels. In a short time, the entire fleet of the enemy surrendered.

Commodore Perry communicated to General Harrison the following intelligence of his victory: "We have met the enemy, and they are ours."

This victory resulted in the evacuation of Detroit, by the British army, which was pursued and overtaken by General Harrison, on the river Thames, about eighty miles from Detroit. At this point was fought, on the 5th of October, the battle of the Thames, one of the most brilliant of the campaign. At this battle, Tecumseh was killed, and the Indian force dispersed.

Preparations were now made by the American army for an attack on Montreal; and for this purpose, the divisions, commanded by Generals Wilkinson and Hampton, were ordered to form a junction on the St. Lawrence. General Wilkinson moved down the river with his troops, early in November, and on the 19th of that month, a severe, but indecisive action was fought at Williamsburgh. Both parties claimed the victory. The American loss in killed and wounded was about 300; the British, about 200. Owing to some misunderstanding, the junction of the two divisions was not effected, and soon after, they went into winter quarters.

In December, General McClure, commanding at Fort George, hearing of the approach of a large British force, dismantled and abandoned the fort, having previously burned the Canadian village of Newark, now called Niagara.

On the 19th of this month, the British crossed the river and carried Fort Niagara by storm; and to revenge the burning of Newark, they proceeded to burn Lewistown, Youngstown, Manchester, now called Niagara Falls' Village, and the Tuscarora Indian village. On the 30th, they crossed again, and burned Black Rock and Buffalo. These villages were only guarded by small bodies of militia, who could oppose no effectual resistance to the marauders.

On the 3d of July, 1814, Generals Scott and Ripley with about 3000 troops, crossed the Niagara river and took Fort Erie, without opposition. The next day, General Brown advanced, with the main body of his forces to Chippeway, about two miles south of the Falls. Here, on the 5th, General Riall, at the head of the British army, advanced to give them battle. The contest was severe, but resulted in favor of the Americans. The enemy lost nearly 500 men; our own troops, 338.

General Riall, after his defeat, withdrew to Queenstown, and afterwards to Burlington Heights. Here he was reinforced by General Drummond, who took the command. The enemy appeared before the camp, just before sunset, on the 25th of July. The American army immediately formed in the order of battle, at Lundy's Lane, about half a mile north west from the Falls; and there, amid the eternal roar of Niagara, the two infuriated hosts continued in deadly conflict, till past midnight.

This was the most hotly contested action of the war; General Scott led the advance, and first engaged a body of the enemy, greatly his superior in numbers, for an hour. Both parties were then reinforced, and the action renewed with greater fury than before. The British artillery was so placed upon an eminence, as to rake every part of the American army; and it became evident that the result of the battle depended on the capture of that battery.

General Scott rode up to Colonel Miller and inquired, "can you storm that battery?" "I can try, Sir;" was the laconic reply; and in a few moments, he was seen at the head of his regiment, impetuously charging upon the artillery, his ranks thinned at every step by the cannon balls.

The enemy resisted bravely, but could not withstand the charge. Three times they returned to the attack, but their battery was turned against them with murderous force; and no sooner did they come within its range, than the deadly rifle, wielded with unerring aim, mowed them down by platoons.

General Drummond was himself wounded, and the army driven from the field. The British force engaged in this battle, was nearly one third greater than the American. The loss of the enemy was 878; of the American troops, 858.

Generals Brown and Scott having both been wounded in the battle, the command devolved on General Ripley, who thought it prudent to retire to Fort Erie. Here, on the 4th of August, he was besieged by General Drummond, at the head of five thousand men. Meanwhile, General Gaines arrived at the fort and took the command, as senior officer. On the 15th, the British made an assault on the fort, but were repulsed with the loss of nearly 1000 men. On the 17th of September, General Brown having recovered and taken the command, a sortie was made from the fort, and the advanced troops of the besiegers defeated.

Soon after, hearing that General Izard was on his way with reinforcements, the enemy raised the siege and returned to Fort George. In November, Fort Erie was abandoned and dismantled by the Americans, who, crossing the river, went into winter quarters, in the neighborhood of the Lakes.

Meantime, events were occurring in the eastern part of the state, which materially hastened the termination of the war. General Wilkinson went into winter quarters at French Mills, now Fort Covington. In the latter part of winter, he broke up his encampment and removed to Plattsburg. On the 30th of March, 1814, he penetrated into Canada, and attacked a body of the enemy at La Colle Mills, on the Sorel river, but was repulsed with some loss, and returned to Plattsburg, where he was soon after superseded in command by General Izard.

Early in September, Sir George Prevost advanced towards Plattsburg with an army of 14,000 men, mostly European veterans, who had served under Wellington. At the same time, Commodore Downie appeared on Lake Champlain with seventeen sail, mounting ninety-five guns, and carrying 1020 men. To oppose this force, General Macomb had only 1500 regular troops, and about 2500 militia; and Commodore McDonough, a squadron of fourteen sail, mounting eighty-six guns, and carrying 820 men.

The two armies engaged in battle on Sunday, the 11th of September. The action between the land forces and the squadrons commenced simultaneously. The British made the greatest exertions to cross the Saranac, but were repulsed at every attempt, with severe loss; and their squadron having been captured, and mostly destroyed, they retreated precipitately, leaving behind them large quantities of military stores. The entire loss of the British, in this action, including killed, wounded, prisoners, and deserters, was estimated at 2500. The remaining battles of the war were fought at the south.

On the 24th of December, 1814, the treaty of Ghent was signed by the commissioners of the two countries, and on the 17th of February, 1815, this treaty was confirmed by the President and Senate.

Of the events which have transpired in this state since the war, there are so many living witnesses, that we shall give but a brief notice.

The canal project, which, during the war, had been forgotten, or neglected, was soon revived. In 1816, some steps were taken for bringing it before the legislature; and in 1817, the petition of more than 100,000 citizens of the state, asking that laws should be passed for its construction, was presented to that body, and action taken thereon. The same year, the Erie and Champlain canals were both commenced and vigorously prosecuted to their final completion, which occurred, the latter in 1823, and the former in 1825.

In 1817, Governor Tompkins was chosen Vice President of the United States, and De Witt Clinton, the ardent and zealous friend of the system of internal improvements, was elected his successor. Governor Clinton was re-elected to the same office, in 1820. In 1821, a convention was called by an act of the legislature, to revise the constitution. This convention met at Albany on the third Tuesday of June, 1821. The result of their deliberations, was the constitution, under which the state has been governed up to the year 1846. This constitution was ratified by the people, in December, 1821, by a majority of more than 33,000.

In 1822, Mr. Clinton having declined the nomination, Joseph C. Yates, at that time Judge of the Supreme Court, was chosen Governor. Mr. Clinton was re-elected, however, to that office, in 1824; and again in 1826. In 1825, the completion of the Erie Canal, and the union of the waters of Lake Erie and the Hudson, was celebrated with great rejoicings.

In 1826, the anti-masonic excitement commenced.

The circumstances which led to it were these.* William Morgan, a Royal Arch Mason, and a printer by trade, said to be a native of Virginia, had taken up his residence in the village of Batavia, Genesee county. Not having been successful in business, he, probably from pecuniary considerations, determined to publish a pamphlet, containing a disclosure of the secrets of Masonry. His intentions were discovered by some of his fellow Masons, who communicated them to others of their own and adjacent lodges.

On the 11th of September, 1826, Mr. Cheesebrough, master of a lodge of Masons at Canandaigua, Ontario county, procured a warrant from Jeffrey Chipman, a justice of the peace in Canandaigua, to arrest Morgan on charge of stealing a shirt and cravat. He with others then proceeded to Batavia, arrested Morgan, and brought him to Canandaigua, before Justice Chipman, who forthwith discharged him, as not guilty.

He was then arrested, on a small debt due to one Aaron Ashley, which Cheesebrough alleged had been assigned to him. The justice rendered judgment against Morgan for two dollars, on which, upon the oath of Cheesebrough, he in-

---

* The account of Morgan's abduction is abridged from Judge Hammond's Political History of New York.

stantly issued execution, and Morgan was committed to close confinement in Canandaigua jail.

During the night of the 12th of September, he was clandestinely taken from jail, by a number of Masons, thrown into a covered carriage, gagged and conveyed, on the evening of the 14th, to the Canada side of the Niagara river, thence taken back to the American side, and left in confinement in the magazine of Fort Niagara. He remained there till the 29th of September, in charge of Colonel King, of Niagara county, and one Elisha Adams, at which time he disappeared, and has never since been heard of. The almost universal impression has prevailed that he was murdered at that time, by the direction of members of the Masonic fraternity.

Measures were instantly taken to investigate this outrage; but the committees appointed for this purpose, found themselves constantly thwarted, by members of the Masonic order, at this time in its most flourishing condition in this state. This opposition to an act of justice, excited the most intense feeling, among those members of community not connected with the Masons; and the excitement, which, in communities less influenced by moral principle, would have prompted to deeds of violence, here found vent at the ballot box; and for a number of years, the anti-masons of Western New York, constituted a formidable political party.

Ere this excitement had reached its highest intensity, Governor Clinton died, very suddenly, while conversing with some friends, on the 11th of February, 1828. This painful event caused a deep sensation throughout the community.

Governor Clinton, though possessing some faults, had been an able and zealous friend of his native state. No man ever did more to promote her best interests. Amid discouragements which would have appalled ordinary men, he steadily advocated and accomplished measures which time has proved eminently conducive to her welfare. It is sufficient proof of his patriotic foresight, that amid the ridicule of his associates, he dared to stake his reputation, on the success of the system of internal improvements. He has left an enduring record of his fame in the hearts of the people, whom his enlightened measures have endowed with plenty and prosperity.

On the decease of Governor Clinton, General Nathaniel Pitcher, the Lieutenant Governor, officiated the remainder of the term. In November, 1828, Martin Van Buren was elected Governor, and Enos T. Throop, Lieutenant Governor. Mr. Van Buren being appointed Secretary of State, in March, 1829, resigned his office, and Mr. Throop became acting Governor.

During the session of the legislature, in the winter of 1828-9, on the recommendation of Governor Van Buren, the Safety Fund Banking Law was passed. The main features of this law were conceived and drawn up by Joshua Forman, Esq. and by him communicated to Governor Van Buren, who by the aid of Thomas Olcott, Esq. of Albany, matured and presented it to the legislature.

In the autumn of 1830, Mr. Throop was elected Governor of the state. During his administration, there were a great number of applications to the legislature, for aid to construct canals in different sections of the state, involving very large expendi-

STATE ADMINISTRATION.

tures, and of doubtful pecuniary profit. Some of these, Governor Throop opposed as premature and unwise; and his opposition to them, though probably judicious, materially affected his popularity and rendered his re-election improbable.

In 1832, William L. Marcy was chosen Governor, and John Tracy, Lieutenant Governor. During the session of 1833, the bill authorizing the construction of the Chenango canal, a work attended with great expenditures, and which was strongly opposed, passed the legislature. Mr. Marcy and Mr. Tracy were re-elected to office in 1834, by a large majority.

A law was passed, in 1835, directing the enlargement and improvement of the Erie canal, and the construction of double locks. This law has involved the state in a debt of some magnitude, but when the proposed improvements are completed, they will unquestionably greatly increase its revenues.

At this session of the legislature, also, the bill to provide the schools of the state with libraries, was passed; a bill which it is hoped, will be of incalculable service to its youth. Governor Marcy and Lieutenant Governor Tracy, were, for a third time, elected to their respective offices.

In 1838, the pecuniary depression of the country produced a change in the politics of the state, and William H. Seward of Orange county, was chosen Governor, and Luther Bradish of Franklin county, Lieutenant Governor.

In 1840, the same gentlemen were re-elected.

In 1842, William C. Bouck, of Schoharie county, was elected Governor.

In 1844, Silas Wright of St. Lawrence county, who for a number of years had represented the State in the United States Senate, was elected Governor, and Addison Gardiner of Suffolk county, Lieutenant Governor.

In June, 1846, a convention, elected by the people, to revise and amend the constitution of the state, commenced its session at Albany, and in October following, reported the constitution which is found in this work, for the action of the people in the ensuing month of November. It was adopted by the people by a majority of more than 20,000 votes.

In November, 1846, John Young of Livingston county, was elected Governor and Addison Gardiner of Suffolk county, Lieutenant Governor.

INTERNAL IMPROVEMENTS.

The system of Internal Improvement, in which New York has taken the lead, forms an important portion of her history. It is interesting to trace the progress of the first of these mighty enterprises, which, in its completion, excited the astonishment and admiration of the whole confederacy, and even of the states of Europe.

In 1784, Christopher Colles proposed to the legislature to improve the navigation of the Mohawk. In 1785, he received $125, to make investigations relative to this enterprise. He again came before the legislature in 1786, but became discouraged from want of success.

The subject was referred to by Governor Clinton, in his speech to the legislature, at the opening of the session of 1791; and an act passed concerning roads and inland navigation, directing the commissioners of the land office, to cause the lands between the Mohawk and Wood creek, in Herkimer county, and between the Hudson river and Wood creek, in Washington county, to be explored, and the probable expense of canals, between these points, estimated.

The commissioners reported in 1792, and Governor Clinton communicated their report, by a message, in which he considered the practicability of effecting the object of the legislature, at a moderate expense, as ascertained.

Mr. Adgate, Mr. Williams, Mr. Livingston and Mr. Barker, were the most efficient advocates of this measure in the legislature. Mr. Elkanah Watson also wrote a number of essays on the subject, and, this year, the Western and the Northern Inland Lock Navigation Companies were chartered. General Schuyler, Thomas Eddy, Jeremiah Van Rensselaer, Barent Bleecker, Elkanah Watson, and Robert Bowne, were among their most efficient advocates.

In 1796, the Western Company completed a canal, two and three fourth miles long, at Little Falls, and another, one and one quarter miles long, at German Flats; and, in 1797, a canal from the Mohawk to Wood creek, one and three-fourth miles long, in all, less than seven miles, with nine locks.

In 1796, finding a reconstruction of their work necessary, they employed Mr. Weston, an English engineer; and when their canal would admit a passage from Schenectady to the Oneida lake, they had expended nearly $450,000. The tolls, however, were so high, that few used their canal. The Niagara company was incorporated in 1798, to make a navigable communication between Lakes Erie and Ontario. It, however, never went into operation.

The distinguished Governeur Morris seems first to have conceived the idea of a continuous canal between the Hudson and Lake Erie. He alluded to it, in a letter to a friend, in 1800, and communicated it to the late Simeon DeWitts, the surveyor general, in 1803. His plan, however, was, to have the canal constructed with a uniform declivity of six inches to a mile, and without locks, except on the slope of the Hudson. This plan afterwards proved impracticable.

In 1807-8, Jesse Hawley, Esq., wrote a series of essays, which were published in the Genesee Messenger, urging the importance of such a canal, and its immediate construction.

In 1808, Joshua Forman presented to the legislature, his memorable resolution, in which, after reciting in the preamble the various reasons for such a step, he proposes the appointment of a joint committee, to take into consideration the propriety of exploring and causing to be surveyed, the most eligible and direct route for a canal, to connect the waters of the Hudson and Lake Erie, to the end that Congress may be enabled to appropriate the necessary sum for the construction of such a work.

This resolution passed, but so little idea had the legislature of the sum requisite for such a survey, that they appropriated only $600 for the purpose. The committee appointed were, Thomas R. Gold, William W. Gilbert, Obadiah German, and James L. Hogeboom, on the part of the house, and John Taylor, John Nicholas, and Jonathan Ward, on the part of the senate. James Geddes, Esq., at that time a land surveyor, made the exploration and survey, under the direction of the surveyor general, and, in 1809, reported in favor of such a route.

In 1810, on motion of Jonas Platt, Esq., Governeur Morris, DeWitt Clinton, Stephen Van Rensselaer, Simeon DeWitt, William North, Thomas Eddy, and Peter B. Porter, were appointed commissioners, to explore the whole route for inland navigation, from the Hudson river to Lake Ontario and Lake Erie.

De Witt Clinton, at that time a member of the senate, was induced to lend a favorable ear to this great project, by the representations of Mr. Platt and Mr. Eddy, the latter of whom appears first to have advised this plan of action.

The commissioners reported, in 1811, in favor of a canal, and estimated its cost at $5,000,000. They recommended that the construction of it should be offered to the national government.

The same year a bill was passed, giving power to the commissioners, (to whom were added Robert Fulton and R. R. Livingston), to consider all matters relative to the inland navigation of the state; to make application to the general government, and to any of the states or territories, for aid or coöperation; to ascertain on what terms loans could be obtained, and at what price the rights of the Western Inland Lock Navigation Company could be purchased.

The general government having declined to offer aid in the enterprise, and the adjacent states and territories affording only their good wishes, the commissioners in 1812, proposed that the state should construct the canal without foreign assistance; and a bill was passed, directing them to procure loans and grants of land on the proposed route, but forbidding them to commence the canal.

During the period from 1812 to 1815, the war with Great Britain diverted all thoughts from this enterprise, to the more urgent one of defending their own firesides from ruthless invasion; but, when peace returned, again this great undertaking engaged the hearts of community. The Holland Land Company had granted to the commissioners more than 100,000 acres of land; and individuals some 7000 or 8000 more, towards the completion of the work.

In 1815, those opposed to the canal were so far in the majority, as to obtain the repeal of the act authorizing the commissioners to borrow $5,000,000.

This was, for the time, a virtual abandonment of the canal policy; but, with the peace, the hopes and energies of its friends revived, and, in 1816, D. D. Tompkins, then governor, recommended the consideration of the enterprise to the legislature, while a host of petitions, ably drawn up, and numerously signed, were brought before that body, praying them to proceed in this great enterprise. Among the most forcible of these, was the petition from New York, drawn up by DeWitt Clinton.

The report of the canal commissioners was full of interest. They recommended the construction of the middle section first, as it would be a source of profit, and would divert the trade from the St. Lawrence.

A bill was proposed to commence the canal immediately, but was modified in the senate, and finally passed, giving the commissioners power to take the preliminary measures, such as causing a thorough survey and estimate of the expense of the route to be made, employing engineers, making further efforts to obtain aid, either from the general, or state governments, and arranging for loans and grants of land.

In 1817, a bill was passed, authorizing the immediate construction of these works; although in view of their magnitude, alternate emotions of hope and fear predominated in the minds of the legislature. There were some who opposed the passage of the bill. Under the new ac , Stephen Van R ns elaer, DeWitt Clinton, Samuel Young, Joseph Ellicott, and Myron Holley, were appointed commissioners.

So much distrust in regard to the result of the enterprise was felt, by those living remote from the line of the canals, that they insisted on the introduction of a clause in the bill, levying a tax of $250,000, upon the lands contiguous to them. This, however, was never collected, as the means provided by the commissioners, proved amply sufficient, without resorting to direct taxation.

The ground was first broken for the Erie canal, on the 4th of July, 1817, at Rome, with appropriate ceremonies. DeWitt Clinton, then governor of the state, was present, and took part in the services on this interesting occasion.

In 1818, the governor congratulated the legislature on the progress of the enterprise, and urged them to persevere in its prosecution. Laws were passed, during the session of this year, authorizing the construction of the Chittenango canal, and a navigable feeder to the Erie canal; also, the examination of Buffalo creek, with a view to the construction of an artificial harbor on the western terminus of the canal.

An act was likewise passed, improving the financial scheme of the previous year, and authorizing the commissioners to obtain a further loan of one million of dollars.

In 1819, measures were taken for the commencement of the Oswego canal. In October, of the same year, that portion of the Erie canal extending from Utica to Rome, was opened for navigation; and the Champlain canal admitted the passage of boats. From this period all open opposition to the enterprise ceased.

In 1820, the property, right and title of the Western Inland Lock Navigation Company was transferred to the state, for the sum of $150,828. Messrs. Young, Holley, Seymour, and Bouck, were designated as acting canal commissioners, and received a salary for their services; while the remainder of the commissioners received no salary, and retained only advisory powers.

An act was passed in 1822, directing the construction of a navigable canal, to connect the Erie canal with the Onondaga lake and Seneca river. This, in connection with the act of 1819, completed the plan of what was afterwards known as the Oswego canal.

In July, 1823, the Erie canal was navigable from Schenectady to Rochester. The price of wheat, west of the Seneca river, in consequence of the facilities afforded by the canal, had already advanced fifty per cent.

In 1824, the Champlain canal was reported as finished. Acts were passed, authorizing further loans for the completion of the Erie canal; for the constructionof a canal to connect Lake Champlain with the St. Lawrence, and for fixing the termini of the Erie canal, at Albany and Buffalo.

<small>Just at the close of the session, by a most ungenerous party manœuvre, De Witt Clinton was removed from the office of canal commissioner. This was a short lived triumph, however, as in the succeeding autumn, he was elected governor, by a large majority, and of course became one of the canal commissioners, *ex officio*.

In 1825, Governor Clinton congratulated the legislature on the prospect of the speedy completion of the Erie canal, and proposed the extension of the system of internal improvements, to render the Susquehanna, the Delaware, and other rivers in the state, navigable, thus affording facilities for bringing into market, the agricultural wealth of the state.</small>

The canal was completed in October, 1826, and on the 4th of November, the first canal boat from Lake Erie, having reached New York, the occasion was celebrated with rejoicings, such, perhaps, as have seldom been equaled in this or any other state of the union.

<small>The different trades and professions of the city, each with suitable badges and banners, joined in the long procession; an immense squadron of ships, steamers, barques, &c., assembled in the bay, to witness the ceremony of the wedding of Lake Erie with the Atlantic; and amid numerous ceremonies, and eloquent orations, the glad shouts of the people went up, as with one voice. Medals were struck, commemorative of the interesting event, and forwarded to the soldiers and officers of the revolution, and to distinguished men, in our own, and other lands.</small>

The whole cost of the Erie and Champlain canals was $9,130,000; the canal debt, at their completion, was $7,738,000; and its interest $413,000. The income arising from tolls, the year after the completion of the canals, was estimated at $750,000, exceeding, very considerably, the interest of the debt. In 1835, the debt of the canal was extinguished, mainly from the tolls.

The year 1826 was the commencement of the railroad policy in the state. In that year, Stephen Van Rensselaer and others received a charter for the construction of a railroad from Albany to Schenectady, with the right of enjoying the profits of the enterprise for fifty years.

<small>The state reserved to itself, however, the power of purchasing the road, by paying to the company the excess of the cost, with interest thereon, over the profits of the work. This feature has been incorporated in all railroad charters since granted.</small>

In 1827, the legislature made an appropriation in aid of the Delaware and Hudson canal, and determined on the most feasible route for connecting the Erie canal and Susquehanna river.

An act was passed in 1832, chartering a company, to construct a railroad to connect the Hudson with Lake Erie, running through the lower tier of counties; and in 1836, a loan of the public credit to the amount of $3,000,000, was granted to the company.

INTERNAL IMPROVEMENTS.

In 1833, an act was passed authorizing the construction of the Chenango canal, a work involving a large expenditure, but which, on its completion, opened a market to a large agricultural region.

In 1835, it was found that the size of the Erie canal was inadequate to the business transacted upon it; and that the locks were worn by use, and required enlarging, and to be made double, to facilitate transportation. The legislature, therefore, the same year, authorized the application of the surplus revenues, arising from the tolls, to be applied to the enlargement of the canal.

In 1836, the legislature directed the construction of the Genesee river and Black river canals, which were soon after commenced. The financial distress in 1837-8, produced some delay and timidity in regard to internal improvements. But, in 1838, $4,000,000 were appropiated to the enlargement of the Erie canal, and the credit of the state loaned to the Catskill and Canajoharie, the Auburn and Syracuse, and the Ithaca and Owego railroad companies, to the amount of $8,000,000. The loan to the New York and Erie railroad company was modified at the same time.

Since that period, several companies have constructed railroads, forming a continuous line between Albany, and Buffalo, and the whole distance (about 400 miles) is run in less than twenty-four hours.

The Black River Canal is as yet incomplete, and the Genesee Valley Canal is only finished as far as Dansville. The New York and Erie Railroad, after long delays, is now in progress of construction, and will be completed, probably, in two or three years. The Harlaem Railroad is also rapidly progressing toward Albany. It is in contemplation to unite this with the Housatonic Railroad.

Railroads have also been projected from New York to Albany along the Hudson river; from Ogdensburg to Plattsburg; from some point on the Harlaem Railroad to New Haven, Conn.; and from Buffalo to Erie, Pennsylvania.

In this connection, too, the Magnetic Telegraph should be mentioned. Telegraph lines have been constructed from Albany and Troy to Buffalo, and by way of the Housatonic Railroad, to New York city, and others are projected. The facilities afforded for business transactions, by this instantaneous mode of transmitting intelligence, appear almost incredible. It is indeed one of the most wonderful discoveries of the present age.

PURSUITS OF THE PEOPLE.

In three of the four great departments of national industry, New York occupies the first rank. Her fertile lands, under the skillful and scientific cultivation they have received, render her preëminent in the culture of the soil; her commerce is greater than that of any other state of the confederacy; her sails whiten every sea, and bring the productions of every clime to her marts; in manufactures, she divides the palm with her sister states, Massachusetts and Pennsylvania; in mining operations, though distinguished, she is inferior to Pennsylvania, and the new states of Missouri, Wisconsin and Iowa.

1. AGRICULTURE. New York, though usually reckoned as one of the grain growing states, might, from the diversity of its surface, and the attention paid to the rearing of cattle, be ranked, with equal propriety, among the grazing states. Its mountainous districts afford rich and ample pasturage for the immense herds of cattle and sheep which dot its hills; and the quantity, or quality, of its dairy products, are exceeded by no state of the union.

Herkimer, Oneida, Orange, Delaware, Jefferson, Chenango, Chautauque, Onondaga, Madison, St. Lawrence, Otsego, Steuben, Dutchess, Erie, Tompkins, Washington, Ulster, Westchester, Oswego, Schoharie, Cayuga, Allegany, Cortland, Monroe, Wayne, Saratoga, Rensselaer and Putnam, are the most productive dairy counties.

The most prolific grain counties are Monroe, Ontario, Livingston, Niagara, Dutchess, Columbia, Orleans, Genesee, Cayuga, Onondaga, Wayne, Oneida, Seneca, Yates, Montgomery, Jefferson and Albany. In most of these counties, wheat is the principal grain; in a few, oats and corn are the chief crops.

The state Agricultural Society, the county societies connected with it, and the numerous and ably conducted agricultural journals, have done much for the improvement of this department of national industry, in the state. The most improved breeds of cattle, horses, sheep, and swine, have been imported; every new implement of husbandry, which possesses real value, and every improvement in farming, is readily adopted.

Under the influence of this commendable zeal, much of that portion of the soil, which is naturally sterile, has been reclaimed; the wilderness has become like a garden, and the desert been made to bud and blossom as the rose.

2. COMMERCE. In commerce, New York not only stands foremost among the American states, but she occupies a very high position among the commercial nations of the world. New York city, her principal seaport, is second only to London in commerce, and when her vast lake and internal commerce is added to this, it will be seen that she has but few rivals in this department.

New York has an extensive trade with all the commercial states of Europe; with Arabia, India, China, Japan, and the dependencies of each; with the various ports on the coast of Africa and South America; with New Holland, and the islands of the Pacific and Indian oceans; with the West Indies, and the various ports of our own country.

The internal commerce of the state is principally confined to the transportation of emigrants and their furniture; the conveyance of the vast amount of agricultural produce of this state, and the western states and territories, to tide water, and the return of goods for this produce. This commerce has increased, with a rapidity far beyond the expectations of the most sanguine, and is yearly increasing, at a ratio of at least ten per cent.

3. MANUFACTURES. New York has not engaged so extensively in the manufacture of the fibrous fabrics, (cotton, woollen and silk goods), as Massachusetts, although the number of manufactories is great, and annually increasing. Yet, in the preparation of those articles which first engage the attention of a new state, after its forests are, in a measure, cleared, and its people begin to provide for their own necessities, she stands foremost among the manufacturing states of the union.

In the manufacture of flour, whether we regard the quantity or the quality, she has no equal in the world. The manufacture of lumber is also extensive, and for some years to come will undoubtedly increase. The tanning and manufacturing of leather is largely carried on, in some counties of the state. Salt is made in larger quantities than in any other portion of the union, and of superior quality.

The production and manufacture of iron is becoming an important interest, yet here she must yield the palm to Pennsylvania. Her foundries are the largest in the United States. Distilled and malt liquors are still produced in very large quantities, amounting to more than five millions of dollars per annum; the amount of these, however, is rapidly decreasing. Brick and lime kilns are very numerous. The other more important manufactures of the state, are glass, soap, candles, paper, hats, caps and bonnets, machinery, hardware and cutlery, carriages, wagons and sleighs, furniture, &c.

4. MINES. The only mines of importance are those of iron and lead. The ores of iron are extensively diffused throughout the state. The magnetic oxide occurs in vast beds in the counties of Essex, Clinton, Warren, and Franklin, and in some portions of St. Lawrence. This is a valuable ore, and furnishes a vast proportion of the malleable iron used in the state. The specular oxide occurs principally in St. Lawrence county, and is mainly used for castings.

There are also, in Putnam and Orange counties, mines of magnetic oxide, and in several of the western counties, particularly those bordering on lake Ontario, are large beds of argillaceous ore, which is well adapted to castings.

The principal lead mines are those of Rossie, St. Lawrence county, and Wurtzboro', Sullivan county, but from the abundance and cheapness of the western ore, they cannot successfully compete with it in market. Sulphurets of copper and zinc have also been discovered in considerable quantities, in St. Lawrence county, and other sections, but have not been smelted to any extent.

Marble, granite, sandstone, serpentine, gypsum, ochres, the limestone of which the hydraulic cement is made, and marl, are all found abundantly in the state, and applied to the purposes of the arts, of agriculture, and of architecture. The geological survey of the state has been of great service, in developing its mineral and agricultural resources.

The statistics of the agriculture, commerce, manufactures, and mines of the state, are exhibited in Tables I., II., III. and IV., at the close of this work.

GOVERNMENT OF NEW YORK.

The Government of the state, like that of the United States, is divided into three departments, viz. the legislative, executive and judiciary.

The legislative department consists of a Senate of 32 members, and a House of Assembly of 128, the former elected for two years, the latter for one.

The executive consists of the Governor and Lieutenant Governor, who are the chief executive officers, and are elected by the people for a term of two years; and the Secretary of State, Comptroller, Treasurer, Attorney General, State Engineer and Surveyor, holding office for two years; three Canal Commissioners, and three Inspectors of State Prisons, holding office for three years. The latter are called administrative officers.

The judiciary comprises the Supreme Court, composed of at least 32 judges, (four in each of the eight districts,) a Court of Appeals, composed of eight judges, and a County Judge for each of the counties of the state, who also, (except by special enactment to the contrary,) performs the duties of surrogate. There are also justices of the peace, and judges in other courts, not of record. These judges are all elected by the people.

Provision was made by the legislature of the state, during the session of 1846, for holding a convention, to revise the constitution of the state; and delegates having been elected by the people, met at Albany, about the first of June, 1846, and in October ensuing, reported a revised constitution, which was adopted by the people, at the election in November of the same year.

The following is the constitution thus adopted.

CONSTITUTION OF NEW YORK.

Adopted November 3, 1846.

We the people of the state of New York, grateful to Almighty God for our freedom, in order to secure its blessings, do establish this Constitution.

ARTICLE I.

Sec. 1. No member of this state shall be disfranchised, or deprived of any of the rights or privileges, secured to any citizens thereof, unless by the law of the land, or the judgment of his peers.

Sec. 2. The trial by jury, in all cases in which it has been heretofore used, shall remain inviolate forever. But a jury trial may be waived by the parties in all civil cases, in the manner to be prescribed by law.

Sec. 3. The free exercise and enjoyment of religious profession and worship, without discrimination or preference, shall forever be allowed in this state to all mankind; and no person shall be rendered incompetent to be a witness on account of his opinions on matters of religious belief; but the liberty of conscience hereby secured shall not be so construed as to excuse acts of licentiousness, or justify practices inconsistent with the peace or safety of this state.

Sec. 4. The privilege of the writ of *habeas corpus* shall not be suspended, unless when, in cases of rebellion or invasion, the public safety may require its suspension.

CONSTITUTION. 103

Sec. 5. Excessive bail shall not be required, nor excessive fines imposed, nor shall cruel and unusual punishments be inflicted, nor shall witnesses be unreasonably detained.

Sec. 6. No person shall be held to answer for a capital or otherwise infamous crime, (except in cases of impeachment, and in cases of militia when in actual service; and in the land and naval forces in time of war, or which this state may keep, with consent of Congress, in time of peace; and in cases of petit larceny, under the regulation of the legislature,) unless on presentment or indictment of a grand jury, and in any trial, in any court whatever, the party accused shall be allowed to appear and defend in person, and with council, as in civil actions. No person shall be subject to be twice put in jeopardy for the same offence; nor shall he be compelled, in any criminal case, to be a witness against himself; nor be deprived of life, liberty, or property, without due process of law; nor shall private property be taken for public use without just compensation.

Sec. 7. When private property shall be taken for any public use, the compensation to be made therefor, when such compensation is not made by the state, shall be ascertained by a jury, or by not less than three commissioners, appointed by a court of record, as shall be prescribed by law. Private roads may be opened in the manner to be prescribed by law; but in every case, the necessity of the road, and the amount of all damage to be sustained by the opening thereof, shall be first determined by a jury of freeholders, and such amount, together with the expenses of the proceeding, shall be paid by the person to be benefited.

Sec. 8. Every citizen may freely speak, write, and publish his sentiments on all subjects, being responsible for the abuse of that right; and no law shall be passed to restrain or abridge the liberty of speech, or of the press. In all criminal prosecutions or indictments for libels, the truth may be given in evidence to the jury; and if it shall appear to the jury that the matter charged as libellous is true, and was published with good motives, and for justifiable ends, the party shall be acquitted; and the jury shall have the right to determine the law and the fact.

Sec. 9. The assent of two-thirds of the members elected to each branch of the legislature, shall be requisite to every bill appropriating the public moneys or property for local or private purposes.

Sec. 10. No law shall be passed, abridging the right of the people to assemble, and to petition the government, or any department thereof; nor shall any divorce be granted, otherwise than by due judicial proceedings; nor shall any lottery hereafter be authorized, or any sale of lottery tickets allowed, within this state.

Sec. 11. The people of this state, in their right of sovereignty, are deemed to possess the original and ultimate property in and to all lands within the jurisdiction of the state; and all lands, the title to which shall fail, from a defect of heirs, shall revert, or escheat to the people.

Sec. 12. All feudal tenures, of every description, with all their incidents, are declared to be abolished, saving, however, all rents and services certain, which at any time heretofore have been lawfully created or reserved.

Sec. 13. All lands within this state are declared to be allodial, so that, subject only to the liability to escheat, the entire and absolute property is vested in the owners, according to the nature of their respective estates.

Sec. 14. No lease or grant of agricultural land, for a longer period than twelve years, hereafter made, in which shall be reserved any rent or service of any kind, shall be valid.

Sec. 15. All fines, quarter sales, or other like restraints upon alienation reserved in any grant of land, hereafter to be made, shall be void.

Sec. 16. No purchase or contract for the sale of lands in this state, made since the fourteenth day of October, one thousand and seven hundred and seventy-five; or which may hereafter be made, of or with the Indians, shall be valid, unless made under the authority, and with the consent of the legislature.

Sec. 17. Such parts of the common law, and of the acts of the legislature of the colony of New York, as together did form the law of the said colony, on the nineteenth day of April, one thousand, seven hundred and seventy-five, and the resolutions of the Congress of the said colony, and of the convention of the state of New York, in force on the 20th day of April, one thousand, seven hundred and seventy-seven, which have not since expired, or been repealed or altered, and such acts of the legislature of this state as are now in force, shall be and continue the law of this state, subject to such alterations as the legislature shall make concerning the same. But all such parts of the common law, and such of the said acts, or parts thereof as are repugnant to this Constitution, are hereby abrogated; and the legislature, at its first session after the adoption of this Constitution, shall appoint three commissioners, whose duty it shall be to reduce into a written and systematic code, the whole body of the law of this state, or so much and such parts thereof as to the said commissioners shall seem practicable and expedient. And the said commissioners shall specify such alterations and amendments therein as they shall deem proper, and they shall at all times make report to the legislature, when called upon to do so; and the legislature shall pass laws, regulating the tenure of office, the filling of vacancies therein, and the compensation of the said commissioners; and shall also provide for the publication of the said code, prior to its being presented to the legislature for adoption.

Sec. 18. All grants of land within this state, made by the King of Great Britain, or persons acting under his authority, after the fourteenth day of October, one thousand, seven hundred and seventy-five, shall be null and void; and nothing contained in this Constitution shall affect any grants of land within this state, made by the authority of the said King or his predecessors, or shall annul any charters to bodies politic and corporate, by him or them made, before that day; or shall affect any such grants or charters since made by this state, or by persons acting under its authority, or shall impair the obligation of any debts contracted by this state, or individuals, or bodies corporate, or any other rights of property, or any suits, actions, rights of action, or other proceedings in courts of justice.

ARTICLE II.

Sec. 1. Every male citizen of the age of twenty-one years, who shall have been a citizen for ten days, and an inhabitant of this state one year next preceding any election, and for the last four months a resident of the county where he may offer his vote, shall be entitled to vote at such election, in the election district of which he shall at the time be a resident, and not elsewhere, for all officers that now are or hereafter may be elective by the people; but such citizen shall have been for thirty days next preceeding the election, a resident of the district from which the officer is to be chosen, for whom he offers his vote. But no man of color, unless he shall have been for three years a citizen of this state, and for one year next preceding any election shall have been seized and possessed of a freehold estate of the value of two hundred and fifty dollars, over and above all debts and incumbrances charged thereon, and shall have been actually rated and paid a tax thereon, shall be entitled to vote at such election. And no person of color shall be subject to direct taxation unless he shall be seized and possessed of such real estate as aforesaid.

Sec. 2. Laws may be passed, excluding from the right of suffrage, all persons who have been, or may be, convicted of bribery, of larceny, or of any infamous crime; and for depriving every person who shall make, or become directly or indirectly interested in any bet or wager depending upon the result of any election, from the right to vote at such election.

Sec. 3. For the purpose of voting, no person shall be deemed to have gained or lost a residence, by reason of his presence or absence, while employed in the service of the United States; nor while engaged in the navigation of the waters of this state, or of the United States, or of the high seas; nor while a student of any seminary of learning; nor while kept at any alms house, or other asylum, at public expense; nor while confined in any public prison.

Sec. 4. Laws shall be made for ascertaining, by proper proofs, the citizens who shall be entitled to the right of suffrage hereby established.

Sec. 5. All elections by the citizens, shall be by ballot, except for such town officers as may by law be directed to be otherwise chosen.

CONSTITUTION. 105

ARTICLE III.

Sec. 1. The legislative power of this state shall be vested in a Senate and Assembly.

Sec. 2. The Senate shall consist of thirty-two members, and the senators shall be chosen for two years. The Assembly shall consist of one hundred and twenty-eight members, who shall be annually elected.

Sec. 3. The state shall be divided into thirty-two districts, to be called senate districts, each of which shall choose one senator. The districts shall be numbered from one to thirty-two inclusive.

District number one shall consist of the counties of Suffolk, Richmond and Queens.

District number two shall consist of the county of Kings.

Districts number three, number four, number five, and number six, shall consist of the city and county of New York; and the board of supervisors of said city and county shall, on or before the first day of May, one thousand eight hundred and forty-seven, divide the said city and county into the number of senate districts to which it is entitled, as near as may be of an equal number of inhabitants, excluding aliens and persons of color, not taxed, and consisting of convenient and of contiguous territory; and no assembly district shall be divided in the formation of a senate district. The board of supervisors, when they shall have completed such division, shall cause certificates thereof, stating the number and boundaries of each district, and the population thereof, to be filed in the office of the Secretary of State, and of the clerk of said city and county.

District number seven shall consist of the counties of Westchester, Putnam, and Rockland.

District number eight shall consist of the counties of Dutchess and Columbia.

District number nine shall consist of the counties of Orange and Sullivan.

District number ten shall consist of the counties of Ulster and Greene.

District number eleven shall consist of the counties of Albany and Schenectady.

District number twelve shall consist of the county of Rensselaer.

District number thirteen shall consist of the counties of Washington and Saratoga.

District number fourteen shall consist of the counties of Warren, Essex, and Clinton.

District number fifteen shall consist of the counties of St. Lawrence and Franklin.

District number sixteen shall consist of the counties of Herkimer, Hamilton, Fulton, and Montgomery.

District number seventeen shall consist of the counties of Schoharie and Delaware.

District number eighteen shall consist of the counties of Otsego and Chenango.

District number nineteen shall consist of the county of Oneida.

District number twenty shall consist of the counties of Madison and Oswego.

District number twenty-one shall consist of the counties of Jefferson and Lewis.

District number twenty-two shall consist of the county of Onondaga.

District number twenty-three shall consist of the counties of Cortland, Broome, and Tioga.

District number twenty-four shall consist of the counties of Cayuga and Wayne.

District number twenty-five shall consist of the counties of Tompkins, Seneca, and Yates.

District number twenty-six shall consist of the counties of Steuben and Chemung.

District number twenty-seven shall consist of the county of Munroe.

District number twenty-eight shall consist of the counties of Orleans, Genesee, and Niagara.

District number twenty-nine shall consist of the counties of Ontario and Livingston.

District number thirty shall consist of the counties of Allegany and Wyoming.

District number thirty-one shall consist of the county of Erie.

District number thirty-two shall consist of the counties of Chautauque and Cattaraugus.

Sec. 4. An enumeration of the inhabitants of the state shall be taken, under the direction of the legislature, in the year one thousand, eight hundred and fifty-five, and at the end of every ten years thereafter; and the said districts shall be so altered by the legislature, at the first session after the return of every enumeration, that each senate district shall contain, as nearly as may be, an equal number of inhabitants, excluding aliens, and persons of color not taxed; and shall remain unaltered until the return of another enumeration; and shall at all times consist of contiguous territory; and no county shall be divided in the formation of a senate district, except such county shall be equitably entitled to two or more Senators.

Sec. 5. The members of Assembly shall be apportioned among the several counties of this state, by the legislature, as nearly as may be, according to the number of their respective inhabitants, excluding aliens, and persons of color not taxed, and shall be chosen by single districts.

The several boards of supervisors, in such counties or this state, as are now entitled to more than one member of Asseblmy, shall assemble on the first Tuesday of January next, and divide their respective counties into assembly districts, equal to the number of members of Assembly to which such counties are now severally entitled by law, and shall cause to be filed in the offices of the Secretary or State, and the clerks of their respective counties, a description of such assembly districts, specifying the number of each district, and the population thereof, according to the last preceding state enumeration, as near as can be ascertained. Each assembly district shall contain, as nearly as may be, an equal number of inhabitants, excluding aliens, and persons of color not taxed, and shall consist of convenient and contiguous territory; but no town shall be divided in the formation of assembly districts.

The legislature, at its first session, after the return of every enumeration, shall re-apportion the members of Assembly, among the several counties of this state, in manner aforesaid, and the boards of supervisors, in such counties as may be entitled, under such re-apportionment, to more than one member shall assemble, at such time as the legislature making such re-apportionment shall prescribe, and divide such counties into assembly districts, in the manner herein directed; and the apportionment and districts, so to be made, shall remain unaltered, until another enumeration shall be taken, under the provisions of the preceding section.

Every county, heretofore established and separately organized, except the county of Hamilton, shall always be entitled to one member of the Assembly, and no new county shall be hereafter erected, unless its population shall entitle it to a member.

The county of Hamilton shall elect with the county of Fulton, until the population of the county of Hamilton shall, according to the ratio, be entitled to a member.

Sec. 6. The members of the legislature shall receive, for their services, a sum not exceeding three dollars a day, from the commencement of the session; but such pay shall not exceed, in the aggregate, three hundred dollars for per diem allowance, except in proceedings for impeachment. The limitation as to the aggregate compensation, shall not take effect until the year one thousand, eight hundred and forty-eight. When convened in extra session, by the Governor, they shall receive three dollars per day. They shall also receive the sum of one dollar for every ten miles they shall travel, in going to, and returning from, their place of meeting, on the most usual route. The speaker of the Assembly shall, in virtue of his office, receive an additional compensation, equal to one-third of his per diem allowance as a member.

Sec. 7. No member of the legislature shall receive any civil appointment within this state, or to the Senate of the United States, from the Governor, the Governor and Senate, or from the Legislature, during the term for which he shall have been elected; and all such appointments, and all votes given for any such member, for any such office or appointment, shall be void.

Sec. 8. No person, being a member of Congress, or holding any judicial or military office under the United States, shall hold a seat in the legislature. And if any person shall, after his election as a member of the legislature, be elected to Congress, or appointed to any office, civil or military, under the government of the United States, his acceptance thereof shall vacate his seat.

Sec. 9. The elections of Senators and members of Assembly, pursuant to the provisions of this Constitution, shall be held on the Tuesday succeeding the first Monday of November, unless otherwise directed by the legislature.

Sec. 10. A majority of each house shall constitute a quorum to do business. Each house shall determine the rules of its own proceedings, and be the judge of the elections, returns, and qualifications of its own members; shall choose its own officers; and the Senate shall choose a temporary president, when the Lieutenant Governor shall not attend as president, or shall act as Governor.

Sec. 11. Each house shall keep a journal of its proceedings, and publish the same, except such parts as may require secrecy. The doors of each house shall be kept open, except when the public welfare shall require secrecy. Neither house shall, without the consent of the other, adjourn for more than two days.

Sec. 12. For any speech or debate, in either house of the legislature, the members shall not be questioned in any other place.

Sec. 13. Any bill may originate in either house of the legislature, and all bills passed by one house, may be amended by the other.

Sec. 14. The enacting clause of all bills shall be, "The people of the state of New York, represented in Senate and Assembly, do enact as follows," and no law shall be enacted except by bill.

Sec. 15. No bill shall be passed, unless by the assent of a majority of all the members elected to each branch of the legislature, and the question upon the final passage, shall be taken immediately upon its last reading, and the yeas and nays entered on the journal.

Sec. 16. No private or local bill, which may be passed by the legislature, shall embrace more than one subject, and that shall be expressed in the title.

Sec. 17. The legislature may confer upon the boards of supervisors, of the several counties of the state, such further powers of local legislation and administration, as they shall from time to time prescribe.

ARTICLE IV.

Sec. 1. The executive power shall be vested in a Governor, who shall hold his office for two years; a Lieutenant Governor shall be chosen at the same time, and for the same term.

Sec. 2. No person, except a citizen of the United States, shall be eligible to the office of Governor; nor shall any person be eligible to that office, who shall not have attained the age of thirty years, and who shall not have been five years next preceding his election, a resident within this state.

Sec. 3. The Governor and Lieutenant Governor shall be elected at the times and places of choosing members of the Assembly. The persons respectively having the highest number of votes for Governor and Lieutenant Governor, shall be elected; but in case two, or more, shall have an equal, and the highest, number of votes for Governor, or for Lieutenant Governor, the two houses of the legislature, at its next annual session, shall, forthwith, by joint ballot, choose one of the said persons, so having an equal and the highest number of votes for Governor, or Lieutenant Governor.

Sec. 4. The Governor shall be commander-in-chief of the military and naval forces of the state. He shall have power to convene the legislature, (or the Senate only,) on extraordinary occasions. He shall communicate, by message, to the legislature, at every session, the condition of the state, and recommend such matters to them, as he shall judge expedient. He shall transact all necessary business with the officers of government, civil and military. He shall expedite all such measures, as may be resolved upon by the legislature, and shall take care that the laws are faithfully executed. He shall, at stated times, receive for his services, a compensation to be established by law, which shall neither be increased nor diminished, after his election, and during his continuance in office.

Sec. 5. The Governor shall have the power to grant reprieves, commutations and pardons, after conviction, for all offences, except treason and cases of impeachment, upon such conditions, and with such restrictions and limitations, as he may think proper, subject to such regulations as may be provided by law, relative to the manner of applying for pardons. Upon conviction for treason, he shall have power to suspend the execution of the sentence, until the case shall be reported to the legislature, at its next meeting, when the legislature shall either pardon, or commute the sentence, direct the execution of the sentence, or grant a further reprieve. He shall annually communicate to the legislature, each case of reprieve, commutation, or pardon, granted; stating the name of the convict, the crime of which he was convicted, the sentence, and its date, and the date of the commutation, pardon, or reprieve.

Sec. 6. In case of the impeachment of the Governor, or his removal from office, death, inability to discharge the powers and duties of the said office, resignation, or absence from the state, the powers and duties of the office shall devolve upon the Lieutenant Governor, for the residue of the term, or until the disability shall cease. But when the Governor shall, with the consent of the legislature, be out of the state, in time of war, at the head of the military force thereof, he shall continue commander-in-chief of all the military force of the state.

Sec. 7. The Lieutenant Governor shall possess the same qualifications of eligibility for office as the Governor. He shall be President of the Senate, but shall only have a casting vote therein. If, during a vacancy of the office of Governor, the Lieutenant Governor shall be impeached, displaced, resign, die, or become incapable of performing the duties of his office, or be absent from the state, the President of the Senate shall act as Governor, until the vacancy be filled, or the disability shall cease.

Sec. 8. The Lieutenant Governor shall, while acting as such, receive a compensation, to be fixed by law, and which shall not be increased or diminished, during his continuance in office.

Sec. 9. Every bill which shall have passed the Senate and Assembly, shall, before it becomes a law, be presented to the Governor; if he approve, he shall sign it; but if not, he shall return it, with his objections, to that house in which it shall have originated; who shall enter the objections, at large, upon their journal, and proceed to reconsider it. If, after such reconsideration, two-thirds of the members present shall agree to pass the bill, it shall be sent, together with the objections, to the other house, by which it shall likewise be re-considered; and if approved by two-thirds of all the members present, it shall become a law, notwithstanding the objections of the Governor. But in all such cases, the votes of both houses shall be determined by yeas and nays, and the names of the members, voting for and against the bill, shall be entered on the journal of each house respectively. If any bill shall not be returned by the Governor, within ten days, (Sundays excepted,) after it shall have been presented to him, the same shall be a law, in like manner as if he had signed it, unless the legislature shall, by their adjournment, prevent its return; in which case it shall not be a law.

ARTICLE V.

Sec. 1. The Secretary of State, Comptroller, Treasurer, and Attorney General, shall be chosen at a general election, and shall hold their offices for two years. Each of the officers in this Article named, (except the Speaker of the Assembly,) shall, at stated times, during his continuance in office, receive for his services, a compensation, which shall not be increased or diminished, during the term for which he shall have been elected; nor shall he receive, to his use, any fees or perquisites of office, or other compensation.

Sec. 2. A State Engineer and Surveyor shall be chosen at a general election, and shall hold his office two years, but no person shall be elected to said office who is not a practical engineer.

Sec. 3. Three Canal Commissioners shall be chosen at the general election, which shall be held next after the adoption of this Constitution, one of whom shall hold his office for one year, one for two years, and one for three years. The Commissioners of the canal fund shall meet at the Capitol, on the first Monday of January, next after such election, and determine by lot, which of said Commissioners shall hold his office for one year, which for two, and which for three years; and there shall be elected annually, thereafter, one Canal Commissioner, who shall hold his office for three years.

Sec. 4. Three Inspectors of State Prisons, shall be elected at the general election, which shall be held next after the adoption of this Constitution, one of whom shall hold his office for one year, one for two years, and one for three years. The Governor, Secretary of State, and Comptroller, shall meet at the Capitol, on the first Monday of January, next succeeding such election, and determine by lot, which of said Inspectors shall hold his office for one year, which for two, and which for three years; and there shall be elected annually, thereafter, one Inspector of State Prisons, who shall hold his office for three years; said Inspectors shall have the charge and superintendence of the State Prisons, and shall appoint all the officers therein. All vacancies in the office of such Inspector, shall be filled by the Governor, till the next election.

Sec. 5. The Lieutenant Governor, Speaker of the Assembly, Secretary of State, Comptroller, Treasurer, Attorney General, and State Engineer and Surveyor, shall be the Commissioners of the Land Office.

The Lieutenant Governor, Secretary of State, Comptroller, Treasurer, and Attorney General, shall be the Commissioners of the canal fund.

The Canal Board shall consist of the Commissioners of the canal fund, the State Engineer and Surveyor, and the Canal Commissioners.

Sec. 6. The powers and duties of the respective boards, and of the several officers in this Article mentioned, shall be such as now are or hereafter may be prescribed by law.

Sec. 7. The Treasurer may be suspended from office by the Governor, during the recess of the Legislature, and until thirty days after the commencement of the next session of the Legislature, whenever it shall appear to him that such Treasurer has, in any particular, violated his duty. The Governor shall appoint a competent person to discharge the duties of the office, during such suspension of the Treasurer.

Sec. 8. All offices for the weighing, guaging, measuring, culling or inspecting any merchandize, produce, manufacture or commodity, whatever, are hereby abolished, and no such office shall hereafter be created by law; but nothing in this section contained, shall abrogate any office created for the purpose of protecting the public health or the interests of the State in its property, revenue, tolls, or purchases, or of supplying the people with correct standards of weights and measures, or shall prevent the creation of any office for such purposes hereafter.

ARTICLE VI.

Sec. 1. The Assembly shall have the power of impeachment, by the vote of the majority of all the members elected. The court for the trial of impeachments, shall be composed of the President of the Senate, the Senators, or a major part of them, and the judges of the court of appeals, or the major part of them. On the trial of an impeachment against the Governor, the Lieutenant-Governor shall not act as a member of the court. No judicial officer shall exercise his office after he shall have been impeached, until he shall have been acquitted. Before the trial of an impeachment, the members of the court shall take an oath or affirmation, truly and impartially to try the impeachment, according to evidence; and no person shall be convicted, without the concurrence of two-thirds of the members present. Judgment in cases of impeachment shall not extend further than to removal from office, or removal from office and disqualification to hold and enjoy any office of honor, trust or profit under this State; but the party impeached shall be liable to indictment, and punishment according to law.

Sec. 2. There shall be a Court of Appeals, composed of eight judges, of whom four shall be elected by the electors of the State for eight years, and four selected from the class of Justices of the Supreme Court having the shortest time to serve. Provision shall be made by law, for designating one of the number elected, as chief judge, and for selecting such Justices of the Supreme Court, from time to time, and for so classifying those elected, that one shall be elected every second year.

Sec. 3. There shall be a Supreme Court having general jurisdiction in law and equity.

Sec. 4. The State shall be divided into eight judicial districts, of which the city of New York shall be one; the others to be bounded by county lines and to be compact and equal in population as nearly as may be. There shall be four Justices of the Supreme Court in each district, and as many more in the district composed of the city of New York, as may from time to time be authorized by law, but not to exceed in the whole such number in proportion to its population, as shall be in conformity with the number of such judges in the residue of the state in proportion to its population. They shall be classified so that one of the justices of each district shall go out of office at the end of every two years. After the expiration of their terms under such classification, the term of their office shall be eight years.

Sec. 5. The Legislature shall have the same powers to alter and regulate the jurisdiction and proceedings in law and equity, as they have heretofore possessed.

Sec. 6. Provision may be made by law for designating from time to time, one or more of the said justices, who is not a judge of the court of appeals, to preside at the general terms of the said court to be held in the several districts. Any three or more of the said justices, of whom one of the said justices so designated, shall always be one, may hold such general terms. And any one or more of the justices may hold special terms and circuit courts, and any one of them may preside in courts of oyer and terminer in any county.

Sec. 7. The judges of the court of appeals and justices of the supreme court shall severally receive at stated times for their services, a compensation to be established by law, which shall not be increased or diminished during their continuance in office.

Sec. 8. They shall not hold any other office or public trust. All votes for either of them, for any elective office (except that of justice of the supreme court, or judge of the court of appeals,) given by the Legislature or the people, shall be void. They shall not exercise any power of appointment to public office. Any male citizen of the age of twenty-one years, of good moral character, and who possesses the requisite qualifications of learning and ability, shall be entitled to admission to practice in all the courts of this state.

Sec. 9. The classification of the justices of the supreme court; the times and place of holding the terms of the court of appeals, and of the general and special terms of the supreme court within the several districts, and the circuit courts and courts of oyer and terminer within the several counties, shall be provided for by law.

Sec. 10. The testimony in equity cases shall be taken in like manner as in cases at law.

Sec. 11. Justices of the supreme court and judges of the court of appeals, may be removed by concurrent resolution of both Houses of the Legislature, if two-thirds of all the members elected to the Assembly, and a majority of all the members elected to the Senate, concur therein. All judicial officers, except those mentioned in this section, and except justices of the peace, and judges and justices of inferior courts not of record may be removed by the Senate on the recommendation of the Governor; but no removal shall be made by virtue of this section, unless the cause thereof be entered on the journals, nor unless the party complained of, shall have been served with a copy of the complaint against him, and shall have had an opportunity of being heard in his defence. On the question of removal, the ayes and noes shall be entered on the journals.

Sec. 12. The judges of the court of appeals shall be elected by the electors of the state, and the justices of the supreme court by the electors of the several judicial districts, at such times as may be prescribed by law.

Sec. 13. In case the office of any judge of the court of appeals, or justice of the supreme court, shall become vacant before the expiration of the regular term for which he was elected, the vacancy may be filled by appointment by the Governor, until it shall be supplied at the next general election of judges, when it shall be filled by election for the residue of the unexpired term.

Sec. 14. There shall be elected in each of the counties of this state, except the city and county of New York, one county judge, who shall hold his office for four years. He shall hold the county court, and perform the duties of the office of surrogate. The county court shall have such jurisdiction in cases arising in justices courts, and in special cases, as the Legislature may prescribe; but shall have no original civil jurisdiction, except in such special cases.

The county judge, with two justices of the peace to be designated according to law, may hold courts of sessions, with such criminal jurisdiction as the Legislature shall prescribe, and perform such other duties as may be required by law.

The county judge shall receive an annual salary, to be fixed by the board of supervisors, which shall be neither increased nor diminished during his continuance in office. The justices of the peace, for services in courts of sessions, shall be paid a per diem allowance out of the county treasury.

In counties having a population exceeding forty thousand, the Legislature may provide for the election of a separate officer to perform the duties of the office of surrogate.

The legislature may confer equity jurisdiction, in special cases, upon the county judge.

Inferior local courts, of civil and criminal jurisdiction, may be established by the Legislature in cities; and such courts, except for the cities of New York and Buffalo, shall have an uniform organization and jurisdiction in such cities.

Sec. 15. The Legislature may, on application of the board of supervisors, provide for the election of local officers, not to exceed two in any county, to discharge the duties of county judge and of surrogate, in cases of their inability, or of a vacancy, and to exercise such other powers, in special cases, as may be provided by law.

Sec. 16. The Legislature may reorganize the judicial districts at the first session after the return of every enumeration under this Constitution, in the manner provided for in the fourth section of this article and at no other time; and they may, at such session, increase or diminish the number of districts, but such increase or diminution shall not be more than one district at any one time. Each district shall have four justices of the Supreme Court; but no diminution of the districts shall have the effect to remove a judge from office.

Sec. 17. The electors of the several towns, shall, at their annual town meeting, and in such manner as the Legislature may direct, elect justices of the peace, whose term of office shall be four years. In case of an election to fill a vacancy occurring before the expiration of a full term, they shall hold for the residue of the unexpired term. Their number and classification may be regulated by law. Justices of the peace, and judges or justices of inferior courts not of record, and their clerks, may be removed after due notice and an opportunity of being heard in their defence by such county, city or state courts, as may be prescribed by law, for causes to be assigned in the order of removal.

Sec. 18. All judicial officers of cities and villages, and all such judicial officers as may be created therein by law, shall be elected at such times and in such manner as the Legislature may direct.

Sec. 19. Clerks of the several counties of this state shall be clerks of the Supreme Court, with such powers and duties as shall be prescribed by law. A clerk for the Court of Appeals, to be ex officio clerk of the Supreme Court, and to keep his office at the seat of government, shall be chosen by the electors of the State ; he shall hold his office for three years, and his compensation shall be fixed by law and paid out of the public Treasury.

Sec. 20. No judicial officer, except justices of the peace, shall receive to his own use, any fees or perquisites of office.

Sec. 21. The Legislature may authorize the judgments, decrees and decisions of any local inferior court of record of original civil jurisdiction, established in a city, to be removed for review directly into the Court of Appeals.

Sec. 22. The Legislature shall provide for the speedy publication of all statute laws, and of such judicial decisions as it may deem expedient. And all laws and judicial decisions shall be free for publication by any person.

Sec. 23. Tribunals of conciliation may be established, with such powers and duties as may be prescribed by law, but such tribunals shall have no power to render judgment to be obligatory on the parties, except they voluntarily submit their matters in difference and agree to abide the judgment, or assent thereto, in the presence of such tribunal, in such cases as shall be prescribed by law.

Sec. 24. The Legislature at its first session after the adoption of this Constitution, shall provide for the appointment of three commissioners, whose duty it shall be to revise, reform, simplify and abridge the rules and practice, pleadings, forms and proceedings of the courts of record of this state, and to report thereon to the Legislature, subject to their adoption and modification from time to time.

Sec. 25. The Legislature, at its first session after the adoption of this Constitution, shall provide for the organization of the Court of Appeals, and for transferring to it the business pending in the Court for the Correction of Errors, and for the allowance of writs of error and appeals to the Court of Appeals, from the judgments and decrees of the present Court of Chancery and Supreme Court, and of the courts that may be organized under this Constitution.

ARTICLE VII.

Sec. 1. After paying the expenses of collection, superintendence and ordinary repairs, there shall be appropriated and set apart in each fiscal year, out of the revenues of the state canals, commencing on the first day of June, one thousand eight hundred and forty-six, the sum of one million and three hundred thousand dollars, until the first day of June, one thousand eight hundred and fifty-five, and from that time, the sum of one million and seven hundred thousand dollars in each fiscal year, as a sinking fund, to pay the interest and redeem the principal of that part of the state debt called the canal debt, as it existed at the time first aforesaid, and including three hundred thousand dollars then to be borrowed, until the same shall be wholly paid ; and the principal and income of the said sinking fund shall be sacredly applied to that purpose.

Sec. 2. After complying with the provisions of the first section of this article, there shall be appropriated and set apart out of the surplus revenues of the state canals, in each fiscal year, commencing on the first day of June, one thousand eight hundred and forty-six, the sum of three hundred and fifty thousand dollars, until the time when a sufficient sum shall have been appropriated and set apart, under the said first section, to pay the interest and extinguish the entire principal of the canal debt; and after that period, then the sum of one million and five hundred thousand dollars in each fiscal year, as a sinking fund, to pay the interest and redeem the principal of that part of the state debt called the General Fund debt, including the debt for loans of the state credit to railroad companies which have failed to pay the interest thereon, and also the contingent debt on state stocks loaned to incorporated companies which have hitherto paid the interest thereon, whenever and as far as any part thereof may become a charge on the Treasury or General Fund, until the same shall be wholly paid ; and the principal and income of the said last mentioned sinking fund shall be sacredly applied to the purpose aforesaid ; and if the payment of any part of the moneys to the said sinking

CONSTITUTION. 113

fund shall at any time be deferred, by reason of the priority recognized in the first section of this article, the sum so deferred, with quarterly interest thereon, at the then current rate, shall be paid to the last mentioned sinking fund, as soon as it can be done consistently with the just rights of the creditors holding said canal debt.

Sec. 3. After paying the said expenses of superintendence and repairs of the canals, and the sums appropriated by the first and second sections of this article, there shall be paid out of the surplus revenues of the canals, to the Treasury of the State, on or before the thirtieth day of September, in each year, for the use and benefit of the General Fund, such sum, not exceeding two hundred thousand dollars, as may be required to defray the necessary expenses of the state; and the remainder of the revenues of the said canals shall, in each fiscal year, be applied, in such manner as the Legislature shall direct, to the completion of the Erie Canal enlargement, and the Genesee Valley and Black River canals, until the said canals shall be completed.

If at any time after the period of eight years from the adoption of this Constitution, the revenues of the state, unappropriated by this article, shall not be sufficient to defray the necessary expenses of the government, without continuing or laying a direct tax, the Legislature may, at its discretion, supply the deficiency, in whole or in part, from the surplus revenues of the canals, after complying with the provisions of the first two sections of this article, for paying the interest and extinguishing the principal of the Canal and General Fund debt; but the sum thus appropriated from the surplus revenues of the canals shall not exceed annually three hundred and fifty thousand dollars, including the sum of two hundred thousand dollars, provided for by this section for the expenses of the government, until the General Fund debt shall be extinguished, or until the Erie Canal Enlargement and Genesee Valley and Black River Canals shall be completed, and after that debt shall be paid, or the said canals shall be completed, then the sum of six hundred and seventy-two thousand five hundred dollars, or so much thereof as shall be necessary, may be annually appropriated to defray the expenses of the government.

Sec. 4. The claims of the state against any incorporated company to pay the interest and redeem the principal of the stock of the state, loaned or advanced to such company, shall be fairly enforced, and not released or compromised; and the moneys arising from such claims shall be set apart and applied as part of the sinking fund provided in the second section of this article. But the time limited for the fulfillment of any condition of any release or compromise heretofore made or provided for, may be extended by law.

Sec. 5. If the sinking funds, or either of them, provided in this article, shall prove insufficient to enable the state, on the credit of such fund, to procure the means to satisfy the claims of the creditors of the state, as they become payable, the Legislature shall, by equitable taxes, so increase the revenues of the said funds as to make them, respectively, sufficient perfectly to preserve the public faith. Every contribution or advance to the canals, or their debt, from any source, other than their direct revenues, shall, with quarterly interest, at the rates then current, be repaid into the Treasury, for the use of the state, out of the canal revenues, as soon as it can be done consistently with the just rights of the creditors holding the said canal debt.

Sec. 6. The Legislature shall not sell, lease, or otherwise dispose of any of the canals of the state; but they shall remain the property of the state and under its management, forever.

Sec. 7. The Legislature shall never sell or dispose of the salt springs, belonging to this state. The lands contiguous thereto and which may be necessary and convenient for the use of the salt springs, may be sold by authority of law, and under the direction of the commissioners of the land office, for the purpose of investing the moneys arising therefrom in other lands alike convenient; but by such sale and purchase the aggregate quantity of these lands shall not be diminished.

Sec. 8. No moneys shall ever be paid out of the treasury of this state, or any of its funds, or any of the funds under its management, except in pursuance of an appropriation by law ; nor unless such payment be made within two years next after the passage of such appropriation act ; and every such law, making a new appropriation, or continuing or reviving an appropriation, shall distinctly specify the sum appropriated, and the object to which it is to be applied ; and it shall not be sufficient for such law to refer to any other law to fix such sum.

Sec. 9. The credit of the state shall not, in any manner, be given or loaned to, or in aid of any individual, association or corporation.

Sec. 10. The state may, to meet casual deficits or failures in revenues, or for expenses not provided for, contract debts, but such debts, direct and contingent, singly or in the aggregate, shall not at any time, exceed one million of dollars ; and the moneys arising from the loans creating such debts, shall be applied to the purpose for which they were obtained, or to repay the debt so contracted, and to no other purpose whatever.

Sec. 11. In addition to the above limited power to contract debts, the state may contract debts to repel invasion, suppress insurrection, or defend the state in war ; but the money arising from the contracting of such debts shall be applied to the purpose for which it was raised, or to repay such debts, and to no other purpose whatever.

Sec. 12. Except the debts specified in the tenth and eleventh sections of this article, no debt shall be hereafter contracted by or on behalf of this state, unless such debt shall be authorized by a law, for some single work or object, to be distinctly specified therein ; and such law shall impose and provide for the collection of a direct annual tax to pay, and sufficient to pay the interest on such debt as it falls due, and also to pay and discharge the principal of such debt within eighteen years from the time of the contracting thereof.

No such law shall take effect until it shall, at a general election, have been submitted to the people, and have received a majority of all the votes cast for and against it, at such election.

On the final passage of such bill in either house of the Legislature, the question shall be taken by ayes and noes, to be duly entered on the journals thereof, and shall be : " Shall this bill pass, and ought the same to receive the sanction of the people ?"

The Legislature may at any time, after the approval of such law by the people, if no debt shall have been contracted in pursuance thereof, repeal the same ; and may at any time, by law, forbid the contracting of any further debt or liability under such law ; but the tax imposed by such act, in proportion to the debt and liability which may have been contracted, in pursuance of such law, shall remain in force and be irrepealable, and be annually collected, until the proceeds thereof shall have made the provision herein before specified to pay and discharge the interest and principal of such debt and liability.

The money arising from any loan or stock creating such debt or liability, shall be applied to the work or object specified in the act authorizing such debt or liability, or for the repayment of such debt or liability, and for no other purpose whatever.

No such law shall be submitted to be voted on, within three months after its passage, or at any general election, when any other law, or any bill, or any amendment to the Constitution shall be submitted to be voted for or against.

Sec. 13. Every law which imposes, continues or revives a tax, shall distinctly state the tax and the object to which it is to be applied ; and it shall not be sufficient to refer to any other law to fix such tax or object.

Sec. 14. On the final passage, in either house of the Legislature, of every act which imposes, continues, or revives a tax, or creates a debt or charge, or makes, continues or revives any appropriation of public or trust-money or property, or releases, discharges, or commutes any claim or demand of the state, the question shall be taken by ayes and noes, which shall be duly entered on the journals, and three-fifths of all the members elected to either house, shall, in all such cases, be necessary to constitute a quorum therein.

ARTICLE VIII.

Sec. 1. Corporations may be formed under general laws; but shall not be created by special act, except for municipal purposes, and in cases where in the judgment of the Legislature, the objects of the corporation cannot be attained under general laws. All general laws and special acts passed pursuant to this section, may be altered from time to time, or repealed.

Sec. 2. Dues from corporations shall be secured by such individual liability of the corporators, and other means, as may be prescribed by law.

Sec. 3. The term corporations, as used in this article, shall be construed to include all associations and joint-stock companies having any of the powers or privileges of corporations not possessed by individuals or partnerships. And all corporations shall have the right to sue, and shall be subject to be sued, in all courts in like cases as natural persons.

Sec. 4. The Legislature, shall have no power to pass any act granting any special charter for banking purposes; but corporations or associations may be formed for such purposes under general laws.

Sec. 5. The Legislature shall have no power to pass any law sanctioning in any manner, directly or indirectly, the suspension of specie payments, by any person, association or corporation issuing bank notes of any description.

Sec. 6. The Legislature shall provide by law for the registry of all bills or notes, issued or put in circulation as money, and shall require ample security for the redemption of the same in specie.

Sec. 7. The stockholders in every corporation and joint-stock association for banking purposes, issuing bank notes or any kind of paper credits to circulate as money, after the first day of January, one thousand eight hundred and fifty, shall be individually responsible to the amount of their respective share or shares of stock in any such corporation or association, for all its debts and liabilities of every kind, contracted after the said first day of January, one thousand eight hundred and fifty.

Sec. 8. In case of the insolvency of any bank or banking association, the bill-holders thereof shall be entitled to preference in payment, over all other creditors of such bank or association.

Sec. 9. It shall be the duty of the Legislature to provide for the organization of cities and incorporated villages, and to restrict their power of taxation, assessment, borrowing money, contracting debts and loaning their credit, so as to prevent abuses in assessments, and in contracting debts by such municipal corporations.

ARTICLE IX.

Sec. 1. The capital of the Common School Fund; the capital of the Literature Fund, and the capital of the United States Deposit Fund, shall be respectively preserved inviolate. The revenue of the said Common School Fund shall be applied to the support of common schools; the revenues of the said Literature Fund shall be applied to the support of academies, and the sum of twenty-five thousand dollars of the revenues of the United States Deposit Fund shall each year be appropriated to and made a part of the capital of the said Common School Fund.

ARTICLE X.

Sec. 1. Sheriffs, clerks of counties, including the register and clerk of the city and county of New York, coroners, and district attorneys, shall be chosen, by the electors of the respective counties, once in every three years, and as often as vacancies shall happen. Sheriffs shall hold no other office, and be ineligible for the next three years after the termination of their offices. They may be required by law, to renew their security, from time to time; and in default of giving such new security, their offices shall be deemed vacant. But the county shall never be made responsible for the acts of the sheriff.

The Governor may remove any officer, in this section mentioned, within the term for which he shall have been elected; giving to such officer a copy of the charges against him, and an opportunity of being heard in his defence.

Sec. 2. All county officers whose election or appointment is not provided for, by this Constitution, shall be elected by the electors of the respective counties, or appointed by the boards of supervisors, or other county authorities, as the Legislature shall direct. All city, town and village officers, whose election or appointment is not provided for by this Constitution, shall be elected by the electors, of such cities, towns and villages, or of some division thereof, or appointed by such authorities thereof, as the Legislature shall designate for that purpose. All other officers whose election or appointment is not provided for by this Constitution, and all officers whose offices may hereafter be created by law, shall be elected by the people, or appointed, as the Legislature may direct.

Sec. 3. When the duration of any office, is not provided by this Constitution, it may be declared by law, and if not so declared, such office shall be held, during the pleasure of the authority making the appointment.

Sec. 4. The time of electing all officers named in this article shall be prescribed by law.

Sec. 5. The Legislature shall provide for filling vacancies in office, and in case of elective officers, no person appointed to fill a vacancy shall hold his office by virtue of such appointment longer than the commencement of the political year next succeeding the first annual election after the happening of the vacancy.

Sec. 6. The political year and legislative term, shall begin on the first day of January; and the Legislature shall every year assemble on the first Tuesday in January, unless a different day shall be appointed by law.

Sec. 7. Provision shall be made by law for the removal, for misconduct or malversation in office, of all officers (except judicial) whose powers and duties are not local or legislative, and who shall be elected at general elections, and also for supplying vacancies created by such removal.

Sec. 8. The Legislature may declare the cases in which any office shall be deemed vacant, where no provision is made for that purpose in this Constitution.

ARTICLE XI.

Sec. 1. The militia of this state, shall at all times hereafter, be armed and disciplined, and in readiness for service; but all such inhabitants of this state, of any religious denomination whatever, as from scruples of conscience may be averse to bearing arms, shall be excused therefrom, upon such conditions as shall be prescribed by law.

Sec. 2. Militia officers shall be chosen, or appointed, as follows:—captains, subalterns and non-commissioned officers shall chosen by the written votes of the members of their respective companies. Field officers of regiments and separate battalions, by the written votes of the commissioned officers of the respective regiments and separate battalions; brigadier generals and brigade inspectors, by the field officers of their respective brigades; major generals, brigadier generals and commanding officers of regiments or separate battalions, shall appoint the staff officers to their respective divisions, brigades, regiments or separate battalions.

Sec. 3. The Governor shall nominate, and with the consent of the Senate, appoint all major generals, and the commissary general. The adjutant general and other chiefs of staff departments, and the aids-de-camp of the commander-in-chief shall be appointed by the Governor, and their commissions shall expire with the time for which the Governor shall have been elected. The commissary general shall hold his office for two years. He shall give security for the faithful execution of the duties of his office, in such manner and amount as shall be prescribed by law.

Sec. 4. The Legislature shall, by law, direct the time and manner of electing militia officers, and of certifying their elections to the Governor.

Sec. 5. The commissioned officers of the militia shall be commissioned by the Governor; and no commissioned officer shall be removed from office, unless by the Senate on the recommendation of the Governor, stating the grounds on which such removal is recommended, or by the decision of a court martial, pursuant to law. The present officers of the militia shall hold their commissions subject to removal, as before provided.

Sec. 6. In case the mode of election and appointment of militia officers hereby directed, shall not be found conducive to the improvement of the militia, the Legislature may abolish the same, and provide by law for their appointment and removal, if two-thirds of the members present in each house shall concur therein,

ARTICLE XII.

Sec. 1. Members of the Legislature and all officers, executive and judicial, except such inferior officers as may be by law exempted, shall, before they enter on the duties of their respective offices, take and subscribe the following oath or affirmation :—

"I do solemnly swear (or affirm, as the case may be) that I will support the Constitution of the United States, and the Constitution of the state of New York ; and that I will faithfully discharge the duties of the office of according to the best of my ability."

And no other oath, declaration, or test shall be required as a qualification for any office or public trust.

ARTICLE XIII.

Sec. 1. Any amendment or amendments to this Constitution may be proposed in the Senate and Assembly ; and if the same shall be agreed to by a majority of the members elected to each of the two houses, such proposed amendment or amendments shall be entered on their journals, with the yeas and nays taken thereon, and referred to the Legislature to be chosen at the next general election of Senators, and shall be published for three months previous to the time of making such choice, and if in the Legislature so next chosen, aforesaid, such proposed amendment or amendments, shall be agreed to, by a majority of all the members elected to each house, then it shall be the duty of the Legislature to submit such proposed amendment or amendments to the people, in such manner and at such time as the Legislature shall prescribe ; and if the people shall approve and ratify such amendment or amendments, by a majority of the electors qualified to vote for members of the Legislature, voting thereon, such amendment or amendments shall become part of the constitution.

Sec. 2. At the general election to be held in the year eighteen hundred and sixty-six, and in each twentieth year thereafter, and also at such time as the Legislature may by law provide, the question, "Shall there be a Convention to revise the Constitution, and amend the same ?" shall be decided by the electors qualified to vote for members of the Legislature ; and in case a majority of the electors so qualified, voting at such election, shall decide in favor of a Convention for such purpose, the Legislature at its next session, shall provide by law for the election of delegates to such Convention.

ARTICLE XIV.

Sec. 1. The first election of Senators and Members of Assembly, pursuant to the provisions of this Constitution, shall be held on the Tuesday succeeding the first Monday of November, one thousand eight hundred and forty-seven.

The Senators and Members of Assembly who may be in office on the first day of January, one thousand eight hundred and forty-seven, shall hold their offices until and including the thirty-first day of December following, and no longer.

Sec. 2. The first election of Governor, and Lieutenant-Governor under this Constitution, shall be held on the Tuesday succeeding the first Monday of November, one thousand eight hundred and forty-eight ; and the Governor and Lieutenant-Governor in office when this Constitution shall take effect, shall hold their respective offices until and including the thirty-first day of December of that year.

Sec. 3. The Secretary of State, Comptroller, Treasurer, Attorney General, District Attorney, Surveyor General, Canal Commissioners, and Inspectors of State Prisons, in office when this Constitution shall take effect, shall hold their respective offices until and including the thirty-first day of December, one thousand eight hundred and forty-seven, and no longer.

Sec. 4. The first election of judges and clerk of the Court of Appeals, justices of the Supreme Court, and county judges, shall take place at such time between the first Tuesday of April and the second Tuesday of June, one thousand eight hundred and forty-seven, as may be prescribed by law. The said courts shall respectively enter upon their duties, on the first Monday of July, next thereafter; but the term of office of said judges, clerk and justices, as declared by this Constitution, shall be deemed to commence on the first day of January, one thousand eight hundred and forty-eight.

Sec. 5. On the first Monday of July, one thousand eight hundred and forty-seven, jurisdiction of all suits and proceedings then pending in the present supreme court and court of chancery, and all suits and proceedings originally commenced and then pending in any court of common pleas, (except in the city and county of New York,) shall become vested in the supreme court hereby established. Proceedings pending in courts of common pleas, and in suits originally commenced in justices courts, shall be transferred to the county courts provided for in this Constitution, in such manner and form, and under such regulation as shall be provided by law. The courts of oyer and terminer hereby established, shall, in their respective counties, have jurisdiction, on and after the day last mentioned, of all indictments and proceedings then pending in the present courts of oyer and terminer, and also of all indictments and proceedings then pending in the present courts of general sessions of the peace, except in the city of New York, and except in cases of which the courts of sessions hereby established, may lawfully take cognizance; and of such indictments and proceedings as the courts of sessions hereby established, shall have jurisdiction, on and after the day last mentioned.

Sec. 6. The chancellor and the present supreme court shall, respectively, have power to hear and determine any of such suits and proceedings ready on the first Monday of July, one thousand eight hundred and forty-seven, for hearing or decision, and shall, for their services therein, be entitled to their present rates of compensation, until the first day of July, one thousand eight hundred and forty-eight, or until all such suits and proceedings shall be sooner heard and determined. Masters in chancery may continue to exercise the functions of their office, in the court of chancery, so long as the Chancellor shall continue to exercise the functions of his office, under the provisions of this Constitution.

And the Supreme Court hereby established, shall also have power to hear and determine such of said suits and proceedings as may be prescribed by law.

Sec. 7. In case any vacancy shall occur in the office of chancellor or justice of the present Supreme Court, previously to the first day of July, one thousand eight hundred and forty-eight, the Governor may nominate, and by and with the advice and consent of the Senate, appoint a proper person to fill such vacancy. Any judge of the court of appeals, or justice of the supreme court, elected under this Constitution, may receive and hold such appointment.

Sec. 8. The offices of chancellor, justice of the existing supreme court, circuit judge, vice-chancellor, assistant vice-chancellor, judge of the existing county courts of each county, supreme court commissioner, master in chancery, examiner in chancery, and surrogate, (except as herein otherwise provided,) are abolished from and after the first Monday of July, one thousand eight hundred and forty-seven, (1847.)

Sec. 9. The Chancellor, the justices of the present supreme court, and the circuit judges, are hereby declared to be severally eligible to any office at the first election under this Constitution.

Sec. 10. Sheriffs, clerks of counties, (including the register and clerk of the city and county of New York,) and justices of the peace, and coroners, in office, when this Constitution shall take effect, shall hold their respective offices until the expiration of the term for which they were respectively elected.

Sec. 11. Judicial officers in office when this Constitution shall take effect, may continue to receive such fees and perquisites of office as are now authorized by law, until the first day of July, one thousand eight hundred and forty-seven, notwithstanding the provisions of the twentieth section of the sixth article of this Constitution.

Sec. 12. All local courts established in any city or village, including the Superior Court, Common Pleas, Sessions and Surrogate's Courts of the city and county of New York, shall remain, until otherwise directed by the Legislature, with their present powers and jurisdictions; and the judges of such courts, and any clerks thereof in office on the first day of January, one thousand eight hundred and forty-seven, shall continue in office until the expiration of their terms of office, or until the Legislature shall otherwise direct.

Sec. 13. This Constitution shall be in force from and including the first day of January, one thousand eight hundred and forty-seven, except as herein otherwise provided.

Done in convention, at the capitol, in the city of Albany, the ninth day of October, in the year one thousand eight hundred and forty-six, and of the Independence of the United States of America, the seventy-first.

In witness whereof, we have hereunto subscribed our names.

JOHN TRACY, *President*,
and Delegate from the county of Chenango.

JAMES F. STARBUCK,
H. W. STRONG,   *Secretaries.*
FR. SEGER.

GOVERNMENT

OF COUNTIES, TOWNS, CITIES AND VILLAGES.

EACH town elects, annually, a supervisor, a town clerk, three or five assessors, a collector, two overseers of the poor, a town superintendent of common schools, not more than five constables, one sealer of weights and measures, as many overseers of highways as there are road districts in the town, and as many pound masters as the electors may deem necessary.

The supervisors of the different towns of the county, thus elected, constitute a board, which meets annually for business, and holds special meetings when necessary. They are authorised to receive, examine, and adjust all accounts against the county, or the several towns, raise money to defray them, make orders concerning the corporate property of the county, elect the county superintendent of common schools, &c.

The other officers of the counties are, the treasurer, county clerk, sheriff, coroner, district attorney, county superintendent of common schools, county sealer of weights and measures, road commissioners, inspectors, &c. By the provisions of the new constitution, most of these officers are chosen for three years.

The cities are governed by a mayor, recorder, and common council. The latter is composed of one alderman, and one assistant alderman, for each ward of the city. These officers have judicial powers conferred on them, in offences not punishable with death. They also perform the duties of supervisors in their respective cities.

There are nine cities in the state; viz., New York, Albany, Troy, Hudson, Schenectady, Utica, Buffalo, Rochester, and Brooklyn.

The incorporated villages are governed by a president and board of trustees, usually five in number. There are about 150 incorporated villages in the state.

PUBLIC EDUCATION.

Origin and History of the Common School System.

Though less zealous in the cause of popular education than the early settlers of New England, yet, ere the forests had been felled, or the Indian war-whoop ceased to be heard, in the neighborhood of the white settlements, the sturdy Hollanders began to provide for the education of their children.

In 1633, Adam Roelandsen, the first schoolmaster of New Amsterdam, arrived in that city. In 1642, the Patroon, Van Rensselaer, sent over a schoolmaster for his "colonie."

The first classical school, or academy, was established in New York city, the teacher being sent out from Holland, by the Dutch West India Company. In all the Dutch settlements, provision was early made for schools.

In 1687, a Latin school was opened in the city of New York, under the sanction of the English government. In 1702, the first legislative action, relative to education, occurred. This act provided for the establishment of a grammar school, and appropriated £50 per annum, for seven years, for the support of a teacher.

Another act was passed, in 1732, to encourage a public school, in the city and county of New York, for teaching Latin, Greek and Mathematics.

Under this act a free school was established, and endowed with £40 a year, for five years; and ten scholars were to be sent from New York, two from Albany, and one from each of the other counties, making twenty in all. This school was the germ of Columbia college.

In 1743, Rev. Mr. Dunlap, of Cherry Valley, Otsego county, established the first grammar school in the state, west of Albany. Between 1746 and 1756, several acts were passed, authorizing the raising of moneys, by lottery, for founding a college in New York, and, in 1754, King's college was chartered.

After the establishment of the state government, the interest of the people was again awakened to the necessity of popular education. On the 1st of May, 1784, an act was passed, changing the name of King's college to Columbia college, and establishing the board of regents of the university of New York.

In 1789, lands were specially set apart, in the several new townships, for the promotion of literature, and the support of common schools. The proceeds of certain lands were also appropriated, in 1790, by the regents, to the institutions under their care. Their income, arising from this source, in 1792, was increased by the grant of £1500 per annum, for five years.

In 1793, the regents, in their report, suggested the importance of establishing schools in various parts of the state, for instructing children in the lower branches of education. These suggestions were renewed for the two years following, and in 1795, a common school system was established.

In 1795, $50,000 annually, for five years, was appropriated from the public revenues, for encouraging and maintaining schools, in the various cities and towns, to be expended much as the public moneys for schools are at the present day.

In 1801, an act was passed, authorizing the establishment of four lotteries, to raise the sum of $25,000 each, one half to be paid to the regents of the university, and the other to the state treasury, to be applied for the use of common schools. This was the foundation of the literature and common school fund.

In 1805, the nett proceeds of 500,000 acres of the public lands, and 3000 shares of bank stock, were appropriated as a fund for the use of common schools, to accumulate till the interest should amount to $50,000 per annum, after which, the interest was to be distributed, as the legislature should direct.

In 1811, preparatory measures were taken to organize the school system, and in 1812, an act was passed for that purpose. Gideon Hawley, Esq., was appointed superintendent of common schools, in 1813. From 1819 to 1827, farther appropriations of lands, stocks, and money, for the increase of the school fund, were made; and $100,000 ordered to be annually distributed, while an equal sum should be raised by tax.

In 1838, the sum of $165,000 per year, from the annual revenue of the United States deposit fund, was added to the amount previously distributed. Of this amount, $55,000 was to be expended yearly, in the purchase of suitable books for district libraries. During this year, the common school system was reorganized, and, with the exception of a few amendments, assumed its present form.

Present Condition of Common Schools.

Funds. By a provision of the constitution, the proceeds of all lands belonging to the state, with the exception of such as may be reserved for public use, or ceded to the United States, together with the fund known as the common school fund, are declared to constitute " a perpetual fund, the interest of which shall be inviolably appropriated, and applied to the support of common schools, throughout the state."

Of these state lands, as yet unsold, there remain about 350,000 acres, lying mostly in the northern part of the state, and valued at about $175,000. These constitute the *unproductive* portion of the school fund.

The *productive* capital of the fund amounts to upwards of two millions of dollars, and consists of bonds, mortgages, bank and state stocks, and money in the treasury, and yields a sufficient revenue to admit of the annual appropriation, and distribution of $110,000 among the several school districts.

An equal amount, viz: $110,000, was, by an act passed in 1838, devoted to the same purpose, from the United States deposit fund. An additional sum of $55,000, was also granted for the purchase of district libraries; by an act passed in 1843, this may be expended, under certain restrictions, for maps, globes, and other school apparatus. The whole sum appropriated, beside the above $55,000, is $220,000, which is applied to the payment of teachers' wages.

The year succeeding any enumeration of the inhabitants, state or national, an apportionment of this sum is made out, among the several counties, towns, and wards, according to their population, and the money paid over to the treasurer of each county, for distribution.

A certified copy of the apportionment is then forwarded to each of the county clerks, to be laid before the board of supervisors, who are required to raise, annually, by taxation, a sum equal to that thus received. They may also raise any additional amount, not exceeding twice the amount of the apportionment, which the electors of any town may vote to raise, for school purposes. The amounts thus raised are to be paid over to the town superintendents, for distribution among the districts.

In addition to these sums, many of the towns annually receive incomes from local funds, arising either from the sale of school lots, reserved in laying out new townships, in 1789, or from bequests, &c. In most of the large cities, large additional amounts are also raised, under special acts, providing for the organization and support of common schools.

The aggregate amount of funds applicable to school purposes, may be stated as follows.

Apportioned from state funds	$275,000
Equal amount raised by taxation	275,000
Sums raised by voluntary vote of towns	20,000
Sums raised under special acts in cities	200,000
Local funds	20,000
	$790,000
Amount raised on rate bills	$450,000
Total amount annually raised, from all sources, for common schools	$1,240,000

This is exclusive of the large amount invested in school houses, furniture, fuel, apparatus, text books, &c.

Districts and their officers. The entire territory of the state has been divided into about 11,000 school districts, each averaging nearly four square miles. The voters of each district choose three trustees, of whom one holds his office for one year, one for two, and one for three years, a district clerk, collector and librarian, who hold their office one year each.

Town Superintendents. The town superintendents of common schools are annually elected, by the people of each of the towns, at their annual town meetings, and have the general supervision of the common schools in their respective towns.

County Superintendents. The county superintendent is the next officer in the gradation of the system, and is appointed, once in two years, by the board of supervisors of each county. Either they, or the state superintendent, may remove him from office, for neglect of duty, or misconduct. Each county is required, by law, to have one county superintendent, and where the number of districts exceeds 150, two may be appointed.

These officers are charged with the general supervision of the schools of the county, or of that section of the county, for which they are appointed. Their compensation may not exceed $500 a year; one half of which is paid by the county, and the other half by the state, out of the annual surplus of the common school fund.

Within a few years past, the county superintendents, in addition to their duties specified by law, have called periodical meetings of the town superintendents, teachers, officers and inhabitants of districts, for the purpose of mutual consultation, and the improvement of the condition of the schools; they have organized and held teachers' institutes, in the spring and autumn, for the purpose of preparing the teachers for the more efficient discharge of their duties.

In conjunction with the town superintendents, they select the pupils, which the county is entitled to send to the state normal school; and deliver familiar lectures on topics connected with public school education, in each district, during their several visitations.

They also meet annually, in convention, for the purpose of mutual consultation with each other, with the head of the department, and with the friends of education, from this, and other states.

State Superintendent. The secretary of state is, by virtue of his office, superintendent of common schools. He maintains a correspondence with all the subordinate officers, and has a general oversight over the whole. To him are referred, for final decision, all questions arising, relative to the common school laws, on appeal from the decisions of the county superintendents.

He is required to report, annually, to the legislature, the condition of the schools in the several counties, and to do all in his power to promote the interests, and extend the benefits, of popular education throughout the state. He appoints one of the clerks of the state department, as his deputy, who aids him in the discharge of his duties, and who, in case of his absence, or the vacating of the office, becomes acting superintendent.

For a full exposition of the duties of all the officers of the common school system, reference may be had to the common school law, a copy of which may be found in each district.

Statistics of the Common Schools. From the last annual report of the state superintendent, made to the legislature, in January, 1846, we gather the following statistics:

Whole number of children between the ages of five and sixteen, in the state, Jan., 1845,	690,914
Whole number, of all ages, under instruction the whole or a part of the year, 1845,	736,045
Average annual increase of children between the ages of five and sixteen, since 1815, is more than	18,000
Average annual increase of children of all ages, receiving instruction,	20,549
Average number of months in which schools have been kept during the year 1845,	8
Amount of public money paid for teachers' wages in 1845,	$629,856 94
Amount paid on rate bills for the same purpose,	458,127 00
Total,	$1,087,983 94
Amount expended for district libraries,	$95,159 25
Number of volumes in district libraries, 1st July, 1845,	1,145,250
Average annual increase of volumes,	100,000
Number of pupils in attendance at private and select schools in 1845,	56,058

State Normal School.

By an act, passed by the legislature of 1844, $9,600 was appropriated for that year, and $10,000 annually, for five years thereafter, and until otherwise directed by law, for the establishment and support of a state normal school, for the instruction and practice of teachers of common schools, in the science of education, and in the art of teaching.

This institution is located in the city of Albany, and placed under the direction of the state superintendent of common schools, and the regents of the university. This board appoint an executive committee, of five persons, of whom the state superintendent is one, *ex officio*, to superintend the general interests of the school, to carry into effect the laws enacted for its regulation, and to report to the board annually.

By the regulations of the executive committee, superintendent, and board of regents, each county of the state is entitled to a number of pupils equal to double its representation in the house of assembly, making in all 256 pupils; to be selected by the county and town superintendents. No charge for instruction or for books is made; and each pupil receives a sum sufficient, on a liberal estimate, to defray his or her traveling expenses, to and from the institution.

The board of instruction consists of a principal, a professor of mathematics, a teacher of vocal music, one of drawing, and six subordinate teachers, in the various branches, deemed requisite to the complete preparation of teachers of common schools.

Connected with the institution are two experimental schools, composed of fifty children each, between the ages of five and sixteen, and under the general supervision of a teacher, specially appointed for this purpose. Into these, the more advanced pupils of the normal school pass, in succession, for a period of three or four weeks each, to test their practical abilities, as educators, before their final graduation.

No definite term of instruction is prescribed. Each pupil is required to complete a specified course of studies, to the full satisfaction of the principal and board of instructors, by whom, and the executive committee, diplomas, setting forth that fact, are conferred, semi-annually, in the months of March and September.

The institution is furnished with a large and well selected library, and all the scientific apparatus requisite to a full and thorough course of instruction, in the various branches of a sound, English education. The number of students, of both sexes, in 1846, exceeded two hundred.

City School Organizations.

1. *City of New York.* In the city of New York, the common schools are divided into three classes, viz: 1st, Public and Primary schools, under the care of the public school society; 2d, Ward schools, under the management of the commissioners, inspectors and trustees of the respective wards; 3d, Corporate schools, conducted by officers, elected under their respective charters.

These are all subject to the general supervision of the county superintendent, and to the inspection and management of the board of education, which consists of two commissioners, two inspectors, and five trustees in each ward. These officers are elected by the people; the commissioners and inspectors hold their offices for two years, and the trustees for five years. They all participate in the public money, and in that raised by the general and special laws, for school purposes.

The *Public School Society* was incorporated by the legislature, in 1805, and up to the year 1843, had the entire control of all the common schools in the city. They have eighteen public, and fifty-four primary schools, beside two public and four primary schools for colored children. In these schools, in 1846, 22,500 children were instructed, at a cost, for tuition, of a little more than $73,000.

There are three normal schools, also, under the control of this society, intended for the instruction of the monitors, and junior teachers of the schools; these normal schools are held on Saturday of each week, and during a portion of the year, in the evenings of the other days of the week. To each of the primary and public schools, a well selected library is attached.

The ward schools occupy from twenty to twenty-five buildings, comprising upwards of fifty schools, and having more than 25,000 children under instruction. There are, beside, thirteen corporate schools, mostly connected with benevolent institutions, and embracing upwards of 2000 scholars.

The aggregate number of children taught in all the public schools, during some portion of the year, exceeds fifty thousand; and it is supposed that about 30,000 more attend the various select schools in the city.

The amount of public money annually expended for common schools, is as follows:

Apportioned by the state	$35,000 00
An equal amount raised by tax	35,000 00
One twentieth of one per cent. on the valuation of real and personal property	114,610 63
Raised under special acts	8,360 66
Total	$192,971 29

2. *City of Rochester.* The common schools of this city are under the control of a board of education, consisting of two commissioners for each ward, annually elected by the people of the several wards, and a city superintendent, chosen by them.

The schools are entirely supported by taxation, no charge being made for instruction or text books. There are in the city, sixteen school houses, all substantial buildings, furnished with ample play grounds, and other conveniences. In these edifices there are between forty and fifty schools, under the care of sixteen male, and thirty female teachers, and comprising about 6000 children, nearly all that are of suitable age, residing in the city.

3. *City of Buffalo.* The mayor and aldermen of the city are, *ex officio*, commissioners of common schools; and are required annually to appoint a city superintendent. The schools are free, being, as in Rochester, entirely sustained by taxation. The number of districts is fifteen, and the schools are under the care of fifteen male, and thirty-six female instructors, having, in attendance, about 7000 children.

4. *City of Hudson.* The members of the common council are here, also, *ex officio*, commissioners of common schools. They appoint three superintendents, who, together, constitute a board of education for the city. An amount, equal to four times the apportionment from the state funds, is raised by tax, and the remaining ex-

penses are defrayed by rate bills, against those who send to the schools.

5. *City of Brooklyn.* Here, too, the common council are, from their office, commissioners of common schools; the general management of which is committed to a board of education, consisting of two members from each district appointed by the common council. They are divided into three classes, one of which annually goes out of office. The schools are free, deriving their support from assessments on the taxable property of the city.

6. *City of Utica.* The board of Commissioners for common schools in this city, consists of six members, two of whom are elected annually. They hold their office for three years. The rate bills may not exceed $2.00 per term. The remaining sums necessary for the support of schools, beyond the state apportionment, are raised by taxes.

7. *City of Schenectady.* The Schenectady Lancasterian school society has the general control of public education, in this city and receives, and disburses the public money applicable to this purpose.

8. *City of Albany.* The public schools of this city are under the supervision of a board of commissioners, nine in number, appointed by the Mayor, Recorder, and such of the Regents as may reside in the city. The members of this board, hold office for three years, one third going out of office each year.

The schools are not entirely free, the sum raised by tax being only twice the amount received from the state; but the indigent are exempted from the payment of rate bills; and a certain number of indigent pupils, who have attended the district schools at least two years, are supported at either of the academies of the city, or at the state normal school. Instruction in vocal music is provided in all the schools. The number of school districts is ten, and children instructed about 3000.

The *city of Troy*, and the villages of *Poughkeepsie* and *Williamsburgh*, have separate local systems, similar to those above described.

UNIVERSITIES, COLLEGES, AND ACADEMIES.

Regents of the University. These institutions are, by law, placed under the supervision, and subject to the visitation of a board, organized by the legislature in 1784, under the title of "Regents of the University of the state of New York." This board consists of twenty-one persons; of this board, the Governor and Lieutenant Governor are, *ex officio*, members, and the others are appointed by the legislature, and hold office, during its pleasure.

Its officers are, a Chancellor, Vice Chancellor, Secretary, and Treasurer, elected by the board. It is their duty to examine, and report to the legislature, the modes of education, discipline, number of students, course of study, funds, debts, &c., of the institutions under their charge.

They are also empowered to fill vacancies in the offices of president or principal of these institutions; to confer degrees, under certain circumstances, above that of Master of Arts; to apportion the annual income of the literature fund, among the several senate districts; and to incorporate academies, on compliance with such terms as they may prescribe.

PUBLIC EDUCATION.

The Literature Fund, appropriated to the support of this class of institutions, amounts to $268,990 57, consisting of state, bank, and insurance stocks, and money in the treasury, besides 9625 acres of land, valued at $4300. It yields an annual revenue of about $75,000.

Of this amount, $40,000 is divided among the academies of the state; $9000 to the university of the city of New York; $7000 to Geneva college, including its medical department; $3000 to Hamilton college; $1000 to the Albany medical college; $2300 to Genesee Wesleyan Seminary; $10,000 to the state normal school, and the balance to the purchase of books and apparatus for the various academies, in pursuance of the provisions of an act passed in 1834.

Universities and Colleges. There are at present, in this state, four incorporated universities, viz: the University of the city of New York, organized in 1832; the Madison University, at Hamilton, Madison county; the Rochester University, and the Buffalo University; the three latter incorporated in 1846.

There are also four colleges; Columbia College, in the city of New York; Union College, at Schenectady; Hamilton College, at Clinton, Oneida county, and Geneva college, at Geneva, in Ontario county.

In addition to these, there are five medical schools, viz; the College of Physicians and Surgeons in New York city; the Medical Department of the University of the city of New York; the Albany Medical College; the Medical Department of Geneva College, and the Medical Department of the Buffalo University, organized in 1846.

Academies. There are 179 incorporated academies in the state, comprising upwards of 25,000 pupils of both sexes. The aggregate value of the land and buildings belonging to these institutions, exceeds $1,000,000; the value of the libraries belonging to them, $60,000, and of their apparatus, $56,600. The aggregate amount paid for tuition, during the year 1845, was over $200,000; the number of teachers employed, over 600; and the number of students gratuitously instructed, over 200.

The branches of study taught, embrace, in addition to those ordinarily pursued in common schools, the higher departments of mathematics and natural Philosophy, with their various applications to practical uses; the languages, ancient and modern; the physical sciences; moral and intellectual philosophy; history in its widest and most comprehensive range; natural theology; political economy; vocal, and occasionally, instrumental, music; drawing, and other accomplishments.

There are several female academies and seminaries; among which, the Albany Female Academy, and Female Seminary, the Troy, Rutgers, in the city of New York, Poughkeepsie, Amsterdam, Schenectady, Clinton, Utica, Auburn, Ontario at Canandaigua, Batavia, Le Roy, Seward, and Rochester Female Seminaries, are the most prominent.

Theological Seminaries. Of these there are nine, viz: the Hamilton Theological Institution, now forming a department of the Madison University, in Hamilton, Madison county, under the patronage of the Baptist denomination, but open, without distinction, to students of every religious denomination, designing to prepare themselves for the gospel ministry; the Oneida Conference Seminary, founded by the Methodists, and located in the village of Cazenovia, Madison county; the Genesee Wesleyan Seminary, at Lima, Livingston county; Auburn Theological Seminary, (Presbyterian;) the Hartwick Theological Seminary, (Lutheran;) the Theological Seminary of the Associate Reformed Church of New York, at Newburgh, Orange county; the General Theological Seminary of the Protestant Episcopal Church in the United States, located in New York city; the Union Theological Seminary, in the same city; and the Roman Catholic Ecclesiastical Seminary, at Rose Hill, in Westchester county.

Collegiate Schools. There are seven of these institutions, located in different sections of the state. St. John's College, a Roman Catholic institution, pleasantly situated at Rose Hill, Westchester Co., about twelve miles from New York city, numbers 115 pupils; St. Paul's College, St. Thomas' Hall, and St. Ann's Hall, at Flushing, Long Island, are under the patronage of the Protestant Episcopal denomination; the latter is specially designed for the education of young ladies; the Poughkeepsie Collegiate School, is located in the flourishing village of Poughkeepsie, and has a high reputation; the Black River Literary and Religious Institute, is a well ordered and flourishing seminary, situated at Watertown, Jefferson county, and averages about 200 pupils; and the New Brighton Collegiate School, situated on the heights, overlooking the village of New Brighton, on Staten Island, six miles from New York.

GEOGRAPHY AND HISTORY

OF THE

COUNTIES.

LAND PURCHASES REFERRED TO IN THIS WORK.

In the description of the several counties, references are made to the Manor of Rensselaerwyck, the Livingston Manor, the Kayaderosseras Patent, the Hardenburgh Patent, Phelps' and Gorham's Purchase, the Holland Land Company's Purchase, the Pulteney estate, the Military tract, Bingham's Purchase, Morris' estate, &c.

The first three of these, are fully described in the general historical sketch, and in the description of the counties of Albany, Rensselaer, Columbia and Saratoga.

The *Hardenburgh Patent* was granted at an early date to a Dutch citizen of wealth, and comprised the larger part of Delaware and Sullivan counties.

Phelps' and Gorham's Purchase included the Holland Land Company's purchase, the Pulteney estate, and the Morris estate.

The history of this purchase is as follows:

The second charter of Massachusetts, granted by William and Mary in 1691, bounded the territory of that colony westwardly, by the Pacific Ocean: thus dividing the present state of New York into two parts, separated from each other, by a section of the width of the state of Massachusetts.

The colony of New York, under the grants made to the Duke of York and Albany in 1664, claimed the whole extent of territory, at present included under her jurisdiction. These conflicting claims gave rise to long and harassing disputes, and protracted legal proceedings, but on the 16th of December, 1786, the controversy was settled, by a convention between the two states, concluded at Hartford, Conn.

By this convention, Massachusetts ceded to New York, all claim to the government, sovereignty, and jurisdiction, of the lands in controversy; and New York granted to Massachusetts, the right of pre-emption, (or first purchase,) from the Indians, and when so purchased, the fee simple of the soil, of all that part of the state, lying west of a meridian drawn through Seneca lake, except a tract one mile wide, along the shores of Lake Erie, and the Niagara river; a territory now comprising thirteen entire counties, and the larger part of Wayne county, and containing nearly 600,000 inhabitants.

On the first of April, 1788, the state of Massachusetts contracted to sell to Oliver Phelps and Nathaniel Gorham, the right of pre-emption, to the whole of this vast tract, for the sum of one million dollars, to be paid in three equal instalments.

On the 8th of July, of the same year, Messrs. Phelps and Gorham made a treaty with the Indians in the neighborhood of Canandaigua, by which the Indian title was extinguished to the tract lying east of the Genesee river, and a tract extending twelve miles west of that river, from York, in Genesee county, northward to the lake. This tract was confirmed to the contractors, by the Massachusetts legislature, in November, 1788.

In February, 1790, Messrs. Phelps and Gorham, having paid $666,666, on the purchase money, and being unable to pay the third instalment, at the time agreed, proposed to the state of Massachusetts, to surrender to the state the remaining portion, to which the Indian title was not extinguished, and should the amount already purchased of the Indians, prove more than one-third of the whole tract, to pay for the excess, at the average price of the whole. This proposition was accepted.

On the 18th of November, 1790, Messrs. Phelps and Gorham sold to Robert Morris, all of their tract east of the Genesee river, except the portion already sold to settlers, and two townships reserved to themselves. The tract thus sold, contained 1,264,000 acres, and Mr. Morris paid about $200,000 for it.

The lands surrendered to the state of Massachusetts were sold to Samuel Ogden, and by him to Robert Morris, who extinguished the Indian title for the sum of $100,000. Mr. Morris, by this purchase, became possessed of the greater part of the tract, originally purchased by Messrs. Phelps and Gorham.

Mr. Morris, soon after, sold to a company formed in Holland, a portion of the land thus purchased, comprising 3,200,000 acres, and including the present counties of Erie, Niagara, Chautauque, and Cattaraugus. This company was known as the Holland Land Company, and their tract as the Holland Purchase. They established a land office at Batavia, and sold the land to actual settlers. Those lands which remained unsold, were, after a time, transferred to other associations, but by far the larger part, are now owned by the inhabitants.

The tract purchased of Phelps and Gorham, by Mr. Morris, was sold by him, to Sir William Pulteney, and hence called the Pulteney estate. It comprised nearly all of Steuben, Yates, and Ontario counties, the east range of townships in Allegany, and the principal part of Livingston, Monroe, and Wayne counties. About one-third of the whole tract had been sold to companies and individuals, previous to Sir William's purchase. Mr. Williamson was appointed his agent, and opened land offices at Geneva and Bath. To his energy, public spirit, and liberality, the people of those counties are much indebted.

The tract lying between this estate, and the Holland purchase, was retained by Mr. Morris, and sold by him to actual settlers. It embraced portions of Orleans, Genesee, Wyoming, and Allegany counties, and contained 500,000 acres.

The *Military tract*, or rather *tracts*, for there were two to which this name was applied, were bounty lands, granted by New York, to her soldiers, who had served during the revolutionary war; an appropriation of 600 acres was made to every private soldier, and larger quantities to the officers.

The act, granting these lands, was passed in 1786, and the grant was made, with the proviso, that the Indian title should first be extinguished. The lands thus granted, comprised the present counties of Onondaga, Cortland, Tompkins, Cayuga, Seneca, and part of Oswego, and Wayne. It contained 1,680 000 acres. As, however, the Indian title was not immediately extinguished, the legislature, the same year, appropriated twelve northern townships in the present counties of Clinton, Franklin, and Essex, containing 768,000 acres, to the location of revolutionary patents. This was called the *Old Military tract*. The Indian title to the other tract, however, being extinguished in 1789, the greater part of the bounty lands were located in Onondaga, and the adjacent counties.

Bingham's Purchase was a tract some twenty miles square, lying partly in Broome county, and partly in the state of Pennsylvania. It was purchased by Messrs. Bingham, Wilson, and Cox, of Philadelphia, in 1785. Immediately north of this, was another purchase, made the succeeding year, by a company from Massachusetts, and containing 230,000 acres. There were sixty proprietors in this company.

Large tracts of land are also held in the counties of Jefferson and St. Lawrence, by the Messrs. Van Rensselaer, and Governeur Morris; and in different sections of the state, by Gerrit Smith, Esq., of Peterboro, Chenango county, and the heirs of the Messrs. Wadsworth, of Livingston county.

I. ALBANY COUNTY.

Square Miles, 515.   Population, 77,268.
Organized, 1683.   Valuation, 1845, $15,603,161.

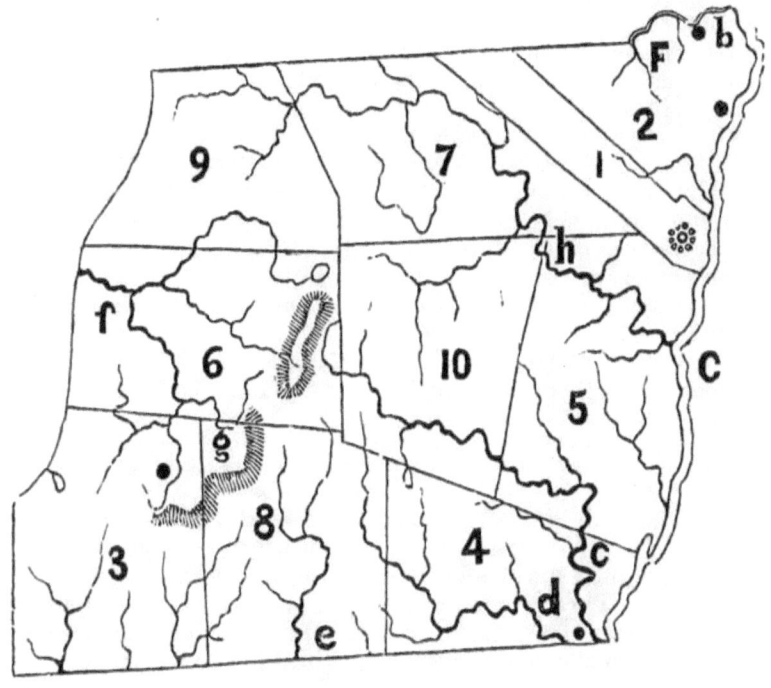

TOWNS.

1. Albany, 1686.
2. Watervliet, 1788.
3. Rensselaerville, 1790.
4. Coeymans, 1791.
5. Bethlehem, 1793.
6. Berne, 1795.
7. Guilderland, 1803.
8. Westerlo, 1815.
9. Knox, 1822.
10. New Scotland, 1832.

Mountains. g. Helderberg Hills.

Rivers, &c. C. Hudson. F. Mohawk. h. Norman's kill. c. Coeymans creek. d. Haivnakraus kill. e. Provost creek. f. Foxes creek.

Falls. b. Cohoes falls.

Cities and Villages. Albany, West Troy, Coeymans, Rensselaerville, Cohoes.

BOUNDARIES. North by Schenectady and Saratoga counties; East by the Hudson; South by Greene; and West by Schoharie county.

SURFACE. The surface is much varied. Along the Hudson, extends an alluvial valley, from a fourth of a mile to a mile in width. From this valley the land rises abruptly, 140 feet, and thence a table land gradually ascends, to the base of the Helderberg hills. Along the Mohawk, the surface is rugged and broken.

The Helderberg hills extend through the western part of the county, uniting, on the south, with the Catskill range.

They are from 400 to 500 feet in height, and very precipitous. Their elevation is quite uniform, displaying no isolated peaks.

RIVERS AND STREAMS. The county is well watered. Besides the Hudson and Mohawk rivers, which partially bound it, the Norman's kill, Coeymans creek, Haivnakraus kill, Provost creek, Foxes' creek, Boza kill, Vlamans kill, and the Patroon's creek, are the principal streams.

Most of these, as well as several smaller streams, have valuable waterfalls, affording great facilities for manufacturing.

The Cohoes, or Great Falls of the Mohawk, at the village of Cohoes, lie partly in this, and partly in Saratoga county.

The river here descends, at a single leap, 70 feet, and then pursues its way, over the rocks, in the channel, which its waters have cut through the solid rock, to the depth of more than 100 feet, to the Hudson. Few cataracts possess more picturesque beauty.

RAILROADS. The Troy and Schenectady, and the Mohawk and Hudson railroads, cross the northeastern section of the county, and the Catskill and Canajoharie, the southeastern.

CLIMATE. The climate is quite variable, being subject to great extremes of heat and cold. Though unfavorable to those affected with pulmonary diseases, it is considered as generally healthy.

GEOLOGY AND MINERALOGY. The geological formation of the county is transition; graywacke and slate are the prominent characteristics of the banks of the Hudson and Mohawk. In the Helderbergs, are fond lime and sandstone, both abounding in organic remains.

In the elevated table lands, lying between the Helderbergs and the Hudson river, are thick beds of blue and yellow marl, of clayey consistence, and destitute of fossils. They are covered with yellow sand.

Bog iron ore is found, in numerous localities, in the county. Marl, and water limestone, also abound. There are several mineral springs, some of which contain sulphuretted hydrogen, others carbonic acid gas, iron, and magnesia.

Epsom salts are found at Coeymans Landing, and petroleum in Guilderland. In the limestone cliffs of the Helderbergs, are several extensive caverns, containing quartz and other crystals, stalactites and stalagmites of great beauty; calcareous spar, bitumen and alum also occur in the county.

SOIL AND VEGETABLE PRODUCTIONS. A portion of the soil is

fertile and productive, and most of that, which was naturally sterile, has, by the skill of the husbandman, been made to yield abundant returns. Considerable tracts, however, are not susceptible of cultivation.

<small>The timber of the county is principally pine, hemlock, oak, hickory, elm, chestnut, and birch.</small>

PURSUITS. *Agriculture* is the pursuit of a majority of the inhabitants. This may be reckoned as one of the grain growing counties, although not one of the most productive.

<small>Oats, corn, rye, buckwheat, and barley, are the principal grains; potatoes are raised in considerable quantities. The western part is favorable to grazing, and butter is there largely produced. The number of sheep in the county is large, and increasing annually.</small>

Manufactures also occupy the attention of a large number of the citizens of the county. In 1845, these considerably exceeded two and a half millions of dollars, of which about two millions were produced in the city of Albany.

<small>The principal articles manufactured were, iron ware, flour, malt liquors, coaches and sleighs, machinery, cotton and woollen goods, brick, cordage, oil and oil cloths.</small>

Commerce. The navigation of the Hudson river, and the Erie and Champlain canals, furnishes employment to large numbers, and this commerce is increasing, in a rapid annual ratio.

<small>Tolls were received, in 1845, in the county, upon produce valued at about twenty-seven millions of dollars. About thirty-five steamers, seventy tow boats, and 630 sloops and schooners, beside scows, &c., are employed in the Albany trade, on the Hudson. The total amount of shipping, belonging to the county, is about 60,000 tons.</small>

STAPLE PRODUCTIONS. Oats, corn, rye, barley, buckwheat, butter and wool.

SCHOOLS. There are, in the county of Albany, 160 district school houses. In 1845, schools were taught, on an average, ten months. During that year, 14,600 children were instructed, at an expense of about $25,000, for tuition. The district libraries contained about 29,000 volumes.

<small>There were also, in the county, the same year, 111 unincorporated private schools, with 3,856 pupils; three academies, and two female seminaries, with 637 pupils; one state normal school, with 294 pupils; and one medical college, with 114 students.</small>

RELIGIOUS DENOMINATIONS. Methodists, Dutch Reformed, Baptists, Presbyterians, Episcopalians, Roman Catholics, Friends, Unitarians, Lutherans, Congregationalists, Universalists, and Jews.*

HISTORY. When Henry Hudson ascended the North river, in 1609, he despatched Hendrick Corstiaensen, with a small

---

<small>* The religious denominations are given, throughout this work, in the order of their numbers, beginning with the most numerous.</small>

crew, in a boat, to ascertain the highest point to which that river was navigable. Corstiaensen penetrated as far as Troy, or Lansingburgh, but landed at the present site of the city of Albany.

In 1611, or 12, he returned and erected a trading house, on Boyd's island, a short distance below the Albany ferry. In the ensuing spring, this was so much injured by the ice and the freshet, that he was compelled to abandon it. He then erected a fort, on a hill, about two miles south of Albany.

In 1623 a fort was erected near the present Fort Orange Hotel, in the city of Albany, mounting eight large cannon.* It was named Fort Orange, in honor of the Prince of Orange, who, at that time, presided over the Netherlands.

This fort was intended to subserve the double purpose, of affording convenient accommodations for the traffic with the Indians, and also of serving as a protection against sudden attacks from them. It was only occupied during the autumn, and winter, by the traders, whose object was trade, not colonization.

In 1630, Kiliaen Van Rensselaer, a wealthy pearl merchant, of Amsterdam, purchased, through his agents, a large tract of land, including most of this, as well as several of the adjacent, counties.

Over this extensive tract, he possessed all the authority of a sovereign, and, anxious to improve it to the best advantage, he sent a colony here, in 1631, well provided with whatever was necessary, to commence a new settlement. To his estate he gave the name of Rensselaerwyck.

It is believed that he never visited his colony. The administration of justice, and the management of its financial affairs, he committed to a commissary general. Fortunate in the selection of these, his colony prospered much more than that at New Amsterdam, and it was to the good offices of Van Curler, or Corlaer, the first commissary, that the colonists at New Amsterdam were indebted, more than once, for their preservation from destruction, at the hands of the savages. This excellent man cultivated the most friendly relations with the Indians, and so strong was their affection for him, that, ever after, they applied the name of Corlaer to the governors of New York, as the highest title of respect.

In 1642, Mr. Van Rensselaer sent over the Rev. Johannes Megapolensis, as minister of Rensselaerwyck, supporting him at his own expense. The first church was erected the succeeding year, and furnished with a bell and pulpit, by the Dutch West India Company. In 1646, the venerable patroon died, at Amsterdam. His son Johannes, then a minor, succeeded him.

During the administration of Governor Stuyvesant, serious difficulties occurred between him and the agent of the patroon, which were finally referred to the states general of Holland, for decision. After New York came into the possession of the Eng-

* *Stone pieces*, they are called in the original Dutch records; meaning, according to Judge Vanderkemp, that they were loaded with stone, instead of iron balls. They were of very large caliber.

lish, the name of Beaverwyck, which had been bestowed upon the settlement, was changed to Albany, that being one of the titles of the Duke of York. The right of soil was confirmed to the patroon, by a new patent, but the government was retained in the hands of the governor of the colony.

In 1686, Governor Dongan granted a charter to the city of Albany, and Peter Schuyler, the friend of the Indians, was elected the first mayor.

In 1689-90, the citizens of this county refused to submit to the administration of Leisler and Milborne, but were at length compelled, by the fears of an Indian invasion, to yield allegiance. No sooner, however, did Colonel Sloughter arrive, than he was welcomed by the people of this county, whose attachment to Leisler had never been ardent, or sincere.

In all the treaties with the Indian tribes, the citizens of Albany bore a conspicuous part, and so entirely had they won the confidence of the savages, that from the date of its settlement, the county was never invaded, by these sons of the forest. The Schuyler family, for several generations, exerted a powerful influence over the Indians.

During the revolution, the Albany committee nobly sustained their countrymen, in their opposition to British sway, and afforded aid, in troops and money, to the suffering inhabitants of Tryon county, to assist them in repelling the frequent attacks of the merciless horde of tories and Indians, who ravaged their settlements.

Burgoyne had boasted, at the commencement of his campaign, that his army should revel upon the spoils of Albany, but he only visited the city as a captive. Sir Henry Clinton twice attempted to invade it, but met with sufficient obstacles to prevent his success.

It became the capital of the state in 1807. Since the introduction of steamboats, and the completion of the canals, the growth of the city and county have been rapid, and the lines of railroads, which connect it with Boston and Buffalo, are giving it a still greater impulse.

The extensive manor of Rensselaerwyck, occupying a territory twenty-four by forty-eight miles in extent, descended, by entailment, to the eldest male descendant of Kiliaen Van Rensselaer. The last proprietor was the late patroon, Stephen Van Rensselaer, a man, whose munificent patronage of every object which could benefit his fellow citizens, or aid in diffusing happiness among men, has embalmed his memory.

At his death, the manor was divided between his two sons, Stephen and William P. Van Rensselaer, the former receiving the portion west of the Hudson, and the latter, that lying east of the river.

The lands had usually been granted on permanent leases, the rental being payable in produce. Some personal services were usually required, by the terms of the lease, but seldom exacted by the patroon. The effort, on the part of the present proprietors, to enforce the collection of the rents, was met by strenuous opposition, on the part of the tenants, who formed themselves into armed organizations, and in their conflict with the officers of the law, several individuals were killed.

These organizations have, of late, assumed a political character. Both the proprietors and the tenants have sought redress from the legislature, but as yet no decisive action has been taken, by that body. The inconsistency of the feudal tenure, with the spirit of our institutions, will be admitted by all; but there is great difficulty in legislating justly upon the subject.

CITIES AND VILLAGES. ALBANY CITY is situated on the west bank of the Hudson, 145 miles above New York. It appears to great advantage, from the river, rising rapidly from the bank, and exhibiting its public buildings in bold relief. The alluvial valley of the Hudson extends about a quarter of a mile from the river bank. From this valley, a bluff rises abruptly, 140 feet, and, in the distance of a mile, about eighty feet more. Upon this bluff, are situated most of the public buildings.

In 1845, the city had 116 streets and lanes. It is divided into ten wards, each of which elect annually, an alderman and assistant alderman, who together form the common council of the city.

The public buildings are, many of them, elegant and costly. The Capitol, erected at an expense of $120,000, is a fine freestone edifice. The State Hall, built of white marble, and fireproof, is an elegant building, of the Ionic order, surmounted by a dome. It cost $350,000. The City Hall stands near it, and is also a fine Grecian structure, of white marble, surmounted by a gilded dome. The Albany Academy, an elegant building of Nyack freestone, opposite the state hall, cost, including the grounds, more than $100,000.

This building, and the capitol have large parks, in front, surrounded by substantial iron fences, and planted with ornamental trees and shrubbery.

The Albany Female Academy is a chaste, marble building, erected at a cost of about $30,000. The Albany Exchange, of massive granite; the Museum, of marble; the Medical College, of brick, and well adapted to the purposes, to which it is applied; the State Normal School; and the State Geological rooms, occupying the old state hall, are the other principal buildings.

Several of the churches, also, are deserving of notice for their architectural beauty. Among these, we may mention the Middle Dutch church, on Beaver street; the Pearl street Baptist church, a finely proportioned structure, in the Ionic style, and surmounted by a splendid dome; the Hudson street Methodist church, one of the most chaste and beautiful models for a church in the United States; the Presbyterian, and Roman Catholic churches, in Chapel street, &c., &c.

Among the hotels the Delavan House, stands preëminent for simple grandeur and chasteness of architecture. It was completed in 1845, and cost about $200,000. The Eagle, Congress Hall, Mansion, Townsend, American, Carlton, Stanwix Hall, and the Franklin House, are also well conducted hotels.

The State Library, founded by the munificence of the state, has an excellent collection of works on history, geography, and general literature. An extensive law library is connected with it. The entire collection numbers over 15,000 volumes, and is accessible to all, without charge.

The Albany Library, founded in 1792, and now numbering about 9,000 volumes, occupies apartments in the Albany female academy. The Albany Institute is a scientific institution, designed to encourage attention to history, and general science, in the city and state. It has a valuable library, of nearly 2000 volumes, in the building of the Albany academy.

The Young Men's Association occupies a fine suite of rooms in the exchange. It has a well conducted reading room, a library of 3200 volumes, and sustains a course of lectures each winter. The number of its members is over 1500. It was the first institution of the kind in the state.

The Alms House has connected with it, a fine farm of 150 acres, cultivated by the inmates. There are in the city, two Orphan Asylums, supported by private charity, which provide for the support and education of about 150 children; and a number of other benevolent societies.

The Albany Academy, founded in 1813, has eight teachers, and about 200 pupils. The Albany Female Academy, founded in 1814, has twelve teachers, and about 275 pupils. The Albany Female Seminary has six teachers. There are numerous other schools, of considerable reputation. The public schools have nine school houses, costing between $30,000 and $40,000.

The Albany Medical College is a flourishing medical school, having an able faculty, and one of the best anatomical museums in the United States. It has seven professors.

The State Geological Rooms, in the old state hall, contain the splendid collection of the state geologists, arranged, in the lower rooms, in the order of the successive strata, and in the upper, in the order of the counties. Here, too, are specimens of the mineral and vegetable treasures of the state, appropriately arranged, and a large collection of the quadrupeds, birds, fishes and reptiles of the state. They are open, free of expense, to all.

At the junction of the Erie canal with the Hudson, the citizens have constructed an extensive basin, to protect the boats from the winds, and give them greater facilities for discharging their cargoes.

The city is largely engaged in manufactures. Its iron foundries are among the largest in the country. More stoves are manufactured here, than in any other city, or town, in the union.

Coaches, sleighs, hats, caps, and bonnets, are also largely manufactured; the three latter articles, to the amount of nearly one million of dollars, annually. It has extensive manufactories of pianofortes. Leather is produced to the amount of more than $400,000 per annum. Population in 1845, 41,139.

West Troy, in the town of Watervliet, is a thriving village, possessing excellent hydraulic privileges, which it derives from the surplus waters of the Erie canal. It is a convenient depot for merchandise, from its facilities for transportation, and is largely engaged in manufactures, having twenty-five or thirty manufacturing establishments. The United States arsenal, established here in 1813, is the largest arsenal of construction, in the United States.

<small>Attached to the establishment, are about 100 acres of land, containing thirty-eight buildings, for workshops and storehouses. It constantly employs about 200 officers, soldiers, and workmen, and manufactures annually, munitions of war, to the amount of about $100,000. The grounds are enclosed by an iron fence in front, and a wall of stone on the sides and rear.</small>

The Erie and Champlain canals form a junction, a short distance above the village, and a bridge and two ferries connect it with Troy. Population in 1845, about 6000.

At *Neskayuna* in the same township, is a community of Shaking Quakers, established in 1776, by Ann Lee, the founder of the sect. This was the first Shaker establishment in the United States.

Cohoes village, also in this town, possesses one of the finest water privileges in the state, and its advantages for manufacturing, are hardly surpassed. It is estimated, that at the lowest stage of the water, there is sufficient to run 1,000,000 spindles. Population in 1845, over 2000.

Rensselaerville, in the town of the same name, is situated on Foxes creek. It has some manufactures, and about 1000 inhabitants.*

Coeymans is a small manufacturing village, having a good landing, and some trade with New York. It has also some manufactures. Population 1000.

<small>* From this town, in 1779, Captain Deitz, and two lads named John and Robert Brice, were taken as captives by the Indians, and suffered all the barbarities which the malice of the savages could inflict. Captain Deitz died at Montreal, from the effect of their cruelties; but the boys were exchanged at the close of the war, and returned home. This is believed to have been the nearest approach made to Albany, by the Indians during the Revolution.</small>

II. NEW YORK COUNTY.

Square Miles, 22.
Organized, 1683.
Population, 391,223.
Valuation, 1845, $239,995,517.

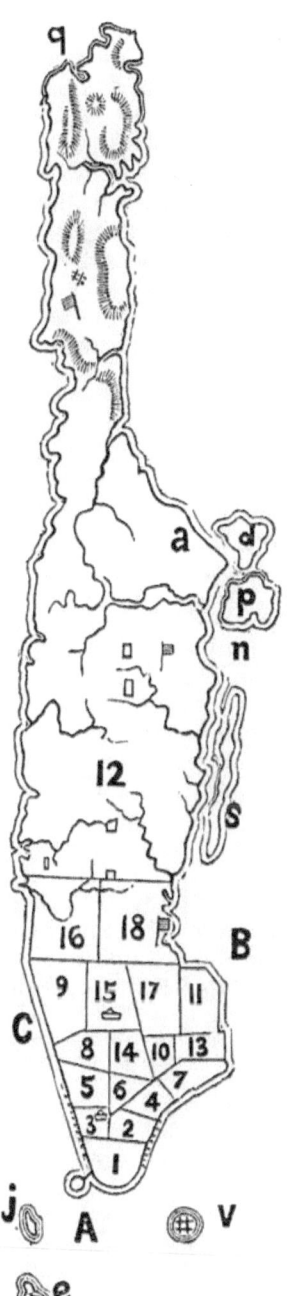

The city and county are of equal extent.*
Rivers. B, East River. C. Hudson River. a. Harlaem River. q. Spuyten Duyvel Creek. n. Hellgate.

Bays. A. New York Bay.

Islands. d. Randall's. p. Barn. s. Blackwell's. v. Governor's. e. Bedlow's. j. Ellis'.

Forts. Castle Garden, or Castle Clinton. Fort Columbus, on Governor's island. Fort Wood, on Bedlow's island.

Battle Fields. Kip's and Turtle Bay. Harlaem Heights. Fort Washington.

Universities. Columbia College. University of New York.

Cities. New York City.

BOUNDARIES. North by Westchester county; East by Westchester county and Long Island; South by Long Island and the waters of New York bay; and West by New Jersey.

Its territory extends to low water mark on the Jersey side of the Hudson, as well as to the same point on the Long Island side of the East river, and the Westchester side of the Harlaem.

SURFACE. The lower part of the county, though originally rough and broken, has been graded and levelled, and now rises gradually, from the shores of the Hudson and East rivers, towards the centre of the city. The upper part is still hilly, and has extensive marshes.

RIVERS. The East river, or strait, and the Hudson, or North river, wash its eastern and western shores, affording fine anchorage, and sufficient depth of water, to permit the largest

* The numbers refer to the wards.

ships to come up to the wharves. The Harlaem river is a narrow strait, connecting by means of Spuyten Duyvel creek, East river with the Hudson. Several small streams water the upper portions of the county, but none of them are of sufficient size to be worthy of notice. The original name of the island was Manhattan, a word of doubtful etymology, but of late years, it has been known by the name of New York Island.

BAYS. The upper, or New York bay, proper, is one of the finest harbors in the world, affording anchorage ground sufficient for the navies of the world. The lower bay, or harbor, is also spacious, but not so completely land locked as the upper. It furnishes, however, convenient and secure anchorage ground.

Kip's and Turtle bays, on the east, and Striker's bay, on the west side of the island, are small inlets, only worthy of notice, for their historic interest.

ISLANDS. Randall's, Barn, and Blackwell's islands, in the East river, and Governor's, Bedlow's, and Ellis', in the harbor, with some smaller islands, belong to the county.

On Governor's island are Fort Columbus, and Castle William; on Bedlow's, Fort Wood. There are also other fortifications, on Long Island and Staten Island, intended, like these, for the defence of the harbor.

CLIMATE. The climate of New York county is, from its situation, more equable than that of the inland counties, generally. The sea breezes waft a refreshing coolness, over the heated streets in summer, and temper the intense cold of the wintry blasts. In healthfulness, it occupies a very high rank, among the great cities of the world. Its ratio of deaths, to the population, is less than that of any of the large cities of Europe.

GEOLOGY AND MINERALS. The rocks of this county, with the exception of a small section at the extreme north, are primitive. Granite characterizes the river banks, and huge boulders of it lie scattered over the surface. Dolomite, (a species of marble), bog iron ore, and oxide of manganese, are the principal minerals, applicable to use in the arts.

Among those interesting to the mineralogist, may be enumerated fine specimens of tremolite, pyroxene, mica, tourmaline, serpentine and amianthus. Some specimens of pyrites, epidote, lamellar feldspar, stilbite, garnet, staurotide, graphite, &c., have also been met with. Marble is abundant, and extensively quarried, in the northern part of the island.

SOIL AND VEGETABLE PRODUCTIONS. The soil is generally fertile, but too costly to be devoted to agricultural purposes. Gardens, of considerable extent, are cultivated, in the upper part of the island.

The island was originally well wooded, but most of the timber is now cut off. Oak, pine, hemlock and chestnut, were the principal forest trees.

PURSUITS. *Manufacturing* is the pursuit of a majority of the inhabitants of the county. The articles manufactured are numerous, and amounted, in 1845, as nearly as can be ascertained, to between eighteen and twenty millions of dollars, giving employment to more than sixty thousand persons.

Commerce. In commerce, this county surpasses every other city or county on the continent, and is the second city in the world, in commercial importance.

In 1845, the registered, licensed and enrolled shipping of the county, amounted to 550,359 tons. The shipping, entered the same year, amounted to over one million tons, and the clearances, to about the same amount.

This commerce is extended to every part of the globe. Not only do the ships of this port visit the various ports of our own country, and Europe, but their sails flutter in the breezes of China, and Japan; their flag is known on the coasts of Arabia, Persia and India, and their trade sought by the swarthy sons of Africa and New Holland, and by the natives of the unnumbered isles, that gem the wide expanse of the Pacific. Wherever there is an opportunity for traffic, there the American flag is the first unfurled.

Directly, or indirectly, this commerce furnishes the means of support, to many thousands of her own citizens, and also to millions in other counties and states.

The great system of internal navigation, so nobly begun and carried on by the state, has also brought immense wealth into the city.

The amount of produce brought to the Hudson, from all the canals, in 1845, the greater part of which came to New York, was over forty-five millions of dollars, and the amount, which was cleared from the Hudson river, the same year, (most of which was from New York), was over fifty-five millions, making a total internal trade, of about one hundred millions of dollars per annum.

Agriculture is not an object of great attention. Horticulture furnishes employment to a considerable number of persons, in the upper part of the island.

EDUCATION. The common school system of the city of New York has been already described. (See page 124.)

It only remains to say, that more liberal and ample provision, for furnishing a thorough education, even to the most indigent, is nowhere made. The child of the poorest emigrant may obtain, free of expense, if he chooses, as full instruction in the sciences, as the son of the wealthiest citizen in the city.

In addition to the common schools, there are twenty-eight incorporated schools and academies in the county, seventeen of which are female seminaries. These are well conducted, and attended by large numbers. There are also several hundred private and select schools, attended, it is estimated, by more than 20,000 pupils.

There are two colleges in the city; viz: 1. Columbia College, founded in 1754, and amply endowed. It has a president and ten professors, 104 students, and a library of 14,000 volumes. The grammar school, connected with it, has between 200 and 300 pupils. The college edifices are located at the foot of Park place.

2. The University of the city of New York, located on Washington square. The university edifice is of white marble, in the collegiate Gothic style, and is one of the finest buildings in the

city. Its cost was nearly $300,000. It has a president, and eleven professors, 143 students, and a valuable library. Connected with it, is a large and flourishing grammar school.

A medical department is connected with the university. It is in a prosperous condition, and occupies a fine granite building, formerly known as the Stuyvesant Institute. This department has seven professors, 407 students, and a valuable museum.

Besides these, there are several professional schools in the city. The College of Physicians and Surgeons, in Crosby street, was founded in 1807, and has always maintained a high rank, among the medical schools of our country. It has seven professors, 279 students, and an extensive and valuable museum and library. The College of Pharmacy is a recent institution, designed for the education of apothecaries.

The General Theological Seminary of the Protestant Episcopal Church in the United States, occupies two elegant gothic buildings, of stone, in the upper part of the city, has five professors, seventy students, and a library of 7300 volumes. It was founded in 1819. The Union Theological Seminary of the Presbyterian Church, situated in University Place, was founded in 1836, has six professors, 112 students, and a library of over 16,000 volumes.

RELIGIOUS DENOMINATIONS. Episcopalians, Presbyterians, Baptists, Methodist Episcopal, Dutch Reformed, Roman Catholics, Methodists not Episcopal, Jews, Congregationalists, Lutherans, Universalists, Friends, Unitarians, New Jerusalem Church, Christians and Moravians. Number of churches 217, of clergymen 282.

HISTORY. The leading facts, connected with the settlement of New York, or New Amsterdam, as the city was called by the Dutch, have been already stated, in the general historical sketch. From the time of its discovery, in 1609, by Henry Hudson, up to the year 1625, no permanent settlement of emigrants seems to have been made.

Companies of adventurers had visited Manhattan Island, erected trading houses, for carrying on the traffic in furs with the natives, and when their objects were accomplished, had returned to Holland. A few, perhaps, fond of this roving life, had remained, and acquired that knowledge of the Indian character, which enabled them, more successfully, to secure his peltries. None, however, settled as colonists, or procured, from its native proprietors, a title to the soil, except for the erection of their trading houses.

In 1614, the Governor of Virginia, Sir Thomas Dale, in order to keep the restless spirits of his colony employed, fitted out an expedition under Captain Argall, against the French settlement at Acadia, (now Nova Scotia.) Returning from his cruise, Argall entered the bay of New York, and compelled the few Dutch traders, whom he found there, to swear fealty to the English crown.

After the formation of the Dutch West India Company, they took immediate measures for establishing a permanent colony, at this important post.

Under their fostering care, bouweries, or farms, were soon taken up, and a substantial fort being erected, the rude dwellings of the settlers began to cluster around it.

Under the administration of Minuit, it prospered and increased in population and importance. The intemperance and quarrelsome tempers of the next two Governors, Van Twiller and Kieft, brought serious evils upon the infant settlement. The injustice of the latter to the Indians, having roused their enmity, had well nigh exterminated it, in 1643 and 44.

Wretchedness and want stared the colonists in the face, and but for the vigor and energy of Governor Stuyvesant's administration, they would perhaps have abandoned the settlement.

In 1642, the Stadt Huys, or city Hall, was erected. It was built of stone, and was taken down in 1700. The same year, the first church, (Dutch Reformed,) was erected in the fort. In 1653, the city of New Amsterdam was incorporated, by the States General of the Netherlands, and its officers were elected by the people.

In 1653, it was rumored that the New England colonists intended to attack New Amsterdam: measures were consequently taken to put the city in a state of defence; and during that, and the succeeding year, a palisade of boards about twelve feet in height was erected, and an embankment of earth thrown up against it.

Fond of their ease, however, the good citizens did not maintain their fortifications, in such perfection, as to make them of any great avail, against an invading foe.

In 1655, Governor Stuyvesant, with the greater part of the inhabitants of the city, capable of bearing arms, engaged in the expedition against the Swedes, on the south, or Delaware river. While they were absent on this expedition, the city was invaded by the Indians, several of the bouweries plundered, and a few killed. The Indians, however, did not venture within the city walls. In 1656, it was laid out into streets, and then contained 120 houses, and 1000 inhabitants.

In 1664, hearing of the approach of the English fleet, Governor Stuyvesant summoned the citizens of New Amsterdam, to aid him in repelling the threatened invasion, but his arbitrary sway had produced so much disaffection, that they were not averse to any change, which promised to increase their civil and religious privileges.

They consequently made but little preparation for the defence of the city, and when Col. Nicolls demanded its surrender, offering favorable terms of capitulation, they insisted upon a compliance with them.

In vain Governor Stuyvesant remonstrated, threatened and refused to sign the treaty of capitulation; the sturdy burghers were bent on submission to English rule, and he was, at length, compelled, though with the utmost reluctance, to affix his signature to the instrument. As has been already stated, (see page 61,) the name of the city and county was changed, immediately after the capitulation, to New York, in honor of the Duke of York.

Under the mild and beneficent administration of Colonel Nicolls, and his successor, Governor Lovelace, the city prospered, and increased in population and wealth.

It was again captured by the Dutch, in July, 1673, and during the administration of Governor Colve, martial law was maintained. The name of the city was changed to New Orange, and of the fort to William Hendrick.

In Oct. 1674, it was again surrendered to the English, and the old name of New York resumed. The assessors' valuation of property in the city, in 1688, was £78.231. (about $320,000.) In 1690, a Congress, of the commissioners of the several colonies, was held at New York. In 1694, there were sixty ships, twenty-five sloops, and forty boats, belonging to the city.

In 1696, Trinity church was built. This building was burned in 1776. The first Lutheran church was built in 1710, on the site lately occupied by Grace church. It was erected by some Palatines, who had fled from persecution in Germany.

In 1711, a slave market was established in Wall street, near East river. The next year, an insurrection occurred among the negroes, and nineteen were executed. In 1725, the first newspaper was published in the state. It was called the New York Gazette. In 1732, the first stage commenced running, between New York and Boston once a month, occupying fourteen days in the journey. The same distance is now traversed, by steamboat and railroad, in nine hours.

In 1740, the New York Society Library was founded. During the two succeeding years, the yellow fever prevailed in the city, to an alarming extent. In 1741, the Negro plot, which has been described, in the general history of the state, occurred. It occasioned great alarm in the city, as, of the 12,000 inhabitants it then contained, one-sixth were slaves. For the succeeding thirty years, the growth of the city was rapid, both in wealth and population. The New York Hospital was founded, by subscription, in 1769.

In August, 1776, the city fell into the hands of the British. It had, at this time, a population of 20,000. In September of this year, occurred a disastrous fire, which consumed one-eighth of the houses of the city. During their stay in the city, the British troops destroyed all the churches, except the Episcopal, or used them for hospitals, prisoner's barracks, or riding schools. They evacuated the city, and General Washington entered it, in November, 1783. A large number of the tory inhabitants, left with the British army, and their estates were confiscated.

In 1788, the adoption of the new Constitution of the United States, was celebrated by a grand procession, and in 1789, Washington was inaugurated, as the first President, in the open gallery of the old City Hall, facing Broad street.

In December, 1790, the population of the city was about 30,000. Free schools were established in the city, in 1797, though not incorporated, till 1805. In 1801, the total valuation of real estate in the city was a little short of $22,000,000.

The erection of the present City Hall was determined on, during the next year, 1802, and the corner stone laid in September, 1803. The population of the city in 1800, was 60,000, having doubled in ten years. In 1807, the first successful attempt at steamboat navigation, was made on the Hudson, by Fulton and Livingston.

In 1810, the population of the city was 96,000, being an increase of 36,000 in ten years. In 1815, the news of peace with Great Britain, was celebrated, with great rejoicings. In 1822, the yellow fever made its appearance. Great consternation was felt by the inhabitants, and large numbers left the city.

In 1826, the completion of the Erie canal called forth an extraordinary triumphal procession. The population, in 1830, was 202,000. In 1832, the cholera raged fearfully in the city. More than 10,000 persons fell, as its victims. In December, 1835, occurred the great fire, which destroyed property, to the amount of nearly $18,000,000. Severe as was this loss, the failures in consequence, were comparatively few.

The same year, (1835,) the citizens voted to construct an aqueduct, from the Croton river to their city, for the purpose of supplying themselves with pure water. This magnificent enterprise was so far completed, in 1842, that water was introduced into the city, on the 14th of October, of that year, amid the rejoicings of the inhabitants. In July, 1845, another disastrous fire occurred, which destroyed property to the amount of about six millions of dollars.

The only important battle, on New York island, was that of Harlaem Heights, on the 16th of September, 1776. After the disastrous battle of Long Island, on the 27th of August, it became evident that the American army must evacuate New York. Accordingly, Washington ordered the troops to retreat, toward the north part of the island.

On Sunday, the 15th of September, the British, after stationing their ships in the East and North rivers, so as to cannonade our lines, commenced landing in force, at Turtle bay: the American troops in the vicinity fled, without making any attempt at resistance. Meantime, several brigades of General Putnam's division were in the city: by his exertions, they succeeded in passing the enemy, with very trifling loss. The intense heat, however, proved fatal to a number.

Washington then ordered the troops to occupy the heights of Harlaem,—a strong position. On the morning of the 16th, several parties of the enemy appeared, on the plains, in front of the American camp. Lieutenant Colonel Knowlton's rangers, who had been skirmishing with an advanced party, came in and reported, that a body of the enemy were under cover of a small eminence, at a little distance.

Willing to raise the spirits of our men, Washington detached Colonel Knowlton with his rangers, (selected, mainly, from the Connecticut regiments,) and Major Leitch, with three companies of choice Virginian troops, to attack them in the rear, while a feigned attack should be made in front.

The action was successful, and greatly inspirited our troops, but the two brave leaders, Knowlton and Leitch, fell early in the conflict. Our loss was four or five killed, and forty wounded; that of the British more than twenty killed, and seventy-eight wounded.

DESCRIPTION OF THE CITY. Streets, squares, &c. The city covers the whole island. The portion which is densely built, lies south of Twenty-third street, being about three miles in length, and varying in breadth, from half a mile, to two and a quarter miles. In this territory, there are over 350 streets, and on the island more than 480.

There are a number of public squares, but not so many as the dense population requires. The principal are; 1st, the Battery, a crescent shaped park, containing about eleven acres, with gravelled walks, and grass plats, well shaded with trees. It affords a fine view of the shipping. Castle Clinton, connected with it by a bridge, has been transformed into a garden and amphitheatre, capable of containing 10,000 persons.

2d. The Bowling Green is a small ellipse, enclosed by an iron fence, having a fine public fountain, which is made to fall over a rude pile of rocks.

3d. The Park is a triangular area, of about eleven acres, laid out with walks, planted with trees, and surrounded by a massive iron fence. It contains a number of public buildings. In the southern angle, is a magnificent fountain, playing within a basin 100 feet in diameter.

4th. Washington Square, or the Parade Ground, contains not quite ten acres. It is neatly laid out and finely shaded.

5th. Union Place is an elliptical area, of considerable extent, at the northern termination of Broadway, adorned with trees and a fine fountain.

Tompkins Square, and Bellevue, in the eastern part of the city, are places of considerable resort. The latter contains the new almshouse.

Hudson Square, or St. John's Park, belonging to Trinity church, is a beautiful park of four acres, highly ornamented, and has a fountain. In the upper part of the city, several squares are reserved, but not yet regulated.

PUBLIC BUILDINGS. Many of these are among the finest models of architecture in the country.

The City Hall, already referred to, located in the Park, is a magnificent structure, and shows to great advantage. It is 216 feet long, and 105 wide.

<small>Its architecture is Grecian, the successive stories being Ionic, Corinthian, and Composite. The front and ends are of white marble, and the rear of brown free stone. From the centre rises a lofty cupola, which overlooks the whole city, where a watchman is stationed, to give the alarm of fire. It contains elegant rooms for the Governor, the Common Council, and the Superior Court, besides numerous offices. Its cost exceeded half a million of dollars.</small>

The Merchant's Exchange, in Wall street, is one of the most imposing and costly structures, on the American continent. It is built of blue Quincy granite, and is absolutely incombustible. Its length is 200 feet, width 144, and height seventy-seven feet, to the top of the cornice, and 124, to the top of the dome.

<small>On the Wall street front is a recessed portico of eighteen massive columns, each of a single block of granite, thirty-eight feet high, four feet four inches in diameter, and weighing about forty-three tons. The exchange or rotunda in the centre, is capable of holding 3,000 persons, being, including the recesses, 100 feet in diameter, and eighty-seven feet high to the top of the dome. The dome rests on eight Corinthian columns, of polished Italian marble, each forty-one feet high, and four feet eight inches in diameter. The cost of the building is estimated at $1,800,000.</small>

The Custom House, extending from Wall to Pine streets, is a magnificent Doric building, of white marble, after the model of the Parthenon, at Athens.

<small>Brick, granite and marble, are its only materials. It has a portico on each front, of eight Doric columns, five feet eight inches in diameter, and thirty-two feet high. The great business hall, is a circular room, surmounted by a dome, that is supported by sixteen Corinthian pillars, each thirty feet high. The cost of the building, including the ground, was $1,175,000. The number of officers employed here, is 354.</small>

The Hall of Justice, on Centre street, is a massive structure, of Hallowell granite, in the Egyptian style of architecture, of which it is an admirable specimen.

<small>Its gloomy and heavy aspect, however, have acquired for it the title of "the Egyptian tombs." Beside rooms for the Police, and other courts of the city, it includes the House of Detention, or prison, containing 148 cells.</small>

CHURCHES. Trinity church, completed in 1846, is one of the most costly and magnificent churches in America. It is constructed of brown sandstone, in the perpendicular Gothic style. Its spire is 283 feet in height, and is of stone throughout.

The length of the building is 192 feet, and its breadth eighty-four.

Grace church, on Broadway, two and a half miles north of Trinity, is a Gothic structure, of rare beauty, erected in 1845.

St. John's church, on Varick street, is one of the finest proportioned churches in the city. It cost $200,000, and has a steeple 220 feet in height.

St. Thomas' church, in Broadway, the church of the Ascension, and the church of the Transfiguration, in the upper part of the city, are also fine edifices. The Dutch Reformed church on Washington square, and that in Lafayette place, are good specimens of church architecture, the former in the Gothic, and the latter in the Grecian style.

The Scotch Presbyterian church, in Grand street, is a handsome edifice of the Ionic order, with a portico of six massive columns. It cost $114,000.

The Rutger's street church, and the Duane street church, are both well proportioned, and imposing buildings. The Beekman street church has a lofty and elegant steeple. The Roman Catholic church, in Barclay street, is a substantial granite structure.

The Roman Catholic Cathedral, in Prince street, is a very large edifice of sandstone. The French Protestant church, in Franklin street, is built of white marble. It is of the Ionic order. The first Baptist church, in Broome street, is a fine Gothic edifice, with a very imposing interior.

The Chapel of the New York University, (usually occupied on the Sabbath, as a place of worship,) is one of the most perfect specimens of Gothic architecture, ever erected in this country.

HOTELS. The Astor House is an immense granite building, with three fronts, one on Broadway, of 201 feet, another on Barclay street, of 154 feet, and the third on Vesey street, of 146½ feet, and cost about $800,000. It contains 303 rooms. The United States Hotel is a fine marble building, seven stories high, containing 225 rooms, and cost $350,000.

The Franklin House, Howard's Hotel, Judson's, Rathbone's, the City, Croton, Carlton, the Pearl street House, and many others, are extensive and elegant buildings, furnishing ample accommodation, for the thousands who visit the city, for business, or pleasure.

RAILROADS, &c. Three lines of Railroads connect directly with New York city: viz. the Harlaem railroad, now progressing rapidly towards Albany; the Long Island Railroad, extending from Brooklyn to Greenport, and the New Jersey, extending to Philadelphia. and forming a part of the great chain connecting with Wilmington, North Carolina. This road has several branches; one to Morristown, and another to Patterson, New Jersey.

Besides these, there are three others, connecting, by steamboats, with the city, and at no great distance from it. These are the New York and Erie railroad, commencing at Piermont; the Camden and Amboy, commencing at Amboy, New Jersey, and the Housatonic, at Bridgeport, Conn.

Lines of steamboats, also, ply between this city and Albany, Troy, Newburgh, Poughkeepsie, Hudson, Catskill, and other places on the Hudson river: Norwalk, New Haven, Hartford, Norwich, Stonington and Providence, Newark, New Brunswick, Elizabethtown, &c. as well as to the several small villages on Long Island, and Staten Island.

Steamers also leave for England, every month, and lines of packets, for London, Liverpool, Havre, New Orleans, Mobile, and Havana, every week.

WATER WORKS. The Croton Water Works deserve to be considered as one of the most magnificent enterprises of modern times. The water is brought from the Croton river, a stream in Westchester county.

A dam 250 feet long, seventy feet wide at bottom, and seven at top, and forty feet high, has been constructed, creating a pond five miles long. From this dam, the aqueduct proceeds, through hills and over valleys, to the Harlaem river, which it crosses on a massive stone bridge, 1450 feet long, erected at a cost of $900,000; thence it crosses several streets, and follows the tenth Avenue down, from 151st street to 107th street; here crossing a square, it follows the 9th Avenue, to 88th street, where it curves and enters the receiving reservoir, in 85th street.

The aqueduct is a hollow cylinder of brick, laid in hydraulic cement. The receiving reservoir is thirty-eight miles from the Croton dam. It covers thirty-five acres, and will contain 150 millions of gallons. From this reservoir the water is conducted in iron pipes, along the 5th Avenue, to the distributing reservoir, on Murray Hill, in Fortieth street.

This reservoir covers four acres, is constructed of stone and cement, is forty-three feet high from the street, and contains twenty millions of gallons. From it, the water is distributed over the city, in iron pipes, laid so deep under ground, as to be secure from the frost. The supply of water is ample, both for the use of the inhabitants, and for fires. There are 1400 fire hydrants, and 600 free hydrants. No city in the world is bet'er supplied, with pure and wholesome water, than New York.

PUBLIC INSTITUTIONS OF THE CITY. The American Institute was incorporated in 1829, for the encouragement of agriculture, manufactures, commerce and the arts.

It has a suite of rooms in the second story of the New City Hall, where it has a library, models for machinery, &c. It holds an annual fair, every autumn, which is visited by not less than 20,000 persons.

The Mechanics' Institute has for its object, the instruction of mechanics and others, in science, and the arts.

The Institute has established annual courses of popular lectures, and has a library, reading room, museum, and collection of chemical and philosophical apparatus. A male and a female school have been established, under the superintendence of its board, the former in 1838, the latter in 1839; both of which, have been eminently successful.

The American Art Union is an incorporated association, for the promotion of the fine arts. Its rooms are at 322 Broadway. The Chamber of Commerce was established for the regulation of trade, &c. in 1768.

SCIENTIFIC SOCIETIES. The most important of these are the Lyceum of Natural History, founded in 1818, for the advancement of knowledge in Zoology, Botany, Mineralogy, Geology, and Conchology;

It has a large library, and extensive and valuable collections, in every department of natural history, which are all arranged for gratuitous exhibition, at its rooms No. 659, Broadway.

The New York Historical Society, occupying rooms in the University building; its library is a very valuable one, of over 12,000 volumes, besides a collection of coins and medals.

The Ethnological Society, founded in 1842, for investigations in history, languages, geography, &c.;

The New York Medical Society comprising the great body of the educated physicians of the city; its object is improvement in medical science.

The National Academy of Design, established for the benefit of living artists. They annually exhibit a large collection of paintings.

LIBRARIES. The New York Society Library was established in 1754. It has a fine building on Broadway, and a library of 40,000 volumes.

The Mercantile Library Association has a fine suite of rooms in Clinton Hall, a library of more than 21,000 volumes, and an elegant reading room.

The Apprentices Library at 32 Crosby street, contains 12,000 well selected volumes.

The New York Law Institute Library was established in 1828, and has a valuable library of about 3500 volumes of select law books.

BENEVOLENT INSTITUTIONS. Hospitals. There are two hospitals in the city. The New York Hospital, founded by subscription, in 1769, is a noble institution. It has extensive buildings and grounds, and good accommodations for 250 patients. It has ten visiting, and as many consulting physicians.

The City Hospital, at Bellevue, is supported by the Municipal government of the city. It has accommodations for between 200 and 300 inmates, and is under the management of a physician, and several assistants.

The City Dispensary affords aid to about 20,000 indigent patients annually. The Northern and Eastern Dispensaries administer relief to from 5000 to 10,000 each. The New York Eye Infirmary treats over 1000 indigent patients, for diseases of the eye. The Bloomingdale Lunatic Asylum, located at Bloomingdale, has about 200 patients. It is connected with the New York Hospital.

The City Lunatic Asylum, on Blackwell's Island, has from 300 to 400 indigent patients. There is also a Lunatic Asylum on Murray's Hill, Fortieth street. The Institution for the Blind, on the ninth Avenue, has about sixty pupils.

The Deaf and Dumb Asylum, on Fiftieth street, has a principal, eight professors, and not far from 150 pupils. Its buildings are large and commodious.

There are also six Orphan Asylums in the city, and several institutions for aged and indigent females.

Societies are also founded, for the protection and benefit of emigrants, who throng, in such vast numbers, to the city.

From its central position, and intimate connexion with other sections of the country, New York city has been made the head quarters, of numerous benevolent institutions, whose measures are intended to benefit the whole country. The most prominent of these are the American Bible Society, the American and Foreign Bible Society, the Methodist Book concern, the American Tract Society, the Home and Domestic Mission Societies, the Seaman's Friend Society, the Society for ameliorating the condition of the Jews, the American Temperance Union, the Moral Reform Society, the American, and the American and Foreign Anti-Slavery Societies, the American, and the American Baptist Home Mission Societies, &c. &c.

PLACES OF AMUSEMENT. These are numerous. Beside two museums, each containing extensive collections of curiosities, there are several public gardens, where there are frequent exhibitions, picture galleries, four large, and two or three lesser theatres, &c. &c.

GOVERNMENT AND POLITICAL DIVISIONS OF THE CITY. For the purposes of government and police, the city is divided into eighteen wards, each of which elects, annually, an alderman and assistant alderman, who, together, form the Common Council, and with the Mayor, administer the government of the city.

The police of the city, whose duty it is to preserve order, arrest criminals, prevent riots, felonies, and other misdemeanors, give alarm of fires, &c., are 800 in number, and are distributed through the wards, according to their population.

In each ward is a station house, and the police force of the ward, are under the control of a captain of police, and two assistants. There are six police justices, who hold courts, in three different sections of the city. The whole police force, is under the direction of a chief of police, whose rooms are in the new City Hall in the Park.

BUSINESS OF PARTICULAR STREETS. Wall street has become the great rendezvous of bankers and brokers. Pearl street, of wholesale dry goods dealers. South street, of wholesale flour and produce dealers. Chatham street, of dealers in clothing. Broadway is a fashionable promenade; and the Bowery, Grand, and Canal streets, contain most of the retail stores.

STORES, &c. There are in the city, 1981 wholesale, and about 4000 retail, dry goods stores, employing a capital of more than sixty millions of dollars. There are twenty-seven banks, with an aggregate capital of $25,563,600, besides four saving banks.

There are sixty-seven fire and marine insurance companies, of which twenty-two are on the mutual principle. The remainder have a capital of about fourteen millions of dollars. There are twelve life insurance companies, four of them on the mutual principle, the remainder have a capital of $19,000,000. There were, in 1846, 106 hotels and coffee houses.

Such is an imperfect view of the great commercial metropolis of our country. Her growth, thus far, has outstripped the expectations, and predictions of the most sanguine; and judging of the future by the past, we are compelled to believe, that ere the close of the present century, she will be, in population and commercial importance, what London now is.

Her resources are unequalled, and her capacity for accommodating and supporting an immense population, unsurpassed; and when the cities of the old world have sunk to decay, New York, fulfilling the promise of her youth, will flourish, queen of cities, and mart of the world.

LONG ISLAND.

Square miles, 1448.   Population, 145,119.

Long Island forms so distinct a portion of the state, that it merits a distinct description. It extends from 40° 34' to 41° 10' north latitude, and from 2° 58' to 5° 3' east longitude. It is 140 miles long, with an average breadth of 12 or 15 miles.

SURFACE. A chain of low hills divides it centrally, north of which, the country is rough and broken, but south of it, is almost a perfect plain, apparently produced by the washing up of the sand from the ocean. This surface is somewhat sterile, but produces heavy pine timber.

RIVERS, BAYS, &c. There are few streams worthy of note, on the island, although as a whole, it is well watered. The Peconic, Connecticut, and Nissiquogue, are the only ones of importance.

Its bays are numerous. On the southern coast, the Great South bay extends from Hempstead to Brookhaven, a distance of more than 70 miles. It is from two to five miles wide, and is

LONG ISLND. 153

separated from the ocean, by a beach of sand, varying in width from a few rods to half a mile, broken only by a few narrow inlets, which are constantly changing in depth, with the action of the waves.

At the eastern extremity of the island, the Great Peconic bay has divided it into two peninsulas, of unequal length. Gardiner's bay, between Shelter and Gardiner's island, furnishes a fine and commodious harbor.

Smithtown bay, on the northern shore, is an open roadstead, of no great depth of water, and unprotected from the winds, by projecting headlands. Huntington bay is smaller, but affords a fine harbor. Hempstead harbor, New York harbor, and Jamaica bay, are the only other bays worthy of notice.

LAKES. There are numerous small lakes, or ponds, scattered over the surface of the island, some of them at short distances from the shore. They are very uniform in their height and temperature, being seldom frozen in winter, and maintaining a most delicious coolness in summer. Ronkonkama, Great Pond, Fort Pond, and Success or Sacut Pond, are the principal.

ISLANDS. A number of islands adjacent to Long Island, are included in its territories. Of these, Shelter, Gardiner's, Plum, Robbin's and Fisher's islands, toward the eastern extremity, and Riker's, Coney, Barren, &c., at the southwestern, are the principal. A part of these are inhabited.

RAILROAD. The Long Island railroad traverses the whole length of the island, and furnishes to its inhabitants easy and speedy access to New York city.

HISTORY. Previous to its discovery and settlement by the whites, Long Island seems to have been densely populated by Indians.

Historians have enumerated the names of fourteen or fifteen tribes, of which the principal were the Canarsee, Rockaway, Merikoke, Marsapeague, Secatogue, and Patchogue tribes on the south side; the Matinecock, Nissaquogue, Setauket, and Corchaug, on the north side; and the Shinecock, Manhasset, and Montauk, from the Canoe Place to Montauk Point. Of these tribes, the Canarsee were subject to the Iroquois; the others were tributaries to the Montauks, whose sachem, Wyandanch, was regarded as the grand sachem of the island. The Pequots, however, had crossed over from the northern shore of the sound, and levied a heavy tribute on these tribes; and after that warlike people were subdued by the English, the Long Island Indians paid tribute to the English, and sought their alliance and protection.

The division of the Island, between the Dutch and English, was long a bone of contention. At length, by the treaty of Hartford, made in 1650, it was settled that the English should hold all of the island east of Oyster bay, and that the remainder should belong to the Dutch. After this date, the eastern part of the island was under the government of Connecticut. till 1664, when the Duke of York claimed it as a part of his patent.

III. KINGS COUNTY.

Square miles, 76.
Organized, 1683.
Population, 78,691.
Valuation in 1845, $30,750,472.

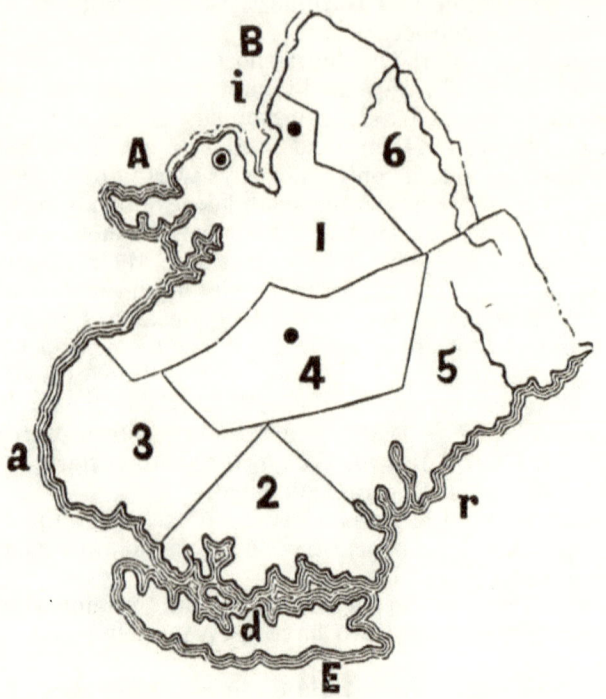

TOWNS.
1. Brooklyn, 1788.
2. Gravesend, 1788.
3. New Utrecht, 1788.
4. Flatbush, 1788.
5. Flatlands, 1788.
6. Bushwick, 1788.

Rivers, &c. B. East River. E. Atlantic Ocean. r. Jamaica Bay. i. Wallabout Bay.
Bays, &c. A. New York Bay. a. Narrows. d. Coney Island.
Forts. Hamilton. Lafayette.
Battle Fields. Battle of Long Island.
Cities and Villages. Brooklyn, Flatbush, Williamsburgh.

BOUNDARIES. North by East river, and New York harbor; East by Queens county; South by the Atlantic; West by New York bay, and the Narrows.

SURFACE. On the northeast, for three or four miles back from the East river, it is hilly. Brooklyn Heights forms the

KINGS COUNTY. 155

termination of the ridge, which runs through the island. On the southeast, a sandy plain extends to the ocean.

RIVERS, &c. There are no streams of importance. The chief bays, or indentations of the coast, are Gravesend bay, Gowanus cove, and the Wallabout bay. Plumb inlet, and Rockaway inlet, on the south, communicate with several ponds in the interior.

GEOLOGY AND MINERALOGY. A considerable portion of the formation of the county is alluvial. The northern portion is granite. Large boulders are found scattered over this, and the adjoining counties. They are mostly granitic.

The principal minerals are hematitic iron ore, iron pyrites, lignite, porcelain clay, magnetic iron sand, and garnet sand. There is also some peat, and a few fossils.

SOIL AND VEGETABLE PRODUCTIONS. The soil of this county is possessed of greater natural fertility, than that of the other portions of the Island, and it is highly cultivated. It is well adapted to horticulture, and fruits and flowers arrive at great perfection. The grape is extensively cultivated, throughout the county. Little timber is found.

PURSUITS. Manufactures are the pursuit of a majority of the inhabitants. The principal articles are distilled liquors, (to the amount of $1,680,000,) cordage, iron ware, oils, flour, oil cloths, leather, glass, ale, &c.

Agriculture, and particularly horticulture, receive considerable attention. Corn, oats, butter, potatoes, fruit, and market vegetables, are produced in large quantities.

Its commerce is large, but being included under the reports for New York city, it is difficult to ascertain its amount with accuracy.

SCHOOLS. There are twenty-four public schoolhouses in the county, in which schools were taught, the whole twelve months, in the year 1845. During that year, 8891 children received instruction, at an expense of $17,095, for teachers wages. The libraries contained about 13,000 volumes.

The school organization of the city of Brooklyn has been already described, (see page 126.)

There are also ninety-nine select schools, containing 3516 pupils; one academy, and two female seminaries, with 150 pupils.

RELIGIOUS DENOMINATIONS. Methodists, Dutch Reformed, Presbyterians, Episcopalians, Roman Catholics, Baptists, Congregationalists, Universalists, Unitarians, and Friends. Number of churches, 75, of clergymen, 85.

HISTORY. The first settlement, in this county, was made by a small party of Walloons, or Waaloons, from the borders of France, in 1625, on the shores of Wallabout bay, (called from them Waalebocht or the bay of the Walloons.)

Here, on the 17th of June, 1625, Sarah, eldest daughter of George Jansen de Rapalje, was born. She was the first child of white parents born within the limits of the state of New York.*

Within the succeeding thirty years, settlements had been made in Brooklyn, Flatbush, Flatlands, Gravesend, New Utrecht, and Bushwick.†

Gravesend was settled by English emigrants, who fled from persecution in New England. Of these, the most distinguished was the Lady Moody, and her son, Sir Henry Moody.

These towns were each organized under a separate government, administered by an officer, or officers, appointed by the Director General.

None of them enjoyed any thing like a representative government, and in the days of Governor Stuyvesant, any attempt on their part, to claim a share in its administration, was frowned down, with the utmost severity. After New York fell into the hands of the English, they were allowed to participate in the imperfect representative government of that period.

During the early part of the Revolution, Kings county was the scene of many interesting incidents. Here occurred, on the 27th August, 1776, the battle of Long Island, which threw such gloom upon the rising hopes of our countrymen, in the outset of the revolutionary struggle.

The British ministry, determined, if possible, to close the war by a single blow, had concentrated a large force in the neighborhood of New York, well equipped, and furnished with all the munitions of war.

Congress had assembled a force of near 27,000 men upon Long Island, but they were undisciplined militia. More than one-fourth of them were invalids, and the remainder but scantily supplied with guns and ammunition.

On the 22d of August, the British fleet approached the Narrows, and landed the troops at Gravesend and New Utrecht, without resistance.

Dividing here, into three sections, under the guidance of inhabitants of these and other towns, who loved the gold of the British, more than their own country, they proceeded, by three distinct routes, to invest the American camp, which lay principally on Brooklyn heights.

---

* There is a tradition extant, that during the infancy of this Sarah Rapalje, Minuit, the Dutch Governor, being on a hunting excursion, with some associates, near the Wallabout bay, entered the cabin of Rapalje, to find something to satisfy his hunger. Finding no one at home, and no food, except an Indian dumpling, they devoured that, when the wife of Rapalje, with her infant in her arms, entered, and berated them soundly for their intrusion, and particularly, for devouring the food she had reserved for her infant. The Governor, to appease her anger, promised her a milch cow, on the arrival of the ships from Holland, as a compensation for her dumpling. On their arrival, in addition to the cow, he gave her twenty morgen, (nearly forty acres,) of land, for pasturage for her cow.

† These towns were named by the Dutch, Breukelen, Midwout, Amersfoort, Gravenzande, Nieuw Utrecht, and Boswyck.

One division of the British army took the road leading along near the Narrows, another, that passing through the village of Flatbush, and the third passed by the way of Flatlands.

Descending, on the morning of the 27th, to the village of Bedford, General Clinton, who commanded one wing of the British army, carried an important point, and an attack was made on the three sides of the camp at once. Suitable precautions seem not to have been taken, by the American officers, to avoid surprise, and although, when thus surrounded, they fought bravely, defeat was inevitable.

Attempting to retreat, they were driven upon the enemy's forces on every side, and those who fought were slain, while those who attempted to fly were made prisoners.

The loss of the Americans was variously estimated at from 1100 to 3300, in killed, wounded, and prisoners. The British loss was less than 400. On the night of the 29th, General Washington silently drew off his troops to New York, and from this time till the close of the war, Kings county was in the hands of the British.

The prison ships, in which the American prisoners of war were confined, during the revolution, were stationed in Wallabout bay. In these ships, nearly 11,000 American citizens perished, from disease and starvation, through the inhumanity of the British officers who had charge of them.

They were crowded into these ships in such numbers that to obtain fresh air was impossible; robbed of their clothing, fed upon the most loathsome and putrid provisions, and scantily supplied even with these, allowed no drink but the most fetid bilge water, and when sick unattended by either physician or nurse.

Yet, amid the horrors of such a condition, the most distressing of which it is possible for the human mind to conceive, our noble countrymen preferred death, with all its horrors, to a traitor's life, with plenty; and very few of them could be persuaded to enlist in the British army, although they were assured that they should be amply provided with food, and suitable clothing. Their heroism, and the brutal inhumanity of their jailors, should go down to the latest posterity.

CITIES, VILLAGES, &c. BROOKLYN city, the seat of justice for Kings county, is situated at the west end of Long Island, directly opposite the lower portion of New York city. Its location is a commanding and delightful one, and its growth, within a few years past, has been rapid, beyond precedent in the state.

It is the residence of very many of the business men of New York city, who prefer its pure air, and quiet streets, to the more crowded and bustling squares of the great metropolis. It is remarkable for the neatness and taste displayed in its private residences.

The city has a number of literary and scientific institutions of a high order. The principal of these are the Brooklyn Institute, formed by the union of the Brooklyn Apprentices' Library Association, the Brooklyn Lyceum, and the City Library; this institution has a large library, and is in a highly flourishing condition; the Lyceum of Natural History, which is engaged with commendable zeal, in the investigation of the physica sciences; the Hamilton Literary Association, and the Franklin Literary Association, both composed of young men desirous of improvement. There are also several academies and female seminaries of distinction.

The United States Government have a navy yard at Wallabout bay, covering forty acres of ground, and well provided with all the necessaries, for the construction of the largest ships of the line. They are constructing a dry dock here, at an immense expense. Connected with the yard, is a Naval Lyceum, composed of officers of the United States navy, and possessing a large library and museum.

The Greenwood Cemetery, situated in the south part of the city, contains more than 200 acres of land. Its situation is delightful, and comprises every variety of surface, which is calculated to make it attractive, as a place of repose for the dead.

The harbor of the city is extensive, and its depth sufficient to allow the largest vessels to come to its wharves. The Atlantic dock, now in progress of construction, is a stupendous work, and one of the most remarkable monuments of private enterprise and wealth, in the country. Population, 62,000.

Williamsburgh, taken from Bushwick, and organized as a distinct town in 1840, is favorably situated for business, and from its proximity to New York, has had a rapid growth. It is the residence of many of the business men of the metropolis, and is fast increasing in population and wealth. It is connected with New York by three steam ferries. Population, about 12,000.

Flatbush, in the town of the same name, is a pleasant though small village. Erasmus Hall, located here, and incorporated in 1787, is one of the oldest and most ably conducted academies in the state. The battle of Long Island was fought mostly within the limits of this town.

IV. QUEENS COUNTY.

Square miles, 396.
Organized, 1683.
Population, 31,849.
Valuation, 1845, $11,568,350.

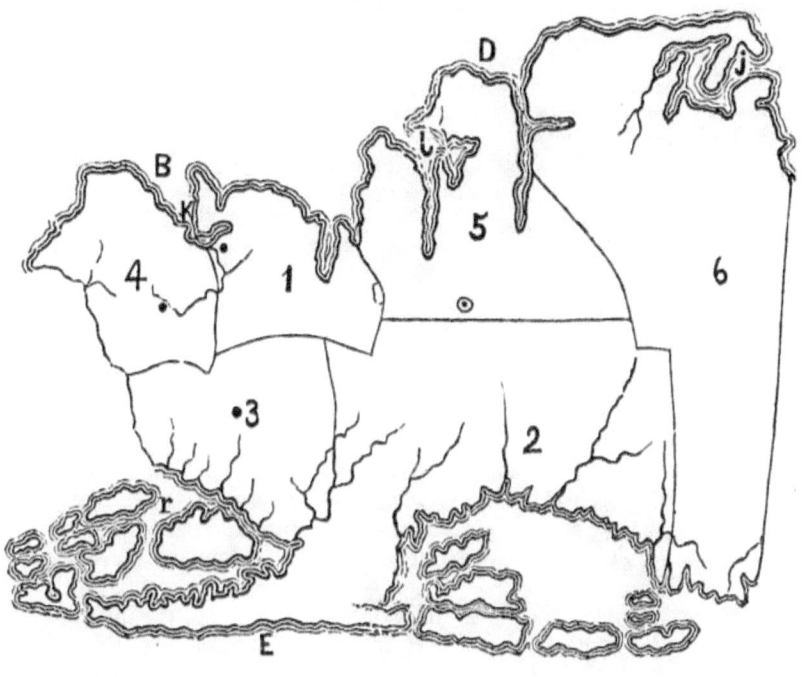

TOWNS.

1. Flushing, 1788.
2. Hempstead, 1788.
3. Jamaica, 1788.
4. Newtown, 1788.
5. North Hempstead, 1788.
6. Oyster Bay, 1788.

Rivers, &c. D. Long Island Sound. E. Atlantic Ocean. B. East River.

Bays. j. Oyster Bay. r. Jamaica Bay. k. Flushing Bay. l. Cow Bay.

Villages. NORTH HEMPSTEAD, Flushing, Jamaica, Newtown.

BOUNDARIES. North by Long Island sound and the East river; East by Suffolk county; South by the Atlantic Ocean, and West by Kings county.

SURFACE. The northern portion of this county is rolling, but with no high hills. Harbor Hill, the highest elevation in the county, is 319 feet above the ocean. The great Hempstead plain extends through the central portion of the county.

RIVERS, &c. The county is well watered, but none of the streams are of considerable size.

BAYS AND HARBORS. These are numerous, both on the northern and southern coasts. The principal on the north, are Flushing, Hempstead, Little Neck, Cow, Oyster, and Cold Spring, bays. On the south, are Jamaica, Rockaway, and part of the Great South bay.

These bays abound with a great variety of fish, oysters, &c., and at certain seasons, large numbers of wild fowl congregate here, the taking of which affords ample amusement to the sportsman.

ISLANDS. Riker's island, on the northern coast, Hog island, Cow island, and several others in Jamaica bay, on the southern, are the principal.

PONDS. Success, or Sacut pond, in Flushing, is the only one worthy of special notice.

This pond is very deep, and its waters of remarkable purity and coldness. Perch are very abundant in it. They were first put into its waters by Doctor Samuel L. Mitchell.

CLIMATE. Like that of the Island generally, it is mild, equable and healthy. The seasons are early, and the frosts occur late in autumn; consequently, fruits attain great perfection.

GEOLOGY AND MINERALS. The geological character of the county alluvial and diluvial, the boulders are mostly granitic. In the southern portion of the county, there are no rocks, nor even stones, of more than a few ounces weight. There are few minerals of importance.

SOIL AND VEGETABLE PRODUCTIONS. The soil of the northern portion is very fertile, and perhaps under as high cultivation as that of any other part of the state. The southern part is sandy and naturally sterile, but by judicious management, it has been made to produce tolerable crops.

The timber is principally oak, hickory, chestnut, and locust in great abundance. The latter was originally introduced from Virginia. In the northern part, the apple, pear, peach, cherry, &c., thrive well. Wheat, corn, and grass, are also favorite crops.

PURSUITS. Agriculture and horticulture are prominent pursuits of the inhabitants of this county. Large quantities of corn and oats are raised. Butter, pork, and wool are produced in abundance. Shrubs, fruit trees, and rare exotic plants are sent from the numerous gardens and nurseries in the county, to all parts of the Union.

Fishing, and fowling, are also the employments of many of the inhabitants. Manufactures are not extensive. The most considerable are flour, woollen cloths, distilled liquors, and leather.

QUEENS COUNTY. 161

The commerce of the county is confined to the coasting trade, and carried on through the ports of Flushing, Glen's Cove, Oyster Bay, and Cold Spring. Steamers ply between New York, and Flushing, Glen's cove, and Rockaway.

STAPLE PRODUCTIONS. Corn, oats, butter, wool, fruit trees, and flowers.

SCHOOLS. The county has seventy public schoolhouses, in which schools were taught, in 1846, an average period of ten months. In them 4960 children received instruction, at an expense of $15,346. The school libraries contained 13,803 volumes.

Beside these there were thirty-six private schools, with 708 pupils, four academies and three female seminaries, with 272 pupils. One of these is a collegiate school, of a high order.

RELIGIOUS DENOMINATIONS. Methodists, Episcopalians, Baptists, Friends, Dutch Reformed, Presbyterians, and Roman Catholics. Total number of churches, 59, of clergymen, 43.

HISTORY. The first settlement made in this county, was at Hempstead, by a company of emigrants from Stamford, Conn., in 1644. This company acknowledged the Dutch jurisdiction, and obtained a patent from Governor Kieft. The place was first called Hemsteede.

In the spring of 1645, a company of Englishmen who had previously resided in Vlissingen, in Holland, emigrated to this country, and locating themselves in Queens county, founded the town of Flushing, called by them Vlissingen. They, too, obtained a patent, from Governor Kieft, for their lands. Between this period and 1656, settlements were commenced at Oyster bay, Newtown, and Jamaica.

A considerable number of Friends having settled in Vlissingen, Governor Stuyvesant, animated by the spirit of intolerance so prevalent at that day, issued an order requiring the people of the town to cease giving them any countenance, or entertaining them.

To this order, the people of that town sent a dignified remonstrance. Gov. Stuyvesant, however, persisted in his intolerant measures, inflicting heavy fines, protracted imprisonment, and severe corporeal punishment, on those who professed the Quaker faith, as well as upon all who assisted or sheltered them. Some thirteen or fourteen prominent individuals were thus made to feel the weight of his displeasure.

One of the sufferers, having manifested more firmness than the rest, in the avowal of his sentiments, was sent by the Governor, a prisoner in chains, to Amsterdam. He was liberated from confinement, and sent back by the West India Company, and made the bearer of a letter from the company to the persecuting Governor, which, for the noble sentiments, in regard to religious liberty, which it avows, deserves to be written in letters of gold.

But the intolerant spirit of the Dutch governor did not stop here. The Lutherans also fell under the ban of his displeasure, and he banished them from the colony.

This bigotry did much toward rendering the people dissatisfied with the sway of the director, and but for the incursion of the English, in 1664, they wo·ld, in all probabilty, have thrown off their allegiance, by a civil revolution. In the exchange of masters, however, there was little else than an exchange of tyrants. Religious intolerance still prevailed, under a new form.

In 1702, Lord Cornbury, having taken refuge in Jamaica, from yellow fever, (at that time epidemic in New York city), occupied the residence of Rev. Mr. Hubbard, the Presbyterian minister of the place, which was courteously tendered him, by its occupant, as the best dwelling in the village.

With characteristic ingratitude, he dispossessed this clergyman of his pulpit, in which he placed an Episcopal minister, whom, on his return to New York city, he ordered to occupy Mr. Hubbard's parsonage. Twenty-six years elapsed, before the Presbyterians were able to recover possession of their church edifice.

In 1707, Lord Cornbury imprisoned two Presbyterian clergymen, in this county, for preaching without his license, and finally liberated them, on the payment of a fine of $500.

During the Revolution, a majority of the inhabitants of this county took the oath of allegiance to Great Britain. British troops were stationed in different portions of the county, and the people were obliged to furnish them with large quantities of wood and provisions.

There were many, however, whose hearts beat with true loyalty to the cause of their country, and who rejoiced, when she succeeded in throwing off the yoke of foreign oppression.

It was rather, perhaps, the misfortune than the fault of the people of this county, that, exposed as they were, without defence, to the hostile power of the enemy, they yielded to a force they could not oppose.

Yet this was made a subject of reproach to them, and in 1784, a tax of £100,000 was levied upon the southern district, to be appropriated, as a compensation, to the other parts of the state, on account of their not having been able to take an active part in the war; and Queens county, in addition to her severe losses from the British, was obliged to atone for her own misfortunes.

VILLAGES. NORTH HEMPSTEAD, the seat of justice for the county, is situated near the southern boundary of the town of the same name. It is an inconsiderable village, and was selected for the county seat, from its being the geographical centre of the county.

Flushing village, in the town of Flushing, situated at the head of the bay of the same name, is one of the most beautiful villages in the state. It is a favorite summer residence of merchants and others, from the city of New York, and has many noble villas and country seats. Population 2500.

Its schools are highly celebrated. St. Ann's Hall, a female seminary of a high order, St. Thomas' Hall, and St. Paul's college, about three miles from the village, a collegiate school for boys, are among the most distinguished. These schools are under the direction of the Episcopalians. The Friends have also a flourishing seminary, and there are several well conducted select schools.

The nurseries and botanic gardens here, have long held the first rank in our country. The Linnean Botanic garden was established, by Mr. Prince, in 1750, and still maintains a high reputation, while the new nursery of the Messrs. Prince, the Bloodgood nursery, the Commercial garden and nursery, and the Floral and Pomological nursery, contend with it for the palm.

In this town is still standing the Bowne mansion, where the celebrated George Fox, the apostle of the Friends, spent much of his time. Near it stands the ancient and venerable oak, under the canopy of which he proclaimed his views, with an eloquence which won many hearts.

Jamaica village, in the town of that name, is situated on the line of the Long Island railroad, twelve miles east from the city of Brooklyn. It is a beautiful village, with many facilities for intercourse with the adjacent towns. The railroad company have here a large manufactory, for the construction and repair of their cars. It also contains Union Hall academy, an old and flourishing institution, a female seminary of some reputation, and several select schools. The Union race course is within the limits of this town. Population about 2000.

Hempstead village is delightfully situated, on the southern margin of the great Hempstead plain, in the town of the same name. For beauty and salubrity, it has few equals. The Hempstead seminary has a fine and costly edifice, and is in a flourishing condition. The village is a favorite summer resort. Population about 1800.

There are several other villages in the town. *Rockaway* beach, or *Far Rockaway*, is a headland projecting from the southern shore of the town, on which the restless surges of the ocean beat, with ceaseless vehemence.

Near Rockaway is a pleasant and thriving little village. Near the Methodist church, stands a marble monument erected to the memory of 139 unfortunate emigrants, whose bodies were washed ashore from the wrecks of the ships Bristol and Mexico, in the winter of 1836-7. In these two melancholy shipwrecks 215 persons were lost.

Newtown, Astoria, Oyster Bay, Glen Cove, and *Norwich,* are villages of some importance. Lloyd's neck belongs to the town of Oyster Bay.

V. SUFFOLK COUNTY.

Square Miles, 976. Population, 34,579.
Organized, 1683. Valuation, 1845, $5,962,618.

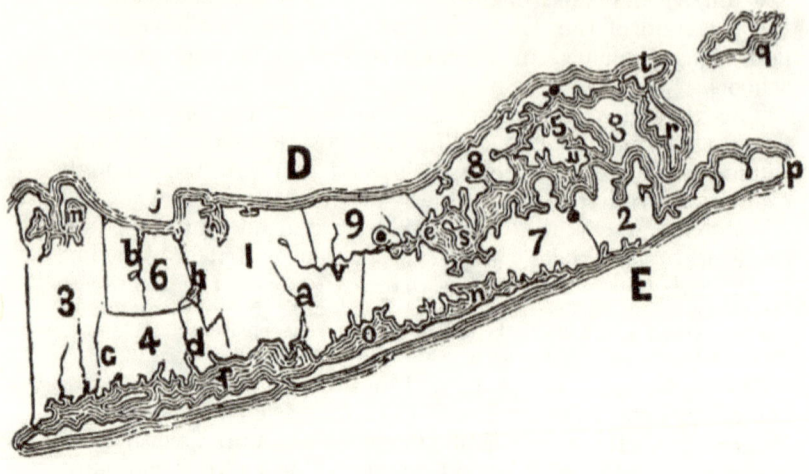

TOWNS.

1. Brookhaven, 1788.
2. East Hampton, 1788.
3. Huntington, 1788.
4. Islip, 1788.
5. Shelter Island, 1788.
6. Smithtown, 1788.
7. Southampton, 1788.
8. Southold, 1788.
9. Riverhead, 1792.

Rivers. a. Connecticut creek. b. Nissiquogue River. c. Sampawan's creek. d. Conesqua River. v. Peconic.

Bays, &c. E. Atlantic Ocean. D. Long Island Sound. f. Great South Bay. e. Great Peconic. g. Gardiner's. j. Smithtown. m. Huntington's. n. Shinecock. o. Great West.

Ponds. h. Ronkonkama.

Islands, &c. q. Fisher's. r. Gardiner's. s. Robbins'. t. Plumb. u. Shelter. p. Montauk point.

Villages. RIVERHEAD. Sag Harbor. Greenport.

BOUNDARIES. North by Long Island Sound; East and South by the Atlantic Ocean; and West by Queens county.

SURFACE. Toward the northern shore, the surface is hilly and broken. The southern portion is level and sandy. There are no hills of considerable altitude in the county. The Great Peconic bay, extending nearly into the centre of the county, divides it into two peninsulas.

RIVERS. The county is not well watered. The Peconic, Connecticut, Nissiquogue, Sampawan's and Conesqua rivers are the principal.

BAYS, &c. The Atlantic Ocean washes its southern and eastern shores, and Long Island sound its northern. Its most considerable bays are Huntington, Smithtown, Gardiner's, Great Peconic, Shinecock, Great West, and Great South bays.

PONDS. Ronkonkama pond lies at the junction of the towns of Islip, Smithtown and Brookhaven.

ISLANDS. Shelter, Gardiner's, Fisher's, Robbins', Plumb, and the Gull islands on the coast belong to this county.

CLIMATE. Similar to that of the Island generally. The prevailing winds are from the southwest. The atmosphere is at all times moist, and the cold of winter is accompanied by a degree of chilliness, which renders it unpleasant. The longevity of its inhabitants is greater, however, than that of any other portion of the state.

GEOLOGY AND MINERALS. The geological formation of this county does not differ from that of the other counties of the island.

It is a disputed point, whether the formation of the whole county is alluvial or not. That of the southern portion is undoubtedly so, and the immense granite and gneiss boulders imbedded in the soil, would indicate that the northern part might be also.

It is the opinion of many eminent geologists, that the northern portion of the island once formed a part of the coast of Connecticut, and that it was rent from the main, either by the force of the waves, or by some convulsion of nature.

Hematite, iron pyrites, lignite, clay, suitable for making porcelain ware, magnetic iron sand, and garnet, are the principal minerals.

SOIL AND VEGETABLE PRODUCTIONS. Portions of the soil of this county are barren wastes of sand, producing little except pitch pine timber. Other portions on the southern shore are composed of sand dunes, or small hillocks of sand, affording no sustenance to any vegetable, except an occasional tuft of coarse grass. There are large tracts, however, of highly fertile land, which, manured with ashes, seaweed, and the fertilizing mossbonker, or whitefish, yield ample crops, to repay the husbandman for his toil.

The timber of the county is chiefly pitch pine, oak, hickory, chestnut and locust. The bay berry, or wax myrtle, abounds in Riverhead.

PURSUITS. *Agriculture* is the pursuit of a majority of the inhabitants. The preparation of lumber and wood, for market, occupies considerable attention, though less now than formerly. Corn and oats are raised to some extent, and in some parts of the county, there are extensive dairies.

The fisheries also afford employment to many of the inhabitants. The whale fishery is extensively prosecuted from Sag Harbor and Greenport. A considerable number of vessels are employed in the codfisheries, and numerous smacks, &c., in the coast fisheries. The entire amount of shipping, enrolled in this district, in 1845, was 28,348 tons.

The *manufactures* of this county are not extensive. Flour, woollen and cotton goods, and leather, are the most important.

STAPLE PRODUCTIONS. Oil, fish, corn and oats.

SCHOOLS. There are in the county 142 district school-houses. The schools were maintained, in 1846, nine months; 9117 children received instruction, at a cost of $17,953. The district libraries contained 19,728 volumes.

<small>There were, in addition, forty-six select schools, with 634 pupils, seven academies and one female seminary, attended by 119 scholars.</small>

RELIGIOUS DENOMINATIONS. Methodists, Presbyterians, Congregationalists, Baptists, Episcopalians, Universalists and Roman Catholics. There are seventy-nine churches, and eighty-two clergymen.

HISTORY. This county was peopled mostly by emigrants from New England, and the inhabitants have retained, in a great degree, to this day, their primitive simplicity of manners and habits.

Southold was the first town settled in the county, and the first to adopt a municipal organization, on the island. Its settlers removed here from New Haven, and remained under the jurisdiction of that colony, until it was included in the charter of Connecticut, in 1662, after which, it became a dependency of that colony, till 1676, when Sir Edmund Andross insisting on his right to jurisdiction over it, the people submitted, somewhat unwillingly.

Southampton and East Hampton were also included under the government of New Haven and Connecticut, until this period.

Smithtown was purchased by Richard Smythe, of Narragansett, Rhode Island, who obtained a patent from Governor Andross, in 1677, and removed here and founded a settlement. Gardiner's Island was settled by Lyon Gardiner, in 1635;[*] Shelter Island in 1652, by James Farrett and others; and Brookhaven in 1655, by emigrants, mostly from Boston.

In 1673, Colve, the Dutch governor of New Netherlands, attempted to reduce these towns to subjection to the Dutch authority at New Orange [New York]. This effort called forth a sharp remonstrance from John Winthrop, the then governor of Connecticut, and a spirited correspondence ensued, which resulted in a partial compromise, on the part of the Dutch governor.

In 1674, however, the English sway was resumed, and in 1676 the county came under the government of the colony of New York. In 1699, the pirate Kidd secreted a portion of his

---

<small>[*] Mr. Gardiner was a man of fine education, and exerted a powerful influence over the Indians, and the white settlers on the island. Wyandanch, the powerful sachem of the Montauks, regarded him with the utmost reverence and affection.</small>

ill-gotten treasures on Gardiner's Island, in this county. These were seized by order of the Earl of Bellomont, the same year.

During the revolution, the people of Suffolk county were decidedly patriotic in their sentiments, and though under the domination of the British, they maintained their affection for their country, and consequently suffered severely from her enemies.

It deserves to be recorded, to the honor of East Hampton, that every man in the town, capable of bearing arms, signed a solemn pledge, on the 6th July, 1775, not to submit to British taxation. The other towns were nearly unanimous in their resistance to oppression.

On the 21st of May, 1777, the British having collected a considerable quantity of provisions and military stores at Sag Harbor, General Parsons formed the design of destroying them, and committed the enterprise to Lieutenant Colonel Meigs.

That officer proceeded directly to Guilford, but on account of the roughness of the weather, could not embark till the 23d, when he left Guilford, at one o'clock, P. M., with 170 men, in thirteen whale boats. They arrived at Southold about six o'clock, P. M., transported their boats over land to the bay, and arrived, at twelve o'clock at night, within four miles of Sag Harbor. Securing their boats under a guard, they marched directly for the village, and attacking the outposts with fixed bayonets, they proceeded immediately to the shipping.

An armed schooner, with twelve guns and seventy-nine men, lying here, fired upon them for three-fourths of an hour, but without effect. Twelve brigs and sloops, (one of which was the vessel above referred to), 120 tons of hay, corn and oats, ten hogsheads of rum, and a large quantity of merchandise, were completely destroyed; six of the enemy were killed, and ninety taken prisoners. Not one of Colonel Meigs' force was either killed or wounded.

At two o'clock in the afternoon, he returned to Guilford, having been absent only twenty-five hours. Congress voted a sword to Colonel Meigs, and Washington addressed him a letter of thanks, through General Parsons.

In retaliation for the capture of Major General Silliman, by the British, in May, 1779, a party of twenty-five volunteers set off from Bridgeport, Conn., on the 4th of November of the same year, to capture Hon. Thomas Jones, then judge of the supreme court, who was noted for his attachment to Great Britain. They succeeded in their object, and captured three other prisoners. These were exchanged, in May, 1780, for Major General Silliman, and other prisoners.

On the 21st November, 1780, Major Benjamin Tallmadge attempted an enterprise against Fort St. George, a British stockade post near Mastic, on the southern shore of the island, in the town of Brookhaven. Embarking at Fairfield, Conn., with eighty men, he crossed the sound to Old Man's harbor, where he remained concealed through the day, and at night marched for the fort, which he reached about two o'clock in the morning, and carried immediately, at the point of the bayonet, taking fifty-four prisoners, and destroying several vessels laden with stores. On his return he stopped at Corum, and burned three hundred tons of hay, which had been collected by the British. He arrived at Fairfield, on the evening of the 22d, with his prisoners and booty, without the loss of a single man.

In October, 1781, Major Tallmadge attacked Fort Slongo, a British post at Tredwell's bank, in Smithtown, and destroyed it, taking a number of prisoners.

During the late war with Great Britain, the enemy repeatedly seized vessels in Long Island sound, and on the coast, and either wantonly destroyed them, or demanded an exorbitant price for their ransom. In one of their incursions for this purpose, at Riverhead, in May, 1814, they were repulsed by the militia, with severe loss.

VILLAGES. RIVERHEAD, the seat of justice for the county, is a small village on Peconic river.

Sag Harbor, the largest whaling port in the state, and the most populous village in the county, is situated on the boundary line between Southampton and East Hampton, the larger portion of it being in the former town. Its site is sandy and sterile, but its harbor is excellent. It was first settled in 1730. In 1845 there were sixty-one ships and barks belonging to this port, engaged in the whaling business, employing a capital of more than $2,000,000, and a number of smaller vessels in the home fisheries and coasting trade. It suffered severely, from a disastrous fire in 1845, but was soon rebuilt, in a better manner than before. Population 3621.

Greenport, the terminus of the Long Island railroad, has sprung up since 1827, and has had a more rapid growth, than any other village in the county. It had twelve ships, engaged in the whaling business, in 1845. Population about 1200.

Huntington, in the town of the same name, is a small but ancient village, with an incorporated academy. It has a fine harbor.

Oyster Ponds, or *Orient*, and *Southold*, are growing settlements.

VI. RICHMOND COUNTY.

Square Miles, 63.
Organized, 1683.
Population, 13,673.
Valuation, 1845, $1,373,279.

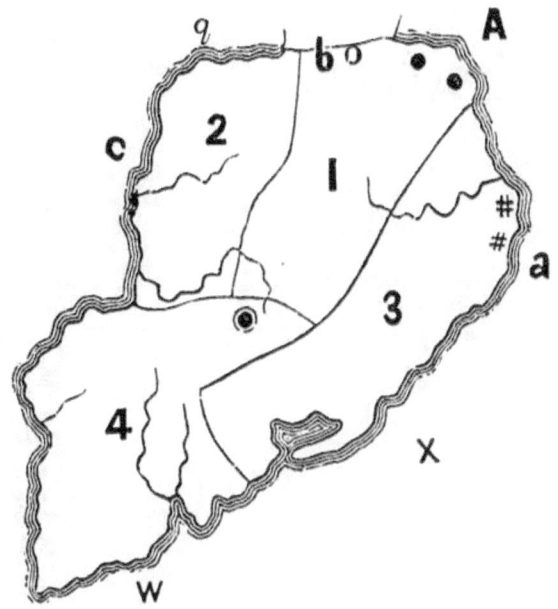

TOWNS.

1. Castleton, 1788.
2. Northfield, 1788.
3. Southfield, 1788.
4. Westfield, 1788.

Bays. A. New York Bay. a. The Narrows. b Arthur Kull Sound. c. Staten Island Sound. q. Newark Bay. w. Raritan. x. Lower Bay.

Forts. Tompkins. Richmond.

Villages. RICHMOND. New Brighton. Tompkinsville. Factoryville.

BOUNDARIES. North by Newark bay and Arthur Kull sound; East by New York bay and the Narrows; South by the Lower bay and Raritan bay; and West by Staten Island sound. It embraces Shooter's island, and the islands of meadow on the west side of Staten island.

SURFACE. Richmond county is quite elevated and much broken. There are a few miles of marsh, however, on the western coast, extending back from Newark bay. The northern shore of the island is very bold, affording some delightful prospects and beautiful sites for building, some of which are occupied. The southeastern extremity is more level.

BAYS, &c. New York bay on the north connects with Newark bay by means of the Arthur Kull sound. Staten island sound, seldom exceeding half a mile in width, bounds it for fifteen miles on the west. New York bay on the east is contracted at Signal hill into the Narrows which divide it into the upper and lower bays. That portion of the upper bay lying northeast of the island is known as the quarantine ground, where vessels from warm climates are obliged to lie at anchor, under quarantine regulations, till permission is given by the health officer for them to proceed to the city.

CLIMATE. The climate is less subject to extremes than in many sections of the state. The sea-breezes moderate alike the heat of summer and the cold of winter. Its inhabitants are healthy.

GEOLOGY AND MINERALOGY. Staten Island is based upon primitive rock, which rises near its centre into a ridge, running longitudinally through it, with a breadth of from one to two miles. Boulders of green-stone, sand-stone, gneiss, granite, &c., appear in some sections sparingly, but on the northeast part of the island in considerable abundance.

Steatite, containing veins of talc, amianthus, and alabaster, covers the granite of the ridge. This approaches in many places within one and a half feet of the surface. Brown hematitic iron ore, of a superior quality, is abundant, as well as a granular oxide of iron. Chalcedony, jasper, lignite, crystalized pyrites, asbestos, amianthus, dolomite, Brucite, Gurhofite, talc and serpentine, are the other principal minerals.

There is a single chalybeate spring, of no great strength, in the county. Marine fossils have been found in the alluvial portions of the island.

SOIL AND VEGETABLE PRODUCTIONS. The soil of the county with proper culture produces fair crops, particularly of oats, corn and grass. Land, however, commands a high price per acre, even when taken in farms.

Oak, hickory, walnut, and chestnut trees are abundant on the ridge, but they are small, and chiefly of after growth.

PURSUITS. The attention of the people is divided between agriculture, manufactures and commerce. Manufactures are almost entirely confined to the dyeing and printing of cloths.

Fisheries are a source of sustenance and profit to many of its inhabitants. Large quantities of fine oysters and clams, shad, herring and mossbonkers, or white-fish, are annually taken from its waters.

Many of its citizens are engaged in business in the city of New York.

SCHOOLS. The public school-houses are fourteen. The schools were taught in 1846 on an average ten months, and were attended by 1915 scholars. The wages of teachers amounted to $5425; the libraries contained 4462 volumes. There are twenty-six private schools with 716 pupils.

RELIGIOUS DENOMINATIONS. Methodists, Episcopalians, Baptists, Dutch Reformed and Roman Catholics. There are twenty-one churches and twenty-four clergymen.

HISTORY. Staten Island was purchased from the Indians, in 1630, by Wouter Van Twiller, as agent for Michael Paauw, one of the directors of the Dutch West India Company, together with a large tract of land in Bergen county, New Jersey. Paauw named his "Colonie" Pavonia,* probably from the abundance of wild turkeys, regarded by the first settlers as a species of peacock.

For some reason, Paauw seems soon to have relinquished his claim to the island, and it reverted to the company. In January, 1639, David Pieterszen De Vries, the pioneer in the settlements on the Delaware, commenced a colony on the island. Through the short sighted policy of Governor Kieft, in regard to the Indians, their revengeful disposition was roused, and in the absence of De Vries, his colony was cut off.

In 1641, Cornelis Melyn, an unprincipled adventurer, claimed the island under an alleged grant from the West India Company, and commenced a colony upon it, but the settlers were soon dispersed by the Indians. In 1651, the Indians sold it again to Augustin Herman, and in 1657, to the Baron Van Capellan, who founded a colony, which was broken up by the Indians.

In 1655, during Governor Stuyvesant's invasion of the Swedish settlements on the Delaware, the Indians made a descent upon Staten Island, and massacred sixty-seven persons, which must have embraced nearly the whole white population.

In 1658, Melyn obtained the exclusive title to the island, and claiming to be independent of New Amsterdam, gave Governor Stuyvesant and the colonists much trouble. In 1659 he conveyed his rights to the company.

In 1664, the county, together with the rest of the colony, fell into the hands of the English, and soon became the home of numerous emigrants. In 1667, the first court of justice was established here. In 1670, it was once more purchased of the Indians by Governor Lovelace. In 1683, it contained 200 families. It was then organized as a county. Soon after this time it received an accession of inhabitants from the Huguenots, who fled from their native land on account of persecution.

On the fourth of July, 1776, Sir William Howe seized the island, and issued from thence his proclamations to the inhabitants of Long Island; and on the 22d of August, landed his troops without opposition, on the Long Island shore, opposite Southfield. The island was held by the British, during the whole revolutionary struggle.

---

* Pavonia signifies the land of peacocks.

On the 21st of August, 1777, Gen. Sullivan, with a force of about 1000 men, undertook an expedition against the English forces on Staten Island He captured about 150 prisoners, but, from the terror of the boatmen who conveyed his troops to the island, he was pressed by the British and thirteen of his men killed, and the rear guard of one division numbering 136 men, taken prisoners, before they could effect a passage to the main land.

In November, 1777, another surprise was attempted by General Dickinson, and in the winter of 1779-80, a third by General Stirling; both were unsuccessful.

Preparatory to the war of 1812, Forts Tompkins, Richmond and Hudson, were erected at the Narrows, which completely command the entrance to the upper bay. On Signal hill, back of the forts, is a telegraph, communicating with New York city.

From the time that the English obtained possession of this island, up to the year 1833, a controversy had existed between New York and New Jersey, relative to the jurisdiction over it. This controversy was at length happily terminated in that year, by commissioners, who decided in favor of New York, but yielded to New Jersey the jurisdiction over a portion of the adjacent waters.

VILLAGES, &c. RICHMOND, the county seat, is a small village in the town of Westfield, near the centre of the county. *Castleton*, upon the Kills and New York bay, is the most hilly town in the county. The great beauty of the prospects, the salubrity of climate, and purity of water which its great elevation secures, and the convenience of access to New York city, has within the last few years much increased the value of its lands. It has three considerable villages, all finely situated; Tompkinsville, New Brighton and Factoryville.

Tompkinsville contains three hospitals connected with the Quarantine department, and the country seat of the late Vice President, D. D. Tompkins. *New Brighton* has a young ladies' seminary and a boarding school for boys. It is distinguished for its beautiful country seats. At *Factoryville* is an extensive dyeing and printing establishment.

In *Northfield* is located the "Sailors' Snug Harbour," founded by Robert R. Randall, in 1801, who left for this purpose twenty-two acres of land, in the fifteenth ward of New York city. The principal edifice, with its wings, is 225 feet in length, and is usually the home of about 100 infirm and aged seamen. Connected with it is a farm of 160 acres. An elegant monument to the memory of the founder fronts the edifice.

VII. WESTCHESTER COUNTY.

Square miles, 470.
Organized, 1680.
Population, 47,578.
Valuation, 1845, $10,036,317.

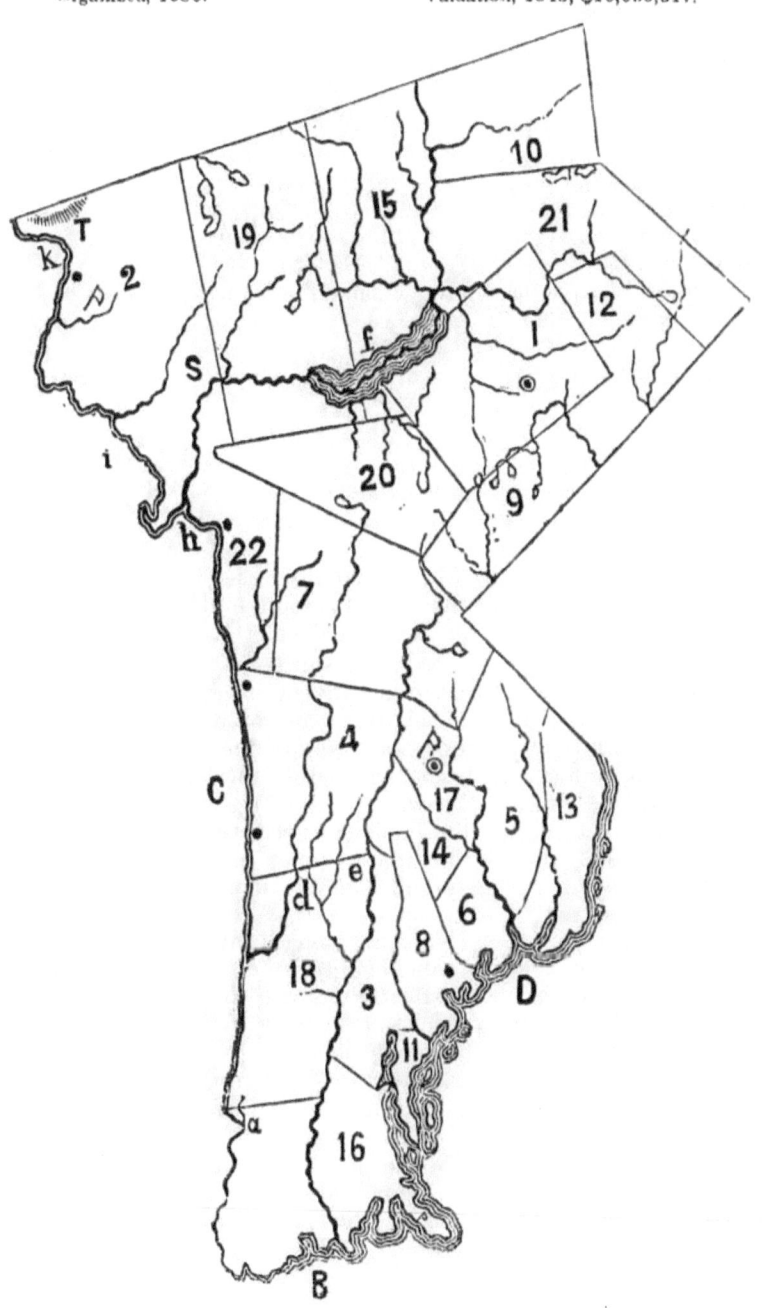

174 STATE OF NEW YORK.

TOWNS.

1. Bedford, 1788.
2. Cortland, 1788.
3. East Chester, 1788.
4. Greensburgh, 1788.
5. Harrison, 1788.
6. Mamaroneck, 1788.
7. Mount Pleasant, 1788.
8. New Rochelle, 1788.
9. North Castle, 1788.
10. North Salem, 1788.
11. Pelham, 1788.
12. Poundridge, 1788.
13. Rye, 1788.
14. Scarsdale, 1788.
15. Somers, 1788.
16. Westchester, 1788.
17. White Plains, 1788.
18. Yonkers, 1788.
19. Yorktown, 1788.
20. New Castle, 1791.
21. Lewisborough, 1788.
22. Ossinsing, 1845.

Mountains. T. Southern termination of the Matteawan mountains.
Rivers, &c. C. Hudson. B. East. S. Croton. a. Harlaem. e. Bronx. d. Sawmill creek.
Bays, &c. D. Long Island Sound. h. Tappan Bay. i. Haverstraw. k. Peekskill.
Ponds. f. Croton.
Forts. Fort Schuyler.
Battle-fields. Verplank's Neck. Stoney Point. White Plains
Villages. WHITE PLAINS. BEDFORD. Singsing. Peekskill Tarrytown. Dobb's Ferry.

BOUNDARIES. North by Putnam county; East by the state of Connecticut and Long Island Sound; South by East river and Harlaem river; West by the Hudson river.

SURFACE. The surface of Westchester county is hilly, being broken by numerous ridges, generally of no great elevation. The general course of these ridges is from south-west to north-east. The Matteawan mountains enter the north-western corner of the county, and from thence cross the Hudson.

A high ridge, forming the watershed of the county, passes from Mount Pleasant on the Hudson, eastward through New Castle, Bedford, Poundridge and Salem, into Connecticut. The south-eastern portion of this county, upon the Sound, becomes more level.

RIVERS, &c. The East river, and Long Island Sound wash the south-eastern shore of the county, and the Hudson the western. The other principal streams are the Croton river, which furnishes a supply of water to New York city, Bronx and Sawmill rivers, and Mamaroneck creek.

BAYS. Tappan, Haverstraw and Peekskill bays are only expansions of the Hudson, upon the western boundary of the county.

PONDS. Croton Pond is a beautiful little lake, five miles in length, formed by the Croton dam, which was erected for the purpose of forming a reservoir, for the water conducted to New York by the Croton aqueduct.

WESTCHESTER COUNTY. 175

RAILROAD. The Harlaem railroad extends through the county to its northern boundary.

CLIMATE. Its climate is mild and healthy.

GEOLOGY AND MINERALS. This county is wholly primitive in its formation. Gneiss and primitive limestone are the prevailing rocks.

The latter furnishes in vast abundance, an excellent building material, which, under the name of Singsing marble, is extensively used in New York city, Brooklyn, Albany and Troy. It is liable, however, to become stained by the action of the sea air, owing in part to its containing minute grains of iron pyrites.

Magnetic iron ore, iron and copper pyrites, green malachite, sulphuret of zinc, galena and other lead ores, native silver in small quantities, serpentine, garnet, beryl, apatite, tremolite, white pyroxene, chlorite, black tourmaline, Sillimanite, monazite, Brucite, epidote and sphene, are the principal among the numerous minerals found within its borders. Peat is found abundantly, and of good quality, in Bedford.

SOIL AND VEGETABLE PRODUCTIONS. As the county is based upon primitive rock, its soil is naturally sterile, but by skillful husbandry it has been rendered productive. It is not adapted to wheat: summer crops succeed well, and by the use of plaster it yields good returns in grass. Much of the land is devoted to the raising of market vegetables.

The timber of the county is principally oak, chestnut, hickory, maple, &c.

PURSUITS. *Agriculture*, and particularly Horticulture, is the pursuit of a majority of the inhabitants. But little wheat is raised; corn is extensively cultivated, and carried in large quantities to New York city, in the ear.

Rye, oats, potatoes and turnips are also largely produced, as well as the garden vegetables adapted to the New York market. The rearing of calves, lambs, pigs and fruits for the same market, is also a source of great profit to the agriculturists. Butter and milk are also produced in considerable quantities.

Manufactures. The facilities for manufacturing in this county are very generally improved, but there is not as much variety in the manufactures as in some other counties of the state. Iron, woollen goods, flour, leather and paper are the principal articles.

Commerce. A considerable coasting trade is carried on between the ports on the Hudson and on the Sound, and New York city. Much of the produce of the county is also transported to New York by the Harlaem railroad, and by steamers on the Hudson.

Mines. Under this head we may enumerate the extensive marble quarries at Singsing, Kingsbridge, and a copper mine in Mount Pleasant, formerly extensively wrought, but now abandoned.

STAPLE PRODUCTIONS. Corn, oats, rye, pork, calves, lambs, fowls, garden vegetables, butter and milk.

SCHOOLS. There are in the county 149 district school-houses. In 1846, schools were taught an average period of nine months, and 8512 children received instruction, at an expense of nearly $23,000. The number of volumes in the district libraries was 26,485.

The same year there were eighty-nine private schools, with 1354 scholars; five academies, and two female seminaries, with 196 pupils, and St. John's College, a collegiate school, with thirteen instructors and 115 students.

RELIGIOUS DENOMINATIONS. Methodists, Episcopalians, Presbyterians, Friends, Baptists, Dutch Reformed, Roman Catholics, Congregationalists, and Universalists. Total number of churches, 111; of clergymen, 101.

HISTORY. The first settlement in this county was probably made in 1642 or 1643, by Mr. Throgmorton, and thirty-five associates, in the town of Westchester. Mr. Throgmorton emigrated hither from New England, and commenced his settlement with the approbation of the Dutch, who named it Eastdorp. The promontory on which Fort Schuyler now stands, received its name of Throg's point from this gentleman. In 1648, the territory now included in the town of Yonkers, was granted to Jonge Heer Van der Donk.*

The boundary line between New York and Connecticut was the cause of almost incessant bickering during the Dutch and the earlier part of the English colonial administration. This settlement of Eastdorp, as well as others in this county, were claimed by Connecticut.

In 1681, a settlement was made in Bedford, at a place called the Hop Ground, under a Connecticut license, and in 1697, a patent was issued for the town by the Connecticut Colonial Assembly. In 1700, however, the settlement was attached to New York by order of King William. A patent was granted to Frederick Philips, for the tract known as Philips' patent, which was south of the Croton river, and was about twenty miles square.

In 1689, Governor Leisler purchased the manor of Pelham, including the present town of that name and New Rochelle, from the heirs of Thomas Pell, to whom it had been granted in 1666, for the Huguenots, who fled hither from France, on account of persecution.

Governor Leisler was warmly supported in his administration by the citizens of this county, and particularly by those of East Chester.

In 1697, the two tracts of land, known as the Cortland manor, lying in this county, and consisting of more than 86,000 acres, were granted to Stephanus Van Cortland. This patent, as

---

* Probably Adriaen Van der Donk, the words Jonge Heer being merely the title of the individual.

usual at that time, gave to the manor the right of representation in the assembly.

Passing over the period from 1700 to 1775, during which few incidents of interest are recorded by historians, we find this county deeply concerned in the events of the revolution. After the disastrous battle of Long Island, and the evacuation of New York city by the American army, in September, 1776, General Washington had entrenched himself in a strong position at Kingsbridge.

Finding it impossible to dislodge him from this post, General Howe, the commander of the British forces determined to cut off his communication with the eastern provinces, and then, if he declined an engagement, to shut him up on the island of New York, or its immediate vicinity, whence it would be impossible for him to retire without serious loss.

Accordingly leaving a sufficient force in New York city, the British General embarked with a large body of troops, for Throg's point. Landing there, and having remained a few days, to receive further reinforcements, and remove obstructions from the roads over which he intended to pass, he marched to New Rochelle, where he left a corps of German troops, to secure the lower road leading to Connecticut. He, himself, proceeded slowly and cautiously towards White Plains, the post of the Highlands, which commanded the other road leading to the east.

Meantime General Washington's army occupied a position parallel to and west of the river Bronx, extending from Kingsbridge nearly to White Plains. During the progress of the British army, he sent out frequent parties to skirmish with the enemy, and thus accustomed his troops to meet a foe, who had hitherto inspired them with dread.

Upon their approach, however, the American commander called in all his troops, and took a strong position near White Plains, on the west side of the Bronx. His right wing, being more exposed than the remainder of the army, was protected by a battery, erected on a hill, about a mile distant from the camp.

On the morning of the 28th of October, the English army advanced in two columns, and having driven in the outposts, attacked the American camp. Perceiving the importance of the battery which protected the right wing of the Americans, the British commander resolved to capture it. After a desperate conflict and severe loss on both sides, it was carried by the enemy.

Night put an end to the conflict. Washington improved the interval in strengthening his entrenchments, and the next morning awaited an attack. The British general delayed for further reinforcements, and when these arrived, a storm prevented an engagement.

Meantime, on the night of the 1st of November, Washington abandoned his encampment, and removed to a stronger position, near North Castle, some seven or eight miles north of White Plains. Finding it impossible to dislodge him from this, the British general withdrew from the pursuit, and determined to reduce the posts, still held by the Americans, in the neighborhood of New York city.

The principal of these were Fort Washington, on New York island, and Fort Lee, on the New Jersey side of the Hudson. Despite Washington's efforts to prevent it, he succeeded in capturing both these forts, though not without severe loss, and the American general was compelled to retreat, with a constantly diminishing army, into New Jersey.

In March, 1777, the Americans having collected a quantity of military stores at Peekskill, General Howe sent a powerful armament up the river, to destroy them. The American troops, finding it impossible to defend them, set fire to the stores and abandoned the place, leaving the British a barren victory.

In August, 1777, while General Putnam's head quarters were at Peekskill, two noted British spies, Strang and Palmer, were detected in the camp of the Americans, and hanged at Oak hill, in the town of Cortland, near Peekskill village. Sir Henry Clinton interfered in behalf of the latter, by sending a flag of truce, demanding his release. General Putnam's reply was characteristic; it was as follows:

Head Quarters, 7th August, 1777.

Sir,—Nathan Palmer, a lieutenant in your king's service, was taken in my camp as a *spy*, he was tried as a *spy*, he was condemned as a *spy*, and you may rest assured, sir, he shall be hanged as a *spy*. I have the honor to be, &c.

ISRAEL PUTNAM.

His Excellency Governor Tryon.

P. S. Afternoon. He is hanged. I. P.

With a view of making a diversion in favor of General Burgoyne, then closely besieged by General Gates, Sir Henry Clinton in October, 1777, ascended the Hudson with a force of between 3000 and 4000 troops, and landed at Verplank's point, a short distance below Peekskill.

From thence he proceeded secretly across the river and gained the rear of forts Clinton and Montgomery, in Orange county. By his adroit manœuvres he succeeded in deceiving General Putnam, and prevented his affording aid to those forts, which might have prevented their surrender.

After the capture of the forts, the British again crossed the Hudson, burned Continental village, where military stores to a considerable amount had been deposited, and proceeded up the river to commit similar ravages upon the towns of the adjacent counties. They were, however, soon compelled to return to New York.

During the whole war of the revolution, this county was neutral ground between the two contending armies—the British lines being generally in the neighborhood of Kingsbridge, and those of the American army in the neighborhood of White Plains.

The territory between these two armies was infested by a gang of marauders attached to each army. That belonging to the British army was principally composed of tories of the most infamous character, who were denominated "Cowboys." The American gang were equally unprincipled, and had received the title of "Skinners." The inhabitants of the county were plundered by each in turn, and dispirited by their sufferings and losses, looked on all whom they met, as foes.

It was in this county that in September, 1780, Andre was captured, on his return from the interview in which Arnold had consummated his treason.

The place of his capture was in the town of Greensburgh, about a fourth of a mile north of the village of Tarrytown. The names of his captors were Isaac Van Wart, John Paulding and David Williams. They were militia men, and had been on an expedition to rescue some property taken the previous night by the Cowboys.

They were concealed for this object, when Andre, disguised as a citizen, passed on the road near them, on horseback. They stopped him, and, losing his presence of mind, he exclaimed, "Gentlemen, I hope you belong to our party." One of them enquired, "what party?" Andre replied, "the lower party." They answered "we do," and Andre at once declared himself a British officer, on urgent business, and begged to be suffered to proceed without delay.

Paulding then informed him that they were Americans, and Andre immediately produced the pass with which Arnold had furnished him, and professed that his former statement] was a falsehood, invented to enable him to escape from arrest by the British patroles.

Their suspicions, were, however, aroused, and they insisted upon searching him, and found papers in his stockings, proving his real character and his purposes. He offered them immense rewards if they would permit him to escape, but in vain.

They delivered him to their commanding officer, Colonel Jamieson, then stationed at North Castle, who imprudently suffered him to apprise Arnold of his arrest. He was tried by a court martial and sentenced to be hung as a spy, and was accordingly executed at Tappan, October 2d, 1780.

Each of his captors were rewarded by Congress with a farm worth $1250, an annuity of $200 for life, and an elegant silver medal with the inscription on one side "Fidelity," and on the other "Amor vincit Patriæ,"—The love of country conquers.

VILLAGES. WHITE PLAINS, one of the county seats, is a pleasant village on the Bronx river. It has an academy and a female seminary, both in a prosperous condition.

BEDFORD, the other half shire village, in the town of the same name, is a small place, only important as being the county seat. It has a female seminary.

Singsing, in the town of Ossinsing, is delightfully situated on the bank of the Hudson. From the village, the prospect of Hudson river, forming Tappan bay, in connection with the distant mountains, and the lofty wall of the palisades, is hardly surpassed by any other in the Union.

The Mount Pleasant academy and female seminary are both excellent institutions, well located, and occupying elegant edifices.

The Croton aqueduct bridge, a noble structure, here crosses the Singsing creek by a single arch of eighty-eight feet span, and is 100 feet in height.

There are several extensive quarries of marble, worked by convicts.

The Mount Pleasant State Prison located here, on the bank of the Hudson, is an immense marble structure. The main building is 484 feet long, forty-four wide, and five stories high, containing 1000 cells. Connected with it are workshops of different kinds, and apartments for the keepers,—all built of marble.

The female prison, also of marble, of the Ionic order, stands on elevated ground, and has nearly 100 cells, besides apartments for the matron. All these buildings were erected by the convicts.

The name given to the town, Ossinsing, is of Indian origin, and signifies "the place of stone." Population about 2600.

Peekskill, in the town of Cortland, is pleasantly situated on Peekskill bay, a beautiful expansion of the Hudson. It is famous for having been the head quarters of both Washington and Putnam. The small one story house occupied by the latter, is still standing. The Peekskill academy, located on Oak hill, near the village, is situated but a short distance from the spot where the tory spies, Strang and Palmer, already mentioned, were executed. The village has some manufactures. Population, 3,000.

Tarrytown, in the town of Greensburgh, is finely situated on the Hudson, and contains the Irving Institute, and the Greenbank female seminary, both schools of high reputation. The village has some trade with New York city. Population about 1000.

The capture of Andre near this village, has been already noticed. Near it too is the far famed "Sleepy Hollow," whose legend, Washington Irving has rendered immortal.

Mr. Irving resides about two miles below the village, in an ancient Dutch mansion, known as the Van Tassel house, which the former proprietor forfeited by his adherence to the British interests.

New Rochelle is pleasantly situated on Long Island Sound, and is a favorite resort for the fashionable from New York, during the summer months. Its first settlers were Huguenots, who named it from their native residence, Rochelle, in France. Many of their descendants still reside here. It has one male and two female boarding schools. Steamboats ply between the village and New York, daily.

Dobb's Ferry is only worthy of notice from its historic interest.

VIII. ULSTER COUNTY.

Square miles, 1096.   Population, 48,907.
Organized, 1683.   Valuation, 1845, $5,398,982.

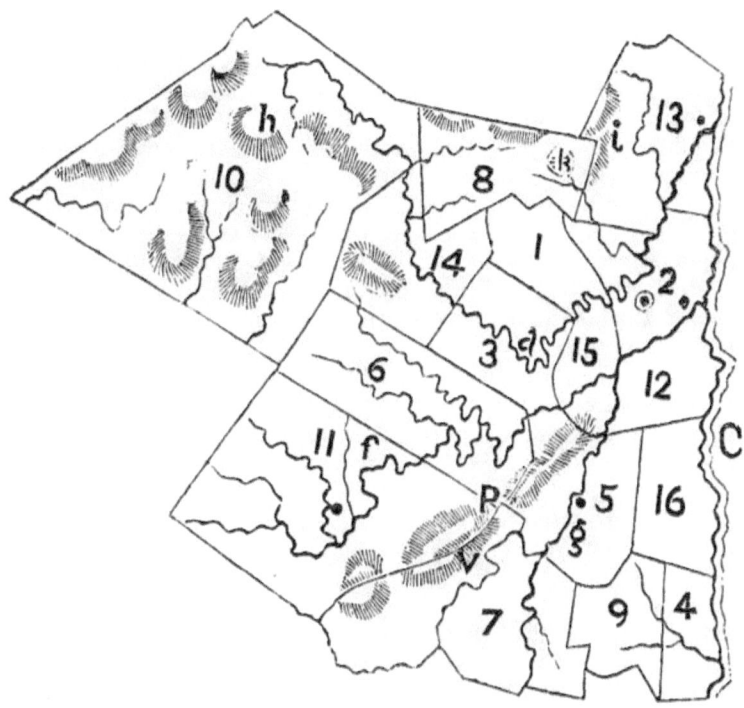

TOWNS.

1. Hurley, 1788.
2. Kingston, 1788.
3. Marbletown, 1788.
4. Marlborough, 1788.
5. New Paltz, 1788.
6. Rochester, 1788.
7. Shawangunk, 1788.
8. Woodstock, 1788.
9. Plattekill, 1800.
10. Shandaken, 1804.
11. Wawarsing, 1806.
12. Esopus, 1811.
13. Saugerties, 1811.
14. Olive, 1823.
15. Rosendale, 1845.
16. Lloyd, 1845.

Mountains. P. Shawangunk mountains. h. Blue. i. Southern termination of Kaatsbergs.

Rivers, &c. C. Hudson river. V. Shawangunk. a. Esopus creek f. Rondout. g. Wallkill river.

Falls. Honk's falls.

Lakes. k. Shin's lake.

Battle Fields. Kingston. Wawarsing.

Villages. KINGSTON. Rondout. Saugerties, or Ulster. New Paltz. Wawarsing.

BOUNDARIES. North by Delaware and Greene counties; East by the Hudson river; South by Orange county; and West by Sullivan county.

SURFACE. Mountainous. The Shawangunk mountains enter the county from Orange, and traverse it in a north-easterly direction, for nearly thirty miles, approaching the Hudson at Kingston.

The Blue mountains, a continuation of the Allegany chain, enter the county from Sullivan county, and spread over its western section, mingling in the northern part with the Catskill range. They are said to rise, in some places, to the height of 2000 feet. Between these and the Shawangunk mountains, is a broad valley through which flows the Rondout creek.

RIVERS. Beside the Hudson which washes its eastern border, the principal streams of the county are the Wallkill and Shawangunk rivers, and Esopus and Rondout creeks, with their tributaries. The Nevisink river also takes its rise in this county.

FALLS. The Rondout, at Honk's falls, descends by a succession of cascades, 200 feet, sixty feet of which is by a single cataract.

LAKES. In the northern and western section of the county are several small lakes or ponds. One of the most important of these is Shin's lake, the source of one of the tributaries of Esopus creek.

CANALS. The Delaware and Hudson Canal extends through the county.

CLIMATE. The mountainous districts are somewhat cold and subject to early frosts. The climate in the valleys is mild and delightful. The county is considered salubrious.

GEOLOGY AND MINERALS. Nearly the whole county belongs to the transition formation, being based upon slate, which is overlaid with limestone. The primary rocks, particularly granite, occasionally appear on the surface, but only in beds of small extent.

The minerals are blue limestone, containing fossils, much used as a building material; hydraulic lime of fine quality, and in great abundance; excellent marble; marl, slate, sulphur, alum, plumbago, (usually called black lead,) zinc ore, several of the mineral pigments, millstones, said to be little inferior to the French, peat, &c. There are also several sulphur springs of some celebrity. A number of skeletons of the mastodon have been discovered in this county.

SOIL AND VEGETABLE PRODUCTIONS. The soil varies with the surface, being barren upon the mountains, fertile on the lower hills, and composed of a deep vegetable mould, of exhaustless fertility, in the extensive valleys. The application of marl, which is abundant in the county, would render those portions naturally sterile, highly productive. It is well adapted to grazing. The timber of the county is oak, hickory, black walnut, pine and hemlock.

PURSUITS. A majority of the inhabitants are engaged in *agriculture*. More attention is devoted to the rearing of cattle and to the dairy, than to the grain culture, although corn, oats, and buckwheat are raised in considerable quantities.

Manufactures are also a popular pursuit. The manufactures of the county amounted, in 1845, to nearly two and a half millions of dollars. Leather, lumber, flour, iron, cotton and woollen goods, hydraulic cement, oil, paper, furniture, white lead, and distilled and malt liquors, are the principal articles manufactured.

Commerce. The Delaware and Hudson canal brings to tide water immense quantities of coal and lumber, most of which is shipped for New York, and other ports. This business gives employment to about 600 canal boats, and eighty sloops and schooners. Several steamboats are also owned in the county, and ply between the ports on the Hudson and New York city.

Mines. The quarries of marble and limestone furnish employment to considerable numbers.

STAPLE PRODUCTIONS. Butter, corn, oats, buckwheat, wool, and lumber.

SCHOOLS. There were in the county, in 1846, 181 district schoolhouses, in which schools were taught an average period of nine months each. 11,547 children received instruction at a cost for tuition of about $20,000. The district libraries contained 26,780 volumes.

There were in the county, the same year, forty private schools, with 811 pupils; two academies and two female seminaries with 135 pupils.

RELIGIOUS DENOMINATIONS. Dutch Reformed, Methodists, Baptists, Presbyterians, Friends, Episcopalians, and Roman Catholics. There are seventy churches, and sixty-one clergymen, of all denominations.

HISTORY. A trading house, or fort, was probably erected in this county as early as 1615 or 16, in the neighborhood of Kingston. At how early a period settlements were made in other sections of the county is uncertain. The frequent references to the settlements at Esopus, as the vicinity of the fort was called in the Dutch records, show that it had early become a location of some importance.

Situated about midway between the city of New Amsterdam and the colony of Rensselaerwyck, whose inhabitants did not always maintain the most friendly relations with each other, and with the Indians, it was more exposed to Indian hostilities than most of the other settlements.

In 1657, Van der Donk, the ex-attorney general, who resided at Esopus, slew a squaw for stealing peaches from his garden, and her tribe revenged the murder by killing several of the white settlers. From this and other causes much ill feeling arose between the natives and the settlers, and in June, 1663, the Indians made a descent upon the settlement, and killed and carried captive sixty-five persons.

Circumstances rendered it probable that a conspiracy had been formed by the Indians to extirpate the Dutch colonists. Governor Stuyvesant summoned the magistrates of the different towns, to consult with him relative to measures of defence. Their views not coinciding with his own, he repaired to Esopus, and took the field in person against the savages, who, on the approach of Martin Creigier, one of his captains, had fled to the mountains.

Sending out parties of wary and experienced soldiers, Gov. Stuyvesant not only kept them in check, but destroyed most of their mountain fastnesses, and so far subdued them that they asked for a truce, and, on the 15th of May following, a treaty of peace was concluded with them.

Wawarsing and some of the adjacent towns were settled by the Huguenots, in the latter part of the seventeenth century, or the beginning of the eighteenth.

The convention, which formed the first constitution of the state, met at Kingston, in a chamber of the house of Mr. James W. Baldwin.

In October, 1777, during Sir Henry Clinton's expedition up the Hudson, for the relief of General Burgoyne, he despatched General Vaughan to Kingston. He landed and burned the village, at that time the third in the state for wealth, population, and elegance. Only one house escaped the flames. Several tories were executed at Kingston during the Revolution.

In 1778, two men, Anderson and Osterhout, were taken captives by the Indians, and carried toward Binghamton. On their way they succeeded in killing their captors, and, after almost incredible hardships, returned to their houses in the town of Wawarsing.

In May, 1779, a party of Indians descended upon a small settlement of the Huguenots, on the Fantine kill in Wawarsing, and killed eleven of the inhabitants and burned several dwellings. They were pursued by Colonel Cortlandt with his regiment, but without effect. Soon after, another family were killed in the same vicinity.

In August, 1781, a large force of Indians and tories, some 400 or 500 in number, made an attack upon the village of Wawarsing, and burned and plundered it. The inhabitants had had timely warning and were in the fort. The Indians in this expedition took but one scalp, while several of their own number were killed, and but for the tardiness of Colonel Cantine, they

ULSTER COUNTY. 185

might have been signally routed. Other similar occurrences took place in some of the other towns of the county.

VILLAGES. KINGSTON, the county seat, is pleasantly situated on a plain, three miles west of the landing on the Hudson. The Esopus creek flows through the village. It was anciently called Esopus, and, as has been already noticed, was early settled by the Dutch.

It was burnt by the British in 1777, but soon re-built. It has considerable trade with New York, and some manufactures. Its business is not concentrated upon one street, but scattered over the whole village plat. It has a flourishing academy, and a female seminary. Population 2500.

Rondout, also in the township of Kingston, is situated on the Rondout creek. It is the place of deposit and shipment of the coal and lumber, brought to the Hudson, by the Delaware and Hudson canal. Nearly 200,000 tons of coal, and several millions of feet of lumber, as well as large quantities of hydraulic cement, and quick lime, are annually exported from this port. A steam ferryboat plies between this place and Rhinebeck, in Dutchess county, and also one to Eddyville, in this county. The United States Government have erected a light house here. Population about 1800.

Eddyville, in the same town, is a small but thriving manufacturing village.

Ulsterville, in the town of Saugerties, is a village of recent growth, being founded in 1826, and incorporated in 1831. Its immense water power, derived from the falls on Esopus creek, has rendered it one of the most flourishing manufacturing villages in the state.

There is an extensive rolling and slitting mill here, employing 250 workmen. Axes, paper, white lead, starch, and bricks are also manufactured in large quantities. A beautiful bridge, with one arch of 260 feet span, crosses the Esopus creek in this village. A steamboat, and several sloops, ply between the village and New York. Population, 2500.

New Paltz, is a small but thriving agricultural hamlet. It has a flourishing academy. New Paltz landing, now included in the town of Lloyd, is a pleasant village, nine miles from the village of New Paltz.

Wawarsing and *Naponoch*, in the town of Wawarsing, are places of some historic interest.

IX. DUTCHESS COUNTY.

Square miles, 765.
Organized, 1683.
Population, 55,124.
Valuation, 1845, $19,784,944.

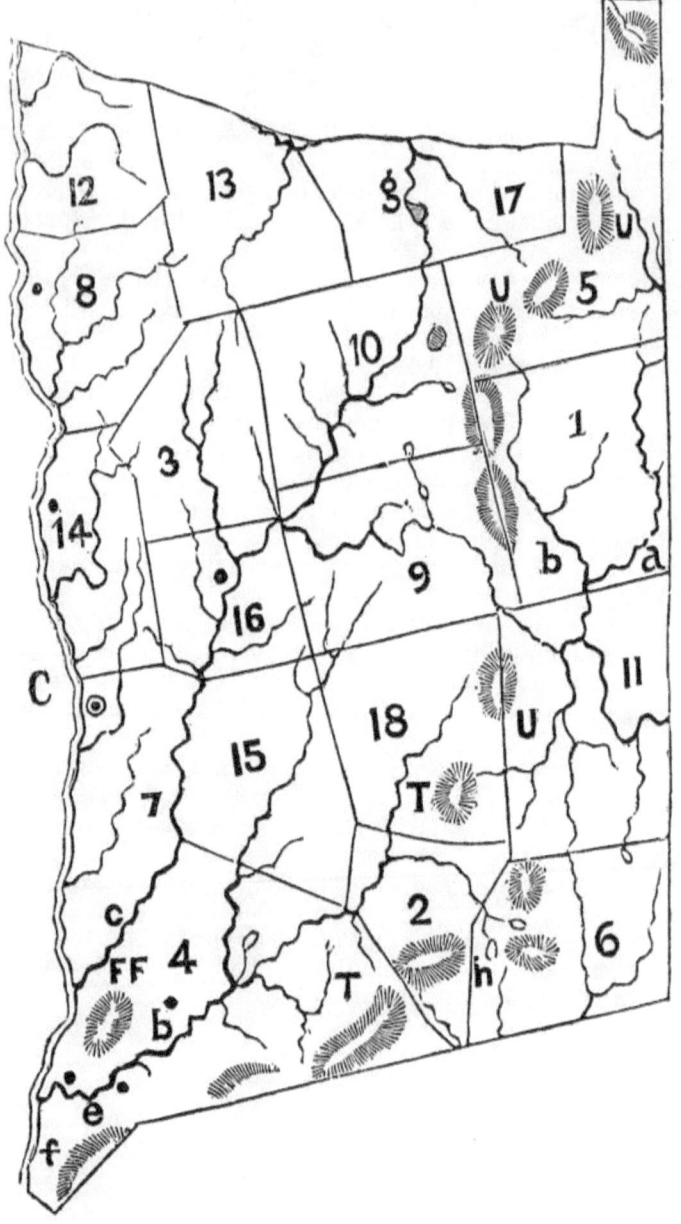

DUTCHESS COUNTY. 187

TOWNS.

1. Amenia, 1788.
2. Beekman, 1788.
3. Clinton, 1788.
4. Fishkill, 1788.
5. Northeast, 1788.
6. Pawling, 1788.
7. Poughkeepsie, 1778.
8. Rhinebeck, 1788.
9. Washington, 1788.
10. Stanford, 1788.
11. Dover, 1807.
12. Redhook, 1812.
13. Milan, 1818.
14. Hyde Park, 1821.
15. La Grange, 1821.
16. Pleasant Valley, 1821.
17. Pine Plains, 1823.
18. Unionvale, 1827.

Mountains. F. F. Highlands. T. Matteawan, or Fishkill Mountains. U. Taghkanic range. e. Old Beacon. f. New Beacon, or Grand Sachem.

Rivers, Creeks, &c. C. Hudson river. a. Ten Mile creek. b. Fishkill. c. Wappinger's.

Lakes, &c. g. Stissing's Pond. h. Whaley's.

Villages. POUGHKEEPSIE, Fishkill, Matteawan, Fishkill Landing, Pleasant Valley, Hyde Park, Rhinebeck.

BOUNDARIES. North by Columbia county; East by the state of Connecticut; South by Putnam county; and west by Hudson river.

SURFACE. The surface is diversified, but generally mountainous, or hilly. Two great valleys intersect the county; the eastern bounded by the Taghkanic and the Matteawan, or Fishkill mountains; the western, lying between the latter and the high banks of the Hudson river. Beside these, there are numerous rolling ridges of less elevation, running through the valleys parallel to the mountain ranges.

The mountains rise in some places to the height of about 1700 feet. The river range presents some of the highest peaks of the Highlands. The Old Beacon, near the Fishkill landing, is 1471 feet, and the New Beacon,* or Grand Sachem, half a mile farther south, 1685 feet, above tide water. The prospect from the top of the latter is very extensive and beautiful.

RIVERS, &c. The principal streams are, Ten Mile, Fishkill, Wappinger's, and Crom Elbow creeks, with their tributaries; several of the smaller streams also possess valuable mill sites. The Fishkill is about twenty miles in length. Wappinger's creek is about thirty-five miles long.

CLIMATE. The climate is agreeable and healthful, though, from the elevations of some portions of the county, it is colder than some of the adjacent counties.

GEOLOGY AND MINERALOGY. The eastern part of the county is primitive. Granite and gneiss are the prevailing constituents.

---

* These mountains received their names from the signal fires lit upon their tops during the Revolution.

West of these, the country belongs to the Taconic system; slate and limestone being the principal underlying rocks, and frequently cropping out upon the surface.

The county abounds in minerals. Iron ore, of rare purity and in extraordinary abundance, exists on the western slopes of the mountains; both the hematitic and magnetic ores occur in the county. Lead and zinc are also found in considerable quantities. Graphite, or black lead, is obtained in great abundance from a mine in Fishkill. Marble, peat, and marl, are found in almost every part of the county. Garnet, green actinolite, talc, anthophyllite, granular epidote, and Gibbsite are the other principal minerals.

In Dover is a cavern which, from its almost perfect Gothic arch, has received the name of "the Stone Church."

SOIL AND VEGETABLE PRODUCTIONS. The soil in general, is very fertile, though portions of the mountainous districts are somewhat sterile.

Gypsum is too much relied upon as a fertilizing agent, while the equally valuable lime and marl upon, and beneath the soil are neglected; a beneficial change is however taking place in this respect. The timber is principally oak and chestnut with some hickory. The county is well adapted to the rearing of cattle and sheep, and the culture of grain.

PURSUITS. *Agriculture* is the pursuit of a majority of the inhabitants of this county. In the production of corn and oats, it stands first in the state, and maintains a respectable rank in the production of other grains. In the growth of wool and the production of butter, it occupies a high rank; in the number of its swine too it exceeds any other county in the state. Flax and potatoes are also raised in great abundance.

Manufactures. Dutchess county is extensively engaged in manufactures. The most important articles are cotton and woollen goods, including prints, iron ware, flour, malt liquors, cordage, leather, oil, paper, &c. The entire value of manufactured products in 1845, exceeded two and half millions of dollars.

Commerce. The whale fishery is prosecuted from Poughkeepsie, and employs several large ships. Some eight or ten steamboats, and a considerable number of sloops, schooners and barges, are employed in the coasting trade.

Mines, &c. In Beekman, Dover, Fishkill, and Pawling, are extensive iron mines; in Fishkill a large mine of Plumbago; in Dover extensive quarries of white and black marble; and in Poughkeepsie numerous and extensive lime-kilns.

STAPLES. Corn, oats, butter, wool, beef, and pork.

SCHOOLS. In the county are 210 district school-houses, in which, in 1846, schools were maintained an average period of nine months. 12,854 children received instruction at an expense for tuition of about $27,962. The district libraries contained about 28,000 volumes.

There were also in the county, eighty-three private schools, with 1155 scholars; four academies, and two female seminaries, with 298 pupils, and one collegiate school, with about 120 pupils.

DUTCHESS COUNTY. 189

RELIGIOUS DENOMINATIONS. Methodists, Friends, Baptists, Presbyterians, Dutch Reformed, Episcopalians, Congregationalists, Roman Catholics, Universalists, and Unitarians. There are 103 churches, and ninety-four clergymen of all denominations in the county.

HISTORY. The precise period when Dutchess county was first settled, does not seem to be satisfactorily ascertained. The first settlement was made at Fishkill, by the Dutch. In 1683, the number of its inhabitants was sufficient to authorize its organization, as a separate county. It was however very small, and, for nearly 20 years, was considered in the light of a dependency upon Ulster county.

In 1689, its inhabitants, like those of Ulster, took part against Leisler, but afterward submitted to his administration.

A large tract, extending from the Hudson to "the Oblong," and some eight or ten miles in width, comprising part of the towns of Hyde Park, Pleasant Valley, Washington, and Amenia, was granted to nine proprietors at a very early date, probably about the commencement of the eighteenth century. It was called the "Great Nine Partners."

In 1711, one Richard Sackett lived on this tract, and with his family remained the only settlers upon it till 1724, when some German families, from the East Camp, on Livingston's Manor, in Columbia county, removed here.

In 1702, the first house was built in Poughkeepsie by Myndert Van Kleek, a Dutchman, and one of the early emigrants to the county.

In 1731, the boundary difficulties which had long existed between New York and Connecticut, were terminated by a compromise; Connecticut relinquishing to New York a tract called "the Oblong," lying mostly in this county, and containing about 60,000 acres, in consideration for which, she received a tract on the southwestern corner of her territory, extending into Westchester county.

Two patents were issued for "the Oblong," one in London the day after the settlement, to Sir Joseph Eyles and others, the other in New York, some few months later, to Hawley & Co. These two patents were the subject of much litigation, and the source of no small amount of party animosity.

In 1741, several families from Connecticut emigrated to the northern part of the county. About the same time a considerable number of Friends from Long Island settled in the eastern section.

In the troublous times which preceded the Revolution, Dutchess county took the side of liberty, and furnished from among her citizens, some of the most brilliant and useful actors in that fearful conflict. Such were Montgomery, the hero of Quebec, the Schencks, and others of imperishable renown.

During the revolutionary war, a part of the American army were stationed for a considerable time at Fishkill, under the command of General Putnam, and afterwards of General Parsons. Their barracks were about half a mile south of the village.*

VILLAGES. POUGHKEEPSIE, the county seat, in the town of the same name, is finely situated on the elevated bank of the Hudson, about equally distant from New York and Albany. During the Revolution, and after its close, the legislature of the state frequently held its sessions here. The convention of the state, which adopted the Federal Constitution, also met here in 1788. The building occupied by that body has since been used as a brewery.

Poughkeepsie is regularly laid out, and has many elegant public and private buildings. It has considerable commerce with New York and other home ports.

It is also largely engaged in manufactures. Of these, machinery, malt liquors, flour, carpets, cutlery, fire arms, silk, pins, iron and brass ware, sash and blinds, and bricks in large quantities and of superior quality, and the principal.

The Poughkeepsie collegiate school is a fine institution, unsurpassed in the beauty of its situation, and the elegance of its edifice. This building is 77 by 137 feet, modeled after the Parthenon at Athens, and surrounded by a massive colonnade. Its cost, exclusive of the extensive and beautiful grounds, was $40,000. The Dutchess county academy, also located in the village, is an excellent chartered institution. Beside these there are four female seminaries. Population about 9000.

Fishkill Landing, in the town of Fishkill, is situated on the Hudson, directly opposite Newburgh. It has much delightful scenery, and is a place of considerable trade. Population about 1000.

Fishkill Village, in the same town, is a picturesque and beautiful hamlet. The Fishkill academy, located here, is a flourishing chartered institution. Population 800.

Matteawan, in the same township, is an important manufacturing village. Large quantities of moleskins, beaverteens, and fustians are produced here. It has also an extensive iron and brass foundry, several machine shops, flouring mills, and other manufactories. The Highland Gymnasium, a celebrated boarding school for boys, is located here. Population about 2000.

---

* In the old stone church in the town of Fishkill, Enoch Crosby the pedlar spy, [the "Harvey Birch" of Cooper's novel, "The Spy,"] was confined, and from thence he made his escape in an extraordinary and mysterious manner.

ORANGE COUNTY. 191

Glenham and *Franklindale*, in the same town, are flourishing manufacturing villages.

Pleasant Valley, on Wappinger's creek, in the town of the same name, is a manufacturing village of some importance. It is principally engaged in the manufacture of cotton goods. Population 700.

Hyde Park is a beautiful village, situated on the Hudson, and has some commerce and manufactures. Population 700.

Rhinebeck, in the town of the same name, is a large and thriving village, with several manufactories. The Rhinebeck academy is a highly flourishing institution. Population 1300.

X. ORANGE COUNTY.

Square Miles, 760.   Population, 52,227.
Organized, 1683.   Valuation, 1845, $11,319,430.

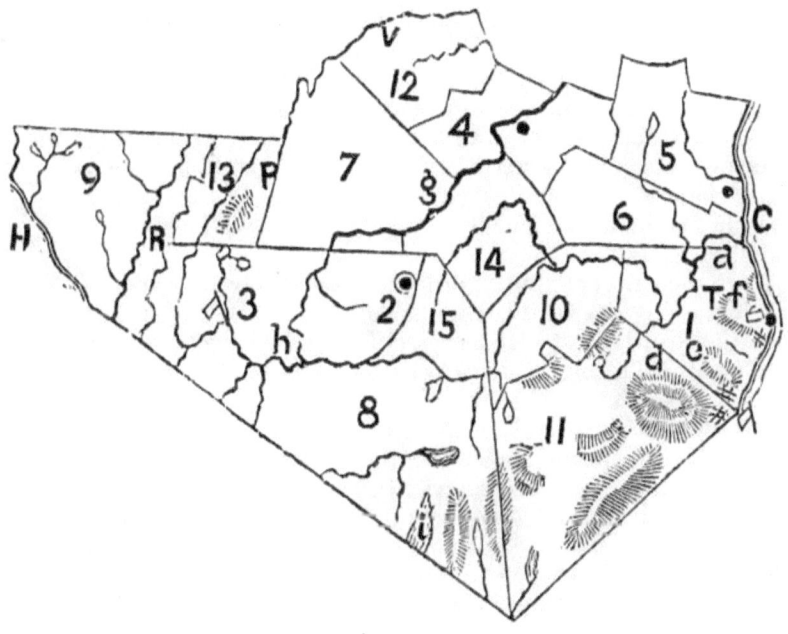

TOWNS.

1. Cornwall, 1788.
2. Goshen, 1788.
3. Minisink, 1788.
4. Montgomery, 1788.
5. Newburgh, 1788.
6. New Windsor, 1788.
7. Wallkill, 1788.
8. Warwick, 1788.

9. Deer Park, 1798. 13. Mount Hope, 1825.
10. Blooming Grove, 1799. 14. Hamptonburgh, 1830.
11. Monroe, 1799. 15. Chester, 1845.
12. Crawford, 1823.

Mountains, &c. T. Matteawan. P. Shawangunk. d. Bare. e. Crow's Nest. f. Butter Hill.

Rivers, &c. C. Hudson. H. Delaware. R. Nevisink. V. Shawangunk. g. Wallkill. a. Murderer's Creek.

Lakes, &c. i. Long Pond. h. Drowned Lands.

Forts. West Point. Clinton. Montgomery.

Battle Fields. Minisink. Montgomery and Clinton.

Colleges. West Point Military Academy.

Villages. NEWBURGH. GOSHEN. West Point. Montgomery.

BOUNDARIES. North by Sullivan and Ulster counties; East by Hudson river and Rockland county; South by Rockland county and the state of New Jersey; and west by Sullivan county and the Delaware river.

SURFACE. Mountains, hills and plains diversify the surface of this county. The Matteawan mountains, or Highlands, cross its southeastern border diagonally; the Shawangunk range stretches along its western boundary; and, parallel to them, run a chain of low hills called Comfort hills. Between these and the Highlands extends a level valley, with occasional marshes.

Upon the banks of the Hudson, in this county, are some of the highest points of the Highlands. Bare mountain is 1350 feet, the Crow's Nest 1418 feet, and Butter Hill 1529 feet above tide water. The eastern face of the latter is an almost perpendicular precipice.

RIVERS. Beside the Hudson, which forms a portion of its eastern boundary, the principal streams are the Wallkill (or Waalkill), the Shawangunk and Nevisink rivers, and Murderer's creek. The Wallkill, for about twenty miles of its course, flows through a marsh, known as the "Drowned lands." The Delaware river just touches a portion of the western boundary.

PONDS. In the south part of the county are several ponds of considerable size. Long pond, on the New Jersey line, is the largest, and is some nine miles in length.

RAILROADS AND CANALS. The New York and Erie railroad passes through the county, affording a daily communication with New York city, while the Delaware and Hudson canal crosses its western border.

CLIMATE. The climate of the county is mild and agreeable. In the vicinity of the Drowned lands, fevers prevail in autumn;

but the county generally is remarkably healthy. The spring opens about two weeks earlier than in the counties west of it.

GEOLOGY AND MINERALS. The southeastern portion of the county, including the Highlands, is of primitive formation, and contains granite, sienite, hornblende, and primitive limestone. The remainder belongs to the transition system, being chiefly composed of slate, limestone and graywacke, of which the first and last are mostly found on the hills, and the second underlying the valleys. The Shawangunk mountains are composed mostly of graywacke, in which the millstone grit prevails.

It abounds in minerals of rarity and value. In the towns of Monroe and Canterbury, are vast beds of magnetic iron ore. Hematitic iron ore is also abundant and of excellent quality.

Among the minerals of interest may be enumerated spinel (a species of ruby) of extraordinary beauty; fine Labradorite, a new mineral; Ilmenite, a rare and interesting mineral, found more abundantly here than in any other known locality; zircon, apatite, fibrous epidote, tourmaline, serpentine, Clintonite, Boltonite, scapolite, idiocrase, Bucholzite, white iron pyrites, sphene, pyroxene, hair brown hornblende, and many others of less importance. Their principal localities are in the towns of Monroe, Cornwall, Warwick and Deer Park. Excellent peat is found in the Drowned Lands and other low lands.

Bones of the Mastodon have been discovered in several places in this county. An entire skeleton of this gigantic animal, by far the most perfect hitherto discovered, was disinterred in Coldenham, in 1845. The locality had evidently once been a marsh, and the animal, in attempting to cross it, had sunk in the mud, and was unable to extricate himself. His length is stated at thirty-three feet; length of tusks ten feet; length of skull three feet ten inches; weight of head and tusks 692 pounds; weight of all the bones 2002. The contents of the stomach were found within the skeleton, consisting of crushed twigs, &c.

This skeleton is now in the museum of the Harvard University. The skeleton of the Mastodon, in Peale's museum, Philadelphia, was taken from the town of Montgomery, in this county, and bones of others have been discovered in Chester and other towns.

SOIL AND VEGETABLE PRODUCTIONS. The soil is chiefly clay and gravelly loam, and is for the most part fertile, but better adapted to grazing than to the culture of grain, except the alluvial lands in the southern part. The vast marsh of the Drowned lands, when drained, furnishes a soil of great depth and fertility, and is annually covered with the most luxuriant vegetation.

The timber of the county is principally oak, chestnut, hickory, maple, black-walnut, elm, &c. The county produces apples and other fruit in perfection, and a great variety of the natural grasses. Owing to the rapid and precipitous course of the Wallkill, before entering the Drowned Lands, and its sluggish progress through them, many plants, belonging to a more southern climate, are found here.*

PURSUITS. *Agriculture* mainly engages the attention of the inhabitants. Orange county stands in the first rank among the dairy counties of the state. More than 4,100,000 pounds of but-

* The first treatise on the Botany of New York, and we believe the first botanical work by an American author, was the Plantæ Coldenhamiæ, by Governor Colden, of Coldenham, near Newburgh. It was published at Upsal, in Sweden, in 1744.

ter were made in 1845, and about seven and a half millions of quarts of milk sent to New York city, the same year. Large quantities of wool and pork are produced. Considerable attention is also paid to the raising of corn, oats, rye and buckwheat.

Horticulture, and especially market gardening, is receiving increased attention.

Manufactures also furnish employment to a considerable number of the citizens of the county. The principal articles are cotton and woollen goods, flour, distilled and malt liquors, leather, iron, oil cloth and paper. In 1845, these amounted to nearly $2,000,000 in value.

Newburgh has considerable *commerce* with New York. Much of the produce of the county is also transported to that city by means of the Delaware and Hudson canal and the Erie railroad.

Mines. The iron mines in the towns of Monroe and Cornwall, are scarcely surpassed in value by any others in the state. Iron mines were worked in the county as early as 1751.

STAPLE PRODUCTIONS. Butter, milk, pork, wool, corn and oats.

SCHOOLS. There are in the county 180 district school-houses. The average length of the schools, in 1846, was nine months. 11,847 children received instruction, at a cost, for tuition, of $26,672. There were in the district libraries 27,629 volumes.

In addition to these, there were in the county seventy-two private schools, with 1335 scholars, eight academies, and one female seminary, with 528 pupils, and one military academy, with about 250 cadets.

RELIGIOUS DENOMINATIONS. Presbyterians, Methodists, Dutch Reformed, Baptists, Friends, Episcopalians, Roman Catholics and Congregationalists. There are ninety churches and ninety-five clergymen of all denominations.

HISTORY. It seems to be uncertain at what date the first settlements were made in this county; but from the early date of the settlement at Esopus, (Kingston), in the adjacent county of Ulster, and the advantages afforded by the soil and surface of Orange, both to the agriculturalist and the trapper, it may be reasonably concluded, that the Dutch emigrants located themselves in the county, at a very early period.

In 1659, the mineral wealth of the county had been so far explored that mines of copper were extensively wrought, probably either in Deerpark or Minisink. The ore was exported to Holland, and with it a large quantity of iron pyrites, which the inhabitants of the county mistook for gold.

In 1669 a bloody battle was fought, in the town of Minisink, between the whites and Indians.

The county was organized in 1683, and then included Rockland. A delegate from the county sat in the colonial house of assembly, organized for the first time that year.

In 1689 the citizens embraced the cause of Leisler, and sent deputies to a convention called by him. Under the colonial government the delegates from Orange county were remarkable for their firm adherence to the principles of liberty. At the commencement of the revolution, a majority of the people embarked with zeal in the cause of their country.

Early in the revolution, Forts Clinton and Montgomery were erected, by the Americans, in the southeast part of this county. They were separated from each other by a small stream, the boundary line between two towns; Fort Clinton being in Monroe, and Fort Montgomery in Cornwall.

They were intended to prevent the British from ascending the river, and in addition to other obstructions in the river, an iron chain was extended from Fort Montgomery to a point on the opposite side, in the county of Putnam. These fortifications were under the command of Gen. Israel Putnam.

In October, 1777, Sir Henry Clinton, being determined to afford succor to General Burgoyne, ascended the river with a force of more than 3000 troops, attacked and carried by storm both these forts, after a brave and prolonged resistance on the part of the garrison (which consisted of only 600 men), and, breaking the chain, proceeded up the river. The British lost in this attack about 250 men, and the garrisons nearly the same number.

The ensuing year the fort and batteries at West point, (a much more eligible position) were erected,* and a larger chain stretched across the Hudson, from that fortress to Constitution Island, under the direction of Captain Machin.

The construction of the fort and batteries was entrusted, it is said, to French engineers, belonging to the army of Count Rochambeau. The work was superintended by Kosciusko, a Polish nobleman, of thorough military education, whose love of liberty had led him to espouse the cause of our country.

After the erection of this fortress, and the extension of the new chain across the river, the British never attempted to pass it. The possession of so important a post, was to them, however, an object of great solicitude; and, in 1780, they had well nigh accomplished it. The command of it had been assigned to

---

* The site of the fort at West Point was selected by General Putnam, and the first ground broken for the fortification in January, 1778, by General Parsons, when the snow lay on the earth two feet deep. It was mainly by the strenuous exertions and great personal popularity of Gov. George Clinton, that the materials for its construction were obtained.

General Arnold, in the autumn of 1779, and it was here that his infamous treason was consummated. Suitable measures were taken, after the discovery of his treachery, to secure it.

In July, 1779, a party of Indians and tories, under Brant, made an attack on the village of Minisink, burning ten houses and several other buildings, and killing and capturing a number of the inhabitants. Those who were able to escape fled to Goshen; where the militia of that and the adjacent towns soon collected, to pursue the enemy, and recapture the prisoners and spoils.

Aware of the subtle character of his foe, Colonel Tusten, their commander, opposed the pursuit, until a larger force should be collected; but his prudent foresight was regarded as cowardice, and it was decided to proceed immediately. The wary Brant had expected pursuit; and, when he ascertained that the militia were approaching, he stationed a part of his troops in ambuscade in such a position, as to enable him to surround them.

Thus hemmed in by a superior force, this unfortunate band fought bravely, but in vain; death met them on every side; and of about 180 men, in the full vigor of life, who started upon that expedition, but thirty escaped from the tomahawks of the enemy. Most of these were from the principal families of the county. Goshen, in particular, suffered severely; forty-four of her best citizens being slain. A monument was erected to their memory on the anniversary of the battle, July 22, 1822.

The American army, never well supplied, either with food or clothing, during the revolution, were, at its close, in a state of great destitution. They were paid in a depreciated and almost worthless currency, and the apathy of congress, in delaying to make suitable provisions to reward their toils and sacrifices, disposed them to revolt.

To prevent so dangerous an event, and at the same time to secure justice for his suffering troops, Washington remained with them in winter quarters at Newburgh, during the winter of 1782-3. The house which he occupied, as his head quarters, is yet standing, and is now the residence of the Hasbrouck family.

The officers of the army, early in the winter, addressed a memorial to congress, stating their necessities, and asking for just compensation. Early in March, 1783, a communication was received from their committee, informing them that their requests had not been granted.

On the 10th of March, an anonymous notice was circulated, calling a meeting of the officers on the following day, "to see what measures should be adopted to obtain that redress of grievances which they seem to have solicited in vain."

The same day an anonymous paper, written with extraordinary ability, and admirably calculated to excite the passions and rouse the indignation of the officers, against the continental congress, was put in circulation.

The writer,—professing to be himself a sharer in their sufferings, depicted, in strong terms, their deplorable condition, and the shameful negligence of congress; and exhorted them " to suspect the man who would advise to more moderation and longer forbearance," to threaten the congress in the event of peace, with civil war—and, if war continued, with an abandonment of their country to its fate.

This eloquent, but dangerous paper (written, as was subsequently ascertained, by Major John Armstrong, afterward secretary of war, at the instigation of General Gates,) had well nigh produced the most serious consequences. It required all Washington's prudence and firmness to check the rising spirit of rebellion incited by it.

To prevent the ill effects of a meeting, assembling under the influence of so much excitement, he issued a general order, disapproving of the meeting on the 11th, and calling one on the 15th of March.

The anonymous writer seized on this incident, to address another letter to the officers,* insinuating that the commander-in-chief sympathized in their views, and was only restrained, by motives of delicacy, from openly expressing that sympathy.

This opinion Washington labored privately to remove, by conversation with the officers, and, at the meeting on the 15th, General Gates being in the chair, he openly canvassed the propositions contained in the anonymous address, showed their folly and wickedness, and so far changed the current of popular opinion, that the officers voted unanimously, that "they viewed with abhorrence, and would reject with disdain, the *infamous* propositions" contained in that address. Thus narrowly did the country escape the horrible calamity of anarchy and civil war.

VILLAGES. NEWBURGH, the larger of the two shire villages of the county, was first settled by German emigrants, in 1701, and named by them from Newburgh, in Germany. The bank of the Hudson, on which it is situated, is quite steep, rising 300 feet in a short distance. When seen from the river, the village presents a fine appearance.

It has many neat public and private buildings, and considerable trade; although a portion of that, which formerly centred here, now reaches New York by the New York and Erie railroad, and the Delaware and Hudson canal. Two or three

---

* This and the preceding address are usually termed the " Newburgh letters."

steamboats, and several sloops and schooners, ply regularly between the village and New York. It has a flourishing academy, a high school, and two female seminaries.

In the village and town, are eighteen or twenty manufactories. The steam cotton mill, at the village, is said, in extent and perfection, to equal any single cotton mill in the United States. Population about 6000.

GOSHEN, the other half-shire village, is justly celebrated for the product of its dairies. The New York and Erie railroad passes through it. The Farmer's Hall academy is a flourishing chartered institution, and has a female seminary connected with it. Population about 1000.

Middletown, in the town of Wallkill, is a new and flourishing village, on the line of the railroad. It has a large iron foundry. Population about 1400.

West Point, in the town of Cornwall, is worthy of notice, not only for its important fortress, to which we have already adverted, but as the seat of the United States Military Academy, established here, in March, 1802. The object of this institution, is to prepare young men for officers in the army.

The course of instruction is very thorough, the discipline rigid, and the examinations severe. The months of July and August, in each year, are devoted solely to military exercises; for which purpose, the cadets leave their barracks, and encamp in tents on the plain, under the regular police and discipline of an army, in time of war.

The course of study comprises, the Latin and French languages, an extended course of mathematics, civil engineering, and the art of fortification. The term of study is four years; and so rigorous are the examinations and discipline, that only about one third of those who enter, complete the course of study, and graduate. The number of instructors is thirty-four; of cadets, about 250. They are entirely supported by the United States government.

Three monuments have been erected here; one to the memory of the Polish hero Kosciusko, whose garden is still shown on the premises; another to Colonel Wood, an early graduate of the institution, who fell at the sortie of Fort Erie, in 1814; and a third, to the deceased officers and cadets of the academy. Population of the village, about 900.

Canterbury, in the town of Cornwall, and *Montgomery*, in the town of the same name, are thriving villages, and are engaged, to some extent, in manufactures.

Walden, in Montgomery, is a manufacturing village. *Chester*, in the town of the same name, is a noted mart for the sale of live stock. Here, too, is an academy of some reputation.

XI. MONTGOMERY COUNTY.

Square Miles, 356.
Organized, 1772.

Population, 29,643.
Valuation, 1845, $3,696,270.

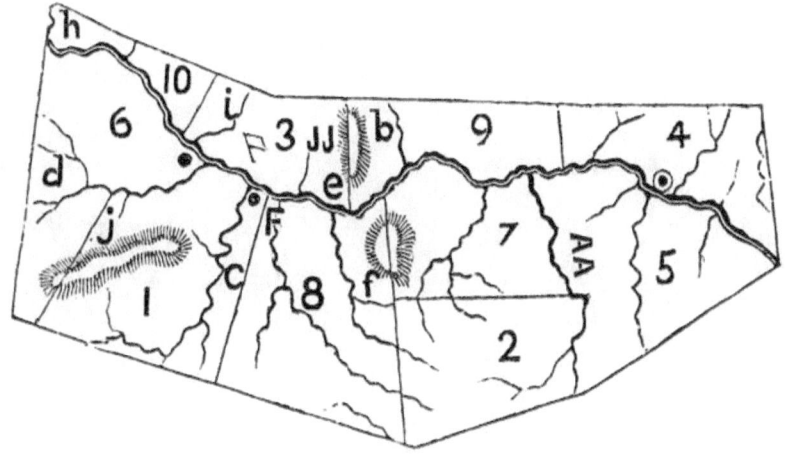

TOWNS.

1. Canajoharie, 1788.
2. Charleston, 1788.
3. Palatine, 1788.
4. Amsterdam, 1793.
5. Florida, 1793.
6. Minden, 1798.
7. Glen, 1823.
8. Root, 1823.
9. Mohawk, 1837.
10. St. Johnsville, 1837.

Mountains. JJ. Au Sable Range. e. Anthony's Nose. f. Flint Hill. j. Otsquaga Hills.

Rivers and Creeks. F. Mohawk River. AA. Schoharie Creek. b. Cayaduta. c. Bowman's or Canajoharie. d. Otsquaga. h. East Canada. i. Garoga.

Battle Field. Stone Arabia.

Villages. FONDA. Amsterdam. Canajoharie. Fort Plain.

BOUNDARIES. North by Fulton; East by Saratoga and Schenectady; South by Schenectady, Schoharie and Otsego; and West by Herkimer, counties.

SURFACE. Hilly and somewhat mountainous. The valley of the Mohawk forms the central portion of the county, while on the north and south, the hills attain a considerable elevation. The Au Sable range enters the county from the north, and forms, on the banks of the Mohawk, the peak known as Anthony's Nose. Crossing the river, this range terminates in the town of Root.

Flint hill occupies the southeastern part, bordering on Schenectady county. In the southwest are the Otsquaga hills. The valleys of the Mohawk, and some of its tributaries, spread out in fertile alluvial plains or flats.

RIVERS. The county is well watered. The Mohawk river, East Canada, Schoharie, Bowman's, Otsquaga, Garoga and Caya luta creeks, are the principal streams.

CANALS AND RAILROADS. The Erie canal runs along the south side of the Mohawk, and the Utica and Schenectady railroad upon the north.

The CLIMATE resembles that of the valley of the Mohawk generally. It is mild and healthful.

GEOLOGY AND MINERALS. The surface rocks of this county all belong to the transition formation. In the southern part, the Lorraine shales, and Hudson river group, (the Taconic system of Prof. Emmons,) are predominant. Along the Mohawk, the Utica slate prevails, and is accompanied by a narrow tract of the Trenton limestone. North of this, the Onondaga salt rocks are seen on the surface.

Pearl spar, calc spar, sulphate of barytes, calcareous tufa, brown spar, quartz crystals, agate, chalcedony, garnet, sulphurets of zinc and lead, and oxide of titanium, are the principal minerals. As yet, none of these have been obtained in sufficient quantities to be of any practical value. In the town of Root, is a large cavern, called Mitchell's cave, containing fourteen apartments, some of them 500 feet below the surface, and profusely adorned with stalactites and stalagmites.

SOIL AND VEGETABLE PRODUCTIONS. The soil is generally productive, consisting of a gravelly or clayey loam, frequently mingled with disintegrated lime or slate. Grass and grains of all descriptions flourish. The forests are composed chiefly of oak, beech, ash, maple, and hemlock.

PURSUITS. *Agriculture* is the leading pursuit of the inhabitants. Considerable grain is raised, and much attention paid to the products of the dairy.

The *manufactures* of the county are limited, consisting mainly of flour, distilled liquors, leather, and woollen goods.

The *commerce* of the county is confined to the transportation of its produce upon the Erie canal, and the Utica and Schenectady railroad.

STAPLE PRODUCTIONS. Oats, corn, barley, potatoes, butter, cheese and wool.

SCHOOLS. In 1846, there were in the county 118 public schools, with 8604 scholars. The annual term of instruction in these schools averaged nine months, and the amount expended for tuition was $15,369. The district libraries contained 18,043 volumes.

There were also in the county, eleven select schools, with 135 pupils; three academies, and one female seminary, with 214 students.

RELIGIOUS DENOMINATIONS. Dutch Reformed, Methodists, Presbyterians, Baptists, Universalists, Episcopalians, Unitarians, and Friends. There are in the county forty-three churches, and forty-six clergymen of all denominations.

HISTORY. The English Episcopalians commenced missions among the Mohawks in this county as early as 1702. The first settlements were made in 1713, or about that time, by German emigrants, a portion of the same band who settled Schoharie county, and by other persons from Albany and Schenectady counties.

It had been the home of the Mohawks, whose three castles were all, it is believed, within the limits of this county. In January, 1693, the French, whose hatred to the Iroquois was inveterate, made a descent upon these castles, and captured them all.

The Indians at Schenectady sent to Albany for assistance to pursue the enemy. Colonel Peter Schuyler, the friend of the Indians, with a body of militia, started for the pursuit, overtook the French, and had a severe skirmish with them. The French lost fifty-nine in killed and wounded. It is related that the Indians ate the bodies of the Frenchmen whom they killed.

Fort Hunter, a somewhat important military post in early times, was erected in 1710, at the junction of the Mohawk and Schoharie rivers, in the town of Florida, by Capt. John Scott. A chapel was erected near the fort which was endowed by Queen Anne, and hence called Queen Anne's chapel. A stone parsonage was also erected near it, to which was attached a glebe of 300 acres, the gift of the Indians.

The fort having become dilapidated at the time of the Revolution, the chapel was fortified, and called Fort Hunter. It was taken down about the year 1820, to make room for the Erie canal.

The first settlement in the town of Amsterdam was made in 1716, by the widow and children of Philip Groat of Rotterdam, who was drowned in the Mohawk, near Schenectady, on his way thither.

In 1722, colonies had been extended along the Mohawk as far as the German Flats, in the county of Herkimer; but few of the settlers, however, had located far from the river.

The subsequent growth and prosperity of the present county of Montgomery, are due, in a great measure, to the enterprise of Sir William Johnson.*

---

* This extraordinary man was born in Ireland, in 1714, of highly respectable parentage. His uncle, Admiral Warren, had acquired a title to a tract of some 15,000 acres, in the present town of Florida, and sent young Johnson over to act as his agent for the disposal of it, about the year 1735.

Soon after arriving in the colony, he was appointed by the British Government,

During the Revolution, this county, (then called Tryon county, and embracing all that part of the state, lying east of a meridian, drawn through the centre of Schoharie county,) suffered severely from the repeated incursions of the tories and Indians, led by Sir John Johnson, the bloodthirsty Walter Butler, and the Mohawk chieftain Brant.

Scarcely a settlement, on either side of the Mohawk, escaped partial or entire destruction; and few families, who had espoused the cause of their country, but were called to mourn over friends and relatives, inhumanly butchered by these savage warriors. Neither age nor sex were spared; neither beauty, wealth, accomplishments, nor amiability of character, served to shield the unfortunate settlers from the tomahawk and the scalping knife.

The towns of Fort Plain, Canajoharie, Palatine, Glen, and Root suffered most severely; many of those who escaped death, being carried into a long and distressing captivity.

At Stone Arabia, a severe and bloody conflict took place in October, 1780, between Sir John Johnson, and the garrison of Fort Paris, (a stockade fort in Stone Arabia.) General Robert Van Rensselaer, of Claverack, (Columbia county,) was in the rear of the enemy, with a force of nearly 1000 men, and ordered Colonel Brown, the commander of the fort, to attack them in front, while he pressed upon their rear.

---

agent for the Iroquois, or Six Nations. Having acquired their language, and adopted to a considerable extent their dress and habits, he soon obtained great influence over them, and was chosen one of their head sachems. This power he used in such a way as to secure their attachment to the British Government, and at the same time to advance his own personal interests.

During the French wars, he was active as an officer, and in 1757, the troops under his command, at Lake George, having repulsed and defeated the French force under Baron Dieskau, he was knighted by the King, and received a donation of £5000 sterling.

In 1759, General Prideaux being killed at the siege of Fort Niagara, Sir William, who was second in command, assumed the direction of the forces, and carried the fortress. In 1760, he led a body of 1000 Indians against Montreal, and was active in an eminent station at the surrender of Canada.

He was twice married. By his first wife, (a German woman,) he had one son and two daughters. His son succeeded to his title as Sir John Johnson. His daughters were married to Colonel Guy Johnson, (a distant relative of the baronet,) and to Colonel Daniel Claus. His second wife was Molly Brant, sister of the celebrated Mohawk chieftain, by whom he had several children.

His first residence was in the town of Amsterdam, about three miles west of the village. It is a massive stone edifice, and is to this day called Fort Johnson. About ten years before his death, he erected a building, which he named Johnson Hall, within the limits of Fulton county, where he resided the remainder of his life.

Fort Johnson, after this period, was occupied by his son, Sir John Johnson. He also erected houses for his sons-in-law, Colonel Guy Johnson and Colonel Claus, in the town of Amsterdam.

Sir William Johnson died very suddenly, in July, 1774, not without suspicion of suicide.

His son and successor, as well as his sons-in-law, and indeed his whole family, embraced the side of the British, in the Revolution. Sir John was the scourge of the Mohawk and Schoharie valleys, during that contest. After the Revolution, their estates were confiscated.

Sir John's force did not amount to more than 500 men, while that of Colonel Brown was about 200, and had General Van Rensselaer fulfilled his part of the duty, the whole British force might have been captured; but through his negligence and cowardice, if not treachery, the brave troops of Colonel Brown were suffered to contend, single handed, with the enemy, till they were nearly all slaughtered, while General Van Rensselaer's troops were within hearing of the action, but were not suffered by him, to afford aid to their suffering brethren, or to pursue the enemy, on their retreat, when, as was afterwards acknowledged by them, they would have surrendered, had they had the opportunity.

A relationship by marriage, which existed between General Van Rensselaer and Sir John Johnson, is supposed to have been the cause of this disgraceful conduct on the part of the former.

Montgomery county received its present name, (in honor of the brave hero of Quebec,) in 1784, soon after which, a large portion of its territory was formed into other counties, and this process of curtailment has continued, till from being the largest, it has become one of the smallest counties in the state.

VILLAGES. FONDA, the county seat, is a small but pleasant village, in the town of Mohawk. It has some manufactures. Population 400.

Amsterdam was incorporated in 1830. It is situated in the town of the same name, on the north bank of the Mohawk, and connected with the little village of Port Jackson, on the Erie canal, by a fine and substantial bridge. It has a flourishing academy, and female seminary, and several manufacturing establishments. Population 1700.

Canajoharie is a thriving village, in the town of the same name, located on the south bank of the Mohawk. It was incorporated in 1829, and has a well conducted academy. Here is an extensive quarry, from whence is obtained an excellent quality of limestone, much used in the construction of locks on the Erie Canal. The village is the proposed terminus of the Catskill and Canajoharie railroad, which is partly finished. Population 1300.

Fort Plain, in the town of Minden, was incorporated in 1834, and is a place of considerable business. Here too, are extensive limestone quarries. Population 1400.

Caughnawaga, in the town of Mohawk, is principally worthy of notice for its stone church, now converted into an academy. This venerable building was erected in 1763, by voluntary contribution.

XII. WASHINGTON COUNTY.

Square miles, 807.
Organized, 1772.
Population, 40,554.
Valuation, 1845, $5,991,847.

TOWNS.

1. Argyle, 1788.
2. Cambridge, 1788.
3. Easton, 1788.
4. Fort Ann, 1788.
5. Granville, 1788.
6. Hampton, 1788.
7. Hebron, 1788.
8. Kingsbury, 1788.
9. Salem, 1788.
10. Whitehall, 1788.
11. Hartford, 1788.
12. Greenwich, 1803.
13. Putnam, 1806.
14. White Creek, 1815.
15. Jackson, 1815.
16. Fort Edward, 1818.
17. Dresden, 1822.

Mountains. U. Taghkanic range. Y. Peterborough range, l. French, or Luzerne mountains.

Rivers, &c. C. Hudson river. a. Wood creek. b. Pawlet river. c. Poultney, or Fair Haven river. d. Batten kill. f. Black creek. g. White creek. k. Hoosick river. i. Moses kill.

Falls. Baker's falls. Great falls.

Lakes. W. Lake Champlain. X. Lake George. j. Big Pond.

Forts. Fort Edward. Fort Ann.

Battle Fields. Kingsbury. Fort Ann. Whitehall.

Villages. SALEM, SANDY HILL, Fort Edward, Whitehall, Union village, White Creek.

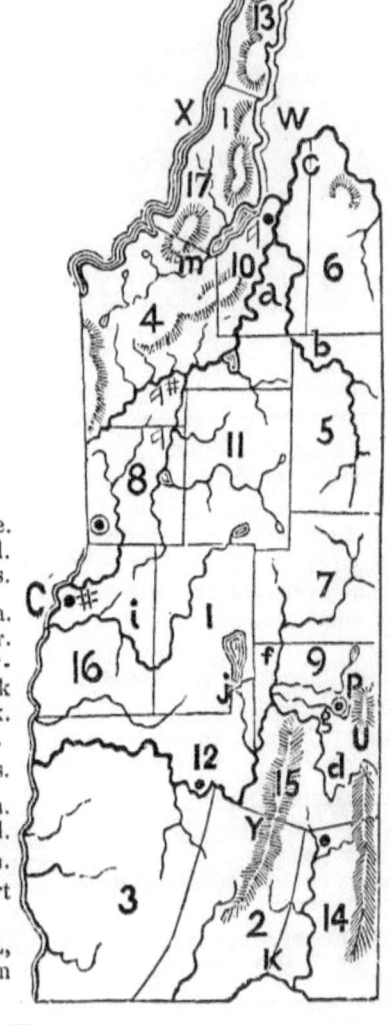

BOUNDARIES. North by Essex county and the state of Vermont; East by Vermont; South by Rensselaer county; West by Saratoga and Warren counties, and Lake George.

SURFACE. Three distinct ranges of mountains are found in

WASHINGTON COUNTY. 205

this county; viz. the Taghkanic, extending along its eastern boundary, with an average width of about five miles; the Peterborough, with a variable height, running from north to south, through the centre of the county, broken through by the Hoosick, Pawlet, and Poultney rivers, and the Batten kill, and maintaining a breadth of from six to eight miles; spurs of this ridge extend toward the river in Greenwich and Easton; and lastly, the Palmertown range, here taking the name of French, or Luzerne mountains, and occupying the narrow peninsula which separates Lake George from Lake Champlain.

These ranges, interspersed with occasional valleys, render the face of the county diversified and picturesque.

RIVERS, &c. The county is abundantly watered. Beside the Hudson, the principal streams are, the Hoosick, Pawlet, and Poultney, or Fair Haven rivers, Batten kill, Wood creek, Moses kill, White and Owl creeks.

FALLS. Baker's falls, on the Hudson, have an almost perpendicular descent of fifty feet, at the village of Sandy Hill. Great falls, on the Batten kill, have a total descent of sixty feet, in the towns of Easton and Greenwich.

LAKES. Lakes George and Champlain form portions of the boundary of this county. Long Lake, in Argyle, is three or four miles in length.

CANALS. The Champlain canal crosses the Hudson at Greenwich, and connects with Lake Champlain at Whitehall, furnishing 32 miles of navigation in this county.

CLIMATE. Cold, but healthful. The spring opens some two weeks later than in Orange, Dutchess, and the lower counties on the Hudson.

GEOLOGY AND MINERALS. The northern part of the county is primitive, and the underlying rock chiefly granite. On the shores of the lakes there is an admixture, and apparent confusion of all the formations, probably the result of some convulsion of nature. In the southern part of the county, the rocks are principally transition, intermixed with occasional patches of primitive. Limestone, graywacke, and slate, alternate upon the surface in this section.

Magnetic and hematitic iron ore, marl, lime, marble, water lime, graphite, lamellar pyroxene, massive feldspar, and epidote, are the principal minerals of the county.

SOIL AND VEGETABLE PRODUCTIONS. The soil is generally good, and produces fine crops of wheat, but is better adapted to grazing than the culture of grain. The principal timber is oak, hickory, chestnut, maple, butternut, pine, and hemlock.

PURSUITS. The people are, for the most part, engaged in *agricultural* pursuits. Oats, corn, flax, and potatoes are largely raised, and considerable quantities of wheat, rye, and barley. Butter, cheese, wool, and pork are produced in great abundance. In the quantity of wool grown, it was, in 1845, the second county in the state.

Manufactures are increasing in importance. Flour, lumber, cotton and woollen goods, leather, and iron, are the principal articles manufactured.

Commerce. The Champlain and Hudson canal affords a convenient mode of transportation to the produce of the county, which is well improved. The tolls received on produce passing through this county in 1845, were about $70,000.

STAPLE PRODUCTIONS. The staples of the county are potatoes, oats, corn, flax, butter, cheese, wool, and pork.

SCHOOLS. The county contained, in 1846, 246 district schoolhouses, in which were taught 13,414 children, at an expense of $16,950 for tuition. The schools were maintained, on an average, eight months each. Number of volumes in the district libraries, 27,656.

It had also twenty-two select schools, with 327 scholars, and five academies, with 345 pupils.

RELIGIOUS DENOMINATIONS. Presbyterians, Methodists, Baptists, Congregationalists, Episcopalians, Roman Catholics, and Universalists. Churches, eighty-eight. Clergymen, seventy-two.

HISTORY. The first settlement in the county was made at Argyle, in 1742, by eighty-three families of Highlanders, who emigrated from Scotland, under the direction of Capt. Laughlin Campbell, who had obtained a grant of 30,000 acres from Governor Clarke. These emigrants were intended to serve as defenders of the frontier, from incursions of the French and Indians.

As they were scantily provided with food and clothing, application was made to the colonial legislature for aid, till they should be able to sustain themselves. This the house of assembly refused to grant, on the ground, it is said, that they had discovered that the Governor and Surveyor General insisted upon their fees and a share of the lands.

Captain Campbell sought redress, but in vain, and with the remnant of his fortune, purchased a small farm in the province. His unfortunate followers were rescued from starvation, by enlisting in an expedition against Carthagena.

In 1755, Fort Edward was erected, by Generals Lyman and Johnson, and in 1756, Fort Ann.

Salem was settled the same year, by two companies of emigrants, one from Scotland and Ireland, the other from New

England. In 1764, Alexander Turner and others, who had received a grant in 1761, settled in the town of Salem. Not far from the same period, settlements were made in Kingsbury.

In 1758, an obstinate and bloody battle occurred, between a body of 500 American troops, under the command of Major (afterwards General,) Putnam and Major Rogers, and a party of French and Indians, under the command of a French officer, by the name of Molaire. The battle ground was two miles north of the village of Kingsbury.

The French commander had stationed a part of his troops in ambuscade for the Americans, and hoped to surprise them; but Putnam, with the coolness which always characterized him, maintained his position, and a fearful conflict ensued. Putnam was taken captive by the Indians, but the bravery of the American troops prevailed, and they finally routed the enemy, who left ninety dead behind them. The Indians bore off Putnam as a prisoner, to Canada, inflicting on him the most cruel tortures; and but for the interposition of the French commander, would have burned him at the stake.

In May, 1775, Whitehall, then called Skenesborough, from its first settler, Major Skene, was seized by a detachment of volunteers from Connecticut. In 1777, the American force stationed there, not being sufficient to protect it against Burgoyne, the fort, stores, and a large number of batteaux loaded with provisions, were burned by the Americans, to prevent their falling into his hands.

In July, 1777, a severe skirmish took place at Fort Ann, between the 8th British regiment and a body of 400 or 500 invalid American troops, under the command of Colonel Long. The British suffered severely, and would have been taken or destroyed but for the want of ammunition on the part of the Americans.

On the 27th of July, 1777, Miss Jane McCrea was murdered by the Indians near Fort Edward.*

---

* The following version of this tragical affair is compiled from Neilson's "Burgoyne's Campaign," and is professedly derived from the most authentic sources. It will be seen that it differs materially from the accounts heretofore published.

Miss McCrea was the daughter of a New Jersey clergyman, and had come, some years before, to reside with her brother on the west bank of the Hudson, five or six miles below Fort Edward. David Jones, her suitor, resided about five miles above, on the same side of the river. He had embraced the royal cause, and was in the army of Burgoyne. On the 26th of July, 1777, Miss McCrea came from her brother's to the house of Peter Freel, who lived close under the walls of Fort Edward, on a visit. She remained there over night, and the next morning went to the house of Mrs. McNeil, afterwards Mrs. Campbell, a cousin of General Frazer, who was at that time in Burgoyne's army. This house was at a distance of about eighty rods from the fort. While at the house of Mrs. McNeil, the commander of the fort sent out a party of fifty men, to reconnoitre the position of the enemy. When about a mile from the fort, this party fell into an ambuscade of Indians, about

VILLAGES. SANDY HILL, in the town of Kingsbury, is a half hire village of this county. It was incorporated in 1810. The village is well laid out, the streets enclosing a triangular area in the centre of the village, which was once the scene of Indian barbarities. The Hudson furnishes an immense water power which is but partially improved. Population 1200.

SALEM, the other half shire village, was incorporated in 1803. It is situated in the midst of a fertile agricultural region, and is celebrated as a mart for wool. The Washington Academy is an old institution, and has sent out a considerable number of eminent scholars. Population 800.

Whi ehall, in the town of the same name, is eligibly situated at the foot of Lake Champlain, of which it is one of the principal ports. It is connected with the Hudson river by means of the Champlain canal, as well as by several lines of stages running to Troy, Albany, and Saratoga; and with Montreal by steamers which ply daily upon the lake. Thus favorably situated for commerce, its growth has been rapid and healthful. Population about 25

Union Village, situated in the towns of Greenwich and Easton, is a thriving and pleasant manufacturing village, with a flourishing academy, and a number of large manufactories. Population 1400.

North White Creek is a pleasant village, in the town of White Creek, in the midst of an agricultural region. It is a great mart for wool. Population 750.

Cambridge, in the town of the same name, is the seat of Washington Academy, a flourishing and highly popular institution.

Fort Edward and *Fort Ann* are small villages, worthy of notice principally on account of their historic interest.

---

200 in number, and fled towards the fort. The Indians pursued and killed eighteen of their number. As they passed the house of Mrs. McNeil, six of the Indians rushed in and seized Mrs. McNeil and Miss McCrea, and hurried with them to the main body of the Indians. Both of the ladies were placed upon horses, which they had probably stolen from the vicinity.

As they ascended a hill about a mile from the fort, Miss McCrea was shot by one of the Indians, and fell from her horse. The savage who shot her, scalped her, and having secured the most valuable articles of her clothing, rolled her body down the declivity of the hill. On the ensuing day her body, and that of a young American officer who had also been killed by the Indians, were found and buried near a small creek about three miles from Fort Edward, by the Americans from the fort. Mrs. McNeil was not killed, but plundered of most of her clothing, and brought to the British camp. Jones, Miss McCrea's suitor, had never sent for her, nor is it certain that he knew that she was in the vicinity of the fort. He is reported to have been killed at the battle of Bemis' Heights, on the 19th of September following.

XIII. COLUMBIA COUNTY.

Square miles, 624.
Organized, 1786.

Population, 41,416.
Valuation, 1845, $8,925,423.

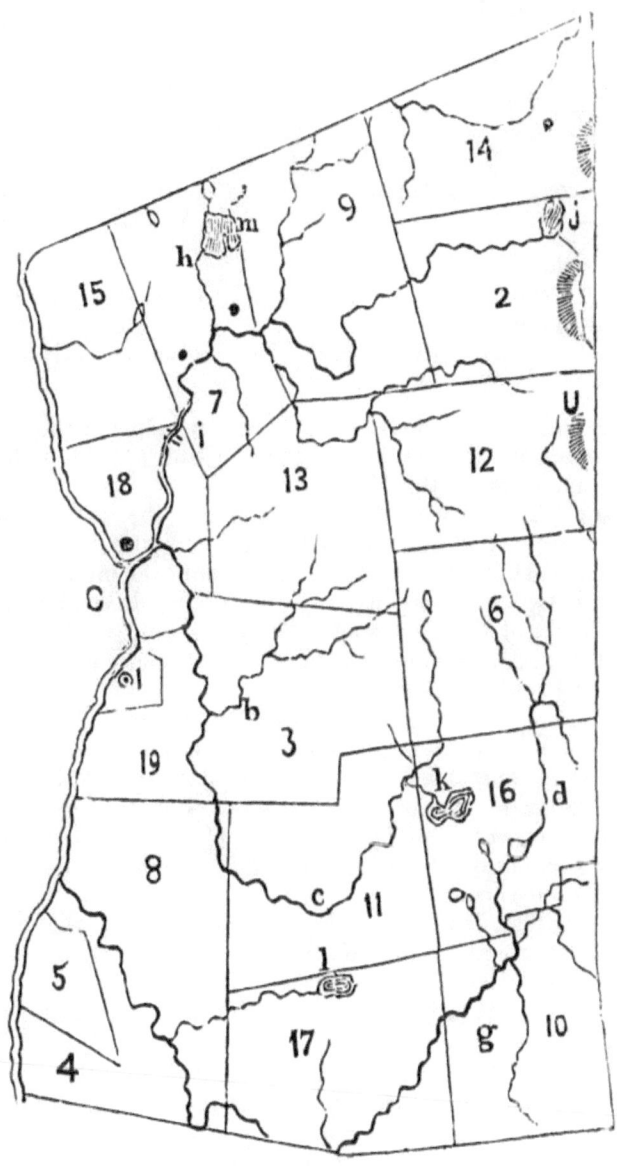

210 STATE OF NEW YORK.

TOWNS.

1. Hudson, 1785.
2. Canaan, 1788.
3. Claverack, 1788.
4. Clermont, 1788.
5. Germantown, 1788.
6. Hillsdale, 1788.
7. Kinderkook, 1788.
8. Livingston, 1788.
9. Chatham, 1795.
10. Ancram, 1803.
11. Taghkanic, 1803.
12. Austerlitz, 1818.
13. Ghent, 1818.
14. New Lebanon, 1818.
15. Stuyvesant, 1823.
16. Copake, 1824.
17. Gallatin, 1830.
18. Stockport, 1833.
19. Greenport, 1839.

Mountains. U. Taghkanic range.

Rivers and Creeks. C. Hudson river. b. Claverack creek. c. Copake. d. Ancram. g. Roeliff Jansen's. h. Vallitje. i. Kinderhook.

Falls. Kinderhook falls.

Lakes and Ponds. k. Copake lake. l. Charlotte. m. Fish. j. Whiting's pond.

Villages. HUDSON. Kinderhook. New Lebanon. Valatie, or Vallitje. Columbiaville.

BOUNDARIES. North by Rensselaer county; East by the state of Massachusetts and Dutchess county; South by Dutchess county; and West by the Hudson river.

SURFACE. The surface of Columbia county is greatly varied, but may be regarded as composed of two long and broken valleys, on the east of which the Taghkanic range forms a natural boundary between the county and the state of Massachusetts; the high banks of the Hudson form the western boundary, and the Peterborough mountains constitute the dividing ridge through the centre of the county.

The western valley rises on the north and south, causing its waters to flow towards the centre; while the eastern, being highest in the centre, sends its streams north and south. The western valley being much the broadest, gives the county the form of a basin, retaining all the waters that rise in it, and discharging them into the Hudson, through the Kinderhook and Roeliff Jansen's creeks.

RIVERS. The Hudson is the principal river; the other streams of the county are Kinderhook, Claverack, Copake, Roeliff Jansen's and Vallitje creeks.

LAKES. Fish, Whiting's pond, Copake and Charlotte, are the only lakes worthy of notice.

RAILROADS. The Hudson and Berkshire, and the Great Western railroad pass through the county; and the route of the Harlaem railroad is laid out through it.

CLIMATE. The climate varies with the surface. In the valleys it is mild and pleasant, with early seasons; on the mountains, it is colder and more backward. The county is regarded as very healthy.

GEOLOGY AND MINERALS. The Taghkanic mountains, in the eastern part of the county, are primitive, and composed mainly of granite, and granular limestone. The remainder of the county is transition, and its principal rocks are graywacke and blue limestone, below which, for the most part, lies a bed of slate.

The minerals are, iron ore of superior quality, lead ore, sulphuret of copper, oxide of manganese, sulphuret of zinc, heavy spar, peat, marl and marble. There are several mineral springs, both sulphurous and chalybeate, in the county. Those at Lebanon are much frequented, and considered as possessing valuable medicinal properties.* The sulphur springs in the town of Stockport are attracting considerable attention.

SOIL AND VEGETABLE PRODUCTIONS. Portions of the county are highly fertile, while others are less productive. The marl and lime which abound in the county, furnish ample means for enriching it, to the highest degree of productiveness. The timber of the county is principally pitch pine, hickory, oak, maple, elm and chestnut.

PURSUITS. *Agriculture* is the leading pursuit. Much attention is given to the culture of grain and the rearing of cattle. The growth of wool is very large.

Manufactures are also an important pursuit in the county. The principal articles are cotton and woollen fabrics, including prints, flour, iron and brass ware.

Commerce. An active trade is carried on from Hudson and the other river towns of the county, with New York and other home ports, employing a number of steamers, sloops and barges. The produce of the inland towns finds its way to a market by the railroads.

Mines. There are some iron mines in the county.

STAPLE PRODUCTIONS. Oats, potatoes, corn, rye, butter, cheese and wool.

SCHOOLS. In 1846, there were in the county, 184 district school-houses, in which schools were taught, an average period of nine months. 11,275 scholars received instruction, at an expense for tuition, of about $22,038. The district libraries numbered 22,540 volumes.

There were, the same year, in the county, twenty-six select schools, with 435 pupils, and four academies with 238 students.

---

* The following is the late Dr. Meade's analysis of the waters of the New Lebanon spring.

	Two quarts of water contain	grs.
	Muriate of lime,	1
Of gases. Nitrogen gas, 13 cubic inches.	Muriate of soda, (common salt,)	1 3-4
Atmospheric air, 8 " "	Sulphate of lime,	1 1-2
	Carbonate of lime,	3-4

RELIGIOUS DENOMINATIONS. Methodists, Dutch Reformed, Baptists, Presbyterians, Friends, Episcopalians, Jews, Lutherans, Shakers, Universalists, Congregationalists, Unitarians, and Roman Catholics. The whole number of churches is seventy-four; of clergymen, sixty.

HISTORY. This county was originally a portion of two manors. The manor of Rensselaerwyck included all except the seven southernmost towns, which constituted the manor of Livingston, granted in 1684, 1685, and 1686, and confirmed to the proprietor in 1714.

In 1710, a company of seventy German families, part of those sent over by Queen Anne, settled in the present town of Germantown, which they called East Camp. In 1725, an arrangement having been made between George I. and the proprietor of the Livingston manor, a tract of 6000 acres was secured to them, of which forty acres were to be reserved for the use of a church and school, and the remainder divided equally among the inhabitants.

The other six towns, Clermont, Livingston, Taghkanic, Gallatin, Copake, and Ancram, still constitute the Livingston manor. The leases are generally long, and payments payable in produce. The northern towns, mostly belong to the manor of Rensselaerwyck.

Difficulties have frequently occurred between the proprietors of these manors and their tenants. In 1766, the military forces were called out to quell the disturbances in the town of Claverack, in the Rensselaer manor, and a conflict ensued in which several lives were lost. Similar occurrences have taken place within a year or two past.

The county was mostly settled by Swedish and Dutch emigrants, with the exception of Germantown, already mentioned, and Hudson, which was founded in 1783, by enterprising citizens of Rhode Island and Nantucket.

The manorial system has perhaps prevented, in some degree, the full development of the capabilities of the county; yet it has, with slight exceptions, uniformly enjoyed a high degree of prosperity.

VILLAGES. HUDSON city, the capital of the county, is pleasantly situated on the banks of the Hudson, here about fifty feet above the level of the river. It was formerly largely engaged in commerce, but the interests of this, as well as all our other commercial ports, were greatly injured by the action of the French and English, relative to neutral vessels, and the course necessarily adopted by our government in return, prior to the late war with Great Britain.

After recovering from the severe losses occasioned by these events, the citizens of Hudson engaged in the whale fishery,

COLUMBIA COUNTY. 213

but with indifferent success. The coasting trade is prosecuted to some extent.

There are some manufactories here, principally of sperm oil and candles, malt liquors, iron, and carriages. The Hudson Academy is an old chartered institution, and the Hudson Female Seminary, is a new and flourishing school. The Hudson Lunatic Asylum is a private institution. but well conducted, and enjoying a large amount of patronage.

The city is supplied with excellent water, by means of an aqueduct. The Hudson and Berkshire railroad adds materially to the business facilities of the city. Population, 5,657.

Valatie is an important manufacturing village, in the town of Kinderhook, situated at the junction of the Valatie (a corruption of Vallitje) and Kinderhook creeks; here are four large cotton mills, two iron foundries, and several other manufactories. Population, 1600.

Kinderhook village, in the town of the same name, is delightfully situated on a plain, five miles east of the Hudson. It has several manufactories, and a flourishing incorporated academy. It is the birth place of ex-President Van Buren, and his beautiful country seat, Lindenwald, is about two miles south of the village. Population, 1500.

Columbiaville, in the town of Stockport, is a manufacturing village of some importance. Its manufactures consist mainly of cotton sheetings. The Hudson River Seminary, a manual labor institution, is located here. There are in the town of Stockport, several other manufacturing villages. The principal are Glencadia, Springville, Hudson Print Works, and Chittenden's Falls.

New Lebanon Shaker Village, in the town of New Lebanon, called by the inhabitants the "Village of the Millennial Church," is situated on the west side of the Taghkanic mountains. This is one of the largest settlements of this singular people. They have here a very large church, arched over throughout its entire extent; ten dwelling houses for their families, or communities, which consist of from 60 to 150 persons each, and numerous workshops and manufactories. Their grounds are highly cultivated, and their society prosperous and wealthy. This settlement was founded a few years after that at Neskayuna, noticed under Albany county. Population about 600.

Two and a half miles from this village, are the New Lebanon springs, which are a fashionable resort for invalids and pleasure seekers, during the summer; the scenery here is very delightful.

XIV. CLINTON COUNTY.

Square miles, 933.
Organized, 1788.
Population, 31,278.
Valuation, 1845, $1,666,140.

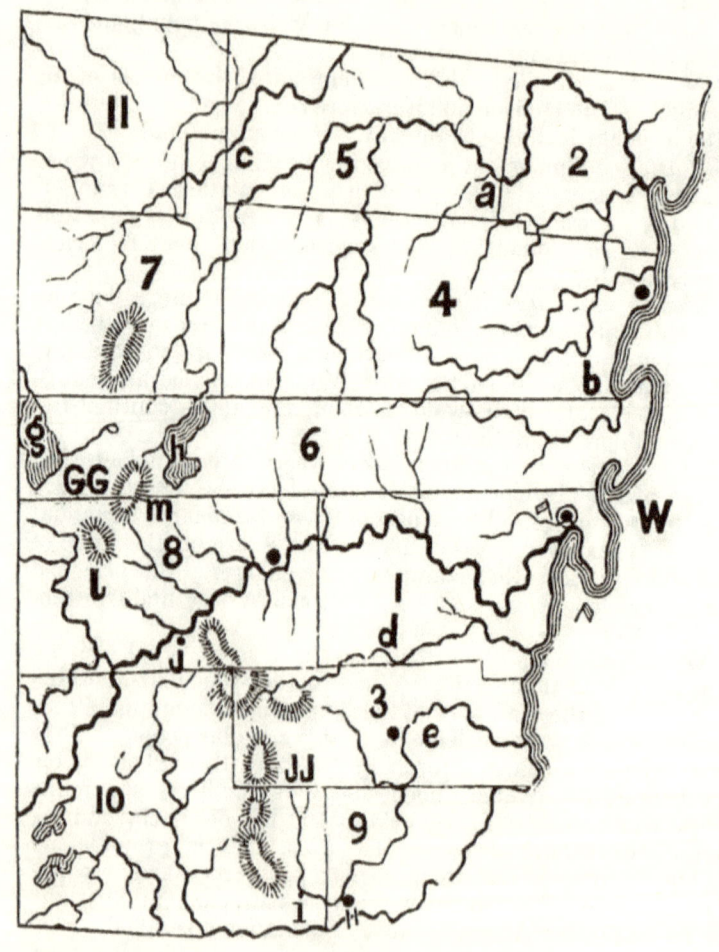

TOWNS.

1. Plattsburgh, 1785.
2. Champlain, 1788.
3. Peru, 1792.
4. Chazy, 1804.
5. Mooers, 1804.
6. Beekmantown, 1820.
7. Ellenburgh, 1830.
8. Saranac, 1834.
9. Au Sable, 1837.
10. Blackbrook, 1837.
11. Clinton, 1842.

CLINTON COUNTY. 215

Mountains. JJ. Au Sable range. GG. Chateaugay. l. Lyon. m. Rand Hill.
Rivers. a. Great Chazy. b. Little Chazy. c. English. d. Salmon. e. Little Au Sable. i. Au Sable. j. Saranac.
Falls. Sheffield.
Lakes. W. Lake Champlain. g. Chateaugay. h. Chazy.
Battle Fields. Plattsburgh. Lake Champlain.
Villages. PLATTSBURGH. Chazy. Redford. Clinton. Peru.

BOUNDARIES. North by Canada East; East by Lake Champlain; South by Essex county; and West by Franklin county.

SURFACE. A plain, about eight miles in width, extends along the eastern border of this county, inclining gently to Lake Champlain. West of this, the surface becomes hilly and broken, giving rise to the Au Sable range of mountains; still farther west, the Chateaugay, which have their origin in Canada, rear their lofty and wooded ridges. Their course is from north-east to south-west.

RIVERS. The principal rivers in the county are the Au Sable, Saranac, Great Chazy, Little Chazy, English, Salmon, and Little Au Sable.

FALLS. The Au Sable has a number of falls within a few miles of its mouth. At Birmingham, the water plunges over a precipice eighty feet in height, and then flows through a ravine of two miles in length, and an average width of fifty feet, with perpendicular walls of granite from seventy-five to 150 feet high. The Saranac has also a number of falls, three of them exceeding in perpendicular descent, forty feet each.

LAKES. Lake Champlain washes the eastern border of the county. The other principal lakes are Chateaugay and Chazy.

CLIMATE. In common with the northern counties generally, it has a rigorous climate. The winters are long, and snow falls to a great depth.

GEOLOGY AND MINERALOGY. The county is wholly of primitive formation, except a narrow strip of limestone, along the shore of the lake. Hypersthene, granite and gneiss, are the prevailing rocks.

Iron is the most abundant and valuable mineral. Both bog and magnetic ores occur in large quantities. Black marble is found near Plattsburgh, of excellent quality. Peat is very plentiful. In Beekmantown, is a sulphur spring, and also one of carbonated water.

SOIL AND VEGETABLE PRODUCTIONS. In the level section upon the lake, the soil is principally a clayey loam, and is very productive. As the country rises, it becomes less fertile.

The summer crops are best adapted to the soil.

The forests are covered with a dense growth of timber, of oak, pine, maple, hemlock, &c. Large quantities of sugar are produced from the maple.

PURSUITS. The inhabitants are for the most part engaged in *agricultural* pursuits. Some grain is raised, but the rearing of cattle and sheep is a more favorite and profitable business. The preparation of lumber for market also furnishes employment to many of the citizens.

Manufactures are increasing in importance, but are, at present, chiefly limited to the manufacture of pig and bar iron, nails, glass, flour, lumber, and woollen goods.

Commerce. The shipping of the Champlain district amounted, in 1845, to 3192 tons, the greater part of which is owned in this county. Several steamers ply on the lake, as well as sloops, schooners, &c.

Mines. There are extensive iron mines in the county. The marble quarries, near Plattsburgh, are in high repute.

STAPLES. Butter, cheese, beef, pork, corn and potatoes.

SCHOOLS. 138 district schools were maintained in the county an average period of six months, in 1846. $8958 was expended for the instruction of 8056 children. The school libraries numbered 14,460 volumes.

There were also in the county, nineteen private schools, with 527 pupils, and three incorporated academies with 191 students.

RELIGIOUS DENOMINATIONS. Methodists, Presbyterians, Congregationalists, Baptists, Roman Catholics, Friends, and Episcopalians. There are thirty-three churches and forty-five clergymen of all denominations.

HISTORY. At the close of the French war, this county was visited by numerous speculators, in quest of pine and oak timber; but no permanent settlements were established till 1765, or 1766, when a grant having been made to two officers of the British Navy, Messrs. Stewart and Freswell, of 2000 acres of land, in two tracts, one situated in Plattsburgh, and the other in Peru, a few families removed here, but were soon driven off by the revolutionary war. The descendants of one of them, however, (Mr. Hay,) still occupy his property.

Grants were also made previous to the revolution, to two gentlemen named Beekman and Deane, with each of whom several partners were associated. A settlement was made in Deane's patent, in 1768, (though not by purchase from him,) by Mr. James Framboise. Being driven out by the enemy in 1776, he served in the American army through the war, and, in 1784, returned to his farm, which is still held by his family.

A German nobleman, Count Vredenburg, who had married a lady of the Queen's household, in England, obtained a grant of 30,000 acres of land, which he located on Cumberland bay, in the present town of Plattsburgh. He resided here, in great splendor, for several years, previous to the revolution, at the commencement of which he sent his family to Montreal, but remained himself, for some time, on his estate, and at length ysteriously disappeared. It was supposed, that he was robbed and murdered. His house, and a saw mill which he had erected, some three miles from his residence, were burned, at the time of his disappearance.

In July, 1782, Lieutenant (afterwards Major General) Benjamin Mooers, with two other officers, and eight men, ascended the Hudson in a boat, from Fishkill landing, and, taking the route by way of Lake George, and Lake Champlain, reached Point au Roche, nine miles above Plattsburgh, on the 10th of August, and commenced a settlement.

In 1784, Judge Zephaniah Platt, and several others, who had formed a company, for the purchase of military warrants, located their lands on Cumberland bay, and laid out the town of Plattsburgh, reserving ten lots, of 100 acres each, as gifts to the first ten settlers, who should remove thither, with their families, and another hundred acre lot for the first male child, born in the settlement.

These gifts were soon claimed, and the settlement prospered steadily from this period. During the late war with Great Britain, one of its severest battles occurred wi hin the limits of this county—we allude to the battle of Plattsburgh, and the simultaneous naval conflict, between the squadrons of Commodore Downie and Commodore McDonough, on the 11th of September, 1814.

In this battle, a force of 1500 regulars, and about 2500 militia, under General Macomb, defeated and routed a force of 14,000 well appointed, and veteran troops, the victors of a hundred battle fields ; and the squadron, under the command of Commodore McDonough, destroyed a force. considerably its superior, on the lake. The loss of the British land forces, was more than 2000, in killed, wounded, prisoners, and deserters; that of the Americans, not more than 150.

On the lake, the English loss was about 1000, in killed, wounded, and prisoners; that of the Americans, 110. The British commander, Commodore Downie, was killed, in the naval action.

The mineral wealth of this county, and its vast forests of valuable timber, will undoubtedly continue to attract emigrants hither, and no where will industry receive a more ample reward.

VILLAGES. PLATTSBURGH, in the town of the same name, is the county seat, and is situated at the head of Cumberland bay. It has numerous manufactories, and is the proposed terminus of the Ogdensburgh and Lake Champlain railroad; several railroads are now in the course of construction, which will probably connect this road with Boston, and other ports on the Atlantic.

Plattsburgh is a United States military post, and the government have erected extensive stone barracks here, and a permanent breakwater for the protection of the harbor.

The Saranac here furnishes a fine water power, descending by a succession of falls, about forty feet. The manufactures of the village are principally cotton and woollen goods. Population, 2500.

<small>Near the village are the ruins of the temporary barracks and breast works, occupied by the troops of General Macomb, during the late war with Great Britain. One mile north of these is the house occupied by the British commander, General Prevost, as his head quarters, during the siege. Between this and the village, the marks of cannon shot can still be seen on the trees and other objects. At a distance of about five miles from the village, on a hill overlooking the village of Beekmantown, is the spot where the British troops met the first repulse in their approach to Plattsburgh, on the 6th of September. In this skirmish, several of the British officers and about 100 men were killed. The British camp was north of the Saranac river.</small>

Clintonville, on the Au Sable river, situated partly in this and partly in Essex county, is a thriving village, largely engaged in the various manufactures of bar and rolled iron, nails, chain cables, &c. which are produced here, in large quantities. The Arnold Hill mine, near the village, furnishes magnetic iron ore of very superior quality. Population, 1000.

Peru is a flourishing village, in the town of the same name. Population, 900.

Redford, in the town of Saranac, is famous for its manufacture of crown glass, which is of superior quality. Population, 700.

Chazy is a small, but thriving village, in the town of the same name. It has some manufactures. The Chazy black marble, quarried near this village, bears a high reputation.

Champlain, in the town of the same name, is a village of some importance. The village of Keeseville, on both sides of the Au Sable, is partly located in this town, and, in point of importance, is only second to Plattsburgh. It is more particularly described in Essex county.

XV. ONTARIO COUNTY.

Square Miles, 617.
Organized, 1789.

Population, 42,592.
Valuation, 1845, $12,624,438.

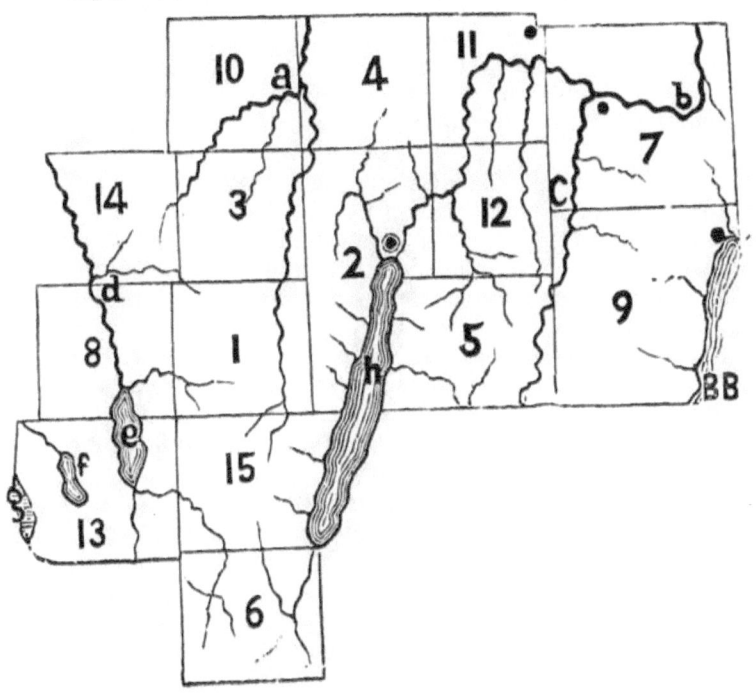

TOWNS.

1. Bristol, 1789
2. Canandaigua, 1789.
3. East Bloomfield, 1789.
4. Farmington, 1789.
5. Gorham, 1789.
6. Naples, 1789.
7. Phelps, 1789.
8. Richmond, 1789.
9. Seneca, 1789.
10. Victor, 1812.
11. Manchester, 1821.
12. Hopewell, 1822.
13. Canadice, 1829.
14. West Bloomfield, 1833.
15. South Bloomfield, 1836.

Rivers. a. Mud Creek. b. Canandaigua Outlet. c. Flint Creek. d. Honeoye.

Lakes. BB. Seneca. h. Canandaigua. e. Honeoye. f. Caneadea or Canadice. g. Hemlock.

Colleges. Geneva.

Villages. CANANDAIGUA. Geneva. Vienna. Port Gibson.

BOUNDARIES. North by Monroe and Wayne counties; East by Seneca county and Seneca lake; South by Yates and Steuben counties; and West by Livingston and Monroe counties.

SURFACE. The surface of Ontario county is diversified, being naturally divided by a north and south line, taking the Canandaigua lake in its course. The whole eastern portion is spread out in beautiful plains and gentle undulations. The western portion comprises numerous swells of rich rolling land, interspersed with fertile vales. In the southwestern portion of the county, these swells form some bold elevations, towering into highlands, having an altitude of twelve or fourteen hundred feet.

RIVERS. Mud creek, Canandaigua outlet, Flint creek and Honeoye, are the principal streams.

LAKES. Canandaigua lake is fourteen miles long, from one to two broad, and surrounded by diversified and beautiful scenery. The other lakes are Seneca, Honeoye, Caneadea and Hemlock.

CANALS. The Erie canal just touches the county at Port Gibson, and the Seneca and Cayuga canal commences at Geneva.

RAILROADS. The Auburn and Rochester railroad has a circuitous course, from east to west, through the county.

CLIMATE. The climate is mild and equable.

In some sections remittent and intermittent fevers prevail in autumn, but the county, as a whole, is decidedly healthy. It is well adapted to the growth and perfection of the peach, apple and other fruits.

GEOLOGY AND MINERALS. Slate is the underlying rock of the county, but it is generally covered with limestone, and, on the higher hills, with graywacke. In the southern part, the clay slate sometimes appears on the surface. In the west it alternates with the limestone, forming an excellent soil. The county lies mostly within the limits of the Ontario group.

Water lime, gypsum and marl are abundant. Iron ore is also found in large quantities. Sulphur springs exist in Manchester. One of the most interesting features in the mineralogical history of this county, is the carburetted hydrogen or inflammable gas, in Bristol and Canandaigua.

The gas forces its way through fissures in the rocks, and in Bristol through the waters of a stream, where it is most abundant; when lighted it burns with a steady, brilliant flame, till extinguished by storms, or by design. The gas has the odor of pit coal, and burns without smoke, but deposits a small quantity of bituminous lampblack. The hillocks where it appears are destitute of verdure, and no plant will live within its influence. There are similar springs in East Bloomfield and Richmond.

SOIL AND VEGETABLE PRODUCTIONS. The constituents of the soil render it quite fertile, and the northern and central towns are peculiarly adapted to the raising of wheat and other grains. It also yields grass and fruits abundantly.

The timber is principally oak, chestnut, hickory, with beech, maple, and some pine in the southern part.

ONTARIO COUNTY. 221

Pursuits. The people generally are engaged in tilling the earth, and find a rich return for their toil, in the abundance it produces. More wheat is raised in this county, than in any other in the state. It also produces more wool. All kinds of fruit congenial to the climate, are produced in large quantities.

The *manufactures* of the county are limited, as it has comparatively little water power. They are chiefly flour, the various woollen fabrics, leather, malt and distilled liquors.

Its *commerce* is confined to the transportation of its produce, and that principally on the Seneca lake.

Staples. These are, wheat, wool, oats, barley and butter.

Schools. In 1846, there were 220 district schools, which were taught an average period of eight months, and contained 14,617 pupils. The amount paid for tuition was $21,519. There were 27,106 volumes in the school libraries.

There were in addition, thirty-five select schools, with 706 scholars, two academies, and one female seminary, with 246 pupils, and one college with eight professors, and, including both departments, 260 students.

Religious Denominations. Methodists, Baptists, Presbyterians, Congregationalists, Episcopalians, Friends, Universalists, Dutch Reformed, Unitarians and Roman Catholics. Total churches seventy-six—clergymen ninety-five.

History. The whole of this county, as well as the counties of Steuben, Genesee, Allegany, Niagara, Chautauque, Monroe, Livingston, Erie, Yates, and the western half of Wayne and Orleans, was included in the lands ceded by New York to Massachusetts, and by that state to Messrs. Gorham and Phelps, in 1787.

In 1788 Oliver Phelps, one of the proprietors, left Granville, Massachusetts, to explore this far distant and unknown country, amid the tearful adieus of his family and friends, who parted with him, not expecting his return.

On his arrival at Canandaigua, he assembled the chiefs of the Six Nations, and purchased from them their title to two and a half millions of acres of land. In 1789, he opened, at Canandaigua, the first land office in America, for the sale of forest lands to settlers.

His system of surveys by townships was subsequently adopted by the United States government, in their surveys of new lands. Almost the whole of the lands of this county were thus sold to actual settlers, a large proportion of whom were from New England.

With a soil of extraordinary fertility, and a thrifty and industrious population; possessing scenery of unrivaled beauty, and removed from the danger of hostile incursions, the growth of this county has been rapid and prosperous, since its first settlement.

VILLAGES. CANANDAIGUA VILLAGE in the town of Canandaigua, was laid out by Messrs. Gorham and Phelps, in 1788, and is the county seat. It is delightfully situated, on an ascent, at the northern extremity of the lake of the same name, commanding a fine view of that beautiful sheet of water. Its buildings, many of them handsome, are principally situated on a single broad street, running north and south, and are surrounded by highly cultivated gardens.

The Canandaigua academy, located here, was founded by the munificence of Messrs. Gorham and Phelps, and is amply sustained by the liberality of the inhabitants. It is also the seat of the Ontario female seminary, an ancient and respectable institution. Population about 3000.

Geneva, in the town of Seneca, was founded by Messrs. Annin and Barton, in 1794. In the beauty of its situation, it is unrivaled among the many beautiful villages of western New York. Situated at the northwest extremity of Seneca lake, its principal street runs parallel with the shore of the lake, at an elevation of about 100 feet, and from many of its residences terraced gardens extend to the banks of the lake.

It has some manufactures, but is chiefly distinguished for its refined society, and for the advantages it affords as a retreat for the scholar, the retired merchant, or the gentleman of fortune. The college, here, has an able corps of instructors, and is rising in reputation and usefulness. In beauty of location it is not surpassed by any institution in the United States. It has a flourishing medical department. There is also in this village a female seminary. Population about 4000.

East and *West Vienna*, in the town of Phelps, are thriving villages, situated one mile distant from each other, on the outlet of Canandaigua lake. They are in the midst of a fine agricultural region and have some manufactories. East Vienna has a female seminary. The Auburn and Rochester railroad passes through the village. Population 1500.

Rushville, partly in this county and partly in Yates, is a village of some importance. Population about 800.

Port Gibson, in the town of Manchester, is the only place where the Erie canal touches the county.

XVI. HERKIMER COUNTY.

Square Miles, 1370.
Population, 37,424.
Organized, 1791.
Valuation, 1845, $6,572,473.

TOWNS.
1. German Flats, 1788.
2. Herkimer, 1788.
3. Schuyler, 1792.
4. Norway, 1792.
5. Fairfield, 1796.
6. Frankfort, 1796.
7. Litchfield, 1796.
8. Warren, 1796.
9. Manheim, 1797.
10. Newport, 1806.
11. Russia, 1806.
12. Columbia, 1812.
13. Winfield, 1816.
14. Danube, 1817.
15. Salisbury, 1817.
16. Ohio, 1823.
17. Stark, 1828.
18. Little Falls, 1829.
19. Wilmurt, 1837.

Mountains. GG. Chateaugay. j. Otsquaga. i. Hassencleaver.

Rivers. F. Mohawk. a. Black. h. East Canada Creek. f. West Canada Creek. b. Beaver. c. Moose.

Falls. g. Trenton. t. Little.

Lakes. d. Moose.

Villages. HERKIMER. Little Falls. Fairfield.

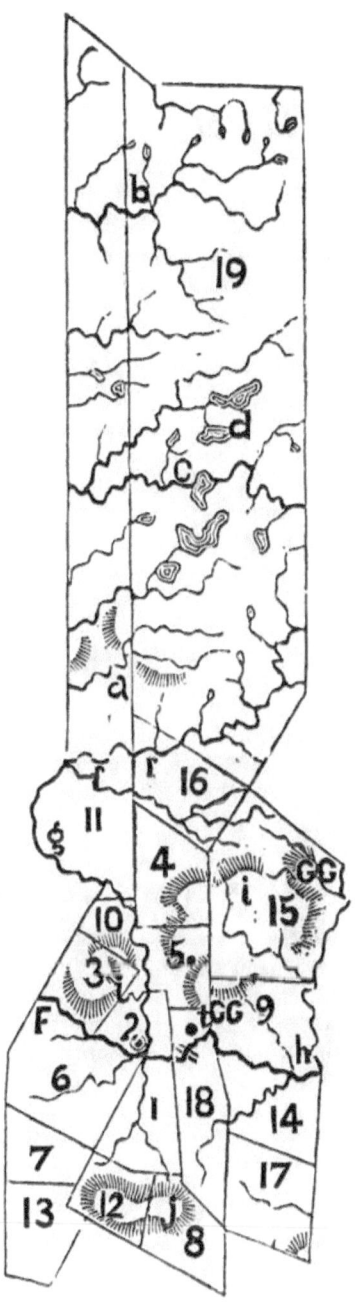

BOUNDARIES. North by St. Lawrence county; East by Hamilton, Fulton and Montgomery; South by Otsego; and West by Oneida and Lewis counties.

SURFACE. The surface is diversified, and crossed by mountains in every direction. The Chateaugay range enters the county from the northeast, and runs southwest and unites with the Otsquaga Hills, which form the dividing ridge between the Mohawk and Susquehanna.

This ridge is broken through, by the Mohawk river, at Little Falls. It varies in height from 700 to 1200 feet. The Otsquaga Hills run from east to west, extending across the whole southern portion of the county. They are about 1000 feet high.

Between the Chateaugay mountains and the western line of the county, are the Highlands of Black river, which are broken through by West Canada creek. The Hassencleaver mountain, an isolated summit, having a base of eight or nine miles, and a height of 800 or 1000 feet, also occupies its central portion.

The northern portion is elevated and rugged, but has not been thoroughly explored. The dividing ridge, between the waters of the St. Lawrence and the Mohawk, crosses it.

RIVERS. The Mohawk passes through the county from east to west. Its principal tributaries are the East Canada and West Canada creeks. The latter, in a course of sixty miles, falls 1220 feet, or on an average twenty-three feet to the mile. The Black, Moose, Beaver, and the head waters of the Oswegatchie river, all aid in draining the northern portion of the county.

FALLS. The Little Falls, at the village of that name, on the Mohawk, deserve notice. They received their name in contradistinction to the Great Falls of the Mohawk, at Cohoes. They extend, upon the river, three-fourths of a mile, the fall in that distance being forty-two feet, divided into two rapids, each of nearly a fourth of a mile in length, and separated by a stretch of deep water.

The beauty of the fall is very much increased by the depth of the river bed, below the adjacent banks of the defile, through which it passes. This defile is about 100 rods wide, two miles in length, and rises from 360 to 400 feet above the river, which has worn for itself this deep channel through the crumbling rocks, which compose the mountain. The scenery is highly picturesque and beautiful.

Trenton Falls, on the West Canada creek, are described under Oneida county.

AKES. There are numerous small lakes scattered over the northern part of the county, among which Moose lake is the largest.

CANALS AND RAILROADS. The Erie canal, and the Utica and Schenectady railroad, pass through the county, on either side of the Mohawk.

CLIMATE. The climate, owing to the numerous mountains, is cold, but healthy.

GEOLOGY AND MINERALS. The northern part of the county is

HERKIMER COUNTY.

primitive, the rocks being either granite or gneiss. On the borders of the East and West Canada creeks, as well as in some other sections, this is overlaid with limestone and slate. South of the Mohawk, the prevailing rock is slate, covered with sandstone, or limestone, except at Fort hill, where the granite again makes its appearance.

Its minerals are quartz, crystals of rare size and beauty, heavy spar, calcareous spar, pearl and brown spar, sulphuret of zinc, galena, iron and copper pyrites, bog iron ore, fibrous celestine, tourmaline, and anthracite, though not in sufficient quantities to be of any practical value. Fossils, of great beauty and perfection, are found in the vicinity of Trenton falls, and petrifactions on the Otsquaga creek, in the town of Stark.

SOIL AND VEGETABLE PRODUCTIONS. The soil is generally arable, and some portions of it highly productive. It is better adapted to grass than to grain. The northern portion is said to be barren and unproducti

The timber is principally oak, hemlock, pine, beech, chestnut, black birch, hickory, butternut, elm and maple. Pine and hemlock are abundant in the northern section.

PURSUITS. *Agriculture* is the pursuit of a majority of the inhabitants. From the hilly character of the surface, more attention is necessarily paid to grazing, than to the culture of grain, and Herkimer stands in the front rank of grazing counties. Its cheese is particularly celebrated, and almost one fourth of the whole amount produced in the state, is made in this county. More than eight millions of pounds mere made in 1845. It also ranks high in the production of butter, wool and pork.

Some attention is paid to *manufactures*, for which the water falls of the principal streams afford fine facilities. The principal articles are leather, cotton and woollen goods, flour, lumber and paper.

The transportation of its produce upon the Erie canal, constitutes the only *commerce* of the county.

STAPLES. Cheese, butter and wool.

SCHOOLS. There are 200 public school-houses, in which schools were taught, in 1846, an average period of eight months, and 11,800 children received instruction, at a cost, for tuition, of $15,459. The district libraries numbered 22,750 volumes.

The county has also thirty-three select schools, with 442 pupils, three academies, and one female seminary, attended by 321 pupils.

RELIGIOUS DENOMINATIONS. Methodists, Baptists, Dutch Reformed, Universalists, Presbyterians, Congregationalists, Episcopalians, Roman Catholics, Unitarians and Jews.

HISTORY. A tract of land, twelve miles square, lying between the East and West Canada creeks, in this county, constituted the royal grant, which Sir William Johnson obtained of old King Hendrick, and which was afterwards confirmed by the king of England.* Another of 94,000 acres, lying in the northern part of the county, was granted in 1770, and called the Jerseyfield patent.

The fertile tract now known as the German Flats, was patented by a company of German Lutherans, in 1725. It consisted of a little more than 9000 acres of excellent land. Their residence was called Burnet's field, after Governor Burnet. A church was erected here, previous to the revolution, and a parsonage of stone, which having been fortified, received the name of Fort Herkimer.

In common with the adjacent counties of Montgomery, Fulton, Otsego, Oneida and Schoharie, Herkimer suffered from the incursions of the savages and tories, during the revolutionary contest. The brave old general whose name it perpetuates, died at his residence, in Danube, in this county, in August, 1777, of wounds received at the battle of Oriskany.

In 1778, the village of Herkimer was burned by the Indians and tories, under the direction of the Mohawk chieftain, Brant. Fortunately their approach had been discovered by the inhabitants, who fled to Forts Dayton and Herkimer, for protection. Two individuals, however, were killed, every house and barn destroyed, and the cattle, horses and sheep driven away by the Indians.

In 1780, a party of Indians and tories visited Little Falls, for the purpose of destroying the mills there, which were of great importance to the inhabitants. They accomplished their object, killed one man, and took five or six prisoners. Two of the occupants of one of the mills, concealed themselves in the raceway, beneath the water wheel, and after the conflagration of the mill, and the departure of the Indians, made their escape.

VILLAGES. HERKIMER, the county seat, is handsomely situated in the valley of the Mohawk, in the town of the same name. It has a fine hydraulic power, sufficient to drive a large amount of machinery. The academy here is in a flourishing condition. The county buildings are on the most improved models, combining security and comfort. Population about 1000.

Little Falls, situated on both sides the Mohawk, in the town of that name, is celebrated for the beauty of its scenery. It is

---

* The way in which this land was obtained, was said to be the following. Sir William having received, from England, several rich suits of uniform, the old Sachem, Hendrick, visited him soon after, and spent the night. In the morning he came to Sir William and said, "Me dream last night." "And what did you dream?" inquired the baronet. "Me dream you give me one fine suit of clothes," was the reply. The baronet, of course, complied with his request.

Not long after, he returned the visit, and in the morning, said to his Indian host, "I dreamed last night." "Ah," said the Indian, "What did you dream?" "I dreamed," replied Sir William, "that you gave me such a piece of land," (describing it). "Well," said the old Sachem, "Me give it you, but me no dream with you again; you dream too hard for me."

HERKIMER COUNTY. 227

largely engaged in manufactures, and has an academy for the education of both sexes, for which the citizens have erected a noble granite edifice. Its houses, mostly of stone, are remarkable for their neat and substantial appearance.

Here is a deep cut on the canal, of two miles, through solid rock, which presented an obstacle to the Erie canal, only surpassed by that at Lockport. The canal constructed by the Western Inland Lock Navigation Company, in 1802, is connected with the Erie canal at this place, by a magnificent aqueduct of white marble. The finest quartz crystals in the United States are found here. Population about 3000.

Fairfield is a pleasant rural village, the seat of an academy of considerable distinction. The college of physicians and surgeons, of the western district, was formerly located here, and occupied a fine building. This medical school, though formerly highly popular, has recently been discontinued.

Mohawk, in the town of German Flats, is situated on the line of the canal. It is a flourishing village, and furnishes a good market for the produce of this section of the county. Population 800.

Newport, in the town of the same name, is a thriving village, with considerable manufactures. Population about 600.

Frankfort, in the town of the same name, has some manufactures. Population 600.

Middleville, in the town of Fairfield, *Winton*, in the town of Salisbury, and *Russia*, in the town of the same name, are villages of some importance.

XVII. RENSSELAER COUNTY.

Square Miles, 626.
Organized, 1791.

Population, 62,338.
Valuation, 1845, $12,624,258.

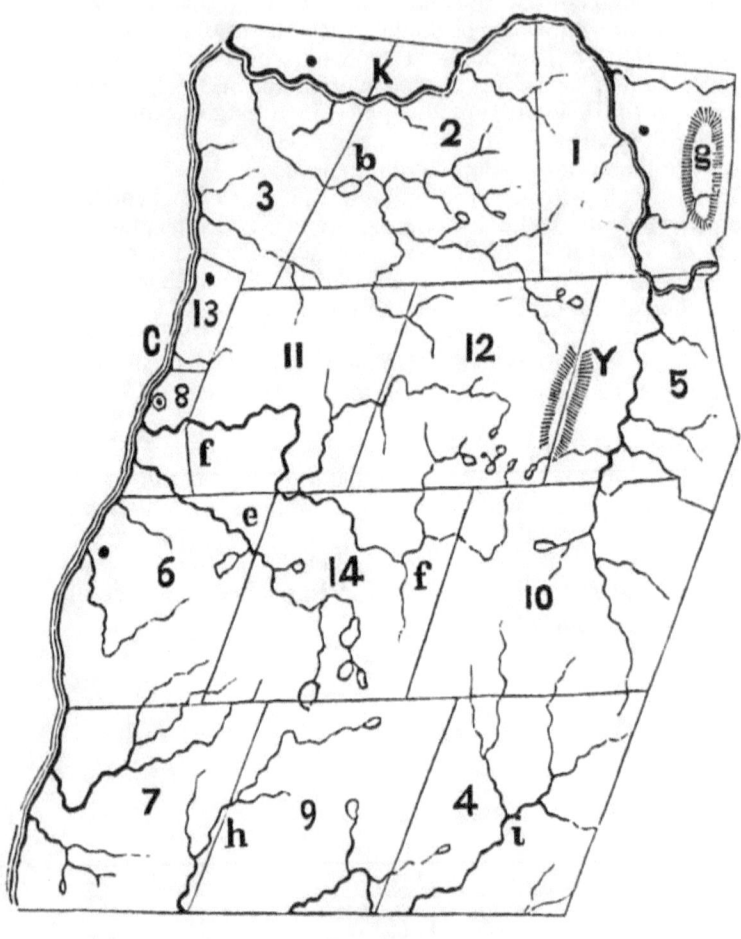

TOWNS.

1. Hoosick, 1788.
2. Pittstown, 1788.
3. Scaghticoke, 1788.
4. Stephentown, 1788.
5. Petersburgh, 1791.
6. Greenbush, 1792.
7. Schodac, 1795.
8. Troy City, 1796.
9. Nassau, 1806.
10. Berlin, 1806.
11. Brunswick, 1807.
12. Grafton, 1807.
13. Lansinburgh, 1807.
14. Sand Lake.

Mountains. Y. Peterborough. g. Williamstown.

RENSSELAER COUNTY. 229

Rivers and Creeks. C. Hudson River. k. Hoosick. b. Tomhenick Creek. i. Kinderhook. h. Vallitje. e. Wynantskill. f. Poestenkill.

Falls. Hoosick.

Villages. Troy City. Greenbush. Lansingburgh. Scaghticoke Hoosick Falls.

BOUNDARIES. North by Washington county; East by the states of Massachusetts and Vermont; South by Columbia county; and West by the Hudson river.

SURFACE. The surface of the county is diversified. From the valley of the Hudson it rises, somewhat precipitously, more than 200 feet. Thence the county is rolling, to the base of the Peterborough mountains. These mountains attain their highest elevation near the centre of the county, subsiding into moderate hills, at the northern and southern extremities. This ridge is separated from the Taghkanic range, here called the Williamstown mountains, by a valley from one to three miles in width.

RIVERS. This county is abundantly watered. Beside the Hudson, its principal streams are, the Hoosick river, Tomhenick, Kinderhook and Vallitje creeks, Wynantskill, and Poestenkill.

RAILROADS. The Western Railroad, which connects Boston and Albany, terminates at East Albany. The Troy and Greenbush Railroad connects this with Troy. The Troy and Saratoga, and the Troy and Schenectady Railroads, both terminate in this county. They cross the Hudson at Troy, on a noble bridge, 1650 feet in length.

CLIMATE. The climate of the county is mild, but exposed to great extremes of temperature. It is considered healthful.

GEOLOGY AND MINERALS. The county is wholly of the transition formation. The basis rock is clay slate, upon which is imposed limestone, graywacke, and some red sandstone.

Roofing slate is extensively quarried in Hoosick, Stephentown, and Troy. Iron is found in several places, but is little wrought. Marl, of superior quality, is abundant in Sand Lake, and Scaghticoke. Epsom salts are found in Lansingburgh; in the same vicinity are quartz crystals of great beauty. There are several sulphur springs in the county.

SOIL AND VEGETABLE PRODUCTIONS. There is considerable variety in the soil, but a loam, composed of sand and clay, and quite fertile, extends over the greater part of the county. Considerable tracts are well adapted to wheat, but grass and summer crops succeed better in the uplands, in the northern and eastern sections. The principal timber is oak, hemlock, spruce, chestnut, and hickory.

PURSUITS. *Agriculture* is extensively and profitably pursued. The productions of the dairy are large. The rearing of cattle, horses, and sheep, receives much attention. It is the largest flax growing county in the state.

The *Manufactures* of the county are numerous and varied. The principal articles are flour, cotton and woollen goods, various kinds of iron ware, leather, carriages and sleighs, railroad cars, malt and distilled liquors, oil, &c.

Commerce. The commerce of the county is quite extensive, and is carried on principally through the ports of Troy, Lansingburgh, and Greenbush.

STAPLES. Flax, oats, potatoes, corn, butter and wool.

SCHOOLS. In 1846, there were in the county, 192 district school-houses, in which schools were maintained an average period of nine months, and 13,040 children received instruction. The wages of teachers amounted to $21,832. The number of volumes in the district libraries was 26,921.

There were also seventy-five private schools, with 1923 pupils, six academies and two female seminaries, with 556 students, and the Rensselaer Institute.

RELIGIOUS DENOMINATIONS. Methodists, Presbyterians, Baptists, Dutch Reformed, Episcopalians, Roman Catholics, Universalists, Unitarians, Friends, and Congregationalists. There are ninety-five churches, and eighty clergymen.

HISTORY. All the towns of this county, except Scaghticoke, Pittstown, Hoosick, the north part of Lansingburgh, and part of Troy, belong to the Manor of Rensselaerwyck. The farms are generally rented at the rate of ten bushels of wheat for the hundred acres.

Pittstown was probably settled at an earlier period than any other portion of the county, emigrants having located there in 1650.

Scaghticoke was also settled by Dutch and German families at an early period, probably about 1700. The first settlement on the present site of Troy, was made in 1720, by Derick Vanderheyden. He obtained a lease of 490 acres, now constituting the most densely populated portion of the city, for three and three-quarters bushels of wheat and four fat fowls annually.

His descendants continued to occupy the land, and from them it assumed the name of Vanderheyden's ferry, which it continued to bear till 1789, when the more classic appellation of "Troy" was substituted for it.

On the 16th August, 1777, a portion of the battle of Bennington was fought within the limits of Hoosick, in this county.

A cantonment was erected at Greenbush, for the United States troops, during the late war with Great Britain.

CITIES AND VILLAGES. TROY CITY, the seat of justice for the county, is pleasantly situated on the Hudson, six miles north of Albany. It was laid out in 1789, and made the county seat in

1791. It is well built, with wide and well shaded streets. The court house, and several of the other public buildings, exhibit great architectural merit.

It is largely engaged in manufactures of almost every description; cast and bar iron, nails, cotton and woollen goods, coaches, sleighs, wagons, railroad cars, flour, distilled and malt liquors, leather, cordage, steam engines, machinery, &c., are the principal. The entire value of its manufactures exceeds $4,000,000 per annum.

The schools of Troy have long maintained a high rank. The Rensselaer Institute, founded by, and named after, the late Patroon, is an excellent practical school, designed to furnish young men with a thorough mathematical education, and to fit them for the practice of civil engineering.

The Troy Female Seminary, begun in Middlebury, Vermont, in 1814, and removed to Troy in 1821, has long ranked among the first institutions of its kind in the country. Nearly 6000 pupils have been educated in it, many of whom have afterwards become teachers in various parts of the Union.

Its former and present principals, have won for themselves the highest reputation as instructors. It has twenty-four teachers and other officers, and more than 200 pupils.

The Troy Academy is also an excellent institution.

The Lyceum of Natural History has a fine library and cabinet, and is well conducted. The Young Men's Association possess a large and well selected library, a cabinet and reading room, and sustain a course of lectures annually.

The city is connected with Schenectady, Saratoga, and East Albany, by railroads, and by means of the last with the great Western Railroad to Boston. Excellent McAdamized roads have also been constructed to Albany and to Bennington; the Erie and Champlain canals, here forming the Junction canal, bring immense quantities of lumber and produce to the city, and receive in return manufactured goods.

The commerce of the city is quite large. Three large and seven or eight smaller steamboats, about sixty sloops and schooners, and twenty-five or thirty barges, are owned here, and employed in transporting produce and manufactured articles to New York. There are also several lines of packets plying to other ports, together with a large number of packet and freight boats, on the Erie and Champlain canals. Population 25,000.

The village of *West Troy*, on the west bank of the Hudson, though in another county, may almost be considered a suburb of Troy, with which it is connected by a fine bridge and two ferries.

Lansingburgh, in the town of the same name, is three miles north of Troy. It was settled before that city, and was for a considerable period the more important village. It has extensive manufactories. By means of a lock, in the state dam across the Hudson, sloops ascend the river to the village. The Lansingburgh Academy was one of the first institutions of the kind established in the state. The village is one of the oldest in the state, having been organized in 1771, and incorporated in 1787. Population 3500.

Scaghticoke Point, in the town of Scaghticoke, is a thriving manufacturing village; cotton, linen, and hemp goods, powder, and powder kegs, are largely manufactured here. Population 1400.

Greenbush is a thriving village in the town of the same name, opposite the city of Albany. The great Western railroad, and the Troy and Greenbush railroad terminate here. The United States barracks, erected in 1814, were on an eminence about a mile southeast of the village. They were very extensive, having been intended for the accommodation of 5000 troops, but are now in ruins. Population 1200.

Hoosick Falls, in the town of Hoosick, is a thriving manufacturing village. Population 500.

Nassau and *Berlin,* in the towns of the same names, are villages of some importance.

Schodac Landing, in the town of Schodac, is a thriving village.

XVIII. OTSEGO COUNTY.

Square miles, 892.
Organized, 1791.

Population, 50,509.
Valuation, 1845, $5,408,040.

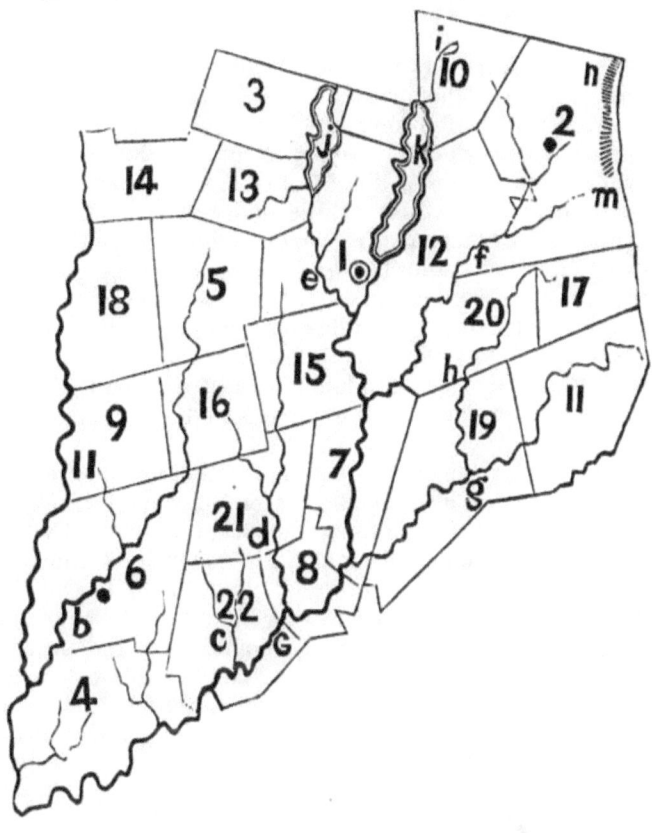

TOWNS.

1. Otsego, 1788.
2. Cherry Valley, 1791.
3. Richfield, 1792.
4. Unadilla, 1792.
5. Burlington, 1792.
6. Butternuts, 1796.
7. Milford, 1796.
8. Oneonta, 1796.
9. Pittsfield, 1797.
10. Springfield, 1797.
11. Worcester, 1797.
12. Middlefield, 1797.
13. Exeter, 1799.
14. Plainfield, 1799.
15. Hartwick, 1802.
16. New Lisbon, 1806.
17. Decatur, 1808.
18. Edmeston, 1808.
19. Maryland, 1808.
20. Westford, 1808.
21. Laurens, 1810.
22. Otego, 1822.

Mountains. m. Kaatsbergs. n. Mount Independence.

Rivers. II. Unadilla. G. Susquehanna. b. Butternut creek. c. Otsdewa. d. Otego. e. Otsego. f. Cherry Valley. g. Schenevas. h. Elk.

Lakes. i. Summit. j. Canaderaga or Schuyler. k. Otsego.

Battle Fields. Cherry Valley.

Villages. COOPERSTOWN. Cherry Valley.

BOUNDARIES. North by Oneida, Herkimer and Montgomery counties; East by Schoharie and Delaware; South by Delaware; and West by Madison and Chenango counties.

SURFACE. The surface is greatly diversified by mountains, hills, valleys and plains. The Kaatsbergs extend along its eastern border, connecting, a little above Cherry Valley village, with Mount Independence, whose summit, more than 2000 feet above tide water, affords a noble prospect, opening, in some directions, nearly 100 miles in extent.

At this elevation, a narrow table land runs along the northern confines of the county, forming the western continuation of the Kaatsbergs, and declines gradually toward the south, divided, however, by the streams, into numerous high ridges and deep valleys.

There are six principal valleys thus formed, viz. Cherry Valley, the valley of the Elk creek, that of Schenevas creek, the valleys of the Otego and Butternut creeks, and of the Unadilla river. The direction of these valleys is generally south-south-westerly.

RIVERS. This county is well watered. The Susquehanna, which forms nearly half its southern boundary, is the principal stream. It takes its rise in Summit lake, whose waters also discharge, in seasons of flood, into the Mohawk. Its course through the county is placid, the descent, in the distance of forty-five miles, probably not exceeding five feet to the mile.

The Unadilla, a branch of the Susquehannah, washes the eastern border of the county. The Cherry Valley creek, on whose banks such deeds of blood were committed, in the early settlement of the county, is also a tributary of the Susquehanna, as are the Schenevas, Otego, Otsdewa, and Butternut creeks.

LAKES. Otsego lake is nine miles long, and from one to three wide. The hills which encircle it are elevated from 400 to 500 feet above its surface. This lake is 1188 feet above tide water. The purity of its waters, and the rich and varied scenery which surrounds it render it an attractive summer resort.

Canaderaga, or Schuyler's lake, is a beautiful sheet of water, five miles long, and from one to two wide.

Summit lake is the source of the Susquehanna. It is a

small body of water, but has an altitude, above tide water, of 1346 feet.

Cromhorn pond, on the Cromhorn mountain, in Maryland, is three miles circumference, and is one of the highest ponds in the state.

CLIMATE. Owing to the elevation of this county the climate is cooler than in some other portions of the state. The diversity of its surface insures a perfect drainage, and renders it highly salubrious.

GEOLOGY AND MINERALS. This county belongs to the transition system. It is underlaid with clay slate, over which is graywacke slate, sandstone, and in the north limestone.

In Cherry Valley and Springfield, gray marble of good quality is found. It is susceptible of a high polish, and abounds with animal fossils. Magnesia is one of its constituents. The graywacke also furnishes an excellent building material. There are some sulphur springs in the county; that at Richfield is highly impregnated, and often visited for its medicinal qualities.

SOIL AND VEGETABLE PRODUCTIONS. The soil is very fertile. The timber of this section is principally oak, white pine, hemlock, beech and maple. Oats, corn, barley, wheat, hops and potatoes are the principal crops.

PURSUITS. *Agriculture*, particularly the rearing of cattle, horses and sheep, and *manufactures* are the principal pursuits. There are no *mines*, but some extensive marble quarries near Cherry Valley.

The Susquehanna is the only navigable stream in the county, and is mainly used for the transportation of lumber, of which considerable quantities are sent to market annually.

The *manufactures* of the county are numerous, and increasing in quantity and value with great rapidity. The most important are flour, lumber, cotton and woollen goods, (including prints,) leather, iron, &c. In 1845, they exceeded $1,100,000 in value.

STAPLE PRODUCTIONS. Wool, beef, pork, butter, cheese, and lumber, are the principal productions.

SCHOOLS. There were in the county, in 1846, 316 district school-houses, in which schools were taught an average period of eight months; 16,859 scholars were instructed during the year, at an expense for tuition of about $19,385. The district libraries contained 31,366 volumes.

There were the same year, in the county, thrity-nine private schools, with 652 pupils, and three academies with 223 students.

RELIGIOUS DENOMINATIONS. Baptists, Methodists, Presbyterians, Episcopalians, Congregationalists, Friends, Universalists, and Unitarians. There were, in 1845, eighty-eight churches of all denominations, and ninety-eight clergymen.

HISTORY. The early history of this county contains many events of thrilling interest. The first settlement in the county, was made in 1739, by Mr. John Lindesay, a Scotch gentleman of some fortune and distinction, who, in conjunction with three other gentlemen, had obtained a patent for a tract of 8000 acres, in the present town of Cherry Valley. The place for several years was called Lindesay's Bush.

Mr. Lindesay sedulously cultivated the friendship of the Mohawks, with whom this section was a favorite hunting ground, and soon had reason to rejoice that he had done so, for in the winter of 1740, his stock of provisions was exhausted, and on account of the depth of the snow, he was unable to procure supplies from the distant settlements, but the friendly Indians brought food on their backs, and thus administered to his wants.

In 1741, by the persuasion of Mr. Lindesay, Rev. Samuel Dunlap, an Irish clergyman of education and talent, was induced to emigrate, with several of his friends, to the number in all of about thirty persons, to this county. Soon after their arrival, provision was made for the erection of a church, a schoolhouse, and a grist and saw-mill.

Mr. Dunlap opened, in 1743, a classical school for boys, the first in the state west of Albany.

The settlement progressed but slowly for the next ten years. Mr. Lindesay was not well adapted to the management of an infant settlement, and after expending his fortune in the enterprise, necessity compelled him to abandon it. He entered the army, and died in New York, after serving a few years as lieutenant.

A few years later, small settlements were made at Springfield, Middlefield, Laurens and Otego.

In 1772, when the county of Tryon was formed, the whole population of Cherry Valley was somewhat less than three hundred; and of the entire western portion of the state, (Tryon county comprising all that portion of the state lying west of a line drawn through the centre of Schoharie,) but a few thousands.

A number of the inhabitants had served in the French war, and had suffered from the hostile incursions of the Indians.

During the Revolution, the inhabitants of this county, as well as those of the frontier settlements generally, were agitated with fear of the tories and Indians, but though often alarmed, they did not suffer from the devastating effects of the border wars, in their own settlements, till the autumn of 1778.

Rumors of an intended attack of the Indians and tories having reached the inhabitants in the spring, they fortified the church, and Colonel Alden, with a portion of an eastern regiment, was stationed to defend the settlement. The summer, and two of the autumn months passed, without the appearance of the enemy, and believing themselves secure, the farmers left the fort, and returned to their homes.

On the 6th of November, Colonel Alden received intelligence from Fort Schuyler, of the approach of a large force of Indians and tories toward Cherry Valley; on the dissemination of this intelligence, the settlers requested permission to remove into the fort, or at least to deposit their most valuable property there.

Colonel Alden denied both requests, and with the most criminal apathy, considering the report unfounded, took no efficient measures to ascertain its truth. He stationed scouts in different districts, but they, actuated by the same feelings with their commander, kindled a fire, lay down to sleep, and were all captured by the enemy.

On the night of the 10th of November, 1778, the enemy, under command of the brutal Walter Butler, and Brant, the Mohawk chieftain, encamped within one mile of the fort, and on the morning of the 11th, approached it.

Colonel Alden, in addition to his other imprudences, had lodged the officers of his garrison in different houses in the neighborhood. By means of their prisoners, the enemy discovered in which houses they were lodged, and took them all captives.

Colonel Alden himself was not in the fort, and on receiving intelligence of the commencement of the attack, was still incredulous, but ordered the guard to be called in, and went toward the fort. Dearly did he pay for his apathy and incredulity; he was among the first victims of the cruel massacre which now took place.

The family of Mr. Robert Wells, consisting of twelve persons, were all murdered in cold blood, and one of the tories boasted that he had killed Mr. Wells while at prayer.

The wife and one daughter of the Rev. Mr. Dunlap, the hardy pioneer of the settlement, already mentioned, were also sacrificed, and himself only spared through the importunity of an Indian. The wife and four children of Mr. Mitchell, were also inhumanly butchered by the wretches. Thirty-two of the inhabitants, mostly women and children, and sixteen continental soldiers were killed, and a large number made prisoners; all the houses and other buildings of the settlement were burned; and the sun, which that morning looked on a quiet and happy village, in that beautiful valley, shed its last rays that evening upon smouldering ruins, and lifeless corses weltering in their blood.

A conference was held at Unadilla in this county, between General Herkimer and Brant, the year previous to this massa-ere, in which the General attempted, though unsuccessfully, to dissuade the Indians from taking part in the contest.

Since the close of the Revolution, the progress of this county has been rapid, and its quiet undisturbed by the warwhoop of the Indian, or the battle-cry of the white warrior.

VILLAGES, &c. COOPERSTOWN, the county seat, is a village in the town of Otsego. It is situated at the southern extremity of Otsego Lake, and in the beauty of its scenery, and the salubrity of its climate, has few equals among the lovely villages of central New York.

The town is largely engaged in the manufacture of cotton goods and paper. Population 1400.

Cherry Valley, whose thrilling story has already been narrated, received its name from its situation, and the great abundance of the wild cherry in its vicinity. It is a pleasant village, situated in a delightful valley.

The Cherry Valley Academy, a flourishing chartered institution, is located here. Population 1100.

Hartwick is principally distinguished for its Lutheran Theological and Classical Seminary, a flourishing and well conducted institution.

Springfield, so called from a large, deep spring in the town, has an agreeably diversified surface, and comprises several villages. It has some quarries of very good marble.

Salt-spring-ville has its name from a small brine spring near it, from which salt was manufactured during the Revolution. It is worthy of notice for its distance from the great salt springs of the state, and its elevation above tide water.

The Chyle is a noted limestone sink, in this town, eighty yards in circuit and about twelve feet deep; it is oval in form. After rains or thaws, it is filled with water, which gradually discharges itself by small orifices below, giving the water a whirling motion.

Unadilla is pleasantly situated on the Susquehanna. It has two fine covered bridges, each 250 feet in length, resting on three arches. It has also conserable lumber trade. A species of sandstone is quarried here for grindstones. Population about 800.

Gilbertsville, on the Butternut creek, is a thriving manufacturing village, and has a flourishing academy.

XIX. SARATOGA COUNTY.

Square miles, 800.
Organized, 1791.

Population, 41,477.
Valuation, 1845, $6,643,513.

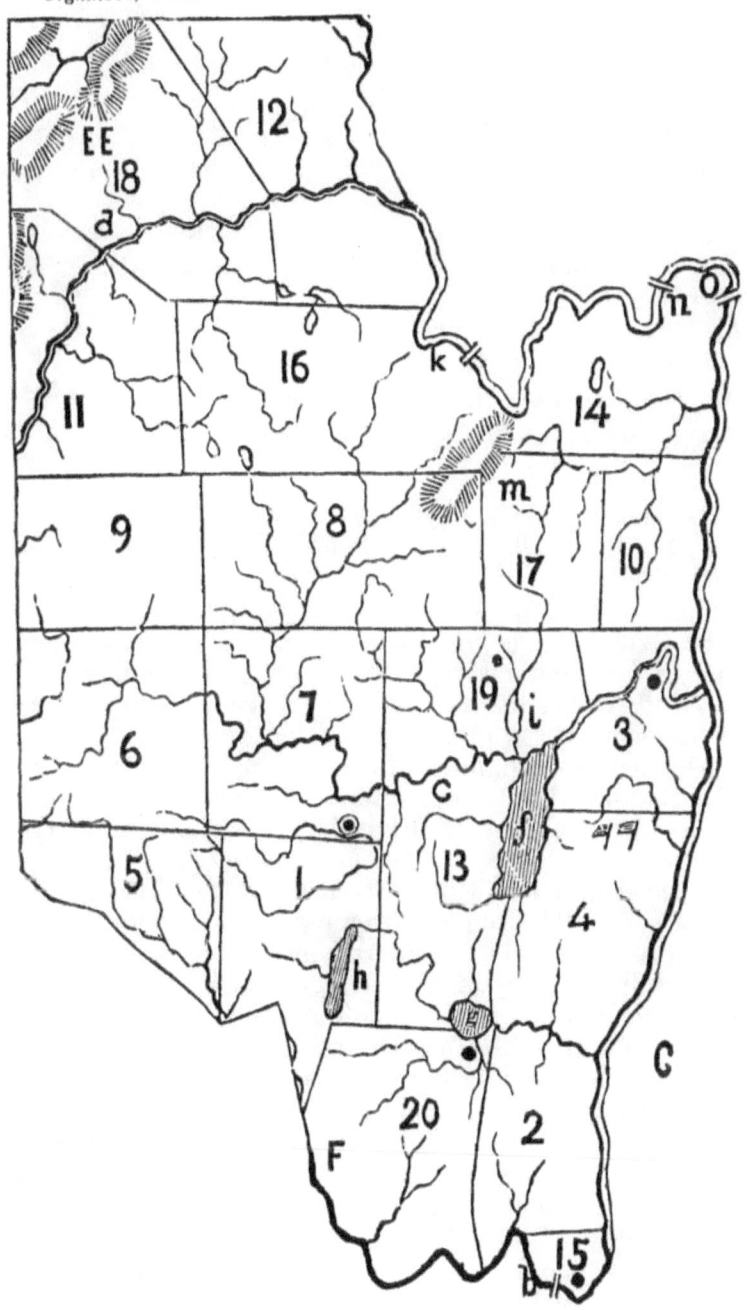

240　　　STATE OF NEW YORK.

TOWNS.

1. Ballstown, 1788.
2. Halfmoon, 1788.
3. Saratoga, 1788.
4. Stillwater, 1788.
5. Charlton, 1792.
6. Galway, 1792.
7. Milton, 1792.
8. Greenfield, 1793.
9. Providence, 1796.
10. Northumberland, 1798.
11. Edinburgh, 1801.
12. Hadley, 1801.
13. Malta, 1802.
14. Moreau, 1805.
15. Waterford, 1816.
16. Corinth, 1818.
17. Wilton, 1818.
18. Day, 1819.
19. Saratoga Springs, 1819.
20. Clifton-park, 1828.

Mountains. m. Palmertown Mountains. EE. Kayaderosseras.

Rivers. C. Hudson River. F. Mohawk. a. Sacandaga. c. Kayaderosseras or Fish Creek.

Falls. b. Cohoes. k. Hadley. n. Glens. o. Bakers.

Lakes. f. Saratoga. g. Round. h. Long. i. Owl.

Battle Fields. Bemis' Heights. Schuylerville.

Villages. BALLSTON SPA. Saratoga Springs. Waterford. Schuylerville. Mechanicsville.

BOUNDARIES. North by Warren county; East by Hudson River; South by Albany and Schenectady; and West by Montgomery, Fulton, and Hamilton counties.

SURFACE. The surface of this county is much diversified and may be divided into mountainous, hilly, and plain lands. The Palmertown mountains enter the county a few miles west of Glen's Falls, and sink to its general level near Saratoga Springs. The Kayaderosseras range crosses the northwestern corner, and is broken through, in the town of Day, by the Sacandaga river. South of that town, a lateral spur, extending in a southerly direction, unites with Flint Hill of Schenectady county. The hilly portion lies east of the mountains, while the level embraces the eastern and southeastern sections of the county.

RIVERS. The Hudson is the main river, forming its eastern and a large portion of its northern boundary line. It receives in its course, from this county, the Sacandaga, Fish creek, and the Mohawk river which waters it on the south.

FALLS. The "Great Falls" of the Hudson are formed by the Palmertown mountains crossing this river in the town of Corinth. After a rapid of a mile and a descent of thirty feet, the river has a perpendicular fall of thirty feet more. There is a remarkable sluice 120 yards above, twelve yards long and four wide, through which the great body of the water flows with great velocity. Parts of Glen's, Baker's, and Cohoes falls are also in this county, particular descriptions of which are given under Warren and Albany counties.

LAKES. Saratoga lake, at the junction of the towns of Malta,

Stillwater, Saratoga and Saratoga Springs, is nine miles long and three wide.

The shore immediately around the lake is marshy, rendering it inaccessible except in a few plac s; the country back rises into lofty ridges and forms a vast m phitheatre f picturesque and cultivated landscape. The fine fi h which inhabit its waters, and the game that frequent its banks, ar objects of much attraction to the spor sman. The visito to the neighboring springs often resort her , and find ample accommodations at the public houses on the western shore. A steamboat plies its waters.

Snake Hill projects into the lake from the east, and rises 200 feet above i su i ce.

Round lake, four miles in circumference, Long lake, in the town of Ballstown, five miles long and one wide, (a beautiful sheet of water, abundantly supplied with fish,) and Owl lake, are the other lakes worthy of notice.

The Champlain canal runs through the eastern border of the county.

CLIMATE. The county is subject to extremes of heat and cold. The sandy nature of the soil, in the eastern and southern sections, renders the heat of summer intense, while its location at the junction of the Mohawk and Hudson valleys, causes the cold of winter to be equally severe. It is however considered healthy. The principal diseases are of a pulmonary nature.

GEOLOGY AND MINERALS. This county comprises primitive, transition, and alluvial formations, and affords to the geologist a rare field of observation and interest. The mountains are primitive in their formation, consisting principally of gneiss, granite, and hypersthene. Fragments of these rocks, corresponding with those in place, in the form of boulders and pebbles, are scattered over the whole county. The transition formation borders the primitive, upon the east and south, and appears in the valley between the great mountain ridges. It consists of pudding stone, sandstone, limestone, argillaceous and graywacke slate, and graywacke. The argillaceous slate, a fragile and crumbling rock, underlies the greater part of the county not included in the primitive region.

At the southern termination of Palmertown mountains, two miles north of Saratoga Springs, occurs a bed of oolitic limestone, extending across the valley which separates the Palmertown from the Kayaderosseras mountains. It is the only known locality of this formation in the state.

The diluvial and alluvial deposites include the pine plains, extending from the northern to the southern limits of the county. They also cover the transition formation, and border the streams. They consist of sand, clay, marl, and rounded fragments of stone, and in many portions of the county are deposited to an unknown depth.

Bog iron ore, magnesia, chrysoberyl, granite, tourmaline, mica, feldspar, apatite, and graphite or black lead, are the principal minerals.

But the most remarkable of the mineral productions of this county, are its springs. These are principally acidulous, saline and chalybeate; there are however a few sulphurous waters. There are fifty or sixty of the acidulated mineral springs. They are quite uniform in their temperature, being generally about 50° Fahrenheit. Their composition is also very similar. They contain carbonic acid, and atmospheric air, from thirty-five to forty cubic inches to the pint of water; and from thirty-five to seventy-five grains of solid matter, consisting of chloride of sodium, (common salt,) carbonates of soda, magnesia, lime, and iron, and generally iodine and bromine in minute quantities. One or two of the springs contain but slight traces of iron, and iodine in larger quantities.

The principal springs are the Congress, Washington, Putnam's, the Pavilion, Iodine, and Union springs at Saratoga; the Public Well, the New Washington, and the Park springs at Ballston Spa. The analysis of several is subjoined.*

---

* The following is an analysis of one gallon (two hundred and thirty-one cubic inches,) of water from the following springs.

Congress Spring.

	Grains.
Chloride of sodium	363.829
Carbonate of soda	7.200
" lime	86.143
" magnesia	78.621
" iron	.841
Sulphate of soda	.651
Iodide of sodium } Bromide of potassium }	5.920
Silica	.472
Alumina	.321
Total grains	543.998
Carbonic acid gas	284.65
Atmospheric air	5.41
Gaseous contents	290.06

Iodine Spring.

	Grains.
Chloride of sodium	137.
Carbonate of lime	26.
" iron	1.
" magnesia	75.
" soda	2.
Hydriodate of soda, or Iodine	3.5
Total grains	244.5
Carbonic acid gas	330.
Atmospheric air	4.
Cubic inches	334.

SARATOGA COUNTY.

Their virtues were known to the Indians, but they carefully concealed them from the whites. In 1767, their affection for Sir William Johnson, who had been a long time ill, led them to communicate them to him. They guided him to the High Rock spring, in the town of Saratoga Springs, and the use of the mineral waters for a few weeks, completely restored his health.

In 1773, the first attempt was made to establish a house for the accommodation of visitors. It was unsuccessful. The following year, one John Arnold established a rude tavern near the High Rock spring. He was succeeded by one Norton, who, during the Revolution, abandoned his tavern and joined the British army. After several changes, it passed into the hands of a Mr. Bryant, who must be regarded as the first permanent settler.

In 1783, General Schuyler opened a road to the High Rock spring* from Fish creek, and the succeeding year built a small frame house near that spring, where he spent five or six weeks every summer, during the remainder of his life.

VEGETABLE PRODUCTIONS. The soil upon the mountainous portion is light and barren, and on the plains, excepting some alluvial bottoms, which are highly fertile, sandy and productive

PAVILION FOUNTAIN.

	Grains.
Chloride of sodium	226.58
Carbonate of magnesia	62.50
" lime	60.24
" soda	4.70
Oxide of iron,	3.10
Iodide of sodium ⎫ Bromide of potassium ⎬	2.75
Silica	.62
Alumina	.25
Total grains	361.74
Carbonic acid gas	480.01
Atmospheric air	8.09
Total cubic inches	488.10

NEW WASHINGTON SPRING, AT BALLSTON SPA.

	Grains.
Chloride of sodium	89.83
Bi-carbonate of soda	18.057
Bi-carbonate of magnesia	42.042
Carbonate of lime	41.51
Hydriodate of soda	0.7
Carbonate of iron	3.71
Silex and alumina	1.25
Solid contents in one gallon	197.099

The gas which it emits in great abundance is pure carbonic acid, probably combined with a small quantity of atmospheric air.

* This High Rock spring is enclosed in a conical rock of tufa (lime) about four feet high and twenty-seven feet in circumference at its base. The water in this is seven feet eight inches in depth, and rises within two feet four inches of the top.

of light crops. The timber of the uplands is oak, hickory, and chestnut; of the plains, maple, beech, ash, elm, white and yellow pine.

PURSUITS. The people are mainly engaged in *agriculture*, and large quantities of grain are annually produced. Most of the improved lands are under a careful and profitable cultivation.

Manufactures. These are chiefly confined to the southern section, yet they form an increasingly important interest. Flour, lumber, cotton and woollen goods, and iron, are the leading articles.

STAPLE PRODUCTIONS. Oats, potatoes, corn, and butter.

SCHOOLS. There were 216 public schools, taught on an average eight months, during the year 1846, having in attendance 11,714 scholars, and paying their teachers $16,005. The number of volumes in the district libraries is 25,532.

The number of private schools is forty-four, attended by 898 pupils. There are also four academies and one female seminary, with 208 students.

RELIGIOUS DENOMINATIONS. Methodists, Baptists, Presbyterians, Episcopalians, Dutch Reformed, Congregationalists, Friends, Unitarians, Universalists, and Roman Catholics. The number of churches of all denominations is ninety-six, of clergymen, eighty-nine.

HISTORY. The settlements in this county were made at a very early date.

Van Schaick's patent, comprising the town of Waterford and the adjacent country; the Saratoga patent north of this, embracing a tract six miles square on the Hudson, and the Apple patent lying on the Mohawk and extending three miles back into the woods towards Ballston lake, were granted about the year 1700.

The patent of Kayaderosseras, embracing nearly the whole of the county not previously conveyed, was granted in 1702, to a company of thirteen individuals, of whom David Schuyler and Robert Livingston were the most prominent.

The exact date of the first settlement on the other patents is uncertain; on the Kayaderosseras they were made as early as 1715.

In 1747, the Indians from Canada attacked the settlement at Fish Creek, now Schuylerville, burned the village, and killed thirty families. After the conquest of Canada, settlements were rapidly made, but confined, for some years, to the neighborhood of the Hudson and Mohawk rivers.

Much of the land in this county is still holden under the annual rent of fifteen or twenty cents per acre, payable to the successors of the company to whom the Kayaderosseras patent was granted.

This county is particularly distinguished for the events of General Burgoyne's campaign in 1777, and his surrender which took place within its limits. The general circumstances connected with this campaign have been already narrated; but a more particular notice of some of the events which transpired in this county may with propriety be introduced here.

After the defeat of Colonels Baum and Breyman at Bennington, General Burgoyne had employed his troops in transporting military stores from Ticonderoga to Fort Edward, until the 12th of September.

Meanwhile General Schuyler, who had retreated from Fort Edward to Stillwater, and thence to the islands at the mouth of the Mohawk, had received considerable reinforcements. On the 19th of August, he was superseded by General Gates, who decided to return to Stillwater, which place he reached with his army on the 9th of September. He immediately selected a strong position on Bemis' Heights, and proceeded to fortify his camp.

On the 13th and 14th, Burgoyne crossed the Hudson and encamped on the heights and plains of Saratoga. On the 17th he approached within four miles of the American camp, and on the 19th advanced against the left wing of the American army, designing if possible to drive them from their position. The action, at first partial, at length became general, and both sides being repeatedly reinforced, the conflict continued till night.

The English remained near the battle field; the Americans retired in good order to their camp, but a short distance from the scene of carnage. Both parties claimed the victory; the English because they held the battle ground; the Americans because they had maintained their position. The British loss, however, was considerably greater than that of the Americans, and in their circumstances, to fight without a decisive victory, was defeat.

The day after this battle, General Burgoyne took a position almost within cannon shot of the American camp, fortified his right wing, and extended his left to the river. Both parties retained their position until the 7th of October; Burgoyne in the hope of receiving aid from Sir Henry Clinton, to whom he had sent the most pressing entreaties for assistance; and General Gates in the confidence of receiving new reinforcements daily.

Receiving no further intelligence from Sir Henry, and finding himself compelled to diminish the rations of his soldiers, the British General determined to test again the strength of his adversary.

Accordingly he selected 1500 choice troops, whom he commanded in person, aided by three of his bravest generals. With these he advanced to the attack, while a corps of rangers, Indians, and provincials were ordered to take a circuitous route, and show themselves in the rear of the American camp.

General Gates perceived the design of the enemy and made such an arrangement of his forces as effectually to defeat General Burgoyne's project; while at the same time, he despatched Colonel Morgan with his corps to a wood which commanded the right flank of the enemy.

Having succeeded in reaching this, unperceived by the British, Colonel Morgan awaited t   moment when they were engaged with the American force in front to pour a deadly and incessant fire upon their right flank.

Meantime, General Gates ordered another division to intercept the retreat of the enemy to their camp. In the attempt to prevent this movement General Frazer, one of Burgoyne's most efficient officers was mortally wounded, and the artillery corps routed. Finding the fortune of the day against him, the British General retreated to his ca   closely pressed by the American army headed by the impetuous Arnold, who, with more than his usual, rashness forced their entrenchments; but being wounded and having his horse killed under him, was compelled to retire. That portion of the British camp occupied by the German troops, was carried by a Massachusetts regiment belonging to Arnold's division.

Darkness put an end to the conflict. The advantage gained by the Americans was decisive. The loss of the British in killed, wounded, and prisoners was heavy, and among the number were several officers of distinction. Their camp too was penetrated by the enemy.

During the night Burgoyne withdrew with his army to a stronger position on the river heights. Aware that his adversary would soon be compelled to surrender from want of provisions, General Gates did not risk another assault, but contented himself with posting strong bodies of troops at every avenue by which retreat was possible, and awaited the result.

Burgoyne attempted a retreat, but could only reach the heights of Saratoga near Schuylerville, where he encamped. Strong bodies of American troops guarded the Hudson and forbade the effort to cross. Driven to desperation, he determined as a last resource to abandon every thing except the arms and provisions which his soldiers could carry, and crossing at or above Fort Edward, press on by forced marches to Fort George.

General Gates had foreseen and prepared for this movement; in addition to the strong guards placed at the fords of the Hudson, he had formed an entrenched camp on the high grounds between Fort Edward and Fort George. On learning this fact, the British General found himself compelled to surrender, and accordingly on the 17th of October the treaty of capitulation was signed, and the British army piled their arms on the plains of Saratoga, east of the village of Schuylerville.

Congress awarded to General Gates and his army their thanks, and presented him with a medal of gold, struck in commemoration of the event.

VILLAGES. BALLSTON SPA, in the town of Milton, the seat of justice for the county, is pleasantly situated, and is celebrated for its mineral waters, which are similar in character to those of Saratoga. It has a number of manufactories, and considerable business. It is connected with Schenectady, Troy, and Saratoga Springs, by railroad. Population, 1500.

Saratoga Springs, situated on a sandy plain, in the town of the same name, is one of the most noted watering places in the world. Broadway, its principal street, is wide and shady, and during the summer, constantly thronged with the gay and fashionable, who resort hither for pleasure and relaxation. It has several fine hotels, which during the summer are crowded with visitors. There are also several academies and female seminaries, and some manufactories. It is connected with Troy and Schenectady by railroad. Population, 3500.

There are eighteen or twenty springs in the town, of which Congress, Putnam's, Pavilion, Iodine, Hamilton, and Flat rock, are the principal. They are regarded as efficacious in bilious and scrofulous diseases.

Waterford, at the confluence of the Mohawk and Hudson rivers, and at the head of sloop navigation on the latter, combines to a great extent, the advantages of railroad, river and canal transportation, and hydraulic power. It is largely engaged in manufactures, which, with its agricultural products, annually amount to between one and two millions of dollars. A bridge 800 feet in length connects it with Lansingburgh. The Waterford sand used for castings, is esteemed the best in the country. Population, about 1800.

Mechanicsville is a small but thriving manufacturing village, in the town of Stillwater. Population, 600.

Stillwater, in the town of the same name, is distinguished for the battles fought between General Gates and Burgoyne, near Bemis' Heights, in 1777, and *Schuylerville*, in the town of Saratoga, for the surrender of the latter, which took place a short distance east of that village.

XX. ONONDAGA COUNTY.

Square miles, 711.
Organized, 1794.

Population, 70,175.
Valuation, 1845, $15,540,164.

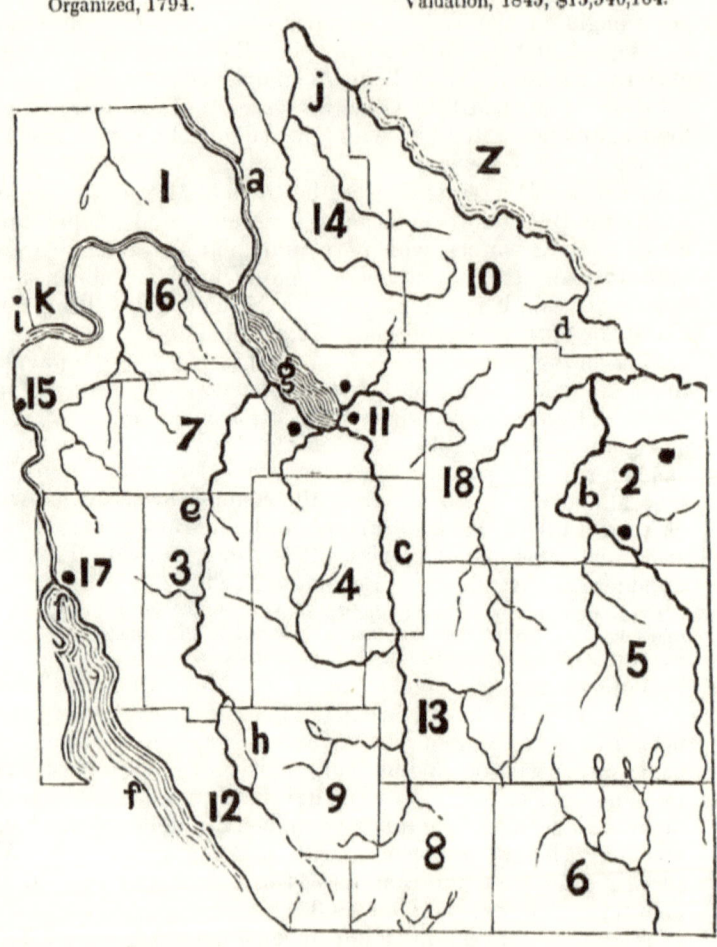

TOWNS.

1. Lysander, 1789.
2. Manlius, 1789.
3. Marcellus, 1789.
4. Onondaga, 1789.
5. Pompey, 1789.
6. Fabius, 1798.
7. Camillus, 1799.
8. Tully, 1803.
9. Otsego, 1806.
10. Cicero, 1807.
11. Salina, 1809.
12. Spafford, 1811.
13. Lafayette, 1825.
14. Clay, 1827.
15. Elbridge, 1829.
16. Van Buren, 1829.
17. Skeneateles, 1830.
18. De Witt, 1835.

ONONDAGA COUNTY.

Rivers. a. Oswego River. d. Chittenango Creek. c. Onondaga. b. Limestone. e. Nine Mile. j. Oneida river. k. Seneca.

Lakes. f. Skeneateles. Z. Oneida. g. Onondaga. h. Otisco. i. Cross.

Villages. SYRACUSE. Manlius. Skeneateles. Salina. Geddes. Jordan.

BOUNDARIES. North by Oswego county and Oneida lake; East by Madison county; South by Cortland; and West by Cayuga counties.

SURFACE. The northern portion of the county is level; the southern hilly, but arable.

The watershed, or height of land dividing the northern and southern waters of the state, passes through the southern portion of this county.

RIVERS. The Seneca, or Oswego river, with its tributaries, drains most of the north-western portion. The other principal streams, flowing northward, are the Oneida River, Chittenango, Limestone, Butternut, Onondaga, and Nine Mile Creeks. The Tioughnioga and Cold Creeks, running southward, have their source in this county.

LAKES. Oneida lake forms a portion of the northeastern boundary. Skeneateles lake, lying mostly in this county, is a beautiful sheet of water, surrounded by picturesque scenery, and abounding in fish. Its trout are particularly celebrated for their size and abundance. The lake is fifteen miles in length, and from half a mile to one mile in width.

Onondaga lake, situated toward the centre of the county, is eight miles long, and from two to four wide. It abounds in fish. Most of the salt springs are near its banks.

Otisco and Cross are the only other lakes of importance.

CLIMATE. The climate of this county is mild and agreeable, more uniform than in some other parts of the state. The diseases of the county are principally of a bilious type.

GEOLOGY AND MINERALS. The northern portion of the county is comprised in that geological formation known as the Ontario group or division, consisting of marly sandstone, soft green shales, and the gypsum and salt rocks, (limestone,) known as the Onondaga salt group. South of this, limestone containing gypsum predominates, and still farther south, slate is the prevailing rock.

Salt is the most valuable and abundant mineral production of this county. The salt is obtained from springs, (probably charged with salt from some deep seated locality of the mineral,) in the town of Salina.

Oxide of iron, gypsum, marl, water limestone, or hydraulic cement, selenite, fibrous gypsum, fluor spar, and serpentine, are also found in the county. Sulphur springs exist in Manlius and many other parts of the county. The marble from the abundance of encrinites and other fossils which it contains, presents a beautiful birdseye appearance, which renders it a valuable building material.

SOIL AND VEGETABLE PRODUCTIONS. The soil is a calcareous loam, intermingled with vegetable mould, and is highly fertile. Maple, basswood, beech, hemlock and pine, are the principal forest trees of the county.

PURSUITS. *Agriculture* is the occupation of a majority of the inhabitants. The soil of the county seems equally well adapted to grazing and the culture of grain. Large quantities of all the grains, as well as flax, potatoes, and other vegetables are raised. In 1845, more barley was raised in this county than in any other in the state. Large quantities of butter, cheese, wool and pork, are also produced.

The county is also largely engaged in *manufactures*. In 1845, they amounted to nearly two and a half millions of dollars, consisting principally of flour, lumber, cotton and woollen goods, iron, distilled and malt liquors, leather and paper.

Commerce. The junction of the Oswego and Erie canals, in this county, gives it a somewhat extensive commerce, both with the Hudson river and the Lakes. The tolls received at Salina, in 1845, amounted to over $52,000, indicating a business of more than $2,000,000.

Mines. Under this head may be included the salt works in the town of Salina. At five different points in this town, salt is produced by the evaporation of brine from the springs.*

In 1840, the amount of salt thus manufactured was 2,622,305 bushels. The springs belong to the state, which receives two mills per bushel for pumping the water, and six cents per bushel duty on the salt. Nearly 11,000 men are employed in the business.

The production of hydraulic cement, so largely used in canals and cisterns, which is extensively prosecuted in this county, also belongs to the head of mines.

STAPLE PRODUCTIONS. Salt, butter, barley, oats, wheat, wool, and hydraulic cement.

SCHOOLS. There were in this county in 1846, 304 school districts. The schools are taught on an average eight months each. $30,857 was expended for the tuition of 24,325 children. The district libraries contained 37,586 volumes. There were also in this county thirty-six unincorporated private and select

---

* The concentration of the brine is accomplished in two ways, viz. 1st, by solar evaporation, for which purpose large shallow vats are constructed, and provided with movable roofs, to protect them from rains ; 2d, by boiling, which is accomplished by means of immense shallow boilers. Crystallization takes place, though in different degrees, by both processes; in the former, the crystals are larger, and the variety known in the markets, as coarse salt, is produced. The latter produces the fine or table salt.

ONONDAGA COUNTY. 251

schools, with 693 pupils, and seven academies, with 338 pupils.

RELIGIOUS DENOMINATIONS. Methodists, Baptists, Presbyterians, Episcopalians, Congregationalists, Roman Catholics, Dutch Reformed, Unitarians, Jews, Universalists, and Friends.

HISTORY. In the town of Pompey, a stone was found some years since, about fourteen inches long, twelve broad, and eight thick. It had a figure of a serpent entwined about a tree, and this inscription.

	tree &c	
Leo X De		L. S.
VIx 1520-		† ∩

This inscription has been interpreted—Leo X. by the grace (or will) of God, sixth year of his pontificate, 1520. L. S. the initials of the person buried, (as it was undoubtedly a sepulchral monument,)—the cross, an indication that he was a Catholic, and the character ∩ perhaps a rude intimation that he belonged to the masonic fraternity. The date is correct, Leo X. having been elected Pope in 1513-14. It seems probable that some Spanish adventurers, in quest of gold or silver, lured by the report of the salt springs, and hoping to find there the object of their search, had wandered hither from Florida, which had been discovered and explored in 1502. One of the number dying here, his companions erected this simple memorial to mark the place of his burial.

In 1655, Father Dablon, a French Jesuit, established himself at one of the Onondaga villages, in the present town of Salina, as a missionary. The succeeding year, the governor of the French possessions in Canada, at his request, sent a colony of fifty men, under the command of the Sieur Dupuys, to settle on the banks of the Onondaga Lake.

For a time the Indians were friendly, but at length they became hostile, and the colonists were compelled to escape by stealth. Having secretly prepared boats sufficient to transport themselves and their effects, one of their number succeeded in inducing the Indians to make a feast, and when, after a hearty repast, all had sunk into a profound slumber, he and his comrades availed themselves of the opportunity to escape, and ere the Indians had awaked, they were beyond their reach.

In 1666, a French settlement was formed, in the northwestern part of the town of Pompey, and flourished for three years, when a party of Spaniards arrived in the village, and quarreling with the French, instigated the natives to destroy them. The Indians, looking with no favorable eye on either, destroyed both, leaving not a survivor to tell the manner of their death.

In the Onondaga Hollow, in the town of Onondaga, formerly stood the town, castle, and council house, of the Onondaga

Indians, the most formidable and highly civilized tribe of the Iroquois confederacy. Here the great council fire was always kept burning, and all matters of importance to the interests of the confederacy were decided. All the leagues and treaties with the whites were made here, and from this tribe was selected the grand Sachem, or principal civil chief, while the Mohawks furnished the principal war chiefs.

Garangula, Thurensera, Decanesora, and Sadekanaghtie, were the most celebrated among their orators, in their early intercourse with the whites.

Black Kettle was the most renowned of their warriors, and more than once he carried war and devastation among the French settlements, even to the gates of their citadels. He was treacherously murdered in 1697, by a party of Algonquins, at the instigation of the French.

In 1696, Count Frontenac, with his usual subtlety, attempted to seduce the Five Nations from their good faith toward the English, and induce them to form a separate treaty of peace with the French. Failing in this, he determined to avenge himself on the Onondagas, whom he regarded as the principal instigators of the opposition to his wishes. Accordingly on the ninth of July, 1696, he set out on an expedition against them, with a large force.

The Onondagas, not receiving seasonable succors from the other members of the confederacy, and finding themselves, (though numbering about 1500 warriors,) unable to cope single handed with so formidable a force, abandoned and set fire to their dwellings, and left to the French commander a barren victory.

The Onondagas, after the return of the French, repossessed themselves of their beautiful valley and reared again their council house and castle. They were the fast friends of the English, and under the direction of Sir John Johnson, took part with them in the revolution. In consequence of their predatory incursions, Colonel Van Schaick was despatched by General James Clinton, to lay waste their towns. As before, they retired at the approach of the invading force, and destroyed their town and castle; only one of their number was slain.

In a few weeks after, they revenged this attack, by an invasion of the settlement of Cobelskill, Schoharie county, in which they butchered several of the unarmed inhabitants. During the late war with Great Britain, they took up arms on the side of the Americans.

The first permanent white settler in the county was a Mr. Webster, who came here in 1786, and settled in Onondaga Hollow, intermarrying with the Indians. In 1788, he obtained permission from the Indians for Messrs. Danforth and Tyler to

ONONDAGA COUNTY. 253

establish themselves in the same valley. This county was originally part of the Military Tract. In the spring of 1788, settlements were made in several towns of the county. In 1790, Manlius was settled. Since the commencement of the present century, the growth of the county has been very rapid.

VILLAGES. SYRACUSE, the county seat, is situated in the town of Salina, on the Erie canal, at its junction with the Oswego canal. It was incorporated in 1825, and owes its rapid growth to the facilities for trade afforded by the canals, and to the extensive salt springs in its neighborhood.

From half a million to a million of bushels of salt are annually produced here; beside iron ware, leather, machinery, flour, &c. Population, nearly 10,000.

It has several extensive and well conducted hotels; its public schools are of a high order; and its substantial buildings and numerous manufactories indicate the enterprise of its inhabitants.

Salina, in the same town, possesses the most productive salt springs in the state, yielding from one to two millions of bushels annually. Its population is about 3000.

Geddes and *Liverpool*, in the same township, the former on the Erie, and the latter on the Oswego canal, are thriving villages, containing productive salt springs.

Skeneateles, in the town of the same name, is pleasantly situated at the foot of Skeneateles lake. Its site commands a fine view of the lake, for a distance of seven or eight miles. Its growth has not been rapid, but healthy, and it is one of the most flourishing villages of the county. Population, about 1500.

Manlius, in the town of the same name, is situated on the Cherry Valley turnpike. It has a flourishing incorporated academy, several manufactories, and about 1200 inhabitants.

Jordan, in the town of Elbridge, is situated on the Erie canal, and is engaged to some extent in manufactures. Population, about 1200.

Onondaga Hollow, in the town of Onondaga, is pleasantly situated on the great western turnpike, four miles south of Syracuse. The Onondaga academy located here, is an old and flourishing institution. Population, about 800.

About three miles south of the village is the Onondaga Indian reservation, where reside the remnant of that once powerful tribe. The legislature, in April, 1846, granted the sum of $300 for the erection of a school-house for the children belonging to this reservation, and a well conducted school is now maintained there.

Fayetteville, in the town of Manlius, has an incorporated academy, and is a thriving village. Population, 900.

XXI. TIOGA COUNTY.

Square miles, 500.
Organized, 1794.
Population, 22,456.
Valuation, 1845, $1,804,211.

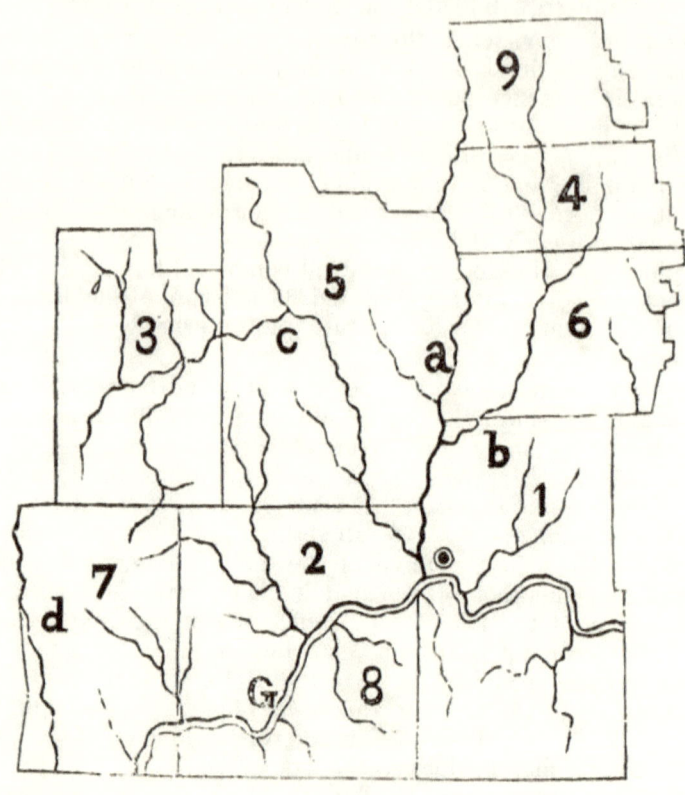

TOWNS.

1. Owego, 1791.
2. Tioga, 1800.
3. Spencer, 1806.
4. Berkshire, 1808.
5. Candor, 1811.
6. Newark, 1823.
7. Barton, 1824.
8. Nichols, 1824.
9. Richford, 1833.

Rivers, &c. G. Susquehanna. a. West Owego Creek. b. East Owego. c. Cattotong. d. Cayuta.

Villages. OWEGO. Rushville.

BOUNDARIES. North by Tompkins and Cortland; East by Broome; South by the State of Pennsylvania; and West by Chemung and Tompkins counties.

TIOGA COUNTY. 255

SURFACE. This, like the other counties bordering on the Pennsylvania line, is elevated. Apparently it was once level, but it is now cut into hills and valleys by the eastern branch of the Susquehanna, and its tributaries, which affords abundance of water for the convenience of the farmer, and in many instances, it may be used for manufacturing purposes. On either side of the Susquehanna, are lofty swells of heavy rolling land, yet the creeks are frequently skirted with broad valleys.

RIVERS. The Susquehanna, having a south-west course through the southern part, and its branches the East and West Owego, Cattotong and Cayuta creeks, flowing southerly, are the principal streams of the county.

RAILROADS. The New York and Erie railroad will probably pass through the valley of the Susquehanna. The Ithaca and Owego railroad is already in operation, connecting the two villages whose name it bears.

CLIMATE. The county has a low temperature, owing to the elevation of its surface. It is regarded as healthy.

GEOLOGY AND MINERALS. This county lies wholly within the Chemung sandstone formation, except a small tract of the old red sandstone upon its southern border.

Its minerals are few. Marl is found in the town of Spencer, which is burned for lime. There are several sulphur springs in the county.

SOIL AND VEGETABLE PRODUCTIONS. The soil is mostly fertile, consisting of a light gravelly loam, with occasional patches of marl and clay. Grass succeeds better than grain in the highlands, but the valleys yield large crops of wheat and corn, while the other crops thrive almost every where. White pine, hemlock, spruce, oak, maple, and beech are the principal timber, and have a dense growth. Maple sugar is produced in considerable quantities.

PURSUITS. *Agriculture.* The people are for the most part engaged in agricultural pursuits. Some grain is raised, and considerable attention paid to the products of the dairy.

Manufactures. The only manufactures of importance are those of lumber and flour.

Commerce. The products of the county find their way to market, by the Susquehanna river, and the Ithaca and Owego railroad.

STAPLE PRODUCTIONS. Oats, corn, potatoes, wheat and butter.

SCHOOLS. This county has 139 district schools, taught in 1846, an average period of eight months each, having 8291 scholars, and paying their teachers over $9,329. The school libraries contained, the same year, 12,744 volumes.

It has nine private schools, with 294 pupils, and one academy, with 125 students.

RELIGIOUS DENOMINATIONS. Methodists, Baptists, Congregationalists, Presbyterians, and Episcopalians. The entire number of churches is thirty-two, of clergyman, forty-two.

HISTORY. Tioga county was taken from Montgomery county in 1694. Its name signifies a point or promontory in the river, a junction of waters. It was the Seneca name for the Chemung river.

The towns of Richford, Berkshire and Newark were part of the tract known as the "Massachusetts ten townships," which were ceded to that state by New York.

Barton, Tioga, Owego, and Nichols, were granted by the state to military claimants. Considerable portions of these townships were sold at eighteen cents per acre.

The county was settled by emigrants from New Hampshire, Massachusetts, Connecticut, New York, New Jersey, and Pennsylvania. The first settlement was made in 1785, at Owego, by James McMaster and William Taylor, who cleared, the first season, ten or fifteen acres, and raised a crop of corn from the same land.

A few years after its first settlement, there was a great famine in this section of country. It occurred just before harvesting, and for six weeks the inhabitants were without bread of any kind. Meanwhile they subsisted principally upon roots, and though they became very much emaciated and feeble, none died of hunger. It was occasioned by the arrival of a greater number of settlers than usual, and a scarcity in Wyoming that season. Famine is at present little dreaded in this region.

VILLAGES. OWEGO VILLAGE, in the town of Owego, is pleasantly situated on the north side of the Susquehanna, and is the county town. It was commenced in 1785, and laid out into lots in 1794 or 1795. It is advantageously situated for trade, has a large water power, and by means of the Ithaca and Owego railroad, and the Susquehanna river, a ready access to market.

Besides the court house, jail, and county clerk's office, it has four churches, an incorporated academy, and a number of stores and manufactories. A bridge a fourth of a mile in length crosses the Susquehanna at this place.

This village takes its name from the Owego creek, which empties into the Susquehanna near it. Population 2500.

Rushville or *Nichols Village*, in the town of Nichols, *Candor*, *Newark*, *Richfield*, and *Spencer*, in the towns of the same names are all thriving villages.

XXII. SCHOHARIE COUNTY.

Square miles, 621.
Organized, 1795.

Population, 32,488.
Valuation in 1845, $1,804,165.

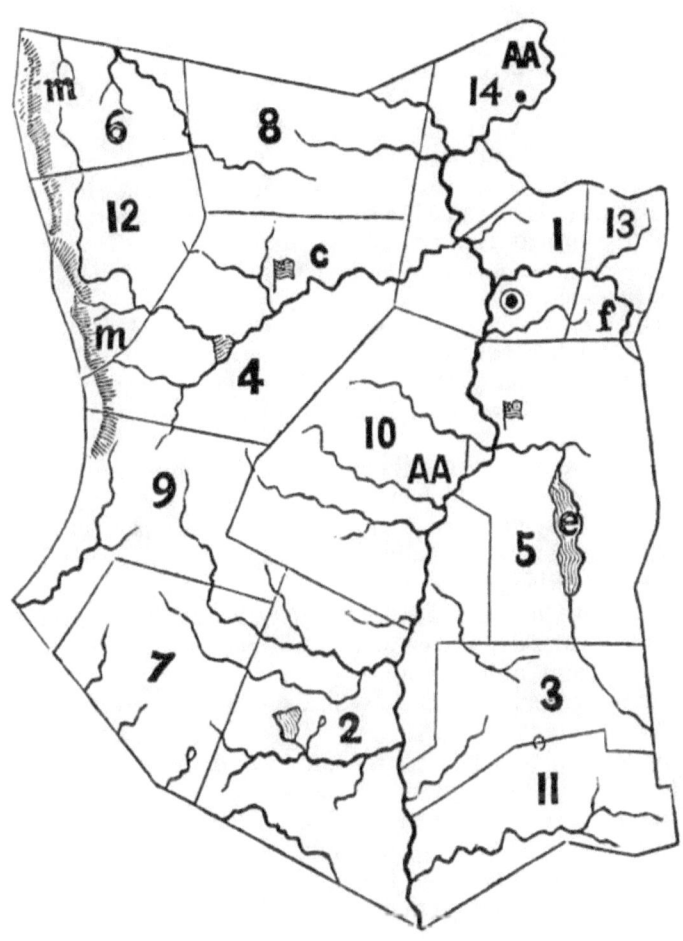

TOWNS.

1. Schoharie, 1788.
2. Blenheim, 1797.
3. Broome, 1797.
4. Cobleskill, 1797.
5. Middleburgh, 1797.
6. Sharon, 1797.
7. Jefferson, 1803.
8. Carlisle, 1807.
9. Summit, 1819.
10. Fulton, 1828.
11. Conesville, 1836.
12. Seward, 1840.
13. Wright, 1846.
14. Esperance, 1846.

Mountains. m. Kaatsbergs.
Rivers, &c. A A. Schoharie Creek. c. Cobleskill. f. Foxes Creek.

Lakes, &c. e. The Vly.
Battle Fields. Cobleskill. Middleburgh.
Villages. SCHOHARIE. Esperance.

BOUNDARIES. North by Montgomery and Schenectady; East by Schenectady and Albany; South by Delaware and Greene, and West by Delaware and Otsego counties.

SURFACE. Mountainous. The county is divided into two unequal sections by the Schoharie kill or creek. The main branch of the Kaatsbergs or Catskill mountains cross the south part of the county, through Broome, Blenheim, Jefferson, and Summit, to the line of Otsego county, broken through, however, by the Schoharie creek.

A spur from the same range passes northward, through Broome, Middleburgh, and Schoharie, into Schenectady and Montgomery counties. This spur is called the Middleberg, from its position between the Helderbergs and the main range of the Kaatsbergs.

The mountains west of Schoharie creek maintain an elevation of from 2000 to 2600 feet. The Middleberg is 1700 feet high, at its most elevated portion, in the south part of the county, but declines gradually towards the east, till it mingles with the Helderbergs.

RIVERS AND CREEKS. The Schoharie creek with its tributaries, the Cobleskill, Foxes and Breakabeen creeks, are the principal streams in the county.

Bowman's creek, and the Catskill and Charlotte rivers, also take their rise in this county.

In the town of Middleburgh is a large marsh, called the Vlaie or Vly, which is the source of the Catskill.

CLIMATE. From the elevation of its surface, the climate of Schoharie county is cold, but healthful.

GEOLOGY AND MINERALS. The rocks of this county are transition, consisting of slate, graywacke, and limestone. The latter, however, predominates, and is generally the surface rock of the county. Portions of the Helderberg series, and the Erie and Catskill groups occupy the county. The last two are confined to the southern part.

Water limestone is found in great abundance in the northern and central portions of the county.

On the west side of Schoharie creek, in the town of Schoharie, are found beds of massive strontianite, of extraordinary beauty. It was regarded by the inhabitants as marble for many years. Arragonite, heavy spar, and calcareous spar, are also found in the water lime formation. Portions of the water limestone have been excavated for lithographic stones, and are said to be equal in quality to the German.

Fine specimens of fibrous sulphate of barytes and carbonate of lime are found in Carlisle, and fibrous celestine, and crystallized iron pyrites, in Schoharie. Bog

SCHOHARIE COUNTY.

iron ore occurs in the same vicinity. Calcareous tufa abounds on the side of the mountains. Anhydrous sulphate of lime has been discovered in Sharon.

Gebhard's cavern, or Ball's cave, in the town of Schoharie, contains numerous apartments abounding in stalactites and stalagmites of great beauty; some of the apartments are large and magnificent.

Otsgaragee cavern, in the same town, has numerous large apartments, highly decorated with spars and stalactites. There are other caves in the vicinity, of less extent.

There are several sulphur springs; those at Sharon have attained considerable notoriety.

SOIL AND VEGETABLE PRODUCTIONS. The flats in the valley of Schoharie creek, are among the most fertile lands in the state. The county generally is fertile, and some sections are adapted to wheat; some portion of the southern towns is sterile and sandy.

The timber consists of oak, maple, elm, linden, ash, poplar, hickory, walnut, white pine, and hemlock. The two latter prevail in the southern part of the county.

PURSUITS. *Agriculture* is the employment of a majority of the inhabitants. Oats, rye, barley, wheat, corn, buckwheat, peas, potatoes, and flax, are raised in large quantities, and butter and wool produced to a very considerable extent.

Manufactures generally have not attained any great importance. The facilities afforded by the hemlock forests, have led to the extensive tanning of leather. The quantity prepared in the county, in 1845, exceeded in value $400,000. Flour and lumber are also manufactured to some extent.

The county has no *commerce* and no *mines*.

The STAPLE PRODUCTIONS are oats, rye, barley, wheat, corn, peas, butter, and wool.

SCHOOLS. There are in the county, 184 school-houses. In 1846, schools were taught, on an average, nine months; 11,043 children received instruction, at an expense for tuition of $13,726. The district libraries contained 17,985 volumes.

There were also in the county, twenty-five private schools, with 334 scholars, and two academies with ninety-four pupils.

RELIGIOUS DENOMINATIONS. Methodists, Baptists, Lutherans, Dutch Reformed, Presbyterians, Unitarians, and Universalists. Number of churches fifty-eight, of clergymen fifty-six.

HISTORY. The first white settlements in this county were made in the spring of 1711.

The benevolent Queen Anne formed the design of establishing a colony of Germans, the families of German soldiers who had served in the English wars, in her transatlantic possessions. She accordingly sent them over to New York, and thence to Albany, and permitted them to select for themselves, from the unoccupied lands of New York, a tract suited to their tastes. They selected the valley of the Schoharie, and the Queen's agent accordingly purchased for them, about 20,000 acres of fertile land, along that creek.

Industrious and frugal, these hardy settlers soon acquired a competence, and perhaps in no part of the state, at the commencement of the troubles which preceded the Revolution, could there have been found a more peaceful and happy settlement. Highly cultivated farms, and substantial dwellings greeted the eye of the traveller in every direction.

But in those exciting times, differences of opinio prevailed, and when the conflict came on, the citizens of Schohaire county were found arrayed in hostility against each other, and, oft times, members of the same family met in deadly strife.

The patriots of Schoharie county seemed, in an especial manner, to have excited the hostility of the enemy. Again and again did the marauding hordes of tories and Indians, under the command of Sir John Johnson, Brant, and the infamous Walter Butler, descend upon the farms of the hapless citizens, murdering and scalping all whom they met, without regard to age or sex, plundering and burning their dwellings, and making that fertile and beautiful valley a desolate and gloomy waste.

On the 1st of June, 1778, a bloody conflict took place at Cobleskill, in which about fifty whites, regular troops and militia, contended with a force of 350 Indians, under the command of Brant, until twenty-two of their number were killed, and eight or ten more severely wounded.

A short distance from Middleburgh village are still visible the remains of the old Middle Fort, which was quite noted in the annals of the border wars in this county. On the 17th of October, 1780, it was attacked by Sir John Johnson with a force of 800 tories and Indians.

The garrison of the fort consisted of about two hundred continental troops, and between one and two hundred militia. Their supply of ammunition was scanty, and the commander of the fort, Major Woolsey, entirely unfitted for his station.

The garrison, however, determined to defend the fort to the last, and when Major Woolsey proposed to surrender, they opposed it, and as he was so much overcome with fear as to be a subject of derision to the garrison, Colonel Vrooman, a militia officer in the fort, took the command.

After continuing the attack through the greater part of the day, without effect, Sir John withdrew down the valley of the Schoharie, burning all the houses and other buildings in his route. In this action the loss of the British was heavy, while that of the garrison was but four wounded, two of whom afterward died.

There were two other forts in Schoharie county, the Upper, five miles southeast from the middle, on the Schoharie creek, in the town of Fulton; and the Lower, near the village of Schoharie.

Many other incidents connected with these incursions are deeply interesting, but pertaining only to individual conflicts, must necessarily be omitted.

Justice, however, requires that we should notice, in passing, the brave and fearless Schoharie rifleman, Timothy Murphy, whose services to the cause of freedom were numerous, and rendered with a cheerfulness and devotion worthy of all praise. Such was his skill in the use of his rifle, that the foeman who came within its range, was always sure to "bite the dust."

After the Revolution, quiet was restored, and the beautiful valley of the Schoharie was soon again lined with farms and dwellings, which indicated the thrift and competency of their owners.

The German language is still spoken by many of the older inhabitants, but their children receive an English education.

VILLAGES, &c. SCHOHARIE, in the town of the same name, is a small village situated in the midst of a region rich in minerals. Its public buildings are neat and substantial. Population about 500.

Esperance, the only incorporated village in the county, is in the town of the same name. It has some manufactures. Population about 500.

Sharon Springs, in the town of Sharon, and near the boundary line of Schoharie, Otsego, and Montgomery counties, has recently become a place of fashionable resort. The sulphur waters are said strongly to resemble those of the White Sulphur springs of Virginia. There is also a chalybeate spring here. The Pavilion, a fine hotel, was erected in 1836, and during the season is usually thronged with visitors.*

---

* The following is Dr. Chilton's analysis of the waters of these springs.

	Grains.
Sulphate of magnesia, (Epsom salts,)	42.40
" lime	111.62
Chloride of sodium	2.24
" magnesia	2.40
Hydrosulphuret of sodium } calcium }	2.28
Total	160.94

Sulphuretted hydrogen gas, 16 cubic inches.

XXIII. STEUBEN COUNTY.

Square Miles, 1400.   Population, 51,679.
Organized, 1796.   Valuation, 1845, $6,172,414.

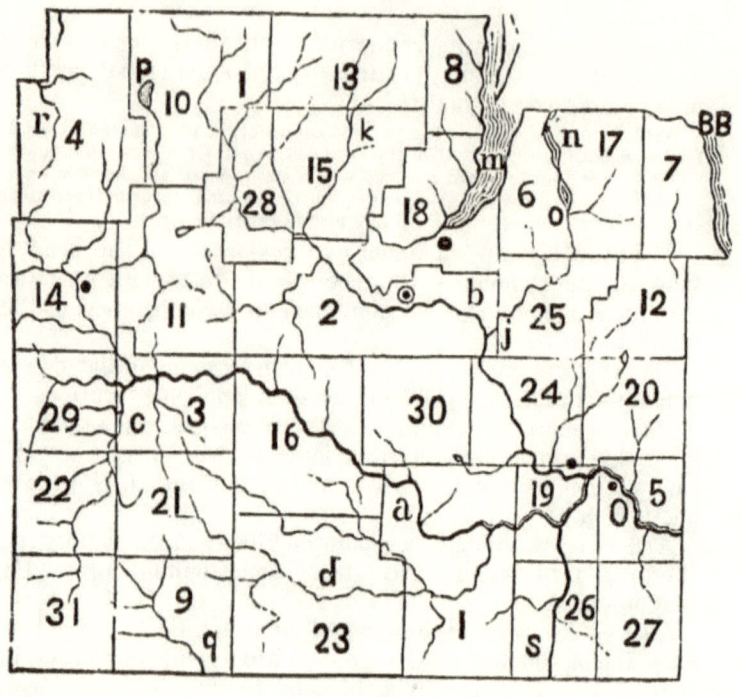

TOWNS.

1. Addison, 1796.
2. Bath, 1796.
3. Canisteo, 1796.
4. Dansville, 1796.
5. Painted Post, 1796.
6. Wayne, 1796.
7. Reading, 1806.
8. Pulteney, 1808.
9. Troupsburg, 1808.
10. Conhocton, 1812.
11. Howard, 1812.
12. Orange, 1813.
13. Prattsburgh, 1813.
14. Hornellsville, 1820.
15. Wheeler, 1820.
16. Cameron, 1822.
17. Tyrone, 1822.
18. Urbana, 1822.
19. Erwin, 1826.
20. Hornby, 1826.
21. Jasper, 1827.
22. Greenwood, 1827.
23. Woodhull, 1828.
24. Campbell, 1831.
25. Bradford, 1837.
26. Lindley, 1837.
27. Caton, 1837.
28. Avoca, 1843.
29. Hartsville, 1843.
30. Thurston, 1843.
31. West Union, 1843.

STEUBEN COUNTY. 263

Rivers, O. Chemung river. a. Canisteo. b. Conhocton. c. Bennett's creek. d. Tuscarora. j. Mud. k. Five Mile. l. Twelve Mile. q. Cowanesqua. r. Canascraga. s. Tioga river.

Lakes. BB. Seneca. m. Crooked. n. Little. o. Mud. p. Loon.

Villages. BATH. Corning. Painted Post. Hammondsport. Hornellsville.

BOUNDARIES. North by Livingston, Ontario and Yates counties; East by Seneca lake and Chemung county; South by the State of Pennsylvania; and West by Livingston and Allegany counties.

SURFACE. This county belongs to the great table land, which extends through the southern tier of counties; owing, however, to the perishable character of the rocks on which it is based, the rivers have worn deep valleys, whose precipitous banks, frequently 400 or 500 feet in height, give it a greatly diversified surface. The general elevation of the table land is about 1500 feet above tide water. An irregular ridge on the west separates the waters of the Susquehanna from those of Genesee river.

RIVERS. The principal stream of the county is the Chemung, formed by the union of the Tioga, the Canisteo, and the Conhocton. The name of the river means "a horn in the water," and is said to be derived from an immense horn or tusk which protruded from the bank of the river many years since. These streams are navigable during the freshet season. Their principal tributaries are Bennett's and Tuscarora creeks, of the Canisteo; and Mud, Five Mile and Twelve Mile creeks, of the Conhocton. The only other streams of any size are the Canascraga and Cowanesqua.

LAKES. Seneca lake forms the eastern boundary of the county for about eight miles. Crooked lake extends into it from Yates for about the same distance. Little, Mud and Loon are the names of the other lakes. The latter has a subterranean outlet half a mile long.

RAILROADS. The Corning and Blossburg railroad entering the county from the south, terminates at Corning, which is situated at the head of the navigable feeder of the Chemung canal. The New York and Erie railroad will pass through this county.

CLIMATE. The surface is so much elevated that the winters are generally cold and severe, and the seasons backward. The county, however, is generally healthy.

GEOLOGY AND MINERALS. The surface rock of this county, to the depth of nearly 1000 feet, is the Chemung group of sandstones and shales. It has some beds of bog iron ore, and several sulphur springs.

SOIL AND VEGETABLE PRODUCTIONS. Most of the soil is productive. The uplands are well adapted to grazing. The alluvial flats of the Chemung river comprise the richest lands in the county, and are said to exceed those of the Mohawk in fertility.

The county north of the Conhocton river, and east of Five Mile creek, is covered chiefly with oak, chesnut, hickory, black walnut, yellow and white pine timber; between the Canisteo and Conhocton, beech, maple, white pine, and hemlock, are the prevailing forest trees, except a narrow tract on the Canisteo, where oak prevails. South of the Canisteo, beech, maple, white pine, and hemlock, are predominant. The oak and yellow pine lands produce excellent wheat; the other lands are better adapted to grass.

PURSUITS. *Agriculture* is the chief pursuit. Grain is largely produced on the alluvial lands. Great numbers of cattle and sheep are raised on the table lands. The lumber business is an important branch of industry.

Manufactures are increasing in importance. Lumber is largely manufactured in the southern part of the county. Flour, leather, and fulled cloths, are also produced in considerable quantities.

The *Commerce* of the county, by means of the spring navigation of the rivers, the navigable feeder of the Chemung canal, and the facilities afforded by the Corning and Blossburg railroad, is quite large and increasing.

STAPLE PRODUCTIONS. Wheat, oats, corn, potatoes, butter, wool, and lumber.

SCHOOLS. In this county there were, in 1846, 326 district schoolhouses, in which schools were maintained an average period of seven months. The number of scholars in attendance was 19,771, and the sum expended for their tuition $20,918. The district libraries contained 30,125 volumes.

There were also twenty-four private schools, with 626 pupils, and one academy and one female seminary, with 148 students.

RELIGIOUS DENOMINATIONS. Methodists, Presbyterians, Baptists, Episcopalians, Universalists, Unitarians, and Roman Catholics. There are seventy-five churches, and 114 clergymen of all denominations, in the county.

HISTORY. This county is indebted to the enterprsie and energy of Mr. Charles Williamson, the agent of the Pulteney estate, for its early settlement and rapid growth. Finding emigrants unwilling to settle upon the elevated lands of this county, while the more alluring flats of the Genesee remained in market, he resolved himself to set the example of emigration to this section. Accordingly, in 1792, with two companions, he cut his way through the forests, and located at Bath. In 1795, the population in the vicinity had increased so rapidly, that Mr. Williamson established a theatre at his new settlement. The succeeding year, the county was organized, and named after Baron Steuben, the Prussian General. The same year a newspaper was established at Bath, and called the Bath Gazette. The population of the county at this time was about 800. The whole county, except the town of Reading, belonged to the Pulteney estate. The emigrants were mostly from Pennsylvania, except in the town of Prattsburgh, which was settled by New Englanders.

In the present town of Erwin, formerly stood the *Painted Post*, so famous in our early Indian annals, erected by an Indian chief, (probably during the first French war,) to commemorate his victory over the whites, and the number of scalps and prisoners, he had taken.

VILLAGES. BATH, the county seat, was laid out by Mr. Williamson in 1792. It is on the north bank of the Conhocton, has regular and parallel streets and two public squares, and is regarded as one of the most pleasant villages of western New York. Here is a flourishing female seminary. Population 1500.

Corning, situated on the south side of the Chemung river in the town of Painted Post, is admirably located for trade, being at the junction of the Corning and Blossburg railroad, with the navigable feeder of the Chemung canal, and also on the proposed route of the New York and Erie railroad. Its coal trade is already very great, and its growth has been rapid. Population 1200.

Hammondsport, situated at the southern termination of Crooked lake in the town of Urbana, is a thriving village. A steamboat plies between this place and Penn Yan. It has also a communication with New York, by means of the Crooked and Seneca lakes, Cayuga, Seneca, and Erie canals. Population 1000.

Painted Post, in the town of Erwin, is a flourishing village at the junction of the Conhocton and Tioga rivers. It has a large amount of hydraulic power, which is in part applied to manufacturing purposes. The painted post above described, is in this village. Population 600.

Hornellsville is a village of considerable importance, situated on the Canisteo in the town of the same name.

XXIV. DELAWARE COUNTY.

Square miles, 1362.
Organized, 1797.

Population, 36,990.
Valuation, 1845, $3,478,012.

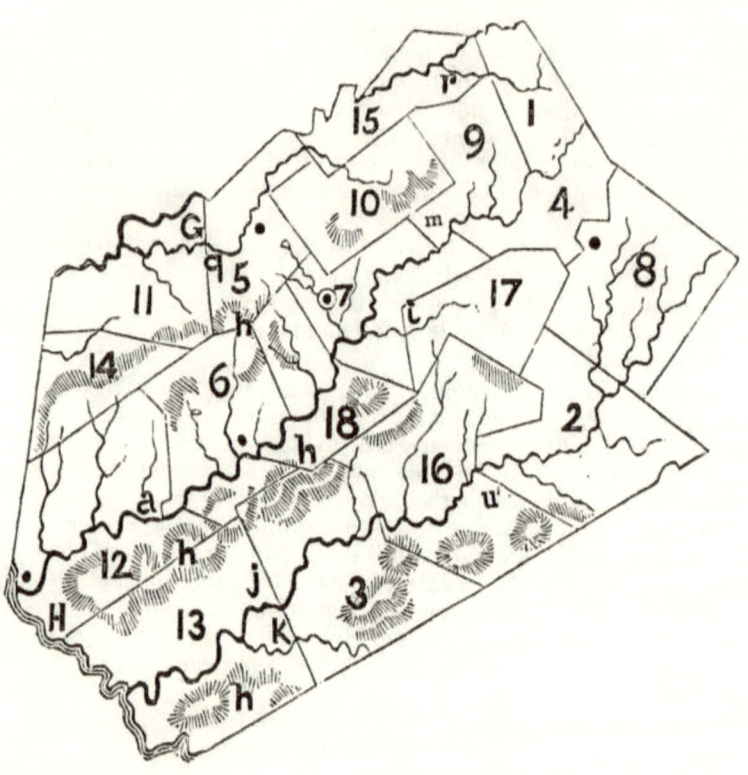

TOWNS.

1. Harpersfield, 1788.
2. Middletown, 1789.
3. Colchester, 1792.
4. Stamford, 1792.
5. Franklin, 1792.
6. Walton, 1797.
7. Delhi, 1798.
8. Roxbury, 1799.
9. Kortright, 1793.
10. Meredith, 1800.
11. Sidney, 1801.
12. Tompkins, 1806.
13. Hancock, 1806.
14. Masonville, 1811.
15. Davenport, 1817.
16. Andes, 1819.
17. Bovina, 1820.
18. Hampden, 1825.

Mountains. h. Blue. m. Kaatsberg. u. Pine.
Rivers. G. Susquehanna. H. Delaware. a. Mohawks or West Branch Delaware. i. Little Delaware river. j. Papachton Branch. k. Big Beaver kill. q. Oleout creek. r. Charlotte river.
Villages. DELHI. Franklin. Hobart. Deposit. Walton.

DELAWARE COUNTY. 267

BOUNDARIES. North by Otsego and Schoharie; East by Schoharie and Greene; South by Ulster and Sullivan, and the state of Pennsylvania; and West by Pennsylvania, Broome and Chenango counties.

SURFACE. Delaware county has three distinct ranges of mountains passing through it from southwest to northeast, rendering its surface very rough and broken. The southeast ridge is a continuation of a range of the Kaatsbergs. The second ridge runs between the Papachton and the Mohawk branch of the Delaware river; while the third, from twelve to eighteen miles in width, is bounded by the Charlotte river and the Susquehanna. The two latter are collectively known as the Blue mountains. A part of the eastern ridge has received the name of the Pine mountains. The surface of the summits and sides of the hills are extremely irregular, and broken by numerous streams.

RIVERS. The Mohawks, or main branch of the Delaware, has its source in Schoharie county, running thence in a southwesterly direction nearly 70 miles, through the center of the county, to Port Deposit, where it takes a southeasterly course, and forms the boundary line between New York and Pennsylvania. Its principal tributaries are the Little Delaware and the Papachton branch; the latter is sixty-five miles long and receives the Big Beaver kill. The Charlotte and Susquehanna form portions of the northern boundary.

RRILROADS. The New York and Erie railroad is in process of construction, through the southeast corner of the county.

CLIMATE. The climate of this county is subject to sudden and extreme changes of temperature, yet it is not unfriendly to health. The cold is severe in winter.

GEOLOGY AND MINERALOGY. The surface rock of this county is the old red sandstone of the Catskill group underlaid by the shales and sandstone of the Portage and Chemung group.

<small>Its minerals are few. Bog iron ore has been discovered in considerable beds; copper extensively diffused, but in small quantities. There are several mineral springs, and a brine spring near Delhi.</small>

VEGETABLE PRODUCTIONS. The soil is as varied as the surface, but generally of a good quality. On the hills it is a sandy loam, and in some places stoney. In the valleys is a rich deep mould, and of lasting fertility. It is better adapted to grass than the raising of grain. The county is densely timbered with beech, birch, maple, ash, elm, basswood, pine, wild cherry, butternut, hemlock, and small quantities of oak.

PURSUITS. *Agriculture* chiefly engages the attention of the people of this county; considerable quantities of grain are produced, and it is exceeded by few counties in the number of cattle reared. It is second only to Oneida in the manufacture of butter.

Manufactures. The water-power of this county is abundant, but little improved. Its principal manufactured articles are leather, flour, lumber, and fulled cloths. The lumber is floated to market on the Delaware and Susquehanna rivers.

The *Commerce* of the county is not large, its rivers being only navigable in the spring.

STAPLE PRODUCTIONS. Butter and cheese, oats, potatoes, rye, wool, and lumber. Increased facilities for conveying them to market will be afforded by the railroad now constructing.

SCHOOLS. In 1846, there were 288 public schools in session, on an average, seven months each, expending for tuition $14,013, and numbering 12,501 pupils. The district libraries contained 24,027 volumes.

There are twenty-three unincorporated private schools, attended by 342 scholars, and two incorporated academies with 124 students.

RELIGIOUS DENOMINATIONS. Methodists, Presbyterians, Congregationalists, Baptists, Episcopalians, Dutch Reformed, and Unitarians. The whole number of churches, is fifty-eight, of clergymen seventy-seven.

HISTORY. The county, west of the Mohawks branch, was originally held by several proprietors, but east of that river was comprised in the Hardenburgh patent. In 1768, William, John, Alexander, and Joseph Harper, with eighteen others, obtained a patent for 22,000 acres of land within its limits. The Harpers soon after moved from Cherry Valley, and founded the settlement of Harpersfield.

In the spring of 1780, a party of Indians and tories under the command of Brant, destroyed this settlement. Most of the inhabitants had previously fled, a few only remained to make sugar. Several of these were killed, and nineteen made prisoners and carried to Niagara. After the war the place was rebuilt, and Colonel John Harper, who had distinguished himself by his bravery and humanity during the war, spent the remainder of his days there.

VILLAGES. DELHI village is the county seat, and contains, besides the county buildings, two churches, an academy, and a number of manufactories. Population 800.

Franklin is the seat of the Delaware Institute, incorporated April 25, 1835. Population 700.

Hobart, in the town of Stamford, is a village of some importance. It has some manufactories.

Deposit, in the town of Tompkins, is a great lumber mart. Much of the lumber which is floated down the Delaware during the spring freshets is deposited here. It is on the proposed route of the New York and Erie railroad. Population 600.

Walton, in the town of the same name, is a small but thriving village on the Delaware.

XXV. CHENANGO COUNTY.

Square miles, 804.
Organized, 1798.
Population, 39,900.
Valuation, 1845, $4,133,256.

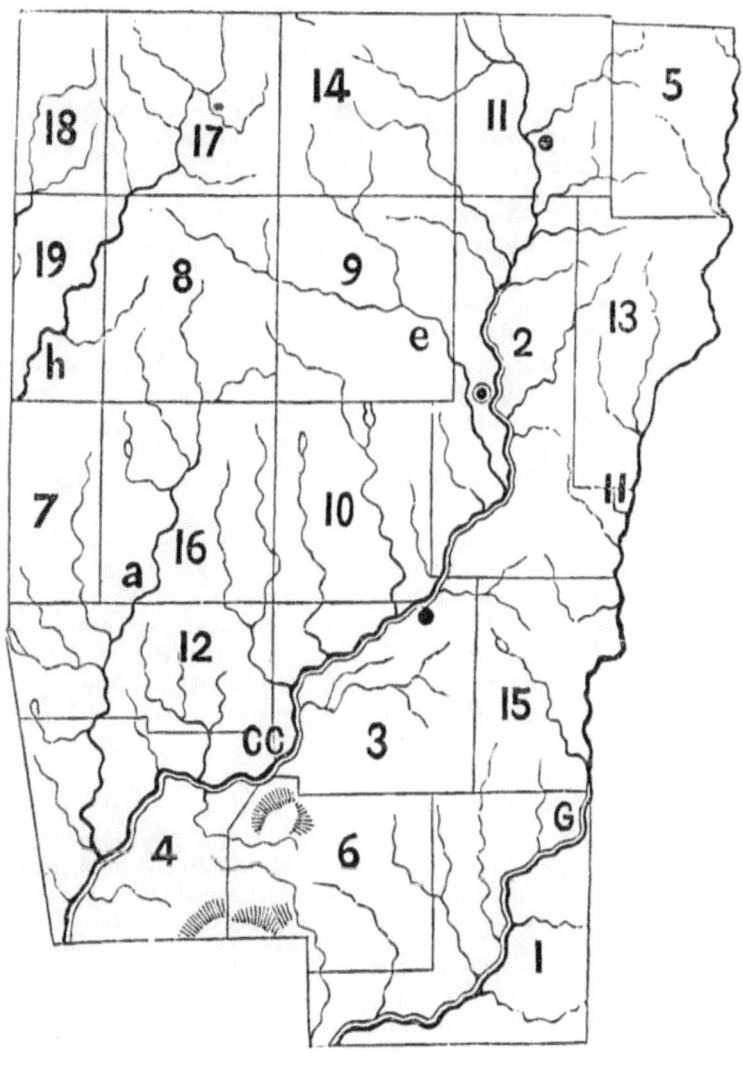

TOWNS.

1. Bainbridge, 1791.
2. Norwich, 1793.
3. Oxford, 1793.
4. Greene, 1798.
5. Columbus, 1805.
6. Coventry, 1806.

7. German, 1806.
8. Pharsalia, 1806.
9. Plymouth, 1806.
10. Preston, 1806.
11. Sherburne, 1806.
12. Smithville, 1806.
13. New Berlin, 1807.
14. Smyrna, 1808.
15. Guilford, 1813.
16. McDonough, 1816.
17. Otselic, 1817.
18. Linklaem, 1823.
19. Pitcher, 1827.

Rivers. II. Unadilla river. CC. Chenango. G. Susquehanna. h. Otselic. a. Geneganslette creek. e. Canasawacta.

Villages. NORWICH. Oxford. Sherburne.

BOUNDARIES. North by Madison county; East by Otsego and Delaware; South by Broome; and West by Broome and Cortland counties.

SURFACE. This county is comprised in the extensive table land, which occupies so large a portion of southern and western New York. The force and velocity of its principal streams, however, have cut deep and broad channels through the rocks, and thus formed wide and beautiful alluvial valleys, giving the county an apparently diversified surface. The table land between the Unadilla and Chenango rivers is 1630 feet above tide water.

RIVERS. The Chenango, a beautiful stream, and its tributaries, the principal of which are the Geneganslette and Canasawacta, drain the central portion of the county. The Unadilla washes its eastern border, while the Susquehanna crosses its southeastern, and the Otselic its northwestern corner.

CANALS. The Chenango Canal passes through the county in the broad valley of the Chenango river, furnishing a convenient outlet for its abundant produce.

CLIMATE. Mild, healthful, and pleasant.

GEOLOGY AND MINERALS. The western part of this county belongs to the Chemung sandstone group; the eastern part to the old red sandstone of the Catskill group, and a small tract at the north to the limestone of the Helderberg series.

There are few minerals in the county, the geological formations not being favorable to their production. There are two or three sulphur springs which have some reputation in the treatment of cutaneous diseases.

SOIL AND VEGETABLE PRODUCTIONS. The soil on the table lands is admirably adapted to grazing; in the alluvial valleys it is a rich, gravelly loam, yielding abundant crops of grain. The principal forest trees are beech, maple, basswood, elm, butternut, black cherry, and in the south, hemlock and pine.

PURSUITS. *Agriculture* is the leading pursuit. Great attention is paid to the rearing of cattle, horses and sheep. Butter and cheese are largely produced, particularly in the southern towns. The county ranks among the first in the state in the production of butter, cheese, wool and flax.

Manufactures are receiving increasing attention. At present, however, the most important are those of flour, lumber, leather, fulled cloths, and cotton and woollen goods.

The *commerce* of the county, through the medium of the Chenango canal, and the Susquehanna river, is large and constantly increasing.

STAPLE PRODUCTIONS. Butter, cheese, wool, flax and oats.

SCHOOLS. In 1846, there were in the county 287 district school-houses, in which schools were maintained an average period of seven months, at an expense for tuition of $16,283; 14,750 scholars attended these schools. The district libraries contained 26,598 volumes.

There were also thirty-five select schools, attended by 658 pupils, and four incorporated academies, with 416 students.

RELIGIOUS DENOMINATIONS. Baptists, Methodists, Congregationalists, Episcopalians, Presbyterians, Universalists, and Friends. The entire number of churches, is eighty-three; of clergymen, ninety-four.

HISTORY. Chenango was formed from the counties of Tioga and Herkimer, in 1798. The first settlement was made in Oxford, in 1790; another was made at Bainbridge, in 1791. The latter township was granted by the state of New York, to Vermont, as a compensation for losses of individuals who had suffered on account of grants made by the state of Vermont, before the settlement of her difficulties with New York. Most of the early settlers of the county were from New England, and a majority of them from Connecticut.

The first settlers in the village of Greene, were a party of French emigrants, some of whom were men of distinction in their own country. After some years, however, owing to pecuniary difficulties, they became discouraged, and removed to Pennsylvania. An academy was established and incorporated at Oxford, in 1794. The town of Sherburne was settled by a party of twenty families, from Connecticut, who organized themselves into a church before emigrating. They arrived at their location on Thursday, and by the succeeding Sabbath had erected a log meeting-house, in which they met for worship, and it is said that not a Sabbath has since passed without divine service.

ANTIQUITIES. In the town of Greene is a remarkable mound, which, before it was disturbed by the plough or spade, was about seven feet high, and nearly forty feet in diameter. It contained human bones, flint arrow-heads, and utensils of the natives; and was probably the place where the slain of some sanguinary battle had been entombed. In Oxford, are the remains of a fort, about three-fourths of an acre in extent. Trees of more than 200 years' growth were standing on this fort when it was first discovered. Its position was admirably calculated for defence. When or by whom it was erected is unknown. The Indian traditions on this subject are by no means definite.

VILLAGES. NORWICH, in the town of the same name, is the seat of justice for the county. It is pleasantly situated on a neck of land formed by the Canasawacta creek and the river. It is surrounded by a rich agricultural district, whose produce finds here a ready market. The Chenango canal connects it with Utica and Binghamton. It has a considerable number of manufactories. Here is a flourishing academy, and a female seminary. Population, 1600.

Oxford, in the town of the same name, is situated on both sides of the Chenango. It is in the midst of a fine agricultural country, and has considerable trade. The academy here is an old and flourishing one, founded in 1794. Population, 1300.

Sherburne, in the town of the same name, is a pleasant incorporated village, on the line of the canal. It has a chartered academy, and considerable trade. Population, 700.

Greene, in the town of the same name is a flourishing village, situated on the Chenango river and Canal. It has considerable manufactures. Population, 800.

New Berlin and *Bainbridge*, in the towns of the same names, are thriving and important villages.

Smithville and *Smyrna*, are also villages of some importance.

XXVI. ROCKLAND COUNTY.

Square miles, 172.
Organized, 1798.

Population, 13,741.
Valuation, 1845, $2,424,553.

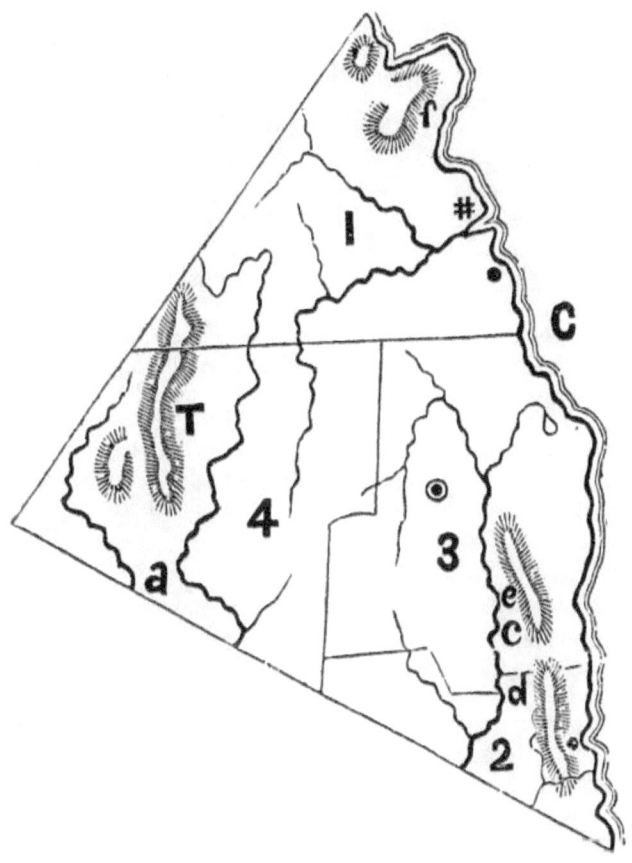

TOWNS.

1. Haverstraw, 1788.
2. Orangetown, 1788.
3. Clarkstown, 1791.
4. Ramapo, 1791.

Mountains. T. Matteawan. d. Closter. e. Nyack Hills. f. Dunderberg.

Rivers. C. Hudson. c. Hackensack. a. Ramapo. Saddle.

Forts. Stony Point.

Villages. NEW CITY. Haverstraw. Piermont.

274 STATE OF NEW YORK.

BOUNDARIES. North by Orange county; East by Hudson river; South by New Jersey; and West by New Jersey and Orange county.

SURFACE. The surface of this county is very much broken, rising in the west and north-west into the Highlands, or Matteawan ridge. The Closter mountain, or Palisade range, enters from Bergen, New Jersey, and receding on the west, forms the Nyack Hills. The summits of some of these rise to the height of 1000 feet. Between these hills and the Highlands, is a valley formed by the Saddle river. Dunderberg and Caldwell mountains, are in the north part, opposite Peekskill.

RIVERS. Rockland county sends forth the Hackensack river and its branches, draining the Nyack valley, and Saddle river, a tributary of the Passaic. The Ramapo, also a tributary of the Passaic, crosses the county in the town of Ramapo.

CLIMATE. The climate of this county is healthy; agreeable in summer, but cold in winter.

MINERALS AND GEOLOGY. The Nyack Hills belong to the Catskill group, being based on red sandstone and capped with greenstone. The Palisades are composed entirely of trap rock. The Matteawan range is primitive; granite, gneiss, mica, feldspar, hornblende, &c. are its principal constituents. South of the Highlands, the whole country is underlaid with red sandstone, supposed by some of the Geologists to be the new red sandstone.

Limestone is abundant in the valleys, and magnetic iron ore in the hills. The other principal minerals are calcareous spar, serpentine, actinolite, zinc ore, green and red copper ores, datholite, stilbite, asbestus, Prehnite, Thompsonite, &c.

VEGETABLE PRODUCTIONS. Notwithstanding the roughness of the surface, the soil is rich and highly cultivated, amply rewarding the labor of the husbandman. This county is well adapted to the culture of both grass and grains.

PURSUITS. *Agriculture* is the leading pursuit, particularly in the more fertile valleys.

Manufactures are also carried on to some extent. Iron wire, nails, sheet iron, and lead, cotton and woollen fabrics are the principal articles.

COMMERCE. Some shipping is owned on the Hudson, by the inhabitants of the county, of whom a considerable number are engaged in commercial pursuits. Ice is extensively exported to New York from this county.

STAPLE PRODUCTIONS. These are corn, potatoes, oats, buckwheat, rye, and ice.

SCHOOLS. In this county, there were in 1846, thirty-nine common schools, averaging nine months' instruction each, at an ex-

ROCKLAND COUNTY. 275

pense of about $7271, and having 2501 pupils. The district libraries numbered 6418 volumes.

There are eight private schools, numbering 149 scholars.

RELIGIOUS DENOMINATIONS. Methodists, Dutch Reformed, Presbyterians, Baptists and Friends. The number of churches, of all denominations, is thirty-two; of ministers, twenty.

HISTORY. This county originally belonged to Orange, and many of the early settlements were made within its limits. Orangetown was originally the county seat, before its division, and remained so till 1737, when Goshen, now in Orange county, was made a half shire town. In 1774, the court-house and jail in Orangetown being burned, the county seat was removed to New City. During the revolution, this little county was the scene of many thrilling events.

On the 27th of September, 1778, Colonel Baylor, the commander of a troop of cavalry, had crossed the Hackensack with his regiment, and taken post at Tappan; on the night of the 28th, they were surprised by a British force, under General Gray, who attacked them in a barn, where they had their quarters, and sixty-seven out of one hundred and four privates were butchered. The orders of the British guard were to give no quarter; about forty were made prisoners through the humanity of one of the British captains. After the capture of Forts Montgomery and Clinton, (the latter of which was in the limits of this county,) by Sir Henry Clinton, in 1777, General Washington directed a fortification to be built at Stoney Point, a commanding promontory on the Hudson, and another at Verplank's Point, opposite the former, on the east bank of the Hudson;— the latter was first completed, and both were garrisoned by the Americans.

In May, 1779, Sir Henry Clinton ascended the river; the fortress at Stoney Point being unfinished, the garrison abandoned it at his approach, and the garrison at Verplank's Point, or Fort Fayette, as it was called, being surrounded by a superior force, were compelled to surrender. Sir Henry immediately caused both forts to be strongly fortified, and manned them with efficient garrisons. General Washington determined to recover them, and accordingly despatched General Wayne, with a sufficient corps of light infantry, on the fifteenth of July, to storm the fortress at Stoney Point. The hill on which the fortress was erected, extends into the Hudson, and is surrounded by it on three sides. The other side was a deep morass, passable only at one point, and this enfiladed by the batteries of the fort. A passage to the fortress was also practicable at low water, along the beach, but this too was commanded by the guns of the fort.

Notwithstanding these obstacles, Wayne and his brave associates commenced the attack a little after nightfall of the sixteenth of July, with unloaded muskets and fixed bayonets, and notwithstanding the terrible fire of the enemy, the two columns which had taken the two routes above described, met in the centre of the fort. The British garrison was captured with a loss to the Americans of fifteen killed and eighty-three wounded, and to the British of sixty-three killed, and 543 taken prisoners, beside military stores to the value of nearly $160,000.

The subsequent attack upon Fort Fayette on Verplank's Point, was unsuccessful, and on this account a larger force than could be spared from the American army, being required to defend Stoney Point, it was abandoned, and soon after occupied by Sir Henry Clinton, who retained it during a considerable period.

In 1780, the trial and imprisonment of Andre took place in the village of Nyack, in this county. He was tried in the old Dutch church, since torn down, and confined in the ancient stone mansion adjacent. His execut took place at a distance of about a quarter of a mile from the village, not far from the New Jersey line. He was buried near the place of his execution. In 1831, his remains were disinterred, by order of the Duke of York, under the superintendence of Mr. Buchanan, the English consul at New York, and transmitted to England.

Dobbs' Ferry, in this county, was also a place of considerable importance during the revolution. Washington's head quarters were for a time near this hamlet.

NEW CITY, in the town of Clarkstown, contains the courthouse, jail, and county offices. It is a mere hamlet.

Piermont, on the Hudson, in the town of Orangetown, is a village of recent growth, and is principally distinguished is the eastern terminus of the New York and Erie railroad. This route of travel is connected with the city of New York by a regular line of steamboats. A larger amount of milk is probably sent to New York from this port than from any other on the river. The steamboat pier is about one mile in length. The Palisades terminate here in a steep and precipitous bluff. Population, 1400.

Haverstraw, in the town of the same name, is a thriving village on the river, engaged in the coasting trade with New York. The fortress of Stoney Point was in the limits of this town.

Nyack, a village in Orangetown, is handsomely situated on Tappan bay, skirted by the Nyack hills on the west. Its celebrity as the place where Major Andre was executed, has been before noticed. Population, about 1000.

XXVII. ONEIDA COUNTY.

Square miles, 1101.
Organized, 1798.

Population, 84,776.
Valuation, $11,807,289.

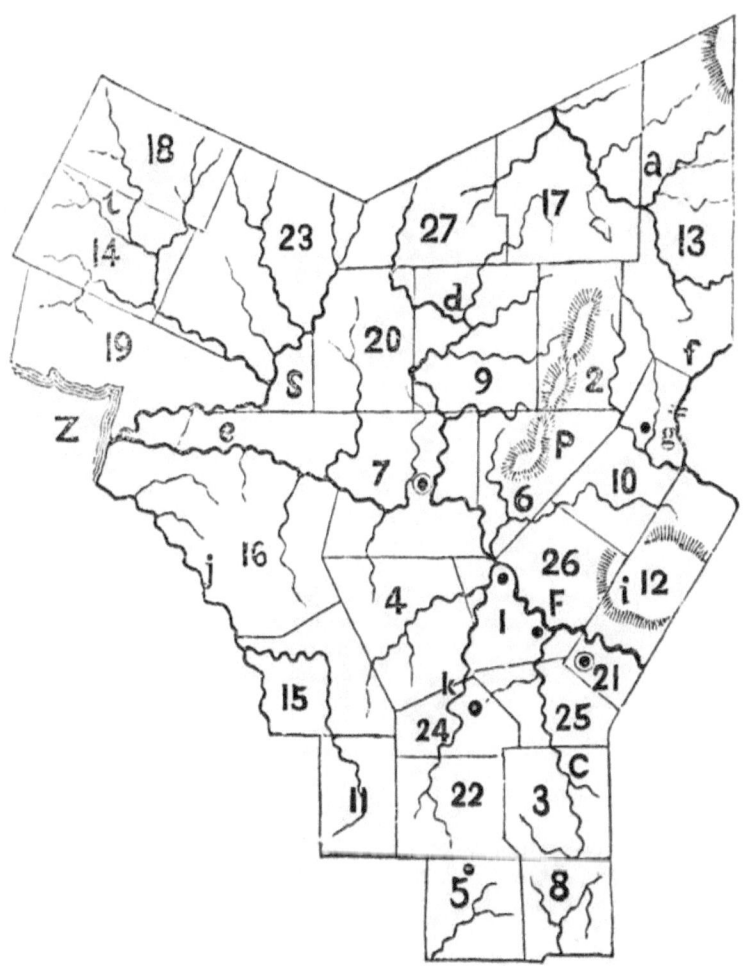

TOWNS.

1. Whitestown, 1788.
2. Steuben, 1789.
3. Paris, 1792.
4. Westmoreland, 1792.
5. Sangerfield, 1795.
6. Floyd, 1796.
7. Rome, 1796.
8. Bridgewater, 1797.
9. Western, 1797.
10. Trenton, 1797.

11. Augusta, 1798.
12. Deerfield, 1798.
13. Remsen, 1798.
14. Camden, 1799.
15. Vernon, 1802.
16. Verona, 1802.
17. Boonville, 1805.
18. Florence, 1805.
19. Vienna, 1807.
20. Lee, 1811.
21. Utica, 1817.
22. Marshall, 1819.
23. Annsville, 1823.
24. Kirkland, 1827.
25. New Hartford, 1827.
26. Marcy, 1832.
27. Ava, 1846.

Mountains. P. Highlands of Black River. i. Hassencleaver mountains.

Rivers and Creeks. F. Mohawk river. a. Black. c. Saghdaquida, or Sauquoit creek. d. Lansing's. e. Wood. f. West Canada. j. Oneida. k. Oriskany. s. Fish. t. West branch of Fish.

Falls. g. Trenton Falls.

Lakes. Z. Oneida.

Battle Fields. Fort Schuyler. Oriskany Creek.

Forts. Fort Stanwix. Fort Schuyler.

Colleges. Hamilton College, in Kirkland.

Cities and Villages. UTICA. ROME. WHITESBORO'. Clinton. Trenton Falls. Oriskany. Waterville.

BOUNDARIES. North by Lewis and Oswego counties; East by Herkimer; South by Madison and Otsego; and West by Madison and Oswego counties.

SURFACE. Oneida county has a diversified surface. The valley of Oneida Lake extends eastward nearly forty miles, through the centre of the county, and the streams which water the county so abundantly, flow for the most part, through broad and beautiful valleys. The Highlands of Black river rise to an elevation of about 800 feet, in the northeastern part of the county, and in the eastern section the Hassencleaver has an elevation of 1200 feet. In the southern part, a ridge of no great height divides the waters of the Mohawk from those of the Susquehanna.

RIVERS, &c. The Mohawk and Black rivers, Lansing's, Fish, Oriskany, Oneida, Saghdaquida, Wood and West Canada creeks, are the principal streams. Several of these furnish, by their rapid descent, valuable hydraulic power.

FALLS. Trenton Falls, on West Canada creek, are much celebrated for their picturesque beauty, and the wild and romantic scenery which surrounds them. The whole descent is 312 feet, and this is accomplished by six distinct falls, all within a distance of two miles.

LAKES. The Oneida Lake forms part of the western boundary of the county. Its shores are low and swampy. Its waters abound with excellent fish.

CANALS AND RAILROADS. The Erie canal passes through the central portion of the county. In its whole course through this and the adjacent county of Madison, there are no locks. The Oneida Lake canal connects the Erie canal with Oneida Lake; the Chenango canal extends from the Erie canal at Utica, to Binghamton, in Broome county; the Black river canal is designed to connect the Erie canal with Black river.

The Utica and Schenectady, and Syracuse and Utica railroads pass through this county.

CLIMATE. The climate is generally mild and quite uniform. The temperature is about an average of that of the state.

GEOLOGY AND MINERALS. From its extent and situation this county embraces a greater variety of geological formations than almost any other in the state. The primary system occupies that portion of the county east of Black river. It consists principally of granite, and Black river and Trenton limestone. Bordering upon these we find the Utica slate and the Hudson river group of shales and sandstone. To these succeed the Oneida slate, which indeed is found in almost every part of the county; the Clinton and Lockport groups of limestone, rich in fossils; the Onondaga salt group, consisting here mainly of red and green shales; the Helderberg limestones; the Oriskany sandstone, forming the surface rock of the valleys of the Saghdaquida, Oriskany, Skenandoa and Oneida creeks; the Marcellus shales appearing at a few points in the extreme southern part of the county; and the Hamilton group of limestones.

Argillaceous iron ore, gypsum, water limestone, peat, marl, calcareous spar, coccolite, blende, or sulphuret of zinc, and tabular spar, are the principal minerals. There are numerous mineral springs, mostly sulphurous, in the county.

SOIL AND VEGETABLE PRODUCTIONS. The soil is every where productive, and in the valleys possesses extraordinary fertility. The crops, both of grass and grain, are abundant, and the county ranks among the first in the state, in its agricultural products. Hops are very successfully and extensively cultivated. The timber of the county is principally maple, beech, birch, elm, black walnut, and basswood, with some oak, hemlock, and pine. Large quantities of sugar are manufactured from the maple.

PURSUITS. *Agriculture* is the pursuit of a majority of the inhabitants. Nearly equal attention is paid to the culture of grain and to the rearing of cattle, horses and sheep. Wheat is not produced in so large quantities as in some of the more western counties, but oats, corn, barley, hops and potatoes are largely cultivated. In 1845, nearly four millions of pounds of butter, and more than three millions of pounds of cheese were made in the county. The clip of wool was also very large.

Manufactures are also a prominent pursuit, being prosecuted to a greater extent than in any other county in the state, except Kings and New York. Cotton and woollen goods are largely manufactured. Flour, lumber, distilled liquors, leather and iron ware, are also produced in very considerable quantities. In 1845, the manufactures of the county amounted to nearly $4,000,000.

Commerce. The commercial relations of Oneida county are quite extensive. The Erie canal affords the means of transportation for its abundant produce; the Oneida lake canal opens a route to Lake Ontario; the Chenango canal brings the agricultural productions of the southern counties hither, on their way to tide water; and the completion of the Black river canal will also add largely to the commerce of the county.

STAPLE PRODUCTIONS. Butter, cheese, oats, barley, corn, hops, potatoes, wool and sugar.

SCHOOLS. There were in the county in 1846, 399 district school-houses, in which schools were taught an average period of eight months each. 23,735 children received instruction, at an expense for tuition of $29,063. The district libraries contained 23,983 volumes. There were also eighty-seven unincorporated select schools, with 912 scholars, ten academies and four female seminaries, with 624 pupils, and one college with nine professors and 126 students.

RELIGIOUS DENOMINATIONS. Methodists, Baptists, Congregationalists, Presbyterians, Episcopalians, Roman Catholics, Friends, Universalists, Dutch Reformed and Unitarians. The total number of churches in 1845, was 160; of clergymen, 202.

HISTORY. This county was the home of the Oneida Indians, one of the bravest tribes of the Iroquois, and the only one which, during the revolution, maintained friendly relations with the United States.

During the French war (in 1758) forts were erected at Rome and at Utica; the former was called Fort Stanwix, the latter Fort Schuyler. Fort Stanwix, on the present site of Rome, was, from its situation at the portage between Wood creek and the Mohawk river, a post of considerable importance, and was fortified at an expense of more than $250,000. At the commencement of the revolution, however, it was very much dilapidated.

In 1766, Rev. Samuel Kirkland, a native of Connecticut, and a graduate of Princeton college, New Jersey, settled among the Oneidas, as a missionary. Through his influence they were restrained from engaging on the side of the British during the war of the revolution.

Mr. Kirkland remained among the Indians during the war, was interpreter to the American officers who visited them, and officiated as chaplain to the army during Sullivan's campaign. After the revolution he settled again in Oneida county, and the legislature of the state granted him the township of Kirkland, as an acknowledgement of his valuable services to the state of his adoption.

Judge Dean, the efficient Indian agent during the revolution, was also an early settler. He was a native of New England, but spent several years of his boyhood among the Oneida Indians, by whom he was adopted. He subsequently graduated at Dartmouth college, intending to become a missionary to that tribe.

The demand for his services during the revolution prevented his fulfilling that intention, and he accepted the office of Indian agent and interpreter, and in that capacity rendered efficient aid to the American cause. The Oneidas granted him, at the close of the war, a tract of land on Wood creek about two miles square, which he subsequently exchanged for a similar tract in Westmoreland. On the extinction of the Indian title, in 1788, the latter was confirmed to him by the state, and he resided upon it during the remainder of his life.*

---

* Two or three years after Judge Dean's removal to Westmoreland, an incident occurred which furnishes a parallel to the often related rescue of Captain John Smith, by Pocahontas.

It was a custom among the Indians, that when one of their number had been murdered by a member of another tribe, the blood of some one of the offending tribe must be shed, as an atonement for the offence. The same custom extended to their intercourse with the whites.

At this period, an Oneida Indian had been killed by some unknown white man, who had escaped. The chiefs assembled to determine what was to be done. After several days consultation, they decided that the life of Mr. Dean must be forfeited, as an atonement for the murder.

Accordingly, the chiefs, eighteen in number, came to his dwelling at midnight, and informed him that they had decided to sacrifice him for the murder of their brother, and that he must now prepare to die. In vain he remonstrated, pleading his past services to their tribe, and urging that he was an adopted son of the Oneidas, and therefore not liable to such a doom. In vain did he represent the hapless condition of his wife and helpless babes.

The old chiefs heard him patiently, but their decision was unalterable. He had nearly abandoned all hope of escape, when his attention was arrested by the pattering of a footstep without the door. Soon the latch was raised and a squaw entered ; she was the wife of the senior chief, and in Mr. Dean's boyhood, had adopted him as her son.

The entrance of a woman into a solemn council was, according to Indian etiquette, at war with all propriety. The chiefs however remained silent. Soon another came, a sister of the first, and the wife of another chief; and presently a third, also the wife of a chief. Each stood near the door in silence, closely wrapped in her blanket.

At length the presiding chief bid them "begone." The squaw who first entered, replied, that they must first change their determination, and not kill the good white man, her adopted son. The command to go was repeated, when each of the squaws threw off their blankets, and brandishing a knife in their extended hands, declared that they would destroy themselves, if one hair of the white man's head was touched. The chiefs were astonished at the whole proceeding, and regarding it as an evident interposition of the Great Spirit in his behalf, reversed their decree, and Mr. Dean's life was spared.

Some years previous to the revolution two men named Roof and Brodock established themselves in the vicinity of Rome, and were engaged in the carrying trade. They were compelled to leave during the revolution, but afterward returned and resumed their farms.

Early in the summer of 1777, news hvaing reached the county that an expedition was intended against the settlements in the Mohawk valley, under the command of General St. Leger, Fort Stanwix at Rome, was repaired, garrisoned, supplied with provisions, and its name changed to Fort Schuyler.

On the 2d of August, 1777, the garrison consisted of 750 men, under the command of Colonel Gansevoort, and they had sufficient ammunition and provisions for a six weeks' siege. At that time the fort was invested by General St. Leger, who demanded its surrender. The demand was indignantly spurned by the garrison. Hearing of the investment of the fort, General Herkimer assembled about 800 militia, and hastened to relieve the beseiged garrison. On the evening of the 5th of August, he arrived at Oriskany creek, and despatched two expresses to Col. Gansevoort, notifying him of his approach, and requesting him to make a sally from the fort at the time of his intended attack.

These expresses arrived safely on the forenoon of the 6th, and a signal cannon having been fired, Colonel Marinus Willet, the second in command, sallied from the fort with 250 men, and succeeded in carrying the camps of Sir John Johnson and the Indians, capturing their stores, baggage, ammunition, &c., without the loss of a single man.

The attack of General Herkimer was less fortunate. St. Leger having heard of his approach, stationed a force in ambuscade on his route. The militia, heedless and self confident, rushed on till their vanguard were surrounded by the enemy. Those in the rear then fled, but the remainder fought with the utmost desperation. Their assailants were mostly Indians and loyalists, and in many cases the two parties were personally known to each other, and private hate was added to national hostility. Rage supplied the place of arms; no quarter was asked or given on either side. Early in the battle General Herkimer was wounded; but seating himself on his saddle, and leaning against the trunk of a tree, he continued to order the battle with the utmost composure. The conflict continued for six hours; at the end of that time the tories and Indians retreated, leaving the militia masters of the field. The loss in killed and wounded on both sides was very great. That of the Americans was nearly 200 killed, and about the same number wounded.

After this battle, St. Leger again summoned the fort, but was again defied. Finding, however, that they must be reinforced or eventually surrender, Col. Willet and Lieut. Stockwell, of the garrison, volunteered to go to the head quarters of General Schuyler, at Stillwater, and obtain aid.

They left the garrison on the night of the 10th of August, creeping on their hands and knees through the enemy's camp, and after numerous hair breadth escapes, succeeded in reaching Gen. Schuyler's camp and procuring the necessary assistance.

General Learned and General Arnold were despatched on this service. The latter, hastening on in advance with 900 troops, captured a tory refugee named Han Yost Schuyler, whom by promises and threats he induced to go to the camp of St. Leger, and alarm the Indians by exaggerating the number of his troops. A friendly Oneida Indian was also sent on the same errand. The stratagem was successful. The Indians, already dissatisfied, abandoned St. Leger at once, on receiving the intelligence of Arnold's approach, and thus deserted, he raised the siege and retreated with the utmost haste, the Indians plundering his troops whenever they found opportunity.

One of the most prominent of the early settlers of this county was Judge White, the founder of Whitestown. He was a native of Middletown, Connecticut, and one of the proprietors of the Saghdaquida patent. He removed here in 1784, with his family.

In 1788 the town of Whitestown was laid out, and comprised all that part of the state lying west of a line drawn north and south through the city of Utica, a tract of country now containing more than 1,100,000 inhabitants. The same year a treaty was made with the Oneidas, by which they ceded to the state the whole of their lands, except a few trifling reservations.

Judge White lived to see the wilderness where he had first located himself, densely populated, and the privations of the settlers exchanged for plenty.* Judge Sanger was another of the early settlers who located in New Hartford.

The town of Steuben was granted by the state to Baron Steuben, for his services during the revolution. He resided here during the latter part of his life, and was buried here.

---

* A little incident which occurred soon after the war, illustrates the Indian character very forcibly. An old Oneida chief named Han Yerry, who, during the revolution, had acted with the British, but who was quite friendly to Judge White, came one day with his wife and a mulatto woman to his house, and asked permission to take the little grand-daughter of the judge home to his cabin for the night, making it a test of the strength of his friendship. Judge White consented, considering it best to manifest confidence in the Indian, although he felt many misgivings, and the mother of the child could hardly be prevailed on to part with it. The succeeding day was one of deep anxiety to the family of the judge—but just at sunset the Indian and his squaw reappeared with the child, clad in a complete Indian dress.

The confidence which the judge manifested in them, secured their warm and permanent friendship.

CITIES AND VILLAGES. UTICA, situated on the south side of the Mohawk, on the site of old Fort Schuyler, is a thriving and business city, in the midst of one of the most fertile and wealthy sections of the state, having a central location. Its locality being on a gentle declivity to the north, commands a beautiful prospect of the Mohawk valley. The streets are spacious, and the buildings neat and commodious. Being connected with Albany and Troy, and with Syracuse, Rochester and Buffalo by railroad and canal; with Binghamton by the Chenango canal, and by stages, with the northern and southern counties of the state, it is the centre of an extensive business. It is also engaged in manufactures. Several large steam mills have recently been erected for the manufacture of cotton and woollen goods.

The New York State Lunatic Asylum, located here, is a noble institution, and when completed will surpass in extent and convenience any other in the United States. A farm of 160 acres is attached to it. The Utica Academy, and the Utica Female Seminary, are both excellent institutions, and have a high reputation. The Young Men's Association possess a good library and have maintained a course of lectures for some years. The museum contains a fine collection of curiosities and antiquities.

The early growth of Utica was slow; in 1794 it contained but three or four houses. It was incorporated as a village in 1798, and received its present name. It was chartered as a city in 1832. Population 12,190.

ROME, on the site of Fort Stanwix (the new Fort Schuyler) is situated at the junction of the Black river and Erie canals. The Utica and Syracuse railroad also passes through it. The village has some manufactories, and is largely engaged in the forwarding trade. The United States government have an arsenal, magazine, and a number of workshops here. The Rome Female Seminary is well sustained. Population 2800.

WHITESBORO', in the town of Whitestown, also a county seat, was incorporated in 1813. It is a pleasant village, finely decorated with shade trees, and is engaged in the manufacture of cotton goods. It has also a very large flouring mill and an extensive pail and tub manufactory.

The Whitesboro' Academy is a large and flourishing institution. The Oneida Institute, a manual labor school of a high order, intended for a boarding school, is also located here; connected with it is a farm of 114 acres. The students are required to labor three hours per day. Population 2000.

Oriskany is a large manufacturing village in the same town. Broadcloths and cassimeres are the principal articles of manufacture. Population 1200.

New York Mills, in the same town is an important village

largely engaged in the manufacture of cotton goods. Population 1000.

Waterville, in the town of Sangerfield, is a thriving village, engaged in the manufacture of woollen goods, carriage springs, starch, and musical instruments. Population 1000.

Trenton Falls is a small village, worthy of notice for the picturesque and beautiful falls on the West Canada creek, from which it derives its name. *Trenton*, in the town of the same name, is a somewhat larger village, incorporated in 1819.

Clinton, in the town of Kirkland, is pleasantly situated on the Oriskany creek, nine miles from Utica. The literary institutions of this village and its vicinity, have given it a wide celebrity. Hamilton College, situated a mile west of the village, was founded by the exertions of the venerable Kirkland, and is now in a prosperous condition. It has four fine stone edifices.

The Clinton Liberal Institute is a chartered institution. The edifice is of stone, ninety-six by fifty-two feet, and four stories high above the basement, for the male department, and a smaller building for the female department. It is conducted by six teachers. There is a farm attached to this institution, for the benefit of such students as may desire to defray the expense of their education by manual labor.

The Clinton Grammar school, and the Clinton Domestic seminary, a female institution of some note, are also located here. In the vicinity are several manufactories. Population 800.

New Hartford, in the town of the same name, and *Oriskany Falls*, in the town of Augusta, are flourishing manufacturing villages.

Vernon, in the town of Vernon, *Sauquoit*, in the town of Paris, and *Hampton*, in the town of Westmoreland, are thriving villages.

Oneida Castleton, a post village in the town of Vernon, occupies the place where the councils of the Six Nations were formerly held,—the large white walnut trees under which they assembled are still standing in full vigor, and often, by the autumnal blasts, sing the requiem of that almost annihilated race of the aborigines.

XXVIII. CAYUGA COUNTY.

Square Miles, 648.
Organized, 1799.
Population, 49,663.
Valuation, 1845, $9,760,050.

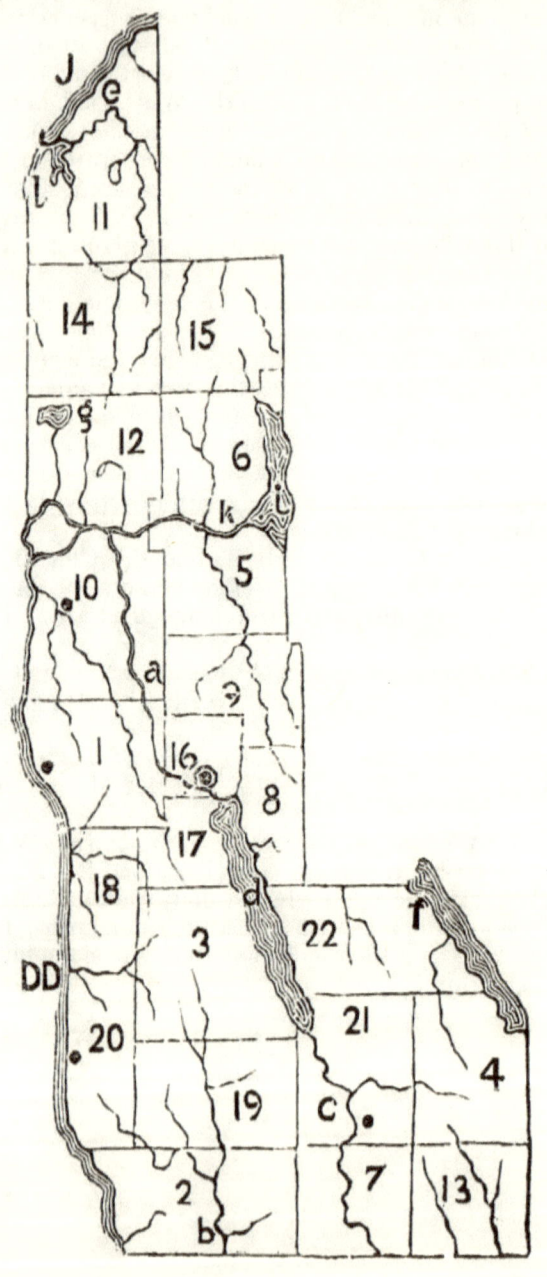

CAYUGA COUNTY. 287

TOWNS

1. Aurelius, 1789.
2. Geneva, 1789.
3. Scipio, 1789.
4. Sempronius, 1789.
5. Brutus, 1802.
6. Cato, 1802.
7. Locke, 1802.
8. Owasco, 1802.
9. Sennet, 1807.
10. Mentz, 1808.
11. Stirling, 1812.
12. Conquest, 1821.
13. Summer Hill, 1821.
14. Victory, 1821.
15. Ira, 1821.
16. Auburn, 1823.
17. Fleming, 1823.
18. Springport, 1823.
19. Venice, 1823.
20. Ledyard, 1823.
21. Moravia, 1833.
22. Niles, 1833.

Rivers. a. Owasco Outlet. b. Salmon Creek. c. Owasco Inlet. e. Little Sodus Creek. k. Seneca.

Lakes, &c. J. Lake Ontario. DD. Cayuga. d. Owasca. f. Skeneateles. g. Duck. i. Cross. l. Little Sodus Bay.

Villages. AUBURN. Aurora. Cayuga. Montezuma. Moravia.

BOUNDARIES. North by Lake Ontario; East by Oswego, Onondaga and Cortland counties; South by Tompkins county; West by Cayuga lake, and Seneca and Wayne counties.

SURFACE. The southern section of the county has an irregular surface, rising into ridges on the shores of Cayuga and Owasco lakes. Poplar ridge, the watershed of the county, is between these two lakes, and has an elevation of 600 feet. The northern part is comparatively level, yet has a rolling appearance, in consequence of numerous gravelly hills, which seem like mounds formed by art.

RIVERS. The principal streams are the Seneca river, Salmon and Little Sodus creeks. The Seneca has a very sluggish course through a marshy country.

LAKES. Cayuga lake on the western border, Skeneateles on the eastern, and Owasco in the centre, are the largest lakes. Besides these it has Cross, Duck and Otter lakes, and Lock pond.

BAYS. Little Sodus bay is an inlet of Lake Ontario.

CANALS. The Erie canal crosses the county a few miles distant from the Seneca river, and parallel with it.

RAILROADS. The great line of Railroad between Albany and Buffalo also passes through this county.

CLIMATE. Mild and temperate, much moderated by the numerous bodies of water around and within it. It is regarded as salubrious.

GEOLOGY AND MINERALOGY. This county embraces quite a variety of formations. On the borders of Lake Ontario is found the Medina sandstone; immediately south of this the Clinton,

Niagara and Onondaga limestone groups; next the Helderberg series, and in the extreme southern part of the county, the Ludlowville slaty rocks.

<small>Gypsum, water limestone, sulphate of Barytes, Epsom salts, fluor spar, sulphate of iron, and pure sulphur are the principal minerals.

Petroleum or mineral oil is found on Cayuga lake. Valuable brine springs occur in Montgomery. Here are also sulphur springs, and a chalybeate spring has been discovered in the town of Sennet.</small>

SOIL AND VEGETABLE PRODUCTIONS. The soil of this county, in consequence of its peculiar geological structure, is rich, and its lands are among the most fertile and highly cultivated in the state. Wheat yields the most abundant crops; and fruits thrive in great perfection. The timber consists of oak, beech, butternut, elm, poplar, basswood, pine and hemlock.

PURSUITS. The attention of the inhabitants is chiefly turned to *agriculture*. Large quantities of the various kinds of grain and wool are annually produced, and considerable numbers of cattle reared.

Manufactures. The principal articles of manufacture are flour, woollen and cotton goods, leather and lumber. Salt is manufactured in considerable quantities.

Commerce. It has a considerable amount of commerce—being connected by the Cayuga lake with the southern counties—by the Erie canal and Auburn and Syracuse railroad with the Hudson and Lake Erie, and by the Cayuga and Seneca canal with the Seneca lake, and the country bordering on it.

THE STAPLES of the county are wheat and other grains, potatoes, butter and wool.

SCHOOLS. The common schools, in 1846, numbered 256. They were taught an average period of eight months, attended by 16,781 scholars, at an expense for tuition of nearly $21,312. The number of volumes in the school libraries was 29,718.

<small>The number of private schools was thirty-five, having in attendance 658 pupils. It has also four academies and one female seminary, with 388 scholars, and one theological seminary with seventy-one students.</small>

RELIGIOUS DENOMINATIONS. Baptists, Presbyterians, Methodists, Friends, Universalists, Congregationalists, Episcopalians, Dutch Reformed, Unitarians, and Roman Catholics. There are in all seventy-seven churches and eighty clergymen.

HISTORY. The first settlements in this county were made in Aurelius, Genoa and Scipio, about the time the Indian title was extinguished, in 1789. The first settlement at Auburn was made in 1793, by Col. John L. Hardenburg, from whom it was named Hardenburg's corners. It received its present name in 1805.

In Moravia, settlements were commenced in 1794. At that

time there were still some Indians residing on the flats. The county has had a rapid and prosperous growth, and in its zeal for public improvements ranks among the first counties in the state.

VILLAGES. AUBURN, the shire town of the county, and one of the most flourishing villages in the state, is situated on the outlet of Owasco lake. Though irregularly laid out, its streets are spacious, and many of its buildings elegant. Besides the county buildings, it contains seven churches, a male and a female seminary, and the Auburn Theological seminary, under the control of the Presbyterians, which has four professors, seventy-one students, and a library of 5000 volumes.

The Auburn State Prison, located here, is a massive granite building, erected at an expense of over half a million of dollars. The main building has a front of 276 feet, and is three stories high besides the basement. The two wings, one on either end, are each 242 feet long, and forty-five wide. The whole is enclosed by a solid stone wall, from sixteen to forty feet high, and three feet thick. The number of prisoners is about 700, who labor in work shops during the day, and are confined in separate cells at night. Population 6171.

Moravia is a thriving incorporated village, in the town of the same name. The Moravian Institute is a chartered institution of some note. Population 600.

Aurora, in the town of Ledyard, lies upon the Cayuga lake, and is hardly surpassed in the beauty of its location, by any village in western New York. The Cayuga academy is a flourishing institution. Steamboats stop here several times a day on their route between Ithaca and Cayuga bridge. Population 500.

Cayuga is a pleasant village on the eastern bank of the Cayuga lake. A daily line of steamboats plies between this place and Ithaca, connecting the Ithaca and Owego and the Auburn and Rochester railroads. A toll bridge, and a railroad bridge, each of them upwards of a mile in length, here cross the Cayuga lake.

Montezuma. A number of saline springs are here found, from which salt of the best and purest quality has been manufactured ever since the earliest settlement of the country. The Montezuma marshes commence about a mile west of the village, and are known as the *Paradise of musquitoes*. Population 700.

Weedsport is a thriving village on the canal in the town of Benton. It has a large amount of business. Population 800.

Port Byron, in the town of Mentz, is a large village, on the Erie canal. It has one of the largest flouring establishments in the state, beside several other manufactories. Population 1000.

XXIX. ESSEX COUNTY.

Square Miles, 1162.
Organized, 1799.
Population, 25,102.
Valuation, 1845, $1,483,136.

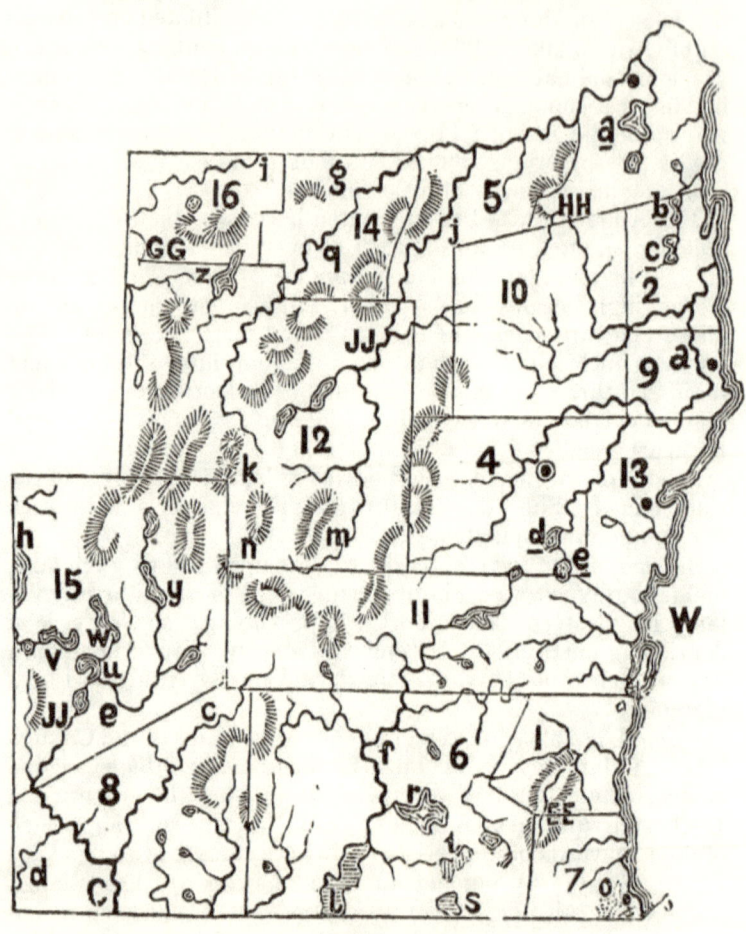

TOWNS.

1. Crown Point, 1788.
2. Willsborough, 1788.
3. Jay, 1790.
4. Elizabethtown, 1798.
5. Chesterfield, 1802.
6. Schroon, 1804.
7. Ticonderoga, 1804.
8. Minerva, 1804.
9. Essex, 1805.
10. Lewis, 1805.
11. Moriah, 1808.
12. Keene, 1808.
13. Westport, 1815.
14. Wilmington, 1821.
15. Newcomb, 1828.
16. St. Armand, 1844.

ESSEX COUNTY. 291

Mountains. EE. Kayaderosseras. GG. Chateaugay. HH. Clinton. JJ. Au Sable.

Peaks. g. White Face. k. Mount McMartin. m. Mount McIntyre. n. Mount Marcy. o. Mount Defiance, (in Ticonderoga).

Rivers. C. Hudson. a. Bouquet. c. Boreas. d. Indian. e. Adirondack. f. Schroon. i. Au Sable. j. Saranac. q. West Branch.

Lakes. W. Champlain. l. Schroon. r. Paradox. s. Pharaoh. t. Crane Pond. u. Harries Lake. v. Rich. w. Delia. h. Teralt. y. Sanford. z. Placid. a. Auger Pond. b. Warm. c. Rattlesnake. d. Black. e. Long.

Forts. Ticonderoga. Crown Point.

Villages. ELIZABETHTOWN. Westport. Keeseville. Ticonderoga. Essex.

BOUNDARIES. North by Franklin and Clinton counties; East by Lake Champlain; South by Warren county; and West by Hamilton and Franklin counties.

SURFACE. The surface of this county is mountainous. Three distinct ranges cross it, and a fourth touches its western boundary. The Kayaderosseras range, beginning at Crown Point, passes over the southeastern towns. The Clinton range extends through the central portion, the Au Sable passes through the northwest section, and the Chateaugay forms a portion of the northwestern boundary.

In the towns of Keene, Newcomb, and Moriah, a group of lofty peaks, known as the Adirondack group, extends from the Au Sable to the Clinton range. Mounts Marcy, McIntire, McMartin, Dial mountain and White face, are the principal of these peaks. Mount Marcy is 5467 feet, or more than a mile, above tide water, Mount McIntire 5183, White face 4855, and Dial mountain 4900 feet high.

It is a characteristic of the mountains of this county, that their sides are precipitous and broken. Between the ranges of the mountains are extensive valleys, through which flow large streams.

<small>The Adirondack pass, about five miles from the Adirondack Iron works, demands a cursory notice. At an elevation of some 2500 feet above tide water, a narrow gorge extends quite through the mountain, whose massive perpendicular walls a thousand feet in height, rear themselves on either hand in gloomy sublimity, as if proudly defying the puny art of man. The pass is nearly a mile in length, and rises in height from 500 to 1000 feet.</small>

RIVERS. The principal rivers of the county are the Au Sable, the Saranac, the Bouquet, the Hudson and the Schroon, with their tributaries, and Putnam creek.

LAKES. No county in the state probably possesses so great a number of lakes and ponds as Essex. The character of its surface is such as to produce this result; in its deep chasms and mountain gorges, its ravines and dells, bounded by walls of ever during granite, the waters which fall upon the hills, or the product of the melting snows upon its lofty peaks, gather and remain, till they have attained sufficient height to overflow the barriers which restrain them.

It is said that there are in the county nearly one hundred lakes and ponds of considerable size. Of these the most important are Schroon, Paradox, Teralt, Rich, Harries, Delia, Sanford, Pharaoh and Placid lakes, and Augur pond.

CLIMATE. The temperature is low, particularly on the mountains. In the valleys it is more mild, but the frosts are early and severe. It is not well adapted to the raising of fruit, or those grains and crops which require a long summer.

GEOLOGY AND MINERALS. The rocks in this county are primary, with the exception of a narrow belt of transition on Lake Champlain. They are principally hypersthene, granite, primary limestone, gneiss, hornblende, and magnetic iron ore.

Iron is found in immense quantities in almost every part of the county. The principal veins are the Penfield, the Adirondack ores, and the Sanford vein. The latter is estimated to contain at least 3,000,000 tons of pure iron. It is in fact a mass of pure iron ore, unmixed with rock or earth. The iron of this county, in all the qualities which render that metal valuable, is unsurpassed by any in the United States, and being situated in a densely wooded country, and with a convenient access to the lake, can be smelted and conveyed to market as advantageously as any in the country.

There are in the county, and particularly on the shores of the lakes, fossil vegetables and shells. The other principal minerals are Plumbago, marble of the Verd Antique variety, Labradorite, calcareous spar, pyroxene, hornblende, serpentine, scapolite, tabular spar, Brucite, apatite, tourmaline, sphene, colophonite, graphite, zircon, garnet, epsom salts, porcelain clay, and pearl spar.

VEGETABLE PRODUCTIONS, SOIL, &c. The soil, though broken, is rich and fertile. The timber is very abundant, and of large size, consisting of white and black oak, white and yellow pine, maple, beech, hemlock, poplar, walnut, butternut, birch, ash, elm, basswood, cherry, fir, spruce, &c.

Upon Mount Marcy, the gigantic beech and hemlock gradually diminish in size to mere shrubs, and the former, unable to sustain the weight of its stem, creeps on the rocky surface of its elevated summit. The forests abound with game, and the waters with fish.

PURSUITS. A majority of the inhabitants are devoted to *agricultural pursuits*. The greater part of the county is adapted to grazing, and in some of the valleys grain succeeds well. Potatoes, oats, together with some wheat, corn and rye are grown. Butter and wool are produced in considerable quantities.

The preparation of lumber for market is a prominent pursuit

with the inhabitants. The amount of lumber and timber exported is very large.

Among the *manufactures*, that of iron is the most important; it is smelted from the ore in large quantities.

The *commerce* of the county upon the lakes is very considerable, and every year increasing.

STAPLES. Iron, lumber, butter, wool, and potatoes.

SCHOOLS. There were in the county, in 1846, 167 school-houses, in which 7925 children were taught an average period of six months, at an expense for tuition of $8758. The district libraries contained 13,774 volumes.

There were also in the county twenty private schools, with 270 pupils, and two academies, with ninety students.

RELIGIOUS DENOMINATIONS. Methodists, Congregationalists, Baptists, Presbyterians, Roman Catholics, and Universalists. The number of churches of all denominations in the county is forty-two, and of clergymen, twenty-nine.

HISTORY. In 1731 a fort, called Fort St. Frederick, was erected by the French, at Crown Point, on the bank of Lake Champlain; it was afterward blown up, but the place was again fortified, and retained as a military post.

In 1756, the French erected Fort Ticonderoga, named by them Carillon. In 1758, General Abercrombie, with a large force, composed of British and provincial troops, attacked the fortress, but was repulsed, with the loss of nearly 2000 killed and wounded. Among the former was Lord Howe, who was universally beloved by the troops.

In 1759, both Ticonderoga and Crown Point were abandoned by the French, on the approach of the English forces. The British general garrisoned Ticonderoga, and caused a fort to be erected at Crown Point, which was likewise garrisoned by English troops.

In 1775, both fortresses were captured by a corps of Connecticut and Vermont volunteers, under the command of Colonels Ethan Allen,* Seth Warner and Benedict Arnold. Crown Point was evacuated the next year.

On the eleventh of October, 1776, the disastrous expedition against Canada was terminated, by the capture of the lake fleet, under the command of General Arnold, near Crown Point.

In July, 1777, Ticonderoga was besieged by General Burgoyne; with great labor and difficulty that officer succeeded in

---

* It is related that when Colonel Allen, who had rushed into Fort Ticonderoga, sword in hand, ordered the commander of the fort to surrender, he enquired "by what authority?" Colonel Allen immediately replied, "I demand it in the name of the great Jehovah and the continental congress."

erecting a battery upon Mount Defiance, which overlooked and enfiladed the fort. General St. Clair, its commander, was thus compelled either to surrender, or evacuate the fort immediately. He chose the latter alternative, and made his escape, though with some loss. It was then garrisoned by the British.

In October, 1777, the garrison, hearing of General Burgoyne's surrender, returned precipitately to Canada. Neither of the fortresses have since been occupied.

This county was chiefly settled by emigrants from Vermont, and other New England states. Considerable portions of it are yet covered with the primeval forests.

VILLAGES. ELIZABETHTOWN is a small village, situated in the midst of beautiful and picturesque mountain scenery. It is the county seat. Population 350.

Keeseville, lying upon both sides of the Au Sable river, and being partly in this county and partly in Clinton, is a large and flourishing manufacturing village. Iron, and woollen and cotton goods, are largely manufactured here. It has also flouring mills, saw mills, a brewery, machine shop, tannery, &c. The falls of the Au Sable give it a fine water power. Here is an incorporated academy. Population 2200.

Westport is a thriving village on the lake. It has a flourishing incorporated academy. Population 700.

Ticonderoga, about two miles from the old fort of that name, is well situated for manufactures, having a valuable and extensive water power, very uniform in its supply, and being advantageously situated for commerce. Population 700.

Essex is a thriving village and has some commerce. Population 700.

Willsborough, in the town of the same name, *Au Sable Forks* and *Jayville*, in the town of Jay, are growing and important villages.

XXX. GREENE COUNTY.

Square Miles, 583.
Organized, 1800.
Population, 31,957.
Valuation, 1845, $2,969,673.

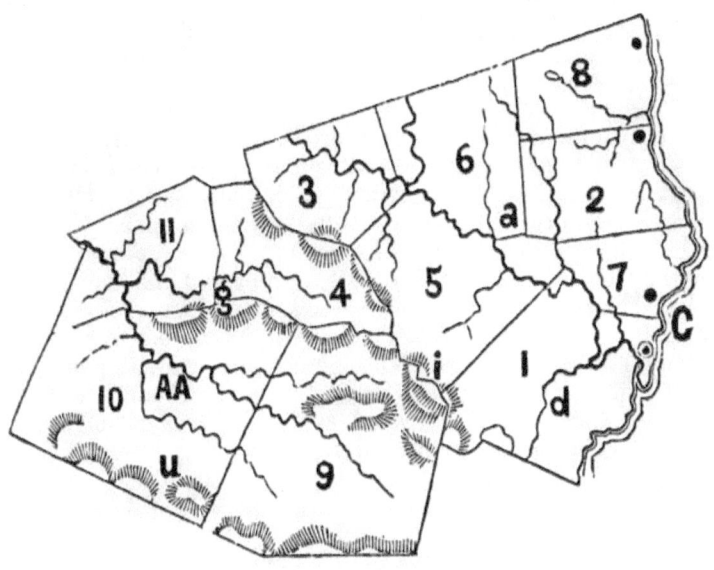

TOWNS.

1. Catskill, 1788.
2. Coxsackie, 1788.
3. Durham, 1790.
4. Windham, 1798.
5. Cairo, 1803.
6. Greenville, 1803.
7. Athens, 1805.
8. New Baltimore, 1811.
9. Hunter, 1813.
10. Lexington, 1813.
11. Prattsville, 1833.

Mountains. i. Catskill. u. Pine.

Rivers. AA. Schoharie kill. C. Hudson. a. Catskill Creek. d. Kaaters kill. g. Batavia kill.

Falls. On the Kaaters kill east branch, three falls.

Villages. CATSKILL. Coxsackie. Athens. New Baltimore.

BOUNDARIES. North by Schoharie and Albany; East by Hudson river; South by Ulster; West by Delaware and Schoharie counties.

SURFACE. The county of Greene has a very hilly and mountainous surface. The Catskill mountains running centrally through the county, divide it into two sections, of which the eastern and northern is the most arable.

The eastern fronts of the mountains are precipitous, while upon the west their declivities are more gentle. The Pine mountain, or Kaatsbergs, form the southwestern boundary. The principal peaks of the Catskill mountains are Round Top and High Peak, which have elevations from 3000 to 3800 feet above tide water.

RIVERS. The principal streams are Catskill creek, Kaaterskill, Schoharie kill, and Batavia kill. The Hudson forms its eastern boundary.

CLIMATE. This county has much diversity of climate. The peaks of the mountains are covered with snow nearly a month later than the valleys, and the summer is shorter, but when vegetation commences, it is more rapid than near the Hudson.

GEOLOGY AND MINERALOGY. The transition and red sandstone formations prevail in this county. The predominant rocks of the Catskill division are conglomerates, red and gray shales, slates, slaty and coarse grits; greenish gray and chocolate colored gray sandstone, known as the Catskill or North river flag stone, is abundant. The Helderberg range, consisting of water and common limestone and pyritous slate, predominates in the north portion of the county. The Hudson river group, composed of slate, shales, shaly and thick bedded grits occupies the eastern and southeastern part.

_{Copper, lead, zinc, iron and coal, have been found in small quantities. Calcareous spar and quartz crystals also occur.}

VEGETABLE PRODUCTIONS. The mountains are sterile—the uplands produce excellent grass, while the valleys are rich, yielding good crops of grain. The timber consists of oak, hickory, cherry, soft and sugar maple, and on the hills beech, birch, and in some places, spruce and hemlock. In the mountainous districts the trees are of great size.

PURSUITS. *Agriculture* is the principal pursuit of the inhabitants. Comparatively little grain is raised. The products of the dairy are large. Many of the farmers are turning their attention to wool growing, for which the county is well adapted.

Manufactures. Leather is manufactured to a greater amount than in any other county in the state. The other manufactures are flour, lumber, paper, fulled cloths, &c.

Commerce. Catskill, Athens, Coxsackie and New Baltimore, are largely engaged in the coasting trade.

The STAPLE PRODUCTIONS of the county are butter, oats, corn and buckwheat.

SCHOOLS. There were in this county, in 1846, 170 common schools, giving instruction to 9071 children, an average period of eight months each, at an expense for tuition of $13,147. The district libraries contained 19,713 volumes.

There were also thirty-three select schools, with 601 scholars; four academies and one female seminary, with seventy-seven students.

RELIGIOUS DENOMINATIONS. Methodists, Presbyterians, Baptists, Dutch Reformed, Episcopalians, Friends, Roman Catholics, Lutherans, and Unitarians. There are in the county, sixty-four churches, and sixty-four clergymen.

HISTORY. Greene county was settled in the latter part of the seventeenth century, by the Dutch. Cairo and Coxsackie were the principal settlements. Shortly before and after the revolution, many families removed from New England into the county, and a majority of the present inhabitants claim a puritan descent.

It is a matter of regret that so little effort has been made to investigate the early history of a county, undoubtedly possessing so much historic interest.

The Hardenburgh patent comprises most of the towns of Windham and Lexington.

Athens was laid out in part, in 1790, by Edward Brockholst Livingston, and E. C. Goodrich.

VILLAGES. CATSKILL VILLAGE, in the town of the same name, was incorporated in 1806. It is the seat of justice of the county, situated on the left bank of the Catskill creek, nearly one mile from the Hudson, and is principally built upon a single street, about half a mile in extent.

It is a port for steamboats and sloops, the creek being navigable from a short distance above the village, to the Hudson, opening a direct communication with the city of New York.

This village is sustained by a wealthy farming community in its own, and adjoining counties; also by a considerable manufacturing interest.

In the business season of the year, Main street, and the wharves indicate great activity in trade and commerce.

The prospect of the Hudson from this village is obscured by a high bluff running parallel with the river, yet this bluff affords desirable sites for residences, some of which are occupied and highly improved.

The location of this village is important, being the terminus of a number of stage routes, some of which communicate with the valley of the Susquehanna. Its public buildings are neat, and its general appearance that of industry. It has an academy, and a select school for young ladies. Population 3000.

Athens, in the town of the same name, pleasantly situated opposite the city of Hudson, was incorporated in 1805,—it is extensively engaged in manufactures, especially of brick and lime.

A considerable number of sloops are owned here, which ply to and from New York. A steam ferry connects it with the city of Hudson. Population 1500.

Coxsackie Landing, in the town of Coxsackie, is a thriving village, engaged in the coasting trade, and in the manufacture of brick. It has an academy of some note. Population 1500.

Prattsville, lying on the Schoharie kill, manufactures more leather than any town in the United States. It received its name from Hon. Zadoc Pratt, who established extensive tanneries here. The village is also engaged in other manufactures. Population 1200.

The "Mountain House," so widely celebrated as a summer resort for travellers, is within the limits of the town of Hunter. It is situated on the Pine Orchard, a peak of the Catskill mountains, twelve miles from the village of Catskill, and at an elevation of 2212 feet above the Hudson.

The prospect from this point is one of the most extensive and beautiful in the world. The majestic Hudson, with its green islets, its numerous sails, its cities, villages, and highly cultivated farms, is visible, on a clear day, for sixty miles in extent, while in the distance, the dim outlines of the Taghkanic mountains bound the horizon.

About two miles west of the "Mountain House" are the Kaaters kill Falls, upon a stream issuing from two lakes in the rear of the hotel. The waters leap over a perpendicular barrier, 175 feet, and pausing momentarily upon a rocky ledge, plunge down eighty-five feet more, and are hid from the view, in the dark ravine through which they seek the valley of the Catskill.

The scenery around, the deep green forests, the rugged cliffs, covered with ivy and summer foliage, and the extended prospect, add to the sublimity of the waterfall, and render this one of the most picturesque and magnificent scenes in nature.

New Baltimore, Cairo and *Coxsackie* are villages of some importance, in the towns of the same names.

XXXI. GENESEE COUNTY.

Square miles, 473. Population. 28,845.
Organized, 1802. Valuation, 1845, $5,873,385.

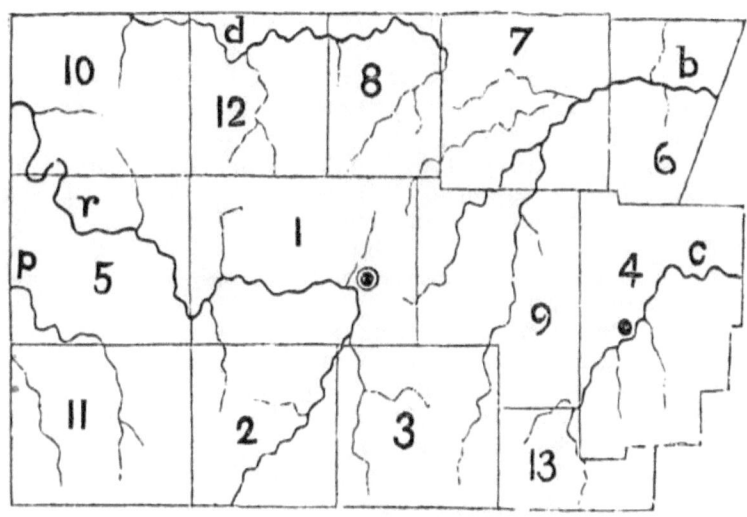

TOWNS.

1. Batavia, 1802.
2. Alexander, 1812.
3. Bethany, 1812.
4. Le Roy, 1812.
5. Pembroke, 1812.
6. Bergen, 1818.
7. Byron, 1820.
8. Elba, 1820.
9. Stafford, 1820.
10. Alabama, 1826.
11. Darien, 1832.
12. Oakfield, 1842.
13. Pavilion, 1842.

Creeks. b. Black creek. c. Allen's d. Oak Orchard. r. Tonawanda.
Falls on Allen's Creek in Le Roy.
Villages. BATAVIA. Le Roy.

BOUNDARIES. North by Orleans and Monroe; East by Monroe and Livingston; South by Wyoming; West by Erie and Niagara.

SURFACE. The surface of this county may be considered as a table land, inclined toward the north, and divided into two sections. The first embraces the northern portion, from five to eight miles in breadth, and includes the Tonawanda swamp. Separated from this by a rocky ridge, the second gradually rises to the southern boundary of the county.

RIVERS. The general direction of its streams is north-east and north-west, of which Tonawanda, Allen's, (so called after

Indian Allen who had his residence in this neighborhood,) Oak Orchard, Black and Murder Creeks, are the principal.

RAILROADS. The Tonawanda railroad, entering the county in the town of Bergen, has a southward course through Batavia, to Attica. The Batavia and Rochester connects this with the eastern lines.

CLIMATE. Mild, temperate and equable. At the early settlement of the county, intermittent and remittent fevers prevailed, but they are now very rare.

GEOLOGY AND MINERALOGY. The whole county is comprised in the transition formation. Its principal rocks are the different varieties of limestone, sandstone and calciferous and marly slate.

The minerals are few in number; the most important are gypsum, argillaceous iron ore, marl and peat.

SOIL AND VEGETABLE PRODUCTIONS. The soil is chiefly a sandy or gravelly loam, highly productive in grass, summer crops, and especially in wheat. The timber of the county is oak, elm, beach, maple, birch, &c. The maple is very abundant, yielding large quantities of sugar.

PURSUITS. The inhabitants are principally employed in *agriculture*. Wheat is extensively raised.

Manufactures. Flour, lumber, leather, woollen cloths, and potash, are the principal articles of manufacture.

Commerce. The railroads furnish the principal means of transportation within the county.

STAPLES. Wheat, potatoes, oats, wool, corn and butter.

SCHOOLS. The county, in 1846, contained 166 district schools, which were in session an average period of nine months each, and were attended by 9,316 scholars. $12,506 was paid to teachers, and the libraries contained 19,458 volumes.

There were also seventeen private schools, attended by 431 pupils; three academies, and two female seminaries, with 360 students.

RELIGIOUS DENOMINATIONS. Methodists, Baptists, Presbyterians, Congregationalists, Episcopalians, Universalists, Unitarians and Friends. The total number of churches is fifty; of clergymen, sixty-seven.

HISTORY. Nearly the whole of this county lies within the Holland Land Company's purchase, from whom the present inhabitants hold their titles. Some small tracts in the southern part of the county, still belong to the successors of that company.

A tract of 87,000 acres, comprising the towns of Sweden and Clarkson, in Monroe county, and part of Bergen and Le Roy, in

GENESEE COUNTY. 301

this county, and known as the Triangle tract, was sold by Robert Morris, to Messrs. Le Roy, Bayard and McEvers.

The first settlement in the county was at Batavia, about the commencement of the present century. The Holland Land Company erected their land office here in 1801. In October, 1804, the settlement contained from twenty to thirty houses, mostly built of logs. It was at that time very sickly. The fertility of its soil and its adaptation to the culture of grain, caused a rapid immigration, and it was organized as a county, in 1802. It then comprised, however, the present counties of Allegany, Chautauque, Niagara, Erie, Cattaraugus, Orleans, Wyoming, and the western portions of Monroe and Livingston.

VILLAGES. BATAVIA village, the county seat, was incorporated in 1823. It is laid out in a plat, two miles square, and has over 300 buildings, a female seminary, the office of the Holland Land Company, and a number of manufactories.

Le Roy, in the town of Le Roy, is a thriving village, situated on Allen's Creek, and incorporated in 1834. The village lots are spacious, and the dwellings are generally built of stone, presenting a very neat appearance. The rapid growth of this village is due to the hydraulic power of the creek, which has three considerable falls.

The first fall at the village, is eighteen feet, the second about a mile below, twenty-seven feet, and the third within two miles, eighty feet, affording great facilities for manufacturing purposes. A number of sites are occupied by flour, oil, and other mills.

It is a remarkable fact that much of the water of this creek disappears before it reaches the highest fall, which is supposed to supply the Caledonia spring in the adjoining town, in Livingston county. It has about 2000 inhabit-ants. Here is a flourishing female seminary.

Alexander is a village of some importance, in the town of the same name. It has an incorporated classical school. Population, 500.

XXXII. ST. LAWRENCE COUNTY.

Square miles, 2,717. Population, 62,354.
Organized, 1802. Valuation, 1845, $3,645,208.

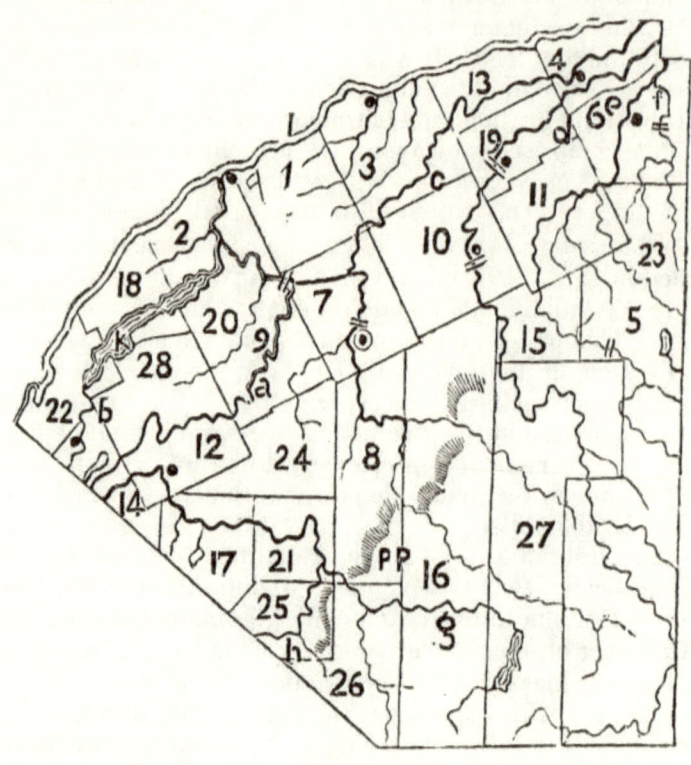

TOWNS.

1. Lisbon, 1801.
2. Oswegatchie, 1802.
3. Madrid, 1802.
4. Massena, 1802.
5. Hopkinton, 1805.
6. Brasher, 1805.
7. Canton, 1805.
8. Russel, 1805.
9. De Kalb, 1806.
10. Potsdam, 1806.
11. Stockholm, 1806.
12. Gouverneur, 1810.
13. Louisville, 1810.
14. Rossie, 1813.
15. Parishville, 1814.
16. Pierrepont, 1814.
17. Fowler, 1816.
18. Morristown, 1821.
19. Norfolk, 1822.
20. De Peyster, 1825.
21. Edwards, 1827.
22. Hammond, 1827.
23. Lawrence, 1828.
24. Hermon, 1830.
25. Pitcairn, 1837.
26. Fine, 1842.
27. Colton, 1842.
28. Macomb, 1842.

ST. LAWRENCE COUNTY. 303

Mountains. PP. Highlands of St. Lawrence county.
Rivers. I. St. Lawrence. a. Oswegatchie. b. Indian. c. Grasse. d. Racket. e. St. Regis. f. Deer. g. East branch Oswegatchie. h. West branch Oswegatchie.
Lakes. k. Black.
Falls. On the St. Regis, in Brasher, Hopkinton and Parishville. On the Racket, at Potsdam, Colton and St. Regis. On the Grasse, at Canton and Pierrepont. On the Oswegatchie, at Canton and Rossie.
Forts. Ogdensburgh.
Battle Fields. Ogdensburgh.
Villages. CANTON. Ogdensburgh. Rossie. Brasher's falls. Potsdam. Gouverneur. Waddington. Massena. Norfolk.

BOUNDARIES. North by the river St. Lawrence; East by Franklin county; South by Hamilton and Herkimer; and West by Lewis and Jefferson counties, and the St. Lawrence river.

SURFACE. The surface of this county is agreeably diversified. Along the bank of the St. Lawrence river, for a distance of seventy-five miles in length, and from thirty to forty in breadth, the county consists of gentle swells, broad valleys, or extensive plains. Farther south it rises into hills, and finally assumes a mountainous character, in the southeast, where are situated the Highlands of the St. Lawrence.

RIVERS. The principal streams of the county besides the St. Lawrence, are the St. Regis, Racket, Grasse, Indian, Oswegatchie and Deer rivers, which by their long and circuitous courses and numerous tributaries, abundantly water it. A natural canal, six miles long, connects the Oswegatchie and Grasse rivers, in the town of Canton.

FALLS. Most of these streams have numerous falls or rapids, furnishing a large amount of water power.

LAKES. Black Lake is the only one of importance. There are many extensive marshes.

CLIMATE. The climate is less variable than in most counties of the state. The air is clear, and the seasons uniform, compensating for the severe cold of winter, and contributing to the health of its inhabitants.

GEOLOGY AND MINERALS. That portion of the county lying along the St. Lawrence, for a width of ten or fifteen miles, belongs to the tertiary, or rather the alluvial formation, consisting of clay and gravel; this is succeeded, at a distance of fifteen or twenty miles from the river, by a belt of Potsdam sandstone, running nearly parallel to the St. Lawrence, and varying in width from five to ten miles; the remainder of the county belongs wholly to the primary formation, and consists of hypersthene, gneiss, granite and primitive limestone.

The Potsdam sandstone forms one of the finest building materials in the world. Specular iron ore is found in this county in immense quantities, and is largely manufactured. The magnetic and bog iron ores are also quite abundant. Graphite or black lead is found in several localities. Lead exists in vast quantities in the neighborhood of Rossie. Zinc and copper occur frequently. Marble, serpentine, and other forms of carbonate of lime are deposited in various parts of the county; steatite or soapstone is plentiful. The other principal minerals are phosphate of lime, sulphate of barytes, quartz crystals, Brucite, talc, pyroxene, hornblende, asbestus, feldspar, albite, Labradorite, mica, spinel, tourmaline, zircon, Babingtonite and sphene.

SOIL AND VEGETABLE PRODUCTIONS. The greater portion of the land is of excellent quality. The soil consists of a dark vegetable mould, often underlaid with lime and marl, and is very productive of grasses, grains, &c. Much of the county is yet covered with dense forests of oak, beech, maple, basswood, butternut, ash, elm, hemlock, white and Norway pine. In the marshes white cedar, tamarack and black ash, are the principal trees. From the maple, large quantities of sugar are manufactured.

PURSUITS. The people are chiefly engaged in *agriculture*. Great numbers of cattle are reared, and much attention paid to the products of the dairy. They are becoming interested in *manufactures*, which at present are mostly limited to flour, lumber, fulled cloths, potash and leather.

Commerce. The commerce of the county is increasing in value and importance. Ogdensburgh is the principal port. The shipping of the Oswegatchie district amounted, in 1845, to about 1500 tons.

STAPLE PRODUCTIONS. Butter, cheese, potatoes, oats, corn, peas, wheat, sugar, wool, potash and lumber.

SCHOOLS. There were 402 common schools in the county in 1846, taught an average period of seven months each, and attended by 22,263 children. The teachers were paid $22,023. The libraries contained 33,191 volumes.

The number of select schools was twenty-three, with 303 scholars; of academies, four, with 346 students.

RELIGIOUS DENOMINATIONS. Presbyterians, Methodists, Congregationalists, Baptists, Episcopalians, Universalists and Roman Catholics. Total number of churches, seventy-five; of clergymen, 125.

HISTORY. The French erected a fort at Oswegatchie, in this county before 1740, which they named Fort Presentation. This fort was captured by General Amherst, in 1760.

The first permanent settlement in the county seems to have been made in 1796, by Judge Nathan Ford, at Oswegatchie. At that time the Oswegatchie Indians had a village near his settlement, and attempted several times to drive him away, but without success. The next settlement was made at Canton, by

ST. LAWRENCE COUNTY. 305

Mr. Stillman Foot, in 1799. These were soon succeeded by others, mostly from New England, and a line of settlements was speedily formed along the river. Much of the land in the county is held by the Messrs. Van Rensselaer, Gouverneur Morris and other wealthy capitalists.

During the late war with Great Britain, some interesting incidents occurred in this county. On the second of October, 1812, the British, in retaliation for the destruction of a large quantity of their stores at Gananoque, Canada, by Captain Forsyth, commenced a heavy cannonade upon Ogdensburgh, from their batteries at Prescott, a Canadian village, on the opposite bank of the St. Lawrence. They continued the cannonade for two days, and on Sunday, the fourth of October, attempted to storm the town.

For this purpose, about 1000 men were embarked in forty boats; as they approached the American shore, General Brown ordered his troops to fire upon them. They did so, and for two hours the British attempted to land, but the galling fire of the Americans was too severe to be endured, and at length they were compelled to retreat to Prescott, with the loss of three boats and a number of men. The American force engaged in this contest, was only about 400 men.

On the twenty-first of February, 1813, the British again attacked Ogdensburgh with a large force, and, though encountering the most determined resistance, succeeded in driving out the American troops, and capturing the village.

Two schooners, two gunboats and the soldiers' barracks were destroyed, and the enemy returned to Canada. The army of General Wilkinson embarked for the campaign of the autumn of 1813, from Morristown, in this county. Since the war, the increase of population in this county has been exceedingly rapid. Its population has nearly quadrupled in twenty-five years; and from its extraordinary facilities for manufactures, mining and agriculture, its future growth must necessarily be rapid.

In 1838, this county and the Canada shore opposite, was the scene of some of the exploits of the Canada Patriots, (so called.) The battle of Prescott was fought at Windmill Point, nearly opposite Ogdensburgh, and several of the citizens of New York, who had aided " the Patriots," were taken prisoners and executed, and others banished to Van Dieman's Land.

ANTIQUITIES. In the town of Gouverneur, is an ancient Indian fortification, consisting of an embankment, enclosing three acres, and containing some remains of rude sculpture.

VILLAGES. CANTON village is the county seat. It is situated on Grasse river, and contains besides the county buildings, an academy, and some manufactories. A fine wooden bridge, with three piers, crosses the river here. Population, 1300.

Ogdensburgh, in the town of Oswegatchie, and at the mouth of Oswegatchie river, was incorporated in 1817. It is a flourishing village of about 4000 inhabitants. It has an academy in a very prosperous condition. It is at the foot of sloop navigation on the St. Lawrence, and is the terminus of the proposed Ogdensburgh and Plattsburgh railroad.

Potsdam, incorporated in 1831, is the seat of the St. Lawrence academy, a chartered institution, with two large stone edifices, each four stories high. It has also several manufactories. Population, 1200.

Rossie is celebrated for its valuable and inexhaustible lead mines. Population, 800.

Brasher's Falls, on the rapids of Deer river, is finely situated for manufacturing purposes.

Waddington is a manufacturing village in the town of Madrid. It was incorporated in 1839, and is rapidly increasing in population. A bridge connects it with Ogden's island, in the St. Lawrence. Population, 600.

Gouverneur is the coldest place in the state. Here is located the Gouverneur Wesleyan Seminary. Population, 600.

XXXIII. SENECA COUNTY.

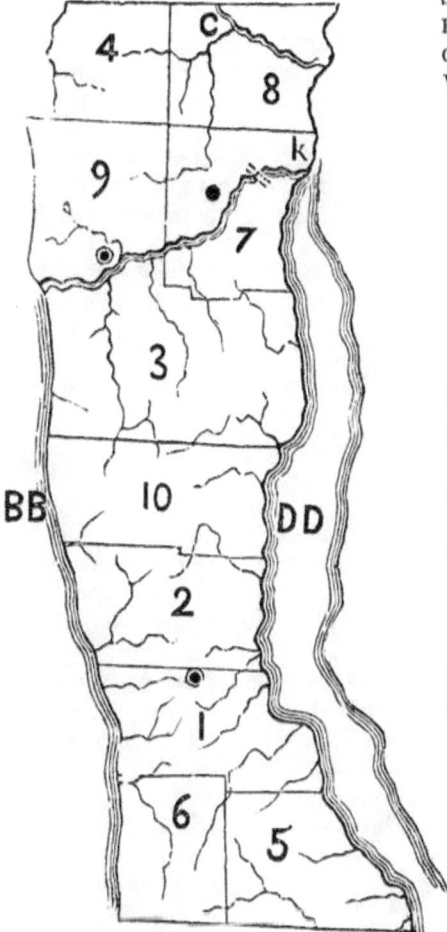

Square miles, 308.
Population, 24,972.
Organized, 1804.
Valuation, 1845, $5,674,034.

TOWNS.

1. Ovid, 1789.
2. Romulus, 1789.
3. Fayette, 1800.
4. Junius, 1803.
5. Covert, 1817.
6. Lodi, 1826.
7. Seneca Falls, 1829.
8. Tyre, 1829.
9. Waterloo, 1829.
10. Varick, 1830.

Rivers. c. Clyde. k. Seneca.
Lakes. BB. Seneca. DD. Cayuga.
Falls. Seneca.
Villages. WATERLOO. OVID. Seneca Falls.

BOUNDARIES. North by Wayne county; East by Cayuga county and Cayuga Lake; South by Tompkins county; and West by Seneca Lake and Ontario county.

SURFACE. The surface of this county rises from the lakes, which bound it on either side, to an altitude of 1200 or 1300 feet above tide water, and presents a pleasing diversity of beautiful valleys and hills.

RIVERS. The Seneca outlet is the principal stream, connecting Seneca and Cayuga lakes. The Clyde crosses its northeastern corner.

FALLS. The Seneca outlet has a descent of forty-seven feet, at the village of Seneca Falls.

LAKES. The lakes are Seneca and Cayuga.

CANALS. The Erie canal passes through the town of Tyre, in the north-east corner of this county, and the Cayuga and Seneca canal crosses the county, through the towns of Seneca and Waterloo, connecting the waters of the Seneca and Cayuga Lakes, and the Erie canal, at Montezuma.

RAILROADS. The Auburn and Rochester railroad passes through this county, most of the distance running parallel with Seneca outlet and canal.

CLIMATE. Mild and temperate. The situation of the county between two considerable bodies of water, prevents the long continuance of snow in winter, and essentially modifies the climate. It is considered healthy.

GEOLOGY AND MINERALS. The rocks of the northern section of this county, belong to the Onondaga salt group; those of the central, to the Helderberg limestones; and the southern to the Ludlowville shales of the Erie group.

Gypsum, or plaster of Paris is found in extensive beds near Seneca falls, and is largely exported. Variegated marble occurs near Seneca lake. Petroleum or Seneca oil is found floating on the Seneca lake, and on springs near it. A pool twenty feet in diameter, near Cayuga, constantly gives off nitrogen gas in large quantities.

SOIL AND VEGETABLE PRODUCTIONS. The soil is mostly a calcareous loam and mould of excellent quality, and well adapted to wheat and grass. Fruit is cultivated to a considerable extent, and attains great perfection. Oak, maple, beech, elm, butternut, and in the highlands, pine and hemlock, are the principal forest trees.

PURSUITS. The people are largely engaged in the culture of wheat and grass, and the rearing of cattle.

Manufactures are increasing. The principal articles are flour, cotton and woollen goods, distilled liquors, and leather.

Commerce. The county has considerable commerce, both by way of the Seneca and Cayuga lakes, and by the Erie canal. Gypsum and agricultural products are largely exported.

STAPLE PRODUCTIONS. Wheat, oats, corn, hops, plaster of Paris, wool and butter.

SCHOOLS. In 1846, there were 110 common schools, taught, on an average, nine months each, and attended by 8065 children. The teachers' wages amounted to $13,022, and the district libraries to 14,956 volumes.

There were also twenty-two select schools, with 298 scholars, and three academies, with 248 students.

RELIGIOUS DENOMINATIONS. Methodists, Presbyterians, Baptists, Dutch Reformed, Episcopalians, Friends, and Roman Catholics. The whole number of churches is thirty-eight, of clergymen, forty-six.

SENECA COUNTY. 309

HISTORY. The first settlers in Seneca county were Messrs. Horatio Jones and Lawrence Van Clief, who located themselves at Seneca Falls, in 1784 or 1785. Mr. James Bennet settled at West Cayuga, in 1787. Colonel Mynderse, who established himself in Seneca Falls in 1795, founded the village of that name in 1816.

The county belonged to the Military Tract, granted to the soldiers of the state, by the legislature, and the land titles are derived from them. The Indian title to these lands was not extinguished till 1789. Its growth has been rapid since its first settlement.

VILLAGES. WATERLOO village, in the town of Waterloo, is a half shire town, lying on the north side of the Seneca outlet, and incorporated in 1824. It is a very flourishing manufacturing village, containing, besides the county buildings, a number of churches and a chartered academy, occupying a fine building, and amply provided with apparatus for the illustration of the natural sciences. Large quantities of limestone are quarried in the vicinity. The Cayuga and Seneca canal, and the Auburn and Rochester railroad, both pass through the village. Population 3200.

OVID, a half shire village, was incorporated in 1816. It is situated on elevated ground, about midway between the lakes, and commands a fine and widely extended prospect. It has a chartered academy. Population 700.

Seneca Falls was incorporated in 1831, and, like Waterloo, is situated on the Seneca outlet, the canal and railroad. It derives an abundant hydraulic power from the Seneca outlet, the water of which is constant and steady, and is applied extensively to manufacturing purposes, by means of four dams having a total fall of forty-seven feet. A flourishing academy is located at this village. Population 3000.

XXIV. LEWIS COUNTY.

Square miles, 1122.
Organized, 1805.

Population, 20,218.
Valuation, 1845, $1,675,000.

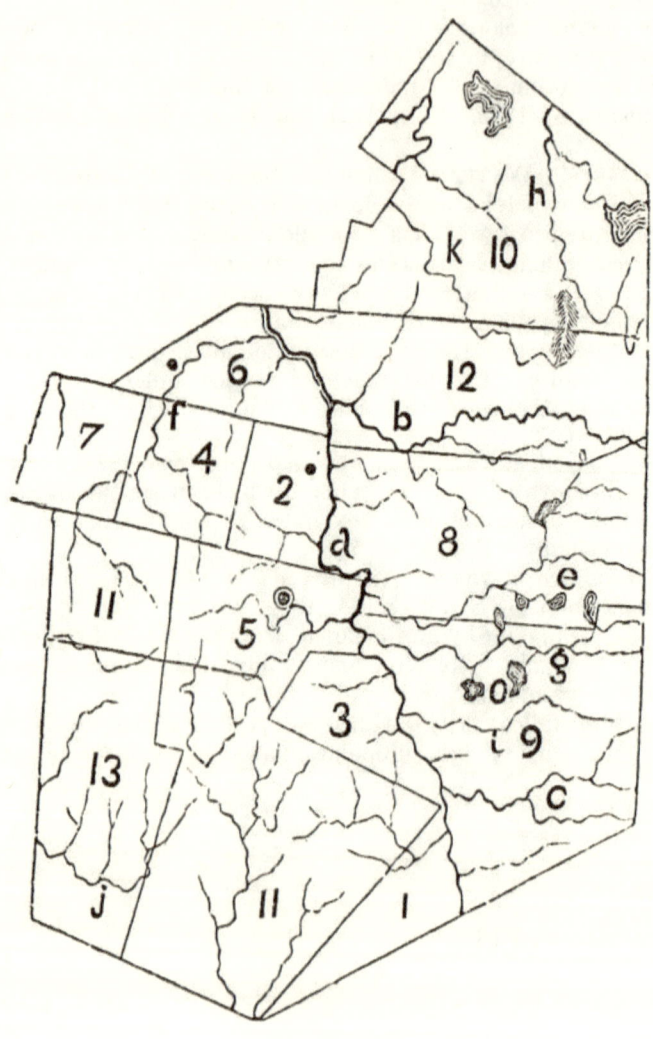

TOWNS.

1. Leyden, 1797.
2. Lowville, 1800.
3. Turin, 1800.
4. Harrisburg, 1803.
5. Martinsburgh, 1803.
6. Denmark, 1807.

7. Pinckney, 1808.
8. Watson, 1821.
9. Greig, 1828.
10. Diana, 1830.
11. West Turin, 1830.
12. Croghan, 1842.
13. Osceola, 1842.

Rivers. a. Black. b. Beaver. c. Moose. e. Independence Creek. f. Deer. g. Otter. i. Fish. j. Salmon. k. Indian. h. West branch of Oswegatchie.

Lakes. o. Fish.

Falls. Falls on the Black river, at Denmark and Greig.

Villages. MARTINSBURG. Lowville. Copenhagen.

BOUNDARIES. North by Jefferson and St. Lawrence counties; East by Herkimer; South by Oneida, and West by Oswego and Jefferson counties.

SURFACE. The county is divided by the Black river into two nearly equal sections. The eastern ascends somewhat rapidly, from the river, to the mountainous region on its eastern line. The western is rolling and frequently hilly, rising from the Black river, for six or eight miles, and then inclining to the south and west. Broad alluvial flats are found along the Black river.

RIVERS. Black and Beaver rivers, Independence, Moose, Deer, Otter, Fish, Salmon, and Indian creeks, and the west branch of the Oswegatchie, are the principal streams.

FALLS. Black river has a fall of sixty-three feet, in the town of Leyden, and Deer creek of 175 feet, in the town of Denmark.

CANAL. The Black river canal, when finished, will unite with Black river just below the high falls at Leyden.

CLIMATE. The climate of Lewis county is cold, but healthy. The winters are long, but the uniformity of the temperature renders them less unpleasant, than would be expected.

GEOLOGY AND MINERALS. The country east of the Black river is primitive in its character. The rock underlying this portion of the county, and frequently appearing on the surface, is granite. West of the river, the whole county is underlaid with a fine compact limestone, which appears every where, on the borders of the streams. The Utica slate also occupies a narrow belt in the western part of the county.

Iron ore is very abundant and of a superior quality; lead ore, (galena,) also occurs in considerable quantities. The other minerals worthy of notice are, sulphuret of zinc, (blende,) very beautiful quartz crystals, scapolite, tabular spar, green cocolite, feldspar, sphene, crystallized pyrites, calcareous and fluor spar, manganese, and Rensselaerite. Probably few counties in the state are richer in mineral wealth.

SOIL AND VEGETABLE PRODUCTIONS. The soil is various, composed of a fertile alluvium, or a gravelly, sandy, and clayey loam. It is susceptible of a profitable cultivation, and furnishes fine grazing. The timber is principally pine, spruce, hemlock, beech, maple, elm, ash, with some white oak and walnut. The eastern section still has extensive forests. From the maple. are manufactured considerable quantities of sugar.

PURSUITS. *Agriculture* is the chief employment of the inhabitants; the products of the dairy are large.

Manufactures. The county has abundant water power, but as yet it is but little improved. Flour, lumber, leather, and fulled cloths, are the chief articles of manufacture.

Commerce. There is little or no commerce; the completion of the Black River canal will aid materially in bringing the produce of their rich and fertile lands to market.

The STAPLES of the county are butter and cheese, wool, potatoes, oats, and wheat. Considerable quantities of barley, buckwheat, flax, hops, and sugar, are also produced.

SCHOOLS. The district school-houses in the county, in 1846, were 150 in number, in which were instructed 6139 pupils. The average length of the schools was seven months. The teachers wages, $6196; the number of volumes in the district libraries, 11,886. There were six private schools with eighty-three scholars, and one academy with sixty-two pupils.

RELIGIOUS DENOMINATIONS. Methodists, Baptists, Presbyterians, Congregationalists, Universalists, Roman Catholics, Episcopalians, and Friends. The total number of churches is thirty-seven, of clergymen, forty-four.

HISTORY. The whole of this county was originally owned by Alexander Macomb. The western part was afterward sold to a company of capitalists in New York city, and the eastern to a French company at Paris. The first settlers were pioneers from Connecticut and Massachusetts, who made their way, in 1797, from Utica and Fort Stanwix, (now Rome,) at that time small settlements, by a line of marked trees, to the falls of Black river, and from thence to the town of Lowville, where they established themselves. Their families followed, the succeeding winter, through snow so deep as to make it necessary to break paths for the cattle and teams, while mothers, shod with snow-shoes, bore their infants in their arms. For some time after, the farmers were obliged to go forty miles to mill, carrying their grain upon their shoulders.

VILLAGES. MARTINSBURG, in the town of the same name, contains the county buildings, a female seminary, and a number of factories. Population 800.

Lowville is a village of some business in the town of Lowville. It has an incorporated academy. Population 800.

Copenhagen, in the town of Denmark, is situated on both sides of Deer river. It is a flourishing village, and engaged in manufactures. Population about 500.

XXXV. JEFFERSON COUNTY.

Square miles, 1125.
Organized, 1805.
Population, 64,999.
Valuation, 1845, $6,536,651.

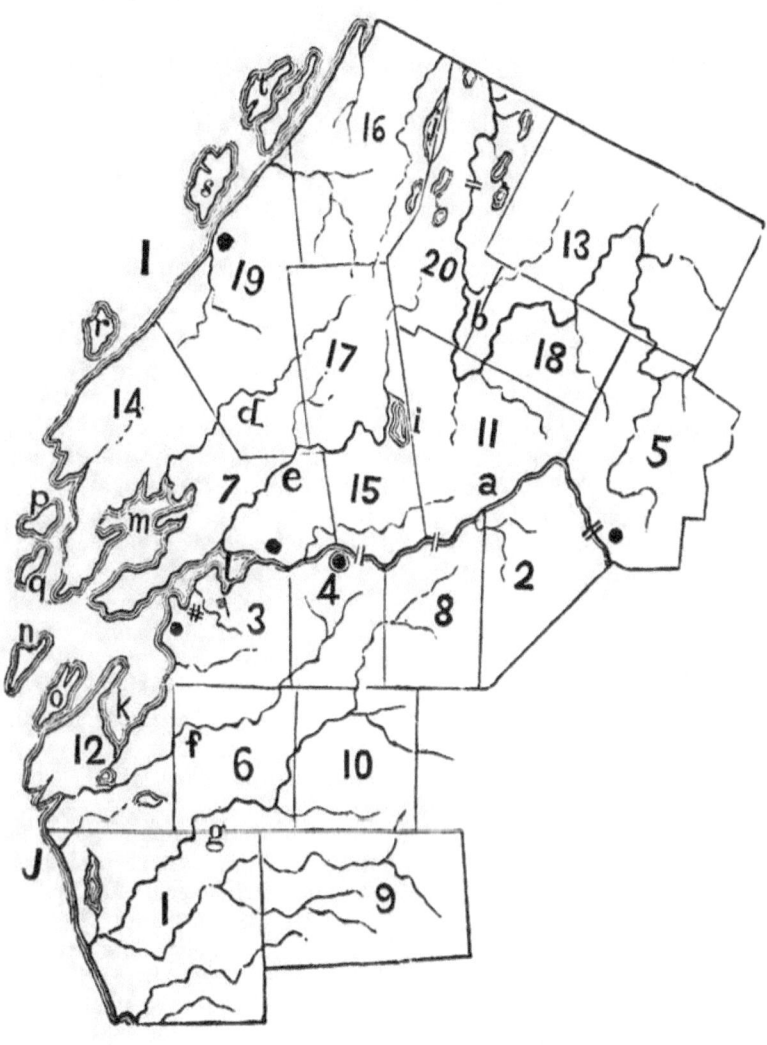

TOWNS.

1. Ellisburgh, 1797.
2. Champion, 1800.
3. Houndsfield, 1800.
4. Watertown, 1800.
5. Wilna, 1800.
6. Adams, 1802.
7. Brownville, 1802.
8. Rutland, 1802.

314 STATE OF NEW YORK.

9. Lorraine, 1804.
10. Rodman, 1804.
11. Le Ray, 1806.
12. Henderson, 1806.
13. Antwerp, 1816.
14. Lyme, 1817.
15. Pamelia, 1819.
16. Alexandria, 1821.
17. Orleans, 1821.
18. Philadelphia, 1821.
19. Clayton, 1832.
20. Theresa, 1842.

Rivers and Creeks. I. St. Lawrence River. a. Black River. b. Indian River. d. Chaumont Creek. e. Perch. f. Stoney. g. Sandy.

Lakes, &c. J. Ontario. i. Perch. j. Yellow. k. Hungry Bay. l. Black River. m. Chaumont Bay.

Islands. n. Gallop Island. o. Stoney. p. Grenadier. q. Fox r. Carlton. s. Grindstone. t. Wells.

Falls. On the Indian river. On the Black river at Champion, Rutland, and Watertown. Long Falls, Wilna.

Forts. Sacketts Harbor.

Villages. WATERTOWN. Sacketts Harbor. Brownville. Cornelia. Carthage.

BOUNDARIES. North by the St. Lawrence River, and St. Lawrence county; East by Lewis county; South by Oswego county, and West by Lake Ontario.

SURFACE. The surface of Jefferson county may be divided into two terraces, the broader of which is on the northwest. The Ridge Road, extending from the Niagara river, at a distance of from six to ten miles from the lake, and undoubtedly indicating the ancient limits of Lake Ontario, is here about 100 feet in height. The surface between this and the lake is level or gently undulating. From this ridge the county has a gentle descent toward the southeast, where an elevated ridge crosses it, and gives it a broken and hilly appearance.

RIVERS. The chief streams of the county, besides the St. Lawrence, are the Black and Indian rivers, Chaumont, Perch, Stoney, and Sandy creeks.

FALLS. There is a series of falls in the Black river, commencing at the Long falls in Carthage.

LAKES. The chief lakes are Ontario, Perch, and Yellow,

BAYS. Hungry, Black River, and Chaumont bays are indentations of greater or less extent, upon the lake coast.

ISLANDS. Along its western line are situated Gallop, Stoney, Fox, Grenadier, Carlton, Grindstone, and Wells islands.

CLIMATE. Equable and healthy. The winters are cold, but without sudden changes. The summer heats are moderated by the lake breezes.

GEOLOGY AND MINERALS. The primary formation is confined to two or three small districts in the county, principally in the

JEFFERSON COUNTY. 315

north and northeast part. In Alexandria, there is a small tract where the primitive rocks are near the surface. They are granite, primitive limestone, gneiss, and hornblende. The greater part of the county, however, belongs to the transition formation.

The order of arrangement of the rocks of this formation, here, is the following, beginning at the northern part of the county: Potsdam sandstone, extending to a point a little south of Theresa falls; calciferous sand rock and birdseye limestone, appearing as far south as the Black river; Trenton limestone, extending through Houndsfield, Adams, Watertown, and Rutland, and succeeded by a narrow belt of the Utica slate; this is followed by the Lorraine shales, lying in Rodman, Lorraine, and Pinckney. In the southern line of towns, the gray sandstone occurs in small quantities.

Bog iron ore, spathic iron, specular iron, arragonite, cacoxene, pyrites, celestine, terenite, tremolite, fluor spar, green malachite, tourmaline, strontianite, idiocrase, apatite, pyroxene, and massive heavy spar, tufa, peat, and graphite in six sided tablets, are the principal minerals.

There is a cave in the town of Pamelia, nearly opposite Watertown, containing a number of apartments, and some fine spars. It has been explored for nearly half a mile.

SOIL AND VEGETABLE PRODUCTIONS. The soil is generally a fertile sandy loam, with some clay and gravel, and susceptible of a high degree of cultivation. In the basin on the northwest, wheat grows abundantly, but the higher lands in the southeast are more favorable to grazing. The forests abound with oak, maple, beech, birch, walnut, ash, elm, hemlock, pine, tamarack, and red and white cedar. The cranberry grows abundantly in the swamps, and forms an article of export.

PURSUITS. *Agriculture* is the leading pursuit of the people. Great numbers of cattle and swine are reared for the eastern market; the products of the dairy are very large. Potatoes, oats, corn, wheat, rye, barley, and flax are produced in great abundance, and the wool-growing interest is not neglected. The county ranks among the first for agricultural products in the state.

The *manufactures* of the county are extensive and rapidly increasing. The principal articles are flour, lumber, iron, leather, distilled liquors, potash, and woollen goods. The value of articles manufactured in the county in 1845, was nearly $2,000,000.

The *commerce* of this county is large and constantly increasing. About one half of its produce finds its way to a market down the St. Lawrence; the remainder through the Oswego and Erie canals, enters the Hudson, or through the Welland and Western canals, and the great lakes, is distributed over the Mississippi valley. The shipping of this county amounts to about 5000 tons. The completion of the Black River canal will open a more ready and convenient conveyance for the produce of portions of the county.

STAPLE PRODUCTIONS. Butter and cheese, potatoes, oats, corn, wheat, wool, flax, barley, and peas.

SCHOOLS. There were 368 district schools in the county, in 1846. The average length of the schools was seven months—number of scholars, 22,866—amount of teachers' wages, $24,141—and number of volumes in the school libraries, 37,552.

There are also fifty-four private schools, with 1089 scholars, and two academies, with 173 pupils.

RELIGIOUS DENOMINATIONS. Methodists, Baptists, Presbyterians, Congregationalists, Episcopalians, Universalists, Roman Catholics, Dutch Reformed, Unitarians, Friends, and Jews. There are ninety-two churches, and 106 clergymen of all denominations in the county.

HISTORY. The first settlement made in this county by whites, was at Ellisburgh, in 1793, by Mr. Lyman Ellis. The next was at Champion, not long after, by settlers from Connecticut. The third was at Watertown, in 1800, by Mr. Henry Coffin, of New Hampshire. In the succeeding year, emigrants from New England settled in Adams, Rodman, Brownville, and Houndsfield; and the year after in Sacketts Harbor and Rutland. Mounds and fortifications of great antiquity, and exhibiting a high degree of architectural skill, are scattered over every part of the county.

At the commencement of the late war with Great Britain, Sacketts Harbor was selected as the principal naval depôt of the lake frontier, on account of the excellency of its harbor.

On the twenty-second and twenty-third of April, 1813, General Dearborn, with a force of 1700 men, embarked from this port, to attack York, (now Toronto,) Canada West. The assault on York was successful, though the brave General Pike, by whom it was led, lost his life by the explosion of the magazine. But the withdrawal of so large a body of troops from Sacketts Harbor, left the important military stores there exposed; and as might have been expected, the British forces at Kingston, availed themselves of the opportunity, to make a descent upon that village.

On the twenty-eighth of May, 1813, they appeared off the harbor, with four ships, one brig, two schooners, two gun boats, and thirty-three flat bottomed boats, containing in all 1200 troops. The alarm of their approach had been given, and General Brown had made every exertion in his power to defend the harbor. The British suffered themselves to delay, in the attempt to capture some boats, coming from Oswego with troops, and thus the militia from the vicinity had time to assemble; but not more than 1000 troops could be collected in all, of whom more than 500 were raw militia, and about 200 more, invalids. General Brown arranged the militia behind a breast work, hastily thrown up, to oppose the landing of the enemy. In the rear of these he had stationed a part of the regular troops. The regular artillerists occupied Fort Tompkins, and Lieutenant Chauncey, with a small corps, defended the naval stores at Navy Point.

The British made an effort to land, but were at first repulsed with severe loss; but after the second fire, the militia became panic struck, and abandoning their breast work, fled in the utmost confusion. Colonel Mills, their commander, was killed in the attempt to rally them.

Meantime the enemy effected a landing, and commenced their march towards the village, but met with the most desperate opposition. Finding, however, that he was likely to be overpowered by the superior force of the enemy, General Brown concerted a stratagem which gained him the day, and compelled the enemy to retreat. Learning that the militia, whose flight had prevented success in the onset, were still in the neighborhood, he hastened to them, put himself at their head, ordered them to follow him, and passing silently through a distant wood, in the direction of the enemy's boats, induced the British commander to believe that he intended to cut off his retreat.

Alarmed at this, and believing the American force superior to his own, in point of numbers, the British general withdrew his forces with the utmost precipitation, leaving his dead and wounded behind him. He was not pursued, because pursuit would have exhibited the weakness of the American force.

While the battle was at its height, intelligence was brought to Lieutenant Chauncey, that the Americans were about to surrender, and accordingly he, in compliance with his orders, set fire to the stores and shipping, to prevent their falling into the hands of the enemy. Learning his error, however, he made the utmost effort to arrest the flames, and succeeded in saving a considerable portion. The British loss was severe in this action, three of their field officers being killed, and not less than 150 wounded, killed and prisoners. The American loss was about the same in number.

After retreating to their shipping, the British demanded the surrender of the village, which was promptly refused.

On the thirtieth of May, 1814, a number of boats coming from Oswego, with cannon and rigging for the new vessels building at Sacketts Harbor, and well manned with sailors, riflemen and Indians, were pursued into Henderson harbor, by five British gunboats, manned with about 200 English marines and sailors.

Captain Woolsey, of the American navy, had command of the American boats, and landing as quickly as possible, stationed a part of his riflemen and Indians in ambuscade on each side of the road, and placed a small body of militia in front of the landing, to contest the passage of the enemy. His stratagem was successful. The British rushed on, and the militia fled before them, but the party in ambush poured upon them so deadly a fire as to compel them to surrender, with the loss of twenty killed, and forty or fifty wounded. The number of prisoners was 137. Five gunboats, armed with heavy cannon, were also captured.

After the war, the extraordinary facilities afforded by the county, for sustaining an abundant population, gave it a rapid growth, and it is now one of the largest counties in the state.

Its population quadrupled between 1810 and 1840, and is still fast increasing.

VILLAGES. WATERTOWN, the seat of justice for the county, is a large and flourishing manufacturing village, situated at the falls of the Black river.

Perhaps no village in the United States possesses more extensive and easily available hydraulic privileges.

The Black river here has a fall in the space of a mile, of eighty-eight feet, over seven artificial dams and five natural cascades, each of which can be used for manufacturing purposes.

The volume of water is estimated at 10,000 cubic feet per second—being sufficient to keep in motion more than one million of spindles. But a small portion of this immense water power, is employed; yet the manufactories of cotton and woollen goods, flour, leather, paper, machinery, pumps, sash, wagons, and carriages are extensive.

The Jefferson County Institute, located here, is a highly flourishing and well conducted seminary. It has about 180 pupils. There are several other schools of considerable reputation.

The village has also a " Young Men's Association for Literary Improvement," which is in a flourishing condition, and has accumulated a respectable library. Population 4200.

Sacketts Harbor, in the town of Houndsfield, is an important village, having one of the best harbors on Lake Ontario. It has also some manufactories, propelled by water power, furnished by a canal, extending from the Black river, near Watertown, to the lake at this place.

The United States government has erected extensive stone barracks here for troops. They occupy a lot of about forty acres, surrounded by a fence, on three sides, and the fourth open to the water. In the military burial ground, attached to the barracks, is a monument to the brave and lamented General Pike, and others, who fell on the northern frontier, during the late war with Great Britain.

The government has also a ship yard, and ship houses, in one of which is the frame of a ship of the line, commenced during the war of 1812.

During the war, Sacketts Harbor increased with great rapidity; but at its close, it experienced a decline, from which, however, it has revived, amid the general prosperity of the county. Population 2000.

Brownville, in the town of the same name, is a thriving manufacturing village, situated on the Black river, four miles below Watertown. Population 1000.

Dexter, in the town of Brownville, is a growing and important village. Its harbor has been improved by the United States government, and it has now considerable commerce and some manufactures. Population 1000.

Adams, in the town of Adams, is situated on both sides of Sandy creek, which here affords a good water power. It has a young ladies seminary, in a flourishing condition. Population 800.

Carthage, in the town of Wilna, is a village of considerable importance. A large quantity of iron is annually manufactured here. Population 600.

In the same town is a natural bridge, twelve feet in width, and six feet above the water, extending over the Indian river. There is a small settlement near it.

Cape Vincent, at the head of the St. Lawrence, is a lake port of some importance.

Belleville and *Ellisburgh*, both in the town of Ellisburgh, are thriving villages.

XXXVI. ALLEGANY COUNTY.

Square Miles, about 1050.
Organized, 1806.

Population, 31,611.
Valuation, 1845, $4,337,756.

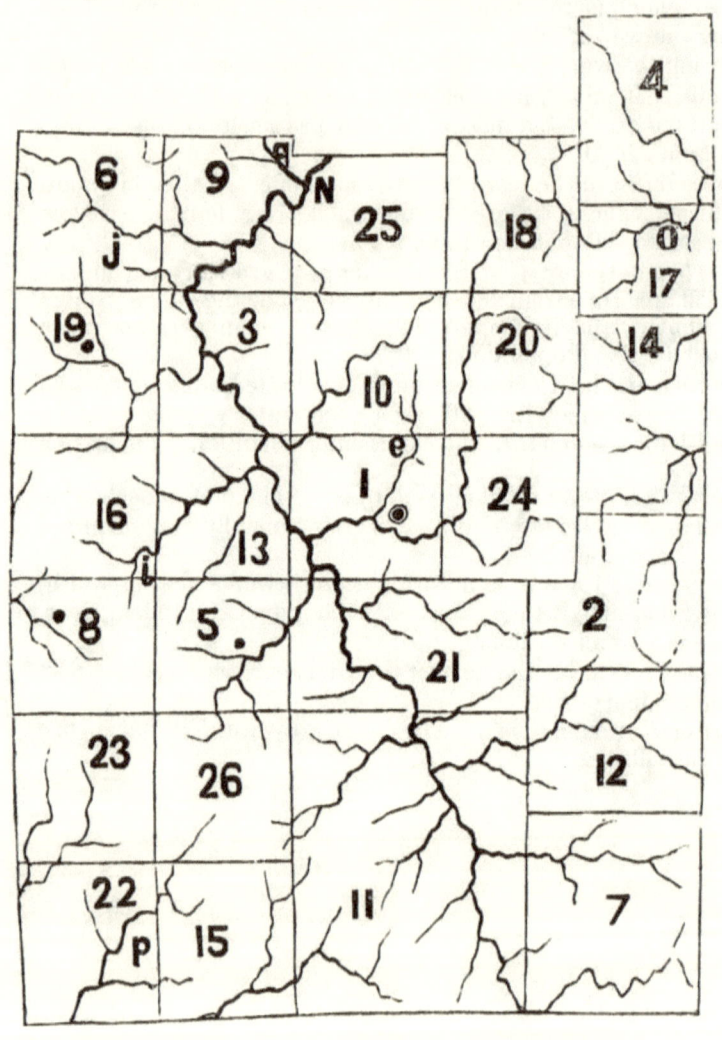

TOWNS.

1. Angelica, 1805.
2. Alfred, 1808.
3. Caneadea, 1808.
4. Ossian, 1808.
5. Friendship, 1815.
6. Centreville, 1819.
7. Independence, 1821.
8. Cuba, 1822.

ALLEGANY COUNTY. 321

9. Hume, 1822.
10. Allen, 1823.
11. Scio, 1823.
12. Andover, 1824.
13. Belfast, 1824.
14. Almond, 1825.
15. Bolivar, 1825.
16. New Hudson, 1825.
17. Burns, 1826.
18. Grove, 1827.
19. Rushford, 1827.
20. Birdsall, 1829.
21. Amity, 1830.
22. Genesee, 1830
23. Clarksville, 1835.
24. West Almond, 1835.
25. Granger, 1837.
26. Wirt, 1837.

Rivers. N. Genesee River.   e. Angelica Creek.   i. Black.   j. Cold.   o. Canascraga.   p. Little Genesee.

Villages. ANGELICA. Friendship. Cuba. Rushford.

BOUNDARIES. North by Wyoming and Livingston; East by Steuben; South by the state of Pennsylvania, and West by Cattaraugus county.

SURFACE. This county forms a portion of the elevated table land which extends through the southern tier of counties, but the deep channels, worn in the rocks which underlie the county, by the Genesee and other streams, and the long narrow valleys thus formed, give its otherwise level surface, a broken appearance. The height of the table land is from 1200 to 2000 feet above tide water. It declines gradually toward the north.

RIVERS. The principal streams are the Genesee river, Angelica, Black, Cold, Canascraga and Little Genesee creeks.

CANAL. The Genesee valley canal has been commenced, but is not yet completed.

RAILROAD. The line of the New York and Erie Railroad has been laid out across its southern portion.

CLIMATE. The elevation of the surface produces a low temperature. The winters are long, and the snows heavy. The county is generally healthy.

GEOLOGY AND MINERALS. This county lies wholly within the Chemung sandstone formation, though the tops of some of the highest hills are capped with the old red sandstone, and conglomerate of the Catskill groups.

Like the rest of this formation, it possesses few minerals of interest. There is, however, some bog iron ore and hydrate of manganese, associated with calcareous tufa. At Cuba is a petroleum, or Seneca oil spring, which has attracted considerable attention. The shales of this vicinity are all bituminous.

SOIL AND VEGETABLE PRODUCTIONS. Much of the soil of the county is fertile, consisting of a clayey and sandy loam; but it is generally moist, and better adapted to grass than grain. The forests are quite dense, and the timber is of large size, consisting of oak, maple, beech, basswood, ash, elm, hemlock, white and yellow pine.

PURSUITS. The people are mainly devoted to *Agricultural* pursuits, particularly to raising cattle and sheep. The products of the dairy are quite large.

Manufactures are principally confined to lumber, flour, fulled cloths, leather, oil and potash.

Commerce. The county has little commerce.

STAPLE PRODUCTIONS. Butter, cheese, oats, potatoes, wheat and wool.

SCHOOLS. In 1846, there were in the county, 234 district schools, averaging seven months' instruction each, expending for tuition, $13,979, and attended by 13,946 children. The libraries contained 20,595 volumes.

The number of private schools was eight, with 142 scholars; of academies two, with 229 pupils.

RELIGIOUS DENOMINATIONS. Baptists, Methodists, Presbyterians, Congregationalists, Episcopalians and Unitarians. Total number of churches sixty, of clergymen, eighty-seven.

HISTORY. Allegany county was taken from Genesee, April seventh, 1806. The two western tier of towns are within the Holland Land Company's purchase. The interest of that company has been purchased by another, since formed. The rest of the county is comprised in the tract constituting the Morris estate.

It was first settled by Philip Church, in 1804. In 1838 a remarkable tornado passed over the western section; of a dense forest of 400 or 500 acres, scarcely a single tree escaped uninjured. The wind for the space of twenty miles left traces of its devastation, yet, strange to tell, though several individuals were buried under the ruins of their houses, none lost their lives.

In 1846, the towns of Eagle, Pike, Portage and Nunda, were taken from this county and added to Wyoming and Livingston counties.

VILLAGES. ANGELICA, located in the town of the same name, is the county seat. It is a pleasant village and has some manufactures. Population 1000.

Cuba is a flourishing village. In this place is a spring, from the surface of which is collected the famed Seneca oil, so much used for rheumatism and sprains. It was highly valued by the Indians, and a square mile around the spring has been set apart for the Senecas. Population 800.

Friendship is a village of considerable importance, on the proposed route of the Erie railroad. Population 800.

Rushford is a thriving and important village. It is increasing in population quite raipidly. Population 1000.

XXXVII. BROOME COUNTY.

Square Miles, 627.
Organized, 1806.

Population, 25,808.
Valuation, 1845, $2,087,167.

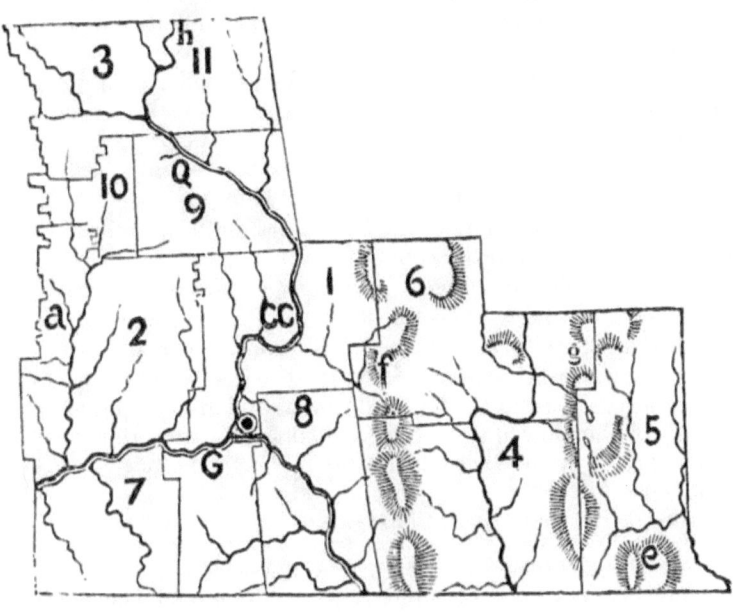

TOWNS.

1. Chenango, 1721.
2. Union, 1731.
3. Lisle, 1801.
4. Windsor, 1807.
5. Sandford, 1821.
6. Colesville, 1821.
7. Vestal, 1823.
8. Conklin, 1824.
9. Barker, 1831.
10. Nanticoke, 1831.
11. Triangle, 1831.

Mountains. e. Oquaga. f. Binghamton. g. Randolph.

Rivers. CC. Chenango River. G. Susquehanna River. Q. Tioughnioga River. a. Nanticoke Creek. h. Otselic.

Villages. BINGHAMTON.

BOUNDARIES. Bounded North by Cortland and Chenango; East by Delaware; South by the state of Pennsylvania, and West by Tioga county.

SURFACE. This county forms the eastern termination of the great table land of the southern tier of counties. Like the other portions of this elevated plain, its surface is much broken by numerous streams, which have worn deep valleys through the soft and perishable sandstones which underlie it. The general elevation of the surface is from 1400 to 1600 feet above tide water, and the valleys are depressed from 300 to 400 feet below this level. In the eastern part the Randolph, Binghamton and Oquaga mountains rise above the general level. The Susquehanna sweeps around the base of the latter, making a very extensive bend.

RIVERS. The Susquehanna, Chenango, Otselic, Tioughnioga and west branch of the Delaware, are the principal rivers of the county.

CANAL. The Chenango canal enters the county with the Chenango river, and terminates at Binghamton.

RAILROAD. The route of the New York and Erie railroad has been laid out through the county.

CLIMATE. The climate is salubrious, but from the great elevation of the county, necessarily cool. Large bodies of snow fall during the winter, and continue late in the spring.

GEOLOGY AND MINERALS. The eastern and southern parts of the county belong to the Catskill group, and are composed principally of the old red sandstone and conglomerate—the western is comprised in the Chemung group, and consists mostly of grey sandstone and slate.

Specimens of garnet, tourmaline, agate, porphyry, jasper, &c., have been collected from the pebbles on the banks of the Susquehanna and Chenango rivers. There are several sulphur and one or two brine springs.

SOIL AND VEGETABLE PRODUCTIONS. The broken character of the soil renders the county generally better adapted to grazing than to the culture of grain. In the valleys of the streams, oats and corn thrive well, and wheat is raised to some extent. The principal timber trees are the white and pitch pine, oak, beech, maple and hickory. Much of the surface of the county is yet covered with wood.

PURSUITS. *Agriculture* is the chief pursuit of the inhabitants. Much attention is paid to the products of the dairy. Some grain is also raised, and summer crops thrive well.

Manufactures. The water power of its many streams furnishes abundant facilities for manufacturing purposes, which the people of this county are beginning to improve. The New York and Erie railroad will, when opened, give a new impetus to its manufacturing interests, by affording increased facilities for transportation.

Lumber and flour, fulled cloths and leather, constitute the chief articles of manufacture.

STAPLE PRODUCTIONS. Butter, oats, corn and potatoes.

SCHOOLS. There are in the county 170 district schools, which in 1846, averaged seven months instruction each. $8676 was paid for tuition; and the school libraries contained 13,800 volumes. The number of children taught was 8285.

<small>There are sixteen select schools, attended by 166 pupils; and one academy, with 212 students.</small>

RELIGIOUS DENOMINATIONS. Presbyterians, Baptists, Congregationalists, Episcopalians, Universalists and Roman Catholics. There are forty-six churches, and sixty-one ministers, of all denominations, in the county.

HISTORY. During Sullivan's campaign, in 1779, he encamped at or near the present site of Binghamton, in this county, for several days, awaiting the arrival of the detachment under the command of General James Clinton. No settlement was made in the county, however, till 1787, when Captain Joseph Leonard removed here from Wyoming, Pennsylvania. He was soon followed by Colonel William Rowe, who emigrated from Connecticut.

The land in the southern part of the county had been granted a few years previously, to Mr. Bingham, an eminent banker of Philadelphia, associated with whom was a Mr. Cox; and that now composing the northern towns of the county, was purchased in 1786, or perhaps earlier, by a company from Massachusetts. The amount of land belonging to this company was 230,000 acres. Having obtained a grant from the Massachusetts legislature, (this being a portion of the ten townships ceded to Massachusetts by New York,) they purchased the title from the Indians, by a treaty, concluded at the Forks of the Chenango.

By the enterprise and good management of General Whitney, the agent of Mr. Bingham, the settlements flourished and increased rapidly in population. In 1806, Broome county was set off from Tioga, as a separate county, and named in honor of John Broome, at that time Lieutenant Governor of the state.

A large proportion of the emigrants were from New England, and probably a majority from Connecticut.

VILLAGES. BINGHAMTON, formerly Chenango Point, is the shire town of the county. It is rapidly increasing in business, and has become already an important inland town. It is much engaged in manufactures, and furnishes a ready market for the produce of the surrounding country, which is mostly shipped by canal to the Hudson, and by the Susquehanna to Philadelphia.

The New York and Erie railroad will soon be opened to this place, and contribute still farther to its prosperity. Toll bridges constructed of wood, cross the Chenango and Susquehanna rivers, from this village. Population, nearly 4000.

Chenango Forks, Windsor and Harpersville are villages of some importance.

XXXVIII. MADISON COUNTY.

Square miles, 582.
Organized, 1806.

Population, 40,987.
Valuation, 1845, $6,490,881.

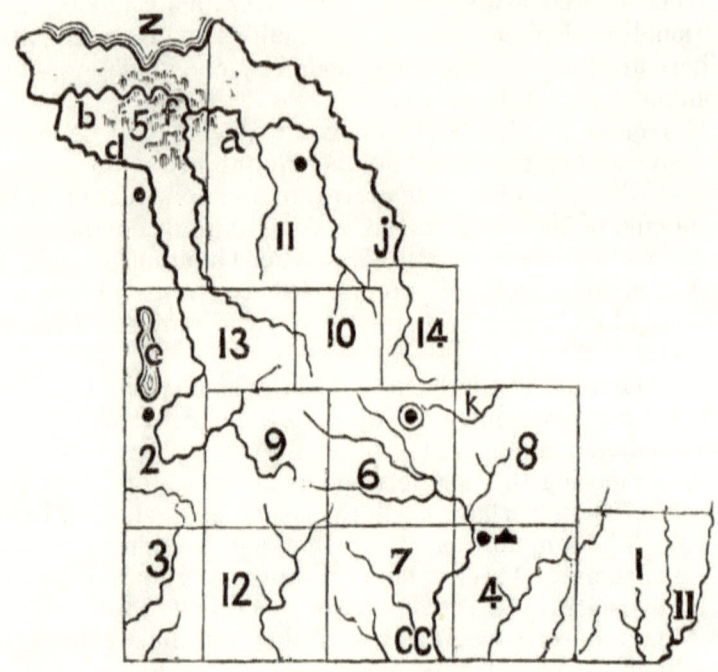

TOWNS.

1. Brookfield, 1795.
2. Cazenovia, 1795.
3. De Ruyter, 1798.
4. Hamilton, 1801.
5. Sullivan, 1803.
6. Eaton, 1807.
7. Lebanon, 1807.
8. Madison, 1807.
9. Nelson, 1807.
10. Smithfield, 1807.
11. Lenox, 1809.
12. Georgetown, 1815.
13. Fenner, 1823.
14. Stockbridge, 1839.

Rivers, &c. CC. Chenango river. II. Unadilla. k. Oriskany Creek. a. Cowasalon. b. Canaseraga. d. Chittenango. j. Oneida.

Lakes. Z. Oneida. e. Cazenovia, or Linklaen.

Marshes. f. Great Swamp.

Universities. Madison University.

Villages. MORRISVILLE. Hamilton. Cazenovia. Canastota. Chittenango.

BOUNDARIES. North by Oneida Lake; East by Oneida and Otsego counties; South by Chenango county, and West by Onondaga and Cortland counties.

MADISON COUNTY. 327

SURFACE. Diversified, and generally hilly, except where the great swamp extends for a distance of eight or ten miles, along the borders of Oneida Lake.

The elevated ridge or watershed, which divides the waters of the Susquehanna from those flowing north, crosses this county near its centre. The hills are, however, generally rounded, and susceptible of cultivation. This ridge is about 1500 feet above tide water.

RIVERS. On the south, the county is drained by the Chenango, Otselic and Unadilla rivers. On the north by the Oriskany, Oneida, Cowasalon, Chittenango, and Canaseraga creeks. The Erie and Chenango canals pass through the county.

LAKES. Oneida Lake forms the northern boundary of the county; Cazenovia, or Linklaen lake, called by the natives Haugena, is a beautiful sheet of water, four miles long by one broad, surrounded by a fine waving country. There are several small ponds on the dividing ridge.

CLIMATE. Healthful, but cool, and very subject to untimely frosts.

GEOLOGY AND MINERALS. Slate is the basis rock of the county. It is, however, overlaid for the most part with limestone, of that formation denominated the Onondaga salt group. Along the Oneida Lake, sandstone appears, and is found in boulders throughout the county. Fresh water limestone, containing fresh water shells, is found near the great swamp.

Argillaceous iron ore occurs in large quantities, in Lenox, and is used for castings; water lime and gypsum are abundant in Sullivan and Lenox; sulphur and brine springs are found in the same towns, and in the former is a magnesian spring, and several others so highly charged with carbonate of lime as to form incrustations on whatever is cast into them. Marl exists in large quantities, in the northern part of the county.

SOIL AND VEGETABLE PRODUCTIONS. The soil is generally fertile; in the valleys highly so: adapted to grain in the north, and to grazing in the south.

The timber is similar to that of the adjacent counties, consisting principally of hemlock, maple and beech. The sugar maple is abundant, and yields large quantities of sugar. In the great swamp, cedar, tamarack, &c. are the principal trees.

PURSUITS. *Agriculture* is the principal pursuit of the inhabitants, whose attention is divided between the culture of grain and the rearing of stock.

Hops, oats, corn and barley, are more largely cultivated than wheat.

Manufactures are considerably extensive, for which the fine water power of the Chittenango and other streams, furnishes ample facilities. Flour, lumber, woollen goods, distilled liquors, leather, iron and potash, are the principal articles manufactured.

The *commerce* of the county is confined to the transportation of its produce and manufactures, upon the Erie and Chenango canals.

STAPLE PRODUCTIONS. Hops, cheese, butter, wool, oats, sugar and potash.

SCHOOLS. There are in the county 234 district school-houses. The schools were taught in 1846 an average period of eight months; 13,523 children received instruction at an expense of $15,721. There were 26,456 volumes in the district libraries.

There were, also, in the county, forty-three private schools, with 1072 pupils, and four academies, with 198 pupils. There is one University in the county, chartered in 1846, and called Madison University. It has in all its departments 209 students.

RELIGIOUS DENOMIN TIONS. Baptists, Methodists, Congregationalists, Presbyterians, Universalists, Friends, Dutch Reformed, and Episcopalians.

There are eighty-one churches, and ninety-four clergymen, of all denominations, in the county.

HISTORY. Madison county originally formed a part of Chenango county, from which it was taken in 1806. The first settlement in the county was made at the village of Eaton, in the town of the same name, by Mr. Joseph Morse, in 1790.

In 1793, Colonel John Linklaen, agent for a company in Holland, settled in Cazenovia. This Holland Company owned a large portion of the county, and their agent sold most of it to New England settlers. The growth of the county was not rapid until the completion of the Erie and Chenango canals by which a market was opened for its produce.

VILLAGES. MORRISVILLE, in the town of Eaton, is the seat of justice for the county. It is situated on the Cherry Valley turnpike. It was settled principally by emigrants from Connecticut, and has some manufactories. Population, about 800.

Eaton, another village in the same town, has a number of manufactories. Population, about 700.

Cazenovia village, in the town of the same name, is pleasantly situated on the south-eastern margin of Linklaen lake. It is well laid out, and has some manufactures and considerable trade. The Oneida Conference Seminary, located here, is under the direction of the Methodist Episcopal church, and is a flourishing and well conducted institution. Here is also a high school and a seminary for young ladies. The village contains nearly 2000 inhabitants.

Hamilton village, in the town of the same name, is principally noted as the seat of Madison University, formerly the Hamilton Literary and Theological Institution. This institution was incorporated in 1819, and commenced operations in 1820. It received a charter as an University in 1846. It is well endowed, has an able corps of professors, and is in a highly prosperous condition.

There is also an academy of some distinction, in the village. Population, about 1600.

Chittenango, in the town of Sullivan, is largely engaged in the manufacture of water-lime, or hydraulic cement. It has also other manufactures. There is a sulphur spring of some note, one mile south of the village. It has also other springs, charged with carbonate of lime, and celebrated for their petrifying quality.

In this village is an academy, under the patronage of the Dutch Reformed Church. Population, 1000.

Canastota, in the town of Lenox, is a thriving and busy village, on the canal and railroad. It derives its name from the Indian appellation, given to a cluster of pines, which united their branches over the creek, which passes through the village. In this village is a high school of some celebrity. Population, about 1300.

De Ruyter is a small but pleasant village, in the town of the same name. Here is located the "De Ruyter Institute," a flourishing literary institution, under the direction of the Seventh Day Baptists. Population, 500.

Madison, in the town of the same name, is a thriving village. Population, 600.

Clockville, in the town of Lenox, and *Bridgeport*, in the town of Sullivan, are villages of some importance.

XXXIX. CATTARAUGUS COUNTY.

Square miles, 1232.   Population, 30,369.
Organized, 1808.   Valuation, 1845, $3,035,315.

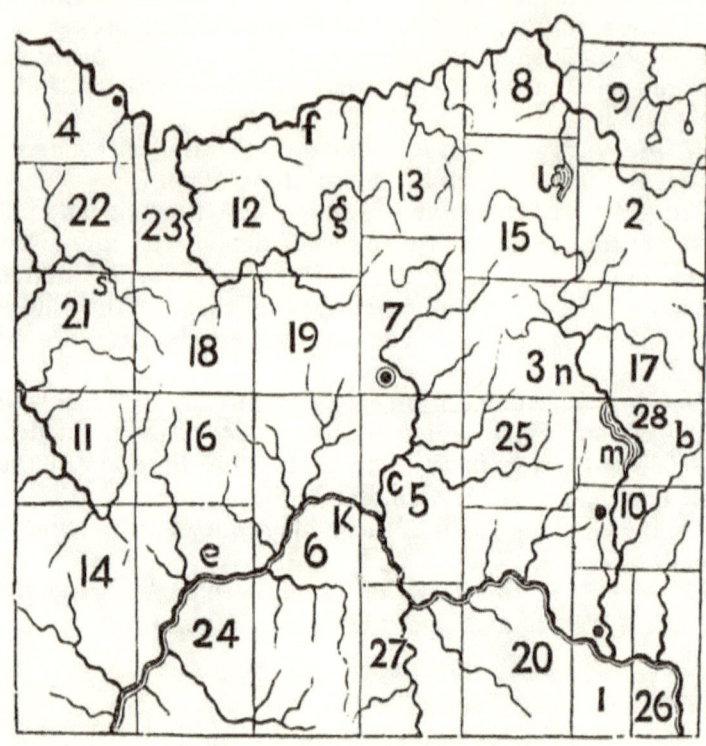

TOWNS.

1. Olean, 1808.
2. Farmersville, 1812.
3. Franklinville, 1812.
4. Perrysburgh, 1814.
5. Great Valley, 1818.
6. Little Valley, 1818.
7. Ellicottville, 1820.
8. Yorkshire, 1820.
9. Freedom, 1820.
10. Hinsdale, 1820.
11. Connewango, 1823.
12. Otto, 1823.
13. Ashford, 1824.
14. Randolph, 1826.
15. Machias, 1827.
16. Napoli, 1828.
17. Lyndon, 1829.
18. New Albion, 1830.
19. Mansfield, 1830.
20. Burton, 1831.
21. Leon, 1832.
22. Dayton, 1835.
23. Persia, 1835.
24. Cold Spring, 1837.
25. Humphrey, 1837.
26. Portville, 1838.
27. Carrollton, 1842.
28. Rice, 1846.

CATTARAUGUS COUNTY. 331

Rivers. K. Allegany. s. Connewango Creek. b. Oil. c. Great Valley. e. Cold Spring. f. Cattaraugus. g. South Branch. n. Ischua.

Lakes. l. Lime. m. Ischua Creek Reservoir.

Villages. ELLICOTTVILLE. Olean. Hinsdale. Lodi.

BOUNDARIES. North by the counties of Erie and Wyoming; East by Allegany county; South by the state of Pennsylvania, and West by Chautauque county.

SURFACE. The surface of the county is elevated and much broken. The high grounds in its centre divide the waters of the Allegany from those of the Chautauque Creek. The valley of the Allegany river is from one to two miles in breadth, and has a depression of 700 or 800 feet below the general surface of the county. North of this river, the land rises for fifteen or twenty miles, and attains the summit of the very irregular ridge which commences at Perrysburgh, on the north-west, and terminates at Farmersville, on the east.

RIVERS. The Allegany river, Cattaraugus, Oil, Great Valley, Cold Spring, South Branch, Connewango and Ischua creeks, are the principal streams of the county.

LAKES. Its lakes are Lime lake and Ischua creek reservoir.

RAILROADS. The line of the New York and Erie railroad crosses the southern part of the county.

CLIMATE. From the elevation of the surface, the climate is cold but healthful.

GEOLOGY AND MINERALOGY. This county is wholly within the Erie group. In the northern part, the Ludlowville slate is the surface rock, with occasional alternations of limestone. In the central and southern portions, the Chemung sandstone predominates. On the highest points in the county, the conglomerate of the Catskill group is occasionally found.

The Rock City, situated seven miles from Ellicottville, and near the line between Great and Little valley, is a remarkable natural curiosity.

The rock here is conglomerate, and by the removal and disintegration of portions of it, large masses from fifteen to thirty-five feet high, have been left standing isolated, and are separated by alleys and passages of various widths. The whole area covered by these blocks is over one hundred acres. The scene is in the highest degree imposing, and impresses upon the beholder the conviction that the name has not been improperly chosen.

The minerals are not numerous; the most valuable are, peat, marl, bog iron ore and manganese. There are also some saline and sulphur springs; petroleum or mineral oil, similar to the Seneca oil, found in Cuba, Allegany county, has been discovered at Freedom.

SOIL AND VEGETABLE PRODUCTIONS. The soil is well adapted to grazing. Grain thrives better in the northern section than in the southern.

Probably no region of equal extent in the United States has produced more valuable timber. The forest trees consist chiefly of pine, oak, hickory, ash, elm, linden, chestnut, walnut, beech, maple and hemlock. The maple is abundant, and affords large quantities of sugar.

PURSUITS. The people of this county are an *agricultural* community, paying more attention however, to the productions of the dairy, and the rearing of cattle, than to the raising of grain.

Manufactures. These are in their infancy, and chiefly confined to lumber, flour, fulled cloths, and leather.

The manufacture of lumber is prosecuted to a greater extent than in any other county in the state, 200 million feet being exported from the county annually.

Commerce. The Allegany is navigable for arks and small steamboats, at high water, to Olean; large quantities of lumber are exported from this county to Pittsburgh and Cincinnati, by this channel.

Its STAPLES are lumber, potatoes, oats, butter and cheese.

SCHOOLS. The county had, in 1846, 234 district schools, which were in session an average period of six months each. The number of children taught was 11,914; the amount paid for tuition $10,870, and the number of volumes in the district libraries, 16,087.

There were twelve select schools, with 264 scholars.

RELIGIOUS DENOMINATIONS. Baptists, Methodists, Presbyterians, Episcopalians, Congregationalists, and Unitarians. The number of churches of all denominations, is thirty; of clergymen, sixty-seven.

HISTORY. This county belonged originally to the Holland Land Company's purchase, and the titles of most of the inhabitants are derived from that Company. The first settlement in the county was made early in the present century, at Olean, by Major Hoops, of Albany, who named it after General Hamilton, "Hamilton on the Allegany."

The next settlement was in the present town of Persia, in 1813. The growth of the county has been quite rapid. Cornplanter and Big Kettle or Ganoth-jowaneh, two of the most distinguished of the Seneca chiefs, resided in this county.

A tract along the Allegany river, extending through the towns of Cold Spring, Little Valley, Great Valley and Carrollton, is still held as a reservation by the Indians.

CATTARAUGUS COUNTY.

The Society of Friends in Philadelphia, have taken great pains to instruct the Indians of this county, in the arts of civilization, sending instructors among them, and establishing settlements in the vicinity. Some of the Indians are now quite wealthy, owning well stocked farms, and large saw mills.

VILLAGES. ELLICOTTVILLE, the county seat, is situated in the town of the same name. It was incorporated in 1837, and contains besides the county buildings two extensive land offices. The scenery around the village is beautiful. The town received its name from Joseph Ellicott, late principal agent of the Holland Land Company. Population, 800.

Lodi is a thriving manufacturing village on Cattaraugus creek, in the towns of Persia and Collins, in Cattaraugus and Erie counties. The water power is abundant, and only in part occupied. Population, 900.

At *Hinsdale*, is to be the junction of the New York and Erie railroad, and the Genesee Valley canal. The state is constructing a large basin here. An incorporated academy is located in this village. Population, 600.

Olean is advantageously situated on the north side of the Allegany river, in the town of the same name. Large quantities of lumber and other produce are annually exported from this place. It is to be the terminus of the Genesee Valley canal. Population, 500.

Franklinville, in the town of the same name, is a thriving village, and has some manufactories. Population, 600.

Cadiz, in the same town, is a village of some importance.

XL. CHAUTAUQUE COUNTY.

Square Miles, 1017. Population, 46,548.
Organized, 1808. Valuation, 1845, $4,586,982.

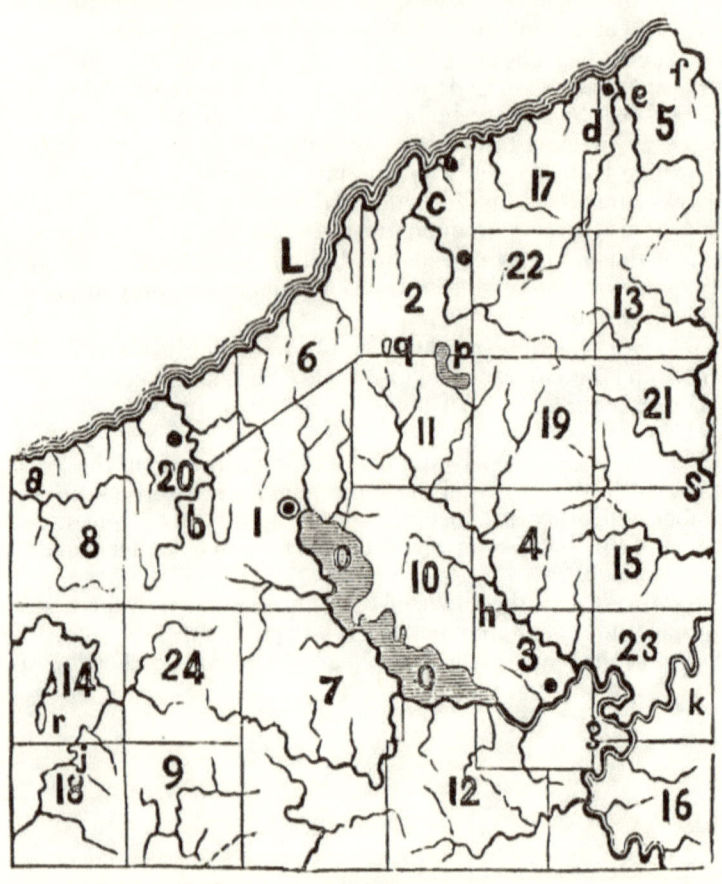

TOWNS.

1. Chautauque, 1804.
2. Pomfret, 1808.
3. Ellicott, 1812.
4. Gerry, 1812.
5. Hanover, 1812.
6. Portland, 1813.
7. Harmony, 1816.
8. Ripley, 1817.
9. Clymer, 1821.
10. Ellery, 1821.
11. Stockton, 1821.
12. Busti, 1823.
13. Villenova, 1823.
14. Mina, 1824.
15. Ellington, 1825.
16. Carroll, 1825.
17. Sheridan, 1827.
18. French Creek, 1829.
19. Charlotte, 1829.
20. Westfield, 1829.
21. Cherry Creek, 1829.
22. Arkwright, 1829.
23. Poland, 1832.
24. Sherman, 1832.

CHAUTAUQUE COUNTY. 335

Rivers. a. Twenty Mile Creek. b. Chautauque. c. Canadawa. d. Walnut. e. Silver. f. Cattaraugus. g Chautauque Outlet. h. Casadaga Creek. j. French. k. Connewango.
Lakes. L. Erie. o Chautauque. p. Casadaga. q. Bear. r Finley.
Villages. MAYVILLE. Jamestown. Westfield. Dunkirk. Fredonia. Fayette. Van Buren.

BOUNDARIES. North by Lake Erie and Erie county; East by Cattaraugus county; South and West by Pennsylvania.

SURFACE. The surface is hilly and elevated. Through its central portion, at a distance of from three to six miles from Lake Erie, and nearly parallel with it, runs the dividing ridge which separates the waters of the lakes from those discharging into the Gulf of Mexico. This ridge is elevated from 800 to 1400 feet above tide water. From this altitude it declines to the northwest, toward the lake, and on the southeast toward the Connewango creek and the Allegany river. The land lying on Lake Erie is a rich and fertile alluvium. The hills throughout the county are nowhere precipitous, but capable of cultivation to their summits.

RIVERS AND CREEKS. The principal streams are the Connewango creek, which drains the eastern and southeastern portions of the county, and uniting with the waters of the Chautauque outlet, in Poland, forms the Connewango river; Cattaraugus creek, which separates this county from Erie; Silver, Walnut, Canadawa, Chautauque, Twenty Mile, North and South branches of French creek, Great and Little Broken Straw and Casadaga creeks. Most of these streams furnish valuable mill privileges.

LAKES. Lake Erie forms the northwestern boundary of the county. Chautauque lake, which gives its name to the county, was so called by the Indians from its form; the Indian name Chautauqua signifying a pack tied in the middle.

It is a beautiful sheet of water, eighteen miles long, and from one to five in width. It is 726 feet above Lake Erie, and 1291 above tide water. Its waters are remarkable for their clearness and purity, and are abundantly stocked with fish. Two steamers ply upon it. It is probably the highest body of water in the world, navigated by steam.

The Casadaga lakes, three in number, each about a mile in extent; Bear lake, and Finley's lake, are the only other lakes in the county.

RAILROADS. The New York and Erie Railroad will pass through this county, and terminate at Dunkirk. Several other railroads have been chartered, but have not been constructed.

CLIMATE. The county has a high reputation for the salubrity of its climate. Fruits thrive well here, and attain great perfection both of size and flavor. From the elevation of its surface, the winters are long, but the cold is somewhat moderated by the proximity of the lake.

GEOLOGY AND MINERALS. This county belongs entirely to the Chemung sandstone group. The rocks of the county consist of alternate layers of sandstone and slaty rocks. In Harmony, Carroll, and some other sections, this sandstone furnishes a fine building material. The crest of the dividing ridge is occasionally crowned with the conglomerate of the Catskill group.

Bog iron ore has been found in several localities, but in no great quantity. Shell marl is abundant in the vicinity of the Casadaga lakes. Alum and copperas are spontaneously formed in the town of Sheridan.

Mineral Springs. Sulphur springs are quite numerous in the neighborhood of Lake Erie. One in Mina is considerably visited. The inflammable springs, or those containing carburetted hydrogen gas, are worthy of notice. There are a number of these along the shores of Lake Erie. The village of Fredonia, in the town of Pomfret, is lighted by this natural gas. It also furnishes material for the light house at Barcelona, and might be employed in the same way at numerous other points along the shores of the lake. It is entirely free from any unpleasant odor.

SOIL AND VEGETABLE PRODUCTIONS. The soil is generally very good. The section on the shores of Lake Erie, extending back for a distance of three or four miles, is a rich alluvium, highly fertile, and well adapted to grains and fruit. The uplands are better fitted for grass, and yield abundant crops.

The timber of the county is oak, maple, beech, black walnut, butternut, hickory, with some pine and hemlock.

On Walnut creek, about a mile from its mouth, formerly stood a black walnut tree, 150 feet in height, thirty-six feet in circumference at its base, and tapering regularly eighty feet, to the first limb. This enormous tree was blown down in 1822. It was supposed to be more than 500 years old. The butt, nine feet in length was excavated, and used for a grocery, at Buffalo. When the Erie canal was opened, it was transported to New York and exhibited to thousands.

PURSUITS. *Agriculture* is the pursuit of a majority of the inhabitants. More attention is paid to the rearing of stock and the produce of the dairy, than to the culture of grain. The principal grains cultivated are corn, oats, wheat, and some barley and buckwheat. Large quantities of flax and potatoes, are also raised. In the latter crop it occupied a high rank among the counties of the state.

Manufactures. The county is not very largely engaged in manufactures. Flour, lumber, leather and iron, are the principal articles, and their entire value is between $700,000 and $800,000.

Commerce. The county has some commerce. Van Buren, Dunkirk, Barcelona and Portland are its principal harbors.

STAPLE PRODUCTIONS. Butter, cheese, wool, pork, potatoes, flax, corn and oats.

SCHOOLS. There are in the county 308 public schools. In 1846, schools were taught an average period of seven months—18,376 children received instruction, at a cost of $17,581. The district libraries contained 30,010 volumes.

There are in the county thirty-one unincorporated schools, with 562 pupils; and five academies, attended by 326 students.

RELIGIOUS DENOMINATIONS. Baptists, Methodists, Congregationalists, Presbyterians, Unitarians, Episcopalians, Universalists and Friends. There are seventy-three churches, and 106 clergymen, of all denominations.

HISTORY. Tradition relates that the French early established a post at Portland, in this county; but at what time is not certainly known. The only Indian settlement within the limits of the county, when first explored, was in the present town of Carroll, on the Connewango creek.

In 1782, a party, consisting of about 800 British and Indians, with a train of artillery and other munitions of war, spent the months of June and July around Chautauque lake, constructing canoes, and making other preparations to descend the Allegany river and attack Fort Pitt, now Pittsburgh. For this purpose they obstructed the channel of the Chautauque outlet, in order to raise the waters of the lake.

The first purchase of lands made in this county, for the purpose of settlement, was in 1801, in the town of Ripley, by Gen. John McMahan. No settlement was effected, however, till 1802, when Col. James McMahan, brother of the general, located himself in the town of Westfield. The same year Edward McHenry settled in the same neighborhood.

In 1796 one Amos Sottle had located in Hanover, but removed in 1800 from the county, and did not return for several years. John McHenry, born in 1802, was the first child of white parents born in the county.

The privations of the early settlers were very great. Often they were compelled to subsist upon the precarious products of the chase, for months, without tasting bread or other provisions.

In 1804, the first town was constituted, and embraced the whole of the present county. In 1808 the county was provisionally organized; but not having a sufficient number of inhabitants to entitle it to a separate organization, it remained attached to Genesee county till 1811.

The whole of this county was included in the Holland Land Company's purchase, and from that company and its successors, the titles to the property were derived.

During the war of 1812, the lake coast was several times invaded by small parties of the enemy, who, however, never accomplished any feats of valor in the county. A party of British landed at Dunkirk, in 1813, to deposite some property which they had plundered from the coast above. Twelve of the boat's crew deserted, immediately on landing, leaving only the officer who commanded the boat, and a single sailor, whom the militia soon compelled to return to their vessel.

In 1814, an armed schooner pursued some lake boats into Canadawa creek, and attempted to capture them, but was repulsed by the militia. About 200 of the Chautauque militia were called out by Governor Tompkins, for the defence of Buffalo; undisciplined and unaccustomed to withstand regular troops, they fled early in the action, but were pursued, and a number killed and scalped by the Indians. Ten or twelve of the citizens of the county fell in this retreat, and others were severely wounded. After the close of the war, the growth of the county was extraordinarily rapid.

In 1835 the Holland Land Company sold out the lands, together with the outstanding and expired contracts, to Trumbull, Carey and others of Batavia. They had made a like sale of their lands in Genesee county, and the new company had compelled such of the settlers as were unable to complete the payments on their farms, to pay an additional sum per acre, as the price of forbearance. This exaction was known as the Genesee tariff. It soon became generally understood, that the principles of this tariff were to be applied to Chautauque county. Meetings were held by the citizens who felt themselves aggrieved, and definite information demanded from the company, as to their intentions.

After some delay the company announced their determination to exact the principal and compound interest from all who would immediately pay for their lands, and to require 25 per cent. advance from those who asked for an extension of time in payment.

These exactions, at this period, would have deprived many of the settlers of their farms, and reduced them to ruin.

Upon learning the demands of the company, resolutions were passed by the citizens, denouncing their course and declaring their determination not to submit to it. On the sixth of February, 1836, a mass of people, mostly from the interior towns, assembled at Barnhart's inn, about two miles from Mayville, about four o'clock in the afternoon, armed with axes, crowbars, &c.; and having organized, proceeded to Mayville, about eight o'clock in the evening. They attacked the office of the Land Company, demolished the wood building, and finally forced open the stone vault, containing the company's books and papers, carried them to Barnhart's, and burned them in the highway.

From this time, till 1838, all intercourse between the Land Company and the settlers ceased. In that year a sale was effected of the property, to Messrs. Duer, Morrison and Seward, (late governor of the state,) and by them an office was opened in Westfield, and the outstanding claims adjusted to the satisfaction of all parties.

VILLAGES. MAYVILLE, the county seat, is a flourishing village, in the town of Chautauque. It was incorporated in 1830. It is beautifully situated, commanding a fine view of the lake. Its public buildings are neat and substantial.

The Mayville academy was incorporated in 1834, and is a well conducted institution. A steamboat plies between this village and Jamestown, daily, during the summer. Population 500.

Jamestown, situated on the outlet of Chautauque lake, in the town of Ellicott, is the largest village in the county. It has a fine hydraulic power, which is extensively used in manufacturing. Lumber, wooden ware, sash, lath, flour, cloth, &c., are manufactured here. The Jamestown academy was incorported in 1836, and is in a prosperous condition. This village was incorporated in 1827. Population 1700.

Fredonia is a beautiful village, in the town of Pomfret, four miles from Lake Erie. It has some trade, but is chiefly remarkable for its inflammable spring, which furnishes a sufficient quantity of gas to light the village brilliantly. It was incorporated in 1829. The academy here, established in 1824, was the first in the county, and sustains a high reputation. Population 1000.

Westfield, in the town of the same name, incorporated in 1833, is situated on Chautauque creek, one and a half miles from Lake Erie. It is a thriving, busy village, and has a fine academy, incorporated in 1837. Population 1000.

Dunkirk, on Lake Erie, in the town of Pomfret, has been designated as the western terminus of the New York and Erie railroad. It is a village of some business. The United States government have expended about $80,000 in the improvement of its harbor, which is now commodious for vessels drawing eight or nine feet water. It is open usually somewhat earlier than that of Buffalo. Population 1000.

Fayette, at the mouth of Silver creek, in the town of Hanover, has a good steamboat landing, and some trade. Pop. 700.

Portland has a good harbor. *Barcelona* has a light house, illuminated with the gas evolved from an inflammable spring near it.

XLI. CORTLAND COUNTY.

Square Miles, 500.
Organized, 1808.

Population, 25,087.
Valuation, 1845, $2,318,208.

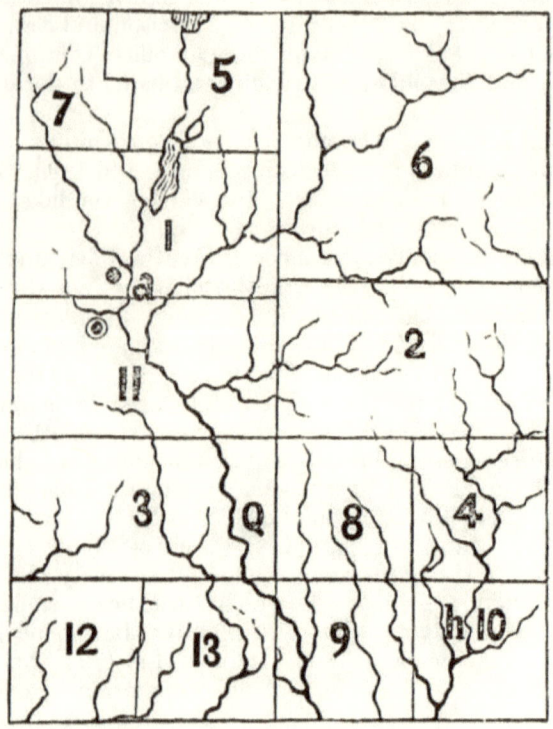

TOWNS.

1. Homer, 1794.
2. Solon, 1798.
3. Virgil, 1804.
4. Cincinnatus, 1804.
5. Preble, 1808.
6. Truxton, 1808.
7. Scott, 1815.
8. Freetown, 1818.
9. Marathon, 1818.
10. Willett, 1818.
11. Cortlandville, 1829.
12. Hartford, 1845.
13. Lapeer, 1845.

Rivers. Q. Tioughnioga. a. Cold Creek. h. Otselic.
Villages. CORTLAND. Homer.

BOUNDARIES. North by Onondaga county; East by Madison and Chenango; South by Broome and Tioga; and West by Tompkins and Cayuga counties.

THE SURFACE is elevated, and gently sloping to the south,

forming a part of the high central section of the state. Its northern boundary lies on the watershed, or dividing ridge between the waters flowing into Lake Ontario, and the tributaries of the Susquehanna river. The broad valleys of the streams, and the rounded and fertile hills, give the surface an agreeably diversified aspect.

RIVERS. The Tioughnioga, rising near its northern boundary, with its tributaries, waters nearly the whole county. The Otselic, its main branch, drains the southeastern section. Both streams are navigable for small boats, when swollen by the heavy rains of spring and autumn.

CLIMATE. Healthy and equable. From the elevation of its surface, the winters are long and much snow falls.

GEOLOGY AND MINERALS. Slate is the basis rock of the county. On the north this is covered with Onondaga limestone, or the limestone and slate of the Helderberg series. On the south and east the Chemung sandstone and shale are the surface rocks.

The minerals of the county are salt, bog iron ore, and marl. There are also some sulphuretted hydrogen springs.

SOIL AND VEGETABLE PRODUCTIONS. The soil is generally a gravelly loam, intermingled with the disintegrated lime and slate, and is quite fertile, yielding good crops of grass and grain. The timber is chiefly oak, maple, beech, basswood, butternut, elm, and chestnut. Groves of pine and hemlock are found in the southern part of the county.

PURSUITS. *Agriculture* is the principal pursuit of the inhabitants. Much attention is paid to the rearing of cattle; considerable quantities of grain are also raised. The products of the dairy are large.

Manufactures are increasing in importance in the county. The principal articles are flour, lumber, cotton and woollen goods, leather and potash.

STAPLE PRODUCTIONS. Butter, cheese, wool, oats, corn, and flax. Considerable quantities of wheat, barley, buckwheat, potatoes, and pork are also produced.

SCHOOLS. The whole number of district schools in the county is 180. In 1846, these were taught, on an average, seven months, and 9,273 children received instruction during the year at an expense of $9470. The district school libraries contained 15,197 volumes.

There are in the county twenty-eight private schools, with 443 pupils, and two academies with 233 scholars.

RELIGIOUS DENOMINATIONS. Baptists, Methodists, Presbyterians, Congregationalists, and Episcopalians. There are in the county forty-five churches, and fifty-four clergymen of all denominations.

HISTORY. Cortland county comprises a portion of the Military Tract, or lands given by the state of New York to her Revolutionary soldiers. It was principally settled by emigrants from the eastern states, who removed here after the Revolution. Homer, the oldest town, was organized in 1794.

The county received its name from General Peter Van Cortlandt, who was a large landholder here. It was taken from Onondaga in 1808.

VILLAGES. CORTLAND, in the town of Cortlandville, is the largest village, and the seat of justice for the county. It is pleasantly situated on the north branch of the Tioughnioga, and has a number of fine public buildings. The Cortland female seminary is a flourishing institution.

The private residences of the citizens are neat, and many of them elegant. Population 1500.

Homer, in the town of the same name, is a beautiful and thriving village on the Tioughnioga. It has an old and flourishing academy of high reputation, with six teachers, and departments for both sexes. In 1846, a large and enthusiastic meeting of its alumni and friends was held, attended with appropriate exercises.

The village is one of the most beautiful in central New York. It is considerably engaged in manufactures. The churches, four in number, and the academy, occupy a public square six acres in extent. Population 1400.

Truxton and *Virgil*, in the towns of the same names, are villages of some importance. The former has some manufactures.

XLII. FRANKLIN COUNTY.

Square miles, 1557. Population, 18,692.
Organized, 1808. Valuation, 1845, $1,584,970.

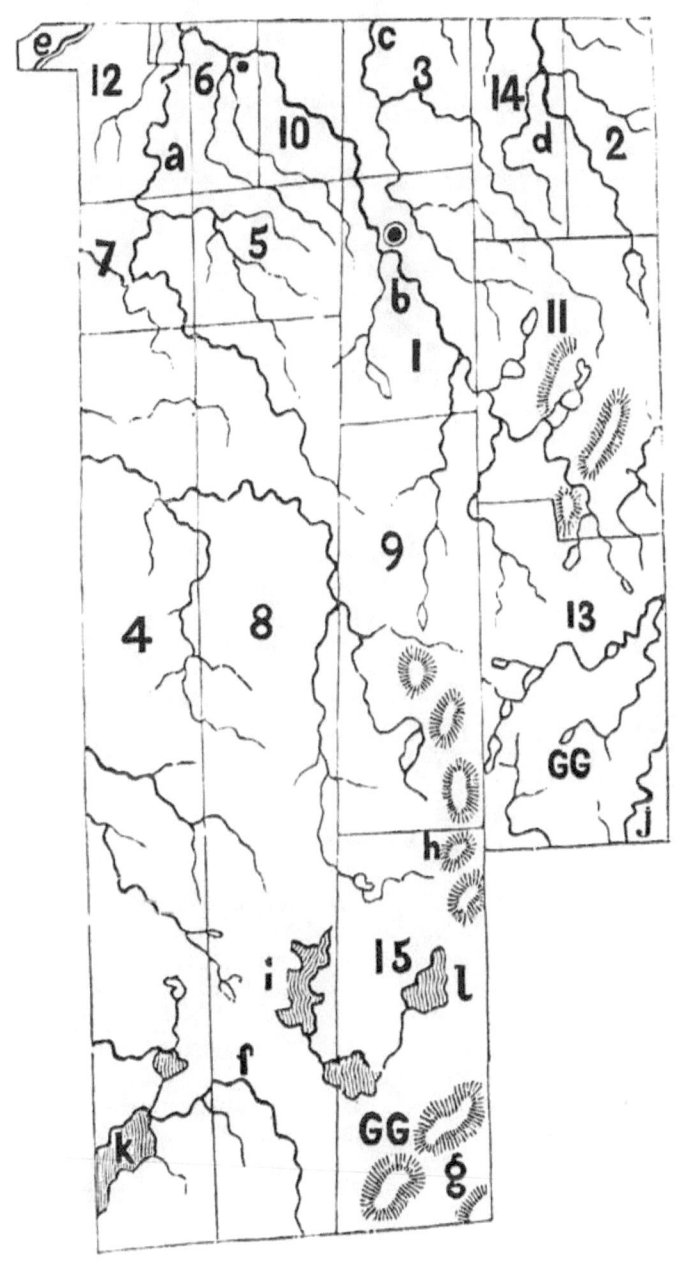

TOWNS.

1. Malone, 1805.
2. Chateaugay, 1805.
3. Constable, 1807.
4. Dickinson, 1808.
5. Bangor, 1812.
6. Fort Covington, 1813.
7. Moira, 1827.
8. Brandon, 1828.
9. Duane, 1828.
10. Westville, 1829.
11. Belmont, 1833.
12. Bombay, 1833.
13. Franklin, 1838.
14. Burke, 1843.
15. Harrietstown, 1843.

Mountains. GG. Chateaugay. g. Seward. h. Adirondack.

Rivers. a. Deer. b. Salmon. c. Trout. d. Chateaugay. e. St. Regis. f. Racket. j. Saranac.

Lakes. i. Upper Saranac. l. Lower Saranac. k. Tupper.

Forts. Covington.

Villages. MALONE. Fort Covington.

BOUNDARIES. North by Canada East; East by Clinton and Essex counties; south by Essex and Hamilton counties, and West by St. Lawrence county.

SURFACE. Elevated and mountainous, in the southern and southeastern sections, where the Chateaugay range crosses it; elsewhere it is undulating or level. Mount Seward, and the Adirondack group, are peaks of this range. Mount Seward has never been ascended, but its height is computed at about 5000 feet.

Numerous lakes are formed in the valleys of the mountain ranges.

RIVERS. The principal rivers are Salmon, Trout, Chateaugay, St. Regis, Deer, Racket, and Saranac.

LAKES. Upper and Lower Saranac, Tupper, and numerous others of less importance.

CLIMATE. The high latitude, and elevated surface of this county render the climate rigorous. The winters are long and severe.

GEOLOGY AND MINERALS. The mountainous district is principally of the primitive formation, and is composed of hypersthene, granite and gneiss. The two latter, indeed, form the surface rocks of a large part of the county. The transition formation, however, extends over the northern slope of the county, and is mainly composed of the Potsdam sandstone, very fine specimens of which are quarried in Malone, Chateaugay, Moira, and Bangor. In the northeast corner of Franklin township, the calciferous sand rock makes its appearance.

The principal minerals are magnetic iron ore, found in Franklin, Duane, and Malone townships, purple scapolite, green pyroxene, graphite in six sided tables, bog iron ore, tufa, peat, and massive pyrites.

SOIL AND VEGETABLE PRODUCTIONS. The soil of the north-

FRANKLIN COUNTY. 345

ern towns is probably equal in fertility to any in the state. The southern townships are less productive. It is mainly a sandy loam, occasionally mixed with clay, and much of it encumbered with stone.

It is not well adapted to wheat, but grass, oats, barley, corn, and the esculent roots, thrive luxuriantly.

The forests, which cover the central and southern portions, are very dense, and consist of white and yellow pine, hemlock, oak, beech, birch, basswood, elm, and white cedar.

PURSUITS. *Agriculture* is the employment of the greater part of the inhabitants, and their attention is particularly directed to the raising of cattle, and the cultivation of summer crops. The *preparation of lumber* for market, is also the occupation of a considerable number of the citizens of the county. There is some *commerce* on the Salmon river, the only navigable stream, and a few *mines*. The iron ores already mentioned will eventually furnish employment to considerable numbers.

STAPLES. Potatoes, oats, wheat, corn, butter and wool.

SCHOOLS. In 1846, there were 120 district schools in the county, in which 6190 scholars were taught. The schools were maintained an average period of seven months, and $6,041 expended for tuition. The district libraries contained 10,230 volumes.

There were also seven select schools, with seventy-four pupils, and two academies, with 113 students.

RELIGIOUS DENOMINATIONS. Presbyterians, Roman Catholics, Baptists, Universalists, Episcopalians, and Congregationalists. There are twenty churches, and twenty-nine ministers of all denominations.

HISTORY. This county was the home of the St. Regis tribe of Indians, who, under the direction of the French, were so often engaged in hostile incursions upon the colonies of New England and New York, in the latter part of the seventeenth and commencement of the eighteenth centuries. The tribe have still a reservation of eleven miles in length and three in breadth, in the county, lying in the towns of Bombay and Fort Covington.

A daughter of Rev. John Williams, of Deerfield, Massachusetts, who, with his family, was taken captive by this tribe in 1704, remained with the Indians, after her father's return, married one of the chiefs, and one of her descendants was a few years since chief of the tribe.

The first settlers were Canadians, who located at French Mills, now Fort Covington about the year 1800.

In April, 1804, Messrs. Benjamin Roberts, of Winchester,

Vermont, William Bailey, and Nathan Beman, commenced a settlement at Chateaugay.

Soon after, Mr. Nathan Wood, of Vermont, settled in Malone. Constable was settled about the same time.

The first standard captured from the enemy, in the late war with Great Britain, was taken at Bombay, by Major G. D. Young, a native of Connecticut, on the 22d of October, 1812.

Major Young was commandant of a detachment of the Troy volunteers stationed at French Mills, (now Fort Covington,) and having learned that a party of the enemy had arrived at the village of St. Regis, and that more were shortly expected, resolved to surprise them before they could be reinforced. He accordingly marched a detachment in the night to the vicinity of the village, surrounded the enemy, and captured forty prisoners, with their arms, equipments, &c., one stand of colors, and two batteaux, without the loss of a single man.

A skirmish took place on the 25th of October, 1813, at Chateaugay, between the British light troops and Indians, and a detachment of American troops, under General Izard, in which the latter were repulsed with the loss of fifty men.

In February, 1814, a detachment of British and Indians, numbering about 2300 men, made an incursion into Malone, and penetrated as far as Chateaugay Four Corners, when, hearing of the approach of American troops, they retreated in great confusion, suffering severely in their flight, from a storm of snow and hail. Upwards of 200 men deserted during this retreat.

Fort Covington, in this county, was erected during the last war, and a part of the army wintered here in 1813—14.

VILLAGES. MALONE, in the town of the same name, is the seat of justice for the county. It is situated on both sides of the Salmon river, which here furnishes a large amount of water power, and is surrounded by a fertile country. In the vicinity are extensive veins of valuable iron ore. The village has several manufactories of cotton goods, leather, scythes, pails, &c. The Franklin academy, located here, is in a flourishing condition. Population 1000.

Fort Covington, located at the head of navigation, on Salmon river, is a flourishing village, largely employed in the lumber trade, and has an incorporated academy and several manufactories. The fort here was an important military post during the war. The village was then known as the "French Mills." It received its present name in honor of General Covington, who was slain at the battle of Williamsburgh, November 13th, 1813. Population 1000.

XLIII. NIAGARA COUNTY.

Square miles, 484.
Organized, 1808.

Population, 34,550.
Valuation, 1845, $4,926,089.

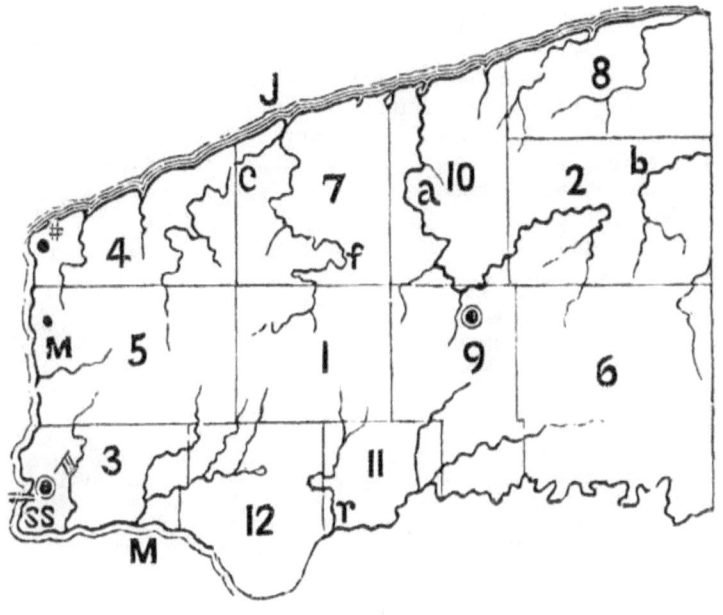

TOWNS.

1. Cambria, 1808.
2. Hartland, 1812.
3. Niagara, 1812.
4. Porter, 1812.
5. Lewiston, 1813.
6. Royalton, 1817.
7. Wilson, 1818.
8. Somerset, 1823.
9. Lockport, 1824.
10. Newfane, 1824.
11. Pendleton, 1827.
12. Wheatfield, 1829.

Rivers, &c. M. Niagara River. a. Eighteen Mile Creek. b. Johnson's. c. Tuscarora. f. Howel's. r. Tonawanda.
Falls. SS. Niagara Falls.
Lakes. J. Lake Ontario.
Battle Fields. Niagara.
Forts. Niagara. Schlosser.
Villages. LOCKPORT. Lewiston. Niagara Falls Village. Youngstown.

BOUNDARIES. North by Lake Ontario; East by Orleans and Genesee counties; South by Erie county, and West by Niagara river.

SURFACE. Like most of the other counties lying on Lake Ontario, Niagara county is divided by the Ridge Road and the mountain ridge, into three terraces, of which the two northernmost rise gradually from the lake shore to the mountain ridge; while the southern declines almost imperceptibly toward Tonawanda creek. The surface is therefore generally quite level, having no more than sufficient inequality to secure its effectual drainage.

RIVERS. The county is well watered. Besides Niagara river, which forms its western boundary, the principal streams are Tonawanda creek, which divides it from Erie county, Tuscarora, Eighteen Mile, Johnson's and Howel's creeks, falling into Lake Ontario; and Cayuga creek, a tributary of Niagara river.

FALLS. This county, conjointly with Niagara district, Canada West, includes the world renowned cataract of Niagara.

To portray fully the wonders of this stupendous waterfall, exceeds the powers of the human mind, and requires a language commensurate with its grandeur and magnificence. We shall therefore only attempt to describe the different elements which combine to render it the most extraordinary of natural wonders, and leave it to the imagination of the reader to group them into one harmonious whole, although nothing but an actual view of the falls, from several points, can give any adequate conception of its surpassing beauty and sublimity.

For a distance of three-fourths of a mile above the falls, the river, over two miles in breadth, hurries forward in a succession of rapids, whose roar, combined with that of the cataract, may sometimes be heard for a distance of twenty miles.

The descent accomplished by these rapids, is between fifty and sixty feet, and their imposing grandeur strikes the beholder with admiration and awe. As the waters approach the fall, the width of the river is compressed to about half a mile. Here it suddenly turns to the eastward, making almost a right angle in its course, and, immediately below the falls, is contracted to a width of only seventy-six rods. In consequence of this bend, the view of the cataract from the American side is more in profile than that on the Canada side, where a short distance below the falls a front view is presented, giving the visitor at a glance an idea of its vast magnificence.

Just above the falls, in the middle of the river, lies Goat or Iris Island, half a mile long, and about one-fourth of a mile wide, containing seventy-five acres. This has been connected with several adjacent small islands, by bridges, and these again with the American shore. Iris island is heavily timbered, and has a number of fine walks, and a large garden.

It extends over the cataract, and presents a wall of perpendicular rock, separating the crescent or Canadian fall, from the American portion of the cataract. This latter is again divided by Luna island. a small islet. There are thus three distinct cascades, one on the Canadian, and two on the American side.

The lower fall, or that nearest the American shore, is more than 300 yards in width, and 164 feet in height. The central fall, extending from Luna to Iris island, has the same height, but is only twenty yards in breadth. Both have a gentle curve in their outline.

From the comparative shallowness of the waters on the American side, they are constantly dashed into foam, ere they reach the precipice.

On the Canadian side of Iris island, is the great Horse Shoe or Crescent fall, over which pour seven-eights of the volume of water composing this mighty stream. It is about 700 yards in width, and 158 feet in height. The deep green of its billows is only relieved by the crests of white foam which surmount them.

To the spectator, standing on Iris island, the cataract is veiled in a cloud of almost impenetrable mist, and all attempts to explore its apparently unfathomable depths seem futile. But in the clear sunlight, this mist is the source of new surprise and admiration; the rainbow, "the crescent of the abyss," with its everchanging hues, spans the impenetrable cloud, and adds new beauty to the scene. The view from Table rock, on the Canadian side, is more distinct, and gives the spectator a better comparative view of the three falls.

Terrapin Bridge, 300 feet from Goat island, extends ten feet over the falls, and near its end, in the water, and upon the edge of the precipice, a stone tower, forty-five feet high, has been erected. The view of the fall from the top of this tower is very grand, but requires some steadiness of nerve.

The banks of the river below the precipice constitute an almost perpendicular wall, nearly 200 feet in height, requiring artificial means for descending to the water's edge. For this purpose, three staircases have been erected. The first is on the main land, on the American side, giving access to the ferry. Recently a railway, moved by hydraulic power, has been constructed, to facilitate the descent. The river is crossed in safety in a row boat, propelled by a single person.

A second staircase was erected in 1829, on the perpendicular face of Iris island, at the expense of the late Nicholas Biddle. A rude but strong flight of common steps leads down a steep declivity of about forty feet, to the head of the Biddle stair case, which is in the form of a hexagon, enclosing triangular steps, that wind spirally round a large and solid oaken shaft. The descent accomplished by these is about 80 feet. Paths lead from the foot of these stairs, to the river brink, to the verge of the British fall, and to the Central fall, and the Cave of the Winds behind it.

The third staircase is on the Canadian side, and conducts the visitor under the overhanging ledge of Table rock. Here he will find a path leading under the Great Crescent fall, by which, if he chooses to venture, he may pass, for a distance of about 150 feet, behind this vast mass of waters.

The depth of the river, a short distance below the cataract, is 250 feet. The quantity of water poured over the falls has been variously estimated. Dr. Dwight computed it at more than 100 millions of tons per hour.

About three miles below the falls, is a whirlpool, produced by the projection of a rocky promontory, against which the waters of the river have, for ages, hurled their angry billows in vain. In this whirlpool, timber and the dead bodies of men or animals, which have been precipitated over the cataract, are often retained for days, and sometimes for weeks, ere they pass the narrow outlet. About a mile below this is a deep ravine, where formerly there was another whirlpool, but the waters, after centuries of unceasing action, wrought out for themselves a more quiet passage. This gloomy dell was, some seventy-five or eighty years since, the scene of a fearful tragedy, which will be related in the historical sketch of the county. It is called "the devil's hole."

LAKES. Lake Ontario forms the northern boundary of the county.

CANALS. The Erie canal passes through the southeastern and southern portions of the county.

RAILROADS. The Buffalo and Niagara falls railroad connects Niagara falls with the lines of railroad from Albany. There is also a railroad connecting Lockport and Niagara falls with a branch extending to Lewiston.

CLIMATE. Owing to the vicinity of the lakes, the climate is mild and equable. It is considered healthful. Here, as in Erie county, fruits flourish in greater perfection, and vegetation is earlier than in the same parallels in the eastern counties.

GEOLOGY AND MINERALS. The Medina sandstone is the basis rock of the county, and makes its appearance near the Lake shore; above this appears the Clinton group of limestones; the Niagara group forms the surface rock of the second terrace, and abounds in fossils; the Onondaga salt group appears as the surface rock of the third terrace, and contains as usual large quantities of gypsum, and numerous brine springs.

<small>Bog iron ore is found in various parts of the county; copper, in minute quantities, has been discovered near Lockport; sulphate of strontian, calcareous spar, anhydrous sulphate of lime, selenite, pearl spar, and occasionally fluor spar, and sulphuret of zinc, are found at Lockport. Sulphur springs are numerous; some of them have considerable reputation. The brine springs are too weak to be of much practical value. There is also a chalybeate spring, and one emitting carburetted hydrogen gas, in sufficient quantity to maintain a steady flame. Shell marl is found in the swamps.</small>

SOIL AND VEGETABLE PRODUCTIONS. The soil is highly fertile, yielding grains and grasses in abundance. Fruit is cultivated here in great perfection. The timber is mainly oak, beech, maple, tamarack, ash, &c.

PURSUITS. A majority of the inhabitants are engaged in *agricultural pursuits*. The culture of wheat and the other grains, occupies the attention of most of the farmers of the county. Butter and wool are also produced in considerable quantities.

The *manufactures* of the county are numerous, and constantly increasing in value and importance. Flour is manufactured in large quantities. Lumber, cotton and woollen goods, iron ware, potash and leather, are the other principal articles produced. Their value, in 1845, was nearly two millions of dollars.

Commerce. The commerce of the county is quite extensive, both on the lake and on the canal. Lewiston is the principal port on the Niagara river.

STAPLE PRODUCTIONS. Wheat is the great staple of this county. The other principal agricultural products, are oats, corn, potatoes, peas, butter and wool.

SCHOOLS. In 1846, there were in the county 158 district school-houses, in which schools were maintained an average period of eight months each. 11,919 children received instruction, at an expense for tuition of $15,034. The number of volumes in the district libraries was 16,612.

<small>822 pupils were instructed in twenty-nine select schools. There were also in the county one academy, and one female seminary, with 185 students.</small>

RELIGIOUS DENOMINATIONS. Methodists, Presbyterians, Baptists, Episcopalians, Friends, Congregationalists, Universalists, Dutch Reformed, Lutherans, and Roman Catholics. There are fifty churches and fifty-nine clergymen of all denominations, in the county.

HISTORY. In 1697, M. de la Salle erected a palisade fort at or near the site of Fort Niagara.

In 1712, the Tuscarora Indians removed to this county from

NIAGARA COUNTY. 351

North Carolina, and united themselves with the Iroquois confederacy, which thenceforth assumed the name of " the Six Nations." They still hold a reservation of about 5000 acres, lying in the town of Lewiston. They are about 200 in number, and are mostly in prosperous circumstances. They have a church and school, both under the direction of the American Board of Commissioners for Foreign Missions.

In 1725, the French erected a fort at the mouth of the Niagara river, in this county, in pursuance of their design of connecting their Canadian settlements with those on the Mississippi, by a chain of military posts.

Here their efficient emissaries, the Jesuit missionaries, won the affections of the simple hearted red men, by their ready compliance with their dress and customs; and extolling the power and grandeur of the French monarchs, incited them to deeds of aggression and bloodshed against the English. Not long after the erection of this fort, a stockade fortress, since known as old Fort Schlosser, situated about a mile above the falls, was also erected.

In 1759, Fort Niagara was captured from the French, by the British army, under the command of Sir William Johnson. It was rebuilt and garrisoned anew the same year.

During the revolution, it was held by the British, and from its time-stained walls, issued numerous bands of Indians and tories, bound on expeditions of bloody revenge, or lawless plunder, to the hapless valleys of the Schoharie and Mohawk. To this place, too, they brought the prisoners and scalps they had taken, to claim the reward which a British ministry offered for these evidences of their own inhumanity.

In 1796, this fort was surrendered to the United States. At that time there was but one white family, beside the occupants of the fort, within the present limits of the county.

During the late war with Great Britain, the American garrison, consisting of 370 men, were surprised by an unexpected attack from a force of more than 1200 British troops, who crossed the river, and after a brief but severe struggle, captured the fort. Sixty-five of the garrison were killed, and twenty-seven pieces of ordnance, with a large quantity of military stores, fell into the hands of the captors. In March, 1815, it was again surrendered to the United States. On the 14th of September, 1826, Morgan, of antimasonic notoriety, was confined in the magazine of the fort.

There can be no doubt that during its occupancy by the French, it was occasionally used as a prison for state offenders; and from that time to the close of the revolution, deeds of crime and blood were committed there, which the light of the judgment day alone will reveal.

On the 17th of September, 1763, a company of troops, numbering with the teamsters, about 175 men, were escorting a quantity of stores to Fort Schlosser, and had reached the ravine known as the Devil's Hole, on the Niagara river, when they were beset by a party of Seneca Indians, who were then in the French interest, and all but two murdered, or dashed to pieces in their fall over the precipice.

One, a drummer, was saved by the strap of his drum being caught in the branches of a tree, in his fall; the other, a man by the name of Stedman, being well mounted, forced his way through the hostile crowd and fled, at the utmost speed of his horse, to Fort Schlosser. His clothes were riddled with balls, but he was unhurt. The Indians considered his escape as miraculous, and gave him a large tract of land, embracing all that he had rode over in his flight.

In December, 1813, the British burned Lewiston, Youngstown, Manchester, (now Niagara Falls village,) and the Tuscarora Indian village, alleging the burning of Newark, in Canada West, by the Americans, as an excuse for their barbarity.

Early in December, 1837, after the failure of the attack of the "Canadian patriots," (so called,) on Toronto, McKenzie and Sutherland, two of their leaders, who had escaped to the United States, together with some twenty-five of their adherents, took possession of Navy island, in the Niagara river, above the Falls, and remained there nearly a month, bidding defiance to the British troops, who were congregated on the Canadian shore, to the number of 3000 or 4000 men.

The ranks of the "patriots" were constantly reinforced by volunteers from the American frontier, until they numbered about 600. The British fired upon them, and killed one man; the fire was returned, and preparations made to cross into Canada, when by the interposition of General Scott, the island was evacuated, and the patriot army dispersed.

It was during the occupation of this island, that Mr. Wells, of Buffalo, the proprietor of a small steamboat, called the Caroline, formed the project of running his steamer as a ferry boat, between Navy island and old Fort Schlosser, in order to accommodate the numbers who wished to pass and repass daily.

Accordingly, on the 29th of December, the boat commenced running, and having made several trips during the day, was moored at night, beside the wharf at Schlosser. Numbers, who had been attracted by curiosity to the place, were unable to obtain lodgings at the tavern, the only dwelling in the vicinity, and sought accommodations on board the boat.

About midnight, the watch on board the steamer observed a boat approaching; he hailed, but before he could give the alarm, a body of armed men from Canada, rushed on board, crying " cut them down, give no quarter ;" no resistance was made on board the boat; all who could do so, escaped to the shore. Five persons were known to be killed.

The boat was cut from her moorings, towed out into the stream, set on fire, and suffered to drift down the river, and over the falls. It was supposed that several persons were on board at the time she went over the cataract. This outrage produced great excitement on the frontier, and had well nigh involved our government in a war with Great Britain.

VILLAGES. LOCKPORT, the county seat, is a large and busy village in the town of the same name. It was founded in 1821, and incorporated in 1829. The Erie canal here descends, by five massive double locks, sixty feet. Before reaching these locks, in its progress eastward, the canal passes, for several miles, through a deep cutting of limestone, where the walls of rock, on either hand, rise twenty or thirty feet above the level of the canal. The descent of the canal furnishes an immense water power, which is partially improved. The village has a great variety of manufactures. Several very large flour mills are in operation. Population, 6800.

Niagara Falls Village is a beautiful and thriving place, deriving much of its importance from its proximity to the cataract. It has been proposed to devote the waters of the Niagara at this place, to manufacturing purposes, but it is to be hoped that such a project may never be carried into execution. Population, 1000.

Lewiston, in the town of the same name, has considerable trade with Oswego, and other ports on Lake Ontario. Here is also a ferry across the Niagara river, to Queenstown. It is the head of steamboat navigation on the river. Population, 900.

Youngstown is a thriving little village in the town of Porter. It has a good steamboat landing, and is connected with the village of Niagara, in Canada, by a steam ferry. Population, 700.

Middleport, in the town of Royalton, is a village of some importance.

XLIV. SULLIVAN COUNTY.

Square miles, 919.
Organized, 1809.

Population, 18,727.
Valuation, 1845, $1,468,283.

TOWNS.

1. Mamakating, 1798.
2. Lumberland, 1798.
3. Nevisink, 1798.
4. Rockland, 1798.
5. Thompson, 1804.
6. Liberty, 1807.
7. Bethel, 1809.
8. Fallsburgh, 1826.
9. Cochecton, 1828.
10. Forrestburgh, 1838.
11. Collikoon, 1842.

Mountains. P. Shawangunk mountains.

Rivers. H. Delaware river. R. Nevisink. a. Collikoon. e. Mongaup. g. Bashe's kill. k. Beaver kill. i. Little Beaver kill.

Falls. On the Mongaup and Nevisink, Fallsburgh and Forrestburgh.

Lakes. h. White Lake. l. Long Pond. m. Round. n. Sand.

Canals. Delaware and Hudson canal.

Villages. MONTICELLO. Bloomingsburgh. Wurtzborough. Fallsburgh. Cochecton.

SULLIVAN COUNTY. 355

BOUNDARIES. North by Delaware and Ulster counties; East by Ulster and Orange; South by Orange county and the Delaware river; and West by the Delaware river.

SURFACE. Hilly and mountainous. The Shawangunk mountains occupy the eastern section of the county. The western face of these mountains is precipitous, but they descend by a gentle declivity on the east. The remainder of the county has an elevated surface, divided into numerous ridges, by the streams which intersect it

RIVERS. The Delaware forms the south-western boundary of the county; the other principal streams are the Collikoon, Mongaup and Nevisink rivers, Bashe's, Beaver and Little Beaver kills.

LAKES. The county abounds with small lakes, among which are White Lake, Long Pond, Round Pond, and Sand Pond.

CANALS. The Delaware and Hudson canal passes through the valley of Bashe's kill.

CLIMATE. Cold but healthy. Vegetation is about two weeks later than in Ulster and Orange counties. In some parts of the county frost occurs every month.

GEOLOGY AND MINERALS. This county comprises several geological formations of interest. The western half, and a portion of the northern section, belong to the old red sandstone formation, or Catskill group; the central and southern portions are composed of the Chemung sandstone and shales; as we proceed eastward we encounter successively the limestones of the Hamilton group, the Helderberg limestones, the gray Shawangunk sandstone and grit, which forms the largest portion of the surface rock of the county; and the Hudson river slate.

_{The number of minerals is not large. In the vicinity of Wurtzborough, and in other parts of the county, mines of lead ore have been opened, which promise to be productive and valuable. Crystallized iron and copper pyrites, sulphuret of zinc, and quartz crystals of great beauty, have been found in connection with the lead at these localities. The red sandstone affords, in some places, a fine building material.}

SOIL AND VEGETABLE PRODUCTIONS. The soil of the uplands is fertile and well adapted to the production of the grasses and more hardy grains. In the valley of the Delaware it is cold and wet. The county is well adapted to grazing. The timber consists principally of pine, hemlock, beech, maple, linden, oak and tulip tree. But little more than one tenth of the soil is under cultivation.

PURSUITS. The people of this county are mostly devoted to *agriculture.* But little grain is raised, and that principally corn, oats and buckwheat. The products of the dairy receive considerable attention.

Manufactures. Leather and lumber are extensively manufactured. The latter finds its way to market by the Delaware river.

Commerce. The Delaware and Hudson canal furnishes an easy mode of transportation for the produce of the eastern section of the county. The Delaware river is navigable in the spring, and immense quantities of lumber are rafted down it.

Mines. There are lead mines near Wurtzborough, in the town of Mamakating.

STAPLES. Oats, corn, butter, beef, pork, lumber and leather.

SCHOOLS. In 1846, there were in the county, 118 district school-houses, in which 6328 children were instructed at an expense for tuition, of $8793. The schools were in session an average period of eight months each. The district libraries contained 10,379 volumes.

There were also eight select schools, with 178 scholars, and one academy with thirteen pupils.

RELIGIOUS DENOMINATIONS. Methodists, Presbyterians, Dutch Reformed, Baptists, Congregationalists, Episcopalians, and Friends. Total number of churches, twenty-eight; of clergymen, twenty-three.

HISTORY. In 1777, or 1778, several persons having been killed by the Indians in Rochester, Ulster county, the commander of the garrison at Honkhill, in Wawarsing, who had two or three hundred troops under his command, determined to intercept the Indians on their return, and punish them for their barbarities. He accordingly called for volunteers, and Lieutenant John Grahams offered his services. They were accepted, and with a lieutenant's guard, consisting of twenty men, he made his way to a place since called Grahamsville, in the town of Nevisink.

Unpracticed in the arts of Indian warfare, they were no match for their wily foes. The Indians decoyed them from their position, induced them to waste their fire upon a single Indian, and then shot them down, and scalped them. But three of the number escaped to carry to the garrison the intelligence of the loss of their comrades.

The town of Mamakating belonged to the Minisink patent, and was settled by the Dutch at an early period. The remainder of the county belonged to the Hardenburgh patent, and was not occupied till near the commencement of the present century. The emigrants, with the exception of those who located at Mamakating, were mostly from the eastern states. The county was named in honor of General Sullivan, of revolutionary memory.

VILLAGES. MONTICELLO, in the town of Thompson, was founded in 1804, by Messrs. S. F. and J. P. Jones, and made the county seat at the organization of the county in 1809. Population, 700.

Bloomingsburgh is a pleasant village, in the town of Mamakating. It is in the midst of a fine agricultural country. It has an academy. Population, 600.

Wurtzborough, in the same town, is a flourishing village, named after the projector of the Delaware and Hudson canal. Near the village is a lead mine of considerable importance. Population, 500.

Liberty, Fallsburgh, and *Cochecton,* in the towns of the same names, are villages of considerable importance.

XLV. SCHENECTADY COUNTY.

Square miles, 186.   Population, 16,630.
Organized, 1809.   Valuation, 1845, $2,739,421.

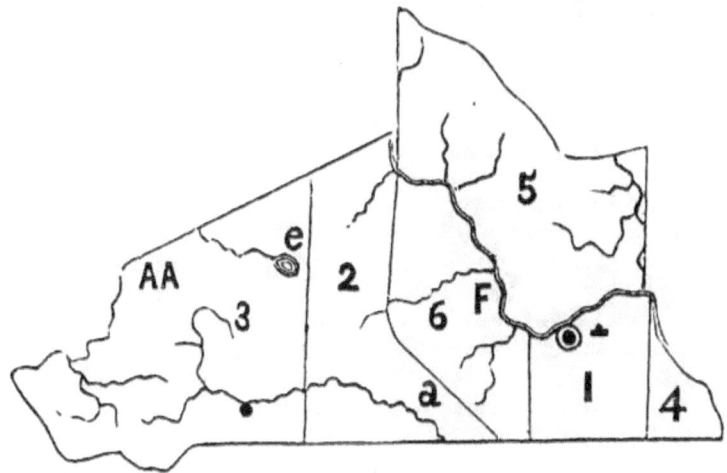

TOWNS.

1. Schenectady, 1684.
2. Princeton, 1798.
3. Duanesburgh, 1801.
4. Neskayuna, 1809.
5. Glenville, 1820.
6. Rotterdam, 1820.

Rivers. AA. Schoharie kill. F. Mohawk river. a. Norman's kill
Lakes. e. Maria.
Cities and Villages. SCHENECTADY. Duanesburgh. Rotterdam.

BOUNDARIES. North by Montgomery and Saratoga; East by Saratoga; South by Albany and Schoharie; and West by Schoharie, counties.

SURFACE. The surface of Schenectady county is agreeably diversified with hills, plains and valleys. Flint hill extends through a part of the southern section, and a spur of the Kayaderosseras range passes through the town of Glenville, nearly to Schenectady. On the banks of the rivers are extensive flats.

RIVERS. The Mohawk, Schoharie kill and Norman's kill, are the principal streams.

LAKES. Lake Maria is a small body of water in Duanesburgh.

CANALS. The Erie canal crosses the Mohawk near the eastern line of the county, and passes along the south west bank of that river.

RAILROADS. It has four lines of railroads, the Mohawk and Hudson, Troy, Saratoga and Utica railroads, all centering in the city of Schenectady.

CLIMATE. The climate of this county is mild and salubrious, but subject to considerable extremes of temperature.

GEOLOGY AND MINERALS. The Hudson river group, consisting of grits and shales, or slaty rocks, is the prevailing surface rock of this county. The Utica slate makes its appearance in the neighborhood of Glenville. The whole county is overlaid by clay and gravel, to the depth of from fifty to one hundred feet.

Bog iron ore occurs near the line of Albany county. There are several localities of calcareous spar, one of which resembles arragonite. Quartz crystals and common jasper are also found in the county.

SOIL AND VEGETABLE PRODUCTIONS. The soil is various. The extensive alluvial tracts along the Mohawk and other streams, are exceedingly fertile. The hills and plains are either a light sandy or clay loam, less fertile, and sometimes barren.

Pine and oak are the principal forest trees.

PURSUITS. *Agriculture* is the leading pursuit of the inhabitants. Wheat and barley are extensively raised. The rearing of cattle occupies some attention.

Manufacturers are quite limited. Flour, cotton goods, iron and leather are the principal articles.

Commerce. By means of its canal and railroads this county enjoys ample facilities for the transportation of its produce.

STAPLE PRODUCTIONS. Oats, potatoes, corn, barley, rye, buckwheat, wheat, butter and cheese.

SCHOOLS. This county had in 1846, seventy-five common schools, with 3614 pupils. They were taught an average period of eight months, at an expense of $4960. The district libraries numbered 7115 volumes.

There were two select schools, with twenty-two scholars; an academy with 108 pupils, and a college, with eleven professors and 242 students.

RELIGIOUS DENOMINATIONS. Dutch Reformed, Presbyterians, Methodists, Baptists, Episcopalians, Universalists, Roman Catholics and Friends. The whole number of churches is twenty four, of clergymen, thirty-four.

SCHENECTADY COUNTY.

HISTORY. This county was one of the first settled in the state. Previous to the year 1620 several Dutch traders established themselves here, to traffic with the Indians for furs.

The first grant of lands was made in 1661, to Arendt Van Corlaer and others, on condition that they purchased the soil from the natives. The deed was obtained in 1672, and signed by four Mohawk chiefs. It comprised a part of the present city of Schenectady.

In November, 1665, Governor Nichols granted to Mr. Alexander Lindsay Glen, a Scotch gentleman of ancient and noble descent, a tract lying on the Mohawk, and comprising most of the present town of Glenville. Mr. Glen resided for a number of years in Albany and Schenectady, and in 1690 removed to his patent, where, in 1713, he erected a country seat, which he named Scotia, and which is still standing.

According to tradition, Neskayuna was settled in 1640. A patent for land in this town was granted to Harmon Vedder, in 1664.

On the eighth of February, 1690, the village of Schenectady, then containing sixty-three houses and a church, was burned, and sixty-three of its inhabitants murdered, twenty-seven carried captive, and others perished, from the severity of the season, in the attempt to escape.

The marauders who thus rushed upon the sleeping and defenceless inhabitants, like wolves upon the sheep fold, were a party of 200 Frenchmen and about fifty Indians, from Canada, who had nearly perished from hunger and cold in their murderous expedition.

Having plundered and destroyed the village, they commenced their return, but were pursued by the Albany militia and the Indians friendly to the English, and twenty-five of their number killed.

In 1748, the Canadian Indians made another hostile incursion into the county, and killed a Mr. Daniel Toll, who had gone about three miles from Schenectady, in search of some stray horses. On receiving intelligence of his murder, about sixty young men, from Schenectady, started in quest of the enemy. They were soon surprised by a party of Indians in ambush, and more than half their number were killed. The remainder succeeded in reaching a house near by, where they kept the enemy at bay, till the Schenectady militia came to their aid, when the Indians fled and returned to Canada. Thirty-two young men, of the best families of Schenectady, fell in this affray.

The county was, with few exceptions, settled by the Dutch, and remained a part of Albany county until 1809.

CITIES AND VILLAGES. SCHENECTADY city, the seat of justice for the county, is situated on the south branch of the Mohawk river, fifteen miles northwest of Albany. As has been already stated, it was founded at a very early period.

Previous to the construction of the Erie canal, it was a place of very considerable business, as goods intended for the western trade were shipped upon the Mohawk at this place. After the completion of the canal, most of this trade was transferred to Albany; but the numerous railroads which now center here, have given it a new impulse, and its business and population have materially increased within a few years past.

The city has some manufactories—the principal are flour, paper, cotton goods, iron, leather, tobacco, malt liquors, &c. Population 6555.

Union College, which is located here, was founded in 1795, and received its name from the fact that its founders were members of different religious denominations. It has a corps of eleven professors, and three principal edifices, two of brick and one of stone. Its apparatus is very complete, and its library large and valuable. It is amply endowed, and has property to the amount of $450,000. Attached to the college building is a tract of land, 250 acres in extent, a part of which is laid out in walks and pleasure grounds. Its situation is highly picturesque.

Rotterdam is a small manufacturing village, in the town of the same name.

Duanesburgh is a village of some importance.

XLVI. PUTNAM COUNTY.

Square Miles, 216.
Organized, 1812.

Population, 13,258.
Valuation, 1845, $2,929,318.

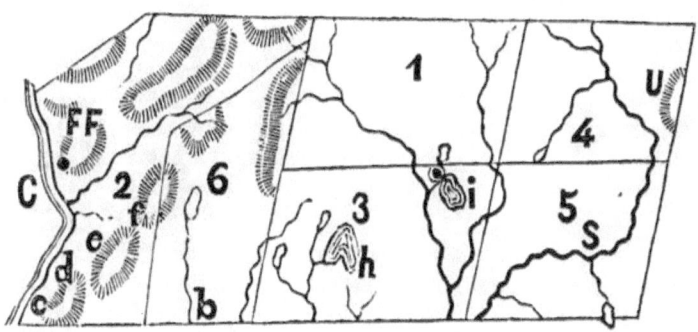

TOWNS.

1. Kent, 1788.
2. Philipstown, 1788.
3. Carmel, 1795.
4. Patterson, 1795.
5. Southeast, 1795.
6. Putnam Valley, 1838.

Mountains. FF. Highlands. U. Taghkanic Range.

Peaks. c. Anthony's Nose. d. Sugar Loaf. e. Bull Hill. f. Breakneck Hill.

Rivers. C. Hudson River. S. Croton. b. Peekskill.

Lakes, &c. Mahopack Pond. i. Shaw's Pond.

Villages. CARMEL. Cold Spring.

BOUNDARIES. North by Dutchess county; East by the state of Connecticut; South by Westchester county, and West by the Hudson river.

SURFACE. Putnam is one of the most mountainous counties in the state. The hills are not, however, generally abrupt or precipitous, but rounded and susceptible of cultivation almost to their summits. It is well adapted to grazing.

The Highlands extend across the western part of the county. The range commences at the river, in the southwest corner of Philipstown, and takes a northeasterly course, extending into Dutchess county. In Philipstown there are several considerable peaks, the most prominent of which are Anthony's Nose, Sugar Loaf, Bull Hill, Breakneck Hill, and High Peak. The highest of these peaks is 1580 feet above the level of the Hudson.

In the eastern part the Taghkanic range extends through the county, from north to south.

RIVERS. Beside the Hudson, which forms the western boundary of the county, the Croton river and its branches, and the Peekskill, are the only streams worthy of notice.

LAKES. Mahopack and Shaw's ponds, in the town of Carmel, are the only bodies of water of importance. The first is nine miles in circumference, and has two islands; the other is much smaller in extent.

THE CLIMATE is healthful, though cool.

GEOLOGY AND MINERALS. This county belongs to the south-eastern primitive district of the state. Granite, gneiss, and primitive limestone are the principal rocks. In the town of Patterson, and at several other points in the county, beds of transition limestone occur. They are, however, of small extent.

The principal minerals of this county are iron ore, of the magnetic and hematitic varieties, in great abundance, and of superior quality; copperas, arsenic, copper ores, chrome iron ore, serpentine, asbestus, dolomite, tremolite, pyroxene, scapolite, epidote, zircon, sphene, albite, graphite, peat, and phosphate of lime.

SOIL AND VEGETABLE PRODUCTIONS. As might be expected from its geological character, the timber is principally oak, chestnut, ash, maple, hickory, &c. The soil is perhaps naturally sterile, but treated with plaster, produces luxuriant crops of blue grass, herds-grass, and clover. The appearance of the farms indicate that the owners are possessed of competence.

PURSUITS. *Agriculture* is the principal pursuit of the inhabitants. Considerable attention is paid to the dairy, and to the rearing of cattle, sheep, swine and fowls. Much of the produce exposed for sale in the New York markets is brought from this county.

Manufactures receive some attention.

The West Point foundry, at Cold Spring, is the largest in the United States, and employs more than four hundred men. There are one or two other foundries in the county. The other manufactures are of comparatively little importance. There are iron *mines* in Philipstown, Putnam Valley and Southeast.

Commerce. There is but one good landing on the Hudson in this county, that of Cold Spring. Some commerce is carried on from this point.

STAPLE PRODUCTIONS. Butter, beef, wool and mutton are the principal staples. Calves, lambs, fowls, &c., are also carried to the New York market in large quantities.

SCHOOLS. There are in the county sixty-three public schools. In 1846, these schools were taught on an average nine months; 3245 children received instruction, at an expense of $6562. The libraries of the district contained 8618 volumes. There were also, ten private schools, with 124 pupils.

RELIGIOUS DENOMINATIONS. Methodists, Baptists, Presbyterians, Episcopalians, Roman Catholics and Friends.

HISTORY. This county was settled at an early period, but remained attached to Dutchess till 1812. At the base of the Sugar

Loaf, in Philipstown, stands Beverly house, formerly the residence of Col. Beverly Robinson, a loyalist, who, during the revolution, went with his family to New York, and thence to Great Britain. His estate was confiscated by the legislature, and his family banished. This house was the head quarters of General Putnam, General Parsons, and the traitor Arnold. It was here that Arnold received the intelligence, that his treason was revealed, and from the landing on this estate he made his escape on board the British sloop Vulture.

From the foot of the peak called Anthony's Nose, to Fort Montgomery, a chain and boom were stretched, by order of the continental congress, in the autumn of 1776, for the purpose of obstructing navigation, and preventing the enemy from ascending the Hudson. This chain was broken the same year, by the British.

In 1778, Captain Machin, the engineer who had constructed the former chain, superintended the making of another, of twice its diameter, which extended from West Point, to a battery at Constitution Island. This was never broken by the enemy, but was taken up every autumn, and replaced in the spring. It weighed 186 tons.

VILLAGES. CARMEL, in the town of the same name, is the seat of justice for the county. In picturesque beauty, and healthfulness of situation, Carmel is surpassed by few villages in the state. Declining gradually to the shore of Shaw's lake, a beautiful sheet of water, it presents one of the loveliest landscapes on which the eye can rest. Population 350.

Cold Spring, on the bank of the Hudson, in Philipstown, is a thriving village, supported mainly by the mammoth iron foundry, about a mile from the landing. Population 1500.

Southeast is a well watered and fertile town. Joe's Hill a noted eminence, extends west from Connecticut, into the centre of the town.

Iron ore is abundant in this town, and of good quality. There are several ponds of considerable size.

XLVII. WARREN COUNTY.

Square Miles, 912.
Organized, 1813.
Population, 14,908.
Valuation, 1845, $976,433.

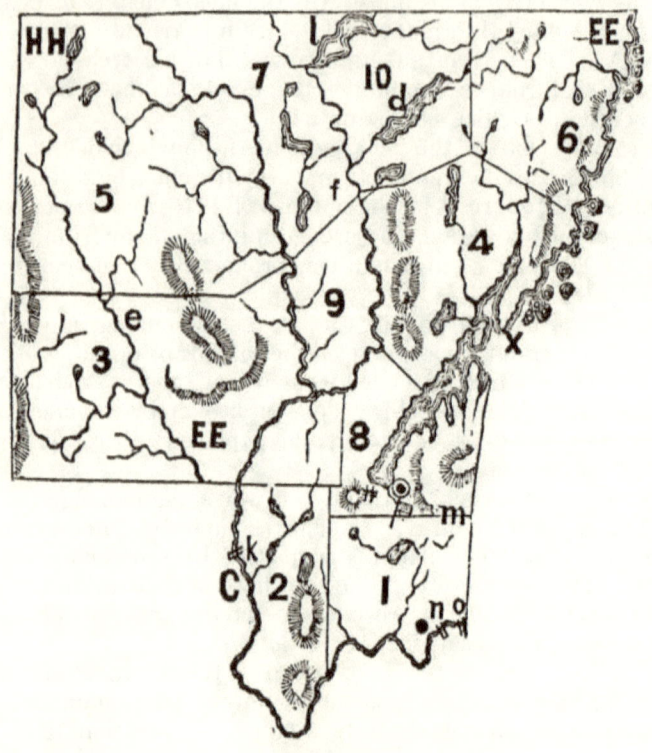

TOWNS.

1. Queensbury, 1788.
2. Luzerne, 1792.
3. Athol, about 1800.
4. Bolton, about 1805.
5. Johnsburgh, 1805.
6. Hague, 1807.
7. Chester, about 1809.
8. Caldwell, 1810.
9. Warrensburgh, 1813.
10. Horicon, 1838.

Mountains. EE. Kayaderosseras. HH. Clinton. m. Luzerne.
Rivers. C. Hudson. e. Jessup's Creek. f. Schroon Branch.
Lakes. X. George. l Schroon. d. Brant.
Falls. k. Hadley. n. Glen's. o. Baker's.
Battle Field. Caldwell.
Fort. Fort George.
Villages. CALDWELL. Glen's Falls.

WARREN COUNTY.

BOUNDARIES. North by Essex; East by Washington; South by Saratoga, and West by Hamilton county.

SURFACE. This county, with the exception of a small portion on the south, has a very elevated and rugged surface. The Luzerne or Palmertown range of mountains traverses the eastern section, the Kayaderosseras the central, and the Clinton range the western portion of the county. Many of their summits attain an altitude of from 800 to 1200 feet. The towns of Warrensburgh and Luzerne, are comparatively level.

RIVERS. The Hudson, Schroon Branch and Jessup's creek, are the principal streams. They have a southerly direction through the county.

FALLS. Hadley, Jessup's, and Glen's falls, are on the Hudson.

LAKES. Lake George, which has already been described, and Schroon lake are the most important.

CLIMATE. Cold but healthy.

GEOLOGY AND MINERALS. With the exception of a small bed of Trenton limestone, in the valleys in the southeast part of the county, the whole county is primitive—composed of gneiss, with some hypersthene, granite and primitive limestone. Serpentine is also found in veins between the predominant rocks.

Iron is considerably abundant. The magnetic ore is frequent, but does not occur in large masses; porcelain clay, black marble of very fine quality, (from the vicinity of Glen's Falls,) verd antique, black lead or graphite, and peat, are the most important of the useful minerals. Besides these, fluor, zircon, pyrites, massive feldspar, tourmaline, rutile, rhomb spar, quartz crystals of great beauty, and calcareous spar occur in several localities.

SOIL AND VEGETABLE PRODUCTIONS. The soil of the greater part of the county is sterile. Some fertile land, however, is found in the narrow valleys, and in the level portions above mentioned. A heavy growth of timber covers its hills, consisting of pine, spruce, fir, cedar, oak, maple, beech, elm and ash.

PURSUITS. *Agriculture* is the leading pursuit; but the settlements are sparse, and in many sections the gigantic timber is not yet felled. Many of the inhabitants are engaged in preparing lumber for market. The county seems to be very well adapted to grazing; corn, oats and potatoes also succeed well.

The *manufactures* are those common to a new country; lumber, leather, potash, flour and fulled cloths. At Glen's Falls, marble is also largely manufactured. The quantity of lumber sent to market from this county is very great.

The *commerce* of the county is mostly confined to the transportation of its own productions to market, by the Champlain canal.

THE STAPLES are lumber, corn, potatoes, oats, butter and wool.

SCHOOLS. In 1846, there were 115 district schools, sustained an average period of six months each, and at an expense for teachers wages of $4869. The number of scholars was 4993, and of volumes in the school libraries 7951. There were eleven private schools, with 525 scholars, and one academy, with ninety-five pupils.

RELIGIOUS DENOMINATIONS. Baptists, Methodists, Presbyterians, Friends, Universalists, and Episcopalians. The whole number of churches is twenty-eight, of clergymen, thirty-four.

HISTORY. In the French war of 1754—63, a number of interesting events occured in this county.

In August, 1755, General Johnson, (afterwards Sir William,) led a force of about 5000 troops, including 1000 Indians, under the command of Hendrick, the celebrated Mohawk chieftain, to attack Crown Point. About the last of the month he encamped at the south end of Lake George, and made preparations to convey his troops, by water, to the foot of the Lake. The Baron Dieskau, the commander of the French forces, meantime, had descended the lake in search of his antagonist. On the 8th of September, General Johnson received intelligence of his approach, and despatched Colonel Williams, with 1200 men, to attack him.

Taking advantage of the dense forests, Dieskau had formed his troops in a crescent, and Williams erelong found himself surrounded by the enemy. He soon fell, as did Hendrick, both fighting with the utmost bravery. Lieutenant Colonel Whiting, of New Haven, Connecticut, the second in command, ordered a retreat, which he conducted with such skill and intrepidity, that his troops returned to the camp without disorder, and took their places in the ranks.

Dieskau pressed on in pursuit, but halting his men, to arrange them for the onset upon the English camp, the English forces recovered their firmness and awaited his attack without disorder. The Indians, in the employ of the French, were soon driven off by the cannon, and fled.

Dieskau led up the main body of his troops, but in vain; they were repulsed again and again, and after an obstinate action of five hours, the English, leaping over the breastwork, engaged the French hand to hand, and soon put them to flight. Dieskau was mortally wounded and taken prisoner. The loss of the French was very severe. The British commander, General Johnson, was wounded in the early part of the conflict, and resigned the command to General Lyman.

For this success, the first which had attended the English arms during the war, General Johnson was rewarded with a baronetcy and a donation of £5000.

The day following the battle, a detachment from Fort Edward attacked the fugitives of Dieskau's army, on French mountain, and killed the greater part of them.

Sir William did not proceed after this victory to Crown Point, which if attacked might have been easily carried, but satisfied himself with erecting and fortifying Fort William Henry at the head of Lake George.

In August, 1757, this fort was taken by the Marquis de Montcalm, the commander of the French forces. Colonel Monroe, who commanded the garrison, made a brave resistance, but the failure of General Webb to send him reinforcements, and the want of ammunition, at length compelled him to capitulate, which he did on the most honorable terms.

No sooner, however, had the French obtained possession of the fort, than the terms of capitulation were most shamefully broken; the Indians rushed upon the defenceless troops, and plundered and murdered them without resistance. Montcalm had promised an escort, but it was withheld, and they were compelled to flee, as best they might, from the murderous assaults of savages thirsting for blood. The wounded and the women and children were the first to fall victims to their barbarity, but the more able-bodied did not escape. It was computed that nearly 1500 were thus butchered.

The fort was destroyed by Montcalm. Fort George was erected as a substitute for it, on a more commanding site, but was never the scene of any important action. Burgoyne deposited most of his stores here in 1777.

Many interesting incidents also occurred during the French war, along the shores of the Horicon lake. At *Sabbath-day Point*, in 1756, a party of Provincial troops defeated a force of French and Indians, who attacked them. Here, too, Lord Amherst, with his army, stopped on a Sabbath morning for refreshment.

Rogers' Rock, is noted as the place where that bold and fearless partizan eluded the pursuit of the Indians, and gave them the impression that he had escaped down the face of the precipice.

The name of *Pierson's Island*, marks the spot where English prisoners were confined during the French war. *Howe's Point*, the spot where that brave and much lamented young nobleman landed, immediately previous to the battle of Ticonderoga, in which he was slain.

The first settlement in the county was made about 1770, at Luzerne and Queensburgh. Johnsburgh was settled in 1790.

The Jessup patent, in the southern part of the county, comprised 40,000 acres of land. It was granted in 1774, to a large company. The town of Caldwell was founded by Mr. James Caldwell, a large landed proprietor. In most parts of the county the population is sparse.

VILLAGES. CALDWELL, the shire town of the county, is delightfully situated on the southern extremity of Lake George. It abounds with interesting associations connected with the early history of this county? Population 300.

Bloody Pond, a short distance southeast of the village, commemorates by its name the bloody conflict of September 6th, 1755. The bodies of nearly 1000 of the slain, mostly Frenchmen, were thrown into it.

Glen's Falls, located on the north bank of the Hudson, in the town of Queensburgh, was incorporated in 1839. It is largely engaged in the manufacture of marble, lime, and lumber. The marble is found on both sides of the river, and is highly prized for the beauty of its color, (black) and its freedom from flaws. The falls at this place have a total descent of fifty feet, affording great hydraulic power, and presenting a picturesque and beautiful landscape. A bridge 600 feet in length crosses the river just above the falls. The navigable feeder of the Champlain canal passes through the village. Here is an incorporated academy, and a female seminary. Population 2500.

Chester, in the town of the same name, is a pleasant village, situated in the midst of a fertile country. The "*Stone Bridge*" in the northern part of the town of Chester, is a great natural curiosity. The stream which it crosses, enters the county from Essex, about thirty rods above the bridge, where it falls over a rocky precipice into a natural basin; thence, turning to the east, it divides into two branches; the northern passing under an arch of granite forty feet high and about eighty feet chord, diminishing in size as the stream descends; this branch may be followed 156 feet from the entrance; the southern and larger branch forces its way through the rock, by a passage which is explored with great difficulty, being at times narrow and confined, and at others opening into caverns of great depth, and thirty or forty feet in diameter. At the distance of 247 feet from the entrance, the two streams, having united during their subterranean passage, again make their appearance, beneath a precipice fifty-four feet high, which terminates the bridge. The arch on this side is five feet high and ten wide.

XLVIII. OSWEGO COUNTY.

Square miles, 923.
Organized, 1816.

Population, 48,441.
Valuation, 1845, $5,332,085.

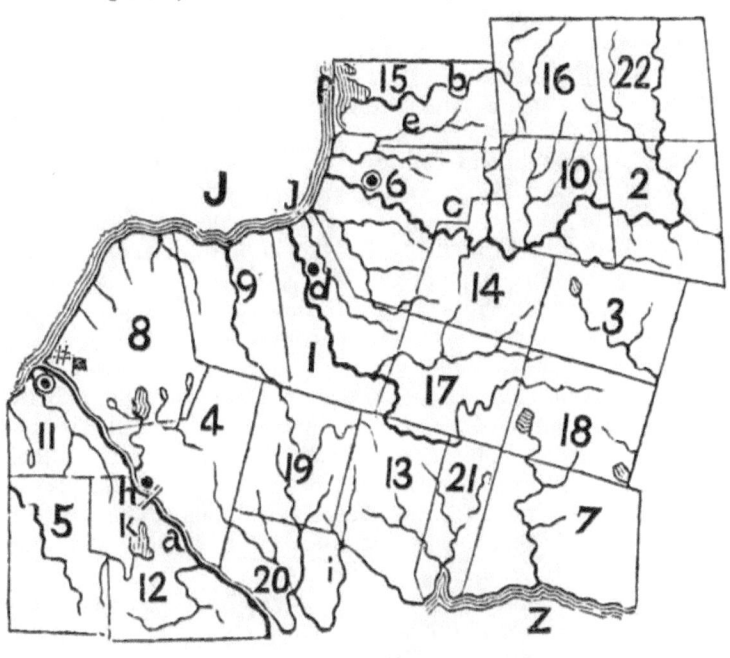

TOWNS.

1. Mexico, 1792.
2. Redfield, 1800.
3. Williamstown, 1804.
4. Volney, 1806.
5. Hannibal, 1806.
6. Richland, 1807.
7. Constantia, 1808.
8. Scriba, 1811.
9. New Haven, 1813.
10. Orwell, 1817.
11. Oswego, 1818.
12. Granby, 1818.
13. Hastings, 1825.
14. Albion, 1825.
15. Sandy Creek, 1825.
16. Boylston, 1828.
17. Parish, 1828.
18. Amboy, 1830.
19. Palermo, 1832.
20. Schroeppel, 1832.
21. West Monroe, 1839.
22. Greenboro, 1844.

Rivers. a. Oswego River. i. Oneida Outlet. b. Little Sandy Creek. c. Salmon River. d. Salmon Creek. e. Deer Creek. h. Oswego Falls.

Lakes and Bays. J. Ontario. Z. Oneida. k. Fish. l. Mexico Bay. f. Little andy Creek Bay.

Battle Fields. Sacketts Harbor.

Forts. Oswego. Ontario.

Villages. PULASKI. OSWEGO. Fulton. Mexico.

BOUNDARIES. North by Lake Ontario and Jefferson county; East by Lewis and Oneida; South by Oneida Lake, Onondaga and Cayuga counties, and West by Cayuga and Lake Ontario.

SURFACE. The southeastern, southern and western portions of the county are level, the interior rolling, and the northern portion rising into hills. A ridge, 110 feet in height, runs westerly through the county, about eight miles north of the southern boundary, forming the watershed or dividing line between the northern and southern waters. The Oswego breaks through this at the great falls at Fulton in the town of Volney.

RIVERS. The Oswego is the principal river of the county. The other important streams are Salmon river, Salmon creek, Little Sandy and Catfish creeks, flowing into Lake Ontario; Scriba and Bay creeks, flowing into Oneida Lake, and Scott and Black creeks, tributaries of the Oswego. The west branch of Fish creek, from Oneida county, drains some of the eastern towns of this county.

LAKES, BAYS, &c. Lake Ontario washes the whole northwestern boundary of the county. Oneida lake forms nearly one-third of its southern boundary. Fish lake, and several other small ponds add to its picturesque beauty. Mexico bay is an indentation of Lake Ontario some ten miles broad. Little Sandy Creek bay is a small land-locked inlet from the lake in the northwestern part of the county.

The Oswego canal, which connects the Erie canal with Lake Ontario, passes through the southwestern portion of the county, following the valley of the Oswego river.

CLIMATE. The climate, influenced by its proximity to the lake, is more uniform than in some of the other counties. Fruits thrive well. It is considered healthful.

GEOLOGY AND MINERALS. The geological formations of this county are v ry simple. The basis rock is a slaty sandstone, making its appearance on the surface in the northwest section of the county. Grey sandstone overlies this on the east, extending into Lewis county. Red sandstone comes next in order, and covers the southern portion of the county, except a narrow strip along the south border. The Clinton group, (limestone,) occurs in several sections of the county, but is generally thickly covered with alluvial deposits.

The county has no minerals of importance. There is a single locality of bog iron ore, and some weak brine springs, in the red sandstone formation.

SOIL AND VEGETABLE PRODUCTIONS. The soil is generally rich and fertile, but better adapted to grazing than the growing of grain. The timber is oak, pine, beech, basswood, ash, butternut and hemlock. The grass crops are very large and of fine quality.

PURSUITS. *Agriculture* is the pursuit of a majority of the inhabitants. The culture of grain and the rearing of cattle, sheep, and swine, each receive a large share of attention. The county is usually reckoned one of the first of the grazing counties. Oats and corn are raised to a greater extent than wheat.

Manufactures. Some attention is paid to manufactures, and such is the amount and convenience of the hydraulic power of the county, that we may anticipate a great increase in this respect, when the county becomes more fully settled. At present, flour, leather, and fulled cloths, are the principal articles produced.

Commerce. The commerce of this county is large, Oswego being one of the best ports on Lake Ontario. Much of the Canada trade enters the state from this direction, as well as that from Lake Erie by the Welland canal. The commerce on the canal is also very large.*

STAPLE PRODUCTIONS. Butter, cheese, wool and oats.

SCHOOLS. There are 272 district school-houses in the county. In 1846, schools were taught on an average eight months. 17,143 children received instruction, at an expense of $17,838. The district libraries contained 24,511 volumes.

There were in the county, twenty-two private schools, with 403 pupils, and three academies, with 178 students.

RELIGIOUS DENOMINATIONS. Baptists, Methodists, Presbyterians, Congregationalists, Episcopalians, Dutch Reformed, and Roman Catholics. There are fifty-two churches, and seventy-two clergymen of all denominations in the county.

HISTORY. In 1722, under the direction of Governor Burnet, a trading hous was erected at Oswego, on the east side of the river. In 1726, in order to prevent the encroachment of the French, Governor Burnet erected old Fort Oswego, on the west side of the river. In 1755, Fort Ontario, on the east side of the river, was constructed, under the direction of Governor Shirley. On the 14th of August, 1756, both these forts, with a garrison of 1600 men, and a large quantity of ammunition, were surrendered to the French, under Montcalm, who had besieged them with a well appointed force of 5000 men, and met with stubborn and long continued resistance.

In 1759, the pentagonal fort, called Fort Oswego, was built. The post was surrendered to the United States, by the British Government, by the treaty of 1794.

During the late war, its garrison, commanded by Lieutenant

---

* TABLE OF COMMERCE OF OSWEGO COUNTY.

Tonnage enrolled and licensed, 1845,	tons, 11,410
Flour shipped at Oswego, 1845,	" 44,560
Property shipped for other states by way of Oswego,	" 71,416
Tolls on the Oswego canal, 1845,	" $58,347

Colonel Mitchell, with an effective force of less than 300 men, sustained an attack from the British force, which consisted of more than 3000 troops, for two days, and finally retreated in good order, with a loss during the whole conflict of o ly forty-four in killed and wounded, while the loss of the enemy was 235. The British, chagrined at their want of success, e acuated the fort in about twelve hours.

Fort Oswego, on the east o t' e river, occupies a station a little north of Fort Ontario, and has recently been repaired by the United States government. It is one of the most important military posts on the lake.

The settlement of the county did not commence till after the Revolution. The towns west of Oswego riv r belonged to the Military Tract, and were granted by the state to officers and soldiers of the New York line.

The townships on the east side of the river constitute a part of "Scriba's patent." These lands were originally granted by the state to Nicholas Roosevelt, of New York, but he not complyi ith the terms of the purchase, a large portion of them were sold to George Scriba, a native of Germany, and then an opulen merchant in New York. The town of Richland, part f Volney, and about o e half of Scriba, were purchased by Messrs. Alexander Hamilton, J. Lawrence, and J. B. Church.

VILLAGES. OSWEGO village, situated on o sides of the Oswego river, in the towns of Oswego and Scriba, is the half shire town of the county. As the terminus of the Oswego canal, it is a place of considerable importance, having an extensive forwarding trade. It has an inexhaustible water power, and is largely engaged in manufactures. Its flour ills are of great size. The harbor is artificial, and is formed by two piers, extendin from the mouth of the river, one 1250 feet long, the other 250. These were erected by the general government, at an expense of $93,000. The village is regularly laid out and well built. Population about 5000.

PULASKI, the other county seat, is a small but thriving village, in the town of Richland. It has valuable water privileges, as yet but partially improved. Population 800.

Mexico, in the town of the same name, is a thriving village, situated on Salmon creek. It has some manufactures, and an academy of some note. Population 600.

Orwell. The falls of the Salmon river at this place are worthy of notice. The stream is about ten rods wide, and after rushing over rocks for about two miles, plunges perpendicularly 107 feet. The banks of the stream are eighty feet high above the falls, and about 200 below them.

Fulton is a large and busy village, in the town of Volney, engaged in manufactures, for which the falls in the Oswego, furnish ample facilities. Population 2400.

XLIX. TOMPKINS COUNTY.

Square Miles, 580.   Population, 38,168.
Organized, 1817.   Valuation, 1845, $4,001,719.

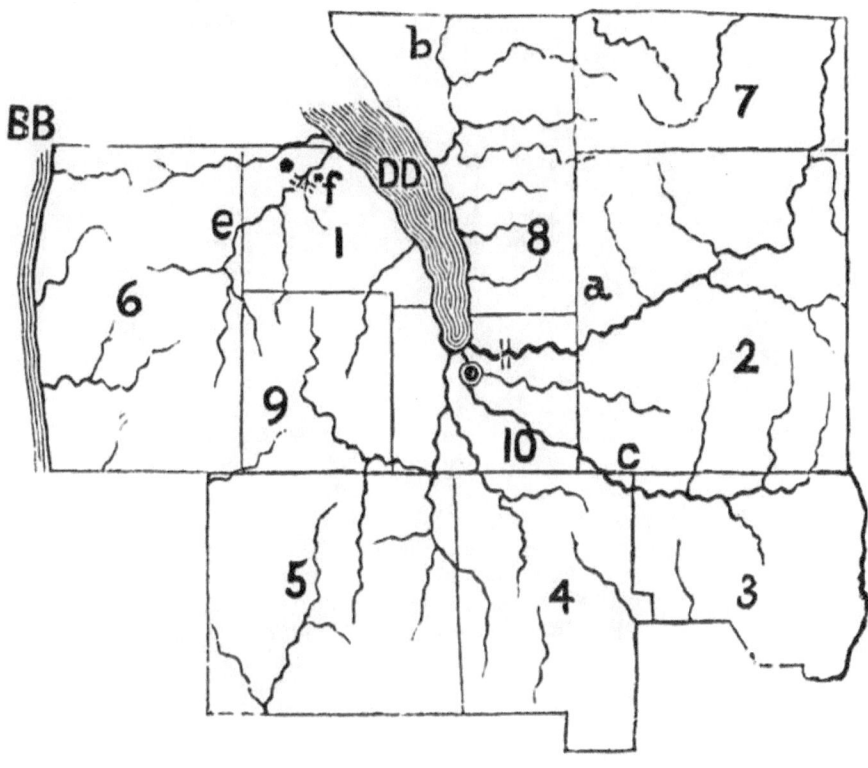

TOWNS.

1. Ulysses, 1801.
2. Dryden, 1803.
3. Caroline, 1811.
4. Danby, 1811.
5. Newfield, 1811.
6. Hector, 1812.
7. Groton, 1817.
8. Lansing, 1817.
9. Enfield, 1821.
10. Ithaca. 1821.

Rivers. a. Fall Creek. b. Salmon. c. Six Mile. e. Halsey's.
Falls. f. Taghannuc falls in Ulysses. Falls at Ithaca.
Lakes. BB. Seneca. DD. Cayuga.
Villages. ITHACA. Trumansburgh.

BOUNDARIES. North by Seneca and Cayuga counties; East by Cortland and Tioga; South by Tioga and Chemung, and West by Chemung county and Seneca lake.

SURFACE. Tompkins county forms a portion of the great table land of Western New York. Its southern portion is most elevated, rising from 1200 to 1400 feet above tide water while on the shores of Cayuga and Seneca lakes it is 800 or 900 feet lower. 500 feet of this depression, however, occurs within two miles of the lakes, where the streams running northward fall over the ledge of the Chemung sandstone, which forms the limit of the highest terrace of the table land.

RIVERS, &c. Salmon, Fall, Six Mile, and Halsey's creek are the only streams of importance. By their rapid descent. they furnish extensive and valuable hydraulic privileges.

FALLS. The most remarkable falls in this county are the Taghannuc, upon Halsey's creek, at the distance of one mile from Cayuga lake. The whole descent, within a short distance, is 300 feet. The water falls, in a single cascade, over a precipice 216 feet in height, with a sheet of water sixty feet wide and two feet deep. The falls around Ithaca also possess great attractions to the lover of the wonders of nature. Fall creek has a descent of 438 feet within one mile. On the Cascadilla, is a fall of 100 feet, in the form of a gigantic stairway.

LAKES. Seneca lake forms a portion of the Western boundary of this county. while Cayuga lake indents it on the north for a distance of about eighteen miles. The scenery at the southern extremity of the latter is highly picturesque.

RAILROADS. The Ithaca and Owego railroad extends from Ithaca to Owego, the county seat of Tioga county. It is twenty-nine and a half miles in length. The proposed route of the New York and Erie railroad is through this county.

CLIMATE. The climate of the county is mild and agreeable, modified in some degree, perhaps, by its proximity to the Seneca and Cayuga lakes. Fruits thrive here in great perfection. It is regarded as healthful.

GEOLOGY AND MINERALS. The whole county, with the exception of two small tracts on the shores of the Cayuga and Seneca lakes, in the towns of Lansing and Hector, belongs to the Erie group, and consists in the north, of the Ludlowville shales, and in the south of the Chemung sandstone. The two small tracts, to which we have referred, are patches of limestone, belonging to the Hamilton group, which appear, beneath the sandstone, near the shores of the lake.

It has but few minerals. Marl and gypsum occur in considerable quantities. Calcareous tufa has been found, near Ithaca, investing moss, &c. and producing, in popular phraseology, petrifactions. There are two or three sulphur springs, of no great reputation, in the county.

SOIL AND VEGETABLE PRODUCTIONS. The soil is, from the geological structure of the rocks, highly fertile, and does not require, in most parts, the addition of any fertilizing agent to maintain or increase its productiveness, the decomposed rocks affording a sufficient stimulus. The hills are productive to their

TOMPKINS COUNTY. 375

summits, and afford luxuriant grazing, while the valleys yield large crops of grain. Fruit is extensively and profitably cultivated. The timber consists of oak, white and yellow pine, hemlock, beech, maple, basswood, elm, ash, poplar, cherry and chestnut.

PURSUITS. *Agriculture* is the pursuit of a majority of the inhabitants. Oats, corn, buckwheat, wheat and potatoes are raised in considerable quantities; the products of the dairy are very large, and much wool is grown by the farmers.

Manufactures also occupy the attention of a considerable number of the inhabitants. Flour, oil, woollen goods, lumber, leather, distilled liquors, paper and potash, are the principal articles produced. The manufactures of the county in 1845, amounted to nearly one and a half millions of dollars.

Commerce. Its commerce is quite extensive. By means of the lakes, it has a direct communication with the Erie canal, while by the Ithaca and Owego railroad the produce of the counties south of it, is brought to a market, and the manufactures of the county distributed over Tioga and Chemung counties, and northern Pennsylvania.

STAPLES. Butter, cheese, wool, oats, buckwheat, wheat and potatoes.

SCHOOLS. In 1846, there were in the county 215 district schools, which were in session an average period of eight months, furnishing instruction to 12,881 children, at an expense for tuition of $21,045. The number of volumes in the district libraries was 24,648.

There were also seventeen private schools, with 497 scholars, and two academies, with 231 pupils.

RELIGIOUS DENOMINATIONS. Methodists, Baptists, Presbyterians, Episcopalians, Congregationalists, Unitarians, Dutch Reformed, Universalists and Friends. The whole number of churches, is seventy-four; of clergymen, seventy-five.

HISTORY. The towns of Newfield, Danby, and Caroline, were purchased of the state, by Messrs. Watkins and Flint. The remainder, (except a small portion in the northeastern part of the town of Dryden, which belonged to the ten townships granted to Massachusetts,) formed a portion of the Military Tract, and the settlers derived their titles through the soldiers' patents. The county was organized in 1817, and was named in honor of the late Daniel D. Tompkins, formerly Governor of the state, and Vice President of the United States. Previous to the completion of the Erie canal, it was in a languishing condition, but since the opening of the canal, its agricultural and manufacturing interests have greatly prospered.

Its early settlers were chiefly from New England. The founders of the town of Lansing, were Germans from Pennsylvania.

VILLAGES. ITHACA village, in the town of the same name, is the seat of justice for the county. It is situated partly on the alluvial flats bordering Cayuga lake, (from which it is about one and a half miles distant,) and partly upon the hills, which form a natural amphitheatre around it. It is regularly laid out, its buildings are neat and tasteful, and its streets well shaded.

It is finely located for trade, communicating freely by means of the lake and canal, with eastern and western New York, and by the railroad and the Susquehanna river, with the coal region of Pennsylvania. The completion of the Erie railroad will still further increase its facilities for business. Its lumber trade is very great.

In available hydraulic power for manufacturing purposes, it is second to no village in New York. It is already largely engaged in manufacturing. Here is located an incorporated academy, with spacious buildings, for the instruction of both sexes, a large Lancasterian school, and numerous select schools, in a flourishing condition. Population, 4200.

Trumansburgh, in the town of Ulysses, is a flourishing village, with some manufactories. Population, 1000.

Danby, in the town of the same name, is a thriving village. Population, 500.

Dryden, in the town of the same name, *Burdette*, in the town of Hector, *Ludlowville*, in the town of Lansing, and *Newfield*, in the town of the same name, are villages of some importance.

L. ERIE COUNTY.

Square miles, 876.
Organized, 1821.
Population, 78,635.
Valuation, 1845, $11,831,969.

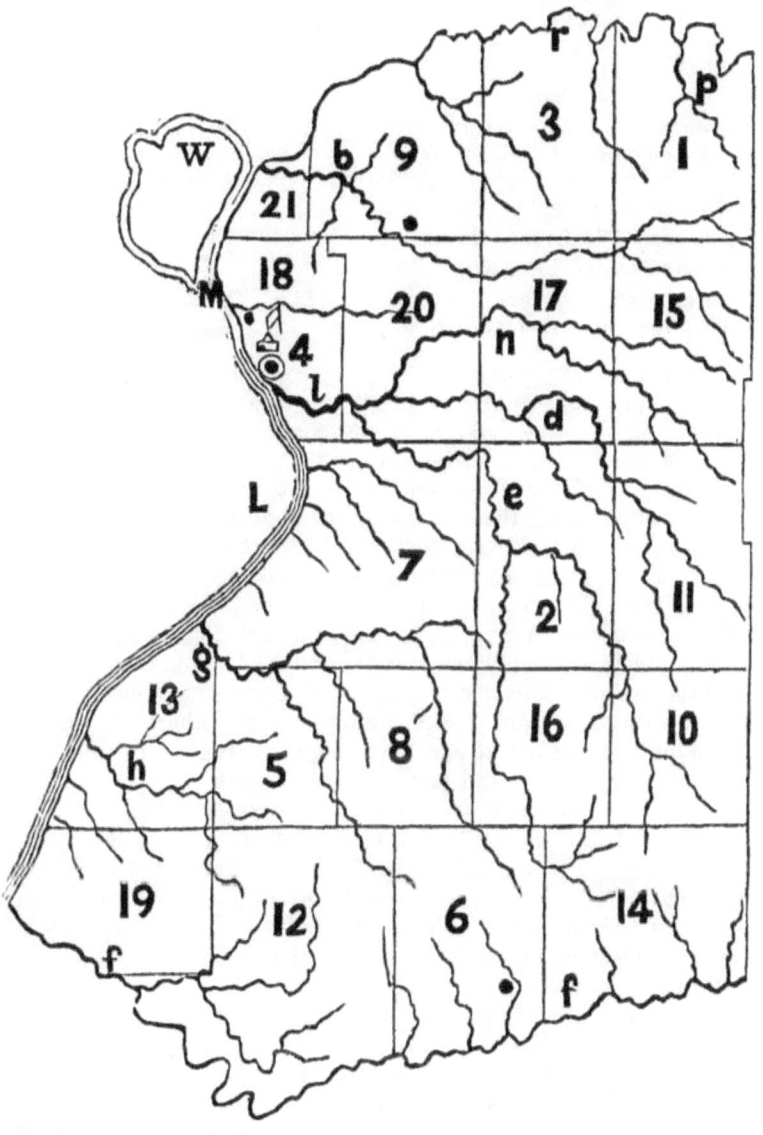

TOWNS.

1. Newstead, 1804.
2. Aurora, 1804.
3. Clarence, 1808.
4. Buffalo, 1810.
5. Eden, 1812.
6. Concord, 1812.

378 STATE OF NEW YORK.

7. Hamburgh, 1812.
8. Boston, 1812.
9. Amherst, 1818.
10. Holland, 1818.
11. Wales, 1818.
12. Collins, 1821.
13. Evans, 1821.
14. Sardinia, 1821.
15. Alden, 1823.
16. Colden, 1827.
17. Lancaster, 1833.
18. Black Rock, 1837.
19. Brandt, 1838.
20. Chictawaga, 1838.
21. Tonawanda, 1838.

Rivers, &c. M. Niagara river. b. Ellicott's creek. d. Seneca. f. Cattaraugus g. Cauquaga. h. Two Sisters. e. Cazenove. l. Buffalo. n. Cayuga. p. Murder Creek. r. Tonawanda Creek.

Lakes. L. Erie.

Islands. W. Grand Island.

Battle Fields. Lake Erie. Buffalo.

Cities and Villages. BUFFALO. Black Rock. Williamsville. Springville. Auroraville.

BOUNDARIES. North by Niagara county; East by Genesee and Wyoming; South by Cattaraugus and Chautauque counties; and West by Lake Erie and Niagara river.

SURFACE. This county lies upon the great western plain. Its northern half is level or gently undulating; the southern is hilly, particularly along the streams; the dividing ridge which separates the waters flowing northward, from the tributaries of Cattaraugus creek, passes through the southern tier of towns.

RIVERS. The county is well watered; Tonawanda creek forms its northern boundary. Its principal tributaries are Murder and Ellicott's, or Eleven mile, creeks. Buffalo creek, formed by the union of Seneca, Cayuga, and Cazenove creeks, waters the central portion of the county. The other streams are smaller: the principal are Cauquaga, or Eighteen mile, Two Sisters, Delaware, and Little Buffalo creeks.

Lake Erie forms a portion of its western boundary.

Grand Island, in the Niagara river belongs to this county.

CLIMATE. From its proximity to the lake, the climate is moist, warmer in winter and cooler in summer, than some other portions of the state. The vegetation is from eight to ten days earlier than in the same parallels in the eastern part of the state.

GEOLOGY AND MINERALS. The Onondaga salt group, (limestone,) is the basis rock of this county. It appears on the surface in the northern tier of towns. The Helderberg series succeed this in the towns of Buffalo, Chictawaga, Lancaster and Alden, and these in their turn give place to the Hamilton group of limestones. In the southern half of the county, the Cashaqua, or Ludlowville shales, and the Chemung sandstones form the surface rocks.

ERIE COUNTY. 379

The limestone is extensively quarried in the neighborhood of Niagara river and the Lake. It is not, however, generally susceptible of a high polish, but makes a fine building material, when hammer-dressed. Water limestone is found on Grand Island. Petroleum springs rise a few miles southeast of Cayuga creek. Iron pyrites, copper ores in small quantities, and water limestone are the principal minerals. There is a sulphur spring about four miles from Buffalo, and one on Grand Island, containing free sulphuric acid in a very diluted state. The bituminous shale, in which the petroleum springs rise, is so thoroughly impregnated with bitumen that it burns freely when ignited. Geodes, or masses of impure limestone, exhibiting fantastic and singular forms, occur in this as well as in some of the other counties.

SOIL AND VEGETABLE PRODUCTIONS. The soil is generally good, consisting of warm, sandy, gravelly loam, occasionally mingled with clay, and well adapted to wheat; in the southern part it is more clayey, and is very productive of grass.

The timber is large and abundant in the southern part, consisting of oak, beech, maple, linden, elm, ash, poplar, hemlock, white pine, butternut, black walnut, wild cherry, &c. In the north it is principally diminutive oaks and underwood. The peach and other fruits attain extraordinary size and perfection.

PURSUITS. *Agriculture* is the pursuit of a majority of the inhabitants. The culture of grain and of grass occupy nearly equal attention.

Manufactures also form the occupation of a large number of the inhabitants. Flour, lumber, cloths, iron, leather, malt liquors, distilled liquors and potash, are the principal articles manufactured. The flour mills produced, in 1845, flour to the value of more than a million of dollars. The entire value of the manufactures of the county, during the same year, was over $2,300,000.

The *commerce* of Erie county is very extensive. Buffalo and Black Rock, the principal lake ports, carry on a large trade with all the states situated upon the upper lakes, and with Canada. The shipping of these ports amounted, in 1845, to 25,000 tons. In addition to this, the immense quantities of produce, manufactures and furniture transported on the Erie canal and its branches, are here transhipped.

STAPLE PRODUCTIONS. Butter, cheese, oats, wheat, corn, wool, beef and pork.

SCHOOLS. There are in the county 291 school districts. In 1846, the schools were taught on an average eight months. The same year, 24,523 children received instruction at an expense of $30,539. The district school libraries contained 31,032 volumes.

There were fifty-seven private schools, with 1304 pupils; and three academies, with 244 students. The school system of Buffalo has been already described, (see page 125.)

RELIGIOUS DENOMINATIONS. Baptists, Methodists, Presbyterians, Congregationalists, Roman Catholics, Friends, Episcopalians, Universalists, Dutch Reformed, Unitarians and Lutherans. There are in the county ninety-four churches, and one hundred and twenty-five clergymen, of all denominations.

HISTORY. The whole county, except a strip a mile wide, on the Niagara river, is within the limits of the Holland Land Company's purchase.

Its settlement dates since the commencement of the present century. Buffalo, the first town in the present limits of the county, was laid out in 1801, but its increase was very slow until 1812, when it became a military post. In December, 1813, the British made a descent upon this county, and burned Buffalo and Black Rock. These villages were soon rebuilt.

In 1816-17, a number of persons from Canada and the United States took possession of Grand Island, in Niagara river, now forming a portion of the town of Tonawanda, and dividing the land between themselves, gave out that they were an independent community, and amenable to neither government. After the question of the boundary was settled, they were expelled by force, under the authority of a law of the state; their houses being destroyed by the sheriff and posse of Erie county.

In 1825, Major Noah, of New York, a learned Jew, and editor of a newspaper in that city, formed the design of building a city of refuge, upon that island, colonizing it with Jews, and making it a resting place for that dispersed people. He erected a monument, which is still in existence, upon the island. But the European Rabbins did not sanction the scheme, and it failed of completion.

Red Jacket, Sagoyouwatha, or Keeper Awake, as his name signifies, the most eloquent and intelligent of his nation, was one of the chiefs of the Senecas, and resided on the Buffalo reservation. He was warmly attached to his tribe, and opposed the whites with the utmost daring, until he saw that resistance was vain. He died in 1832.

Mary Jemison, the Seneca white woman, was buried in this reservation.

The completion of the Erie canal, in 1825, brought a vast tide of emigration into this county, and it has now become the fourth county in the state in population.

CITIES AND VILLAGES. BUFFALO city, the county seat of Erie county, as has been already stated, is a city of modern growth, laid out at the commencement of the present century, and contained in 1817, but one hundred houses. It owes its growth to its advantageous commercial position on the lake, rendering it the depot of the immense quantities of produce, which find their way through that channel, from the boundless prairies of the west, to tide water, and to the great western railroad which connects with Boston.

In 1845, the amount of produce coming from other states by way of Buffalo, was 233,135 tons, of which 118,614 tons were flour. Probably about one half this amount of goods, furniture, &c. was shipped at Buffalo, for other states. The tolls received at Buffalo, in 1845, amounted to $482,000.

The harbor of Buffalo is spacious and convenient for vessels of light draught: it is obstructed by the ice in the spring, till a later period than the ports on the Canada side. It has been proposed to construct a ship canal across the isthmus, from the lake to Buffalo creek, which would in a measure obviate this difficulty.

The United States government have expended nearly $100,000 in the improvement of this harbor, the construction of a mole, pier, &c. and the erection of a light house. Considerable sums have also been expended, for the same purpose, by the citizens. Buffalo is largely engaged in manufactures of various descriptions. The present population of the city is somewhat over 30,000. It was chartered as a city in 1832.

Black Rock, a village in the town of the same name, is about three miles north of Buffalo, on the Niagara river. The harbor is formed by an immense stone pier, or mole, more than a mile in length. By means of this the Erie canal is supplied with water for nearly half its length. This work was erected by the state of New York, at an expense of $300,000. It also furnishes a fine water power, which is employed for flouring mills, saw-mills, &c. Black Rock is extensively engaged in manufactures. The lower or northern terminus of the Erie canal is here: the town increases rapidly in population, and now numbers about 5000 inhabitants. It was burned by the British in December, 1813.

Auroraville, in the town of Aurora, possesses fine water power on the Cazenove creek, as yet, however, not fully improved. The Aurora seminary is a flourishing institution. Population, 1000.

Williamsville, in the town of Amherst, is a thriving village. Large quantities of water lime, (hydraulic cement,) are manufactured here. Population, about 1000.

Springville is a flourishing manufacturing village, in the town of Concord. It has a number of factories, and an incorporated academy. Population, 1200.

Tonawanda is a new town, comprising Grand Island and a portion of the main land, as well as some other small islands. The island was purchased some years since by a company called

STATE OF NEW YORK.

the East Boston Company, who erected here extensive sawmills, for the purpose of preparing ship timber, but in the general depression of business in 1836-7, they were forced to suspend operations. The village of Whitehaven was built mainly by this company.

LI. LIVINGSTON COUNTY.

Square miles, about 563.
Organized, 1821.

Population, 37,345.
Valuation, 1845, $8,572,869.

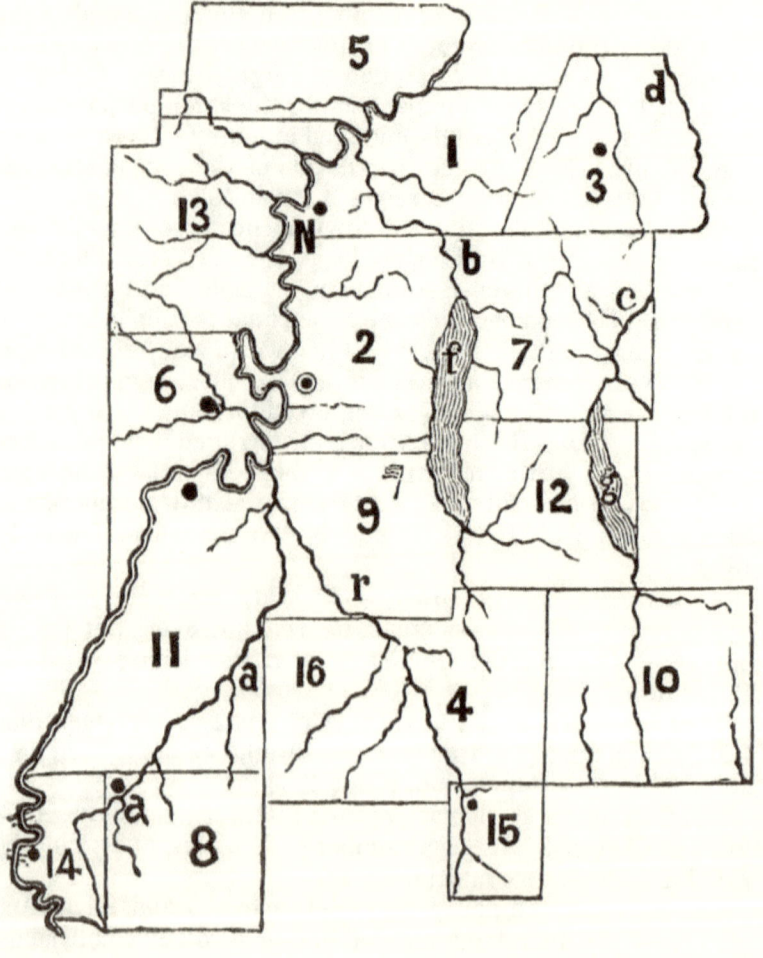

LIVINGSTON COUNTY. 383

TOWNS.

1. Avon, 1789.
2. Geneseo, 1789.
3. Lima, 1789.
4. Sparta, 1789.
5. Caledonia, 1802.
6. Leicester, 1802.
7. Livonia, 1808.
8. Nunda, 1808.
9. Groveland, 1812.
10. Springwater, 1816.
11. Mount Morris, 1818.
12. Conesus, 1819.
13. York, 1819.
14. Portage, 1827.
15. North Dansville, 1846.
16. West Sparta, 1846.

Rivers. N. Genesee. a. Cashaqua. b. Conesus Outlet. c. Outlet of Hemlock Lake. d. Honeoye Creek. r. Canascraga.

Lakes. f. Conesus. g. Hemlock.

Battle Fields. Beardstown.

Villages. GENEEO. Mount Morris. Dansville. Avon Springs. Portageville. Nunda. Moscow. Lima.

BOUNDARIES. North by Monroe; East by Ontario; South by Allegany and Steuben; and West by Wyoming and Genesee counties.

SURFACE. This county is situated on the northern slope of the great dividing ridge which separates the tributaries of the Susquehanna and Ohio, from the waters flowing into the lake.

The southern portion of the county is about 800 feet above Lake Ontario, and the descent toward the lake, though for the most part gradual, is divided into two terraces, the one, nearly on a line with the Portage falls, in Wyoming county; the other, a continuation of the mountain ridge of Ontario. This inclined plane is, however, intersected by the valley of the Genesee river, which, with a width o from two to four miles, has a depth, in the southern part of the county, of not less than 400 feet. A ridge of still greater elevation, traverses the section between the Conesus and Hemlock lakes, bearing northeast.

RIVERS. The Genesee river is the great stream of this county, and receives all the waters which rise in, or flow through it. Its principal tributaries are the Canascraga and Cashaqua creeks, and the outlets of the Conesus and Hemlock lakes.

The Honeoye outlet forms a portion of the eastern boundary of the county.

LAKES. Conesus and Hemlock are the only lakes of importance in the county. The former is nine miles long and nearly a mile broad. It is well stocked with fish, and is said to be more than 300 feet deep.

Hemlock lake is six miles long and one mile wide. It lies partly in Ontario county.

CLIMATE. The climate is mild and temperate; more uniform than in some other sections of the state. It is regarded as very healthful.

GEOLOGY AND MINERALS. About two-thirds of the county, upon the north, belong to the Ontario group, consisting principally of the limestone of the Onondaga salt group, which, in some cases, approaches very near the surface. In the southern portion, the Ludlowville and Cashaqua shales are the prevailing rocks, though intermingled with limestone.

Bog iron ore occurs in the county. Gypsum is abundant. Some brine springs have been discovered, though not of great value. The sulphur springs of Avon* have a high and deserved celebrity, in numerous diseases, and rank among the best sulphur springs in the United States.

SOIL AND VEGETABLE PRODUCTIONS. The soil is generally highly fertile, and well adapted to the growth of grain. In the north it consists principally of sandy loam, intermingled with decomposed limestone, which renders it perpetually fertile.

In the north, the oak prevails, but is occasionally interspersed with other timber; in the south, oak, maple, elm, basswood, butternut, walnut, ash, hemlock, white pine, &c., are the principal forest trees.

PURSUITS. *Agriculture.* The culture of grain, and the rearing of cattle and swine, form the principal pursuits of the inhabitants of this county. *Manufactures* are, however, rising in

---

* The following are analyses of the sulphur springs of Avon. That of the Upper spring was made by Professor Hadley, of Fairfield, and that of the Lower, by Dr. S. Salisbury, Jr. of Avon.

UPPER SPRING.

	Grains.
Carbonate of lime,	8
Sulphate of lime,	84
" magnesia,	10
" soda,	16
Muriate of soda,	18.4
Amount of saline ingredients.	136.4

One gallon contains per volume.	cub. in.
Sulphuretted Hydrogen,	12
Carbonic acid gas,	5.6
Gases,	17.6

LOWER SPRING

	Grains.
Carbonate of lime,	29.33
Chloride of calcium,	8.41
Sulphate of lime,	57.44
" magnesia.	49.61
" soda,	13.73
Amount of saline ingredients,	158.52

	cub. in.
Carbonic acid gas,	3.92
Sulphuretted hydrogen,	10.02
Nitrogen,	5.42
Oxygen,	56
Gases,	19.92

LIVINGSTON COUNTY. 385

importance. The principal articles manufactured are flour, paper, lumber, distilled liquors, cloths, &c.

Commerce. The Genesee Valley canal furnishes a convenient mode of transportation, for the produce of the county, to tide water. There are no *mines* in the county.

STAPLE PRODUCTIONS. Wheat, pork, and cattle are the great staples of the county. Large quantities of butter, wool, oats, and corn are also exported. Hemp and flax are grown largely in the Genesee valley.

SCHOOLS. There are 193 school-houses in this county. The schools were taught, on an average, nine months during the year 1846, and 12,677 children were instructed, at an expense of $19,502. There were 25,121 volumes in the district libraries.

There were twenty-four private schools, with 136 pupils, and three academies, with 165 students.

RELIGIOUS DENOMINATIONS. Presbyterians, Methodists, Baptists, Episcopalians, Dutch Reformed, Universalists, Unitarians, Congregationalists, Lutherans, Roman Catholics, and Jews. There are seventy-two churches, and ninety-two clergymen of all denominations.

HISTORY. The banks of the Genesee river in this county, were the favorite residence of the Seneca Indians, for a long period before the white man had trod that beautiful valley. In civilization, this tribe were more advanced than the Indians generally, and were considered foremost in the arts of peace, among the allied tribes. They cultivated their fields, built cabins for themselves, and when they could not obtain a supply of food from the forests or the lakes, looked to the products of their soil for sustenance.

In 1687, the Marquis de Nonville, governor of Canada, enraged at the firm adherence of this tribe to the English, collected a large force of French and Indians, and commenced an expedition against them. Following the course of the Genesee, he approached their villages with the intention of destroying them, and subjecting the captives he might take to the torture; but the wily Senecas were too crafty for the French commander. They stationed 500 warriors in ambuscade on his route, and having thrown his troops into disorder, by a well directed volley of musketry, rushed upon them, tomahawk in hand. The battle was fierce and bloody; the Senecas were at length repulsed, but not without severe loss on the part of the French. De Nonville could not be persuaded to follow them till the next day, and then found that they had destroyed their villages, and removed their wives and children beyond his reach. Two old men, all that remained, were carried away, killed and eaten by his savage allies.

De Nonville returned to Canada, establishing, in his route, a fort at Niagara, which he garrisoned with 100 men. This fort was so closely invested by the Indians, that eighty-eight out of the hundred perished from starvation, and but for the aid of a party of friendly Indians, the rest would have shared the same fate.

In 1779, General Sullivan terminated his campaign on the banks of the Genesee, in this county, after sending a detachment to Little Beardstown, now Leicester. It was in this town that the brave Lieutenant Boyd met with his melancholy fate, being executed with the most horrible tortures by the Indians, at the instigation of the infamous Butler, after his life had been guarantied by Brant.

Ebenezer Allen, known as Indian Allen, the first miller of Rochester, a monster of wickedness, settled here soon after the revolution, but in a few years removed.

The principal founders and benefactors of the county were William and James Wadsworth, who emigrated from Connecticut in 1790. They purchased large tracts of land, which, by the rapid tide of immigration, soon became very valuable. Many of the early settlers were from Connecticut, and their enterprise and industry has made them wealthy.

VILLAGES. GENESEO, in the town of the same name, is the seat of justice for the county. It is pleasantly situated, about a mile from the river, on the terrace back of the flats. It is well built, and has considerable trade. The Geneseo academy, formerly the Livingston county high school, of which Mr. Wadsworth was the chief benefactor, is located here. It has a spacious building, and is well endowed.

In this town are situated the Wadsworth farms, located on the broad alluvial flats of the Genesee, and celebrated for their fertility and superior cultivation. The mansion of the late James Wadsworth is, perhaps, unsurpassed in the state for the beauty of its location. Population 1600.

Avon, in the town of the same name, has become a favorite resort of late for invalids and pleasure seekers, from all sections of the country. The healing virtues of its justly celebrated springs were known to the Senecas, long before the country was visited by the whites. Red Jacket, a distinguished Seneca chief, was accustomed to resort to them. Population 800.

Upon the Genesee flats in this town, the Mechoacan, wild potatoe vine, or man of the ground, (Convolvulus panduratus,) is found abundantly. It has a large bulbous root, three or four feet in length, and frequently six or eight inches in diameter. It is a mild cathartic, resembling rhubarb in its effects.

There is a pond on the flats irregularly circular in form, a neck of land runs into it and expands within the circle, and upon this are remains of Indian fortifications.

Lima, situated in the town of the same name, is a beautiful village, remarkable for the neatness of its dwellings. The Genesee Wesleyan seminary, located here, is under the control of the Methodists. It was incorporated in 1834, and placed under the visitation of the Regents of the University in 1836. It is well endowed, and in a highly flourishing condition. Population 600.

Mount Morris, in the town of the same name, is a finely situated, thriving village, settled in 1804, by emigrants from Connecticut. It is considerably engaged in manufactures. Population 1400.

Dansville, in the town of North Dansville, at the head of the Genesee valley, forty-five miles from Rochester, is a large, thriving and busy village. It is extensively engaged in manufactures, and has an abundant supply of hydraulic power. Paper, flour, leather, iron, cloth, and lumber, in large quantities, are among its principal manufactures. A branch of the Genesee Valley canal extends to this village. Population 1800.

Nunda, in the town of the same name, on the proposed line of the Genesee Valley canal, is a place of considerable business. It has a flourishing academy, and several manufactories. The town in which it is situated was annexed to Livingston county, by the legislature, in 1846. Population 1100.

Portageville is in the town of Portage, on the west bank of the Genesee river, where it enters the gorge, and is surrounded by beautiful and picturesque scenery. It has great facilities for manufacturing. This town, like the preceding, was taken from Allegany in 1846. The falls and tunnel here are worthy of notice. Population about 1000.

LII. MONROE COUNTY.

Square miles, 607. Population, 70,899.
Organized, 1821. Valuation, 1845, $14,351,436.

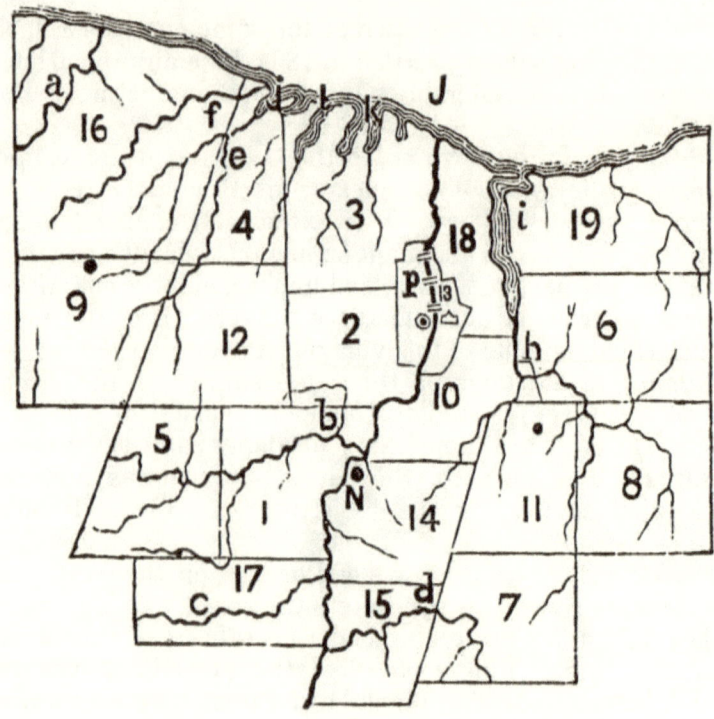

TOWNS.

1. Chili, 1802.
2. Gates, 1802.
3. Greece, 1802.
4. Parma, 1808.
5. Riga, 1808.
6. Penfield, 1810.
7. Mendon, 1812.
8. Perrinton, 1812.
9. Sweden, 1813.
10. Brighton, 1814.
11. Pittsford, 1814.
12. Ogden, 1817.
13. Rochester, 1817.
14. Henrietta, 1818.
15. Rush, 1818.
16. Clarkson, 1819.
17. Wheatland, 1821.
18. Irondequoit, 1837.
19. Webster, 1838.

Rivers. N. Genesee. a. Sandy Creek. b. Black Creek. C. Allen.
  d. Honeoye. e Salmon. f. Little Salmon. h. Irondequoit.
Falls. p. Genesee Falls. Honeoye Falls.

MONROE COUNTY.

Lakes and Bays. J. Ontario. i. Teoronto, or Irondequoit Bay. j. Braddock's Bay. k. Duck Pond. l. Long Pond.

Cities and Villages. ROCHESTER. Pittsford. Brockport.

BOUNDARIES. North by Lake Ontario; East by Wayne county; South by Ontario and Livingston counties, and West by Genesee and Orleans counties.

SURFACE. This county, like Orleans and Niagara, is divided into terraces by the Ridge-Road, and the mountain ridge, which cross it from east to west. The surface as a whole declines gradually towards the lake. The terrace, at Rochester, is 270 feet above Lake Ontario, and sixty-four feet below the upper terrace, which is nearly on a level with Lake Erie.

On the shores of Irondequoit bay, and Irondequoit creek, are numerous conical sand hills, sometimes single, at others united, and rising to an average height of 200 feet.

RIVERS. The Genesee is the principal stream. Its tributaries are the Honeoye creek, from the east, and Black, and Allen's creeks, from the West.

Sandy, Salmon, Little Salmon, Rush, and Irondequoit creeks, flow directly into the lake.

BAYS. Teoronto or Irondequoit Bay, Duck Pond, Long Pond, and Braddock's, or Bradlow's Bay, are the principal of the numerous inlets of the lake, upon the coast of this county.

The name of the first (Teoronto) is of Indian origin, and signifies "the place where the waves gasp and expire."

CLIMATE. The climate of this county, influenced by the nearness to the lake, is mild and equable, and the thermometer has a less average range, than in most parts of the state. Pulmonary affections are, however, becoming increasingly prevalent.

GEOLOGY AND MINERALS. The basis rock of the county is the Medina sandstone, which is widely expanded, and makes its appearance at the surface along the shore of the lake. Above this lies the Clinton group, thinner than in Wayne; next the Niagara group, abounding in fossils; next the Onondaga salt group, which is well developed in some parts of the county, and contains numerous beds of gypsum.

There are several salt springs in the county, but the brine is not sufficiently strong to render them valuable. Sulphur springs are numerous, but few of them are visited. The Monroe springs, five miles from Rochester, are the most celebrated. There are also springs strongly impregnated with sulphur in the town of Ogden. There is a mineral spring at Riga containing iron.

Marl is abundant in Wheatland, Chili, and Riga. Gypsum occurs in large quantities in Wheatland. A bed of argillaceous iron ore extends from the Genesee river to the eastern limit of the county, but it is little worked.

Blende and galena, the sulphurets of lead and zinc, are also found in the county in small quantities. Fire stone, a magnesian earth used for lining stoves and fire-places, is found abundantly in Ogden and Sweden. There is some limestone suitable for building.

SOIL AND VEGETABLE PRODUCTIONS. The soil is gravelly loam, usually of great depth, and by the aid of disintegrated limestone, is rendered perpetually fertile.

The timber is mainly oak, beech, and maple, frequently very dense, but in the oak openings more sparse. In the swamps are black oak, pine, and tamarack.

The Genesee wheat, so abundantly raised in this county, is found, on analysis, to contain more saccharine matter than that of the southern states, and to combine with less water in the composition of bread. The superiority of its flour is too well known to need remark.

PURSUITS. *Agriculture* holds a high rank among the pursuits of the people of this county. It is the largest grain county in the state. In 1845, there were raised in the county 1,338,000 bushels of wheat, besides large quantities of other grains.

Manufactures are also in a highly flourishing condition. The county contains, perhaps, the largest flouring mills in the world, and produces flour annually to the value of more than two and a half millions of dollars. Lumber, cloths, iron, paper, and leather are also extensively manufactured.

Commerce. A steamer plies on the Genesee, between Rochester and Avon, in Livingston county. Steamers from the lake ascend the Genesee to Carthage, which is the port of Rochester; the Erie canal receives a large portion of its immense freights from this county. There are no *mines* of importance.

THE STAPLE PRODUCTION is wheat. Considerable quantities of butter, wool, and pork are also produced.

SCHOOLS. There are in the county 240 school-houses. The schools were taught, during the year 1846, an average period of nine months. 19,448 children received instruction, at a cost of $33,994. The libraries of the districts contained 34,468 volumes.

There were sixteen private schools in the county, attended by 297 children, and eight academies and female seminaries, with 432 pupils.

The organization of the Rochester city schools has been described at page 125. The Rochester university was incorporated in 1846.

RELIGIOUS DENOMINATIONS. Baptists, Methodists, Presbyterians, Congregationalists, Friends, Universalists, Episcopalians, Roman Catholics, Unitarians, Dutch Reformed, and Lutherans.

HISTORY. This county was settled principally by emigrants from New England, with a few from other states, and other sections of New York.

In 1726, a station was established at Teoronto or Irondequoit bay, to secure the Indian trade.

In 1796, the first permanent settlement was made at Hanford's landing, where was erected the first house in this county, west of Genesee river. Indian Allen, so notorious in the history of this region, erected a grist mill and saw mill on the hundred acre lot on which part of the city of Rochester now stands, in 1789, receiving a deed of a hundred acres of land adjoining, from Messrs. Phelps and Gorham, the proprietors, for his encouragement.

In a few years, these decayed and were abandoned. Rochester was not settled till 1811, and was laid out as a village in 1812.

In 1813, the Seneca Indians held a great sacrifice and thanksgiving of several days continuance, on the present site of Rochester.

The terror inspired by the incursions of the British and their savage allies, during the late war, prevented the rapid settlement of the county.* After the close of that war, however, its growth was astonishingly rapid. The completion of the Erie canal, by opening a market for the productions of its fertile soil, gave a new impulse to its prosperity, and it is now one of the most populous counties in the state.

CITIES AND VILLAGES. ROCHESTER city lies on both sides of the Genesee river, seven miles from Lake Ontario. It is finely situated and handsomely built. The streets are generally wide and well paved. The two sections of the city are connected by several bridges, and by the splendid aqueduct of the Erie canal. It has many fine edifices, among its churches and public buildings.

---

* In 1814, Sir James Yeo, with thirteen vessels of various sizes, appeared off the mouth of the Genesee river, threatening the destruction of the infant settlement. There were but thirty-three people in Rochester capable of bearing arms. They assembled, together with the few who could be gathered from the other settlements, and hurried down to the mouth of the river. The militia were undisciplined and not in uniform, but they were brave and determined. They were marched and counter-marched through the woods, in order to deceive the enemy in regard to their numbers. Presently an officer was sent from the British fleet with a flag of truce. He was received by ten of the most soldier-like of the militia, who, in order to be ready for action, kept fast hold of the triggers of their muskets. The British officer expressing his surprise at this, the officer, to rectify his mistake, ordered his men to ground arms. This astonished the British officer still more, and believing their ignorance to be feigned, he hurried back to the fleet, fully satisfied that a plot was laid for them.

In the afternoon of the same day another officer was sent with a flag of truce, the object of the enemy being, if possible, to obtain the provisions stored there, without endangering their own safety. Captain Francis Brown was deputed with a guard to receive the flag. The officer was still suspicious, and finally asked that the military stores and provisions should be given up, on the condition that the settlements were spared by Sir James Yeo. "No," was the prompt reply of the patriotic Brown, "Blood knee deep first." While this parley was in progress, an American officer with his staff, on their return from Fort Niagara, were accidentally seen, passing from one wooded point to another. This confirmed the suspicions of the British officer, and on his return to the fleet, a vigorous attack was made *upon the woods* with bomb shells and balls, which were returned with some effect by a rusty old six pounder, which had been furbished and remounted for the occasion.

After a few hours, Admiral Yeo slipped his cables and ran down to Pulteneyville, where, to his mortification, he learned how he had been outwitted by a handful of militia.

This city owes its rapid growth to the vast hydraulic power created by the falls of the Genesee river, which amount to 268 feet within the bounds of the city, there being three falls of ninety-six, twenty, and 105 feet, besides rapids. The passage of the Erie canal through the city, and the navigability of the Genesee river, above and below the falls, render it a central point for the immense trade of the fertile counties by which it is surounded.

ester was laid out in 1812 by Nathaniel Rochester, Charles Carrol and William Fitzhugh, and received the name of the senior proprietor. In 1816 it numbered but 331 inhabitants; and in 1817 it was incorporated as a village, under the name of Rochesterville. In 1834 it received a charter as a city, and now (1846) has a population of more than 25,000 inhabitants.*

The quantity, as well as the quality of the flour manufactured here, entitle the city to rank among the first flour markets in the world. Between one and two millions of dollars are invested in this business.

Brockport, a village in the town of Sweden, is pleasantly situated on the line of the canal. It has a large trade, particularly in grain. The collegiate school edifice, erected by the citizens at an expense of $25,000, is a noble stone building, five stories high. Population 2000.

Wheatland is appropriately named; the fertility of its soil and its adaptation to the culture of grain is such as to render it the granary of the county. It is rich also in gypsum and marl.

Scottsville, in this town, was founded by Isaac Scott, in 1800. It is a thriving village, and has some manufactures. Population 600.

Mumfordsville and *Garbellsmills* are small villages in the town.

West Mendon, in the town of Mendon, is a manufacturing village of some importance.

Port Genesee, at the mouth of the Genesee river, in the town of Greece, has a customhouse, lighthouse, several large warehouses, &c. Its harbor is good, having thirty feet water within the bar. It has some trade.

Pittsford, in the town of the same name, is a thriving village on the canal. Population 800.

---

* About the commencement of the present century, it was proposed in the legislature of New York, to build a bridge across the Genesee river, at the present site of Rochester. The project was strongly opposed, and one member remarked that it was "a God-forsaken place, inhabited only by muskrats, and visited only by straggling trappers, through which neither man nor beast could gallop without fear of starvation, or fever and ague."

LIII. YATES COUNTY.

Square miles, 320.
Organized, 1823.

Population, 20,777.
Valuation, $4,207,936.

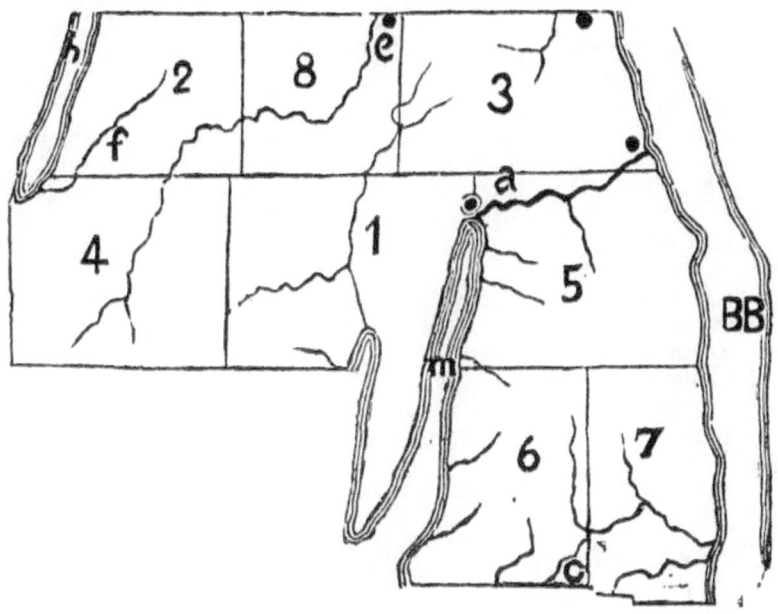

TOWNS

1. Jerusalem, 1789.
2. Middlesex, 1789.
3. Benton, 1803.
4. Italy, 1815.
5. Milo, 1818.
6. Barrington, 1822.
7. Starkey, 1824.
8. Potter, 1832.

Rivers. a. Crooked Lake Outlet. c. Big Stream. e. Flint Creek. f. West.

Lakes. BB. Seneca. h. Canandaigua. m. Crooked.

Villages. PENN YAN. Rushville. Bellona. Dresden.

BOUNDARIES. North by Ontario county; East by Seneca lake; South by Steuben county, and West by Crooked and Canandaigua lakes, and Ontario county.

SURFACE. The surface of this county is greatly elevated. It lies on the northern declivity of the ridge which separates the waters of the Susquehanna from those flowing into the lakes and the St. Lawrence. The southern extremity of the county is elevated from 1200 to 1300 feet above tide water, and in the town of Barrington attains the height of 1600 feet. From this height it descends to the surface of the Canandaigua and Seneca lakes—the former of which is 670, and the latter about 420 feet above the level of the ocean.

The hills, however, are never abrupt, but generally gently waving, and rounded at their summits.

RIVERS AND CREEKS. The principal streams of the county are Flint creek, Crooked lake outlet, connecting Crooked and Seneca lakes; West river, a tributary of Canandaigua lake, and Big and Rock streams flowing into Seneca lake. The Crooked lake canal follows the course of the outlet.

LAKES. Seneca lake forms the entire eastern boundary of the county. Two-thirds of Crooked lake lie within its limits, and Canandaigua lake forms its northwestern boundary.

CLIMATE. The climate is temperate and healthful, and for the cultivation of fruit is not surpassed by that of any county in the state.

GEOLOGY AND MINERALS. The Ludlowville shale is the prevailing rock, and approaches the surface in the southern part of the county. The soil above this is a marly clay, highly fertile, and particularly favorable to grass crops. The northern portion of the county belongs to the great central limestone formation, but the limestone alternates with slate.

Sulphate of iron (copperas) is found native in the eastern part of the county. There is a valuable sulphur spring near the foot of Crooked lake. An inflammable gas spring has been discovered near Rushville, and a very productive brine spring has been found at the Big stream falls, near Dundee, in the town of Starkey.

VEGETABLE PRODUCTIONS. The timber of the county is large, but not so dense as in some other sections. It consists of oak, hickory, chestnut, black and white walnut, wild cherry, maple, beech, linden, poplar, ash, &c. The apple, pear, plum, cherry, melons and grapes, are all very successfully cultivated here.

PURSUITS. *Agriculture* is the pursuit of a majority of the inhabitants—the elevated and diversified surface of the county renders it well adapted to grazing. In portions of it, however, grain is successfully cultivated.

Manufactures are attracting some attention. The principal articles manufactured are flour, lumber, woollen cloths, oil, distilled liquors and leather.

The *commerce* of the county is confined to lake and canal navigation, and is not very extensive. There are no *mines* of importance.

STAPLE PRODUCTIONS. Wheat, oats, corn, barley, butter, wool and pork.

SCHOOLS. There are in the county 106 public school houses. In these, schools were taught an average period of seven months, in 1846. The number of volumes in the district libraries is 13,644; 6536 children were instructed during the year, at an expense of $8789.

There were in the county eighteen private schools, with 218 pupils, and one academy, with twenty-six scholars.

RELIGIOUS DENOMINATIONS. Methodists, Baptists, Presbyterians, Episcopalians, Congregationalists and Dutch Reformed. There are forty-five churches, and forty-one clergymen, of all denominations, in the county.

HISTORY. This county was entirely included in the Massachusetts grant, and formed a portion of the Pulteney estate. The first inhabitants were from New England and Pennsylvania.

This county was the residence of the celebrated Jemima Wilkinson, during the latter part of her life.*

VILLAGES, &c. PENN YAN, the seat of justice for the county, is a village in the town of Milo. It is pleasantly situated at the foot of Crooked lake, and received its name from the circumstance that its original inhabitants were Pennsylvanians and Yankees, in equal numbers. Population 2500.

Jerusalem, one of the earliest settled towns in the county, is fertile and well cultivated. Bluff point is a high bold tongue of land extending between the arms of Crooked lake. The landscape, which spreads itself before the beholder, from this lofty headland, is one of the most picturesque and beautiful afforded by the scenery of the smaller lakes.

Starkey is a hilly but well watered town. The falls of Big stream, in this town, are worthy of the attention, both of the geologist and traveller. The stream, after dashing over a rapid half a mile in length, leaps down 140 feet, into a basin eight or ten rods in diameter, from whence its foaming waters find their way to the lake, by a channel some eighty rods in length.

Dundee is a busy and thriving village in the town of Starkey. It has some manufactures. Population 1000.

---

* Jemima Wilkinson, or as she styled herself, the "Universal Friend," was born in Cumberland, Rhode Island, about the year 1753. She was educated among the Friends. When about twenty-three years of age, she was taken sick, and during her illness an apparent suspension of life occurred. After her recovery she professed to have been raised from the dead, and to have been invested with divine attributes, and authority to instruct mankind in religion. She also pretended to foretell future events, and to possess the power to heal the sick and to work miracles; and if any person who made application to her was not healed, she ascribed it to a want of faith. She asserted that those who refused to believe her claims, would be forever punished for their incredulity. She possessed extraordinary beauty, and though illiterate, discovered great tact in maintaining her extraordinary pretensions. Her memory was said to be very retentive. She settled at Milo, in this county, with her followers, in 1790, and subsequently removed to Bluff Point, where she died, in 1819. The settlement at Milo numbered about forty familes, and was then the largest in the whole Genesee country. A few of her disciples still remain at Bluff Point.

LIV. WAYNE COUNTY.

Square miles, 572.
Organized, 1823.

Population, 42,515.
Valuation, 1845, $6,818,533.

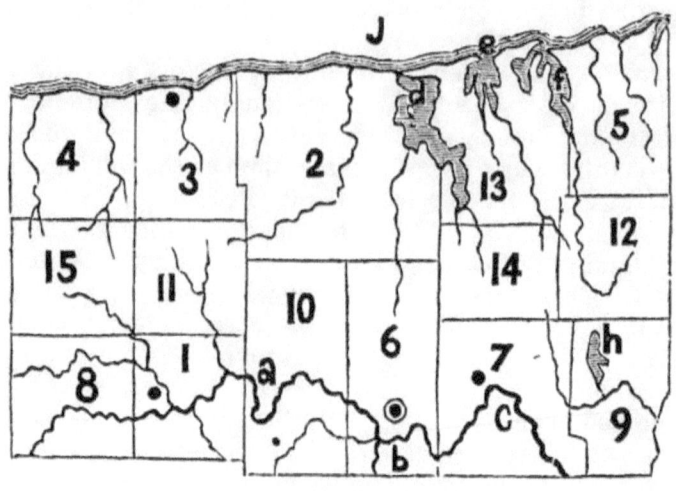

TOWNS.

1. Palmyra, 1789.
2. Sodus, 1789.
3. Williamson, 1802.
4. Ontario, 1807.
5. Wolcott, 1807.
6. Lyons, 1811.
7. Galen, 1812.
8. Macedon, 1823.
9. Savannah, 1824.
10. Arcadia, 1825.
11. Marion, 1825.
12. Butler, 1826.
13. Huron, 1826.
14. Rose, 1826.
15. Walworth, 1829.

Rivers, &c. a. Mud Creek. b. Canandaigua River. c. Clyde.

Lakes and Bays. J. Ontario. d. Sodus Bay. e. Port Bay. f. East Bay. h. Crusoe Lake.

Villages. LYONS. Palmyra. Newark. Clyde. Pulteneyville.

BOUNDARIES. North by Lake Ontario; East by Cayuga county; South by Seneca and Ontario, and West by Monroe.

SURFACE. The surface is much diversified. The Ridge Road extends through the county, from east to west, at a distance of from four to eight miles from the shore of Lake Ontario, and at an elevation of 140 feet above it. North of this road, the descent to the lake is gradual and nearly uniform; south of it, and extending to the mountain ridge, the surface is raised into low hills of gravel and sand, seemingly by the action of the waves of the lake, which, perhaps, at some remote period, covered this whole region.

The mountain ridge forms, here, the watershed of the county,

WAYNE COUNTY. 397

dividing the waters which flow into the lake from those which run southerly.

RIVERS. The principal streams of the county are Mud creek and the Canandaigua river or outlet. The length of each of these streams is about fifty miles. They unite in the town of Lyons and form the Clyde, a tributary of the Seneca river.

BAYS. The lake coast is indented by three considerable bays, viz: Sodus bay, Port bay and East bay. The first of these affords a very good harbor for vessels of light draft.

Crusoe lake, in the town of Savannah, is a shallow pond, one and a half miles in circumference.

CLIMATE. The temperature is rendered agreeable by the extent of surface exposed to the lake. The county is generally considered healthy.

GEOLOGY AND MINERALS. The Medina sandstone appears on the surface along the shore of the lake. As the land rises, this is succeeded by the Clinton, Niagara and Onondaga groups—all limestones. South of the Ridge-Road, the county is traversed by numerous long, narrow, parallel ridges of sand and gravel, from twenty-five to thirty feet high.

Lenticular iron ore and bog iron ore are found in considerable quantities. Gypsum, marl, gypseous marl, and water limestone are abundant. Sulphur springs and weak brine springs occur in several localities. The latter were formerly of considerable importance. In 1810, 50,000 bushels of salt were manufactured from them. In Wolcott, specimens of heavy spar have been discovered.

SOIL AND VEGETABLE PRODUCTIONS. The soil of this county is very fertile, and experience has proved, that the process of cultivation renders it increasingly so, by producing disintegration and decomposition of the earths of which it is composed. The timber is similar to that of the other counties on the lake, consisting of beech, maple, elm, black and white oak, white walnut, some hemlock and pine, black and white ash, &c.

PURSUITS. *Agriculture* is the principal pursuit of the inhabitants. The diversity of the surface renders grazing and the culture of grain nearly equally profitable, and both are practiced extensively.

Manufactures are increasing in importance in the county. Large quantities of flour and lumber are produced, and the manufactures of iron, glass, leather, distilled and malt liquors, pot and pearl ashes, employ a considerable amount of capital.

The *commerce* of the county is not large, vessels of light draft only being able to cross the bar, at the mouth of the Sodus bay, on which the principal landings are situated.

There are some iron *mines*, or quarries, as they are denominated, in which considerable quantities of the lenticular iron ore are obtained.

STAPLE PRODUCTIONS. Wheat, corn, oats, potatoes, flax, wool, butter, cheese and pork.

SCHOOLS. The whole number of school-houses in the county is 227. The public schools were maintained on an average eight months during the year 1846; 15,296 children received instruction, at a cost of $17,635 for tuition. The district libraries contained 25,760 volumes.

There were in the county thirty-one private schools, with 871 pupils.

RELIGIOUS DENOMINATIONS. Methodists, Baptists, Presbyterians, Friends. Episcopalians, Congregationalists, Dutch Reformed, Universalists, Unitarians and Lutherans. There are in the county seventy-two churches, and eighty-nine clergymen, of all denominations.

HISTORY. The settlement of this county dates since the revolution. About two-thirds of its territory, including one quarter of the towns of Galen, Rose and Huron, and all west of these, was included in the Massachusetts grant to Messrs. Phelps and Gorham, and formed a part of the Pulteney estate. The other third belonged to the Military Tract. The emigrants were from New England, New Jersey, Pennsylvania, England, Scotland, and Germany. During the late war with Great Britain, Sodus, and Pulteneyville, (a village in the town of Williamson,) were invaded by the British, and the former burnt. They were repulsed in each instance, before obtaining the provisions, which were the object of their incursions.

In 1829 or 30, the Mormon delusion originated at Palmyra, in this county. Joseph Smith, the reputed prophet and founder of that system, resided in the town of Manchester, in Ontario county, and his leading disciple, Martin Harris, was a thrifty farmer of Palmyra. By money furnished by this man, Smith was enabled to publish the first edition of the book of Mormon, or the Mormon Bible, as it has since been called. In the autumn of 1830, Smith removed to Kirtland, Ohio, afterward to Missouri, and finally to Nauvoo, Illinois.

VILLAGES. LYONS, the county seat, is a pleasant village in the town of the same name. It was first settled in June, 1798, by Mr. Van Wickle and about forty other emigrants from New Jersey and Maryland. It has a fine hydraulic power, obtained by a canal of half a mile in length, from the Canandaigua outlet. The mill privileges afforded by this canal are well improved. The High school here is an excellent institution, surpassed by few academies in the state. Population about 2000.

Palmyra, one of the earliest settled towns in the county, has a village of the same name within its limits, situated on the Erie canal. It is a place of considerable business, and extensively engaged in the lumber trade. It is considered one of the most beautiful villages on the canal. Its streets are ornamented with fine shade trees. Here is an incorporated academy. Pop. 2200.

Clyde, on the river of the same name, a village in the town of Galen, is a thriving, busy place. It has a number of manufactories. The high school here is incorporated and comprises two school districts, which have united for greater efficiency. It is in a flourishing condition. Population 1200.

Sodus contains within its limits the principal harbor of the county. At the mouth of the bay in this town, the United States government have erected a pier, a mile in length, for the improvement of the harbor. The town was burned during the late war with Great Britain. Population about 500.

Pulteneyville, a village on Lake Ontario, in the town of Williamson, was also invaded by the British, but their fears of the American riflemen prevented them from doing much injury. Population 500.

LV. ORLEANS COUNTY.

Square Miles, 372.
Organized, 1824.
Population, 25,845.
Valuation, 1845, $4,761,054.

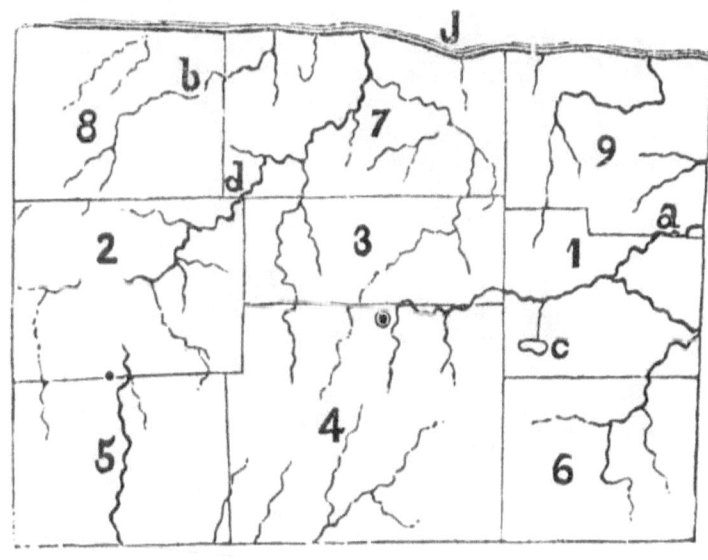

TOWNS.

1. Murray, 1808.
2. Ridgeway, 1812.
3. Gaines, 1816.
4. Barre, 1818.
5. Shelby, 1818.
6. Clarendon, 1821.
7. Carlton, 1822.
8. Yates, 1822.
9. Kendall, 1838.

Rivers, &c. a. Sandy Creek. b. Johnson's. d. Oak Orchard.
Lakes. J. Ontario. c. Jefferson.
Villages. ALBION. Medina.

BOUNDARIES. North by Lake Ontario; East by Monroe county; South by Genesee, and West by Niagara, counties.

SURFACE. The county has three distinct terraces, the first rising gradually from the shore of the lake, to the height of 130 feet, is about seven or eight miles broad, and is terminated by the Ridge-Road. The second, from one to three miles in breadth, rises from the ridge more precipitously, to about the same height, and is terminated by a ledge. The third extends into Genesee county; its ascent, of about 140 feet, is quite rapid. The elevation of this highest terrace above the lake, is, therefore, about 400 feet.

RIVERS AND CREEKS. Oak Orchard, Johnson's, and Sandy creeks, are the only streams of importance in the county. The first is about fifty miles in length.

By an open aqueduct four and a half miles in length, cut for most of the distance through solid rock, the canal commissioners have turned the upper waters of the Tonawanda creek into Oak Orchard creek, thus increasing the volume of the latter, and rendering it more valuable for hydraulic purposes, and for supplying the feeder of the Erie canal.

LAKES. There are no lakes or ponds of any importance in the county. Jefferson lake, in the town of Murray, is the largest, but does not contain more than fifty acres.

MARSHES. The great Tonawanda Swamp, which extends over portions of Genesee and Niagara counties, lies partly in this county. It is twenty-five miles in length from east to west, and from two to seven in breadth. It is bounded on all sides by plains a little elevated above its surface.

CLIMATE. The exposure of the whole northern boundary of the county to the lake, has the effect of producing a more uniformly mild climate, than that of some of the more southern counties. The county is generally considered healthy.

GEOLOGY AND MINERALS. In the northern portion of the county, the Medina sandstone prevails, affording in many places, an admirable material for building. In the central and southern portions, the Niagara, Clinton and Onondaga limestones form the surface rock.

The mineral productions are principally bog iron ore, and some brine and sulphur springs.

SOIL AND VEGETABLE PRODUCTIONS. The soil is mostly clay and argillaceous loam, and is highly fertile. The timber of the county, is beech, maple, linden, elm, red, black and white oak,

ORLEANS COUNTY. 401

hickory, hemlock, pine, black and white ash, &c. The southern part of the county is more heavily wooded than the northern.

PURSUITS. *Agriculture* is the principal pursuit, and the attention of the farmers is divided between the culture of grain and the rearing of cattle. The county, however, may properly be ranked among the grain counties.

Manufactures receive some attention, particularly those of flour, lumber, leather, fulled cloths, iron, and distilled liquors.

There is but one harbor on the lake, and very little *commerce*, nor are there any *mines* of importance.

THE STAPLE PRODUCTIONS of the county are wheat, oats, corn, potatoes and lumber; a considerable quantity of butter and cheese are also produced.

SCHOOLS. There are in the county 134 public schools, taught, during the year 1846, an average period of eight months. In these schools, 9841 children received instruction, at an expense for tuition of $11,226. The district libraries contained 16,895 volumes.

There were in the county the same year, sixteen private schools, with 313 pupils; three academies and one female seminary, with 330 students.

RELIGIOUS DENOMINATIONS. Methodists, Baptists, Presbyterians, Unitarians, Universalists, Episcopalians, Congregationalists, Friends, and Dutch Reformed.

There are forty-one churches, and fifty-nine clergymen, of all denominations, in the county.

HISTORY. This county was first settled by emigrants from New England. It was all included in the grant to Massachusetts; the towns of Barre, Carlton, Gaines, Ridgeway, Shelby, and Yates were comprised in the Holland Land Company's purchase; whilst Murray, Clarendon, and Kendall, belonged to the Pulteney estate.

Murray, the oldest town in the county, was organized in 1808, In a settlement so recent, there is of course little of historical interest.

In Ridgeway and its vicinity are remains of Indian fortifications.

VILLAGES. ALBION, a village in the town of Barre, is the seat of justice for the county. It is pleasantly situated upon the canal, near the centre of the county.

A flourishing female seminary is here located, and an incorporated academy. It is surrounded by a rich and fertile country, and is a neat and thriving village. Population, 1600.

Holley is a pleasant village in the town of Murray. It has some manufactures. A short distance east of the village, is the Holley embankment, one of the largest on the canal, elevated seventy-six feet above the creek. Population 400.

Medina, a thriving village in the town of Murray, was incorporated in 1832.. It has some manufactures. Population, 1200.

Knowlesville, in the same town, is a growing village. Population, 600.

Gaines, in the town of the same name, has an incorporated academy. Population, 700.

LVI. CHEMUNG COUNTY.

Square Miles, 530.
Organized, 1836.
Population, 23,689.
Valuation, 1845, $2,464,634.

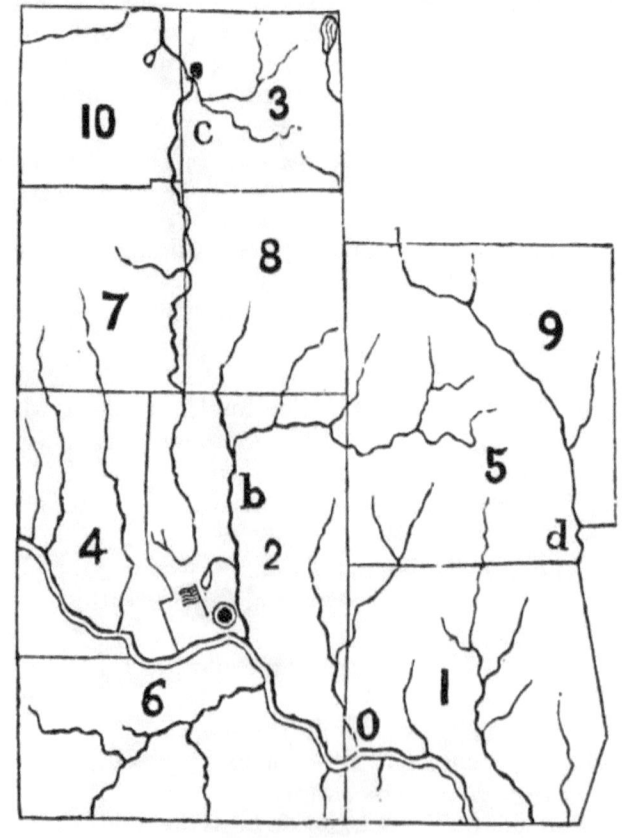

TOWNS.

1. Chemung, 1791.
2. Elmira, 1792.
3. Catharines, 1798.
4. Big Flats, 1822.
5. Erin, 1822.
6. Southport, 1822.
7. Catlin, 1823.
8. Veteran, 1823.
9. Cayuta, 1824.
10. Dix, 1835.

CHEMUNG COUNTY. 403

Rivers. 0. Chemung. b. Newtown Creek. c. Catharine's. d. Cayuta.
Battle Fields. Elmira.
Villages. ELMIRA. Havana.

BOUNDARIES. North by Steuben and Tompkins; East by Tompkins and Tioga; South by the state of Pennsylvania; and West by Steuben county.

SURFACE. This county forms part of the great table land extending from the counties of Ulster and Greene, to the vicinity of Lake Erie. Its mean elevation is about 1600 feet above tide water, but the northern portion declines gradually toward Seneca Lake, whose waters are but 456 feet above the level of the ocean. The streams which pass through the county divide this otherwise level surface into ridges, their banks being very high and precipitous.

RIVERS. The Chemung or Tioga river is the principal stream of the county. The other streams are, Cayuta Creek, forming part of the eastern boundary, Wynkoop, Baldwin's and Newtown Creeks, tributaries of the Chemung, and Catharine's Creek, an inlet of Seneca Lake.

LAKES. Cayuta Lake, in the northeastern part, is the only pond of importance in the county. Seneca Lake forms a portion of the northern boundary.

CANALS. The Chemung canal connects the village of Elmira with Seneca Lake.

RAILROADS. The route of the New York and Erie railroad is laid out through this county.

CLIMATE. The climate, like that of the table land generally, is cool, but salubrious. The vicinity of Seneca Lake exerts some influence in modifying it.

GEOLOGY AND MINERALS. The basis rock is secondary graywacke slate, sometimes mingled with shale, at others compact, and forming fine building stone. It is covered with a fine, close grained sandstone. In the northern part of the county are beds of limestone. The surface rocks belong to the Chemung sandstone, except a small tract around Seneca Lake, where the Helderberg limestone makes its appearance.

The mineral productions of Chemung county are few, and generally unimportant. There is some marl, in various parts of the county, and gypsum in Catharines and Catlin.

VEGETABLE PRODUCTIONS. The soil is generally fertile; the pine plains in the towns of Big Flats and Elmira, which were formerly deemed worthless, are found by the application of plaster, to yield abundant crops The timber of the county is white pine, hemlock, spruce, oak, maple, elm, beech, ash, linden,

&c. The maple is very abundant, and yields large quantities of sugar.

The soil of the uplands is better adapted to grass than grain, but the valleys yield abundantly the various grains, peas, beans and hops.

PURSUITS. The people of the county are mostly devoted to *agriculture;* attention being paid to grazing in the uplands, and to the growing of grain in the more fertile valleys.

Manufactures are also increasing in importance. Flour, lumber, cloth, iron and leather, are the principal articles.

The opening of a navigable communication between the Hudson and Susquehanna, through the Seneca Lake and Erie canal, by means of the Chemung canal, has opened a market to the inhabitants of Chemung county, and been productive of extensive inland commerce.

The Corning and Blossburg railroad, which pours a portion of the mineral wealth of Pennsylvania into New York, has also been of great advantage to the county.

STAPLE PRODUCTIONS. Oats, wheat, corn, buckwheat, butter, and cheese.

SCHOOLS. There are in the county 128 schools, maintained during the year 1846, an average period of seven months, affording instruction to 7962 children, at an expense for tuition of $10,336. The district libraries contained 12,197 volumes.

There were in the county, the same year, twenty-four unincorporated private schools, with 283 scholars, and one academy and one female seminary, with 134 pupils.

RELIGIOUS DENOMINATIONS. Methodists, Presbyterians, Baptists, Episcopalians, and Friends. There are twenty-six churches, and forty-one clergymen, of all denominations.

HISTORY. The first white settlers in this county located in Elmira, Southport and Big Flats, between 1786 and 1792, having become acquainted with the country while engaged in General Sullivan's expedition, in 1779. They were mostly from Pennsylvania, and from Orange county in this state. Catlin, Catharines, and Veteran, were settled soon after, by emigrants from Connecticut; Erin by Dutch and Scotch emigrants from New Jersey and Delaware county; and Chemung by emigrants from Lancaster county, Pennsylvania. During General Sullivan's campaign in 1779, of which we have spoken in the historical sketch of the state, he encountered the enemy's force, consisting of somewhat more than 1000 Indians and tories, under Brant and Colonels Butler and Johnson, at Elmira, in this county. The battle which ensued, called "the battle of the Chemung," was a severe and bloody one. It terminated in the defeat of the enemy, and the destruction of their towns. The land in this county was sold to the settlers, in 1788, at eighteen cents per acre.

VILLAGES, &c. ELMIRA, the county seat, is admirably situated for the purposes of trade, being in the midst of a fertile valley of considerable extent, and connected with Pennsylvania and Maryland, by means of the Susquehanna river, and with almost every part of New York, by the Chemung canal. It is also on the route of the New York and Erie railroad, and from its commercial facilities, must eventually become a place of considerable importance. The first settler in the town was Colonel John Hendy, a veteran who had served under General Sullivan. He united, in a remarkable degree, extraordinary courage and great physical power, and in his conflicts with the Indians, often exhibited both. Population, 3300.

In 1790, a treaty was negotiated at this place between the Indian tribes and the United States. Over 1000 Indians were present, and among them most of the principal chiefs. In 1797, Elmira was visited by Louis Phillippe, the present king of the French, accompanied by the Duke de Nemours, and the Duke de Berri. They had travelled on foot from Canandaigua to Elmira, a distance of seventy miles. Mr. Tower, whom they visited, fitted up an ark or flat boat, on board which he conveyed them to Harrisburg.

The village has an incorporated academy and female seminary, both in a prosperous condition. There is also a mechanics' association, which has a commodious hall and a public library.

It is largely engaged in the manufacture and exportation of lumber, ten million feet of marketable planks and boards being exported annually.

Chemung, the earliest organized town in the county, has a hilly and broken surface, but much of it is fertile. In the south part of the town, is a mound called "Spanish hill," which but for its extent might be considered a work of art. It is elevated 110 feet above and near the river's brink, and has upon its summit vestiges of fortifications which display much skill and judgment. The entrenchments are regular and command the bed of the river. By whom they were constructed is unknown.

Catharines, one of the early settled towns, was named after Catharine Montour, the wife of an Indian sachem. This extraordinary woman was a native of Canada, a half breed, and had been carried into the Seneca country when only ten years of age, and adopted by one of its families. She possessed a good address and had great influence with her tribe, frequently accompanying the chiefs to Philadelphia and other places where treaties were made. Her town, consisting of thirty houses and farms in a high state of cultivation, was destroyed by General Sullivan, in 1779.

Havana, in the town of Catharines, is a thriving village on the Chemung canal. It has some manufactures. Population, 1000.

Fairport, formerly called Horseheads, from the fact that General Sullivan here killed some seventy or eighty of his pack horses, to prevent their falling into the hand of the Indians, is a thriving village in the town of Elmira. It is considerably engaged in the lumber trade. Population, 600.

Millport, in the town of Veteran, is a village of some importance. It has a fine hydraulic power. Population, 500.

LVII. FULTON COUNTY.

Square miles, 500.
Organized, 1838.

Population, 18,579.
Valuation, 1845, $1,308,724.

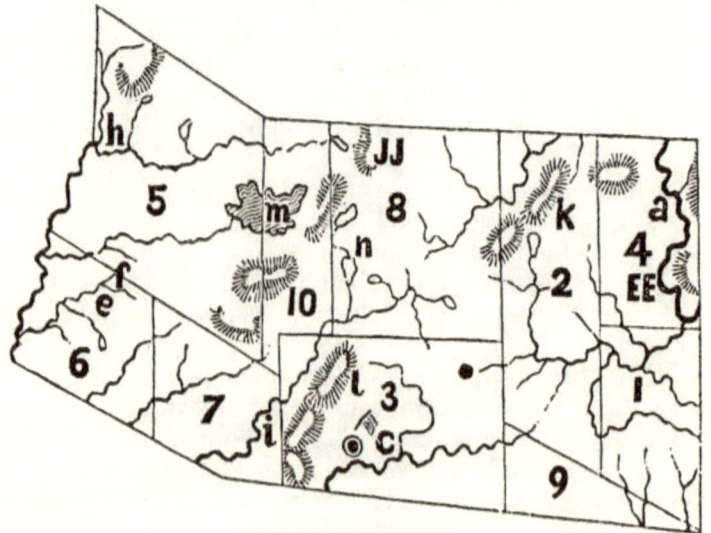

TOWNS.

1. Broadalbin, 1793.
2. Mayfield, 1793.
3. Johnstown, 1798.
4. Northampton, 1801.
5. Stratford, 1805.
6. Oppenheim, 1808.
7. Ephrata, 1827.
8. Bleeker, 1831.
9. Perth, 1838.
10. Garoga, 1843.

Mountains. EE. Kayaderosseras. JJ. Au Sable range. k. Mayfield mountain. l. Klip Hill.

FULTON COUNTY. 407

Rivers. a. Sacandaga. c. Cayaduta or Little Canada Creek. f. Fish. h. East Canada. i. Garoga.

Lakes. m. Fish Lake. n. Garoga Lakes.

Battle Fields. Johnstown.

Villages. JOHNSTOWN. Kingsborough.

BOUNDARIES. North by Hamilton county; East by Saratoga county; South by Montgomery county, and West by Herkimer county.

SURFACE. Mountainous. The Kayaderosseras and Au Sable ranges traverse the county. Mayfield mountain and Klip hill are local names given to spurs of these ranges.

RIVERS. On the east the county is drained by Sacandaga river and its branches, West Stoney and Mayfield creeks. On the south by Chuctenunda, Cayaduta, Garoga and Zimmerman's creeks, all flowing into the Mohawk, and on the west by East Canada Creek and its tributaries, Ayres, Fish and Sprite Creeks.

LAKES. Fish Lake and the Garoga Lakes are the only considerable sheets of water in the county.

CLIMATE. Healthful, but from the elevation of much of the surface, cool.

GEOLOGY AND MINERALS. The rocks of the northern part of the county are primitive, consisting of gneiss, in some of its forms. As we approach nearer the Mohawk, the calciferous or earlier limestone makes its appearance, particularly in the eastern part of the county. In Mayfield, the limestone denominated by Geologists, birdseye, is found, and on the southern limits of the county, the Trenton limestone.

<small>The county does not appear to be rich in minerals. Mica, garnet, green feldspar, and porphyritic gneiss, are the principal yet discovered. Quartz, in fine transparent crystals, occurs in the southern part of the county.</small>

SOIL AND VEGETABLE PRODUCTIONS. The soil of the southern portion of the county is rich and fertile, and well adapted to grain. Oak, hickory, ash, maple, &c. are the principal forest trees. In the northern part of the county the hemlock and oak are found, and the land is less fertile.

PURSUITS. *Agriculture* is the pursuit of a majority of the inhabitants. In the southern towns a considerable quantity of grain is raised; in the northern, more attention is paid to the rearing of cattle, sheep and swine, and to the products of the dairy.

Manufactures also form an important pursuit in the county, and are annually increasing in value. The principal articles of manufacture are leather, (for which the hemlock forests of the northern portion afford great facilities,) buckskin gloves and mittens, which are made here in larger quantities than any where else in the United States; flour, lumber and paper.

There is no *commerce* from the want of navigable streams. There are no *mines*.

THE STAPLE PRODUCTIONS are butter, cheese, wool, oats, rye, flax, potatoes and corn.

SCHOOLS. There are 105 public schools in the county. The average number of months during which schools are maintained is seven. The expenses of public school instruction in 1846, were $7168, and the number of scholars 5593. The district libraries contained 11,292 volumes. Three private schools had nineteen pupils, and two academies eighty-five scholars.

RELIGIOUS DENOMINATIONS. Presbyterians, Methodists, Baptists, Dutch Reformed, Unitarians, Episcopalians and Universalists. There are in the county thirty-two churches, and twenty-nine clergymen, of all denominations.

HISTORY. The first settlements in this county, appear to have been made by German emigrants, in 1724, at Oppenheim and Ephrata. The settlements about Johnstown were made between 1760 and 1770, through the influence of Sir William Johnson and his family. In 1764 or 1765, Sir William erected the residence known as Johnson Hall, one mile west of the village of Johnstown, and resided there till his death. A sketch of his life has already been given, under Montgomery county. The possessions of the baronet in this, as well as in Montgomery county, were confiscated after the revolution, and sold.

On Sunday, the 21st of May, 1780, Sir John Johnson made an incursion into Johnstown, and burned thirty-three houses, killed eleven persons and wounded a number more. Colonel Visscher, one of those who were wounded, was scalped and left for dead, but finally recovered.

In October, 1781, the battle of Johnstown was fought, on the Hall Farm, in Johnstown.

A body of tories and Indians, about 700 in number, under the command of the inhuman Ross and Walter Butler, had made a descent upon the valley of the Mohawk, to plunder and butcher its inhabitants. They had proceeded thus far, marking their course with fire and blood, when Colonel Marinus Willet, with a body of Mohawk valley troops, attacked them, and after a severe action compelled them to retreat. They were closely pursued, and it was during their flight, that the infamous Butler met with the fate he so justly merited, at the hand of an Oneida Indian.* The loss of the Americans, in this conflict, was about

---

* It is related that when Butler was wounded, and the Oneida Indian who had shot him, rushed upon him, tomahawk in hand, the wretch, who had never shown

forty. Nearly the same number of the enemy were killed, and about fifty taken prisoners.

VILLAGES. JOHNSTOWN is a fine and thriving village, in the town of the same name. Its location was selected by Sir William Johnson, and several of its public edifices erected by him.

It has a flourishing academy, the bell of which was the gift of Queen Anne, to a chapel called after her, which was destroyed during the revolution. It is the county seat. Population 1000.

Kingsboro' is another village in the same township, famous for the manufacture of deerskin gloves and mittens. It has an academy of some note. Population 400.

Gloversville, in the same township, is also celebrated for the manufacture of mittens, gloves and moccasins, of buckskin. Population 400.

At the confluence of Mayfield creek with the Sacandaga river, is the *Fish House* village, so named from Sir William Johnson's summer residence, which stood at this point, and at which he was accustomed to spend a considerable portion of each summer, in hunting, fishing and rural amusements.

About 1000 acres of the Vlaie, or great marsh, extending over some 5000 acres, lie in this vicinity, and afford a valuable range for cattle in the dry season, and a fine fishing and hunting ground for the sportsman.

Rawsonville, in the town of Broadalbin, is a village of some importance. Population 500.

---

mercy to any, however innocent and helpless, who had implored it at his hands, begged for quarter from the Indian. "Me give you Sherry valley quarters," was the broken reply of the savage; alluding to the bloody massacre of Cherry valley, in which Butler had acted so conspicuous a part. With this answer, he buried his tomahawk in the brain of the murderer.

LVIII. HAMILTON COUNTY.

Square Miles, 1064. Population, 1882.
Organized, 1835. Valuation, 1845, $339,228.

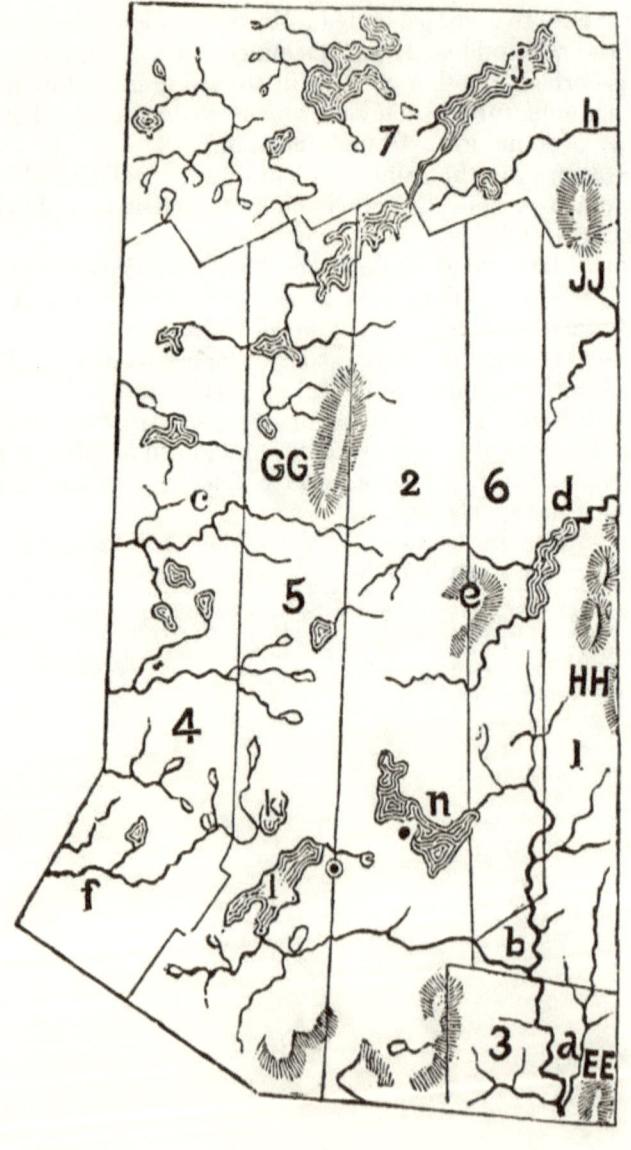

HAMILTON COUNTY. 411

TOWNS.

1. Wells, 1805.
2. Lake Pleasant, 1812.
3. Hope, 1818.
4. Morehouse, 1835.
5. Arietta, 1837.
6. Long Lake, 1838.
7. Gilman, 1839.

Mountains. EE. Kayaderosseras. GG. Chateaugay. HH. Clinton range. JJ. Au Sable range.
Rivers. a. Sacandaga. b. Oxbow. c. Moose. d. Indian. f. West Canada Creek.
Lakes. h. Teralt. j. Long. k. Oxbow. l. Piseco. n. Pleasant.
Villages. PISECO. Lake Pleasant.

BOUNDARIES. North by St. Lawrence and Franklin counties; East by Essex Warren and Saratoga; South by Fulton and Herkimer, and West by Herkimer, counties.

SURFACE. The surface of this county is mountainous, four chains of mountains traversing it, viz: the Kayaderosseras, Clinton, Chateaugay and Au Sable ranges. Much of it is covered with dense forests and lakes, presenting to the eye an appearance very similar, probably, to that of New England, two hundred years ago. The hills are generally susceptible of cultivation, the soil being strong and productive, and considerable tracts as arable and fertile as the timber lands of the west.

RIVERS. The principal streams which drain the county are the Racket, Indian, Sacandaga, Oxbow, Moose and Beaver rivers, and West Canada creek.

LAKES AND PONDS. These are almost innumerable, and in the purity of their waters, the picturesque and majestic scenery which surrounds them, the abundance of trout and other fish which they afford, are equal to any in the world.

Long, Indian, Racket, Transparent, Clinch, Crotchet, Pleasant, Round, Piseco. Elm, Oxbow, Beaver and Squaw lakes, are the principal. The forests abound with deer and other game, not excepting panthers, bears, catamounts and wolves.

CLIMATE. From its elevation, as well as the density of its forests, the climate is cold, and the winters long.

GEOLOGY AND MINERALS. The county belongs almost entirely to the great northeastern primitive formation; and its rocks are mainly granite, gneiss and hypersthene.

Iron has been discovered, and probably the other metals and minerals of a primitive country exist. The ore of iron discovered is the magnetic, and of excellent quality.

VEGETABLE PRODUCTIONS. The timber is principally beech, maple, black birch, butternut and elm; the lower range of hills produces pines of gigantic growth. Portions of the county are well adapted to the culture of grain.

Pursuits. The inhabitants are mostly devoted to *agricultural* pursuits and fishing. The county possesses much land suitable for grazing.

The *manufactures* are principally domestic.

Staple Productions. Butter, cheese, lumber, corn, oats, buckwheat and potatoes.

Schools. There are twenty-six schools in the county, attended by 690 children. The number of months in which schools were taught, during the year 1846, was five, and the amount paid for teacher's wages $677. The number of volumes in the district libraries was 1043.

There is one private school in the county.

Religious Denominations. Baptists and Methodists. There are three churches and three clergymen, of all denominations, in the county.

History. Very little can be said of the early history of this county. The first settlers probably removed from the counties of Montgomery and Fulton, into the wilderness. The first town was organized in 1805. In some sections of the county considerable bodies of Welch emigrants have located themselves.

Villages. Piseco, on the Piseco lake, in Arietta, has been designated as the county seat. It is a small but pleasant village.

Lake Pleasant, on the lake of the same name, is a small village. It is a favorite resort for sportsmen and anglers.

LIX. WYOMING COUNTY.

Square Miles about 590.
Organized, 1841.

Population, 31,526.
Valuation,* 1845, $3,652,782.

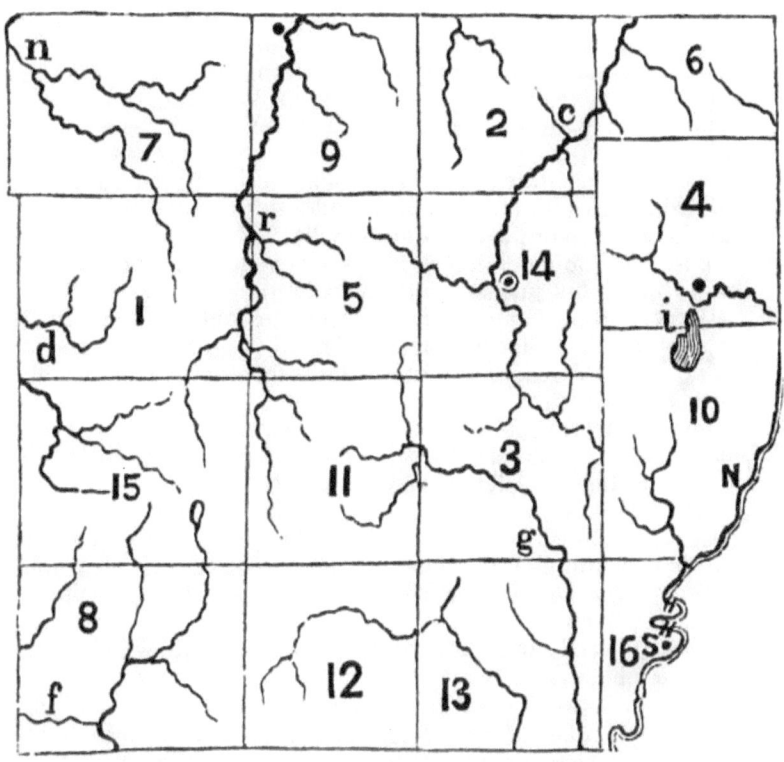

TOWNS.

1. Sheldon, 1808.
2. Middlebury, 1812.
3. Gainesville, 1814.
4. Perry, 1814.
5. Orangeville, 1816.
6. Covington, 1817.
7. Bennington, 1818.
8. China, 1818.
9. Attica, 1821.
10. Castile, 1821.
11. Wethersfield, 1823.
12. Eagle, 1823.
13. Pike, 1827.
14. Warsaw, 1828.
15. Java, 1832.
16. Genesee Falls, 1846.

Rivers. N. Genesee River. c. Allen's Creek. d. Seneca. f. Cattaraugus. g. Nunskoy. n. Cayuga.

Falls. s. Portage Falls.

Lakes. i. Silver.

Villages. WARSAW. Attica. Genesee Falls. Perry.

BOUNDARIES. North by Genesee; East by Livingston; South by Allegany and Cattaraugus; and West by Erie.

---

* This sum is exclusive of the three towns of Eagle, Pike and Genesee Falls, added in 1846, from Allegany county.

SURFACE. This county occupies, for the most part, the second of those elevated tableaux, or plains, which stretch from Lake Ontario to the southern border of the state, and which are divided from each other by steep and almost perpendicular precipices. The table land on which most of Wyoming county lies, commences with the ledge, which runs through the southern towns of Genesee county, and over which the waters of Allen's creek are precipitated in Le Roy, and rises with an ascent not exceeding ten or twelve feet to the mile, to the ledge over which the Genesee river falls, at Portageville.

There are no mountain ridges in the county, and the declivity of the land is but just sufficient to drain it.

RIVERS. The Genesee river forms the southeastern boundary of the county, for a distance of nearly twenty miles, and in its fall over the ledge, at Genesee falls, furnishes a valuable hydraulic power.

The other principal streams of the county are Allen's creek, (named from the ferocious villain known, for many years, in this region, as Indian Allen,) Tonawanda, Cayuga, Seneca, Wiskoy, and Nunskoy creeks.

LAKE. Silver lake, lying partly in Perry and partly in Castile, is a beautiful little sheet of water, five eighths of a mile wide, and three miles long, elevated several hundred feet above the Genesee river.

The CLIMATE is generally salubrious. The prevailing diseases are of a bilious type.

GEOLOGY AND MINERALS. The county lies almost entirely within the bounds of the Erie group. In the north the Ludlowville shales predominate. In the south the Chemung sandstone is the prevailing rock.

_{Carbonate of lime, crystallized in fantastic and sometimes beautiful forms,* sulphate of lime, or gypsum, and iron pyrites are abundant. There is some sulphate of barytes, and small seams of anthracite, but, as might be expected in the geological formation of this section, in too small quantities to be of any practical value.}

_{The fossils are mainly vegetable, consisting mostly of fucoides, or mosses. There are also, in some portions of the county, fossil shells, but not in great variety.}

SOIL AND VEGETABLE PRODUCTIONS. The soil is generally fertile, particularly along the Genesee valley. The forest trees of this county are, in the north part, the beech, maple, hemlock and elm, with some oak. In the southern portion, pine, basswood and ash.

The principal crops are oats, wheat, potatoes, corn, flax, barley, peas and buckwheat.

* Among the most singular of these forms are masses, weighing from ten to three hundred pounds, bearing a striking resemblance, in form, to the turtle. Their homogeneous structure, and some peculiarities in their form, preclude the supposition that they are fossil animal remains.

WYOMING COUNTY. 415

PURSUITS. *Agriculture* is the principal pursuit. The eastern and northern towns are largely engaged in the culture of grain, particularly wheat and oats. The southern towns are better adapted to grazing.

Manufactures are increasing in the county, but as yet are in their infancy. Flour, leather, lumber, pot and pearl ashes, and woollen goods are the principal articles. The entire value of the goods manufactured in the county, in 1845, was estimated at $412,000.

There are no *mines* or quarries, of importance, in the county.

The Genesee river canal, affords a convenient mode of transportation for the produce of the eastern towns of the county.

STAPLE PRODUCTIONS. Oats, wheat, potatoes, butter, cheese, wool, beef, pork and lumber.

SCHOOLS. There were, in 1846, 198 district schools, in this county. The average amount of instruction given in these was eight months. 20,479 volumes were reported in the district school libraries; and $12,946 was the amount paid for the instruction of 11,517 children.

There were also eight private and select schools, with 220 pupils, in the county, and three incorporated seminaries, with 132 students.

RELIGIOUS DENOMINATIONS. Baptists, Methodists, Presbyterians, Congregationalists, Universalists, Episcopalians, Roman Catholics and Dutch Reformed. There are in the county fifty-four churches and sixty-four clergymen, of all denominations.

HISTORY. The first settler in this county was Mr. Elizur Webster, who removed from New England, and settled in the present town of Warsaw, in 1803. His daughter, (now the wife of Hon. A. W. Young of this county,) was the first child born in the county. Many of the early settlers were from Washington and the adjacent counties in Vermont. These generally settled in the vicinity of Warsaw.

As a part of the Genesee valley, its fertility attracted a host of emigrants to its borders, and though the youngest county in the state in its organization, it occupies a middle rank in population.

Much of the land was formerly owned by the Holland Land Company, but it has, within a few years been very generally purchased by actual settlers.

The Gardeau tract, or flats, was a tract of about 10,000 acres, lying on the Genesee river, partly in the town of Castile, which the Indians reserved in a treaty with Robert Morris, in 1797, as a gift to the Seneca white woman, Mary Jemison.*

---

* This extraordinary woman was a native of Ireland, and was taken prisoner by the Indians, when a child twelve or thirteen years of age. She was adopted by an Indian family, and embraced the Indian faith, habits and customs. She was

Wyoming county formed part of Genesee county, till 1841, when it was organized as a separate county, and, in 1846, the towns of Eagle and Pike, and that portion of Portage lying west of Genesee river, were taken from Allegany county and annexed to it. The last town received the name of Genesee Falls.

VILLAGES, &c. WARSAW, the county seat, in the town of the same name, was settled by emigrants from New England, who were highly intelligent and religious, and to this day it is characterized by the intelligence and morality of its inhabitants. It is situated in the midst of a fine agricultural district, and has some manufactures. The first church edifice erected west of the Genesee river, was standing in Warsaw a few years since. Population 800.

Perry is a thriving and busy town, considerably engaged in manufactures. There are two villages in the town, *Perry* and *Perry Centre*. There is an academy at Perry, of some note, and a number of manufacturing establishments. Population 1200.

At Perry Centre a literary institution, called the Perry Centre Institute, has recently been established.

Middlebury has a flourishing academy, incorporated in 1817, located in the village of *Wyoming*, which is situated in a pleasant valley, and has a population of about 600.

Genesee Falls, in the town of the same name, formerly called Portageville, is situated at the falls of the Genesee river, one of the most romantic and interesting locations in western New York. In the space of two miles there are three distinct falls, of 60, 90, and 110 feet, each possessing beauties of a character peculiar to itself. The banks of the river tower up in stupendous perpendicular walls, more than 400 feet in height, and are crowned with gigantic evergreens, which, from their venerable appearance, seem to have maintained their position for ages.

Notwithstanding the immense depth to which the bed of the river has been worn, its turns are short and graceful, giving the admiring visitor new, though limited views, at every stage of his progress.

In June, 1817, a land slide of about fifteen acres took place from the side of a hill in this town, into the river, which for some time completely dammed it, leaving a perpendicular bank more than 100 feet in height.

The hydraulic power furnished by the falls of the Genesee, is improved to a considerable extent. Population 800.

---

married twice to Indian chiefs, and died in September, 1833, at the age of ninety or ninety-one years. Since her death, most of her extensive property has been sold by her heirs.

STATISTICAL TABLES.

The following Tables compiled with great care, from the state census of 1845, and other authentic sources, present the principal agricultural and horticultural products of each county, and of the state, and the number of cattle, sheep, horses and swine, together with the amount of butter, cheese, and wool produced; the principal manufactures; and the commercial statistics of the different districts of the state.

TABLE I.

Agricultural and Horticultural Products.

COUNTIES.	Wheat.	Rye.	Corn.	Oats.	Buck-wheat.	Barley.	Peas.	Beans.	Potatoes.	Turnips.	Flax.
Albany,	Bushels, 44,149	163,694	208,254	624,039	183,274	120,978	51,252	4,487	404,594	12,220	lbs.34,985
Allegany,	260,190	31,144	101,140	503,134	61,995	38,132	48,250	2,378	575,196	32,197	95,268
Broome,	81,388	37,049	172,713	331,425	75,019	1,032	2,929	1,458	182,461	13,349	32,144
Cattaraugus,	177,927	934	96,540	459,770	24,026	13,671	18,370	1,830	506,919	20,813	42,886
Cayuga,	652,896	4,415	479,151	652,281	94,067	143,516	56,755	3,524	536,933	22,567	139,126
Chautauque,	268,261	3,158	313,121	448,834	20,000	32,833	28,746	3,183	686,969	22,143	129,749
Chemung,	180,095	10,780	177,965	287,146	104,567	25,265	5,069	1,148	146,901	4,957	27,163
Chenango,	104,562	40,148	241,205	597,508	70,803	20,147	5,845	1,897	396,096	22,464	114,911
Clinton,	114,570	37,998	104,831	268,258	51,564	21,018	25,823	6,601	620,028	29,246	4,266
Columbia,	75,065	302,508	526,629	1,093,850	129,001	9,271	2,653	1,092	415,035	12,812	32,182
Cortland,	96,855	4,532	123,186	400,342	50,157	32,214	12,237	1,276	259,364	25,075	101,344
Delaware,	50,685	113,114	85,128	648,982	133,235	2,404	3,783	550	467,582	30,152	30,110
Dutchess,	86,264	165,782	814,153	1,283,718	89,199	5,671	1,347	692	387,124	84,134	34,633
Erie,	251,781	11,007	238,295	637,593	31,593	40,485	51,401	4,636	552,091	17,899	36,819

COUNTIES.	Wheat, Bushels.	Rye,	Corn,	Oats,	Buckwheat,	Barley,	Peas,	Beans,	Potatoes,	Turnips,	Flax, lbs.
Essex,	84,217	32,160	96,429	241,514	20,690	1,869	31,885	3,144	515,650	25,707	7,385
Franklin,	97,999	21,746	70,109	148,378	24,780	6,518	19,622	1,981	623,844	25,459	9,250
Fulton,	17,118	42,623	105,424	287,221	48,694	26,596	22,384	943	166,162	6,287	50,812
Genesee,	695,107	2,033	225,615	406,594	19,713	60,716	75,966	3,866	380,710	7,314	19,440
Greene,	19,713	84,380	178,027	347,891	106,524	11,209	8,467	3,503	265,978	13,932	14,647
Hamilton,	253	956	4,536	14,625	5,058	810	357	40	26,104	2,422	863
Herkimer,	60,700	22,367	180,340	690,413	44,193	101,805	27,507	1,689	263,999	3,976	51,179
Jefferson,	421,819	55,457	467,230	709,232	42,128	159,872	153,374	6,974	1,235,139	18,538	208,545
Kings,	26,992	9,724	124,688	64,786	2,997	360	9,345	4,821	178,434	57,038	
Lewis,	87,406	9,278	53,180	202,515	25,803	23,119	21,925	678	498,849	22,340	85,281
Livingston,	821,762	5,200	257,346	351,233	34,148	93,959	33,429	2,371	268,161	6,742	32,510
Madison,	190,364	5,888	230,781	512,789	24,445	229,606	31,312	2,063	393,989	7,399	42,232
Monroe,	1,338,583	3,198	453,463	538,063	31,345	57,102	66,342	4,272	667,491	38,581	10,796
Montgomery,	69,589	80,962	187,700	717,212	119,843	161,396	70,205	2,666	187,905	1,841	72,191
New York,	60		6,325	2,135	300	30		25	6,085	600	
Niagara,	713,318	98	188,166	292,099	20,101	58,340	84,627	2,186	333,658	26,464	9,412
Oneida,	115,927	19,676	423,753	971,608	76,614	162,235	26,497	4,159	685,168	31,452	38,000
Onondaga,	636,177	10,107	516,496	829,002	51,198	360,421	106,875	4,294	573,896	22,503	107,035
Ontario,	918,616	9,569	357,747	533,062	43,690	211,653	50,941	3,773	414,090	13,967	20,240
Orange,	82,881	191,864	603,167	417,388	111,672	1,907	30	332	173,018	24,623	15,350
Orleans,	692,127	219	213,203	236,743	8,528	16,872	45,589	3,001	276,432	11,119	13,681
Oswego,	98,880	1,594	285,366	359,767	57,926	16,130	30,648	3,497	541,737	25,529	57,034
Otsego,	109,551	87,925	201,031	1,004,541	117,265	112,261	21,999	2,789	620,921	32,517	89,589
Putnam,	4,913	31,275	120,858	81,416	37,516	62		318	74,430	24,506	2,832
Queens,	99,374	61,680	438,661	324,218	67,571	2,600	38,219	20,299	229,876	90,710	1,416
Rensselaer,	75,708	201,314	403,548	763,841	64,362	12,382	9,985	4,552	604,025	21,631	282,690
Richmond,	10,337	7,501	66,421	27,704	3,016	3,231	269	272	44,230	7,559	100
Rockland,	1,705	26,283	95,698	45,120	37,289	133	33	49	59,080	6,207	863
Saratoga,	104,661	145,777	512,361	620,395	98,208	30,975	29,070	2,312	611,919	22,613	30,619
Schenectady,	19,754	56,205	103,729	254,455	54,682	91,451	16,351	1,432	112,842	5,342	19,840
Schoharie,	79,175	120,030	85,173	683,560	147,709	208,321	77,946	2,406	319,914	6,177	70,672

STATISTICAL TABLES.

Seneca,	483,773	4,094	204,940	292,397	37,611	50,071	6,335	895	169,081	4,690	39,220
St. Lawrence,	264,832	51,716	304,403	646,556	47,014	48,100	101,555	5,496	1,592,723	56,577	40,508
Steuben,	457,304	16,378	194,064	635,304	195,165	59,817	52,949	2,680	551,723	29,885	59,413
Suffolk,	77,423	60,376	501,939	278,820	51,193	13,791	131	3,302	190,830	97,750	6,328
Sullivan,	3,252	64,869	62,362	150,300	67,267	146	41	276	79,786	13,318	6,541
Tioga,	113,165	9,433	168,100	265,922	80,767	2,032	9,391	890	167,339	6,148	35,575
Tompkins,	375,646	8,493	248,752	528,763	158,460	23,873	32,407	2,438	316,334	7,838	55,091
Ulster,	39,323	218,281	356,201	429,713	151,130	257	326	271	201,064	19,912	56,025
Warren,	16,469	32,319	92,746	107,112	22,474	509	8,171	1,038	236,344	9,761	6,952
Washington,	75,497	116,834	471,756	593,423	97,279	9,470	37,676	7,400	969,501	10,436	149,550
Wayne,	587,818	4,178	441,543	476,422	57,188	48,236	38,553	3,675	531,941	21,974	98,498
Westchester,	23,613	100,016	498,019	316,156	68,944	7,883	304	479	488,534	92,837	3,491
Wyoming,	331,111	811	102,139	456,160	21,935	42,281	41,771	2,699	368,640	12,889	108,193
Yates,	403,069	4,564	135,999	224,673	35,933	71,144	6,146	1,184	177,740	5,189	11,579
Total,	13,391,771	2,966,322	14,722,115	26,323,051	3,624,679	3,108,705	1,761,504	162,188	23,653,418	1,350,332	2,897,062

TABLE II.

Agricultural Products.

COUNTIES.	No. of Neat Cattle.	No. of Horses.	No. of Sheep.	No. of Hogs.	No. of lbs. of Butter.	No. of lbs. of Cheese.	No. of lbs. of Wool.
Albany,	26,840	10,780	66,536	32,807	950,009	111,329	142,747
Allegany,	51,900	10,261	184,901	23,573	1,563,054	887,113	349,759
Broome,	30,307	4,540	66,133	15,267	1,153,484	148,752	127,506
Cattaraugus,	45,256	6,908	103,780	19,844	1,284,635	567,867	196,903
Cayuga,	41,584	13,932	175,148	43,546	1,696,764	394,001	412,668
Chautauque,	66,885	10,506	225,403	32,013	2,130,303	974,474	485,816
Chemung,	22,516	5,085	55,498	16,800	724,135	71,553	107,559
Chenango,	63,745	10,416	223,453	23,949	2,816,291	1,145,057	503,937
Clinton,	24,006	6,378	63,533	13,476	677,348	184,440	135,613
Columbia,	35,718	9,814	172,579	54,477	1,519,610	246,384	252,739
Cortland,	39,068	7,049	108,862	18,155	1,588,696	682,201	227,034
Delaware,	62,535	8,585	135,623	24,374	3,117,649	135,562	272,220
Dutchess,	47,258	11,242	199,993	66,828	1,772,770	164,525	471,097
Erie,	57,506	12,527	148,732	38,087	1,728,021	1,288,780	274,638
Essex,	23,895	5,118	90,495	12,083	673,366	212,475	198,104
Franklin,	20,069	3,878	47,790	10,343	554,441	240,415	102,830
Fulton,	20,311	4,548	38,546	11,141	733,958	432,051	81,097
Genesee,	25,689	10,096	156,578	27,264	888,396	313,491	360,998
Greene,	27,383	6,258	48,541	20,606	1,122,526	123,718	91,318

STATISTICAL TABLES.

County							
Hamilton,	2,133	288		788			4,608
Herkimer,	53,440	10,053	2,641	23,578	1,480,628	10,032	158,769
Jefferson,	85,934	16,397	75,964	53,068	3,080,767	8,208,796	380,633
Kings,	7,449	4,360	184,526	9,515	80,059	2,802,314	250
Lewis,	32,793	4,570	108	15,813	1,266,933	606	89,229
Livingston,	28,808	10,910	40,657	28,819	1,027,611	1,420,368	5 4,741
Madison,	45,216	11,774	218,258	28,540	1,531,205	265,140	5 1,274
Monroe,	39,305	16,811	263,132	48,493	50,397	2,022,855	402,927
Montgomery,	30,202	9,010	173,952	24,850	26,986	366,782	120,218
New York,	831	13,346	56,260	8,591	12,080	911,292	
Niagara,	27,835	8,614	22	30,968	861,300	50	180,687
Oneida,	85,464	17,303	80,549	45,723	3,876,276	154,976	409,748
Onondaga,	49,495	16,968	194,589	52,907	2,123,787	3,277,7 0	423,864
Ontario,	32,544	2,625	190,429	36,986	1,286,119	749,838	620,739
Orange,	59,712	10,226	257,821	57,265	4,108,840	424,742	120,708
Orleans,	21,207	7,696	45,819	10,399	781,467	6,717	207,960
Oswego,	41,300	9,008	90,525	27,736	22,144	216,950	168,100
Otsego,	61,706	14,183	76,698	38,485	2,436,719	933,922	548,868
Putnam,	16,083	2,049	70,564	12,833	7,780	1,595,407	28,981
Queens,	16,271	7,395	14,062	21,148	533,110	24,361	41,348
Rensselaer,	34,734	10,594	21,054	39,262	1,409,312	10,209	375,902
Richmond,	3,669	1,222	170,552	3,085	81,982	738,841	156
Rockland,	6,458	2,495	148	6,242	267,178	31	5,771
Saratoga,	36,784	10,028	2,830	37,882	1,498,986	336,085	213,464
Schenectady,	12,043	3,884	99,706	10,971	545,404	155,979	39,989
Schoharie,	36,902	9,512	19,461	29,625	1,545,889	122,532	122,887
Seneca,	17,521	7,267	75,131	22,023	816,061	71,781	168,400
St. Lawrence,	77,979	13,470	71,965	38,150	2,529,741	1,281,972	356,713
Steuben,	55,482	12,310	168,314	35,987	1,838,420	311,314	424,340
Suffolk,	24,728	6,558	217,658	21,623	584,281	22,501	81,721
			49,851				

TABLE II.—Continued.

COUNTIES.	No. of Neat Cattle.	No. of Horses.	No. of Sheep.	No. of Hogs.	No. of lbs. of Butter.	No. of lbs. of Cheese.	No. of lbs. of Wool.
Sullivan,	20,507	2,958	19,545	9,858	795,607	17,307	40,731
Tioga,	23,999	4,746	54,293	15,764	822,220	170,755	108,695
Tompkins,	38,174	11,191	135,787	28,488	1,785,604	142,594	3,242
Ulster,	36,513	8,643	46,522	42,627	1,35,45	8,946	9,102
Warren,	13,631	2,734	28,831	7,49	415,496	9,628	7,868
Washington,	43,527	11,115	254,866	42,189	1,639,416	3,736	579,056
Wayne,	32,891	12,258	130,562	35,873	1,466,124	305,067	281,257
Westchester,	32,848	6,935	21,567	35,609	1,4,242	29,197	54,567
Wyoming,	34,039	8,104	16,365	21,607	1,1,141	763,208	362,015
Yates,	18,978	6,523	130,134	18,882	841,643	130,187	285,296
Total	2,072,330	505,155	6,443,855	1,584,344	79,501,723	36,744,976	13,861,828

TABLE III.

Manufacturing Statistics.

COUNTIES.	Value of articles produced in Grist Mills.	Saw Mills.	Oil Mills.	Fulling Mills.	Carding Machines.	Cotton Factories.	Woollen Factories.	Iron Works.	Trip Hammers.	Distilleries.
Albany,	$526,921	$104,885	$62,563	$18,046	$16,722	$96,000	$193,935	$600,500		$14,500
Allegany,	336,461	215,243	8,600	86,996	45,195		76,975	19,500	$3,200	
Broome,	118,779	175,833	150	24,448	26,205			6,500		4,000
Cattaraugus,	122,243	202,116		28,193	28,770		9,865	900	1,300	500
Cayuga,	576,937	701,745	5,900	36,737	51,000	59,000	139,165	29,800	15,750	25,220
Chautauque,	315,959	174,518	7,700	42,686	56,300		32,800	59,050	13,000	26,250
Chemung,	185,846	162,753	1,800	14,626	12,162		14,000	44,000		200
Chenango,	185,220	99,081	5,900	51,847	53,183	39,183	13,388	13,761	4,865	
Clinton,	149,378	176,005		56,799	15,730		56,740	721,450	14,500	
Columbia,	392,059	22,749		43,694	44,764	262,250	132,095	119,647	17,760	
Cortland,	180,316	55,529	13,000	19,013	2,337	17,500	6,000	5,300	2,400	5,000
Delaware,	161,018	152,654		68,105	70,561		35,300	1,000	2,400	
Dutchess,	519,128	44,144	24,000	8,103	13,365	418,550	409,250	195,915	25,430	2,256
Erie,	1,016,624	347,622	1,200	51,363	53,443	18,000	52,290	338,119	680	43,647
Essex,	171,707	336,152		53,614	24,350		40,500	431,390	3,700	
Franklin,	119,960	58,824	4,000	16,025	25,782	20,000	40,500	5,010	4,740	6,495
Fulton,	77,002	63,841	2,000	15,097	11,163		8,784		6,371	4,553
Genesee,	242,878	41,932	5,550	22,699	19,756		25,587	33,220	4,890	7,300

TABLE III.—Continued.

COUNTIES.	Value of articles produced in Grist Mills.	Saw Mills.	Oil Mills.	Fulling Mills.	Carding Machines.	Cotton Factories.	Woollen Factories.	Iron Works.	Trip Hammers.	Distilleries.
Greene,	$268,694	$70,360		$28,208	$30,126		$30,200	$27,100		$2,500
Hamilton,	2,400	10,528								
Herkimer,	197,543	97,336	$5,000	45,534	36,449	50,581	151,750	43,900	$28,600	23,434
Jefferson,	468,318	212,815	6,100	73,828	70,313	42,500	139,345	179,500	20,650	54,150
Kings,	298,175		321,453					355,400		1,682,530
Lewis,	117,838	52,759	4,200	9,730	17,910		9,000			
Livingston,	426,170	46,890	3,500	15,832	30,196		6,600	38,200	700	21,324
Madison,	364,267	105,805	5,600	25,362	38,312	47,540	204,470	32,620	8,700	122,094
Monroe,	2,539,687	147,353	12,500	74,102	31,770		111,849	404,355	8,500	38,941
Montgomery,	286,535	71,923	400	25,433	9,355		9,111	19,280		103,867
New York,	52,291	785,700	750,000			82,200	16,191	2,193,417	60,000	894,700
Niagara,	776,148	122,899	2,500	35,875	29,184	28,317	3,000	27,595		16,050
Oneida,	466,515	255,350	550	41,892	51,376	680,374	502,593	178,586	28,100	436,446
Onondaga,	775,842	203,108	13,975	29,722	28,046	40,251	240,110	98,850	9,200	120,778
Ontario,	568,347	50,892	700	21,754	33,753		72,800	10,400		20,596
Orange,	475,378	45,653	87,600	10,457	40,810	115,124	242,088	139,550		31,878
Orleans,	446,550	57,578	6,500	15,462	21,172		16,100	16,850		20,150
Oswego,	1,677,725	207,558	4,075	53,944	47,618	13,000	20,196	18,100	1,400	
Otsego,	298,548	109,418	2,500	55,972	53,273	192,959	8,365	41,950	9,220	35,239
Putnam,	67,888	11,755		6,452	8,120			397,867	128,212	600
Queens,	221,784	15,655		15,818	10,644	5,000	127,680			40,000
Rensselaer,	793,285	79,317	36,060	18,631	18,170	373,157	306,426	285,500	9,900	106,400
Richmond,	19,300	200						4,800		
Rockland,	51,219	22,417		200	1,093	80,936	47,250	519,836		4,402
Saratoga,	422,474	170,468		19,115	23,899	163,023	82,030	12,000	80,700	2,900
Schenectady,	50,518	10,134	10,139	3,675	4,570	27,000	2,500	113,000		
Schoharie,	131,379	61,609		37,743	46,811		26,312	10,500	5,300	

STATISTICAL TABLES. 425

Seneca,	$381,929	$52,520	$61,175	$4,691	$10,150		$171,010	$27,375		$30,000
St. Lawrence,	450,719	205,297	3,000	95,828	85,503		45,298	110,173	$19,300	28,870
Steuben,	286,965	381,073		29,151	111,795		33,300	3,000	900	8,008
Suffolk,	166,181	10,815		3,005	4,453	$17,000	24,500			
Sullivan,	100,542	144,620		9,781	8,770					32,00
Tioga,	163,935	182,982	2,150	35,543	27,668		17,700	9,500	2,500	22,255
Tompkins,	485,781	120,618	25,760	29,357	33,847		133,137	33,920	800	44,226
Ulster,	360,273	89,275	160,426	24,384	23,621	55,000	35,965	381,500	33,100	8,616
Warren,	38,569	120,942		8,212	8,589		16,000	9,600		
Washington,	248,937	127,636		37,927	30,402	49,559	145,225	25,736	4,260	49,947
Wayne,	376,269	448,596		19,143	19,274			53,930	3,500	3,050
Westchester,	197,797	49,058	4,900	6,648	9,468	15,680	154,270	348,780		4,383
Wyoming,	196,893	35,703		24,549	32,093		31,133	13,315	1,500	32,400
Yates,	273,675	56,328	21,800	19,818	18,932		9,600	10,000		
Total,	$22,794,474	$7,577,154	$1,695,026	$1,660,881	$1,678,320	$2,979,087	$4,281,257	$8,402,587	$586,328	$4,222,155

19*

TABLE III.—Continued.
Manufacturing Statistics.

COUNTIES.	Asheries.	Glass Factories.	Rope Factories.	Chaincable Factories.	Oil Cloth Factories.	Dyeing and Printing Factories.	Clover Mills.	Paper Mills.	Tanneries.	Breweries.
Albany,	$850		$73,127		$34,000		$90		$110,008	$351,800
Allegany,	34,203				600		2,680		42,825	2,000
Broome,	6,920				30				50,670	
Cattaraugus,	41,835								43,514	
Cayuga,	26,311		75		600		5,378	$20,000	66,857	7,000
Chautauque,	37,011		250					3,700	83,155	
Chemung,	2,710								15,530	
Chenango,	16,561		9,820				1,000	9,600	86,524	5,300
Clinton,	18,345								40,102	3,000
Columbia,	13,815		625			$325,000		21,630	33,060	4,000
Cortland,	8,317		2,750			19,000	570	6,000	25,905	1,800
Delaware,							150		165,034	
Dutchess,	23,266		22,000			301,200		13,800	92,183	125,400
Erie,	388		13,200						271,660	61,826
Essex,	64,750						535	12,000	15,200	
Franklin,	675		775						25,355	
Fulton,	24,270		520				2430	18,300	122,597	4,000
Genesse,									24,230	

STATISTICAL TABLES. 427

County										
Greene,	$658								811,790	
Hamilton,					$7,000				180	
Herkimer,	5,000	$36,000	$5,125				$14,600	35,000	217,244	$2,500
Jefferson,	64,482	130,000	639,500	$5,000			60	5,000	100,774	8,080
Kings,			3,000		121,000	$6,000			182,880	25,380
Lewis,	16,971		900						28,374	675
Livingston,	10,362						900	74,500	20,726	1,000
Madison,	28,230						1,000	9,750	79,208	2,800
Monroe,	20,365		900		30		2,943	61,540	244,907	45,800
Montgomery,	1,429						1,285		62,416	
New York,	6,000	4,800	20,870						132,000	287,109
Niagara,	43,885	8,000			15,000	50,000		20,000	36,650	6,665
Oneida,	13,496	15,300	3,400			37,116	515	22,000	208,446	29,300
Onondaga,	22,779						7,648	22,383	88,056	21,556
Ontario,	15,080	32,000					8,995	1,000	33,078	22,804
Orange,			7,600		52,500		2,700	27,000	121,274	90,000
Orleans,	13,239								4,137	3,600
Oswego,	13,769	20,000	225					18,800	156,399	2,386
Otsego,	12,704		2,737			82,680	20,823	12,000	153,401	4,500
Putnam,									17,690	
Queens,			1,900		38,000	20,000		32,500	22,000	
Rensselaer,		25,000	63,640			710		69,395	185,611	114,950
Richmond,						945,280			10,900	
Rockland,						300,0 0	840	20,864	80,100	
Saratoga,	300		2,150				2,150		30,100	
Schenectady,									400,641	3,500
Schoharie,	4,146						17,402	3,600	30,274	$13,760
Seneca,	$9,816						11,075	5,000	68,275	6,500
St. Lawrence,	213,741			$1,000			1,440	10,000	72,516	
Steuben,	15,715						150	7,000		

COUNTIES.	Asheries.	Glass Factories.	Rope Factories.	Chain cable Factories.	Oil Cloth Factories.	Dyeing and Printing Factories.	Clover Mills.	Paper Mills.	Tanneries.	Breweries.
Suffolk,	20						4,103	6,629	9,100	
Sullivan,	475								466,751	
Tioga,									39,950	
Tompkins,	15,203		1,800		1,000		4,726	27,000	47,602	5,000
Ulster,		40,000	150				2,533	57,500	742,943	
Warren,	62						500		111,176	
Washington,			1,000				1,050	8,000	43,070	1,220
Wayne,	14,791	26,000	5,600				2,427		65,054	11,300
Westchester,			8,000		500			17,000	34,150	
Wyoming,	22,974		801				480		42,176	672
Yates,	2,875						1,490		20,670	
TOTAL,	$909,195	$378,700	$918,540	$5,000	$270,260	$2,086,986	$124,567	$702,505	$6,585,006	$1,313,273

TABLE III. B.

MANUFACTURING STATISTICS.

Domestic Manufactures.

Number of yards of fulled cloth manufactured in the families of the state, in 1844,	1,664,366
Number of yards of cloth not fulled,	2,650,116
" " linen, cotton, or other cloth,	2,775,657

TABLE III. C.

The following table comprises articles not enumerated in the census of 1845, but reported in the United States census for 1840. In most of the items there has been considerable increase. The statistics are for the whole state.

Hardware and cutlery were manufactured in 1840 to the amount of	$1,566,974
Machinery,	2,895,517
Carriages, wagons and sleighs,	2,364,461
Sugar,	385,000
Confectionary,	386,142
Hats and Caps,	2,914,117
Bricks and lime,	1,198,527
Precious metals,	1,106,203
Other metals,	2,456,792
Tobacco,	831,570
Pottery,	159,000
Gun Powder,	142,000
Musical Instruments,	472,910
Furniture,	1,071,776
Soap,	596,991
Tallow and Wax Candles,	565,836
Drugs and Paints,	877,816
Turpentine and Varnish,	431,467
Cannon,	5,600
Small Arms,	124,600
Granite, Marble, &c.	966,220
Chocolate,	5,000
Total,	$22,424,519

TABLE IV.

COMMERCIAL STATISTICS.

A. Total registered, enrolled and licensed tonnage of each district in the state, 1845.

	Tons.
Champlain,	3,192
Sackett's Harbor,	3,419
Oswego,	11,410
Niagara,	12
Genesee,	235
Oswegatchie,	1,456
Buffalo,	24,770
Sag Harbor,	28,348
New York city,	550,359
Total,	623,201

B. Commerce of the State.

Ships cleared in 1845,	tons, 1,340,968
Crews,—Men,	86,770
Boys,	1,362
Ships entered in 1845,	tons, 1,450,711
Crews,—Men,	86,430
Boys,	1,449
Tons of shipping built in 1845,	29,432

C. Imports and Exports.

Imports of New York in 1846,	$70,269,811
Exports " "	36,423,762

D. Arrivals of Shipping.

Vessels arrived from foreign ports, 1846,	2,289
Coastwise arrivals,	4,663
	6,952
Number of passengers from foreign ports, 1846,	115,230

E. Internal Navigation,—Canals.

Number of tons of products of the forest transported on all the canals of the State in 1845,	881,774
Value of do.	$6,472,237
Number of tons of agricultural produce transported on all the canals of the State in 1845,	555,160
Value of do.	$29,479,488
Number of tons of manufactures transported on all the canals of the State in 1845,	160,638
Value of do.	$6,994,932
Number of tons of merchandise carried, &c.	151,450
Value of do.	$52,542,336
Number of tons of other articles,	228,543
Value of do.	$5,140,866
Total number of tons,	1,977,565
Total value,	$100,629,859
Property cleared from the Hudson river on all the canals in 1845,	$55,453,998
Property which came to the Hudson from all the canals in 1845,	$45,452,301
Total arrived and cleared,	$100,906,299*
Tolls on all the canals from September 30, 1845, to September 30, 1846,	$2,764,121

TABLE V.

MINING STATISTICS, 1840.†

Cast Iron,	tons, 29,088,	Value,	$872,640
Bar Iron,	" 53,693,	"	4,295,440
Lead,	lbs. 670,000,	"	20,100
Other metals,		"	84,564
Granite and other stone,		"	1,541,480
Salt,	bushels, 2,867,884,	"	716,971
		Total value,	$7,531,195

---

* This includes those canals which are not the property of the State.
† These statistics are for the most part far below the truth.

TABLE VI.

Governors of the State.

1. UNDER THE DUTCH.

1. Peter Minuit, - - 1624—33
2. Wouter Van Twiller, 1633—37
3. William Kieft, - - 1637—47
4. Peter Stuyvesant, - 1647—64

2. UNDER THE ENGLISH.

1. Richard Nicolls, - 1664—67
2. Francis Lovelace, - 1667—73

DUTCH ADMINISTRATION RESUMED.

5. Anthony Colve, - - 1673—74

ENGLISH ADMINISTRATION RESUMED.

3. Edmond Andross, - 1674—83
4. Thomas Dongan, - 1683—88
5. Edmond Andross, - 1688—89
6. Jacob Leisler, - 1689—91
*7. Henry Sloughter, - 1691
8. Richard Ingoldsby, - 1691—92
9. Benjamin Fletcher, - 1692—98
*10. Richard, Earl of Bellomont, - - 1698—1701
11. John Nanfan, - - 1701—02
12. Lord Cornbury, - 1702—08
*13. John, Lord Lovelace, 1708—09
14. Richard Ingoldsby, - 1709—10
15. Gerardus Beekman, - 1710
16. Robert Hunter, - 1710—19
17. Peter Schuyler, - 1719—20
*18. William Burnet, - 1720—28

*19. John Montgomery, - 1728—31
20. Rip Van Dam, - 1731—32
*21. William Cosby, - 1732—36
22. George Clarke, - 1736—43
23. George Clinton, - 1743—53
*24. Sir Danvers Osborne, 1753
25. James De Lancey, 1753—55
26. Sir Charles Hardy, - 1755—57
*27. James De Lancey, - 1757—60
28. Cadwallader Colden, 1760—61
29. Robert Monkton, 1761
30. Cadwallader Colden, - 1761—65
*31. Sir Henry Moore, - 1765—69
32. Cadwallader Colden, - 1769—70
33. John, Lord Dunmore, 1770—71
34. William Tryon, - 1771—77

INDEPENDENT GOVERNMENT.

1. George Clinton, - 1777—95
2. John Jay, - - 1795—1801
3. George Clinton, - 1801—04
4. Morgan Lewis, - 1804—07
5. Daniel D. Tompkins, 1807—17
6. De Witt Clinton, - 1817—22
7. Joseph C. Yates, - 1822—24
*8. De Witt Clinton, - 1824—28
9. Nathaniel Pitcher, 1828—29
10. Martin Van Buren, - 1829
11. Enos T. Throop, - 1829—33
12. William L. Marcy, - 1833—38
13. William H. Seward, - 1838—42
14. William C. Bouck, - 1842—44
15. Silas Wright, - 1844—46
16. John Young, - - 1846

* The administration of those Governors marked by an asterisk, (*) was terminated by death.

NOTE. A few errors escaped notice till the last sheet was in press. The only ones of importance are the following. Page 17. 3d paragraph, for "The first four are navigated," read, "They are all navigated." Page 51 5th paragraph, for "1626," read "1629." Page 81, 7th paragraph for "1778," read "1779." Page 84, 6th paragraph, for "1785," read "1795." Page 127, 4th paragraph, St. John's College at Rose Hill, Westchester County, should have been added to the list of Colleges and omitted on the next page. Page 192, Map of Montgomery County, the County Seat should be in 9, instead of 4. Page 224, 5th paragraph for "from east to west," read "from west to east." Page 248, last line, for Otsego read Otisco. Page 290, Map of Essex County, 5 should be 3, and the north-eastern town should be 5. Page 310, for XXIV, read XXXIV.

www.ingramcontent.com/pod-product-compliance
Lightning Source LLC
Chambersburg PA
CBHW030259080526
44584CB00012B/370